The Social Psychology of Stereotyping and Group Life

𝔅

The Social Psychology of Stereotyping and Group Life

Edited by Russell Spears, Penelope J. Oakes, Naomi Ellemers, and S. Alexander Haslam

BLACKWELL
Publishers

Copyright © Blackwell Publishers Ltd, 1997

First published 1997

2 4 6 8 10 9 7 5 3 1

Blackwell Publishers Ltd
108 Cowley Road
Oxford OX4 1JF
UK

Blackwell Publishers Inc.
238 Main Street
Cambridge, Massachusetts 02142
USA

British Library Cataloguing in Publication Data

A CIP catalogue record for this book is available from the British Library.

Library of Congress Cataloging-in-Publication Data

The social psychology of stereotyping and group life / edited by
   Russell Spears . . . [et al.].
      p.   cm.
   Includes bibliographical references and index.
   ISBN 0–631–19772–9 (hbk. : alk. paper). — ISBN 0–631–19773–7
(pbk. : alk. paper)
   1. Social psychology.   2. Stereotype (Psychology)   3. Group
identity.   I. Spears, Russell.
HM251.S6753
302—dc20

96–11401
CIP

Typeset in 10$\frac{1}{2}$ on 12 pt Ehrhardt
by Graphicraft Typesetters, Hong Kong
Printed in Great Britain by Hartnolls Ltd, Bodmin, Cornwall

This book is printed on acid-free paper

Contents

Acknowledgements

It would be most inappropriate in a book about 'group life' not to acknowledge the group effort that has brought it to life. The fact that as editors we have managed to work together on opposite sides of the globe, and have been brought even closer together through our collaboration, proves again that the group is much more than the sum of its parts. However, many who have contributed to this product have been working hard behind the scenes. In particular, we would like to thank Alison Mudditt at Blackwell Publishers for her usual efficiency, good humour and her faith in our ability to deliver (almost) on schedule. Thanks are also due to Tony Grahame, our desk editor, and to the production team at Blackwell for making up any time which we lost. Thanks also to Mark Nolan and Janet Tweedie at ANU for compiling the index. The Australian Research Council provided welcome support for a meeting of the editors in Amsterdam and the Kurt Lewin Institute supported this joint venture in many ways. Finally we would like to express our gratitude to all the authors for their contributions to this collective enterprise – thanks to them, editing this volume has been a real pleasure.

Russell Spears
Penny Oakes
Naomi Ellemers
Alex Haslam
Gmunden, 18 July 1996

Contributors

Phyllis Anastasio   Holy Family College, USA
Betty Bachman   Siena College, USA
Richard Y. Bourhis   Université de Quebec à Montreal, Canada
Susan Condor   University of Lancaster, UK
Anne-Marie de la Haye   Université René Descartes, Paris, France
Bertjan Doosje   University of Amsterdam, The Netherlands
John Dovidio   Colgate University, USA
Naomi Ellemers   Free University, Amsterdam, The Netherlands
Samuel Gaertner   University of Delaware, Newark, USA
André Gagnon   Université de Quebec à Montreal, Canada
S. Alexander Haslam   Australian National University, Canberra, Australia
Nick Hopkins   University of Dundee, UK
John T. Jost   University of Maryland, USA
Karen Long   University of Sussex, Brighton, UK
Craig McGarty   Australian National University, Canberra, Australia
Penelope J. Oakes   Australian National University, Canberra, Australia
Stephen Reicher   University of Exeter, UK
Katherine J. Reynolds   Australian National University, Canberra, Australia
Steve Rocher   Catholic University, Louvain-la-Neuve, Belgium
Hank Rothgerber   Texas A & M University, USA
Georges Schadron   Catholic University of Lille, France
Bernd Simon   Universität Münster, Germany
Russell Spears   University of Amsterdam, The Netherlands
Charles Stangor   University of Maryland, USA
John C. Turner   Australian National University, Canberra, Australia
Ad van Knippenberg   University of Nijmegen, The Netherlands
Stephen Worchel   Texas A & M University, USA
Vincent Yzerbyt   Catholic University, Louvain-la-Neuve, Belgium

1

Introduction: The Social Psychology of Stereotyping and Group Life

Russell Spears, Penelope J. Oakes, Naomi Ellemers and S. Alexander Haslam

In recent years there has been a steady growth of interest in social psychological research into stereotyping processes, as reflected in the ever increasing number of journal articles, monographs and edited books on the subject. One obvious question readers may ask themselves then is 'Why yet another book on this topic?'. There are a number of answers to this question. Perhaps the most obvious or facetious answer is that the work presented can be seen as simply part of this upsurge of interest in this issue. A more serious and substantive justification concerns our ongoing interest in understanding the social psychological processes involved in intergroup relations, ethnocentrism and prejudice, and the important role that stereotyping plays in these social phenomena. However, many other books on this topic doubtless make similar general claims. There has to be a more specific reason to produce a *book* on the subject, rather than simply promulgating the work in journals. Rather than just providing another outlet for our work and that of colleagues the inspiration for us (the editors) in embarking on this project was partly a *response* to this very upsurge of interest in the topic, the form this has taken, what it neglects, and what an alternative view might offer.

We felt that despite the important developments and wealth of research in this field, much of this work has been funnelled in less diverse theoretical directions than might be desirable. In particular, much of the recent flux of research has tended to emphasize the information processing mechanisms responsible for producing and maintaining stereotypes, from a relatively individualistic theoretical perspective, and based on particular meta-theories of cognition. As two of our contributors put it, current stereotyping research can be seen as 'the child of a one parent family' (Worchel and Rothgerber, this volume). That is, more emphasis is laid on the cognition than the social within 'social cognition'. It would be a mistake to see the social and the cognitive as somehow separate or even conceptually separable, but what this remark conveys is that many models and approaches seem to have a rather asocial view of the social. The social often merely defines the object or target of perception, rather than the very source and medium of cognition itself. We would argue that how the social is conceptualized has profound consequences for the way cognition itself is regarded. To frame our project more positively, then, we felt there was (and is) plenty of scope to bring together work emphasizing the more social (but no less social psychological) dimensions of stereotypes, which might perhaps be better placed to explain the very social nature of the phenomena in which they are embedded (e.g., intergroup relations, ethnocentrism and prejudice).

This is not to say that work in these more 'social traditions' (which we hope to define more clearly below) has been entirely neglected. Indeed this book would not be possible if that were the case, and the collected contributions are testimony to the opposite. However, it is true to say that information processing in the social cognition mould has become the mainstream motif for research on this topic. The rationale for this book then is therefore partly to provide a meeting point for scholars attempting to provide alternatives to information processing accounts of the stereotyping process. Hopefully this volume should provide a diverse but distinctive source-book for readers interested in sampling these alternative views. At the same time it is not our aim to be inward-looking and concern ourselves with intra-disciplinary disputes for their own sake. This would take our eyes off the prize of the real world issues of concern to those outside as well as inside the discipline. To the extent that there are intra-disciplinary debates conducted within the pages of this book, it is hoped that exposing the theoretical issues will lead to better understanding of the stereotyping process. Sometimes we have to look inwards in order to be able to look outwards.

This is not an introductory textbook, nor is it a monograph. In various ways the various contributors not only advance the explanation of stereotyping, but also address or initiate debates with other often more accepted positions in the field. However, the authors have attempted to write accessibly so that familiarity with the issues and debates should be an outcome rather than a prerequisite. The volume is not a monograph in the sense that there is no one single guiding theoretical framework. There is both commonality and difference between the approaches adopted in the various chapters. However, it has been a deliberate part of this project to create a distinctive volume with different positions to those taken elsewhere, rather than provide an eclectic volume aimed at covering all the ground, and overlapping with other collections.

In this introductory chapter we try to elaborate further a number of themes that motivated work on this volume, and to show how the various chapters relate to these themes. As we have already suggested, the dominant theme which infuses and informs all others is the emphasis on a social level analysis of the stereotyping process that is at the same time psychological. In this we continue the tradition set out by Tajfel, both in his development of social identity theory, and also in his insistence that stereotypes serve social as well as cognitive functions (Tajfel, 1981a). Indeed his 1981 chapter is probably one of the most commonly cited in the present volume. In this Tajfel questions the utility of an overly or exclusively cognitive focus, that he, among others, was largely responsible for initiating with his earlier (1969a) article on the cognitive aspects of prejudice (cf. Hamilton, 1979, 1981). As we have implied, if research on stereotyping was already dominated by a 'cognitive' theoretical emphasis in 1981, this is probably just as true today (although some are retreating from this position). Our focus on the social level can be contrasted with what might loosely be termed the 'cognitive approach' (Hamilton, 1979, 1981). However the fact that the authors in this volume are still every bit as concerned with ('cognitive') psychological processes involved in stereotyping makes clear that the contrast is one of theoretical emphasis. A social level analysis of the psychological processes involved in stereotyping also implicates cognitive processes, but it does tend to ascribe a different explanatory status to them, and to the role of social context than the 'cognitive approach'. The point here is not to divide theorists or research into different camps, especially as the metatheory guiding much social stereotyping research is often implicit, or draws on both cognitive and more social themes. However, we feel it is important to characterize, if not caricature this theoretical distinction for analytic purposes, to make our own goals clearer.

In its purest form, the cognitive approach tends to view stereotyping as perception of social objects (e.g., groups) that is in principle little different to categorization and perception of other 'physical' objects. More generally, this view of 'social cognition' regards the social context as an external stimulus field. Stereotyping arises from information processing biases caused by the need to simplify this complex stimulus environment. Social categorization and associated stereotypes can thus be regarded as either constituting, or resulting from, cognitive heuristics used to deal with the richness and complexity of these stimuli. Part of the project of some advocates of the cognitive approach was to try to push the cognitive information processing mechanisms 'as far as they would go' in accounting for the development of stereotypic and prejudiced beliefs, without having to recourse to motivational principles (Hamilton, 1981; cf. Nisbett and Ross, 1980), almost as if the image of the cognitive miser which provided the central metaphor for research should be reflected in the parsimony of the theory. More recently, social cognition research has begun to consider the role of affect in relation to stereotyping and categorization processes (e.g.,

Mackie and Hamilton, 1993), but this is often treated as an incidental independent variable (e.g., mood state), and so still tends to be divorced from the more 'integral' emotional and socio-motivational processes considered within a more social level analysis (see e.g., Haslam, Oakes, Turner and McGarty, 1996). The addition of affect does not, therefore, necessarily transform the 'theoretical' nature of the cognitive approach. The cognitive approach does not of course deny that stereotyping is functional and adaptive. However in keeping with the cognitive focus, the adaptive functions of stereotyping are often seen to reflect their cognitive functions for the individual, namely simplification of the complex stimulus environment, easing information processing and so forth, functions that are adaptive in the sense that an organism whose mental load is lightened is better able to cope with that environment. As with the heuristic and biases literature, a bit of bias or error is small price to pay for general efficiency.

It is important to acknowledge that this 'heuristic' approach of social cognition has been of tremendous heuristic value. To view categorization and stereotyping as the product of everyday processes used in the perception of everyday objects introduced an important paradigm shift that moved stereotyping out of the realm of psycho-dynamic or socio-cultural pathology into the psychological mainstream. Social cognition research has also introduced a whole range of methods and paradigms for researching stereotyping that have enriched our understanding of this process. On the other hand, the theoretical message of the cognitive approach would seem to be a pessimistic one. If we can do nothing about the complexity of the social world, and the nature of our information processing systems, this would imply stereotyping and bias are more inevitable than they were when considered the preserve of prejudiced personality types, or bigoted groups and subcultures. We would agree that social categorization and stereotyping are essential and thus inevitable features of social perception and judgement. However, the conclusion is only pessimistic if stereotyping is defined at the outset as biased and pernicious. From a more social perspective this is by no means clearly the case.

Whilst cognitive processes are no less central to social level analyses (here we can think of research in the social identity and self-categorization tradition, but also other approaches included in this volume) it is still possible to make a theoretical contrast with the more cognitively analytic focus. Although it would not be denied that the categorization and perception of social objects shares much in common with the processes used to characterize physical objects (cf. Tajfel, 1969a, 1981a, b), there are also fundamental theoretical differences between these sorts of perception. First and foremost, the notion that the perceiver is implicated in and is part of the context is a key difference that needs to be theoretically acknowledged. An important feature, then, is that perception is socially structured by virtue of the involvement and interests of members of the social groupings involved. In important respects the social context is therefore constitutive of us and of how we perceive: the self is fundamentally *interested* in the social context (in both senses of the word). One of the consequences of this is the necessity for a non-individualistic theoretical approach; once the self is socially defined and the group is a part of the self, it becomes easier to consider stereotyping as part of shared group life, in which we ourselves form a part of the social context. Two immediate practical implications of this theoretical emphasis on self-reference and self-relevance are a greater interest in intergroup contexts, rather than simply the stereotyping of outgroups, and the notion that we not only habitually stereotype others, but also ourselves. This degree of self-reference and self-relevance also tends to undermine the notion of there being a fixed or objective vantage point from which to observe a single reality. The flexible and context-specific nature of the self suggest that this perspective is not necessarily even stable within the perceiver. Thus, attempts at a clear analytic separation between individual and an external social context become problematic from this theoretical perspective.

Like cognitive approaches this view sees stereotyping as functional and adaptive (as well as often dysfunctional), although often for additional or different reasons. Research in the social tradition acknowledges the organizing function of social categorization and stereotyping. However, it tends to identify more social level functions that correspond to the social bases and consequences of social stereotyping as a shared or group activity. For the cognitive approach, both the phenomenon to be explained and the explanation tend to have a cognitive regulative character. For a more social level psychological analysis, the phenomenon may be no less cognitively encapsulated, but the 'explanans', the different functions that stereotyping can serve (Tajfel, 1981a), are more likely to have socially defined origins and aims. This means that rather than seeing stereotyping as an undesirable outcome of otherwise adaptive but occasionally biased perception, we can regard it as a deliberate and purposeful activity aimed at capturing the relevant aspects of social reality for certain perceivers in certain contexts.

Describing these theoretical themes would seem abstract, even somewhat rhetorical, without relating them to the concrete data and arguments presented in the book. Let us therefore take a tour through the structure of the volume and flesh out some of the themes mentioned above. There is no easy way to structure the order of the chapters. Although some contributions draw on classical social cognition paradigms whereas others are more concerned with intergroup behaviour, an attempt to divide the chapters into such neat taxonomies might end up lending credence to the various dualisms which we view as problematic. Intergroup behaviour is impossible without social cognition, and we would argue that social cognition is closely tied up with both past and potential behavioural practice. Instead we have ordered things by beginning with chapters concerned with conceptual and definitional issues. A key argument of the book is to challenge some of the accepted notions of the stereotype and the stereotyping process.

These first chapters (2 to 6) question the way we should think about stereotypes, how they come to be, and what functions they serve. These themes are also evident in later chapters, but their central focus moves on to other concerns. Two chapters at the centre of the book (7 and 8) look at issues of stereotype formation and the reasons why we stereotype by addressing perhaps the two dominant cognitive approaches to stereotyping in social cognition. Illusory correlation has become the paradigm case of the cognitive approach, suggesting that stereotypes can form purely on the basis of an information processing bias. The following chapter also addresses the heuristic theme and addresses the cognitive miser view of stereotypes as energy saving devices. The remaining chapters of the book (9 to 13) all in various ways pursue the theme that stereotyping is structured by our group identities, and the variable social context in which we are located. We now go through the chapters highlighting some of these recurring themes.

The opening chapters begin by tackling the central conceptual issues of what stereotypes are, with questions of the causes and functions of stereotyping never far away. The classical view of stereotypes is of 'pictures in our heads' about other social or ethnic groups (Lippmann, 1922), and they are usually conceptualized as a constellation of personality traits that characterize these groups (e.g., Katz and Braly, 1933). Although research in the cognitive tradition has adopted a more process-oriented view of these perceptions and beliefs, and of how they come about and are maintained (e.g., Hamilton, 1981), it has by and large not questioned this general conceptualization of stereotypes (but see e.g., Stangor and Lange, 1994). In the opening chapter Yzerbyt et al. make a serious attempt to dig beneath the surface of stereotypes, and reveal their underlying 'essence'. Rather than defining them as mere pictures, associations or beliefs, they view stereotypes as explanatory devices linked to groups and located in intergroup relations, serving to explain and justify these social relations. Categorization, rather than being a simple perceptual activity of grouping like with like, involves more complex understandings of the nature of groups, which are closely bound up with the functions these theories serve. Once again, links with Tajfel's work on the social functions of stereotyping are central here.

This sense of stereotypes being used to justify and explain social relations raises some familiar issues of stereotypes as being biased generalizations, related to prejudice and so forth. However, to the extent that stereotyping is critically evaluated by Yzerbyt, Rocher & Schadron it is not so much that it constitutes some information processing error, which then produces false beliefs (or 'false consciousness'). If there is 'bias' here this is handed down from the social level, reflecting the group interests and perspectives involved. As in other types of ideology critique, it is important to ask what underlies stereotypes – what is the underlying dynamic that accords essentialism to categories? Yzerbyt et al. argue that system justification is an important function of the stereotyping process. In these terms, stereotypes are not simply dependent variables or outcomes, but independent variables or vehicles to achieve social or systemic ends. They function to rationalize and justify, forming a sort of 'social cement' that holds group and group relations in place. This work is also reminiscent of ideas pointing to the 'performative' effect of stereotypes (qua 'speech acts') in producing and reproducing particular social relations (cf. Condor, 1990; Graumann and Wintermantel, 1989). This contribution, therefore, clearly emphasizes the social embedding and structuring of cognition; the social precedes and helps to explain cognition and perception rather than the reverse (Tajfel, 1981a, p. 163). Moreover, these authors show that stereotyping, just like explanation generally, requires cognitive work, an observation which leads them to question certain aspects of the cognitive miser analysis of stereotyping, a theme further developed by Spears and Haslam in chapter 8.

Having displaced the issue of bias from the cognitive to the social tier, this issue is then addressed head on in the chapter by Oakes and Reynolds who consider the thorny issue of stereotype accuracy that has resurfaced in recent years (e.g., Judd and Park, 1993; Lee, Jussim and McCauley, 1995). In contrast to recent attempts to assess bias by defining and refining stereotype measurement, these authors problematize the whole conception of calibrating stereotypes. They argue that the idea that stereotypic accuracy can be measured, and related to a kernel of truth, rests to a large extent on the individualistic assumption that stereotypes are static properties of groups that can be measured, rather than dynamic properties of group relations that vary with both the social context and the perceiver's relation to that context. From a self-categorization perspective the authors argue that stereotypes reflect valid social perception attuned to the intergroup reality of the social arena. To the extent that stereotypes reflect and constitute these group realities they are not generically reactionary or flawed either in process or content terms. If stereotypes perpetuate prejudice in the interests of powerful groups, then this has to be understood in relation to the real interests of these groups and their ideologies but does not necessarily reflect a biased cognitive process. Oakes and Reynolds argue that the validity of stereotypes can better be seen in the context of this political struggle (cf. chapter 5) which is not to say that we (from our own group perspectives) are not in a position to take sides and judge whose positions we agree with and whose stereotypes we accept. Thus, in line with the arguments of the preceding chapter, stereotypes can be viewed as serving ideological functions. However, whereas Yzerbyt et al. emphasize the function of stereotypes in stabilizing and justifying particular social relations, Oakes and Reynolds' account is open to more of a social conflict analysis with the prospect that stereotypes may also play a part in *challenging* aspects of stability or the status quo. This is a position that is taken up in greater detail in chapter 5 by Reicher, Hopkins and Condor.

Meanwhile, continuing with the conceptual themes in chapter 4, Worchel and Rothgerber argue for broadening the scope of stereotyping and the stereotype concept. Noting the cognitive emphasis, they point to a number of neglected domains and dimensions of the stereotyping process, and outline a framework for analysing stereotyping from a more integrated perspective. In particular, the temporal and cultural dimensions of their analysis are important aspects that have received little attention in current research. Their work on group development shows that stereotypes are not only an important part of shared group life, but that they develop over time along with the interests and aims of the group. Once again this gives the lie to stereotypes as fixed images, and locates them in the contexts of group goals. The cultural dimension continues to emphasize the theme of sharedness at an even higher level of abstraction, reminding us that our culture itself constitutes an all-embracing group with its own *weltanschauung*. As with the social context, culture should not be seen as a backdrop against which individuals perceive and stereotype others or within which groups play out their struggles. It is also a part of ourselves, a part of a more abstract identity, which make its subtle influences all the harder to spot and thus to challenge. The relation to ideological functions discussed in the preceding chapters is therefore an important point of contact here. Although we live in a very individualistic western culture, it is part of the aim of this book to show that individualism is not a fixed property of our culture, and that collective being and behaviour are features of all social life. However, this individualism has probably contributed to a collective cultural denial of the appropriateness of perceiving people in terms of group stereotypes.

The theme of stereotype sharedness is further extended and elaborated in the next two chapters that also relate this property of stereotyping to the process of social influence. Sharedness has, from the earliest writings by Lippmann, been a defining feature of stereotypes. However, the cognitive revolution, associated refinements in measurement, and more individualistic meta-theory have changed this. Some theorists have argued that sharedness should not be included in stereotype definition (Hamilton, Stroessner and Driscoll, 1994; Judd and Park, 1993), whereas others have proposed we should distinguish individual and cultural stereotypes (Devine, 1989; Gardner, 1993). However, even this last concession would seem to neglect an important middle ground, namely those stereotypes shared by more specific social groups. As should be clear from the theme of this volume, sharedness is more than an important dimension to stereotypes, it is what makes them social – idiosyncratic 'stereotypes' are likely to be of little social consequence and to play only a marginal, if any, role in group life. Moreover, sharedness is more than a definitional issue, it is the assumption that drives collective perception and behaviour. The chapters by Reicher et al., and Haslam show that stereotyping is not just a private perceptual activity, but also a social activity in which we expect to agree with other members of our group about stereotypes that define both ingroup and relevant outgroups. When we disagree, this is a site for both struggle and social influence.

Reicher et al. continue the conceptual critique of traditional approaches at both a theoretical and a methodological level. Focusing on 'self-stereotyping' in the definition of 'Scottishness', these authors question simplistic assumptions of fixed or uniform definitions of identity or 'self-stereotypes'. In common with Worchel and Rothgerber, they highlight neglect of the both temporal and historical dimensions of stereotyping as well as the role of interpretation and meaning in relation to a social-functional analysis. Once again the debt to Tajfel (1981a) is acknowledged and his chapter forms a point of departure for an approach that aims to be true to some of his intentions. Reicher et al. show that interpretations vary widely about what the national category 'Scottish' actually means, with very different consequences for the sort of behaviour it prescribes. Whereas Worchel and Rothgerber characterized the process of interpretation, within their continuum framework, largely as an individual psychological activity, Reicher et al. go one step further and argue that interpretation of category content is a matter of social struggle and debate. The meaning of category content is not pregiven, a point made all the clearer in this fiercely partisan political context. Viewing the stereotyping process as a struggle over meaning also informs the method chosen to investigate it. The more discourse analytic approach Reicher et al. employ is well suited to getting at the dynamic rhetorical dimensions of this struggle in a way that would be more problematic for an experimental approach in which the categories are predefined and in which the temporal and historical dimension would be inadequately represented. This approach reminds us that it can be important to follow (meta)-theoretical critique through into research methods and practice, and that our choices of methods should follow theoretical questions and not drive them.

Nevertheless, the chapter by Haslam shows that the issues of stereotype sharedness, although neglected by the cognitive experimental approach, is still amenable to experimental research. Just as perceptual similarity can be seen as a judgemental effect of the stereotyping process, rather than its basis (cf. Yzerbyt et al., this volume), analogously Haslam sees shared group membership as the starting point of the stereotyping process, rather than viewing the shared nature of stereotypes as arising from common individual experiences. Once again the difference between these contrasting models of stereotype acquisition and social consensus reflect meta-theoretical differences between a relatively individualistic notion of information processing on the one hand, and the socially structured nature of perception on the other. The point Haslam makes is not to deny the possibility of common individual experience, but to argue that sharedness begins with shared self-definition, the assumed similarity of ingroup members and the expectation of agreement with them. Social influence within group boundaries is the process that regulates this agreement, and produces real and not just perceived homogeneity within these boundaries. The interactive process of influence described in this chapter, and the interactive struggle over category meaning in the previous one, thus emphasize the

the point that stereotyping is social in the *interactive* as well as in the psychological sense. Research on the issue of sharedness and social influence in the context of stereotyping is still in its relative infancy, but the self-categorization approach, which links influence to self- and other-stereotyping, offers one framework within which to make this relation explicit.

The next two chapters move on to address two issues and areas that have defined perhaps the most productive and influential paradigms of theory and research within the cognitive approach. These concern the illusory correlation explanation of stereotype formation, and the analysis of stereotype function and use in the face of cognitive load. In both cases the authors try to provide a new twist on these paradigms, once again questioning the stereotyping process as a heuristic information processing bias resorted to in the face of stimulus complexity.

In chapter 7 McGarty and De la Haye reappraise the cognitive analysis of stereotype formation provided by work within the illusory correlation paradigm. This paradigm proposes that stereotypes may form because of the distinctiveness and 'availability' of associations between infrequently occurring behaviours in infrequently encountered minority groups. A first remark, then, is that this paradigm applies primarily to the stereotyping of outgroups. However, in keeping with the thread of the social approach, and as Ellemers and van Knippenberg discuss in chapter 9, research has increasingly shown that the illusory explanation tends to break down when the perceiver is implicated in the target groups involved. Nevertheless, to the extent that this paradigm provides robust evidence of the generation of stereotypic associations where there is apparently no basis for them in the presented data, this would seem to present difficulties for any analysis claiming that stereotyping is rational, unbiased, or socially functional. McGarty and De la Haye try to demonstrate that rather than deriving from an information processing mechanism based on distinctiveness and availability, it may be possible to explain the illusory correlation effect as resulting from an attempt to make sense of the task at hand through meaningful categorical differentiation. They argue that both situational demands, and actual patterns of 'fit' present in skewed frequency distributions contribute to the illusory correlation effect. In other words it is suggested that stereotyping in the illusory correlation paradigm may result from the same meaningful sense-making categorization process argued to underlie stereotyping generally, rather than being the product of a cognitive bias.

In the following chapter Spears and Haslam attempt to apply a similar argument to the analysis of stereotyping under conditions of cognitive load. A number of studies conducted within the 'cognitive miser' framework over the last decade or so would seem to provide support for the notion that reliance on categories and stereotypes is likely to increase as a function of mental load. To the extent that this reveals categorization as primarily rendering cognition more efficient, rather than serving any direct social function, this is once again a clear example of a 'cognitive' account of stereotyping as outlined earlier. However, whilst not disputing the fact that categorization and stereotyping can be efficient, these authors question whether this is their primary function or goal. As well as questioning whether cognitive economy has more than an incidental role in the broader categorization and stereotyping process, this chapter also argues that these processes themselves may often involve considerable interpretative activity and effort. Evidence is presented for more complex (curvilinear) relationships between load and categorization and stereotyping than a cursory review of this literature might suggest. Whilst not denying the focus on cognitive processes, it is the attempt to relate these to more rational social functions which distinguishes the approaches taken in chapters 7 and 8 from the traditional cognitive approach.

This is also true of the subsequent contribution in which Ellemers and van Knippenberg reappraise a number of other cognitive paradigms that have tended to neglect aspects of the social context, and the implications for perceivers in that context. For example, the argument that information about ingroups and about outgroups is organized differently, and therefore that each type of information has its own associated cognitive structures (i.e., more attribute-based organization for outgroups, more person-based organization for ingroups) is questioned. Rather, Ellemers and van Knippenberg suggest that the cognitive organization of information may be sensitive to social context, and specifically whether information is judged in an intragroup context or an intergroup context. Similar arguments have been made about other related stereotyping phenomena such as outgroup homogeneity and ingroup heterogeneity which have tended to be seen as fairly stable features of how we structure our social worlds (e.g., Haslam, Oakes, Turner and McGarty, 1995). An approach that shows these effects are sensitive to shifts in the social context of judgement not only undermines the notion of these effects as stable cognitive structures, but also shows that perception is meaningfully structured by the reality of groups and group life.

Despite some of the more mechanistic implications of the information processing metaphor which grounds a large amount of research in the cognitive tradition, this approach has often, in fact, characterized the person as an active information interpreter and not just a passive recipient of information. Despite this acknowledgement, we have argued that there is a tendency in the cognitive tradition to regard this perceiver as an outsider, looking in on the social context. To some extent this may be a consequence of experimental methodologies where participants are presented with pre-packaged stimulus sets, a shortcoming to which Reicher et al. provide perhaps the most radical solution. However, like Haslam, Ellemers and van Knippenberg show that involvement in the social context is also open to controlled experimentation in the classic paradigms of the cognitive tradition. Involvement and identification with groups and with stereotypic attributes will affect information processing. Thus, following on from the chapter by McGarty and De la Haye, the classical pattern of distinctiveness-based illusory correlation starts to look quite different when involvement and identification with relevant groups are introduced. This is important because involvement and group identification are likely to be chronic features of those social contexts where stereotypes matter and are meaningful (Tajfel, 1982a). There is also a second issue here relating to the external validity of effects dependent on particular stimulus configurations. The 'biases' obtained may be much less robust considered across the longer time frames of continuous sampling, and with more representative 'object sampling' of the stimulus domain (cf. Brunswik, 1943; Hammond, 1978). Evidence that the illusory correlation effect may be undermined by subtle deviations from standard paradigm features is also discussed by Spears and Haslam in chapter 8.

As well as demonstrating how identification can motivate group based perceptions, Ellemers and van Knippenberg also show how social reality can constrain it. This reintroduces the theme of social reality that arises in a number of chapters, perhaps most explicitly in Oakes and Reynolds (chapter 3). Our socially motivated judgements are not only balanced by a concern for them to be accepted as valid by others (often by outgroups as well as ingroups), but we have to accept them as valid ourselves. However, we should be reminded that acceptance of stereotypic or status differences (for example) also constrain what is deemed to be valid (cf. chapter 2, this volume), so these can be contested and become the matter of social struggle and social change (Reicher et al., this volume). The fact that we appreciate that the perspectives of ingroups and outgroups may differ, and that we cannot always get away with presenting our preferred view of reality to outgroups, highlights the strategic dimensions of stereotyping and the level of meta-cognitive insight involved in its expression. The ability to frame social perception as well as action in terms of ongoing social goals forms an important dimension of a more social analysis. Others coming from more cognitive traditions have also noted the strategic as well as the motivated bases of social cognition (see e.g., Fiske, 1993a). The value of supplementing a strategic analysis with a social identity framework is that it defines the levels of self (e.g., individual vs. collective) that prescribe the appropriate strategic goals of relevance to the agents involved (Reicher, Spears and Postmes, 1995; Spears and Lea, 1994; Turner, 1991).

In chapter 10, Anastasio et al. use their common ingroup identity model to address in greater detail the question of the relation of stereotyping to self-definition, and show how this relation can transform the nature and object of stereotyping. This approach has close commonality with the social identity and self-categorization principles that permeate many of the chapters in the volume, and also extends seminal work on realistic group conflict theory. In a series of experimental and quasi-experimental studies in laboratory and field Anastasio et al. draw on the socio-motivational tendency to favour the ingroup to demonstrate that redefining the ingroup to include the outgroup in a broader ingroup category can undermine negative outgroup stereotypes. Recategorizing the self and other, ingroup and outgroup, is thus shown to mediate co-operative versus competitive relations with the outgroup. As well as underlining the flexible nature of self-definition and stereotyping, these authors also make clear that any approach to stereotyping needs to incorporate the motivational component that gives stereotyping much of its impetus in the first place. Their analysis in terms of social identity makes clear that this motivational component is social in nature in so far as it influences perception and behaviour via the social or group self.

This work emphasizes the social nature of the stereotyping process and suggests that reducing or changing the focus of (negative) stereotyping requires social reorganization ('recategorization') rather than simply changing cognitions or beliefs. Once again the social definitions in terms of categorization are the starting points that mediate the other cognitive and behavioural consequences that characterize stereotyping and discrimination. This point also addresses the apparent contradiction between an attempt to reduce negative stereotyping or 'prejudiced' beliefs about outgroups, with earlier contributions that emphasize the basic validity and pervasiveness of the stereotyping process (e.g., Oakes and Reynolds, this volume). It can be argued that the approach advocated by Anastasio et al. does not so much eliminate negative stereotyping as replace (negative) outgroup stereotyping with (positive) ingroup or self-stereotyping, and thereby move negative stereotyping to another level. That individuation is not enough to break stereotypes shows that stereotypes cannot simply be eliminated by presenting new information – they have to be replaced by other stereotypes that apply at the group level if generalization is to occur.

As in a number of the other chapters (notably Ellemers and van Knippenberg and Doosje and Ellemers), Anastasio et al., question the view of stereotypes as fixed properties of groups, or fixed pictures held by them. They are partly strategic devices serving group ends. This is evident in terms of the variable stereotype content and is expressed through variations in the importance or emphasis ascribed to aspects of stereotypic content. For example, lower status groups tend to emphasize their superiority on alternative (e.g., social) dimensions, which illustrates the way in which people use creativity strategies to make positive comparisons possible within the restrictions of a generally unfavourable social reality.

This idea is central to the following chapter (11) by Doosje and Ellemers which also examines the identity management strategies employed by low status groups to cope with their plight. These authors show that a crucial variable that moderates the effects of perceived status is the degree of identification with the group (see also chapter 9, this volume). In line with social identity principles, Doosje and Ellemers demonstrate that identification may determine whether those involved in the intergroup situation opt for more individualistic strategies of differentiating themselves from the group (cf. social mobility) or try to preserve the coherence and distinctiveness of the group, thereby offering the prospect of collective action and social change (cf. Tajfel and Turner, 1986). This research advances previous work in this tradition by stressing the role of group identification in combination with threats to identity, and by demonstrating their effect on two important dimensions of stereotyping, namely group variability judgements and self-perceived prototypicality. The same basic interaction is demonstrated across a range of studies: whereas threats to identity lead to more heterogeneous group perceptions and less self-stereotyping for low identifiers, high identifiers actually display an accentuation of intragroup homogeneity and enhancement of self-stereotyping when their identity as group members is threatened. In terms of self-stereotyping, these data clearly reveal the collectivist perceptions that arguably provide an important bridge between classical social cognition measures on the one hand, and the more behavioural domain of intergroup relations on the other. In sum, this research specifies the conditions under which the contrasting strategies outlined in social identity theory can be expected to obtain. Together with the preceding chapter it clearly shows that stereotyping should not be divorced from the behavioural domain, since it forms an important springboard for shaping social behaviour.

This movement towards more explicit consideration of stereotyping as an aspect of intergroup behaviour is further developed in the following two chapters, which focus on intergroup differentiation and discrimination between groups. Once again, and in line with social identity theory, it is argued that the cognitive process of categorization is insufficient as an explanation of ingroup favouritism, and needs to be supplemented with the socio-motivational principles and a social level of analysis. The classical social identity theory account of discrimination refers to the enhancement of social identity resulting from intergroup differentiation, and in chapter 12 Bourhis, Turner and Gagnon defend this explanation of ingroup favouritism against a recent critique. In chapter 13, Long and Spears also re-examine the utility of an analysis in terms of 'self-esteem' in the face of critics, and try to distinguish and disentangle the effects of personal and collective dimensions of this construct in the intergroup context.

If the cognitive approach can sometimes be accused of being mechanistic (cf. the computational information processor metaphor), overly mechanistic and reductionist approaches also have their social level equivalents. Interdependence theories based on rational utilitarian self-interest have been used to argue that ingroup bias can be explained simply in terms of the assumed material rewards deriving from one's group. The idea that intergroup discrimination, and the negative stereotyping that accompanies and facilitates it, can reflect material group interests is of course not new. Realistic group conflict theory makes this very point and as such provided an invaluable social level explanation of conflictual intergroup relations, prejudice and ethnocentrism that was in stark contrast to the individualistic explanations of the day (Sherif, 1967). It also provided and still provides a timely reminder of the importance of the material dimension. We would argue that materialist analyses must form an important part of any complete social psychology, reflected in the fact that social reality has been a recurring consideration throughout a number of the chapters (cf. Oakes, Haslam and Turner, 1994). Social identity theorists have always acknowledged an intellectual debt to realistic conflict theory and social identity theory was always intended to supplement rather than to replace this analysis (Tajfel and Turner, 1986). However, if social identity effects of the kind found in the minimal group paradigm were entirely explicable in terms of interdependence-relations and rational self interests associated with the group, there would be little need for an analysis in terms of social identity and social competition, or for the theory of the self and the group entailed by this approach (cf. Tajfel and Turner, 1986). Ironically, because interdependence analyses tend be contrasted with explanations that emphasize psychological identification with and interest in social group memberships, they ultimately end up being individualistic and reductionist. Bourhis et al. provide a body of compelling evidence that behaviour can be structured by our group definitions, and that ingroup favouritism is not reducible to self-interest defined in any abstract or individualistic sense. In these terms, the group is not just an external source of reward, it is an internal dimension of self-definition, which forms the source of intentional rather than constrained behaviour.

Perhaps an even more significant controversy besetting the social identity explanation of intergroup relations in recent years concerns the 'self-esteem' hypothesis – seen by many as the cornerstone of this theory. This controversy is due in no small part to the rather mixed support for the hypothesis that has emerged after at least two decades of research. In various ways this apparent failure is as much conceptual as it is empirical and can arguably be traced to both subtle and more explicit tendencies to individualize the original formulation. Accounts of social identity theory that place self-esteem as the prime motor driving intergroup differentiation, rather than being its outcome, arguably put the cart before the horse and have perhaps inevitably led to readings which reduce intergroup phenomena to a quest for self-esteem. Treating self-esteem as a personality or individual difference variable was then a logical outcome that brought this analysis full circle from its social origins back to the individualistic hydraulic mechanisms that social identity theory set out to contest.

The individualistic conception of self-esteem has been addressed by recent research, although the concept of collective self-esteem does little to counter individualism when it is conceived as an individual difference variable driving intergroup discrimination. Nevertheless, in chapter 13, Long and Spears show that it is important to consider the interactive effects of collective and personal self-esteem in the intergroup context. These authors argue that the two levels of self-esteem can have very different, if not opposing, influences on the tendency to express ingroup bias, precisely because they refer to different levels of self-definition. Whereas low collective self-esteem may be threatening to social identity in itself, being judged in terms of this category may compound this threat if it obscures the credit associated with one's own (high) sense of personal worth. These authors, therefore, propose that there may still be much mileage in analyses of self-esteem, and that reformulation and refinement of self-esteem as a predictor of intergroup differentiation is required. If the original point of social identity theory was to show that intergroup effects cannot be reduced to interpersonal or intra-psychic dynamics, the present analysis tries to take this argument a step further and show how aspects of the intergroup comparative context may actually impact on these intra- and interpersonal processes, only to rebound in terms of intergroup discrimination (cf. Tajfel, 1981a). Like the research reported by Doosje and Ellemers, this contribution suggests it is time to move on from the evaluation of basic 'main effects' hypotheses to study more complex interactive interrelationships from an integrative theoretical perspective. It also confirms that identity threat is an important predictor of classic intergroup discrimination, as well as self-stereotyping processes. In these terms, negative reactions be they encoded in stereotypes or in discrimination should not be regarded as simply automatic or gratuitous, but as responses to real intergroup tensions.

Drawing the substantive contributions to a close, in chapter 14 Simon continues with the theme of social self-definition, and indeed makes this the central focus. In so doing he explicitly questions many of the dualisms that are the source of implicit and explicit critique throughout the book. Although it is possible to distinguish an individual and collective self, the former is clearly no less socially defined, and may itself vary with the comparative context. The notion that individuals or their attributes are to be contrasted with social categories is thereby undermined, as these are themselves social categories used to meaningfully and functionally define ourselves and others in social situations. In this sense, stereotyping and self-stereotyping are not just a feature of our group life, they form an all-pervasive dimension of social perception at all levels. This analysis suggests that attempts to privilege the individual over the social self, characteristic of much individualistic social psychology, becomes essentially meaningless once this dualism is resolved.

Despite this however, Simon is aware of the powerful spectre of the 'individual' in contemporary western culture. Indeed, its impact in social psychological theory makes it clear that this level of self cannot easily be ignored. He suggests that we therefore need to acknowledge these historical and cultural pressures to see ourselves first and foremost as individuals, reminding us of the importance of a cultural dimension to stereotyping (cf. chapter 4, this volume). However, culture (and cultural difference) can be something of an empty analytic category which itself requires unpacking if it is to do any useful explanatory work. The pressures towards individualism in the west are to some extent founded in the material sphere of economic social relations given particular form by the enlightenment and the industrial revolution, spawning the liberal individualism characteristic of western society today. It is no accident that the title of Simon's chapter is reminiscent of Marx's Eleven theses on Feuerbach, which among other things contained a scathing critique of Bentham's individualism. To the extent that many of the contributions suggest the promise of a more realist approach to the study of social stereotyping, it follows that a materialist understanding of the social relations in which self-definition and stereotyping take place is also indispensable. Aspects of such an analysis are evident in chapters considering themes of system justification and ideology (2, 3 and 5), relativism and realism (3), social reality and social constraints (3, 9 and 11), and interpretation and social change (5). The final discussion chapter by Stangor and Jost in integrating the various themes, also re-emphasizes the importance of the more superordinate societal and system levels of analysis in helping us to understand the nature and functions of stereotypes. Although the contributions within this volume do not claim to move beyond a social psychological analysis, the scope for more interdisciplinary work with sociology, economics, politics, social theory, ideology critique, cultural studies (to name but a few) should be clear.

Hopefully some of the aims and themes that motivated this book should now be more apparent, and should become even more so in reading the chapters. The various contributions try to provide a social approach to stereotyping that is also fundamentally psychological. Although both cognitive and social level analyses of stereotyping can be seen as functional, we would argue that a focus on more cognitive and individual functions divorced from social reality may be problematic, at least in explaining the wider social features and effects of stereotyping. We would argue that it is the cognitive system that serves social needs and functions (in terms of selectivity in focus and level of perception for example) rather than driving the stereotyping process. If the perception of people as group members (unlike perception of people as individuals) did indeed uniquely or disproportionately reflect the limits of our information processing systems, this would seem to set us as social animals at a peculiar disadvantage in major areas of social life. An analysis of active perception is inextricably tied to social interests and goals, and is in this sense socially structured by our place in the intergroup arena.

Greater integration of the social analysis of perception, cognition, and action, helps to resolve an individual-social dualism, that tends to theorize the individual as apart from and outside the social context (see also Hardin and Higgins, 1996). Assumptions that define the individual as the real building block of social life, or the basic unit of accurate perception are also untenable from a social perspective. If the group is not only more than the sum of the individuals, but also a part of the individual, then it makes sense to perceive people as group members, and in terms of their shared stereotypic features, in situations where this is relevant. A social level analysis also helps to resolve the dualism of cognition and motivation, because at a social level these are often united by similar goals and objectives to the point where the distinction becomes hard to sustain. Social categorization and social identification are inextricably bound up with each other, and simultaneously define the self or ingroup, and thereby the outgroup or 'other'.

The perspective of our social position tied to group identities also suggests a solution to classical philosophical debates relating to issues of relativism and realism, as applied to the question of stereotyping. If stereotypes depend on a group perspective, they can be both relative to position but also real in the sense that the reality is also partly determined by our group values and interests (Spears, 1995). As we have seen, social positions, and the power relations associated with them, also include the power to impose one's own preferred stereotypic agendas on others and get these accepted (cf. chapter 2, this volume). It is important here not to confuse the product (stereotypes) with the process (stereotyping), and remind ourselves that negative stereotypes will often say more about the realities and interests of the groups holding them than their targets. It should be clear by now that we think that the nature of specific stereotypes has as much to do with the social system as with the cognitive system. A realist underpinning to the process of social perception does not therefore rule out the possibility of reification and ideological processes (e.g., system justification), but this should perhaps best be seen as a product of social relations based on power, rather than due to any inherent weaknesses or biases in our cognitive systems.

Nor does a social realist analysis mean that stereotypes or their content are inscribed in stone. As Reicher et al. argue they are open to contestation and social change, as part of the inevitable and necessary struggles over meaning in argument and practice. In other words, the actual content of stereotypes and not just the context in which they are judged, can be in a state of flux (although this is less likely where social relations are stable). That these struggles over stereotypic meaning are often struggles for political control (the self-determination of stereotypes, the freedom to be seen as individuals) again argues clearly for the social basis of stereotyping. Although it is often the majority groups with power that have the luxury not to be seen as group members (Doise, 1988; Simon, 1993), for low status minorities it may make sense to resist at a collective level, so that self-stereotyping may be both the most politically viable and psychologically healthy strategy (cf. Doojse and Ellemers, this volume). On this view, stereotyping can be evaluated as either good or bad depending on who indulges in it and what they do with the stereotypes. Thus, as well as being devices for representing reality, stereotypes should perhaps be judged in terms of the performative 'use value' of their self-ascribed or imposed contents for realizing group goals. They can be used to prefigure change as well as to interpret the world.

We do not claim of course that this book or the various contributions resolve all current debates about stereotyping. On the contrary we see this as an attempt to *open up* new debate, and we hope that the various contributions will at least stimulate thought, if not always agreement, about how to best to conceptualize and research issues of stereotyping and group life. Given the pace at which stereotyping research is advancing, we would conclude only by asserting that these contemplations are both vital and timely.

2

Stereotypes as Explanations: A Subjective Essentialistic View of Group Perception

Vincent Yzerbyt, Steve Rocher and Georges Schadron

Tel peuple a l'esprit lourd et stupide, tel autre l'a vif, léger, pénétrant. D'où cela vient-il, si ce n'est en partie, et de la nourriture qu'il prend, et de la semence de ses pères, et de ce chaos de divers éléments qui nagent dans l'immensité de l'air?

La Mettrie, 1748, 1981, pp. 100–3[1]

The show we endure year in, year out on our TV screens provides us with far too many opportunities to be shocked by the behaviour of our fellow human beings. Wars and massive killings have become a common dish on the menu of our evening news. As human beings, but even more so as social psychologists, we feel something ought to be done to better understand the unfolding of relationships between human groups. Very early indeed, social psychologists displayed a great interest for intergroup relations and the various factors affecting their dynamics. Central among the variables involved are the views that people entertain about one another: stereotypes. Stereotypes can be defined as 'shared beliefs about person attributes, usually personality traits, but often also behaviours, of a group of people' (for reviews, see Duckitt, 1992; Leyens, Yzerbyt and Schadron, 1994; Messick and Mackie, 1989; Oakes, Haslam and Turner, 1994; Stroebe and Insko, 1989). Early research tended to locate stereotypes in the minds of those who suffered frustration (e.g., Dollard, Doob, Miller, Mowrer and Sears, 1939), underwent deficient parental education (e.g., Adorno, Frenkel-Brunswick, Levinson and Sanford, 1950), or displayed a personality prone to prejudice and ethnocentrism (e.g., Rokeach, Smith and Evans, 1960). Stereotypes were nothing but errorful generalizations made by prejudiced individuals, or under abnormal circumstances. Because of their shameful status, stereotypes long remained out of mainstream social psychology. Interest in intergroup relations and in person perception were mostly disconnected from each other.

The situation changed dramatically in the late seventies when social psychologists, highly influenced by the cognitive revolution in experimental psychology, looked at stereotypes in a different light. Actualizing early insights by Lippmann (1922), Allport (1954) and Tajfel (1969a), the basic tenet of the social cognitive approach was that social information is much too complex to be dealt with satisfactorily. As a consequence, human information processors need to simplify the environment. Categorization offers a means to treat individual stimuli as instances of larger groups about which prestored knowledge is available. Looking back at 25 years of scientific endeavours, there is little doubt that what has been called the cognitive miser view of social perceivers greatly contributed to our knowledge of the way people handle information about groups and individuals (Fiske and Taylor, 1984, 1991; Hamilton, 1981; Markus and Zajonc, 1985; Stephan, 1985; Taylor, 1981b; Wyer and Srull, 1984).

In the first three sections, we argue that stereotypes do not only stand as handy devices to facilitate our dealings with a puzzling environment. Stereotypes also serve another important function: they provide subjective meaning to the world (Bruner, 1957b; Leyens, Yzerbyt and Schadron, 1992, 1994; Fiske, 1993b; Oakes and Turner, 1990; Tajfel, 1981b; Yzerbyt and Schadron, 1994). In our view, stereotypes work as *enlightening gestalts*; they supply perceivers with extra information by building upon a rich set of interconnected pieces of data. Moreover, stereotypes comprise more than the list of attributes that help describe a particular social category. They also, and perhaps most importantly, include the underlying explanation that links these attributes together (Schadron and Yzerbyt, 1993; Yzerbyt and Schadron, 1994, 1996).

As we will show, the explanation view has long intruded the research on person and group perception. While people may well view others in terms of simple lists of attributes, they more likely represent them in terms of well-organized sets of features. We examine the work on hypothesis confirmation and suggest that perceivers build up a causal scenario that allows them to integrate incoming information according to their specific views about people and groups. We also ascertain the relevance of an explanation view for the issue of inconsistency management and provide some new data from our laboratory clarifying the impact of the explanatory activity in the maintenance of stereotypes.

In the following sections, we outline our subjective essentialistic view of stereotypes and propose that stereotypes enable perceivers to understand why the instances of the category are what they are and thus justify their being treated the way they are (Yzerbyt and Schadron, 1994). The first idea, what is it that makes the group a group, may be linked to the idea of subjective essentialism, as it has recently been developed by some cognitive psychologists. The second one, how to account for what happens to the group, refers to the function of rationalization of the stereotypes. We will argue that these two ideas are, in fact, highly interconnected.

We first review the current debate on categorization in cognitive psychology, showing that the validity of classic similarity approaches is largely questioned and that the use of essentialistic theories is now offered as an alternative account for categorization learning and use. Turning back to the field of stereotyping, we then examine a series of theoretical (and sometimes old) contributions showing the importance of essentialistic explanations in social categorization. Next, we suggest that a functional view of explanations as they underlie stereotypic beliefs has come of age. We argue that stereotypes play a key role in the rationalization of the existing social order. We then spell out possible differences between essentialistic versus non-essentialistic categorization. We examine how subjective essentialism relates to group perception phenomena such as beliefs about group entitativity or group homogeneity and prejudice. We suggest a continuum of social categorization and conclude by proposing a syndrome of essentialistic categorization. Our final section brings subjective essentialism and the rationalization function of stereotypes together. Drawing again on research insights in the field of person perception, we suggest a series of mechanisms that may contribute to create and perpetuate existing social theories. We also offer empirical evidence that an essentialistic definition of social groups may polarize observers' impressions and thus lead them to neglect situational constraints that impinge on the groups.

1   Lessons from Impression Formation Research

When Solomon Asch (1946) launched his research on impression formation, his goal was very clear. As a faithful gestaltist, he thought that the processes by which people perceive others needed to be understood even if such mental constructions proved to be globally inaccurate. Asch asked his subjects to imagine that a short list of traits belonged to a real person. Subjects were asked then to produce an open description of the person and to checkmark one of two traits in a series of pairs. Using this simple paradigm, Asch managed to demonstrate two of the most robust effects in social psychology namely the primacy effect and the centrality effect. The primacy effect corresponds to the fact that the initial traits in a list influence the general meaning more than the final traits. Asch either presented a list comprising positive traits in the beginning and negative traits in the end or the same list in the reverse order. For both lists, the resulting impression was somewhat positive but, more importantly, the impression was more positive for the first than for the second order. The centrality effect refers to the fact that some traits in a given list may more or less influence the impression. So, for instance, replacing the trait 'warm' in Asch's list by its opposite 'cold' had a huge impact on the final impression. In comparison, using 'polite' instead of 'blunt' changed the impression to a lesser extent.

For Asch, these effects stem from the active construction of an impression by observers as they gather information. His interpretation was soon to be challenged. In 1954, Bruner and Tagiuri launched the concept of implicit theories of personality (ITP) to indicate that people possess a working knowledge of the way various traits of personality go together. So, for example, if a person is warm, then that person is also generous. In this associationistic view, people would form impressions on the basis of trait covariation (Wishner, 1960). With the advent of new statistical tools, researchers examined the ITP from a somewhat different perspective. The main idea was to uncover global underlying dimensions that would organize the set of personality traits. Most well-known is the work by Rosenberg and colleagues using Multidimensional Scaling techniques (Rosenberg, Nelson and Vivekanathan, 1968; Rosenberg and Sedlak, 1972). Subjects rated the extent to which two traits are similar and the resulting matrix is then submitted to MDS. Typically, two evaluative, almost orthogonal dimensions emerged: one concerned sociability and the other intelligence. This dimensional view seemed quite an improvement over the associationistic view. It was now possible to explain the centrality effect as uncovered by Asch on the basis of the composition of the list. A pair of traits would be central to the extent that they are extreme on a dimension not touched on by the other traits in the list. So, for instance, the traits warm and cold both concerned sociability whereas the remaining traits pertained to intelligence (for an insightful presentation, see Brown, 1986).

Anderson and Sedikides (1991; Sedikides and Anderson, 1994) recently challenged both the associationistic and the dimensional views of implicit theories of personality. According to their typological view, people think about others in terms of person types. Each person type comprises several personality traits and the knowledge of a given trait within a person type can be used to infer the presence of other traits in the same person type. In other words, people perceive traits within person types to be interconnected through causal bonds. Anderson and Sedikides (1991) presented their subjects with a list of personality traits. The task consisted of grouping the traits into piles according to their degree of similarity. Cluster analysis was then used to uncover the various person types underlying subjects' solutions. Let us make things concrete with a simple example. One person type identified by Anderson and Sedikides is Extroverted, defined as being *ambitious, outgoing, enthusiastic, energetic and confident*. Although the trait *confident* belongs to the cluster Extroverted, the average correlation between *confident* and the other members of the type is lower than a number of alternative traits, such as *intelligent, humorous, friendly, warm, helpful or pleasant.* Still, compared to its competitors, the trait *confident* performs better on a series of important criteria. To take but one significant measure, subjects who read the four strong members of the type, that is, *ambitious, outgoing, enthusiastic and energetic*, more often generate the trait *confident* than any of its competitors. Clearly then, this approach highlights the fact that first-order correlations are not always a reliable predictor of the link between a trait and a person type. A typological view thus offers an ideal means to understand how two apparently inconsistent traits can be assigned to the same individual. Although laziness correlates negatively with intelligence, both these two traits prove quite compatible with our view of an artist. The type 'Artist' makes these two characteristics appear consistent because, we would argue, a general explanation makes it possible to reinterpret the semantic clash between these two traits.

The question remains as to what extent each perceiver brings in an idiosyncratic view concerning the particular pieces of information collected about a specific target person. Is it the case that people uniquely combine different pieces of information, thereby building up different impressions of the same target? Park, DeKay and Kraus (1994) recently addressed this question in a study that relied on Kenny's variance partitioning technique (Kenny and LaVoie, 1984). The basic idea of the study is fairly simple. Subjects read a series of behaviours performed by five target people in five different settings, that is, a total of 25 behaviours. In the 'unknown' condition, the 25 behaviours were randomly ordered and subjects were left to think that each behaviour was performed by a different person. Subjects' task was to rate each behaviour on 10 trait dimensions. In the 'known' condition, subjects were given the same 25 behaviours but, this time, the 5 behaviours performed by the same target person were always presented as a set. After writing their impression of the target person on the basis of the set of five behaviours, subjects then rated each behaviour on the 10 trait dimensions and, finally, gave their global rating of the person on the same 10 traits before moving to the next target person. There are two central questions. First, do subjects combine the behavioural information in such a way that targets appear more consistent across situations in the 'known' than in the 'unknown' condition? In other words, are ratings concerning the same target more consistent when the target's identity is known? Second, do perceivers form idiosyncratic views about target people? In other words, is it the case that different subjects' ratings of the same target person are different from one another? Park et al.'s (1994) data fully support both predictions and confirm the idea that perceivers construct different models of what the target person is like. Supposedly, these models enable explanations of events in a manner parallel to narrative explanations (Fiske, 1993b; Read, 1987; Sedikides and Anderson, 1994).

The work by Anderson and Sedikides (1991) and Park et al. (1994) stresses the importance of perceivers' naive theories and the role of causal connectedness in impression formation. Of course, due to the specific methodology adopted by these authors, it is not really the case that perceivers find themselves confronted with inconsistent sets of information. As it turns out and without the benefit of current methodological and sophisticated statistical tools, Asch had already tackled the issue of inconsistency and demonstrated people's extraordinary ability to construct theories in order to explain the association between various apparently inconsistent traits. In one variation of his classic set of studies, Asch (1946) confronted subjects with only three of the six traits used to demonstrate the primacy effect. After having written the description sketches and chosen the traits on the checklist, subjects were given the remaining three traits as applying to a new person and asked for a new description and for another choice of traits. No difficulty seemed to emerge in building up these two (very different) impressions. Asch then told his subjects that the six traits actually belonged to the same person and requested a new impression. Integration of the entire set of information seemed very difficult. Most likely, perceivers who integrated the two sets of three traits could not reconcile the two models into one (Burnstein and Schul, 1982). At this stage, it is important to remember how easily subjects built up an impression when they were told right away that all traits belonged to the same person (Asch, 1946). In a subsequent piece of research, Asch looked at the various strategies people rely upon to reconcile the inconsistent information contained in a description (Asch and Zukier, 1984). He was able to show that people easily explain how a target person may possess two semantically opposed traits such as cheerful and gloomy. For instance, perceivers select one trait to stand as the focal feature of the person and the other trait as only complementing the global picture (Park et al., 1994). Asch and Zukier's (1984) findings directly speak to perceivers' fantastic ability to reconcile apparently inconsistent pieces of information.

2 From Persons to Groups

The various efforts described above concern research on impression formation, a topic that is traditionally seen as separate from stereotyping. We would like to argue that a similar view gains credence in research on stereotypes. We therefore document the evolution of theoretical perspectives from purely associationistic to a more schematic conception of stereotypic knowledge.

The oldest methods for studying stereotype content mainly relied on the idea of association. Influenced by Katz and Braly's (1933) seminal work on the measurement of stereotypes, social psychologists devoted a lot of time and energy to examining those features that subjects saw to be highly correlated with specific groups of people. The royal path to a better understanding of inter-group perceptions was to uncover the co-occurrence of a given feature and a group. To be sure, we have learned a great deal from the checklist approach. For instance, the successive waves of research among Princeton students allowed us to grasp the representational concomitants of historical events (Gilbert, 1951; Karlins, Coffman and Walters, 1969; Katz and Braly, 1933).

Despite its obvious merits and its continuing success, the checklist approach now tends to be complemented by a number of newer techniques building on what may be called the typological view of stereotypes. We owe the first empirical work in this perspective to Brewer and colleagues (Brewer, Dull and Lui, 1981). These authors verified that their American subjects distinguish elderly persons in 'grandmotherly', 'elder statesman' and 'senior citizen' types. In one study, subjects received a stack of photographs representing elderly people of the three types. Their task was to sort the pictures into what they thought were appropriate groups. Subjects' sortings closely corresponded to the authors' a priori classification. In a second study, subjects examined six clusters of three photographs forming either meaningful or non-meaningful subsets. Specifically, all pictures in a given subset belonged to the same type or each subset comprised one picture from each type. Subjects were provided with an adjective checklist and asked to assess the various attributes that corresponded to each subset. Results indicate that meaningful subsets led subjects to produce richer and more consensual descriptions than non-meaningful subsets. Brewer and colleagues (1981) built upon these findings as well as related information processing data to argue that psychologically meaningful cognitive representations of groups are likely to be organized into basic level categories, a level of abstraction below that of general categories such as age, race or sex (Deaux and Lewis, 1984; Taylor, 1981b). To summarize, people seem to rely on a series of types to infer the presence of other, related, characteristics (Devine and Baker, 1991). Moreover, research also indicates that stereotypes of groups or social roles, being richer and more concrete, are generally preferred to types based on abstract personality traits (Andersen and Klatzky, 1987; Andersen, Klatzky and Murray, 1990; Brewer and Lui, 1989; Grant and Holmes, 1981).

To recap, the research on impression formation witnessed a shift from associationistic views to typological views. The main feature of the latter perspective is the role of the relationships between the components of the schematic representation. We argue that a similar view has come of age in the field of stereotyping. Without denying the importance of looking at the discrete characteristics comprising stereotypes of various social groups, we promote the idea that stereotypes are better seen as an interconnected set of components. A key aspect of a typological conception of stereotypes is the importance of the coherence among the various pieces of information comprising the stereotype (Fiske, 1993b; Yzerbyt and Schadron, 1994, 1996; see also, Worchel and Rothgerber, this volume).

3 Stereotypes as Explanatory Frameworks

The traditional view that stereotypes are labels associated with a list of features has generated an enormous amount of research (for reviews, see Hamilton and Sherman, 1994; Stangor and Lange, 1994). We now have evidence aplenty to show that people's stereotypic beliefs influence the encoding and the retrieval of information (Darley and Gross, 1983; Bodenhausen, 1988; Bodenhausen and Lichtenstein, 1987; Kunda and Sherman-Williams, 1993; Sagar and Schofield, 1980; Srull and Wyer, 1989; Wyer and Srull, 1980, 1981, 1989). Without denying the importance of these findings, our explanation view of stereotypes stresses a somewhat different aspect of confirmation processes. We argue that the internal causal structure of stereotypes plays a crucial role in guiding explanation and attribution processes. That is, people try to integrate the individual pieces of information in order to come up with a coherent story about the target person or the group and, in so doing, they quite heavily rely on their naïve theories to organize incoming information (e.g., Deaux and Emswiller, 1974; Duncan, 1976; Taylor and Jaggi, 1974; Jaspars and Hewstone, 1984). In sum, stereotypes serve as enlightening gestalts (Fiske, 1993b; Leyens, Yzerbyt and Schadron, 1994; Yzerbyt and Schadron, 1994).

Several lines of research illustrate the importance of the explanatory activity in stereotyping. Wittenbrink, Gist and Hilton (1994) recently identified two major causal models that white Americans hold about African Americans. In the first model, African Americans are seen as being responsible for their current lot. An absence of motivation and proper values stands as the major reason for their being unable to achieve success in society. The second model states that structural disadvantages, that is, lack of job opportunities, inadequate education system, and so forth result in economic failure and lower social status. Whereas the first models characterizes African Americans as the perpetrators of racial problems, the second model sees them as the victims of discrimination. Importantly, although a series of features of African Americans may be present in both models, the underlying account is likely to provide them with a very different meaning. So, for instance, African Americans may be characterized as uneducated people in both models. Still, the 'perpetrator view' emphasizes the intellectual and motivational limitations of African Americans and so questions the impact of better school environments in critical neighbourhoods. In sharp contrast, the 'victim view' insists on the objective potential of African American people and stresses the shortcomings of public investment in the school system. To test the idea that people would rely on their stereotypic conceptual knowledge to construe the incoming information, Wittenbrink presented subjects with a jury decision task about an interracial assault. Clearly, high and low prejudiced subjects interpreted the evidence in line with the perpetrator or the victim view, respectively. As expected, subjects' judgement of guilt and sentence reflected their level of prejudice. In our opinion, the specific contribution of Wittenbrink's study, however, lies in its reliance on open descriptions which were then coded for locus of causality. Subjects made up very different stories depending on their specific views about African Americans.

Anderson and colleagues (Anderson, 1982, 1983; Anderson, Lepper and Ross, 1980) also demonstrated the impact of explanation on stereotype maintenance, something they call belief perseverance (see also, Koehler, 1991). For instance, Anderson et al.'s (1980) subjects were given two detailed case histories of fire-fighters suggesting that risk-seeking behaviour predicted either future success or failure. When informed that the descriptions were fictitious, subjects continued to believe in the relationship they had been presented with. Interestingly, half of the subjects were asked to generate causal explanations for the scenarios given to them, the others were not. Subjects who engaged in causal processing showed more belief perseverance than subjects who did not perform this kind of cognitive work. One important asset of Anderson's work is that both theories linking risk preference to job performance as a fire-fighter were provided to subjects who knew little or nothing about this issue. The findings underscore the impressive ability of theories to self-perpetuate if they are adequately backed up by an explanatory framework (Anderson, Lepper and Ross, 1980; Ross, Lepper and Hubbard, 1975). Anderson (1983) demonstrated that concrete data, that is, case histories, were much more efficient in feeding causal scenarios than abstract data, that is, statistical information, despite their obvious lack of reliability.

Not surprisingly, the explanatory activity is most tangible when people are presented with a person who combines seemingly conflicting features (Asch and Zukier, 1984). When a target individual turns out to belong to several social groups, is it the case that attributes are simply added up to a growing list of features or do people generate new explanations and come up with original materials to account for the surprising mix? In an ingenious set of experiments, Kunda and colleagues (Kunda, Miller and Claire, 1990) showed that people are capable of forming a unified impression of a person who belongs to a surprising combination of social categories. Subjects were asked to write a description of their expectations about a person who belonged to one of two constituent categories (such as Harvard-educated and carpenter; blind and lawyer) or to both categories. Results supported Kunda et al.'s (1990) hypothesis that people would engage in causal reasoning and rely on broad world knowledge in order to reconcile the apparent contradictions. A specific finding was that subjects often came up with emergent properties not contained in the definition of the constituent categories. So, for instance, some subjects perceived a Harvard-educated carpenter as being non-conformist and non-materialistic, two features mentioned neither for a Harvard-educated person nor for a carpenter.

Recent work on subtyping also exemplifies the role of explanation in the maintenance of stereotypes. Interestingly, the cognitive approach to the issue of stereotype change very quickly relied on the typological view of stereotypes (Gurwitz and Dodge, 1977; Hewstone, Macrae, Griffiths, Milne and Brown, 1994; Johnston and Hewstone, 1992; Rothbart, 1981; Weber and Crocker, 1983; for a review, see Hewstone, 1994). The classic pattern of results is that the concentration of stereotype inconsistent information in a few members of the target group leads perceivers to form a subtype. As a result, the stereotype of the group as a whole is hardly affected. In contrast, when inconsistent information is distributed over several if not all of the members of the target group, subjects take the contradictory evidence into account. Judgements reveal a much more important modification of their stereotype of the group. The bottom line of this kind of research is that very inconsistent members of an otherwise consistent group are encapsulated into a subtype and seen as irrelevant to the rest of the group. One important question remains however as to the nature of the processes involved in subtyping. More recent work by Kunda and Oleson (1995) provides additional insight in this regard. These authors stress the role of construal processes, a strategy highly similar to what we call explanatory activity. According to Kunda and Oleson (1995), encounters with a deviant member of a group should not lead to generalization at the level of the group stereotype if other available information allows the perceiver to account for the inconsistency. The authors use the stereotype of lawyers, perceived by control subjects to be highly extroverted. In one condition, subjects are presented with a brilliant *introverted* lawyer. Compared to the control subjects, these subjects generalize to the group as a whole and evaluate lawyers to be less extroverted. In two other conditions, subjects also learn that the introverted lawyer works in a small or in a large firm. Importantly, pretests show that the size of the firm is totally unrelated to lawyers' introversion/extroversion. This time, however, no generalization takes place. Compared to the control subjects, subjects in these two conditions do not rate lawyers in general as being less extroverted. Additional data collected by Kunda and Oleson (1995) suggest that the size of the firm, an initially neutral piece of information, is used by subjects in order to account for the introversion of the target person and to stick to their view of lawyers as being extroverted people. Results such as these show that perceivers maintain their stereotype even in the face of inconsistent information. More importantly, they suggest that stereotype maintenance depends on the existence of a subjectively valid explanation (Crocker, Hannah and Weber, 1983; Kulik, 1983).

The lesson from subtyping research is that encounters with deviant members of a social category affect the expectations to the extent that a strong connection is forced between the information presented to the perceiver and the explanation that underlies group membership in the perceiver's mind. In other words, we suspect that not being able to rely on a biased account of the newly encountered evidence will force the perceiver to take stock and modify whatever stereotypic view is entertained. To the extent that explanation is at the heart of what it means to hold a stereotypic view, we would argue that accounting for the presence of inconsistent information must be a time- and energy-consuming job. As a consequence, people will likely maintain their stereotypes in the face of inconsistent information to the extent that they can manage to reconcile it with their a priori views.

In a recent study, we addressed these important issues using a paradigm that combined Kunda and Oleson's procedure and more traditional cognitive business methodology (Yzerbyt, Coull and Rocher, 1995). Specifically, we decided to expose our subjects to a deviant member of a stereotyped category under distraction versus no-distraction conditions. We selected the category of computer engineers because it seemed highly associated with the idea of introversion. In contrast to Kunda and Oleson, subjects in all conditions were presented with a successful computer engineer who was attributed a number of consistent (i.e., rational), inconsistent (i.e., extroverted), and neutral (e.g., married) characteristics. Information about the target person was conveyed by means of a two-minute informal interview played on audio tape. Half of the subjects had to play a very simple video game on a computer screen while listening to the interview. The remaining subjects just listened to the tape. Immediately after the interview, half of the subjects had to rate the computer engineers in general on a series of personality traits including extroversion–introversion. The other half rated the target person. An additional group of subjects provided us with a baseline for the category of computer engineers.

Results supported our hypotheses (see figure 2.1). Whether distracted or not, subjects who rated the target person proved sensitive to the inconsistency of the information that was presented to them. This result indicates that our distracted subjects were not impaired to the point that they did not encode the relevant target information. Indeed, additional analyses indicated that there were no differences in recall of the target information between distraction and no-distraction subjects. Our main hypothesis concerned the evaluation of the group as a whole. As expected, non-distracted and baseline subjects rated the group in a similar way. This result is totally compatible with Kunda and Oleson's findings and suggests that non-distracted subjects were able to reconcile the inconsistent information with the stereotype of the category as a whole. Finally, compared to the non-distracted, subjects who were presented with the distracting video game rated the category as a whole to be less introverted. These findings are congruent with the view that stereotype maintenance is resource-consuming and that distraction prevents subjects from explaining inconsistent information away, thereby stressing the crucial role of explanatory activity in stereotype maintenance. In addition, our results suggest that one would be well-advised not to take the cognitive economy metaphor too literally (Spears and Haslam, this volume).

To be sure, people have been shown to benefit greatly from the existence of such devices as stereotypes in their dealing with incoming information (Macrae,

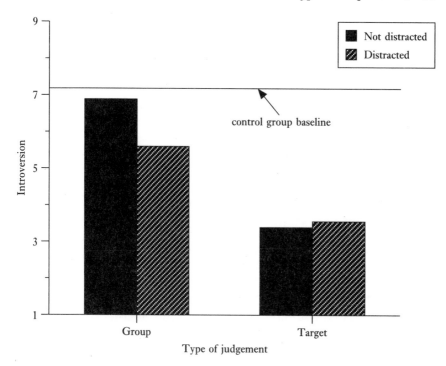

Figure 2.1 Judgement of introversion as a function of type of judgement and level of distraction.

Milne and Bodenhausen, 1994). However, the presence of a stereotypic label inconsistent with the remainder of the information may force subjects into resolving internal inconsistencies and finding appropriate explanations. As a result, the presence of a stereotypic label, compared to its absence, may actually increase the demands on the cognitive system and deteriorate performance on concurrent tasks. Yzerbyt, Rocher and Coull (1995) recently tested this hypothesis and confirmed that the provision of a stereotypic yet inconsistent label greatly impaired subjects' performance on a probe reaction time measure. Such a perspective has implications for the issue of stereotype change and one promising line of research for stereotype alteration would be to underline the link between inconsistent information and the explanation underlying group membership.

In our opinion, researchers should consider abandoning the simplistic view of stereotypes as simple lists of attributes and take more seriously the idea of stereotypes as well-organized theoretical structures. Interestingly, recent work on categorization has been dealing with related issues. In the next section, we review the current arguments relating to this issue proposed by cognitive psychologists. As it turns out, a number of conceptual and empirical advances now stress the importance of explanation in object categorization. Similarity of surface characteristics is denied its primary role in the categorization process. Instead, object features are given a collaborative role in the organization of semantic memory along with perceivers' explanatory theories. In the fifth section, we examine the implications of a subjective essentialistic approach to categorization for research on stereotypes and stereotyping.

4   Categorization: From Similarity to Essence

The work on stereotyping and social categorization owes much to the research endeavours of a number of cognitive psychologists. For instance, most social psychologists would agree that the work by Rosch (1978) allowed them to re-examine with great success prevailing conceptions about person perception (Andersen and Klatzky, 1987; Brewer, 1988; Cantor and Mischel, 1977, 1979; Fiske and Taylor, 1984, 1991; Taylor, 1981b; Turner, Hogg, Oakes, Reicher and Wetherell, 1987). Similarly, insights of a number of cognitive psychologists about the role of exemplars in semantic memory were quickly adopted by social psychologists in order to challenge the dominant prototype model (Linville, Fischer and Salovey, 1989; Linville, Salovey and Fischer, 1986; E. R. Smith and Zaràte, 1990). We think that the ongoing debate in the cognitive literature points to a new conception of the categorization process (Komatsu, 1992; Murphy and Medin, 1985; Medin, 1989; Medin, Goldstone and Gentner, 1993; Medin and Ortony, 1989; Wattenmaker, Nakamura and Medin, 1988) and that the time is ripe for social psychologists to take advantage of these insights (Corneille and Leyens, 1994; Yzerbyt and Schadron, 1994).

According to the Roschian perspective of categorization, the classical view that concepts have necessary and defining features needed to be challenged for a variety of reasons. For one thing, it proved to be impossible to specify the list of features that define psychologically meaningful categories. Wittgenstein (1953) made this argument very vividly when he used the example of games. One simply cannot establish a definitive set of characteristics that only games would have and the absence of which would indicate that the object to be categorized is not a game. A second problem is the fact that some members of a given category seem to be better representatives of the category than others. So, for instance, a cow seems to be a better example of a mammal than a dolphin. A classical view of categories cannot account for such typicality effects. Finally, the fact that members may be difficult to assign to a category is hardly compatible with the classical view of categories in which the membership is simply decided by looking for the presence of defining features.

As it turns out, the above effects can easily be accounted for by the probabilistic view of categories which holds that categories are 'fuzzy' or 'ill-defined' concepts (for a review, see Smith and Medin, 1981). In their pioneering work, Rosch and Mervis (1975) showed that category members were perceived to be better representatives of a category to the extent that they possessed a high number of characteristic features. Characteristic features are defined as those features that most, but not necessarily all, members of the category possess. Abandoning a strict definitional conception of categories, the probabilistic view of categories argues that people form abstract summaries of the category, prototypes, and that prototypes are the basis for categorization. People decide about category membership on the basis of the similarity between the object and the various prototypes stored in memory.

Closer scrutiny of the probabilistic view indicates that it tends to stress the role of the perceived object and to downplay the importance of the perceiver. In other words, the external world is ruling much of the categorization process. An example will help clarify this point. People see birds and mammals the way they do because the members of each of these two categories share a high number of attributes and the overlap between categories remains minimal. The argument here is that the members of one category are similar to one another and different from members of another category in some observer-independent sense (Medin and Ortony, 1989). A cow and a horse are members of the same category, mammals, because they are the 'same' in an absolute sense. Even the exemplar view, the most successful competitor to the prototype view, gives the external world the central role. Specifically, the exemplar view states that perceivers categorize not on the basis of similarity to an abstract prototype that summarizes the evidence relevant for the category but on the basis of the similarity to any specific member using the entire set of category members stored in memory. In other words, the exemplar view holds that perceivers categorize a new instance by comparing it with stored knowledge and choose that category which contains the closest resembling exemplar (Hintzman, 1986; Medin and Shaffer, 1978).

By showing that categories can be created on the basis of pragmatic goals, Barsalou (1987) introduced the idea that perceivers' goals can shape the categorization process. So, for example, subjects seem quite capable of sorting out the kind of objects that one would like to give as birthday presents. Smith and Zárate (1992) similarly elaborated the exemplar view by arguing that the set of exemplars that are activated in order to categorize a specific instance are highly sensitive to the transient goals of the perceiver. While these two approaches question the imbalance of the dominant views in favour of the external world and give perceivers some importance in the categorization process, they hardly address the issue of the underlying comparison process: how is similarity between a new object and a prototype or a set of exemplars computed? Indeed, turning back to our mammals example, a real problem emerges when one questions the selection of features underlying the decision about membership. Why is it that these features instead of others were selected for consideration (Murphy and Medin, 1985)? Strictly speaking, any two objects can always be made to differ from one another. All it takes is to select the right set of features. Conversely, any two objects can be made similar if the appropriate set of features is retained. Last but not least, similarity is highly sensitive to the comparative context (Tversky, 1977; Tversky and Gati, 1978). So, Austria is seen to resemble Sweden more than Hungary or Poland. In contrast, Austria looks more similar to Hungary than to Sweden or to Norway. As cognitive psychologists now widely recognize, what this all means is that the (perceptual) similarity of surface characteristics as a basis for category coherence is most slippery and unconstrained (Medin, Goldstone and Gentner, 1993).

Taking the above problems into account, Medin (1989; Medin, Goldstone and Gentner, 1993) suggests that we would be better off considering similarity as a product rather than a cause of conceptual coherence. Two things are seen to be similar because perceivers have a good theory that justifies seeing them as members of the same category. Such a theory would work at the level of deeper features of the category members and would explain why the surface characteristics are the ones that people witness. Such a knowledge-based categorization process not only stresses the role of the perceiver as opposed to a strict objectivist position but it also highlights the importance of conceptual coherence in semantic knowledge. In one illustrative study, Medin and Shoben (1988) found that people rated the terms 'white hair' and 'grey hair' to be more similar than 'grey hair' and 'black hair' but the terms 'white clouds' and 'grey clouds' to be less similar than 'grey clouds' and 'black clouds'. Supposedly, the presence of a theory of ageing in the first case and a theory of weather in the second accounts for the findings (Medin and Shoben, 1988). Thus similarity does not provide conceptual coherence but theories do. The basic idea here is that categories seem to be organized around an underlying explanation that links the features together (Wattenmaker, Nakamura and Medin, 1988).

Despite his questioning the status of similarity, Medin (1989) argues against throwing the baby out with the bath water. Were we to eliminate the notion of similarity, categories would be explained strictly in terms of perceivers' theories. Obviously, we would be left in no better condition as far as the constraint problem is concerned. One way out of this problem is to give similarity the important role of constraining our theories (Frazer, 1959). In this sense, theories and similarity join together and guide the categorization process. The interplay between surface and deeper features leads us to the notion of psychological essentialism. According to Medin (1989, p. 1476), 'people act as if things (e.g., objects) have essences or underlying natures that make them the things that they are'. In other words, we function on the basis of surface level similarities as if some deeper properties of the object supports the decision process. When people adopt a psychological essentialistic stance, their working hypothesis is that things that look alike tend to share deeper properties. We directly build upon this work to argue for a subjective essentialistic view of social categories.

5 Subjective Essentialism in Early Stereotyping Research

'Stereotypes are not objectionable because they are generalisations about categories; such categorisations are valuable when they are true. Stereotypes are not objectionable because they are generalisations that have been proven false; for the most part we do not know whether they are true or false – in their probabilistic forms. Stereotypes are not objectionable because they are generalisations acquired by hearsay rather than by direct experience; many generalisations acquired by hearsay are true and useful. What is objectionable about them? I think it is their ethnocentrism and the implication that important traits are inborn for large groups.' (Brown, 1965, p. 181)

Minimizing the significance of some of the most debated features of stereotypes, Brown's quote suggests that the usual evil aspects of stereotypes may not be so detrimental after all. What is seen as being more important, however, is that stereotypes entail a very special aspect: they link specific attributes to the very essence of what people are. A strong concern for essentialism in the stereotyping area can be traced back to Walter Lippmann, the father of the concept of stereotype. Lippmann not only anticipated the major developments of later research, he also outlined the danger of linking certain kinds of explanation to specific stereotypic contents. The clearest example of this view can be found in a debate about the relative role of nature versus nurture in the development of intelligence. Indeed, Lippmann strongly disputed Terman's (1923) use of intelligence tests. Of course, he worried about the validity of the measure itself. More importantly, however, his fears concerned Terman's conception about innateness. According to Lippmann, the power of the tester becomes dangerously exaggerated if the measure of intelligence is used to rank every member of the society and if the hereditary explanation is thought to justify the ranking once and for all. 'If the impression takes root that these tests really measure intelligence, that they constitute a sort of last judgement on the child's capacity, that they reveal "scientifically" his predestined ability, then it would be a thousand times better if all the intelligence testers and all their questionnaires were sunk without warning in the Sargasso Sea' (Lippmann, 1922, quoted in Gould, 1981). As a matter of fact, Terman (1916) considered education to be of little help in modifying people's level of intelligence and agreed with the idea that differences between various social groups are biologically based. Claiming that Indians, Mexicans or blacks all suffered from an hereditary deficit, he expressed explicit regrets that there was 'no possibility of convincing society that they should not be allowed to reproduce although from a eugenic point of view they constitute a grave problem because of their unusually prolific breeding' (pp. 91–2). To sum up, before empirical research on stereotypes even began, Lippmann was already warning against the terrible consequences of prejudice when it is backed up by a powerful explanation.[2]

The prominent advocator of the socio-functional perspective on stereotypes, Sherif, also alluded to the notion of essence. In his book *An Outline of
Social Psychology*, he invites students of prejudice to pay attention to what
he calls the 'substantive mode of mentality'. As Sherif (1948, p. 361) notes,
'by substantive mode of mentality, we mean the tendency to account for or
describe events (social and otherwise) in terms of the "essence" of things
instead of in terms of related processes. The great mass of bourgeois respectability shows a tendency to deal with human and social events in terms of an
eternal "human nature", qualities inherent in this or in that group . . . This
unscientific substantive mentality is clearly indicated in the Middletown attitudes concerning masculine and feminine characteristics. In spite of the facts
that the masculine and feminine roles and statuses have actually undergone considerable changes in the United States since the Revolution, the prevailing
conceptions of men and women are held to be *inherent*, immutable qualities of
the sexes' (emphasis in original). A few years later, Allport (1954), in his classic
treatise on prejudice, similarly stresses the role played by essential beliefs in
the generation of prejudice. Presumably, a belief in essence develops because
perceivers fall prey to 'the principle of least effort'. So, for instance, Allport
(1954, p. 173) mentions that 'there is an inherent "Jewishness" in every Jew.
The "soul of the Oriental", "Negro blood", Hitler's "Aryanism", "the peculiar
genius of America", "the logical Frenchman", "the passionate Latin"'. All
these comments concern the belief in essence. In fact, Allport (1954) spoke of
the 'principle of least effort' not so much to describe the use of categories per
se but, rather, to refer to the essentialist attitude.

Clearly, the question of the nature of the link between the group label and
the stereotyped features surfaced in early social psychological views on prejudice and stereotypes. But how do contemporary positions deal with this aspect
of stereotyping? A recent contribution by Rothbart and Taylor (1992; Anderson
and Sedikides, 1991) can be seen as the most explicit attempt at stressing the
role of essentialistic thinking in social categorization. These authors build upon
the distinction between natural kind categories (such as mammal, gold, etc.)
and human artefacts (such as furniture, car, etc.). Whereas for human artefacts
category membership is based on the possession of a set of arbitrary defining
characteristics, natural kind categories are thought to be organized around
underlying essences. According to Rothbart and Taylor (1992), social categories are considered to be like natural kind categories rather than like human arte-
fact categories. Social groups may easily be perceived as natural categories when
they can be identified on the basis of physical features such as sex, race, age,
etc. Supposedly, surface characteristics echo deeper, essential, features. In other
words, psychological essentialism is likely to prevail when objective indicators
are available. The idea of an underlying essence suggests that perceivers appraise
category membership of social targets as reflecting their true identity, their real
nature. Associated is a strong feeling of unalterability: membership to an essentially

defined social category can hardly be modified. Also, members of natural kind categories are perceived to be relatively homogeneous, thereby allowing for rich induction and complex theoretical construction to take place. Rothbart and Taylor's (1992) analysis gives a new insight about a number of issues in the area of social categorization and may explain the power of stereotypes.

This brings us to the final part of our journey concerning the 'stereotypes as explanations' model. After all, the critical question really is to understand why it is that people tend to adopt a subjective essentialistic approach about social categories. By asking such a question, we find ourselves reasserting the functional approach of stereotypes. In the remainder of this chapter, we argue that the stabilization of the current state of affairs is one important goal of people's reliance on stereotypic knowledge in general and essentialistic categorization in particular. After we outline what could stand as the essentialistic syndrome, we examine the mechanisms linking subjective essentialism to rationalization.

6 Stereotypes as Tools for Rationalization

Even a cursory look at the research carried out under the cognitive banner confirms the common intuition that characteristics encountered in the environment play a crucial role in the emergence of stereotypes. Some researchers stress the fact that we meet members of outgroups less often than members of the groups to whom we belong (Linville, 1982; Linville, Salovey and Fisher, 1986). Because people's knowledge basis is less complex and less differentiated for outgroups as compared to ingroups, judgements about outgroups end up being more extreme. The social learning approach to stereotypes as it has been promoted by Eagly and colleagues also emphasizes the role of direct observation in the emergence of stereotypes (Eagly and Kite, 1987; Eagly and Steffen, 1984). According to Eagly (1987), we hold stereotypes about groups of people because we observe individual members in a limited set of circumstances. So, for instance, our stereotypes of women and men are a simple consequence of observing these two categories of people occupying different social roles. Borrowing from research on prototypes (Rosch, 1978) as well as from earlier work on accentuation (Tajfel and Wilkes, 1963; Tajfel, 1972), Stangor argues that people select those traits that maximize category differentiation (Stangor and Lange, 1994). Using intelligence and friendliness as the underlying trait dimensions, Ford and Stangor (1992) provided their subjects with behavioural information about members of two groups, a 'blue' group and a 'red' group. Subjects preferentially described the groups in terms of the trait dimension for which the mean difference between the two groups was largest (Expt. 1) or the within-group variability was smallest (Expt. 2). These data suggest that stereotypes develop to help differentiate groups from each other. As far as the notions of comparative fit and meta-contrast ratio build upon the relative importance of inter- and intracategory differences, self-categorization theory is partially grounded in this same tradition (Oakes, 1987; Oakes, Haslam and Turner, 1994; Haslam, Turner, Oakes, McGarty and Hayes, 1992).

From the perspective of the initiators of the cognitive approach of stereotypes (Allport, 1954; Tajfel, 1982), the monopolistic status of the cognitive economy function comes out as a surprise. For example, Tajfel (1982a) noted that the cognitive processes involved in categorization serve a higher purpose. Indeed, by selecting, accentuating and interpreting information, the process of social categorization actually 'fulfils its function of protecting the value system which underlies the division of the surrounding social world' (Tajfel and Forgas, 1981, p. 118). We think that most students of stereotypes would agree that stereotypes are here for some other reasons than strict information processing constraints. The fact is though that functional approaches have been forced into a long recess as the cognitive wave reoriented researchers' interests (Wyer and Srull, 1984). However, these concerns surface again and could well benefit from the findings accumulated over the years by the social cognition approach (Spears, Oakes, Ellemers and Haslam, this volume).

A number of findings substantiate the rationalization function of stereotypes. In a recent analysis, Jost and Banaji (1994) identify three versions of the functional approach, the ego-justification approach, the group-justification approach and the system-justification approach. The ego-justification function can be best illustrated by the work of Adorno and colleagues (1950). The basic thrust of this approach is that stereotypes stand as some sort of defence mechanism allowing the individual to rationalize conduct in relation to specific social categories. As it turns out, some renewed interest for this line of thinking can be observed in the area of attitudes and attitude change (Snyder, 1992; Snyder and DeBono, 1989; Snyder and Miene, 1990). By far the most popular, the group-justification approach stresses the fact that stereotypic thinking must be viewed in the context of group interest (Sherif, 1967). In this context, stereotypes are essentially tuned to the nature of the relations between and within social groups. In other words, one would expect group interactions to be of utmost importance in the variation of the content of the stereotypes (for reviews, see Leyens, Yzerbyt and Schadron, 1994; Oakes, Haslam and Turner, 1994). That stereotypes are sensitive to changes in relations between groups is in fact no new finding (Avigdor, 1953; Buchanan, 1951; Gilbert, 1951; Karlins et al., 1969; Katz and Braly, 1933; Meenes, 1943; Prothro and Melikian, 1955; Seago, 1947; Sherif, 1967). The work of Tajfel and colleagues (Tajfel and Turner, 1979; Turner, 1975; Turner, 1987b) also illustrates the view that stereotypes stand as an ideal means to justify the ingroup treatment of the outgroup members. Negative views of outgroups offer the possibility to derogate the outgroup in an attempt to differentiate positively from outgroup members and thus serve the group members at the level of their social identity. When a group is not providing its members with reasons for positive social identity, people may want to alter the relative status of the group or, alternatively, to leave the group for a better one (Tajfel and Turner, 1979). The choice between a strategy of social change or individual mobility largely depends on the subjective belief that group boundaries are or are not permeable (Doosje and Ellemers, this volume; Ellemers, 1993; Tajfel, 1978a).

According to Jost and Banaji (1994), the group-justification approach in general and social identity theory in particular has some difficulty explaining the phenomenon of 'outgroup favouritism' (for an example, see Hinkle and Brown, 1990). Members of disadvantaged groups are expected to strive for a better image. However, evidence exists aplenty that people internalize positive but also sometimes negative views of themselves and the groups to whom they belong. With respect to these issues, the system-justification approach suggests that stereotypes are best understood as a means to maintain the social structure in its current state. Indeed, social arrangements often involve several groups not all of which enjoy a satisfactory status. To the extent that the system perpetuates itself, one is forced to conclude that either some violent coercive power is exerted by those who enjoy a privileged position in society or that some form of acceptance characterizes the members of the disadvantaged group. System-justification thus refers to these processes whereby members of a given social system accept and justify prevailing social, economic, political, sexual conditions simply because they happen to exist. This means that, to the extent that a system-justifying attitude is encountered among members of the dominated group, they will put aside self or group-interest and value the maintenance of the existing arrangement. It then becomes easy to understand why group members sometimes entertain negative views of the ingroup and positive views of outgroups. In fact, the notions of 'legitimacy' and 'stability' of the system as they have been proposed by social identity theorists concur with the plausibility of the system-justification approach as a sensible account of stereotyping phenomena (see Ellemers, van Knippenberg, De Vries and Wilke, 1988; van Knippenberg and Ellemers, 1990). This view of system-justification is of course highly reminiscent of the notion of ideology (Althusser, 1970; Beauvois and Joule, 1981; Ibañez, 1994; Marx and Engels, 1846/1968).

Along the same line, we argue that stereotypes are best seen as explanatory devices that serve a rationalization function: stereotypes allow people to provide an account for why things are the way they are. In that respect, our approach capitalizes on Jost and Banaji's (1994) work. However, we would like to take the argument one step further and suggest that rationalization is best served by an essentialistic approach to social categories.[3] When such a subjective essentialistic belief prevails, the differences between groups are seen to be phenotypic surface characteristics resulting from the existence of genotypic deeper features defining the groups. In a thoughtful analysis of the social classes composing various societies, Sherif (1948) stressed the fact that the dominated group often adopts the views of the dominant group. He further noted that 'the caste system in India . . . was not the idea of the ignorant or the frustrated "untouchables." It was the philosophical Brahmins and the British masters of the local

Indian princes and rulers who were interested in keeping these delineations intact. The psychological correlates of theses delineations in the form of alleged inherent capacities and "traits" corresponding to the politico-economic scales have certainly been effective at times in keeping various groups "in their place," sometimes of their own volition' (1948, p. 343). This quote represents very well what we mean by an essentialistic mechanism of rationalization. Members of a given social situation are likely to refer to some intrinsic feature of the parties involved in order to strengthen social stability.

A study by Hoffman and Hurst (1990) provides tentative support for the role of essentialism in stereotyping. These authors disagree with the idea that stereotypes acquire their meaning on the basis of a kernel of truth (Eagly, 1987) and argue instead that stereotypic views are ideal means to rationalize and justify intergroup relations. Subjects were to imagine that a fictitious planet was the home of two different species (depicted by way of drawings revealing family resemblance) versus two different subcultures (depicted by way of drawings revealing different clothing habits). Whereas, subjects were told, the majority of the members of one group work in the city (a masculine activity), the majority of the members of the other group raise children (a feminine activity). Instructions indicated very clearly that there were no sex differences within groups. Subjects received three pieces of information about each of the 15 members of each group, one consistent with the occupation of the member, one inconsistent and one irrelevant. Half the subjects were told to think about and write down a reason for the prevalence of a specific role in each of the two groups. Results show that subjects later associated feminine traits more with the child-rearing group than with the city-worker group. The reverse was found for masculine traits. Also, this pattern came out stronger when biology rather than culture was the basis of the categorization. Even more interesting is the fact that explaining the category-role correlation led to the formation of stronger stereotypes. This finding provides support for the idea that the explanatory function (rationalization) plays a major role in the formation and use of stereotype. In Hoffman and Hurst's (1990, p. 206) terms, 'stereotype formation of the kind at issue here is not purely an information processing phenomenon . . . role-based category stereotypes originate in a rationalisation process that operates by positing intrinsic differences between the categories in question'. In sum, stereotypes about a specific category of people will most likely be used when the underlying theory seems to account for the traits that happen to describe the group and when perceivers feel that they know a lot about the members of the group.

7　A Syndrome of Essentialistic Categorization

A number of criteria may help define essentialistic categorization (see also Rothbart and Taylor, 1992). At a core level, subjective essentialism is based on the belief that the social category has a specific ontological status. In this respect, Campbell (1958) long suggested that perceptual factors and Gestalt principles govern the extent to which people consider others to comprise a 'real' entity. Both the similarity and the proximity of group members foster the idea that a significant social group is at stake. The common fate enjoyed by group members also contributes to increase group entitativity. Strong links thus exist between Campbell's (1958) early analysis of groups in terms of their entitativity and the current subjective essentialistic view of social categories. In our view, people who face a group having the nature of an entity tend to believe that there is a feature common to all category members. This happens despite the fact that people often remain unable to point out the exact nature of the underlying essence. A second aspect is that perceivers believe a member of a given category cannot cease to be a member. This seems to be somewhat trivial with respect to the most obvious categories such a gender, race and age. People's commitment to the unalterability of group membership plays a role in many contexts where categories are clearly the consequence of social definition. In Europe, working class people always seem to remain working class people, even if they become successful and rich business people. The sharp distinctions between castes in India may be an extreme version of this belief in unalterability. In that case, only the death of an individual authorizes a switch from one social category to another. The third characteristic of an essentialistic social categorization is the inductive potential. Informed about the category of a target person, perceivers feel that they know a lot about the person. A fourth related feature is the interconnectedness of the various features. Because the underlying essence provides an explanation for the category, all associated features are reinterpreted in light of one unifying theme. The fifth and final feature we would like to point out concerns the way essentialistic categorizations exclude other possible categorizations of the target. It is as if people with an essentialistic approach about others have a hard time thinking of them in alternative categorical terms. This aspect can be linked to a series of findings about the chronic accessibility of schemata (Higgins and King, 1981; Stangor, 1988).

Whereas all five features of a subjective essentialistic stance about categories have been framed in terms of the perceivers' beliefs, the same analysis can be applied to the targets' beliefs. Hypothesis confirmation (Snyder, 1984) and behavioural confirmation (Snyder, Tanke and Berscheid, 1977; Word, Zanna and Cooper, 1974) both contribute to make stereotypes become reality. This would appear as a very simple mechanism to account for the so-called kernel-of-truth hypothesis. Finally, all these notions are very much linked to the issue of prescriptive stereotypes and normative beliefs as defended by Fiske and colleagues (Fiske, Bersoff, Borgida, Deaux and Heilman, 1991; Fiske and Stevens, 1993). Indeed, members of dominated categories may embrace successful pathways but the major drawback remains the way other people expect them to behave. So, for instance, high-level female executives will be expected to conform to their stereotyped role. This would involve being feminine, socially caring, responsive to male seduction, etc. One prediction in line with prescriptive stereotyping would be that people in the privileged position would be more willing to endorse an essentialistic view of existing social categories than members of the non-privileged groups. Data collected by Smith and Russell (1984) provide some evidence for this hypothesis. These authors found that boys were more likely to attribute sex differences to biological factors whereas girls were more likely to cite social factors. Of course, the perceived legitimacy of the social arrangement as well as the lack of permeability of group boundaries may lead members of a non-privileged group to share the views of the dominant group.

A recent study by Martin and Parker (1995) examined people's naïve theories about sex and race and provides empirical evidence concerning the role of an essentialistic syndrome in prejudice. These authors assessed their subjects' beliefs about the role of biological, social and circumstantial factors in sex and race differences, the difficulty of eliminating differences between sexes and races, and the variability within and between sexes. They also measured people's intolerance of ambiguity. In line with our reasoning, the more subjects thought that sex or race differences rested on biological factors, the less they believed that these differences could be eliminated. Not surprisingly, Martin and Parker found that a positive correlation emerged between the beliefs that sex differences could be eliminated and the variability within each sex. Still, the more subjects thought that men and women differed between as compared to within sexes, the more they thought that differences would be difficult to eliminate. More importantly, perceived differences between women and men were positively correlated with the belief that biological factors play a role in sex differences. Finally, Martin and Parker (1995) also found that intolerance of ambiguity correlated positively with the belief that biology is an important factor in sex and race differences and the perceived difference between women and men but correlated negatively with the perception of differences among women and among men.

The above pattern of results is consistent with our idea that subjective essentialism induces the belief that social categories differ from one another. To be sure, category differentiation may largely depend on actual group differences. In that case, the impact of essentialism would be limited to an increase of the difference in the eye of the essentialistic categorizers as compared to that signalled by the non-essentialistic categorizers. In more traditional terms, this corresponds to the well-known accentuation phenomenon (Eiser and Stroebe, 1972; McGarty and Penny, 1988; Tajfel and Wilkes, 1963; Wilder, 1986). A stronger hypothesis also entails the possibility that differences in perception arise despite the absence of a factual basis or that actual differences remain unnoticed simply because they do not fall under the umbrella of a unifying theory. Hoffman and Hurst's (1990) results can be seen as an illustration of the first of these two situations.

Examples abound in the literature that biology is not the only essence to play a major role in stereotypic thinking. A long time ago, Aristotle considered the uniqueness of the geography of Greece to be the main reason for the superiority of the Greeks over other people. In other words, the subjective essentialistic view on rationalization need not take the form of genetic essentialism. What is important, however, is the extent to which the various features of the essentialistic syndrome characterize the specific theory used by people. If anyone who comes to live in Greece may benefit from the weather and 'improve' as a person, category membership is fairly alterable. If no matter what, the birth under a given climate determines the person once and for all, there is not much that can be done to alter category membership. The latter case more closely reveals the influence of subjective essentialism.

A more recent illustration of subjective essentialism can be found in a fascinating study by Steinberg (1974) about the relation between religion and university fields selected by North American professors. This author collected impressive evidence to show that Protestants outnumber other religious groups in traditional scientific fields (such as agriculture, technical schools, chemistry, geography, etc.), that one finds more Catholics than members of other religious groups in the humanities (such as art, philosophy, foreign languages, religion, history, etc.), and that Jews are relatively more numerous in medical schools and behavioural sciences (such as law, economics, sociology, psychology, etc.). For Steinberg (1974), the cultural values put forth in the various religious groups may account for this state of affairs. Such an explanation actually builds upon a long tradition in sociology relating the choice of curricula and religious background (cf. Weber, 1964). According to Boudon (1990), an alternative account of Steinberg's data could very well be that a conjunction of random factors together contribute to generate the observed pattern. What the cultural explanation illustrates is the fact that people are reluctant to explain important facts of life by referring to trivial, not to say meaningless, variables. Because the choice of a scientific field is a consequential behaviour, it ought to be grounded in factors that truly and significantly differentiate between the three groups. In other words, deep features of the groups appear to be the only acceptable way to account for such a critical phenomenon. Interestingly, Friedman (1983) showed that a combination of collective mobility of Protestants, Catholics and Jews in North American society and the successive waves of expansion within the academic world, two phenomena that prove to be largely independent, provides an excellent account for the observed data. In other words, it was when positions in behavioural sciences were made available that young generations of Jews had access to higher education. In our view, one could suggest a similar analysis of the advent of computer science and mathematics and the influx of Asian students on American campuses. It is to be noted here that people tend to rely on one cause to explain critical phenomena instead of considering several possible (e.g., situational) causes. Steinberg's (1974) viewpoint not only shows the desire of researchers to isolate one plausible and preferably essentialistic cause for consequential behaviour but also the power of cultural, religious or ethnic explanations.

It is interesting to see how scientists and, more generally, experts in a given field may subscribe to the essentialistic view with even more faith than lay people. As it turns out, the very scientific status of a number of theories resides in the fact that the theorists have been able to account for surface differences anyone can observe in a way that none could ever suspect. Most often, the so-called 'real' difference boils down to some version of an essential difference between the categories. A well-known theory of personality, Eysenck's trait-type model (1983), provides a nice example of such a position. Lay people are very good at telling apart surface characteristics of introverts and extroverts. Eysenck, however, has the theoretical sophistication that allows him to account for these phenotypic differences in terms of more basic, more essential, genotypic differences. Our view regarding these claims is that one ought to be extremely cautious. In fact, showing that scientific and lay knowledge may not be so far apart from each other provides an elegant way to question the status of scientific claims. In a simple but fascinating study, Semin and Krahé (1987) presented their subjects with genotypic depictions of an introvert or an extrovert and asked them to evaluate the typicality of a series of introvert and extrovert phenotypic characteristics. Results indicated that subjects were quite able to make sense of the genotypic descriptions in the way Eysenck predicts. Indeed, all phenotypic characteristics were seen as being typical of their appropriate genotypic counterpart. A second study showed that the reverse inference resulted in near perfect correspondence as well. This work thus stresses the fact that scientific claims about essentialistic features and naïve conceptions are not alien to each other.

To recap, different essentialistic theories may underlie the division of humans into various social groups. Still, we think that one would generally invoke genetic or ethnic differences among people to account for observed inequalities because surface features more readily point to genetic or ethnic explanations. One should thus approach the issues of essentialistic theories in terms of a continuum on which the various features defined above vary. In combination with perceptual factors such as similarity and proximity, the significance of the behaviour and the specific group division for the larger social system are likely to influence the degree of essentialistic characterization of groups. When people are confronted with major social events, they are prone to rely on inherent features to characterize the groups involved. We expect an essentialistic view of groups to maintain the social status quo. The more members of certain categories find themselves in a dominant position or in what appears to be a legitimate system, the more they embrace an essentialistic view about the social system. Ironically, the extreme opposite stance, that is, a revolutionary agenda, could very well adopt a similar perspective about essentialism only it would concern a different hierarchy and possibly different categories: As the terrible events of Cambodia illustrate, it is not rare to see oppressed people become oppressors.

8 The Mechanics of Subjective Essentialism in Stereotyping

One important item on our research agenda is to better understand the processes involved in rationalization. We now present preliminary empirical evidence about the possible implication of subjective essentialism in the development of stereotypes and in the way they fulfil their function of rationalization. Before we address the issue of group perception, let us first illustrate the phenomenon at the interpersonal level. In a neat study, Humphrey (1985) told subjects that the study concerned the way people work in an office setting. Relying on an ostentatiously random procedure, some participants were assigned the role of 'managers' and the others the role of 'clerks'. The particular tasks to perform took about two hours. Managers and clerks then rated themselves and each other on a series of work-related traits such as intelligence, leadership, etc., and made several behavioural predictions for the future. Except for the prediction of hard-workingness, managers were consistently rated better than clerks. Clearly thus, the high-skill tasks and the directive role of the managers on the one hand and the low-skill, repetitive jobs and the lack of autonomy of the clerks on the other led all participants to believe that they were facing two different kinds of people (see also Sande, Ellard and Ross, 1986). So, people tend to attribute personality characteristics that are coherent with the observed occupation, allowing themselves to rationalize the behaviours specific to the various roles. But for such a correspondence to be possible, people must neglect the situational determinants of behaviour. We know that they do. Two lines of work are particularly suggestive in this respect: the work on the fundamental attribution error, on the one hand, and the research on compliance, on the other. In fact, both traditions of research concern the way people provide accounts of other people's and their own behaviour.

Researchers in the field of person perception have indeed documented the fact that, when people explain behaviours, they largely underestimate the impact of situational factors and, in contrast, overestimate the weight of person characteristics (for reviews, see Gilbert and Malone, 1995; Jones, 1990; Ross, 1977; Ross and Nisbett, 1991). Ross, Amabile and Steinmetz (1977) offered a deceptively simple illustration of this 'fundamental attribution error' or 'overattribution bias'. Randomly designated questioners, contestants and observers all took part in a quiz game. As predicted, both contestants and observers later rated the questioner to be more knowledgeable than the contestant despite the fact that role assignment was explicitly random. In fact, the questioner was the only one to take into account the privileged position of being allowed to ask rather than to (try to) answer the questions (Sande, Ellard and Ross, 1986).

Cognitive dissonance and self-perception work and, more generally, the work on compliance illustrate how people's own behaviours stand as a very powerful weapon in order to modify (in the case of attitude-discrepant behaviour) or to reinforce (in the case of attitude-consonant behaviour) existing attitudes (for reviews, see Eagly and Chaiken, 1993; Cialdini, 1988). The well-known studies on the forbidden toy suggest that mild as opposed to strong situational pressures can lead people to appraise their behaviours as being the consequence of their own decision (Aronson and Carlsmith, 1963; Freedman, 1965). Cognitive dissonance findings on insufficient-justification (Festinger and Carlsmith, 1959) and on effort-justification (Aronson and Mills, 1959) make a similar point. To the extent that external constraints remain in the background, the author of the behaviour is seen as the primary culprit for whatever course of action has been taken. Turning to attitude-consonant behaviours, the foot-in-the-door technique nicely shows that people can take their own behaviour at face value. By first asking people to go along with a small request, one increases compliance with a larger request (Freedman and Fraser, 1966; for reviews, see Cialdini, 1988; Joule and Beauvois, 1987; for a frightening illustration, see Milgram, 1974). Again, people are shown to overlook situational pressures and favour instead the decisive role of the author of the behaviour.

Both lines of work thus prove useful to understand how people come to characterize the various groups in their environment and integrate particular beliefs about how things and people are in a given social context. Indeed, the question is to know what will happen when groups are at stake? We suggest that the above findings at the interpersonal and intrapersonal level can easily be reinterpreted at the intra- and intergroup level, that is people will also tend to perceive groups in a way that helps rationalize their situation. Of course, an attribution to the group has to be plausible. Such an attribution will be facilitated by the belief that the group is an entity for which a good explanation is available. We thus argue that rationalization is well-served by some sort of essentialistic stance. To the extent that stereotypes link specific behaviours to underlying dispositions of the members of the group, one should be able to find evidence for a pervasive tendency for perceivers to infer underlying dispositions among members of a group despite the fact that circumstantial factors offer an alternative account of the observed behaviours. As Jones (1990, p. 96) noted, 'converting the possibility of illusory correlation into damaging stereotypes, however, requires more than the association of particular actions with particular groups of people. It requires that these actions be attributed to the underlying dispositions defining the basic identity or nature of group members . . . This tendency toward "correspondence bias" is undoubtedly a crucial link in the formation of discriminatory stereotypes.' Moreover, these mechanisms likely explain why people may entertain views about themselves and others that are not particularly self-serving in an absolute sense.

In our subjective essentialistic view of stereotyping, groups' 'inherent' characteristics are some sort of social creations, that is, arbitrary qualities, that are attributed to social entities in order to explain their behaviour in a given cultural and historical context and to perpetuate the social system. Put simply, we talk about others and define them in ways that are relevant for the social system we live in. The present argument is not alien to work by Beauvois and colleagues on the norm of internality (Beauvois, 1984; Jellison and Green, 1981; for reviews, see Beauvois, 1995; Dubois, 1994). These authors show that the reference to dispositional features of individuals as a means to account for behaviours is a norm that people acquire during their socialization (Beauvois and Dubois, 1988; see also Newman, 1991). Moreover, Beauvois and colleagues suggest that social status is associated with different levels of skill with regard to this norm: high-status children more often rely on dispositions than their low-status counterparts. Other research suggests that people may be differentially sensitive to dispositional inferences because they entertain different theories about human nature (Gervey, Chiu, Hong and Dweck, 1993; Dweck, Hong and Chiu, 1993; Newman, 1993) and that people's readiness to reason in terms of dispositional entities is culture specific (Miller, 1984; Morris, Nisbett and Peng, 1994; Morris and Peng, 1994; Newman, 1991; see also Quattrone, 1982; Krull, 1993). It thus appears that people's proneness to rely on individual overattribution and the relative status of individualism and personal freedom go hand in hand. By analogy, we suggest that a more collectivistic orientation or, for that matter, a judgemental context that promotes categorization in terms of group membership may foster a subjective essentialistic approach to categories.

The above reasoning led us to hypothesize that a subjective essentialistic approach to group membership would facilitate people's reliance on stereotypes to explain unrelated events that happen to the group. We tested this conjecture in a series of studies using a new paradigm (Schadron, Morchain and Yzerbyt, 1994; Yzerbyt, Schadron and Morchain, 1994). Subjects' task was to form impressions about six alleged participants in another study who were videotaped during a discussion. For half of the subjects, the six persons had been randomly selected among 200 students ('aggregate' condition) . The other half was told that the answers to a series of personality and social background questionnaires had been used in order to constitute a very homogeneous group of six people ('group' condition). A second manipulation concerned the future fate of the six persons. In the 'positive fate' condition, subjects learned that these six persons had been randomly assigned to a special education programme: this very favourable program provided the students with closer attention from the staff members, better classrooms, unlimited access to computers, etc. In the

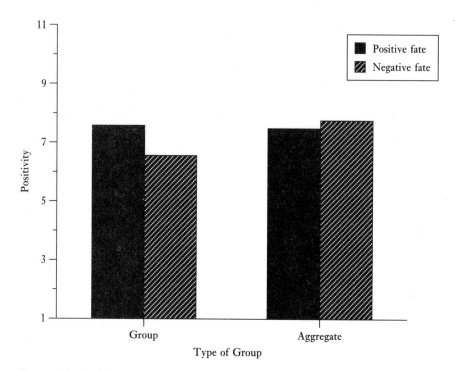

Figure 2.2   Positivity of judgement as a function of type of group and fate.

'negative fate' condition, the six persons were supposed to be the losers of the lottery: in spite of the existence of the special programme, they were to be the 'control group' who would have rather unfavourable educational conditions. To allow subjects to form an impression, all subjects then saw a 5-min discussion involving the six students. At the end of the tape, subjects evaluated the target people on a series of personality traits.

It is important to remember that the target people were clearly shown to be selected for one or the other educational context on a strictly random basis. There was thus no objective reason for subjects to perceive people differently in these two contexts. In line with our predictions, however, people saw the unfavourable context students in a less positive light that the favourable context students (see figure 2.2). We predicted that this difference would emerge only when the students were thought to belong to a meaningful group, to an entity (Campbell, 1958). As expected, the above difference emerged only when subjects believed that the students were distributed into homogeneous groups on the basis of personality and social background variables. Interestingly, our data also reveal the observed effects are mainly due to the unfavourable context students in the group condition. In other words, our subjects were especially prone to account for the fate of the people in terms of their inner characteristics when the targets were both a homogeneous group and faced with an unfavourable fate. This pattern of results can be linked to similar findings in person perception. So, for instance, Lerner (1980) found that people easily attribute negative characteristics to victims. He further suggests that, in order to feel reassured as to their own lot, perceivers need to justify the occurrence of misfortune, accidents or any other bad event by putting some of the responsibility on the sufferer. Our results show a similar pattern for social groups only when a strong underlying theory was suggested to the subjects. These data demonstrate that the (random) fate of a group is translated into inherent features of the members of a category.

To recap, we propose that the rationalization function of stereotyping is well-served by an essentialistic approach to social categories. In other words, the best way to account for the existing social situation is to promote the idea that it stems from the nature of things. Extending well-established findings in the field of attribution and social influence, we suggest that people may overestimate the extent to which the current situation of group members is the consequence of their deep, inherent features. We have presented evidence from an ongoing research programme that an essentialistic stance about groups may facilitate the emergence of group overattribution. Indeed, our data reveal that what happens to a group tends to be attributed to characteristics of the group members particularly when the groups were defined in an essentialistic way. The rationalization function appears to be an important factor in determining people's use of stereotypes whenever some essentialistic reasoning applies.

9 Conclusions

Most researchers in the information processing tradition have stressed the cognitive economy function of stereotypes. We emphasize the fact that stereotypes are more than lists of features associated to a group label. To use more functional terms, stereotypes also help perceivers orient themselves in the environment as they provide them with rich knowledge about the social world. Based on recent developments in cognitive psychology and on a series of insights in the field of stereotyping, we argued that the 'stereotype as explanation' view may not only stress the existence of strong relationships between the components of the stereotypes. Any underlying explanation also accounts for why it is that these components hold together and why it is that the group is a group, to be differentiated from other groups. In this respect, a crucial function of stereotypes may be to rationalize the current social arrangement. The new and central message of our chapter is that the rationalization function of stereotypes is likely to be linked to a strong tendency for perceivers to fall prey to subjective essentialism.

Notes

We thank Olivier Corneille, Jacques-Philippe Leyens, Anouk Rogier and the editors of the present volume for their insightful comments on earlier drafts of this chapter. The first author is also indebted to Bogdan Wojciszke and to the students of the Social Categorization group at the EAESP Summer School held in Serock, July 1994.

1 This quotation could be translated as follows: 'One people has a stupid and heavy mind, Another one enjoys a sharp, quick, and insightful mind. Where does this come from, if it is not partly from the food, from the seeds of its fathers, and from the chaos of various elements floating in the immensity of the air?' (La Mettrie, 1748/1981, pp. 100–3)

2 As a matter of fact, sterilization laws were enacted in sixteen US states between 1907 and 1917. Criminals in particular categories as well as epileptics, drug addicts, the insane and idiots were sentenced to compulsory sterilization. Shipman (1994) reports that 36,000 people had been operated upon by 1941.

3 By linking the system-justification view to the notion of 'false consciousness', Jost and Banaji (1994) question the veracity of stereotypes. Their position implicitly acknowledges the existence of 'true consciousness', something we do not take for granted. We would favour an intermediate stance that neither claims that stereotypes are correct nor that they are necessarily incorrect. In fact, the view that stereotypes are 'socially valid' (Oakes et al., 1994) or that they are 'pragmatic' (Fiske, 1993b; Leyens et al., 1994; Yzerbyt, Schadron, Leyens and Rocher, 1994) better suits our taste.

3

Asking the Accuracy Question: Is Measurement the Answer?

Penelope J. Oakes and
Katherine J. Reynolds

How accurate are social stereotypes? We might believe that Germans are scientifically-minded, Australians pleasure-loving and the English polite, but to what extent (and in what sense) do these stereotypical images reflect the true nature of these groups?

This question has had an interesting history in the stereotyping literature. It preoccupied researchers in the pre–cognitive era, but almost completely disappeared from the research agenda during the 1970s and 1980s. Just recently it has again become the focus of vigorous interest (e.g., Judd and Park, 1993; Lee, Jussim and McCauley, 1995; Oakes, 1993; Oakes and Turner, 1990; Oakes, Haslam and Turner, 1994; Stangor and Lange, 1994; Swim, 1994).

During the earlier period of interest in stereotype accuracy many argued that the only way to resolve the issue was through the comparison of reported stereotypes with criteria assumed to reflect the actual characteristics of group members (e.g., see Fishman, 1956). This argument has recently been revived by Judd and Park (1993), who aim 'to make explicit in a systematic and thorough fashion the issues involved in asking the accuracy question' (p. 110). They, too, advocate comparison of stereotypes with 'the true attributes of the group' (p. 110), and outline careful empirical procedures for optimal accomplishment of this task, together with a discussion of the specific forms potential stereotype *in*accuracy might take.

In this chapter we take a new look at the issue of stereotype accuracy. More specifically, we approach the accuracy issue from a primarily theoretical rather than empirical perspective. In our view, some fundamental theoretical questions – what are stereotypes? what is their purpose in social perception and group life? what is the nature of the processes responsible for them? – need to be asked *before* we can decide whether stereotype accuracy can be measured. We conclude that, while the measurement of stereotype accuracy may be compatible with some understandings of the process, from our own theoretical perspective the accuracy question can never be resolved through measurement.

We begin with a brief discussion of the empirical tradition in stereotype accuracy research. We then place the accuracy question in its current theoretical context, outlining two approaches to stereotyping, one based on the cognitive miser analysis of social cognition (e.g., Fiske and Neuberg, 1990; Hamilton, Stroessner and Driscoll, 1994), and the other on self-categorization theory (Oakes et al., 1994; Turner, 1985; Turner, Oakes, Haslam and McGarty, 1994). From the latter perspective, we suggest a new way of thinking about the validity and accuracy of social stereotypes.

1   Accuracy as an Empirical Issue: The 'Kernel of Truth' and the Criterion Problem

In reaction to some fairly dogmatic statements about the supposedly self-evident evils of stereotyping (e.g., Schoenfeld, 1942; Zawadzki, 1942), several commentaries published in the 1950s (e.g., Allport, 1954; Bogardus, 1950; Fishman, 1956; Klineberg, 1951) argued that the only fair basis upon which to pass judgement on the character of stereotyping was to examine '*every* stereotype . . . in order to determine its relation to external reality' (Klineberg, 1951, p. 511).

This call to empirical action did not arise in a theoretical vacuum. One important idea which informed attempts to assess rather than simply assume the extent of stereotype (in)accuracy was that stereotypes may have a kernel of truth – they may be based on real and important differences between groups. The strong form of this argument was that stereotypes could only be useful, and would only survive, to the extent that they reflected such a kernel and therefore did not 'differ sharply from everyday perceptual data' (Prothro and Melikian, 1955, p. 4; see also Brigham, 1971). Other researchers argued that *some* stereotypes *may* have their origins in actual group differences, but that they tended to exaggerate and otherwise distort such real differences (e.g., LeVine and Campbell, 1972), and that 'irrational' (Allport, 1954) stereotypes which did not correspond to reality at all were perfectly possible.

Perhaps the most interesting discussion of the kernel of truth idea is that presented by Campbell (1967). He argued that stereotypes have at least a 'grain of descriptive truth' (p. 824) because they develop from and reflect substantive differences between groups. Indeed, he hypothesized quite explicitly that the features most likely to appear in stereotypes would be those which most clearly differentiate between stereotyped and stereotyping groups. He reported anthropological evidence supporting this idea, and a similar argument was recently presented and confirmed experimentally by Ford and Stangor (1992; see also P. Brown, 1994).

Campbell comments that the kernel of truth idea 'seems obvious when one starts from the anthropological position that groups, cultures, etc. do in fact differ' (p. 823), but it is rejected by many psychologists, social psychologists included, who tend to argue that 'all stereotypes of group differences are false, and, implicitly, that all groups are on average identical' (p. 823). In elucidating the difference between these perspectives, he stressed that while his aim was to 'emphasize the stimulus component in stereotypes' (p. 825), this referred to the 'social reality' at the level of intergroup relations, rather than 'intrinsic and essential' differences between members of racial or cultural groups. In other words, he suggested a qualitative distinction between individual level and group level characteristics, and argued that it was the latter, *not* the former, that were reflected in stereotypes. He felt that stereotypes were erroneous in various ways, but that social psychologists should find some way to 'state the errors, without claiming that all groups are identical' (p. 824). Similarly, Vinacke (1949) objected to the erroneous biological attributions contained in some stereotypes, rather than their description of group differences per se. He suggested that 'militant liberals' (p. 285), understandably vigilant for characterizations of groups which could be used to justify discrimination, should make the arguments of biological essentialism and genetic inescapability contained in some stereotypes their targets, 'rather than refusing to admit any group differences' (Vinacke, 1949, p. 285; see also R. Brown, 1965, p. 181; Campbell, 1967, p. 825).

Interestingly, we need look no further than the classic paper by Katz and Braly (1933, p. 289) to find one of the clearest statements of this rejection of group differences which Campbell and Vinacke had noted. Katz and Braly derided the 'group fallacy attitude' which stereotypes seemed to reflect. They stated unequivocally that 'there are no racial or national groups which exist as entities and which determine the characteristics of the group members'. From this perspective, they seriously doubted the utility of 'strictly objective surveys' of stereotype accuracy, because the already exisiting 'fiction' may well 'produce distorted and fallacious observations'. Clearly, from the earliest days of stereotyping research, theoretical disagreements about the nature of social reality and the role of stereotypes led to divergent perspectives on the correct approach to answering, indeed the very utility of asking the accuracy question.

The empirical issue for those who did wish to explore the kernel of truth hypothesis was stated thus by Prothro and Melikian (1955, p. 3): 'are there characteristics of the stereotyped group which influence the image?' Several studies carried out during the 1960s attempted to answer this deceptively simple question (e.g., Abate and Berrien, 1967; Schuman, 1966; Triandis and Vassiliou, 1967; see Oakes et al., 1994, chapter 2 for detailed discussion). Notwithstanding Campbell's distinction between group and individual level 'truth' alluded to above, most researchers understood the task to be the comparison of stereotypes with information about the *personality characteristics* of group members, usually as revealed by self-report measures. For example, Abate and Berrien (1967) assessed the stereotypes held by American and Japanese students of both their own nation (self-stereotypes) and the other nation (hetero-stereotypes). They compared these with the responses of a separate sample of American and Japanese students on the Edwards Personal Preference Schedule (EPPS), which was assumed to 'provide an approximation of the target's real characteristics' (p. 435). Thus, 'accuracy' was defined as correspondence between the stereotypes and the EPPS scores (the 'vereotypes').

While there was considerable agreement between self- and hetero-stereotypes (e.g., both groups believed that the Japanese showed more deference to authority than Americans), there was less correspondence between the EPPS responses and both the national self-stereotypes and the national hetero-stereotypes. This was especially the case for the Japanese, whose personal characteristics were apparently portrayed quite inaccurately in the Japanese stereotypes reported by the Americans and, moreover, in the Japanese stereotypes they themselves reported. Considering the overall pattern of stereotype–vereotype correlations, Abate and Berrien find it 'somewhat surprising . . . that in nearly all cases, the respondents were no more accurate in perceiving their own national group than in perceiving the foreign group' (p. 437). Indeed, they begin to question the relevance of the vereotypes to the national stereotypes, finally concluding that 'accuracy correlations between vereotypes and stereotypes are difficult to interpret' (p. 438).

This is, of course, the outstanding 'thorny issue' (Judd and Park, 1993, p. 113) in this area: the validity of the chosen accuracy criterion. Why should we assume that self-reports of personality, such as the EPPS, are *necessarily* more accurate than stereotypic images (see Stangor and Lange, 1994)? Both represent *perceiver-mediated impressions of an aspect of reality* (myself as an individual, myself as an American, the Japanese as a group . . .), from that perceiver's perspective. To some extent, the simple fact that measures such as the EPPS assess individual-level rather than group-level characteristics is thought to render them more 'accurate', but this idea can be seen to reflect a meta-theoretical assumption that the truth about people is to be found in their personality rather than their group memberships – an assumption we would dispute (cf. Asch, 1952; Oakes et al., 1994, chapter 4; see Simon, this volume; Spears, Oakes, Ellemers and Haslam, this volume).

As an alternative accuracy criterion, some studies took the convergence of a self-stereotype with that held by another group as indicating that the stereotype must reflect a real 'kernel'. Recall that this convergence was quite high in Abate and Berrien's study. However, such findings have also been interpreted as evidence that a stereotyped group has simply internalized the image held of it by the stereotyping group. For example, Bayton (1941) attributed black and white college students' agreement that blacks were superstitious, lazy, happy-go-lucky, ostentatious and loud to propaganda influences rather than 'accuracy' (see also Prothro and Melikian, 1955, p. 4). Similarly, Cauthen, Robinson and Krauss (1971, p. 117) suggested that minority acceptance of and agreement with majority stereotypes was a serious *problem* associated with stereotyping (see also Brigham, 1971; Tajfel, 1972). Indeed, whether or not given patterns of convergence are taken to indicate 'accuracy' seems to be affected by the ideological acceptability of the specific findings reported (see below; Mackie, 1973, and see Kruglanski, 1989 for a discussion of the experimenter's role in criterion-setting). It has been argued, for example, that increased contact between groups improves stereotype accuracy (e.g., Prothro and Melikian, 1955; Triandis and Vassiliou, 1967). Prothro and Melikian reported that increased contact between American and Arab students led to the addition of the attributes sociable, jolly, superficial and simple to the American stereotype, and were happy to conclude that this indicated 'the presence in the stereotype of a kernel which constitutes the social stimulus value of the stereotyped group' (1955, p. 9). On the other hand, Mussen (1950) did not attribute his finding of increasing hostility in white children's stereotypes of blacks over the course of a mutliracial summer camp to increasing 'accuracy'.

Although far from resolved, the '"kernel of truth" impasse', as Fishman (1956, p. 29) put it, had been more or less abandoned by the early 1970s. In addition to the fact that identifying reliable criteria for stereotype accuracy had become a research nightmare, the hypothesis attracted theoretical criticism. Most significantly, Sherif (1967) questioned the basic utility of the concept of a kernel of truth. Drawing on relevant findings from his field studies, he emphasized the complex (see also Vinacke, 1949) and variable nature of stereotypes conceptualized as representations of intergroup relations:

> The choice and salience of particular attributes . . . reflect the stance of our own group in past and/or current relationships with the particular group in question. Both the generalized and vague descriptive character of the attributes and their *singular point of view* make the search for 'kernels of truth' in stereotypes unrewarding. (1967, p. 37, emphasis added)

Add to this the continuing impact of Cronbach's critique of accuracy research in person perception (Cronbach, 1955; Gage and Cronbach, 1955), and it is not surprising that interest in the empirical assessment of the accuracy of stereotype content declined sharply. Indeed, interest in stereotype content declined altogether with the shift towards process models which followed Tajfel's (1969a; see also Allport, 1954) call to a cognitive analysis. One outcome was that the accuracy question was approached and answered in a different way. As Kruglanski comments, 'process models . . . soon acquired prescriptive or "normative" overtones . . . and the emphasis shifted from the study of process per se to the study of bias or inaccuracy' (1989, p. 398). These developments were as evident in the stereotyping literature as elsewhere, and the models of error, bias and illusion which characterized the 'cognitive miser' period (Taylor, 1981a; see Fiske and Taylor, 1991, p. 13; Spears and Haslam, this volume) provided an at least implicit answer to the old accuracy question – the *process* of stereotyping leads us into inaccuracy. These ideas are considered in more detail in the next section.

More recently, however, Judd and Park (1993) have revived the content accuracy issue, and have done so from the perspective of stereotypes as 'probabilistic generalizations about a group or class of people' (p. 109) with no mention of the kernel of truth hypothesis at all. They define the accuracy issue as a matter of determining 'the correspondence between personal beliefs and the true attributes of the group' (p. 110), and do not attempt to shy away from the criterion problem. They discuss it in some detail and suggest several sources of criterion information, together with indications of likely problems associated with their use, such as response biases and sample selection biases. Their suggested criteria include standardized personality tests, self reports assessing personality dispositions and attitudes, and the opinions of expert judges (e.g., clinical psychologists) who should remain 'truly blind to [the] group membership' of interest when making their judgements. They conclude that all criteria are potentially biased, and that researchers must use multiple criteria in full awareness of the problems associated with each. They then outline their 'full-accuracy design', conscious of the fact that they have not solved the criterion problem in any final sense but for present purposes 'assum[ing] that a valid criterion is available' (p. 114).

Judd and Park's paper also includes a theoretical discussion of the potential forms that stereotype *in*accuracy might take. They identify three ways in which stereotypes may deviate from a faithful representation of reality. These are stereotypic inaccuracy, dispersion inaccuracy, and valence inaccuracy. Briefly, stereotypic inaccuracy follows distortion of the group's central tendency on stereotypic attributes relative to counterstereotypic attributes (e.g., overestimating the average politeness of the English whilst underestimating their fashion consciousness, or vice versa), dispersion inaccuracy involves distortion of the variability of the group on stereotypic attributes (e.g., seeing the English as more or less homogeneously polite than they in fact are), and valence inaccuracy 'reflects the tendency to view the group as more or less positive than it actually is' (p. 111). Where this distortion is in the direction of a *less* positive image (e.g., if English narrow-mindedness is overestimated to a greater extent than English politeness) the outcome is prejudice. Judd and Park refer to research on information processing biases and the use of judgemental heuristics (e.g., Rothbart, Evans and Fulero, 1979; Snyder and Swann, 1978), and to psychodynamic analyses of prejudice (Adorno, Frenkel-Brunswik, Levinson and Sanford, 1950; Bettelheim and Janowitz, 1964) to support their expectation that:

well-known information-processing effects and motivational processes may lead to stereotypic, valence and dispersion inaccuracies in the direction of exaggeration, prejudice, and overgeneralization. (p. 112)

In summary, Judd and Park's stated aim in their paper is to provide researchers with 'a set of tools for accuracy assessment' (p. 127), to sharpen awareness of and suggest some solutions to *methodological* problems which may have been retarding the accuracy assessment mission. They conclude that the assessment of the accuracy of stereotype content is a difficult task, but one that is 'feasible using the procedures we have outlined' (p. 127). In other words, the difficulty is defined at an empirical level – establishment of criterion values, sufficiently controlled and balanced research designs, elimination of sample selection biases and response language confounds. A *theoretical* consensus is more or less assumed, one which endorses the assumption that it is possible and reasonable to establish the validity of social stereotypes by comparing stereotype content with standardized personality assessments, individualized clinical judgements, private self-reports, statistical information and so forth.

In our view, this approach inevitably distils into a kernel of truth assumption. It suggests that there may be intrinsic differences between the members of different groups (including differences in *value*; see the definition of valence inaccuracy), to be revealed through the use of apparently objective tools which examine the 'essence' of the individual person, such as personality assessments and clinical judgements. An 'accurate' stereotype, it is assumed, should reflect these 'intrinsic and essential' (Campbell, 1967) individual differences.

Let us apply this idea to the current (July, 1995) situation in the former Yugoslavia. If personality tests or the judgements of unbiased clinicians revealed that individual Bosnian Serbs were, on average, towards the non-aggressive end of the 'aggressiveness' scale, would this render a Bosnian Government-held stereotype of the Serbs as 'highly aggressive' inaccurate? If the Serbs' *self*-stereotype did not confirm their characterization as 'aggressive' (they might describe themselves as 'principled' 'strong', and 'uncompromising', but not 'aggressive'), would this invalidate the Bosnian Government's view of them? Would it be reasonable to tell the government side that their perception of the Serbs as aggressive was inaccurate and wrong?

Might it be more fruitful to agree with Campbell that the validity of stereotypes refers to the 'social reality' of group life and intergroup relations, rather than the individual characteristics of group members? Perhaps the role of stereotypes is to express and explain (Yzerbyt, Rocher and Schadron, this volume) 'the stance of our own *group* in past and/or current relationships with the particular *group* in question' (Sherif, 1967, p. 37, emphasis added), rather than to summarize dispassionately or 'objectively' the individual-level characteristics of group members. If this is the case, it may be, at best, 'unrewarding' (Sherif, 1967, p. 37), at worst highly misleading, to define and attempt to assess the validity of stereotypes through their correspondence with criteria of the type discussed above. Rather than focusing the accuracy question on issues of methodology and measurement, we would suggest that there is a logically prior requirement to clarify just what stereotypes are, and the role they play in social perception. The next section briefly reviews current conceptualizations of stereotypes, with an emphasis on implications for stereotype accuracy.

2   The Current Theoretical Context: Stereotyping and Psychological Validity

There is widespread theoretical agreement that the categorization process is critically implicated in social stereotyping. As Hamilton and Trolier put it, 'the basis for all stereotyping is the differential perception of social groups. Without such differentiation between groups, stereotyping cannot occur' (1986, p. 134). There is less agreement, however, about just how, when and (perhaps most importantly) *why* we categorize people into groups. We have reviewed these perspectives in detail elsewhere (Oakes, in press; Oakes et al., 1994; Oakes and Turner, 1990; see Spears and Haslam, this volume). Our aim in this section is briefly to outline the theoretical context which currently frames the accuracy question. How are the nature and role of stereotyping being defined within social psychology, and what are the stated implications of these views for stereotype accuracy?

On the one hand, a substantial body of work argues that stereotyping is, at base, an *information processing error*, 'a necessary, if unfortunate, byproduct of our cognitive makeup' (Fiske and Neuberg, 1990, p. 14; e.g., see Hamilton and Sherman, 1994 for a review). 'Necessary' because of the limited capacity of our information processing systems, and the associated 'need of economizing attention' (Lippmann, 1922, p. 60). This need is, in part, met by the categorization process which, in this view, works as an information reduction mechanism that allows us to draw upon predigested, generalized images of social categories rather than go through the capacity-draining process of appreciating the actual uniqueness of each individual. The essence of this view is summarized in the following statement by Fiske and Neuberg:

> We have neither the cognitive capacity nor the time to deal with all the interpersonal information we have available to us . . . Given our limited cognitive resources, it is both simpler (requires less effort) and more efficient (requires less time) for a perceiver to use stereotyped information to make inferences about individuals belonging to a group than it is to analyze each person on an individual basis. (1990, p. 14)

The idea that, in stereotyping, the perceiver sacrifices accuracy for efficiency has become widely accepted. In the interests of efficient, economical processing, we sacrifice the rich detail of individuated, non-stereotypical person perception (see also Brewer, 1988, pp. 28–9). Individuation is the 'accurate' but capacity-draining standard *in comparison to which* group-based, stereotypical impressions are seen as an oversimplified distortion.

This argument has been made explicit in the continuum model of impression formation developed by Fiske and Neuberg (1990), and in related work on the effects of outcome dependency and accuracy goals on person perception (e.g., Neuberg and Fiske, 1987; Riley and Fiske, 1991; Ruscher and Fiske, 1990; Ruscher, Fiske, Miki and van Manen, 1991). One major premise of this work is that some impression formation involves categorization processes and some does not. Specifically, stereotypical impressions involve categorization processes, whereas individuated impressions are formed through piecemeal, attribute-by-attribute processing. For example, Fiske (1993a) comments, 'category-based or stereotypic responses *contrast with* fully individuated, attribute-by-attribute consideration of another person' (p. 623, emphasis added). In the latter case impressions remain 'relatively uncontaminated by category-based generalizations' (Fiske and Neuberg, 1990, p. 8). These attribute oriented, individuated impressions are considered to be '*more accurate* but less efficient' (ibid., p. 62, emphasis added) than category-based, stereotypical impressions. Thus, accuracy is equated with individuation, and with an impression formation process which does not involve categorization but rather an almost unmediated ('uncontaminated') appreciation of others' 'true' characteristics. In summary, the continuum model quite unambiguously argues that stereotyping involves, through the very nature of the process responsible for it (categorization), a loss of accuracy.

Similarly, Judd and Park's (1993) theoretical definitions of potential stereotype inaccuracies are founded on the assumption that the effects of the categorization process skew impressions away from an accurate representation of reality. As noted above, Judd and Park define three forms of stereotype inaccuracy. Concentrating for the moment on the first two (stereotypic and dispersion inaccuracy), Judd and Park suggest that these are most likely to take the form of exaggeration and overgeneralization, respectively. In other words, the tendency is for perceivers to exaggerate the absolute level of politeness amongst English people, and to overestimate the homogeneity of politeness amongst the English. Although Judd and Park make no reference to the category accentuation literature, the exaggeration and overgeneralization effects they discuss would appear to equate with the accentuation of inter-category difference (exaggeration instance of stereotypic inaccuracy) and intra-category similarity (overgeneralization instance of dispersion inaccuracy). Judd and Park discuss these effects as, by definition, errors. They suggest that, in order to qualify as accurate, perception of a group must be *indistinguishable* from perception of its members in isolation. Thus, our conceptualization of the English *as a group* (and standing in a specific relationship to membership groups of our own) should be no different from a statistician's aggregated information about individuals who happen to be English. However, we know that categorization into groups is reliably associated with accentuation effects (McGarty and Penny, 1988; McGarty and Turner, 1992), so by Judd and Park's definition stereotyping is, again, highly likely to be inaccurate.

Clearly, interpretations of the function and effects of the categorization process are critical to these theoretical perspectives on the relative (in)accuracy of stereotypical perception. It is not surprising, therefore, that adopting a different view of the categorization process has led us to reconceptualize the accuracy issue. From the perspective of self-categorization theory we have argued that *all* person perception (indeed, all perception; Bruner, 1957a) involves categorization (Turner et al., 1994; see Spears and Haslam, this volume). One reason for this is that all stimuli derive their meaning, at least in part, from the context in which they are perceived, and the paramount significance of categorization as an aspect of the perceptual process is that it endows stimuli with *context-dependent identity*. It is the crucial process which brings together our general understanding of and theories about the world and the material reality in which we live (Medin, Goldstone and Gentner, 1993), and includes apprehension of the *relations between* stimuli as part of their representation.

Categorization is essentially concerned with the perception of context-specific similarity and difference (see Oakes et al., 1994, pp. 95–100). Because of this, the basic data for categorization are not single, isolated stimuli but rather the *comparative relations between stimuli* within the current context. This idea is formalized in self-categorization theory in the concept of meta-contrast, the relative similarity of stimuli within and between potential categories. We have argued that what drives the categorization process is not a matching of isolated pieces of data with fixed cognitive structures (see Medin, 1989; Medin et al., 1993, for discussion of problems with this simple similarity-judgement approach to categorization) but *relative* similarity and difference within the stimulus context as a whole.

Self-categorization theory emphasizes the idea that there is a constant and normal variation in the *level of inclusiveness* at which social categorization occurs, and argues that this reflects constant *real* variation in the patterning of social behaviour. The theory takes for granted that there is some social reality that is distinctively represented by perception at different levels of social categorization. It assumes, for example, that individuals can and do act as both individual persons and social groups under different conditions. These conditions are specified through the variables of comparative (meta-contrast) and normative fit (Oakes, 1987). Where behaviour varies with group memberships, categorization at the ingroup–outgroup level becomes salient, and perception is stereotypical. More specifically (and in interaction with the effects of perceiver readiness; Oakes, 1987), ingroup–outgroup categorization occurs where behaviour differs within groups less than it differs between groups, and perceived differences are consistent with the perceiver's background theories about the nature of distinctions between those groups. On the other hand, where behaviour varies with individual identity, where it differs within more than it differs between groups on relevant dimensions, categorization operates at the level of individual differences, and perception is individuated (e.g., Blanz, 1995; Hogg and Turner, 1987; Oakes, in press; Oakes, Turner and Haslam, 1991; Oakes and Reynolds, 1995; Reynolds and Oakes, 1995; van Knippenberg, van Twuyver and Pepels, 1994; see Ellemers and van Knippenberg, this volume). Thus, the distinction between individuated and stereotypical perception is not in terms of the presence or absence of categorization, but rather in terms of the *level of inclusiveness at which the categorization process is operating*.

To summarize the accuracy implications of current theory: the limited capacity approach in general, and the continuum model specifically, argue that (a) whilst stereotypical perception involves categorization, individuated perception does not, so it is more 'direct', 'uncontaminated', and (b) by definition, individuated perception is more accurate (closer to reality) than group-level, stereotypical perception. Similarly, Judd and Park's (1993) treatment of stereotype accuracy identifies certain perceptual outcomes (exaggeration, overgeneralization) which are known to result from the basic functioning of the categorization process as, by definition, inaccurate. Self-categorization theory (a) argues that individuated and stereotypical perception involve categorization in equal degree (see also Cantor and Mischel, 1979; McCauley, 1988), (b) identifies a process (fit, in interaction with perceiver readiness) through which variation in levels of categorization is lawfully related to variations in social reality, and (c) emphasizes the psychological and social reality of group identifications, rejecting the idea that to perceive people as unique individuals is, in general, to represent them more accurately (see Asch, 1952; Oakes et al., 1994, chapter 4; Simon, this volume).

On this basis, self-categorization theory argues that stereotyping is *psychologically valid*, in the sense that the process responsible for it (categorization) is designed to provide the perceiver with an accurate representation of reality.[1] From this perspective there is no reason to assume that stereotyping is, by definition, less accurate than any other type of impression formation. Since both individuals and social groups exist objectively, both personal and social categorizations are necessary for the accurate representation of social life. Indeed, given that groups are real, not to represent them would be inaccurate (see Asch, 1952, p. 238).

3   Accentuation: Distortion or an Accuracy-oriented Sensitivity to Context?

Is it the case, however, that through social categorization we simply 'represent' groups? Surely the evidence is that the unavoidable effects of the categorization process lead us to 'accentuate' characteristics of group members, distorting actual similarities and differences in the manner identified by Judd and Park in their definitions of exaggeration and overgeneralization (we shall turn to valence inaccuracy presently).

Self-categorization theorists have been arguing for some time that the interpretation of accentuation effects as distortions is inappropriate (see Turner and Oakes, 1989, p. 269; also, Haslam and Turner, 1992, 1995; Oakes et al., 1994, chapter 6). Accentuation only appears to be distortion if we assume that there is a fixed, absolute 'standard' (a kernel of truth, perhaps) in comparison to which alternative judgements can be defined as 'accentuations', and that accuracy inheres in reporting the 'standard' value (cf. Swann, 1984, for a discussion of this issue in terms of 'stimulus constancy' in person perception). In contrast, SCT explicitly links the validity of person perception with the extent to which it provides *contextually appropriate*[2] representations which take into account the inherently variable *relations between* stimuli (including the perceiver him or herself). We have argued that valid perception is made possible by a categorization process which is highly context-specific and variable, but always (whatever the level of abstraction) lawfully related to *real stimulus variation*. Thus, we do not endow any one level of perception (e.g., individuated perception) with the status of a 'standard' in comparison to which other types of representation (e.g., stereotyping) are seen as accentuated distortions. Each is equally likely to be an accurate representation of *current stimulus relationships*.

An example may serve to clarify this point. Imagine an informal gathering of local Greenpeace activists which is suddenly invaded by a group of pro-nuclear testing French citizens. An intragroup context has become an intergroup context, and this real change in social relations would produce a shift in the salient level of categorization. Interpersonal differences between the Greenpeace members, salient before the invasion, would be displaced by salient intergroup differences (between Greenpeace and the pro-nuclear group) and intragroup similarities (within the two groups; see Haslam, Oakes, Turner and McGarty, 1995a and b). A forewarned social psychologist who had administered an appropriate questionnaire just before and just after the invasion would register an increase in perceived intragroup similarity and intergroup difference, and it is this *shift in the salient level at which similarity and difference are defined* that has been called 'accentuation' – the perception of individuals-as-group-members as more similar within and more different between categories than individuals perceived as individuals. However, only this particular shift, from interpersonal to intergroup, is referred to as accentuation. Let's imagine now that the Greenpeace members repel the invaders, return to their earlier interpersonal harmony, and yet again complete our measure of perceived similarity and difference. Surely our findings now indicate an 'accentuation' of interpersonal differences relative to the intergroup situation. It is the individualist tradition that has defined interpersonal differences as the baseline (indeed, as 'uncategorized'), and intragroup similarity as an accentuated distortion. We would argue, however, that ingroup–outgroup differences are no more of a distortion than the *lower level accentuations* of individual differences (see Reynolds, 1995, study 5, and see Mischel's 1981 discussion of the consistency issue in personality theory as an example of accentuation in individuated perception).

The self-categorization analysis suggests that patterns of accentuation appropriately (accurately) reflect the contextual properties of stimuli that derive from the relationships between them; more specifically, intragroup similarity and intergroup difference appropriately reflect *properties of individuals that derive from their group memberships*. This follows from our arguments about the reality of the group and the context-specificity of valid perception (see Oakes et al., 1994, chapter 6 for more detailed discussion). In fact, we see the very term 'accentuation' as misleading because it suggests that the 'accurate' representation of any stimulus should reflect properties apparent when it is judged in isolation, independent of any category to which it might belong. As noted above, in place of this notion of an abstract, context-free 'standard' of accuracy, we consider the appropriateness of perception at all levels of abstraction to be fully relative to the social context. So, to return to our example, if the pro-nuclear people arriving at the Greenpeace gathering see the activists there not as individuals but as people who share a group membership with each other, but not with them, the emphasis of this difference on relevant dimensions of comparison is a veridical reflection of contextually significant social realities. It is not a distortion, whereas to insist upon consideration of and behaviour towards all present *in ignorance of their group identities* would be.

Finally, we should note that this re-analysis of accentuation is not restricted to conditions where group influences do in fact transform the character of individual 'stimuli', such as where conformity processes produce relatively homogeneous behaviour within groups (Turner, 1991). This is, of course, part of a clear dynamic within which stereotyping processes operate (see Vinacke, 1956), but even where the stimulus is incapable of effecting change itself (as in most studies of social judgement), veridical perception will still involve accentuation (at some level of categorization), because accentuation simply reflects cognizance of the *relational* properties of stimuli within the current context. Consider, for example, the results of the classic study by Tajfel and Wilkes (1963). Subjects presented with eight lines categorized into two groups of four apparently distorted reality by, amongst other things, representing the difference between the longest of the four short lines and the shortest of the four long lines as 1.9 cm when the 'actual' difference was 0.9 cm. It can be argued, however, that 0.9 cm is a judgement of distance made in isolation, using a classification device – a ruler – designed and consensually employed to make judgements at that singular, isolated level of abstraction. This judgement is not, under all conditions, more valid, accurate or useful than judgements which reflect the category memberships of those lines. The 'accentuated' judgements reflect the fact that there were *important and meaningful* differences between the two categories of lines, a significant higher level structural property of the stimulus situation that *cannot be conveyed* by use of a ruler.

Similarly, we would argue that while personality inventories may (just like the ruler) provide us with useful information about people at one particular level of abstraction and in particular, limited contexts, stereotypes are describing important and meaningful differences between groups, significant higher level structural properties – aspects of *intergroup reality* – which cannot be conveyed by the use of personality tests.

To summarize, self-categorization theory argues that the 'accentuation' effects of the categorization process are essential to, rather than enemies of accurate perception. Our emphasis here on contextual specificity, and on the contribution of *relational* properties to accurate perception, throws serious doubt on the feasibility of establishing abstract, context-independent accuracy criteria. Further, we cannot agree that the aspects of stereotyping described by Judd and Park under the headings of stereotypic and dispersion inaccuracy are examples of perceptual distortion. In our view, Judd and Park have described (and renamed) two aspects of the perceptual selectivity which enables *contextually valid* perception.

4   Relativity, Relativism, and the Political Dimension of Stereotype Validity

Thus far we have argued for the psychological validity of stereotyping as a means of representing people in terms of contextually salient group relationships. It is obvious, however, that stereotypes also serve motivational and social functions (Tajfel, 1981a) which can sometimes make them appear to be little more than self-serving rationalizations of intergroup discrimination (cf. Yzerbyt et al., this volume). It is this evaluative aspect of stereotypes which often creates a final stumbling block for those trying to move towards an understanding of their validity (e.g., Stangor and Lange, 1994). How can it be 'valid' to characterize and, even more importantly, treat a group of human beings as lazy, ignorant and dirty? Perhaps part of the appeal of 'deficit' theories of stereotyping (from the authoritarian personality through to the cognitive miser) is that they allow us to treat such characterizations of human groups as errors, mistakes, side-effects, by-products. If we accept the psychological validity of stereotyping, we have to deal squarely with the real social and political sources of intergroup discrimination and hatred (cf. Sherif, 1967). In this section we address this issue, developing arguments presented initially in Oakes et al. (1994, chapter 8).

Of course, it is almost exclusively the *negative* evaluation of and associated discrimination against *minority groups* which is seen as compromizing stereotype validity. Sociologist Marlene Mackie suggests that 'the liberal sympathies of social scientists' (1973, p. 431) have retarded our understanding of stereotype accuracy because we have been unprepared to even ask questions about the potential accuracy of negative stereotypes of ethnic groups. On the other hand, social scientists do appear to be quite happy to present extremely negative characterizations of groups such as bureaucrats (Merton, 1957) and hospital administrators (Goffman, 1961). In the same vein, Fishman makes this fairly ascerbic comment about the influence of our own values in our approach to stereotypes and their validity:

> Is the view that White Protestant Americans possess certain laudable group-related traits necessarily any less an instance of stereotyping because scientifically oriented liberals hold it to be true and can supply some supporting 'evidence' when challenged? (1956, p. 32)

Clearly, the evaluative nature of stereotypes presents difficulties for the accuracy argument. In their recent chapter advocating a kernel of truth approach to the accuracy question, Ottati and Lee (1995) find it necessary to sound a 'cautionary note' against the implication that all stereotypes, including disparaging ones, are accurate. Some have attempted to deal with this by suggesting that the accuracy of a stereotype and its evaluative implications should be treated as separate issues (e.g., McCauley, Jussim and Lee, 1995). Thus, a belief that the English are polite could be either accurate or inaccurate, and may have either positive or negative attitudinal implications. More daringly, however, Judd and Park confront the issue head-on with the concept of 'valence inaccuracy'. Recall that this was defined as 'the tendency to view the group as more or less positive than *it actually is*' (Judd and Park, 1993, p. 111, emphasis added). This definition incorporates the rather controversial idea that there are absolute, inherent differences in value between human groups, expressed in the absolute valence of their 'true attributes' (p. 110). If those true attributes (potentially, the kernel of truth) turn out to be widely viewed as negative, what do we conclude? Is 'prejudice', rejection of that group, then justifiable?

Katz and Braly (1935) came face-to-face with this question in a follow-up to their more famous 1933 study. They asked 65 subjects (white, Princeton undergraduates) to rate the eighty-four checklist traits in terms of their 'desirability . . . in friends and associates' (p. 183). These subjects had no knowledge of the 1933 study, or the idea that the traits had anything to do with social groups, so these ratings stand as relatively 'objective' non-group-related assessments of trait valence. Using the stereotypes elicited in 1933, the overall favourability of the traits thought to characterize each of the ten stimulus groups (Americans, Germans, Turks, etc.) was then calculated, and the groups rank ordered accordingly. This rank ordering, based on separately judged trait favourability, revealed that Americans and English people were perceived most favourably, and Turks and 'Negroes' least favourably.

A further 60 subjects were asked to rank order the ten *groups* 'in terms of your preference for association with their members' (p. 185). This ordering, suggested Katz and Braly, represented 'rankings on the basis of prejudice' (p. 190). It was almost identical to that based on separate evaluation of relevant attributes. Again, Americans and the English headed the list, with 'Negroes' and Turks at the bottom.

Katz and Braly comment that 'one possible interpretation of this similarity is that racial prejudice is . . . a response to *the actual characteristics of races*' (p. 190, emphasis added). In other words, if Turks' 'true attributes' are cruel, physically dirty and sensual (i.e., if this aspect of the stereotype taps a kernel of truth), and these are evaluated negatively, then prejudice against Turks simply reflects the rational evaluation of their characteristics. But Katz and Braly were not claiming to have assessed the 'true attributes' of their target groups, so they are not bound to this explanation of prejudice. Indeed, they 'prefer . . . to interpret their findings differently' (p. 190), arguing that prejudice, as an emotion, is 'bolstered' by complex racial attitudes, including stereotypes which *need* bear no relationship at all to the 'true characteristics' (p. 190) of groups.

But the researcher who did lay claim to a valid, objective criterion for valence accuracy, or indeed to any type of objective criterion, could not so easily avoid the idea of prejudice as 'a response to the actual [negative] characteristics of races'. Aware of this danger, Ottati and Lee (1995) argue that we should distinguish between *belief in* a kernel of truth and *actual* accuracy, noting that 'undue confidence' in the kernel 'may serve to justify deep-seated prejudice, bias, and discrimination against victimized groups' (p. 50). However, these authors do accept the notion of a kernel of truth, of actual accuracy as defined and measured from one, absolute common perspective, and they suggest that 'only when we understand intergroup differences *objectively and accurately* can we change or minimize intergroup conflict' (p. 50, emphasis added). If that 'objective and accurate' understanding of another group reveals it to be vicious and immoral, will that minimize intergroup conflict? There are clearly many opportunities for 'objective' assessment to portray groups very negatively (McCauley et al., 1995), and proponents of the kernel of truth hypothesis and the measurement approach need to be prepared for the *political* response aspects that their research will provoke. Witness, for example, current reactions both within and beyond psychological science, to Herrnstein and Murray's (1994) revelations of supposed group differences in intelligence in *The Bell Curve* (e.g., Dorfman, 1995; Fraser, 1995; see below). This 'objective' understanding of group differences has certainly not minimized intergroup conflict.

We have already discussed the difficulties of establishing valid, reliable criteria with which to compare reported stereotypes. In the case of valence the problem is magnified, and obvious. In addition to the ideological and meta-theoretical problem just outlined, we would argue that value is an outcome of human judgement rather than an inherent property of any stimulus, and value judgements are therefore particularly prone to contextual variation. There is, for example, clear evidence that judgements of the valence of group attributes vary with group context and perspective (e.g., Doosje, Spears, Haslam, Koomen and Oakes, 1995; Mummendey and Schreiber, 1983; Mummendey and Simon, 1989; see also Reynolds, 1995, study 2). Further, all human perception (not just stereotyping) is motivated, purposeful, goal-driven and value-laden. It is not that there is perception distorted by value on the one hand, and accurate, value-free perception on the other, and there can be no absolute judge to say that one evaluation is accurate, another inaccurate. Consider, for example, the suggestion made by Bogardus (1950), that stereotypes could be rescued from invalidity through the collection and dissemination of what he called 'sociotypes' which, in contrast to stereotypes, would be 'socially representative and socio-logically valid', based on 'empirically-tested data', 'objective method', and the avoidance of 'value judgements' (pp. 286–91). In other words, the ideal would be for everyone to define and perceive the social world in the same way as, and from the perspective of, social scientists. This is patently absurd, clearly involving the simple substitution of perceivers' own personal and group-based values and perspectives for the values and perspective (albeit 'objectified' as empirical and sociologically valid) of another group.

Human judgements are value judgements, and attempts to establish 'valence accuracy' can only ever involve comparing one human value judgement (e.g., a stereotype) with another human value judgement (e.g., the judged valence of its constituent attributes). We are not omniscient beings, who see all things at all times from all perspectives, nor neutral computers that analyse exhaustively and mechanically with no social purpose or emotional investment. If we, as social psychologists, characterize and, at least implicitly, condemn judgements as 'inaccurate' because they do not measure up to these inhuman ideals, we may present a seriously misleading picture of what human social judgement is all about. Instead, we can better understand the role of values in stereotyping if we see them as the *premises* from which psychologically valid, but admittedly and unavoidably *relative* judgements are made.

To take an example, consider the possible stereotypes which might develop to describe and explain real differences between the groups 'employed people' and 'unemployed people'. The perceiver who believes in liberal politics and the welfare state may characterize unemployed people as unfortunate victims for whom the state, and those in work, should take responsibility. On the other hand, a conservative economic rationalist may blame the unemployed themselves for their fate, and perceive them as lazy exploiters of others' efforts. Each group would reject the other's stereotype of the unemployed as 'inac-curate', but for each it is 'true' from the perspective of the value (liberalism/

conservatism) which functions as the premise for the group judgement (see Guimond, Begin and Palmer, 1989, p. 128). Most importantly, the psychological processes through which both the liberal and the conservative arrive at their stereotype are identical. In both cases, the stereotype represents aspects of an intergroup relationship *from the perspective of the perceiver* (cf. Sherif, 1967; see above), and the value judgement involved is part of that intergroup relationship. Part of the stereotype's function, usefulness, and psychological validity resides in its ability to represent that value judgement. As we noted above, neither the liberal nor the conservative is likely to abandon their stereotype on being presented with an objective, empirically assessed, social scientific 'sociotype' of unemployed people (Bogardus, 1950). Such information would be of little use to a perceiver with specific political values and motives.

Must we conclude, then, that all stereotypes are equally accurate? If they are all psychologically valid, based on rational processes designed to provide the perceiver with an accurate representation of reality *from that perceiver's own vantage point, and relative to that perceiver's own values*, then do all stereotypes have an equal claim to 'accuracy', and are all equally acceptable? Should we 'allow a bigot to continue to use his or her stereotypes, [because] those beliefs seem to them to be accurate' (Stangor, 1995, p. 289)?

Any discussion of stereotype accuracy must eventually face these twin issues of relativity and relativism. We have accepted perceptual relativity, arguing that it is unavoidable, and indeed that it contributes to psychologically valid social perception. We do not, however, endorse the relativism which tends to follow from the 'pragmatic' perspective on relativity and accuracy, the idea that 'judgements are accurate if they are useful' (Fiske, 1993b, p. 157). Clearly, there are many 'useful' stereotypes which we would be most unwilling to define as accurate, and bigotry is, as Stangor insists, indefensible. As well as their psychological validity, stereotypes must be considered in terms of their *social validity* (see Oakes et al., 1994, chapter 8), in the context of the social, ideological, political and historical processes which influence stereotype formation, validation and rejection. Stereotypes which are fully psychologically valid may, nonetheless, be challenged as socially invalid, indeed as *inaccurate*, by perceivers who reject the value premises on which those stereotypes rely.

In this way, stereotypes become *political weapons* (see Haslam et al., 1995b; Reicher, Hopkins and Condor, this volume). As active participants in the social process, and confident of the psychological validity of our views (of the fact that they are *not* based on a failure to pay attention, or some other psychological inadequacy; see Oakes et al., 1994, pp. 209–10), we defend and promote our own values and associated stereotypes while at the same time rejecting and attempting to change those with which we disagree. From an opposed political position, we may protest that the economic rationalist's stereotype of the unemployed is self-interested and cruel, and use whatever means we have to demonstrate the validity of our own view. On the basis of the principle of human rights we argue that the stereotypes used to justify the practice of 'ethnic cleansing' are inaccurate distortions, while at the same time developing and promulgating our own politically motivated views of the perpetrators. In the context of a 'moral sense of humanity's essential oneness' (Mackie, 1973, p. 444), we reject many stereotypes of minority groups as discriminatory and false, whereas assertions of equality on the basis of race, gender, sexual preference, marital status and so forth are accepted as self-evidently true.

Taking issue with the objectivity of apparent 'evidence' of group differences *when this 'evidence' conflicts with our values* is part of this political process. If its implications are unacceptable to us, we often challenge evidence produced on a supposedly objective basis, such as through psychometric testing or statistical reporting – surely front-running candidates, from the measurement perspective, for the role of objective criteria for stereotype accuracy. One current and noteworthy example of this process occurring is the commentary on *The Bell Curve* (Herrnstein and Murray, 1994) in a recent edition of *Contemporary Psychology* (Bouchard, 1995; Dorfman, 1995; see also Fraser, 1995). Donald Dorfman attacks both the scientific respectability and the value premises of the 'evidence' of group differences in intelligence. He asks, 'Who are the authors of *The Bell Curve*? Are they right?' (p. 419), and part of his answer is to invite us to judge the *political values* of Charles Murray, who 'wants[s] to end welfare', works for 'a conservative research group' and publishes in 'a neoconservative magazine' (Dorfman, 1995, p. 419). Dorfman concludes that the book is 'not a scientific work . . . it has a specific political agenda' (p. 419), and that whether or not you see any value in its findings 'depends on your point of view' (p. 421). In other words, as far as Dorfman is concerned, it is a matter of *politics*. It depends upon whether you want to accept the politically conservative values that he has argued supply the work's premise.

This example suggests that the identification of objective indicators of group difference may affect stereotype accuracy in a way quite other than that intended by its proponents. Far from non-controversially resolving the accuracy question through measurement, it may tend to act as a catalyst to the processes of social influence, including political argument, through which society attempts to move towards more socially valid stereotypes – stereotypes which are valid from the perspective of the whole community. Stereotypes linking race and intelligence are currently, thanks to Herrnstein and Murray, undergoing renewed and intense social scrutiny. Like other social beliefs, stereotypes are subject to a continual process of social influence through which their subjective validity can be either bolstered or challenged. Identity and group relationships are crucially implicated in this process (Turner, 1991; see Haslam, this volume; Reicher et al., this volume). The elucidation of the role of identity in stereotype validation and change is currently a major focus of our empirical work (Haslam, Oakes, McGarty, Turner, Reynolds and Eggins, in press), and we see this as crucial to the development of our as yet rudimentary understanding of the social aspects of stereotype validity. Importantly, self-categorization theory argues that it is the hierarchical nature of self-categorization which enables 'human perception . . . to bootstrap itself out of its own relativity' (Oakes et al., 1994, p. 210):

> at one level, ingroup and outgroup may disagree about stereotypes without uncertainty, but at the higher level of a superordinate social identity (as a member of 'civilized society', 'Western culture', 'humanity'), even ingroup and outgroup will feel the need to reach agreement and reduce the uncertainty which arises from conflict. Our desire, despite being members of different social groups, to assert one stereotype over another as true for all, our belief that a level of validity higher than purely relativistic judgement is possible, can be derived from the hierarchical character of self- and social identity . . . It is the fact that we share higher-order identities that makes it possible to define validity at a level higher than the judgement of a single group. (Oakes et al., 1994, pp. 209–10)

It is this possibility, the fact that we *can* define and experience validity at a higher level and therefore do not rest content in our relativity, that renders relativism social-psychologically (as well as politically) inadequate and unacceptable. Relativity is never eliminated, but the combination of perspectives, the correction of individual relativity at the level of the group, of group relativity at the level of society and beyond holds the potential to *replace the false with the valid*.[3] In other words, some 'relativities' win, others lose, and this is as much a matter of true social influence as it is of power – millions of people do not, now, stereotype women, Jews, gays, the unemployed, as they did just a few decades ago. It is not that shared identity supplies a basis of harmonious, higher level agreement in which we can lose sight of real differences, but rather that it motivates us towards the interactive struggle through which subjective validity is challenged and beliefs, values and ideologies are changed. The confrontation of alternatives cannot guarantee progress, but it involves a process of political argument, open conflict and struggle which many have seen as a precondition for progress towards truth and 'accuracy' (see the writings of Marx and Hegel; e.g., Berlin, 1978, p. 41).

5   Conclusions

In this discussion of stereotype accuracy, we have drawn a distinction between the psychological and the social validity of stereotypes. We have argued (in contrast to other current theory) that stereotypes, as context-specific representations of intergroup relationships, are psychologically valid and therefore carry a full potential for accuracy. They emerge from processes designed to provide the perceiver with an accurate, though relative, representation of reality.

The concept of social validity emphasizes the social, political and ideological aspect of stereotyping. We have suggested that social values, which serve as premises for the perceived accuracy (and therefore acceptance and use) of stereotypes, cannot be deemed 'objectively' true or untrue, but rather can be either validated or challenged through processes of social influence and political action. Modern versions of the kernel of truth hypothesis attempt to maintain the plausibility of the measurment approach and to evade the political dimension of stereotyping by divorcing content from evaluation, actual accuracy from belief in accuracy and so forth. But ultimately, the human, social defintion of a stereotype as accurate or not is a political act. It is not, we would argue, achieveable through the measurement techniques of psychological science.

Notes

Grateful thanks to Yueh-Ting Lee and Chuck Stangor for making available material that was unpublished at the time of writing, and to Naomi Ellemers, Alex Haslam, Bernd Simon, Russell Spears and John Turner for comments on an earlier draft of the chapter.

1 Note that the term here is *psychologically* valid, not phenomenologically valid (cf. Stangor, 1995). The validity is defined in terms of the nature of the underlying psychological processes, *not* subjectively. We agree entirely with Stangor's argument that it is not sufficient to accept a pragmatic definition of accuracy: if it works for the perceiver, and they therefore feel it is 'accurate', it is. This type of view leads directly to relativism, which we reject, but we do not see 'objectivism', the kernel of truth idea, or the measurement tradition as the only, or indeed as a feasible or acceptable alternative approach.

2 Note, again, that our aim here is not to equate 'accuracy' with 'pragmatics', with the context-specific *usefulness* of stereotyping (cf. Fiske, 1993b; Swann, 1984). We are arguing that *as the nature of stimulus relations changes* across contexts, i.e., as relevant aspects of *reality* change, then the validity of representations at different levels of abstraction and on different dimensions varies.

3 Questions of epistemology and philosophical orientation inevitably enter into this complex issue (e.g., see Cook, 1984, p. ix; Hastie and Rasinski, 1988). Our rejection of relativism is clearly related to a rejection of philosophical idealism. Like Hastie and Rasinski, we assume that the social perceiver is 'attempting accurately to judge the real properties of . . . [a stimulus which] exists independently of them' (1988, p. 194), taking into account our emphasis on the reality and importance of the relational properties of social stimuli (Oakes et al., 1994, chapters 4 and 5).

4
Changing the Stereotype of the Stereotype

Stephen Worchel and
Hank Rothgerber

Long before I (S.W.) cracked the pages of books on stereotyping, I received a lesson on the subject that, having the distinct advantage of primacy, has shaped my thinking and research on group perception. The classroom was the gridiron (the American football field) and the teacher was Billy Joe Canter (I'll change his name slightly in case the true Billy Joe should chance upon this chapter), a 280-pound left tackle from West Texas. Football, like most team sports in the southern United States, was segregated (no blacks allowed) in 1963, and this situation 'was how the Lord intended' according to Billy Joe. To put his view in printable terms, Billy Joe described African Americans as lazy, dangerous, dumb, sexual and musically inclined, all views held by his friends back in west Texas. African Americans were 'OK in their place', and that place was not on a football team with white boys.

Most of us tolerated Billy Joe because any sign of disagreement unleashed a torrent of quotes from books (including the Bible) in support of Billy Joe's view and a threat of bodily harm if the disagreement continued. Our team was winning, and most of us were more interested in basking in the glory than doing battle with Billy Joe. But as fate would have it, integration of college athletics was ordered by the courts. My team's colour barrier was broken the next year with the recruitment of Johnny Gray, a wonderfully talented African-American running back who not only had Olympic-speed, but who was an honour student with an ambition to be a lawyer.

The impact of this historical event on the team was surprisingly muted; most of us were cautious and curious. But Billy Joe was anything but muted. After first threatening to quit the team (but abandoning the idea when he realized there was no place he could play on a segregated team), Billy Joe spent the first month trying to make Johnny as uncomfortable as possible. He taped newspaper stories of black criminals on the walls, tried to taunt Johnny into fights, and refused to sit at the team dining table with Johnny. But the heat of summer practices and Johnny's sparkling play seemed to take the starch out of Billy Joe.

The first change came after an especially tough game when Johnny had a spectacular game despite playing with two broken fingers and a broken nose. After the game Billy Joe, nearly drunk with the joy of victory, yelled to Johnny, 'I knew you people were bad and dangerous! *I'm glad you're bad and I'd rather have you with me than against me.*' Although the terms 'bad' and 'dangerous' held their place in Billy Joe's stereotype, he had subtly changed their meaning to indicate 'tough' and 'courageous'. The next change came when mid-term grades were posted in the training room. Johnny had the second highest grades on the team, whereas Billy Joe ranked in the middle. One of the team members playfully reminded Billy Joe of his characterization of African Americans as 'dumb'. The remark, which would have been grounds for a fight six months earlier, brought a matter-of-fact response from Billy Joe that '. . . not all blacks are dumb, only most of them.' This response showed that there was no change in the content of Billy Joe's stereotype of 'blacks', but there was now a subtle suggestion that all blacks were not alike. The final incident came at the end of the season when Billy Joe introduced Johnny to his parents, announcing that Johnny's mother was Jamaican, and because of this accident of heritage, Johnny was '. . . not like those blacks at home'.

The seemingly ironic conclusion to the story was that when Billy Joe Canter graduated in 1967, the world of sports had changed, but little had changed in Billy Joe's hometown in west Texas or in the unflattering terms Billy Joe used to describe African Americans. He told one of his friends, 'We've got to watch out for those blacks. They're lazy, dumb, dangerous . . .' Then he went out to dinner with Johnny Gray and his wife. After four years Billy Joe's stereotype had not changed, or had it?

1   The Many Faces of a Stereotype

Answering this question leads us deep into the history of social psychology. The study of stereotypes has been embraced by investigators with a variety of motives. Originally, the interest in stereotypes grew out of the suspected relationship between stereotypes, prejudice and discrimination (Katz and Braly, 1933, 1935). There was a general view that stereotypes were both evil and erroneous, and represented flawed thinking (or more correctly, lack of thinking).

More recently, stereotypes have found their way into the social cognition camp. Like a reformed sinner, much of the evil nature of the stereotype has been washed away; some investigators (Judd and Park, 1993) have even suggested the heretofore unspeakable position that there may be accuracy to stereotypes. Social cognition researchers have been intrigued by the relative stability of stereotypes, and stereotypes have been seen as presenting an exciting opportunity to examine how social information is stored, processed and acted upon (Messick and Mackie, 1989; Hamilton and Sherman, 1989; Rothbart, Evans and Fulero, 1979).

Although much has changed in the study of stereotypes, the view of what constitutes a stereotype has remained relatively stable. Most investigators accept the definition that portrays stereotypes as sets of characteristics ascribed to people on the basis of their group membership (Oakes, Haslam and Turner, 1994). The emphasis in this definition is on the *content* of stereotypes. Traits such as intelligent, aggressive, kind and ambitious are the building blocks that form the stereotype. In many cases, the content may also include a general perception of the group as being either good or bad. A stereotype is measured by examining the traits an individual uses to describe a group. According to this point of view, stereotypes are changed when a trait is deleted, added or replaced by another trait.

This definition of stereotypes fits the bill if one is concerned only with the content and process involved in an individual's perception. However, this view is not compatible with two positions that we will advance in this chapter. First, we will argue that stereotypes are strongly influenced by the perceiver's group; they are not simply the creative product of an isolated individual. Second, we suggest that stereotypes are multidimensional, with traits (content) ascribed to the target group being only one dimension. Stereotypes, like diamonds, have many faces in addition to content. Expanding the definition of stereotypes to accommodate these positions should allow us to relate research on stereotypes to the broader area of intergroup perception and ignite a search to identify the other components of the stereotype.

Tajfel (1981b) and Turner (1982) anticipated one of these components in their theory of social identity and social categorization. Tajfel argued that people create their social identity by defining the groups to which they belong and the outgroups of which they are not members. The first stage toward a social identity is identifying the relevant groups and the people who comprise these groups. The group is, therefore, not a given but a social judgement. The judgement process allows the individual wide latitude in constructing social reality. Individuals can create, change and recreate their social world by changing the membership of groups or creating new groups. Turner and his colleagues (1985, 1991; Turner and Oakes, 1989; Oakes, et al., 1994) suggested that categories can be broken into subcategories, and these subcategories can be further dissected into even more refined subcategories. Carrying this view a step further, we would argue that one component of stereotypes is the group to which traits are ascribed. Any representation of a stereotype must, therefore, include reference to the target: *the social category*. This inclusion is critical because stereotypes can be changed by recategorizing (Gaertner et al., 1989; Anastasio, Bachman, Gaertner and Dovidio, this volume) or by creating new subtypes (Weber and Crocker, 1983; Johnston, Hewstone, Pendry and Frankish, 1994) that fall outside the group that was the focus of the original stereotype. My old friend Billy Joe demonstrated this point when he severed Jamaican blacks from his category of black.

A third component of stereotypes that has also been the focus of considerable research in intergroup relations is the *perceived homogeneity of the target group*. Research supporting the exemplar model of representation (Linville, Fischer and Salovey, 1989) demonstrated a tendency for outgroups to be seen as more homogeneous than ingroups (Linville and Jones, 1980; Park and Rothbart, 1982). However, other research has demonstrated that this perceived homogeneity is exactly that, *perceived*, and is, therefore, subject to change (Linville et al., 1989: Worchel, Coutant-Sassic and Wong, 1993). Perceptions of group homogeneity are based on psychological reality, and readily influenced by a variety of group conditions (Simon and Brown, 1987; Ellemers and Van Knippenberg, this volume; Doosje and Ellemers, this volume). This plasticity of perceptions opens another door for changing stereotypes while holding basic content constant; stereotypes can be changed by the psychological manipulation of the perceived homogeneity of the target group. The belief that all blacks are dangerous is very different from the belief that although blacks are generally dangerous, this is not a homogeneous group (e.g., 'not all blacks . . .'). Therefore, it is important that any description of a stereotype include an indication of the perceived homogeneity of the target group.

Another component of stereotypes that is often overlooked is the individual's *interpretation* of each term or trait. Cognitive consistency theorists (Anderson, 1965; Feldman, 1968) have commented on the gymnastic ability of the mind to maintain consistency by manipulating the meaning of traits, rather than changing the traits themselves. If we apply this view to stereotypes, we discover another component of stereotypes, *and* another route by which stereotypes can be changed. In the opening example, Billy Joe maintained his description of blacks as 'dangerous', but the interpretation of the concept shed its negative connotation when it assumed the cloak of being tough and powerful. Interpretation, then, becomes the chameleon quality of stereotypes, allowing broad changes in meaning without requiring change in the traits that comprise the content. Any description of a stereotype must, therefore, include the interpretation given to each trait in the content, and any study of stereotype change must be sensitive to the interpretation component (Reicher, Hopkins and Condor, this volume).

A close cousin to interpretation is the *salience or weighting* given to the various components of the content. Allport (1961) suggested that one's personality is defined both by one's traits and the prominence (centrality) of those traits. So, too, may the meaning of a stereotype be affected by the prominence one gives to the traits that comprise the stereotype. A high percentage of people may agree that Jews are ambitious, but for some this might be viewed as a central term in the stereotype, whereas for others it is seen as more peripheral. An individual can dramatically change the meaning of a stereotype by shuffling the deck of content, placing some traits in the central position and moving others to a less prominent position.

Our preamble to this point leads us to argue that a new, more broad, definition of stereotype is necessary. Rather than simply being a 'collection of attributes believed to characterize the members of a social group' (Oakes et al., 1994, p. 1), a stereotype is a collection of traits along with the meaning and position of centrality of each trait and a description of the target group along with an estimation of the degree of homogeneity within that group. Any meaningful measure of stereotypes must be multidimensional. This expanded definition of stereotype not only describes, it also guides research into areas that are not typically viewed under the umbrella of stereotyping. It places research on group homogeneity, categorization, language, interpretation and meaning at the same level as research on stereotype content. It argues that research on these issues is not only concerned with the process of stereotyping, but that these studies are also concerned with the nature and structure of stereotypes.

The expanded picture of stereotypes has important implications for the process involved in changing stereotypes. One intriguing possibility is based on the cognitive miser position (Taylor, 1981b). According to this position, change in stereotypes should occur on one dimension. If this position is correct, a strong case can be made for measuring all dimensions of stereotypes because change may be overlooked if some dimensions are not examined. A second alternative is that change may occur in numerous dimensions, with greater change being recorded in some components. Research is needed to determine how change results. However, regardless of the position that is supported, a challenge for a working model of stereotypes is to identify the conditions that lead to changes in certain dimensions. One step toward developing this model is to determine the foundations (sources) of each of the stereotype components.

2   The Roots of Stereotypes: Group and Individual

In an effort to identify the roots of stereotypes, we began our search by digging in the fertile soil of early investigations, and then proceeded to collect new data. Let us begin by presenting the case suggested by the early research, and then offer some supporting data at the end of this chapter. Katz and Braly (1933) identified stereotypes by asking 100 Princeton students to select adjectives that defined select groups. The result of this method was a list of traits *and* the percentage of people who included each trait in their stereotype. For example, Katz and Braly report that 83 per cent of their subjects indicated that Negroes were 'superstitious', while 38 per cent listed 'ignorant' in their stereotype. The percentage of subjects that indicate a specific trait gives an indication of the shared nature of that trait. Two messages are communicated in these data. First, stereotypes are composed of specific traits (content). And second, stereotypes have a social or shared component (Haslam, this volume). In other words, stereotypes have roots in the social group; they are, to borrow Bar-Tal's term, group beliefs (Bar-Tal, 1990). A similar message is found in research on prejudice and discrimination. For example, Adorno and associates (1950) argued that high Authoritarians were most prone toward prejudice. However, this personality type also had a distinctive social component that disposed the individual to defer to power, whether that power resided in a leader or in a group. These studies suggest that if we were to perform a definitive DNA test to identify the parents of stereotypes (and prejudice), we would find they result from a union of individual *and* social forces.

More recently, however, the stereotype has become a child in a single-parent family, that parent being social cognition which focuses on individual information processing. The results from this approach have been exciting and illuminating (Hamilton, 1981; Judd and Park, 1993; Brewer, 1988), but the approach has not been as sensitive as it could be to Tajfel's (1969a) admonition that 'much of what happens to us is related to the activities of groups to which we do or do not belong . . .' (p. 81). As a result of the focus on the individual, the stereotype has been viewed as a description (a schema, if you will) that is developed, processed, stored, massaged and changed by the *individual*. The stereotype is social only in the fact that its target is people rather than rocks, trees or animals. This limitation largely ignores the broader social component of stereotypes, a component that does not contradict the individual focus, but expands and complements it.

We would argue that the time is ripe to give at least the rights of visitation to the 'social' parent. One area where the cognitive and social approaches can be comfortably intertwined involves examining stereotypes in light of the expanded model we presented earlier. We suggested that a stereotype is multidimensional and includes information about content, categorization, group homogeneity, interpretation and weighting. If we dissect each of these components, we find that each has both an individual/cognitive base and a group base, but the impact of these influences is different for each component. In other words, some of the components arise from the social experiences and/or group membership, while others are more closely related to individual experience, personality and cognitive processing. Some components are, therefore, shared while others are more unique to the individual. If we develop a continuum ranging from uniquely individual to shared or group-based, we can locate the components of a stereotype.

The basis for our reasoning is the view of groups having two competing

Figure 4.1   Source of components of a stereotype.

pressures. On one hand, in order for the group to survive, there must be some shared links that bind the members together. It is this shared ground that ensures that members will see themselves as belonging together, and be prepared to behave in a relatively uniform manner. The shared linkages must be easily identified by both ingroup and outgroup members. On the other hand, the corset which the group places on its members cannot be so rigid that it eliminates all uniqueness and individual freedom. Total uniformity results in a stagnant group, and individuals will rebel against a structure that allows no individual freedom of thought or action. Stereotypes are critical for a group because they guide members' interpersonal relationships with outgroup members. However, interpersonal relationships (involving both ingroup and outgroup members) are also of central interest to the individual whose personal comfort, and possibly survival, is intertwined in these relationships. In order to placate these competing forces, we argue that stereotypes are composed so that some components meet the group uniformity needs, while others are more sensitive to the individual's need for personal freedom of thought and action.

As figure 4.1 indicates, we argue that the content of a stereotype is the most strongly group-based component. Bar-Tal (1990) defines group belief as 'convictions that group members (a) are aware that they share and (b) consider as defining their "groupness"' (p. 36). Being a member of a group often involves sharing common beliefs.

Publicly stating these beliefs demonstrates that the individual is part of the group. Content, we argue, is the best candidate for the group belief because it is the most broad (crude) component of stereotypes, and it is most easily communicated by groups. By dictating content, the group defines the normative position while still leaving individuals some freedom to incorporate personal experience. Supporting the group foundation of the content component is the fact that individuals often hold stereotypes of target groups of which they have no first-hand knowledge. The traits applied to these target groups represent the position of their ingroup. Indeed, Katz and Braly (1933) identified stereotypes by the degree to which the content was shared by members of the perceiving group. The content of stereotypes is most likely to be stated in the form of 'we believe' rather than 'I believe'. In suggesting a group foundation for content, we are not ignoring the possibility that content can also reflect individual experience; we simply want to emphasize the strong social influence on this component (Haslam, this volume). The group base for content also helps explain why stereotypes (or more precisely, the content of stereotypes) are often resistant to change. If the content of a stereotype is the product of one's group, it is understandable that it is unlikely to change because of an individual's unique experience or persuasive communications aimed at the individual. Rather, as we will discuss later, the content is most likely to be changed by experiences shared by all or most of the perceiving group members; such shared experiences may involve changes in the relationship between ingroup and target group, or broadly recognizable change within either the ingroup or target group.

Moving across the group/individual continuum, we would argue that categorization and perceptions of group homogeneity have a more equal contribution from group and individual bases. Turner (1987b) makes an elegant case for the role of the self in the categorization process, showing how individuals can structure their social world through categories and subcategories. He argues that issues of self-identity and social concerns guide the fingers of the mind as they craft categories. Although categorization has deep roots within the individual's perceptions and cognitions, individuals are not completely free of group influences in the formation of these categories. There is a tendency toward social comparison when developing categories, and finding that one's categories are significantly different from those of other ingroup members should cause discomfort and may initiate ridicule from the group. Group influences help determine the rules by which categories can be established and, to some extent, the members placed in these categories. The role of the group in defining categories is seen most clearly in cases where categories are explicitly defined. For example, the apartheid laws in South Africa were accompanied by legal definitions of 'blacks' and 'coloureds'. Similarly, 'Negroes' in post Civil War Louisiana (USA) were considered to be anyone who was one-sixteenth Negro. The Olympic Committee turned to DNA tests to define categories of male and female.

Sliding further toward the individual side of the continuum, we suggest that interpretation and weighting, while not being free from group influences, are largely left to the individual's discretion. Although there is clearly 'shared meaning' of concepts and traits (Ng and Bradac, 1993), and specific aspects of a stereotype are more or less widely held by group members (Katz and Braly, 1933), the group influence is more evident at the macro level of content. There is more of an 'I' flavour to meaning and weighting. These components are more often influenced by aspects of the individual and his or her situation than by that of the group. Indeed, several investigators (Brewer, 1979; Worchel, 1979) have found considerable variation in the way individuals interpret contacts with outgroup members as representing individual or collective contacts. Likewise, other investigators (Taylor and Fiske, 1978; Wilder, 1978) have shown that conditions unique to the immediate situation affect the salience of information about an ingroup or outgroup member.

The basic point is that the components of a stereotype are differentially rooted in individual and group bases, and that the roots of the components influence the degree of resistance a particular component has to change and the conditions which are most likely to foster change in that component. In order to explicate this latter point, let us engage in a bit more speculative license to identify the conditions that should create change in various components of a stereotype.

3   The Winds of Change: Relating Group and Individual Variables to Change in Components of a Stereotype

Conceiving a stereotype as multifaceted and recognizing that the facets are differentially rooted along a group–individual continuum sets the stage for identifying the conditions that are most likely to create change in the various components. Any discussion of changing stereotypes requires some attention to the functional nature of stereotypes. Tajfel (1981a) suggested that there are five functions, two operating at the individual level and three at the group level. At the individual level, stereotypes help organize and simplify the social environment and they represent and preserve social values. At the group level, stereotypes explain large-scale social events, justify various forms of collective action and create positive intergroup distinctiveness.

Research on impression formation suggests additional functions and processes involved in stereotypes (Jones and Pittman, 1982). Conflicting storms often beset stereotype formation. On the one hand, there is the desire to organize and simplify the world, which is tempered by the desire to perceive the world in an accurate way. This latter force is strongest when the individual is faced with acting in the environment, rather than being a passive observer. Jones and Pittman (1982) identify a third motive in the impression formation process: presenting one's self (we will take the liberty of adding one's group) in the most positive light possible. Therefore, stereotypes can be used to present a positive impression of one's group.

Both the social identity and impression formation positions endow stereotypes with cognitive and motivational characteristics, individual and social functions, and both approaches identify strong forces lobbying for stability (organizing and simplifying functions) and flexibility (justifying action and accuracy). To these insightful analyses, we add one additional function: stereotypes help establish and maintain one's membership in groups. Shared stereotypes establish a common bond between group members, and create a reluctance on the part of the individual to tamper with certain dimensions of stereotypes, lest he or she weaken the bond with the group. Individuals can demonstrate their loyalty to a group by voicing group beliefs (stereotypes) (Noel, Wann and Branscombe, 1995; Reicher, Spears and Postmes, 1995).

With these functions in mind, we can venture into the question of the conditions that are likely to create change in stereotypes. Given our multidimensional model of stereotypes, our concern with change draws attention to the characteristics of the information/situation instigating change rather than the individual process involved. Two characteristics of the situation seem critical for our purpose. The first is whether or not the situation is shared by most or all of the perceiving group members (e.g., likely to create group change) or unique to the individual (unlikely to create group change in stereotype). The second, but related factor, is whether or not the situation involves intergroup relations (between the perceiving and target group), the condition of the group (perceiving group or target group), or the condition of the individual. Because we argue that stereotypes are developed to meet both group and individual needs, changes on any of these dimensions should influence the stereotype. However, different types of situation/information change should affect different dimensions of the stereotype.

Looking at the intergroup arena, we find that groups can be interdependent (either cooperative or competitive), or they can be independent. Numerous investigators (Brewer, 1986; Worchel, 1986; Gaertner et al., 1989; Anastasio et al., this volume) have argued that the nature of interaction between groups affects and is, to some degree, affected by the salience of group boundaries. Given that one function of stereotypes is to justify collective action and that changes in the relationship between groups are evident to all members of the perceiving group, any change in the nature of interaction between groups should set the stage for change in stereotypes. However, the change should be most profound within the more group-based dimensions of the stereotype (content, categorization and perceptions of outgroup homogeneity). This analysis does not preclude changes in the other dimensions, but it does predict the most likely seats of change. In addition, it argues that the change in these dimensions of stereotypes will occur in most (or all) members of the perceiving group, rather than in isolated individuals.

The second category of events that instigates stereotype change focuses more directly on the group, either the perceiving group or the target group. Looking first at the target group, there are several events that can impact stereotypes. One may find information about a group on a dimension that was not originally included in a stereotype. For example, it may be announced that blond-haired children in the US won 90 per cent of the academic awards in a year. Previously, intelligence (high or low) may not have been part of the stereotype, but the new information creates the need to re-examine the stereotype. Second, the condition of a target group may change on an existing stereotype dimension: for example, women's scores on the maths section of college entrance exams increased 20 per cent. As we will see, even information about the changes in the size of a target group can affect stereotyping. When changes in the condition of the target group are evident to all or most members of the perceiving group, we would argue that these changes are most likely to affect the content, the categorization and the perception of homogeneity components of stereotypes.

For example, in previous research (Worchel et al., 1992), we had difficulty creating conditions under which subjects in the perceiving group would change the content of their perceptions of a target group, even in the face of disconfirming information. We reasoned that this result occurred because subjects were not made aware that the information they received about the target group was shared by other group members. In a recent study we (Rothgerber and Worchel, 1995) attempted to rectify this problem by giving subjects information about the target group in a group setting and allowing them to observe the reactions of their ingroup members when they received this information. We were also interested in whether or not subjects would change their perceptions of a target group that originally had many of the characteristics of their own ingroup.

In the study, subjects were informed that two other groups in addition to their own would work on several tasks. They were told that one of the other groups would work under optimal environmental conditions. The other group was similar to their own group in that they had to labour under relatively impoverished environmental conditions. During the course of the study, subjects received information that the 'advantaged group' performed consistently well and that their ingroup performed consistently below average. However, the information about the other disadvantaged group indicated that the group either showed an accelerating pattern of improved performance, consistently performed below average or showed a decelerating pattern of increasingly poor performance.

Measures of perceptions of the outgroups formed an interesting pattern. Content ratings of the disadvantaged group changed as the performance of that group varied. Similarly, the disadvantaged group was perceived as being more homogeneous when their performance quality increased. The advantaged group was perceived as less homogeneous when the disadvantaged group performed well. These last two findings support our speculation that when positive changes occur within a target group, they are perceived to be more homogeneous. Overall, this study supports the idea that shared information affects the content and homogeneity components of stereotypes.

Weber and Crocker (1983) offer additional support for this prediction. In their study, individual subjects received information about either 6 or 30 members of a target group. In some cases, information inconsistent with existing stereotypes was dispersed across the entire sample, while in other cases the inconsistent information was confined to a few members of the target group. When the subjects received the widely dispersed stereotype-inconsistent information they changed both the content of their stereotype of the target group and developed subtypes (subcategories) within the target group. This effect was especially strong when they received information on 30 group members. On the other hand, when the inconsistent information was concentrated in a few target group members, there was relatively little change in the content of stereotypes or in the number of subtypes they created. This study shows that when subjects receive widespread information about a target group, group-based components (stereotype and categories) are changed. Unfortunately, the investigators did not measure the other dimensions (homogeneity, salience, interpretation) of stereotypes. According to our model, changes in these dimensions might have been found in the concentrated information conditions.

It is equally unfortunate that in many stereotyping studies (Weber and Crocker, 1983; Rothbart et al., 1979; Johnston and Hewstone, 1992), the investigators did not take measures of how widely shared within the ingroup subjects believed the information to be. We would expect that if subjects believed that other members of their group (other subjects) received stereotype-inconsistent information, there would be a greater tendency for them to change the content and category components of their stereotypes than in cases where they believed that they were the only ones privy to the inconsistent information. Indeed, in the condition where inconsistent information was spread across a large number of the target group members, subjects may have inferred that other subjects were likely to receive inconsistent information. This assumption may have contributed to their willingness to change stereotype content and categories. In fact, we would hypothesize that in cases where individual subjects believed that their inconsistent information about the target group is unshared, the change in the stereotype initiated by this information will be in the interpretation and weighting components rather than in the other three dimensions. We are presently conducting research to test this hypothesis.

In addition to information about the target group, we also suggest that changes to one's ingroup can influence stereotypes about target groups. Change to the ingroup may be in the form of increasing (or decreasing) fortune, such as experiencing an economic windfall or the group experiencing a scandal. A second category of group change falls under the heading of group development. We (Worchel, Coutant-Sassic and Grossman, 1992; Worchel et al., 1993; Worchel, 1994) have argued that groups go through a predictable series of developmental stages (group identification, productivity, individuation, decay) as part of their natural life cycle. Each stage is dominated by a specific focus and internal group dynamic. And the stage of development which the group is undergoing may influence the perceptions of the ingroup and the outgroup. At first glance, it may seem curious to suggest that the condition of the perceiving group influences individual's stereotypes of target groups. However, there is considerable evidence showing that internal group conditions influence members' desires to compete with outgroups or to engage in social comparison. For example, Hovland and Sears (1940) reported that there was an increase in the number of lynchings of blacks in the South as the price of cotton decreased. They argued that the declining prices frustrated whites and increased their perception that blacks were a threat. Forsyth (1990) suggests that deteriorating ingroup cohesiveness may instigate efforts to derogate outgroups, and/or may motivate leaders to represent these outgroups as a threat in order to repair ingroup cohesiveness. Given our position that several of the dimensions of stereotypes are group-based, it is not much of a leap to suggest that changes in the internal conditions of ingroups can result in changing stereotypes.

When changes within the ingroup affect most or all of the members, the impact on stereotypes should be in the domains of content, categories and outgroup homogeneity. When such changes are confined to a small segment of the members of the ingroup, the impact will be most noticeable in the domains of categorization, perceived homogeneity in the outgroup and interpretation of trait terms. Based on research suggesting that increased arousal is associated with the restriction of attention to fewer aspects of the environment (Easterbrook, 1959), we would suggest that negative internal events (declining group prosperity, scandal) will result in more negative portrayals of outgroups (content), fewer subcategories and a tendency to perceive high homogeneity in the outgroup. However, positive changes within the ingroup will enhance the view of the outgroup, increase the number of subcategories involved in the stereotype, and reduce the perceived homogeneity in the outgroup.

A third set of events that should affect stereotypes involves the condition of the individual. This is a broad category that may include the individual developing personal contact with members of outgroups or receiving information about the outgroup that is not shared by other members of the ingroup. This category would also include situations that affected the individual's fortune (increasing or declining) and/or position within the ingroup (higher or secure position vs. low or insecure status). In all these cases, the conditions affect only the specific individual. Therefore, any change that results in the stereotype should be most evident on dimensions with a more individual base, specifically, the weightings given the traits and interpretations (meaning) of these traits.

A final category of situations concerns social identity. We use the social identity concept in a more limited sense than that employed by Tajfel and Turner (1986). Here we refer to the individual's actual or desired membership in a group. Given our proposal that groups 'instruct' members on the 'appropriate' structure of many of the dimensions of a stereotype, we suggest that stereotypes will change when the individual changes group membership. And this impact of group change will occur in those dimensions that are most deeply rooted in the group: the content, the categories and the perception of target group homogeneity. Changing groups occurs when, for example, an individual changes citizenship, moves to a new neighbourhood or town, accepts a job in another company or joins a different football team. In addition to actual

Table 4.1   Changing stereotypes

Condition		*Stereotype Components**
I	Intergroup Relationship (cooperative/competitive)	a. Content b. Categorization c. Homogeneity
II	Information about Outgroup	a. Homogeneity b. Categorization c. Content d. Salience e. Interpretation
III	Ingroup Condition (development, success/failure)	a. Homogeneity b. Categorization c. Content d. Salience e. Interpretation
IV	Personal Contact with Outgroup Member	a. Interpretation b. Salience c. Homogeneity d. Categorization
V	Individual Changing Groups (social identity)	a. Content b. Categorization c. Homogeneity d. Salience e. Interpretation

* listed in order most likely to change

membership, we would also include 'desired' group membership. For example, a Dutch citizen may aspire to being a citizen of New Zealand; a student at Texas A&M University may aspire to being a student at the University of Texas. In the cases of desired membership, we would anticipate that the individual's stereotype (especially content, categories and perception of homogeneity) will reflect that of the desired group.

In order to give some form to our meanderings, we offer the following general model of stereotype change (see table 4.1). The model indicates which conditions are most likely to lead to change in the various components of a stereotype. While the model appears to draw rigid distinctions, it is important to recognize that we are suggesting emphasis rather than mutually exclusive events. For example, changes to the conditions of the ingroup should have its greatest impact on perceptions of group homogeneity and categories, but this does not preclude changes in content, interpretation and weightings.

4   An Eye Toward Context: The Role of Culture in Stereotyping

Our emphasis on the shared nature of many of the components of stereotypes opens up another vista that has escaped the watchful eye of stereotype researchers. Individuals and groups scurry through their routines like ants within an ant hill. Nibbling further on this analogy, we find that the ants have considerable latitude in their behaviour, but that some constraints are imposed by the structure of the ant hill and the terrain in which the hill is constructed. A similar situation is faced by individuals who have considerable freedom of action and belief, but encounter the quiet shaping of their larger social environment: their culture. There is considerable evidence showing that culture affects all human activity ranging from emotions and cognitions (Markus and Kitayama, 1991) to group behaviour (Brislin, 1993). Only a small step is needed to propose that culture will impact stereotypes and stereotyping.

The possible influences of culture on stereotyping could be the topic of a complete chapter or book. Here, however, we will deal with only one point of intersection. Hofstede (1991) and Triandis (1994) present an impressive array of data suggesting that cultures vary along a collectivism/individualism dimension. One feature involved in this variation is the role of groups within the culture. In collective cultures, the group is the unit of focus, and the individual is viewed as a representative of the group. Group boundaries are clearly marked, and membership in groups is often a lifetime commitment. In individualistic cultures, individual independence rather than interdependence is the focus, and groups are the products of individuals rather than the reverse. Group membership is more fluid, and individuals move in and out of groups with relative frequency.

This distinction has a number of important implications for stereotyping if we allow the social perspective of stereotypes a seat at the table. For example, we have suggested that content, categories and perceptions of group homogeneity have a strong base in the group. Sharing common positions on these dimensions promotes group harmony. We would, therefore, predict that these features would be more strongly shared in collective cultures than in individualistic cultures. That is, we should find greater similarity in the content, categories and perceptions of homogeneity between members of a common group in collective cultures than between members of a common group in individualistic cultures. For example, if subjects were asked to list the traits that described a target group, we would expect greater agreement on the descriptive traits from subjects in a collective culture than in an individualistic culture. On the other hand, if subjects were asked to identify the salience of specific traits, we would not expect more agreement within the collective culture than in the individualistic culture.

Culture should also influence the approaches that are most likely to lead to change in stereotypes. Overall, we would expect that in collective cultures, efforts to change an individual's stereotype will be most effective if they are designed to change the stereotype held by the individual's group. On the other hand, efforts aimed at the individual (such as supplying the individual with disconfirming information) will be most effective in individualistic cultures, and such interventions will have little impact in collective cultures. Beyond these 'main effects', the impact of culture should show differential effects on the various dimensions of stereotypes. For example, while changes in intergroup relations and changes within groups should affect stereotype content, categories, and perceptions of homogeneity, the effect should be most evident in collective cultures. Changes in the individual's condition or standing within the group, should significantly affect the interpretation and weighting dimensions of people in individualistic cultures. However, because stereotypes have a stronger group base and because the condition of the individual is less important in collective cultures, change of interpretation and weighting will be more muted in collective cultures even when the individual's condition changes.

We could continue along this line, but the basic point should be clear. Because culture helps define the basic relationship between the individual and his or her group, culture should also play a role in determining the process involved in forming and changing stereotypes. Culture should not only affect the content of stereotypes, but it will influence the basic processes involved in all aspects of stereotyping. The role of culture in stereotyping, therefore, should be included more centrally in examinations of stereotypes, and existing research should be interpreted with this caveat in mind.

Before leaving this topic, let us briefly examine how culture intersects our model of stereotypes. Descriptions of collective cultures by Triandis and others suggest that while the group is paramount, individuals have a considerable degree of personal freedom once they have accepted the supremacy of the group. In other words, individuals have the opportunity to develop personal attributes within the group context. Along these lines, it is interesting to note that some of the most powerful forms of individual growth were developed in highly collective cultures; these highly personalized activities include meditation, yoga and Tai Chi. In light of this unique dichotomy, we suspect that in collective cultures, those components (content, perceptions of target homogeneity, categories) that have a strong group base will be displaced further toward the group side of the continuum. However, individual components (interpretation, salience) will be located more on the individual side of the continuum in collective cultures than in individualistic cultures. According to our model, then, culture is an orthogonal factor that will influence the foundation of each component.

5   From Speculation to Support: A Research Paradigm and Some Supporting Data

Much of our model of stereotypes and stereotyping has been based on interpretations of existing theory and research spiced with a liberal dose of speculation. However, we have not ventured out on this journey without provisions from our own laboratories. Over the last decade, my students and I (S.W.) have collected considerable data that gives some support to our approach. In some cases, the research has been aimed directly at examining group perceptions, while in other cases, the research is more indirectly related to the area of stereotyping. Given space limitations, we will briefly present some of these studies and their results.

The structure and foundation of stereotypes

We suggested that a stereotype is a multidimensional construct, having some components more influenced by group variables, whereas others are more closely tied to the condition of the individual. Some support for this position comes from an ongoing programme designed to examine group development and intergroup relations over time (Worchel et al., 1992; Worchel et al., 1993; Worchel, 1994; Worchel et al., 1994). The general motivation for studying group development was our concern that most research on groups employs 'groups' in only the most limited sense. Groups in much of the research involve strangers who meet for a limited time, and the members have no experience with each other and no expectations of future interaction. Measures of behaviour are often taken at a single point in time, so that there is no opportunity to examine how behaviour changes over time or how changing group conditions affect behaviour. These issues are also important for the study of stereotypes because stereotypes take time to develop and individuals are generally faced with changes in their own situation and the situations of their group and outgroups. We began our model building by examining archival data of ongoing groups, and followed this approach with a series of laboratory studies. In the laboratory, we typically recruited subjects to be members of work groups that would meet together several times over a three- to six-week period. During the experimental sessions, the groups faced several situations, such as the introduction of new members or an influence attempt by a minority, which were introduced at different periods during the group's life. We collected data on individual and group behaviour, as well as behaviour towards and perceptions of outgroups.

Therefore, we were able to examine group and individual task performance as well as relations with outgroups. Because our groups were formed with specific task goals, there may be some question as to whether our results could generalize to social categories that involve no direct interaction or have no defined task goal. However, it should be mentioned that our original archival research did include several 'social categories' such as the Women's Movement and the Civil Rights Movement in the United States. In general, the patterns we observed in our small task groups were similar to those found in the larger social movement.

Based on a combination or archival, field and laboratory research, we concluded that groups develop through a series of repeating cycles involving group identification, productivity, individuation and decay. Each stage is characterized by a particular group focus, and each is accompanied by predictable intrapersonal, intragroup and intergroup behaviours. Groups, we argue, begin by attempting to establish their identity and independence. This stage is accompanied by strong pressures toward uniformity within the group, centralized leadership, intolerance of deviants, high arousal, perceptions of ingroup homogeneity and a sense of optimism. Groups next focus on productivity where attention is paid to setting and achieving goals, identifying task-relevant skills in members and seeking strategic alliances with other groups which will enhance productivity. From this stage, groups enter a period of individuation in which the focus shifts to the individual. Individuals demand recognition and reward, equity rather than equality and an opportunity for social comparison. Finally, groups begin a stage of decay in which the group is blamed for failures, members explore joining other groups and individual contact with outgroup members increases dramatically. Although some members leave the group, the group continues and a precipitating event often invigorates the group to begin anew in the stage of group identification.

Although the model focuses on group development, a vital consideration is intergroup relations. Not only do developmental changes within the group impact relations with outgroups, but changes in the relations with outgroups can affect ingroup dynamics. For example, Worchel et al. (1993) found that members of groups in the stage of Group Identification desire conflict and competition with outgroups, while groups in Individuation and Decay stages desire cooperation with the outgroup. Likewise, ingroups revert back to the Identification stage when an outgroup threatens independence of the ingroup. The results from a number of studies examining the relationship between groups over extended periods of time have direct implications for the proposed conceptualization of stereotypes and stereotyping.

In one case, Worchel et al. (1992) had groups of eight subjects work together on a common task. These subjects were then divided into two separate groups that competed on one or two tasks. In a control condition the two separate groups were formed at the beginning, never allowing all subjects to work together as a single unit. The groups were asked for their perceptions of their group and the competing group immediately after the division into groups occurred, after competing on one task or after competing on two tasks. Most germane to the issue of stereotyping was the finding of relatively small changes across conditions in content ratings of the outgroup (intelligence, friendliness, appearance, talkativeness). However, perceptions of the similarity of outgroup members on these traits were significantly different, with greatest outgroup homogeneity seen when the groups competed on two tasks and in the control condition when the groups never worked as a single group. Thus, the content of the stereotype was not affected by our manipulations, but the perceptions of homogeneity of the target group did change. Even more interesting to the present concern were the results of pretest conditions that were eventually excluded from the study. In these conditions, ingroup subjects were given an opportunity to discuss the task and the outgroup before completing the questionnaire. These conditions were eliminated because of our concern that the nature of the discussion was an uncontrollable variable that could confound the interpretation of the results. However, data obtained in these 'discussion' conditions indicated striking changes in the content ratings of the outgroup and more muted changes in the homogeneity ratings. These data demonstrate the social or shared quality of stereotype content, and they would argue that the different dimensions of stereotypes might be affected by different conditions.

In another study we (Worchel, Wong, Shackelford and Coutant) investigated how students at two rival universities (University of Texas and Texas A&M) perceived each other, and how these perceptions changed over time. The data were divided along lines of the subject's ingroup (University of Texas and Texas A&M) and the subject's longevity in the group (just entering the group: Freshman; midstream membership: Sophomore and Junior; and final year in group: Senior).

The results indicated that the highest agreement within schools occurred on the *content* of the outgroup stereotype; for example, there was considerable uniformity in the way Texas A&M students described University of Texas students. Further, subgroupings within the larger ingroup influenced the degree of agreement on content; for example, greatest agreement on content was found in the Sophomore and Junior group. Although there was less overall uniformity in the perceptions of outgroup homogeneity, the outgroup was perceived as being most homogeneous by Freshmen and least homogeneous by Seniors. Finally, subjects were asked to indicate their interpretation (positive/ negative) of each term used in the description of the outgroup. It was on this dimension that we found the highest variability both within and between each category of subjects. On some terms such as intelligent and friendly, there was relatively high agreement, although it was clear that some subjects felt that 'too much of a good thing' was not so positive; being too friendly could be overbearing. On other terms such as 'religious' and 'uses alcohol', the responses were bimodal indicating that some subjects viewed them as positive, while others viewed them as negative. The pattern of results from this study makes a number of points. First, within a perceiving group, the degree of uniformity may differ on the different dimensions of a stereotype. The present study found greatest agreement on content and least uniformity on interpretation. This pattern fits nicely with our suggestion that content of stereotypes is more strongly founded in the group, while interpretation is more subject to individual control. What is interesting is that agreement was not simply a function of length of time the subject had been in the group or the amount of interaction he/she had with the target group. Greatest agreement was found when subjects had a moderate amount of time in their ingroup (Sophomore/ Junior) and a moderate amount of contact with the target group. This point has important implications for understanding how stereotypes are formed and how they can be reduced. Second, the stereotype of the target group may be influenced by conditions of the perceiving group and the individual group member; the present study implicates length of time the individual has been in the group, while the Worchel et al. (1992) study suggests longevity of the group and/or nature of intergroup relations as critical factors.

The impact of culture on self and group perceptions

We have argued that the process of stereotyping must be considered within a cultural context, because culture determines the centrality of groups in the individual's social horizon. A direct test of this position would be to compare stereotyping and the nature of stereotypes across a variety of cultures. We are presently engaging in a study of this nature which is based on a preliminary study that examined self-descriptions and descriptions of one's country using subjects from eight countries. In one analysis of these data (Worchel and Hills, 1995), the countries in the sample were placed into Hofstede's (1980) dimensions of collective/individualistic and masculine/feminine. As we mentioned, collective cultures view the group as paramount, whereas individualistic cultures emphasize the independent role of the individual. Hofstede argues that masculine cultures emphasize masculine values (for example, competition) and traditional group structures that often place males in leader roles. More feminine cultures, on the other hand, emphasize values such as cooperation and nurturance that are more often associated with women, and the more androgynous orientation offers a wider variety of opportunities for women.

From the present standpoint, the most interesting results were those that dealt with the relationship between perceptions of the self and the country. In collective cultures, there were significant correlations between subjects' comfort with themselves and their perceptions of the fortunes of their country. There was no relationship between self-comfort and perceptions of their *personal* progress. On the other hand, in individualistic cultures, comfort with one's self was only related to perceptions of personal progress. Likewise, women's reported self-comfort and personal and country progress were most closely related in feminine cultures, while these relationships were found for men in masculine cultures. In other words, culture affects the nature of the relationship between the individual's perception of the self and the group. Individuals in collective cultures align their individual perceptions closely with their perceptions of the group. It should be noted here that our research related perceptions of the personal condition with those of the country. Presumably, we would find an even stronger relationship between personal and group condition if we examined groups that subjects considered primary, such as the family or tribe. Although our design precluded this type of analysis, it is important for future research to examine this relationship. From the standpoint of stereotyping, it is likely that while some stereotypes may be rooted in the larger group, others are most directly linked to individuals' ingroups within the culture. However, our data do suggest that people in collective cultures perceive a relationship between their personal situation and that of their country. Their personal satisfaction and comfort is tied closely to the progress of their group. Therefore, we might expect a high degree of shared perceptions, including stereotypes, in collective cultures. The relationship between individual comfort and perceptions of progress of the group was nonexistent in individualistic cultures, suggesting less need to hitch personal perceptions with those of the group.

6 Conclusions

Our aim has been to re-acquaint stereotypes with their social roots. Much of the previous research on stereotypes has approached the topic from the standpoint of the individual. From this position, a natural course is to explore how individuals develop stereotypes, the functions stereotypes have for individuals, and the conditions that can entice individuals to change those stereotypes. If we approach stereotypes from the position of the group, we must begin by determining the functions stereotypes (or any other belief) have for groups. We recognize that stereotypes reside deep within the mind of the individual. But the group focus goads us to explore the shared nature of stereotypes. In other words, we must consider the social as well as the cognitive sides of the issue.

Taking this group approach opens up a host of new avenues that are not evident from a strictly intrapersonal perspective. If we assume that shared stereotypes have a function for the group (Tajfel, 1981a), it is logical to ask to what degree sharing, or to question what is shared. It is this question that leads to placing the concept of stereotype under a microscope to identify its parts. And it is this process that leads us to suggest that the stereotype is actually a multi-component concept, some of the dimensions are more group-based (shared) while others are more individual in origin and control. Our aim is not to contradict or criticize results found from the individual/cognitive approach. Rather we are grasping the elephant at a different location, and describing the beast from our vantage point. Our aim is to complement the description of stereotypes offered by other approaches. We are suggesting that including the group perspective raises new questions and suggests additional methods for studying stereotypes. Indeed, we argue that these new questions and methods should invigorate the search to understand stereotypes and stereotyping.

Note

A large number of graduate and undergraduate students have worked on various studies within this programme. We would like to recognize the contributions of Dawna Coutant, Michele Grossman, Frankie Wong, Judy Ouelette, Leah Worchel, William Webb and Stacey Jackson. Thanks are due to Wendy Wood for her insightful comments on earlier drafts of this manuscript. Some of the research reported in this chapter was supported by a research grant from the Texas Coordinating Board of Higher Education.

5
Stereotype Construction as a Strategy of Influence

Stephen Reicher, Nick Hopkins and Susan Condor

> I write now in English and now in Scots
> to the despair of friends who plead
> for consistency; sometimes achieve the true lyric cry,
> next but chopped up prose; and write whiles
> in traditional forms, next in a mixture of styles.
> So divided against myself, they ask:
> how can I stand (or they understand) indeed?

Hugh MacDiarmid from 'The Caledonian Antisyzygy' (1948)

1 A new approach to the study of stereotyping

Developing the implications of functionality

The British Poet Laureate, Ted Hughes, once referred to poems as 'my sad captains' which, once set out, ended up in places undreamed of and certainly unwilled by the author. There is a similarly winsome note in Tajfel's (1981a) chapter on 'social stereotypes and social groups'. While his own early work was devoted to examining the cognitive aspects of prejudice (Tajfel, 1969a, b, 1973; Tajfel and Wilkes, 1963) he expresses some surprise at the way in which this has turned into an account of prejudice in general and stereotyping in particular as purely cognitive phenomena.

Even in its own terms, Tajfel characterizes the social cognition approach to stereotyping as a retreat from its roots. On the one hand, there is a tendency to ignore the evaluative dimension which renders a categorical distinction between 'fruits' and 'vegetables' very different from one between 'blacks' and 'whites'. On the other hand, there is little concern with the nature and determination of the dimensions which are used to differentiate one group from another. More broadly, however, Tajfel argues that if stereotypes are treated as purely cognitive phenomena, then their social nature is systematically ignored.

As we, amongst others, have previously pointed out, the word 'social' is one of the most ambiguous, contested and polysemic terms that we use (Condor, 1990; Jahoda, 1986; Reicher, 1995). In the 1981 chapter, Tajfel describes stereotypes as social in at least two senses. In the first place he stresses that a key characteristic of stereotypes is that they are shared rather than simply being idiosyncratic individual representations. Secondly, he argues that stereotypes do not only serve individual functions such as ordering the world so as to make it manageable and defending personal values, they also serve collective and ideological functions such as making sense of large-scale social events, justifying the actions of one's own group against others and defining one's own group as positive in relation to outgroups. These functions are named, respectively, social causality, justification and differentiation.

Tajfel is not simply interested in adding a social dimension to the study of stereotypes. He insists on the need to integrate the social and the individual functions of stereotypes and suggests two paths to this end. The first is social identity theory and, crucially, its insight that people may define themselves through their place in a system of group relations (Tajfel, 1978a, 1982b; Tajfel and Turner, 1986). The second is the work on social attribution which suggests that the way in which people explain events may be a function of the categorical relationship between actor and perceiver (Hewstone and Jaspers, 1982; Taylor and Jaggi, 1974).

Tajfel acknowledges that he is not in a position to offer a theory which covers the individual and social nature of stereotyping; he sees his position more as theoretical criticism of where we have been than a model of where we should go and describes his contribution as 'no more than a hazy blueprint for future research' (p. 167). But here, once again, Tajfel's words are in danger of suffering the same fate as Ted Hughes' poems. As is the fate of many key texts, the 1981 chapter is often ritually intoned only to be all the more effectively ignored. It is as if acknowledging a need to study the social functions of stereotyping (and how social and individual are inextricably intertwined) substitutes for the study itself. It is not only that passing reference to the social dimension can be used to distract attention from its omission in the substantive analysis, it is also that mentioning Tajfel's argument without following through its implications can cover for problems of commission. The general aim of this chapter is, therefore, to extend and to illustrate a functional approach to stereotyping. In so doing, the aim is also to explore the implications of such an analysis for stereotyping research in general.

Of course, we are not the first to argue that Tajfel's arguments have been oft quoted but rarely heeded. There are a number of publications which focus on the social and ideological uses of stereotypes and they provide an important service in stressing the job that remains to be done (Condor, 1990; Huici, 1984; Jost and Banaji, 1994). However, in the main this work is limited to a critical review of existing work. It was 1981 when Tajfel, quoting Hinde (1979), suggested that the present stage is one of critique – of clearing the old ground in order to provide space for the new. Fifteen years on, those who are being criticized might fairly complain that it is time to put up or shut up. It is high time that we moved from outlining the need for the project to providing a more developed analysis of the social functioning of stereotypes and to showing how such an analysis provides a more adequate understanding of the issues.

What is more, while these reviews are united in arguing that stereotype research needs to include the social functional dimension, not all of them follow through all the conceptual shifts such inclusion would entail. We would highlight two shifts in particular. The first concerns the extent to which social stereotypes should be seen as shared within a group. The second concerns our very conception of the content of such stereotypes.

Once it is acknowledged that stereotypes are linked to such things as the ways in which groups explain and justify their actions and their projects, then one is forced to face the fact that groups are rarely if ever completely united. When social identity theorists illustrate the concept, they tend to repeat similar types of group memberships: national, religious, political and gender. Since the study we will be reporting further on deals with national identity, we will limit our comments here. Suffice it to say that analyses of nations and of national identity, whether they be contemporary or historical, relating to advanced industrial societies or developing countries, all show that beneath visions of national destiny rooted in timeless national pasts lies a plethora of visions of what the nation has been, what it is and where it should go (Billig, 1995; Condor, 1995; Reicher, 1993a; Reicher, Hopkins and Condor, in press).

When it comes to religion, it is hard to divorce the word church from that of schism. Cohn (1970) charts the intricate divisions and subdivisions over interpretations of the faith and how it should be organized. Indeed, Umberto Eco's novel *The Name of the Rose* (Eco, 1984) uses these same splits in order to make the general point that dogmatic interpretation will always be self-destructive unless tempered by humour and irony. Lest it be thought that such splits lie in the past, it is worth reflecting that the Church of England, fresh from a dispute about the ordination of women (and hence the very nature of its ministry) is now embroiled in controversy over faith and sexuality.

If the term schism originates in religion, it is now as much associated with politics. In Britain, the Tory party is split down the middle over Europe, the Labour Party only seems comparatively more united since it has just succeeded in expelling much of its left wing and the Liberal Democrats have just gone through three organizational redefinitions in a decade leaving splinters all over the place. Lest it be thought that one will find calm once one leaves the arguments raging in nations, religions and politics, then a glimpse at gender and gender identity will rapidly disabuse one. What it means, say, to be a woman is fiercely contested (Williams and Giles, 1982). The most obvious division is between 'traditional' and 'feminist' women, but the meanings of each of these are equally open to dispute (Condor, 1986, 1989).

All in all, the tranquil picture promoted by social identity theory (and also the other major perspective in European social psychology, social representations theory (Moscovici, 1961; Moscovici and Farr, 1984)), whereby all members of a group share identical understandings simply by virtue of being in the group, seems hopelessly naïve. The histories of most if not all groups are marked by coalition, schism and recombination (Sani, 1995; Sani and Reicher, 1995). To the extent that group stereotypes are in any way tied to group actions past, present and future then a consensualist account of them is clearly simplistic.

So social stereotypes vary within a group, they are contested by group members. But what is the contest all about? Since Katz and Braly (1933), stereotypes have tended to be conceptualized as lists of trait adjectives: women are emotional and irrational; the English are repressed and polite; Jews are mean and sly. Even those who promote a dynamic view of stereotypes as defined through the relationship between groups in a specific comparative context still operationalize stereotypes much as Katz and Braly and demonstrate change as the shift in response on trait scales (Haslam and Turner, 1992; Haslam, Turner, Oakes, McGarty and Hayes, 1992; Oakes, Haslam and Turner, 1994). Such a contradiction between process and content – whereby stereotypes are defined as a function of social relations but are measured in terms that exclude them – is particularly stark. It may be that the continued use of traits is less a matter of theoretical commitment than of practicality. Trait scales are a simple means of obtaining clear quantitative results. However, there is a danger in letting methodological convenience drive our conceptual perspective. In a climate where everybody sees stereotypes in terms of traits this serves to perpetuate such a viewpoint. Nor is it adequate to declare oneself agnostic as to whether a trait definition is adequate. While it is arguable that the matter of how stereotypes are defined is not always crucial, it is certainly so that a trait conception limits our understanding to certain key aspects of stereotypic phenomena.

We have argued elsewhere that the trait conception is inadequate to deal with the phenomenon of stereotype change (Reicher, 1996, in press). Most conventional work on change involves the presentation of disconfirming information to passive subjects (e.g., Hewstone, 1989; Hewstone, Hopkins and Routh, 1992; Hewstone, Johnstone and Aird, 1992). Yet this is to ignore the fact that change predominantly occurs through the activity and interaction of groups. Such activity not only affects hetero-stereotypes. We also may change our own self-conceptions through collective action and it is difficult to see how action on the basis of a static set of attributes may in itself change those attributes.

Our interest here is more in the functional and strategic uses of stereotypes. Having already looked at the implications of stereotyping as justification, it is worth adding in a consideration of stereotyping as an account of social causality. If stereotyping is bound up with the explanation of important social events, then it becomes very limiting to conceptualize them purely in trait terms. Take the present conflict in the former Yugoslavia – one of the major issues in the world of 1995. Certainly one could explain it in terms of the characters of those involved: the brutality of the Bosnian Serbs, the innocence of the Bosnian Muslims, the heartlessness and pusillanimous nature of the world leaders who refuse more active interventions. However one could equally explain the conflict in other terms: as the expression of an invariant human nature where people will inevitably fight for territory and against those who are different to them; as the outcome of social forces unleashed by the break up of Yugoslavia; as an ideological contest between liberal and fascist visions of society; or as the expression of divine (or else demonic) intervention.

Even in a society as individualistic as our own, there are many different levels upon which one can explain how collectivities behave. Therefore stereotyping must allow for these different levels of explanation rather than being exclusively associated with one in particular – the trait account. Equally, it is more flexible and more profitable to see stereotypes as involving models of how groups act and interrelate rather than reifying them in terms of some invariant form of model. What is more, the very choice of categories whose actions are to be explained is itself part of the explanation. To continue with the Bosnian example, we have referred to the groups (in common with much media coverage) as Bosnian Serbs versus Bosnian Muslims. Yet to do so is to suggest an ethnic/religious principle of organization and conflict. Others contest this fiercely and argue that this principle of organization is itself the focus of conflict. If the Serbs seek to divide people along ethnic lines, their opponents do not. They believe in and practice a model of society where people of different faiths and origins live together. Hence the opposition should be termed the Bosnian government, not the Bosnian Muslim, side.

All this is not to deny that stereotypes may involve traits. But even when they do, it is necessary to recognize them as a particular model of group action and intergroup relations. As Kidder and Stewart (1975) noted long ago and as Jost and Banaji (1994) reaffirm more recently, the stereotypic traits associated with oppressed groups tend to have much in common and serve to explain (if not explain away) their subordinated position. If traits are divorced from the context of explanation in which they are used, they become ambiguous or even meaningless. The same trait may mean different things or else different traits may mean the same thing. Thus Schwarz (1982) notes that the description of the English as 'freedom-loving' alters its significance considerably according to whether one is explaining opposition to the Nazis in 1940 or else opposition to Asian immigration in the 1970s.

Between psychological reductionism and psychological nihilism

Thus far we have argued that current research misconceptualizes the nature of stereotypes, but what are the broader theoretical implications of this? To date, critiques such as ours have been associated with a broader anti-cognitivism. Thus Potter and Litton (1985) argue forcefully that a view of social groups sharing common social beliefs is at best tautological since common social beliefs are often used as the grounds on which groups are defined. Potter and Wetherell go on to show that variability is a defining feature of human expression. Not only do people in the same group vary in what they say within the same context, but the same individual may express contradictory understandings even within the space of a single phrase. Billig (1987, 1992; Billig et al., 1988) makes argument the principle of human thought in general and social categorization in particular. First of all, he suggests that the nature of categories is always open to contestation on a number of levels: how the category is defined, how instances relate to categories, even what the argument itself is all about! Secondly, he contends that argument is not only public but that private thought involves the interplay of contrasting ideas. Thirdly, ideas in themselves are inherently dilemmatic in that they contain contradictory themes. Thus we believe things only in relation to the existence of conflicting ideas. While stereotypes may be only one example of these principles they certainly are no exception (cf. Condor on 'race' (1988), 'gender' (1993) and English national identity, in press).

In putting stereotypes in argumentative context, Billig also dwells on their explanatory function. This is most developed in his work on nationalism (Billig, 1995). Billig argues that national identities and national stereotypes are far more than character descriptions. They are theories about how the world is and how it should be. But theory relates to practice, for they are also about ways of being and ways of striving within the world. Wetherell and Potter (1992) in a study of Pakeha ('white' New Zealander) views of Maoris show in considerable detail how stereotypes are used to tell stories about the relations between groups and explain both the nature, the prognosis and the ways of resolving these relations.

What renders such arguments radical is not simply that they look at the ways in which people talk about, debate and contest the nature of social groups but that they refuse any other level of analysis. Discourse analysts in particular (Edwards and Potter, 1992; Potter and Wetherell, 1987) suggest that language should not be treated as a surface from which one can discover underlying psychological constructs (of attitude, belief, stereotype or whatever) but rather it is through language usage itself that reality (including psychological reality) is created. As to whether a cognitive level of analysis is viable, the response is either agnostic (there may be such a level, but it is only apparent to the researcher when it is communicated and therefore only the communicational/discursive level is researchable) or else nihilistic (all psychological constructs such as identity, trait, stereotype – and even the very idea of psychological explanation – are ideological perspectives, achieved through language, of specific cultural/historical contexts).

Our perspective is somewhat different (cf. Reicher and Hopkins, in press, a, b; Reicher, 1993b, 1995a). On the one hand, we argue that certain psychological constructs such as the notion of self and other as well as the need to ascribe stereotypic content to such categories is both existentially and socially necessary irrespective of the particular society in which people live. We root this assertion in the prerequisites of social action. First of all the planning of action depends upon a representation of how the world works, of where one stands in that world and of how one is able to act within/upon that world. Identity, in the sense of a model of self in social relations is necessary for practice. Secondly, the motivation to act now for outcomes that will be in the future depends upon some notion of the continuity of the self (cf. Foote, 1951). Thirdly, the possibility of any social organization which defines boundaries of action depends upon being able to hold people to account at one time (the trial) for action at another (the crime). Again, some notion that there is continuity of identity is required. Even on the level where identity is a myth, it is not confined to some societies but is a necessary feature of social being.

Insofar as identity is a constituent element of practice it follows that the way that identity is defined will have implications for how people will act (and vice versa). Thus, whether others are included in a common identity or not will determine whether they are seen in terms of similarity or difference, as allies or potential opponents, while the terms of that identity (for instance 'Bosnian Muslim side' or 'Bosnian government side') will determine the dimensions around which opposition will be organized. Where identity is defined on a collective level, the stereotypic content ascribed to the categories will determine the possibilities and priorities of action: not only what one's own group is able to do and what ends it seeks but also how the outgroup is likely to behave and how it needs to be responded to. Finally, the extent to which individuals are defined as consonant or dissonant with group stereotypes will determine the extent to which they are seen as able to speak for and define group action.

Much of this will be familiar for it largely accords with the claims of social identity and, more particularly, self-categorization theory (SCT) concerning the consequences of defining group identity (Tajfel and Turner, 1986; Turner, 1982, 1991; Turner, Hogg, Oakes, Reicher and Wetherell, 1987; Turner, Oakes, Haslam and McGarty, 1994). Insofar as the initial focus of SCT has been on extending the logic of the social identity concept (the idea that people may define themselves and their relationship to others on a categorical level – 'we' vs. 'they' – as well as an individual level – 'I' vs. 'you' – or indeed other levels of abstraction) to intragroup processes it has mainly been concerned with self-stereotyping rather than hetero-stereotyping. We too will focus on self-stereotypes although much of our argument applies to hetero-stereotypes as well. Indeed, as both Tajfel (1981b, 1982b) and Turner with his colleagues (Haslam and Turner, 1992; Haslam, Turner, Oakes, Mcgarty and Hayes, 1992; Oakes, Haslam and Turner, 1994) recognize, the one can only be defined in relation to the other.

Where our emphasis differs from SCT is on the issue of how category definitions are arrived at. As our arguments would suggest, we strongly agree with self-categorization theorists when they insist that the process and content of stereotyping does not derive from a need to simplify the stimulus complexity of the social world (even if at the cost of some distortion) but rather is rooted in the nature of social reality (Spears and Haslam, this volume). However, even if some acknowledgement is given to the active role of the perceiver, the overwhelming emphasis in SCT to date has been on the way in which stereotypes arise within any given situation through processes of internal computation. As Condor (1990) puts it, such a stress may portray the organism as active in the sense that a computer's central processing unit actively deals with input, but it underplays the idea of people as thoughtful, reflexive and creative actors. It is hard to square such a view with the general idea that stereotypes are used to achieve social functions for that suggests that they are constructed and deployed with conscious intentionality. More specifically, we would argue that there is an implicit tension (in SCT at least) between the way in which the consequences of self-categorization are conceptualized and the way in which their antecedents are explained.

In terms of consequences, one way of rephrasing our foregoing argument is to say that the nature of collective action will flow from the definition of social categories: the extent of who forms part of the collective and who the collective acts against will relate to the boundaries of ingroup and outgroup; the direction which the collective takes will relate to the content of group identity and ability to gain influence over the collective will relate to who is prototypical. Moreover, insofar as the social identity approach is explicitly formulated to explain extended groups as well as small face-to-face groups (Tajfel, 1978a, 1982b; Turner, 1982), then this argument applies at a macro- as well as a micro-social level, to the mass as well as the coterie. In short, the definition of social categories becomes the very stuff of politics. It is central to mass mobilization whether electorally or around specific initiatives. To observe that there will be different political projects around any given issue is a truism, but it follows that there should be attempts to define the categories involved in different ways.

There is a plaintive saying that 'I said the world was mad, while they said

I was mad and, by damn, they outvoted me'. If psychological theories exclude the very possibility of something which is undeniably so then it is for the theory to be revised rather than the phenomena to be denied. We would argue that there is a danger for SCT if (as in some of the studies) social reality is taken as self-evident and hence categorization is seen to follow from it in a one-way direction of causality. Although a consensus around the nature of context – including what the relevant context is – may sometimes obtain, this is not always so especially around novel events. When Iraq first invaded Kuwait was it a squabble between middle eastern states or a threat to world peace? Who was involved: just Iraq and Kuwait; Saudi Arabia as well; or the whole world? Context is contestable and therefore categories are not self-evident. While we accept the important claim of SCT that the two are interrelated we would stress that the relations of causality must be explored in both directions rather than just one.

In taking this step we allow for a position that stands between SCT and discourse analysis. For while, as we have stated, we accept the psychological reality (indeed necessity) of self-stereotypes we also accept that these will always be given substance in society where the concept of society must not only include macro-social structures and ideologies but also the micro-social processes of debate and argumentation in which identities are defined. Such a step also suggests an additional strategic consideration which will frame this process of argumentation. Functionality is not simply retrospective: to explain what has happened and to justify what has been done. It is also pro-active. Stereotypes will be used to achieve desired futures. Tajfel lists differentiation in this regard, but that is only one aspect of group action. We propose that those with different political projects will define identities in order to shape mass action. More particularly, they will define ingroup stereotypes in different ways so as to present their projects as consonant with group identity and hence appropriate for group members. In short, we argue that a key aspect of self-stereotyping is the use of identity definitions in order to achieve mass social influence. Sometimes these definitions may take the form of traits and sometimes they may not – but even when they do, the meanings of any definition can only be ascertained in relation to the wider project and hence what the definitions are being used to achieve.

The following study concerns the way in which the various political parties in Scotland sought to define the stereotypic content of 'Scottishness' in the context of the British general election of 1992. Its purpose is to illustrate the nature of self-stereotyping as a strategy of influence. To be more specific, we wish to show (a) how the self-stereotype of 'Scottishness' was variable and contested; (b) how this variability can be explained in terms of the strategic use of self-stereotypes in order to define the direction of collective action; (c) that in order to capture the strategic use of self-stereotyping to achieve mass social influence it is inadequate to conceptualize self-stereotypes in trait terms.

2   A Study of Scottishness

Background to the study

The 1992 General Election in Scotland: Scotland lost its status as an independent state when it joined with England through the Act of Union in 1707. According to the Act, the Scottish parliament was dissolved in return for guarantees concerning the continuation of the Scottish legal, educational and ecclesiastical institutions and the provision for Scottish Members of Parliament (MPs) to sit in the Westminster parliament.

Although the Union has endured, it has always been opposed by a section of the Scottish people. In the early days this took the form of riot and uprising (Berresford Ellis and Mac a'Ghobhainn, 1989). More recently, the independence movement has adopted a more constitutional path culminating in the formation of the Scottish National Party (SNP) in 1934 (Marr, 1992).

Since the 1960s, the SNP have been a constant presence in both local government and at Westminster. Moreover their influence has been outwith their numbers since they have forced the national question to the top of the political agenda. The Labour Party and the Liberal Democrats both went into the 1992 election committed to a devolved Scottish parliament (even if these parties do not go as far as the SNP policy of full independence within the European Community). The Conservative Party remain the only major party to oppose both devolution and independence (Marr, 1992; McCrone, 1992).[1]

A number of factors conspired to place the constitutional issue centre stage in the 1992 general election. In January 1992, an opinion poll indicated that support for independence stood at over 50 per cent. Even if this was later seen as a freak result it transformed the political debate. Alex Salmond, SNP leader, went so far as to claim that 'this will be Scotland's independence election' (Marr, 1992).

The Conservative Prime Minister, John Major, also chose to focus on the national question – albeit to highlight his party's distinctive pro-unionism. In a keynote election speech to the Conservative Central Council on 14 March 1992 in Torquay (a most English of English towns) he declared that the constitutional issue was 'more than a Scottish concern. It matters in Gloucester as it matters in Glasgow'. Indeed in Birmingham on 30 March, Major went further and described it as 'quite literally, *the* national issue'. Most famously, at a mass rally in Wembley Arena, the Prime Minister declaimed: 'if I could summon up all the authority of this office I would put it into this single warning – the United Kingdom is in danger. Wake up my fellow countrymen. Wake up *now*, before it is too late' (emphases in original, all quotes taken from Major, 1992).

Materials and analytic conventions: The following analysis is based largely on public meetings and interviews. Throughout the period of the election campaign we attended and tape-recorded a total of 20 public meetings addressed by candidates from all of the main political parties. After the election we tape-recorded speeches given at a range of mass rallies and demonstrations organized to mobilize extra-parliamentary support for a Scottish parliament (10 in total). We conducted a total of 40 interviews with prominent figures from the major parties (Scottish National Party (SNP), Labour, Liberal Democrat and Conservative) which included 25 of the 72 Scottish MPs covering all four parties. Some of these MPs were interviewed more than once. This is but one part of a larger corpus of materials collected in the context of the research. In the following analysis (for details of procedure, see Reicher and Hopkins, in press, a, b) extracts from our texts are numbered for ease of reference. Where the text was publicly available (e.g., an election meeting or post-election rally) the context is identified and the speaker is named. Where the text derives from private interviews only the party affiliation and general status of the speaker is given. In all cases the general nature of material (interview or meeting) is identified.

Arguments over Scottish identity

Variability and mobilization: Here are four different quotes from Scottish speakers which address the question of what Scottishness means:

1. The trouble with the Scots is that without their own government they therefore don't have a political system which actually reflects the true nature of the Scottish psyche . . . My argument would be that the Scottish attitude to our institutions is fundamentally different from that in England. We still have a sense of community in Scotland. We don't have any fear of the National Health Service or the education system because it is of the people. It belongs to the people. We would look for democratic control of it, more accountability from it. Whereas in England, especially under the Thatcher years, there was a complete contrast when it was all self, the individual . . . It's just the Scottish way. It's very difficult to pin it down to anything, but we do have a sense of community. 'We're all Jack Tamson's bairns'[2]

2. The English in general would tend to be far more inclined towards, you know, the, if you like, not the capitalist so much as free enterprise and capitalism: keeping the taxes low and being distrustful of the public sector. I think the Scots are far more at ease with the idea of the public sector or the state interfering. The Scottish tradition is far more egalitarian. There is very little private health in Scotland for example. Very little private education. There is a much wider reliance on the state in Scotland and people don't get uncomfortable with the idea with things being under public ownership which seems to be the case much more in England.

3. I don't conceive the Scottish character as being subject to the kind of narrow nationalism that in my judgement the Scottish National Party promote . . . I think the narrowness is the assumption that everything that comes out of Scotland is by definition good. I mean if you listen, if you take, don't just listen

or read one speech, but if you actually look at the whole corpus of nationalist Scottish National Party thought for the last 20 years it is not difficult to discern the old sort of 'who's as good as we are?' This sort of breast beating self-belief which goes far beyond self-confidence to arrogance and I don't think that's part of the Scottish character. There is a robustness, but it's not arrogant and I think that's where nationalism fails to understand properly the nature of the Scottish character.

   4. I think Scots are recognised, and I would like to think that I was recognised in this light, as being a strong-willed nation: people who are steadfast and when we make our mind up, we'll go and do something and do it properly. We are also a nation who believe in paying our way in the world and this has been the case over many generations. I think sometimes down the road now we're getting a slight change in that. But we've always been brought up to spend what we can afford to spend and don't go over the top – and I think that's held Scots in good stead for many years. When you think of the Poll Tax situation[3] and the way in which people have been portrayed as not wanting to pay their way – I'm just thinking about local government – it goes against the grain in many Scots and I think that will come out in this general election, possibly, that people will say 'no, no, no, that's not the stuff that Scots are made of'.

From these four quotes alone it is clear that there is no consensus over the stereotypic definition of Scottishness. In the first Scots are inherently communitarian, in the second they are egalitarian and socialist, in the third they are robust without being arrogant and in the fourth they are steadfast and thrifty. These differences become more intelligible when one realizes their origins. Each comes from an interview with a representative from one of the four major parties contesting the election: in order, an SNP MP, a Labour MP, a Liberal Democrat MP and a Conservative parliamentary candidate. In each case, the definitions of Scottishness promote the politics of the party. Thus, the SNP speaker suggests a fundamental contradiction between Scottish identity and English institutions such that an entirely new institutional arrangement (which would go far beyond the limited powers of a devolved parliament) is necessary. The Labour politician also suggests a contradiction between Scottishness and Englishness but stresses policies rather than institutions and also emphasizes the inherent socialism of the Scots. The Liberal Democrat MP also goes against separatism and does so much more explicitly than the Labour figure; however, he eschews any socialist dimension to Scottish identity. Finally, the Conservative candidate portrays Conservative economic policy as an expression of Scottishness and opposition to that policy as incompatible with such an identity. In each case, the definition of identity serves to make party policy prototypically Scottish.

   The differences between these quotations is, therefore, at least compatible with our position that stereotypes are variable constructs that are used strategically in order to achieve influence. However, it could be argued that these quotes do not demonstrate members of the *same* national group differing over the nature of their self-stereotype but rather members of *different* political parties holding different hetero-stereotypes. Thus, we have not shown intra-group variability in stereotypes (which would be theoretically challenging) but rather intergroup variability (which everyone accepts).

There are a number of difficulties with such a criticism. To start with, variability does not only exist between political parties but can also be found within the same party. Thus, some Labour people emphasize the distinctive nature of Scotland and insist that it is Scottishness which makes people vote for the left – as is clear from the following interview with an activist:

> 5. I think we have a long history in Scotland of saying – of not saying – 'I'm all right jack'. We are far more caring about those that aren't for whatever reason less fortunate, in inverted commas than ourselves. We care more about the poor, we care more about the disabled, we put our caring into operation and this is reflected, I think, in voting patterns. It is reflected through religious medias, it is reflected through the media itself, it's reflected through our culture in Scotland.

In contrast, a Labour MP being interviewed rejects any notion of Scotland's distinctive nature:

> 6. There was a time in the 1950s when Glasgow, of all cities, actually had a majority of Tory MPs, while now we all enjoy the fact that we don't have a single Tory MP in Glasgow. But I think what we have done in Scotland in driving the Tories down to being a minority party can also be done in England. I think it is a myth that we are somehow different, that different blood runs in our veins. How could it, we're not some of pure race distinct from the English – we too are a mix of peoples.

Interestingly, there is a similar debate in the Conservative party as to whether Scots are distinctively Tory or not distinctive at all. Thus the Labour MPs words are almost uncannily echoed during an interview with a Tory MP:

> 7. Nothing could be more different as a Glaswegian from an Aberdonian or a Borderer from an Invernesian . . . They're totally different in their personality characteristics and their views. So if there is a tension between being Scottish and being British there must be a tension between all parts of Scotland. It's absolute nonsense.

Thus the notion that different parties hold consistent but different positions on Scottishness is undermined both by the evidence that there is variability within parties and also that some of the positions expressed in one party coincide with those expressed in another. Of course, one could respond to the first point (if not the second) by arguing that this variability reflects the positions of subgroups within the parties and hence there is still heterogeneity within any group. But such an argument is dangerously near to tautology insofar as one simply invokes a new group division as soon as one encounters any difference over stereotypes. What is more, it involves grouping people according to the categories which the analyst sees as relevant rather than in terms of actors' own expressed self-categorizations – a violation of the basic tenets of SCT.

This leads on to a third, and crucial, point. It isn't just that speakers don't define themselves in terms of political subgroups when talking of Scottishness, they don't define themselves in terms of political parties either. Both in the interviews and in more public domains, speakers position themselves as part of what they are defining. When people wish to say what is distinctive about Scottish identity they talk of the Scots as 'we'. Occasionally (as in extract 4 where the MP states that 'I think Scots are recognised, and I would like to think that I was recognised in this light . . .') they go further and make explicit claims to Scottishness.

The cynic might respond that, whatever they say, these people are politicians who, almost by definition are not to be trusted ('the politician is an acrobat, he keeps his balance by saying the opposite of what he does' according to Maurice Barres). They may purport to speak in terms of the nation but they actually do so from a party perspective. Quite apart from the fact that this brings us back to the problem of how we define group membership, such an objection would miss the point. Obviously, parliamentary politicians vie for votes and obviously they will do so by claiming to fulfil voters' self-interests. The interesting thing is that all the major parties choose to do so by claiming to fulfil the voters' interests as Scots. Thus they are appealing to the same audience in terms of the same collective identity. Likewise, their arguments are conducted through offering different definitions of this one identity. It may well be that not all definitions have the same impact. But the very fact that the political debate is constituted through the battle of definitions indicates that the heterogeneity of self-stereotypes is not only thinkable but commonplace.

Even if it is accepted that the definition of social identities is a domain of disputation, some might still object that it remains to be shown whether the variability can be explained strategically: all right, people within groups differ over what group membership means, but do they do so in order to promote or else oppose particular forms of action? At least three forms of evidence suggest that they do.

First of all, speakers frequently deploy particular definitions of Scottishness in order to support their own policies. We have remarked upon this in general terms around extracts 1 to 4. Sometimes there is a more explicit link between identity and particular detailed policies. Thus a Conservative MP, interviewed just after the election, talks about controversial government health policies which involved giving individual General Practitioners (family doctors) their own funds which they could use as they wished (to send patients to hospital, to improve their surgeries etc.) and forming hospitals in 'trusts' which also had control of their own budgets:

> 8. I think there is a great pioneering thing that goes through Scottish people. I think that we have in some respects, let's take something political, talk about health. Things like GP fundholding and things like – and even this is not common throughout Scotland, this is a compact area of Scotland where GP fundholding took off much quicker than anywhere else. Trusts, the first trust hospital, one of the first two, Aberdeen. Far more willing to try new things, to seize opportunities and to go forward. And I think that is something which is typical of Scotland. Give us a chance and we will grab it.

Such explicit links between group identity and ingroup policies are, however, somewhat rare – perhaps because whole speeches are often implicitly organized around the consonance of party policy and Scottishness while to speak explicitly about this consonance makes it clear that the point is arguable and hence open to rejection. By contrast, many speakers seek to contest outgroup policies by showing how they are dissonant with Scottish identity. We have already shown in extract 1 the SNP arguing that Thatcherism was alien to Scottishness; in extract 3, the Liberal Democrats arguing that independence is alien to Scottishness; and, in extract 4, the Conservatives arguing that not paying the Poll Tax (supported by the SNP and sections of the Labour Party) is alien to Scottishness. The following two extracts from interviews are even clearer: first of all a Labour politician arguing that SNP policy is alien to the inherent socialism of Scottish identity then a Conservative MP arguing that Labour policy is alien to the inherent anti-socialism of Scottish identity:

> 9. The idea, for example that it's Scotland's oil, I think that's a very Thatcherite idea that Scotland can garner all the revenues from North Sea oil and keep [it] in Scotland to raise the standards of working people here, when that would be to the expense of the living standards of working people in England and Wales and Northern Ireland. I think that is abhorrent and not part of the Scottish tradition in fact, that the Scottish tradition is more Labour orientated, more socialist orientated and would wish to share these resources.
>
> 10. Scots are people who are intelligent and perhaps slightly aggressive in the way they attack things and if they have a job to do they'll attack it aggressively. That's the natural way for Scots to perform. I think in some ways there's been a culture developed over recent times that's taken that away and we've got to change away from it . . . I regret the fact that within Scotland for some there's been a dependency culture developed. I believe that's come about through socialism in actual fact. I believe that one of the problems we've had since the war in particular is socialism at local government level, which tried to ensure that everybody would rely on the local authorities and that to me was probably foreign to Scottish natural feelings.

Thus far, our focus has been upon the way in which speakers deploy different constructions of Scottishness in order to establish consonances with ingroup policies and dissonances with outgroup identity. However – and this is our second form of evidence – there are also instances where speakers argue not over Scottishness but over the relationship between policies and Scottishness. In Billig's terms, these are arguments over the relationship between instances and categories rather than over categories per se (Billig, 1987).

If extract 9 involves a Labour MP attacking SNP policy for being anti-socialist and therefore anti-Scottish, the next extract involves an SNP representative attacking Labour policy for it's own anti-socialism. It is taken from the speech of Bill Houston, an SNP candidate in a constituency with a sitting Labour MP, to an election meeting. After telling a story about a disabled worker mistreated by the local (Labour) council, he continues:

> 11. But it's not just that it's in Falkirk district, it's at central region, it's everywhere the Labour Party have got decisions to make. The decisions they make are based on the values that we are trying to shake out of our country. Victorian mill owner values, that's what is applicable to the Labour Party of today, and the choice you are faced with in this election is between the kind of reborn conservatism of the Labour Party that doesn't know how to get rid of Thatcherism. I lend, I reminded Jim Sillars [*an SNP leader also speaking at the meeting*] that I was born and brought up in Govan, and I served an engineering apprenticeship in Clydeside, and it was one of the first political comments I ever heard was one of the shop stewards said to me 'there's only one thing worse than a Tory and that's two Tories'.

Another way of arguing that the opposition is dissonant with ingroup identity is to claim that, even if in the abstract they appear consonant, in practice they are incapable of being realized by the opposition (and hence impede their realization by one's own party). Thus the Labour Party MP John McAllion, speaking at a public meeting in the industrial town of Dundee, makes the following appeal:

> 12. The Labour Party is the only party which is capable of taking on and defeating the Tories in this election. It's the only party which can deliver what I believe the majority in Dundee and Scotland want to see and that's radical, political and constitutional change. And the objective truth is this: that the SNP cannot win these seats. They will not win the 16 seats in which they currently stand in second place. They will not win their target of 37 seats and they will not be negotiating for independence at the end of the day. Because though they claim they will be, they are really lying through their teeth and of course they can improve on their present position. They can advance in a parliamentary seat, here and there, across Scotland. But the price that will have to be paid for that will be to undermine the only party in Scotland that is capable of taking on and defeating the Tories.

The same logic was used by Jim Sillars on the night of the election when he argued that votes for Labour, however well intentioned are useless, since the English are inherently Conservative and will always vote accordingly. This speech is quoted by a losing SNP candidate speaking to a mass rally in Glasgow three days after the election:

> 13. Scotland can't wait another five years for change [*five years is the maximum length of a parliamentary term in British politics*]. We've been hammered (applause) we've been hammered by the Tories for thirteen years and we can't wait five more . . . if we wait now, it may be longer than five years because the Labour Party cannot win another government in Westminster (applause). The Scottish people have to reconcile themselves to that fact before they can solve the paradox that Jim Sillars mentioned on Thursday night, the paradox of Scotland voting Labour and England voting Tory (applause).

However it is achieved – whether through arguments over the nature of identity, arguments over the meanings of policies or arguments over the capability of policies to be realized – the link between identity definitions and arguments over party prototypicality is almost ubiquitous. The fact that speakers devote so much time and such rhetorical sophistication to showing how their party can realize the values and priorities of Scottishness – while other parties at best fail in doing so and more commonly contradict them – demonstrates at the very least that speakers realize and use self-stereotype definitions to strategic ends.

It is still logically conceivable that our speakers are merely opportunistic. They simply take advantage of the set stereotypes they believe in rather than constructing these stereotypes to strategic ends. However even this possibility is undermined by our third and final source of evidence which concerns the ways in which the same speaker may use different constructions of identity. The same person may use different (and even contradictory) constructions in order to achieve the same end. Thus, the Tory MP who, in extract 7, denied the existence of a Scottish identity, later on in his interview gives it a specific meaning:

> 14. I mean it's, it has a national identity. It has no reason to have a government identity. And Scots resent authority. They don't like being talked down to and told what to do and therefore, now, I've never found anybody who thought governments were better if they were closer.

What unites both quotes is that they both serve to argue against a Scottish parliament, either devolved or independent. Either the Scots don't have an identity in which case they don't merit distinctive institutions or else their identity is distinctively anti-parliamentarian in which case it is against their interests (and wishes) to have one. The fact that the speaker produces different constructions in the same context (arguing against opposition parties) undermines the notion that people have set stereotypes or even that they have contextually determined stereotypes. The fact that strategic function remains constant while identity usage varies suggests that strategies of influence may determine the variability in stereotypic constructions. Such a conclusion is further reinforced by evidence that speakers may alter their constructions as their strategic purposes change. A past president of the Scottish Conservative Party whom we interviewed was asked why Scots are more pro-Labour than the English. He replied:

> 15. Maybe Scots allow their hearts more to rule their heads perhaps more than people in England do. People in England are perhaps more taken with 'we've got to balance the books, we can do what we can but we have to balance the books'. In Scotland, no. We give to those who have not got and to hell with balancing the books.

However, when talking about whether electoral unpopularity was inevitable, he said:

> 16. Incorporated or encapsulated within the Scottish psyche is a degree of carefulness. Carefulness about money for example, not frugalness, perhaps in some senses, carefulness about being able to balance the budget, an absence of any sort of liking for debt.

Thus, in the context of explaining the reality of past defeat, the Scots are inherently profligate ('to hell with balancing the books') and it is not the Conservatives fault. In the context of future prospects, the Scots are inherently careful ('being able to balance the books') and hence should vote Tory. Almost the mirror image is provided by an SNP MP. At an eve of poll public meeting he was asked why his party did well in the area. He replied:

> 17. If you look at places like that, Buchan and Angus, they are independent people, they make up their own minds. The people here are very independent. Every burgh in Angus is distinct in character and different and you will find that that is what people have in common when they have voted SNP.

After electoral defeat for the SNP, the same MP provided the following explanation in an interview:

> 18. Something very Scottish happened at that election. We called canny. Don't know if you know that expression, but we tend not to go to the extreme . . . and therefore people I think at the election said 'yes, we'd like independence,

but let's go for the easier option of independence'. And I think that's precisely what happened: we called canny. It's the cautious part of the Scottish nature.

Thus, with the prospect of victory ahead, Scottishness is consonant with independence especially in the local area. With the reality of defeat behind, the Scottish nature goes against independence. It isn't the SNP's fault. As before, self-stereotypes vary and they follow strategic needs.

Self-stereotypes and trait descriptions: In the foregoing extracts, we have come across many descriptions of Scots in terms of traits – they are canny, they are independent, they resent authority, they are egalitarian and so on. However, not all descriptions are in such terms. Often Scots are described in terms of characteristic actions rather than qualities: the Scots are willing to try new things, they act aggressively, they care more about those who are disadvantaged. This might derive from personality but it might also derive from culture or else from the way Scots live. Thus the SNP's Jim Sillars, speaking at a public meeting, insists that Scotland's fear of poverty, and hence its radical priorities, derive from Scottish priorities:

> 19. All of us in here have [*only*] our ability to work physically, mentally or intellectually. Our whole lives are determined by whether we can sell ourselves in the labour market. If there's a labour market which has thirty workers chasing one job, you are in a weak position and you live in a society riddled with anxiety – that describes Scotland.

So, to characterize self-stereotypes as if they are necessarily defined in trait terms is only to tell part of the story. More importantly, and as we argue in section 1, however stereotypes are characterized – as traits, as cultures or as practices – they are always part and parcel of an explanation of what has happened, what is happening or else what might happen in the social world. If the Scots are communitarian it explains why they oppose the Conservatives and favour autonomy, if they are robust (but not arrogant) it explains why they are not for independence, if they are canny it explains why they reject independence even while favouring it; traits like everything else are part of arguments. The same trait may therefore change its meaning entirely when placed in different contexts and therefore to abstract traits from their argumentative context is to render them meaningless. We have already made this point conceptually, however it is particularly clear in our election material. Two illustrations will suffice.

On the one hand, speakers frequently summarize Scottish character through the means of prototypically Scottish sayings – most notably the Burns quotation 'a man's a man for all that' and 'we're all Jock Tamson's Bairns'.[4] These sayings were frequently used in the election but they acquired very different meanings in different hands. To take the Burns quote first of all, both SNP and Labour speakers use it to reinforce the notion of an egalitarian and hence socialist Scotland. Extract 5, from a Labour activist, stresses the caring nature of Scotland. The speaker continues in the following terms:

> 20. Robert Burns after all, with many of his poems trying to expand on that with 'a man's a man for a' that' etc . . . And a lot of his works went down very well with socialist, in inverted commas, countries and I think that again epitomises our attitude towards the corporate community which is Scotland.

In the hands of a Conservative activist the same phrase is turned against corporatism:

> 21. Robert Burns expressed so many things about Scottish culture with his poetry . . . 'A man's a man for a' that'. We may be achievers, we may get here and we may get to the top, but there are those quintessentially human characteristics that the Scot does not lose sight of. My mother lives in a small village in Fife. There's a fantastic system of informal social support. They care for one another and it's very much, you know, 'do unto others as you would have done unto yourself'. And I've seen her both as a giver as well as a recipient of that informal social support which I happen to think is infinitely better than anything that would be provided by the council's social work department.

Moving on to Jock Tamson, it has already been used by an SNP MP in extract 1 as further support for radical communitarianism. Once again, as used by a Conservative MP, it acquires entirely different connotations when he asserts that Scotland is:

> 22. A very small country and everyone knows everyone else. It's only in the larger countries that the Duc de Normandie is not known by the burghers of Calais that you get an aristocratic structure. There is a perfectly good aristocratic structure in Scotland but the – it's rather like a big pub, Scotland. You know, everyone talks to everyone else and no-one minds who you are particularly. We're all Jock Tamson's bairns.

The difference is between what McCrone (1992) calls the 'activist' and the 'idealist' interpretations of Scottish egalitarianism. On the one hand, the idea that we are all the same is used to advocate an active opposition to manifestations of inequality or privilege. On the other, the idea that we are all equivalent in terms of our humanity is used to say that we should accept surface differences and live together as we are in a stratified society. The practical implications of the two – even if they start from the same phrase – are diametrically different.

Our second illustration involves a shift from commonplaces, which are used to validate traits, to the traits themselves. Already, the extracts relating to 'a man's a man' (5 continued as 20 and 21) involve two different meanings of the idea that Scots are caring. For Labour this means institutional structures to support the poor and weak, for the Conservatives it means the substitution of informal for institutional structures. A similar diversity can be found in the meanings ascribed to other commonly used Scottish traits.

The Scots are anti-authority. In extract 14, a Conservative uses this to mean that they don't want a parliament nearby. But, according to an interview with a Labour activist:

> 23. There's a famous line that Scott[5] does in his novels about the Union of the parliaments, where a woman says standing outside the Scottish parliament building after the vote for the Union, and she says in Scots: 'well at least when tha wi' here, we could pelt 'em wi' stanes when they were nae good bairns, but nabody's nails can reach the length a' London'. And that's another example. There was a great practice of mob riots outside the Scottish parliament building when folk were nae passing laws that the people wanted. So there's a healthy disdain, I think for authority.

In this case, being anti-authority is used to argue that Scots *do* want a parliament nearby which they can hold to account.

The Scots are internationalist. For a Conservative MP this means that it was natural for Scots to be involved in the British empire:

> 24. I think that the Scot as a person is a much more tolerant, much more international person than the Englishman. And I think that if you go back into history that comes over: some of the great men of the empire were Scots. During the days of empire if you go to any far flung part of the British empire there would be a Scot whether in the Raj in India or in the far east.

By contrast, for an SNP MP, it means the SNP policy of independence in Europe:

> 25. Scotland has always had an internationalist outlook. I mean sovereignty is actually a problem for the English. It's not a problem for us. We pooled our sovereignty with the English in a common market 300 years ago and what we are now saying is we wish to regain that sovereignty to once again pool it in a wider 300 million European Community. A growing changing community in which Scotland must be there in her own right participating in those changes.

It would be possible to continue with further examples, but the point should be clear by now. An abstracted notion of trait which can equally well mean expanded social services or no social services, a Scottish parliament or no Scottish parliament, serves only to obscure the meaning of stereotypes. Just as it is essential to examine the argumentative uses of stereotyping, so it is essential to describe the content of stereotypes within that argumentative process.

3 Conclusions

The immediate aims of this study were threefold. First of all, we wished to show the variability of self-stereotypes. This has been apparent from our first extracts. Different people define Scottishness in very different – often directly contradictory – ways. So do the same people at different times. Secondly, we wished to show how this variability could be accounted for as a strategy of mass influence. Once again, this was apparent from the start. Whether in terms of different speakers at the same time or the same speaker at different times, variable constructions of Scottishness invariably present the speaker's position or policy as prototypical for Scots in general. Finally, we wished to show that such a strategic stance requires us to abandon a trait conception of stereotypes. Stereotypes, we showed, are always explantions of where people were, are or should be going. Even where they are used, trait terms are meaningless when divorced from this explanatory context: the same term may mean different things; different terms may mean the same thing. In the isolated form of a trait scale, items are at best ambiguous and at worst indecipherable.

More generally, this chapter has been primarily a call for the functional and strategic dimensions of stereotyping to be taken seriously. We have argued that, even if lip service is frequently paid to them, these dimensions are characteristically ignored in studies of stereotyping. First of all, the conceptual implications of a functional analysis for stereotyping in general are never followed through and, secondly, such analyses may be encouraged but they are never actually carried out.

Our analysis should therefore be seen as but one example of what a functional/strategic approach might look like. Clearly, it is very far from an attempt to exhaust the field since it flows from a distinctive functional analysis, it is addressed only to self-stereotyping and it deals with political discourse. Nonetheless, even this situated analysis highlights some important general theoretical and methodological points. In fact the two are intertwined. It is, perhaps, due to the abstracted way in which stereotypes are studied that they become conceptualized in such abstracted ways. Long ago, Israel and Tajfel (1972) made a plea that we place psychological phenomena in their proper social context. Well the context of stereotyping is in arguments over the nature of the social world. Therefore, stereotyping needs to be studied as it is being used and tussled over by various parties. Our first plea is for research into stereotypes to move beyond the laboratory and for more studies of stereotyping in its context of usage. This is not to say that we would scrap the laboratory. We would argue that it can be useful to use experiments in particular circumstances where stereotypic definitions are set and where the consequences are at issue (Reicher, in press; Spears, 1994). However, experiments are notoriously bad at exploring dynamics and, therefore, we shouldn't 'fetishize' them as the only legitimate method of psychological research. What is more, even where experiments are used we should beware of employing operationalizations, such as trait scales, which distort the phenomena we are investigating.

On a conceptual level, we hope that our analysis opens up a dialogue between the hitherto opposed self-categorization and discursive camps – and points to the fruitfulness of such a dialogue. If our analysis shows clearly that self-stereotypes are constructed and deployed discursively and in argument, it is equally true that the nature of self-identity is a key theme in all our texts. Not only do speakers deliberate over the nature of Scottishness when we ask them to do so in interviews, they also do so spontaneously in public meetings, leaflets and press releases (though we have not included such written texts in the present analysis). It is hard to explain on a simply discursive level why the construction of identity should be such an omnipresent and such a passionate theme. Hence, it is more expedient to use a psychological account of why identity is so important and what flows from the way it is defined. In short, if identity is constructed in discourse, it is psychology which explains the discursive focus on identity. This approach not only applies to stereotypic content of self-categories. It can also be used to look at the question of category salience, category boundaries, prototypicality and a host of other key issues in the analysis of group behaviour. The exploration of these various issues is our current project.

We have only just made a start in this domain. However, even at such an early stage we would echo and extend the words of MacDiarmid with which we began. All identities (not just Scottish), and all aspects of identity (not just the content of stereotypes), are marked by diversity. If social identities define who we are and what we are to do, then we are always at least potentially caught in the cross-fire of different constructions – literally divided against ourselves. Of course this is only a starting point and there are many other issues to be addressed. Most notably, a study of elite discourse begs the question of popular understanding. In crude terms, it may be that politicians argue over identity but does it have any effect on the electorate. The study of whether and how arguments work lies in the future. However, one thing that becomes obvious when studying stereotyping in public meetings and mass rallies is that the arguments of speakers can engage the passions of their audience. People can adopt the constructions offered to them with great enthusiasm. Of course, it depends upon the performance and therefore it is apposite to finish with the speech of a theatrical figure. On 24 April a mass rally was held in Glasgow's George Square. David Hayman, a director of the radical drama group 7:84 theatre (so-called because 7 per cent of Scots own 84 per cent of the land) came to the stage and engaged the crowd in call and answer:

Hayman: Hello!
Crowd: Hello

H:	I just want to ask you a few questions. On Thursday April 9th did you vote Conservative?
C:	No
H:	On Thursday April 9th did you vote for the destruction of our health service?
C:	No
H:	On April 9th did you vote for the dismantling of our industry?
C:	No
H:	Did you vote for the decay of our educational system?
C:	No
H:	Did you vote for greed?
C:	No
H:	Did you vote for selfishness?
C:	No
H:	[pointing to the south] The English did
C:	Loud applause
H:	For the fourth election in a row the people of England have voted for greed and self-interest. And I'll tell you something. There's nearly 50 million of them and only 5 million of us so we don't stand a snowball's chance in hell of ever having the parliament we deserve unless we have our own. Right?
C:	Applause and cheering
H:	Right?
C:	Applause and cheering
H:	Right?
C:	Applause and cheering

Notes

1 In broad terms, in 1992 the Labour Party represented the left of mainstream British politics with strong structural links to the Trades Unions; the Liberal Democrats represented the centre with a combination of liberal social policy but more pro-market economic policy and the Conservatives, or Tories, represented the right wing. The position of the SNP is harder to define. Historically dubbed the 'tartan Tories' by their opponents, a left-wing leadership had assumed power by 1992. This leadership, of whom Alex Salmond and Jim Sillars (an ex-Labour left-winger) were the best-known figures, was in many ways more radical than the Labour Party in policy terms and in advocating mass action. However, it lacked influence within working-class organizations – the unions in particular.

2 A well-known Scottish saying meaning, literally, 'we are all the children of Jack Tamson' and suggesting that Scots all share a common humanity.

3 The Poll Tax (officially named the 'community charge') was a new form of flat rate

local taxation introduced by the Conservative government and levied in Scotland a year before England. The tax attracted widespread opposition – and a large non-payment campaign – on the grounds of abandoning progressive principles of taxation. It was eventually dropped after John Major replaced Margaret Thatcher as Conservative Prime Minister.

4　The 'Jock Tamson' saying has already been explained in note 2. The saying 'a man's a man for a' that' is taken from Burns' poem 'Is there for honest poverty'. The relevant verse reads:

> What though on hamely fare we dine
> Wear hoddin grey an' a' that?
> Gie fools their silks, and knaves their wine –
> A man's a man for a' that.
> For a' that and a' that
> Their tinsel show and a' that,
> The honest man, tho' e'er sae poor,
> Is king o' men for a' that.

Although our point is that the precise significance of this is contested it is agreed that, in general terms, the phrase points to the way in which all, whatever their station in life, are equally human.

5　Sir Walter Scott, the famous author of the Waverley novels and a key figure in the creation of Scottish tradition.

6
Stereotyping and Social Influence: Foundations of Stereotype Consensus

S. Alexander Haslam

1   Introduction

In the most basic terms, stereotypes can be thought of as sets of beliefs about the characteristics of groups of people that serve to mark those groups out as distinct entities (e.g., Ashmore and del Boca, 1981, p. 20; Judd and Park, 1993; McCauley and Stitt, 1978, p. 935). More specifically, they often present homogeneous, extreme and value-laden images that define the place of groups and individual group members within a broad social system and which in this capacity are an alternative to perceiving people as unique, idiosyncratic individuals.

However, beyond this, many (but not all) researchers agree that *social* stereotypes achieve their force, and thereby become a significant topic for research, because they are *widely shared* by large groups of people. It is not difficult to realize that the course of history would have been very different if the English-held stereotypes of the Irish, or the Nazi-held stereotypes of the Jews or the first European settlers' stereotypes of Australian Aborigines had been shared only by a few members of each group, or even if they had been shared by a majority of group members unbeknown to each other. In each case though, the stereotypes became potent because, within the groups who held them, they came to reflect and express a particular world view which dictated that group's *collective* behaviour towards particular targets of oppression.

In light of this point, it is interesting to remark that while an enormous amount of stereotyping research has been directed towards understanding the psychological substrates of the individual features of stereotypes (e.g., their homogeneity and extremity), very little work has addressed their collective, inter-subjective properties (Gardner, 1993; Stangor and Schaller, 1996). This is not to say that stereotype sharedness has not been recognized as a relevant issue. Indeed, discussion of the role of inter-subject agreement in stereotype content is a feature of most treatments of stereotype definition (e.g., Ashmore and del Boca, 1981; Brigham, 1971; Tajfel, 1981a; see also Reicher, Hopkins and Condor, this volume; Worchel and Rothgerber, this volume). However, it would appear that rather than debate leading to any theoretical or empirical progress, it has largely focused on attempts either (a) to promote sharedness as a research topic, (b) to encourage separate investigation of shared (social) and idiosyncratic (personal) stereotypes (e.g., Ashmore and del Boca, 1981; Karlins, Coffman and Walters, 1969; McCauley and Stitt, 1978) or, (c) to argue that sharedness be ignored altogether.

Illustrative of the latter view, Hamilton, Stroessner and Driscoll (1994) suggest that:

> Stereotypes are belief systems that reside in the minds of individuals . . . In this view, therefore, neither the definition nor the measurement of stereotypes should be constrained by the necessity of consensual agreement. (p. 298)

Similarly, Judd and Park (1993, p. 110) contend that 'a stereotype is defined at the level of the individual perceiver and it need not be consensually shared'.

This position has been countered by those who argue that sharedness is the *sine qua non* of properly social stereotypes and that this should be the primary focus of social psychological enquiry. This point was made particularly strongly by Tajfel (1981a, p. 147), when he argued that:

> Stereotypes can become *social* only when they are *shared* by large numbers of people within social groups or entities – the sharing implying a process of effective diffusion.

His view has since been echoed by a number of other researchers, most of whom express some level of discontent with the direction in which research into the stereotyping process has developed in the last fifteen or so years (e.g., Condor, 1990; Gardner, 1993; Hogg and Abrams, 1988; Leyens, Yzerbyt and Schadron, 1994; Oakes, Haslam and Turner, 1994). Yet, while sharedness has thus proved useful as a means of demarking alternative traditions of stereotype research – traditions that we might refer to as 'individual cognitive' and 'societal' respectively (cf. Spears, Oakes, Ellemers and Haslam, this volume) – it appears that demarcation is the principal (if not the only) advance that the analysis of stereotype sharedness has achieved to date.

The objective of this chapter is to go beyond the simple (and hitherto largely unfruitful) question of whether or not it is important to investigate stereotype consensus but to show instead that by seeking to develop an integrative (or more strictly, an interactive) analysis of the individual cognitive and the shared social underpinnings of stereotypes, we can not only enhance our understanding of both, but also move towards a properly social cognitive understanding of the stereotyping process as a whole. It follows from the arguments presented above that the ultimate test of this integration will be its ability to account for both the individual *and* the collective aspects of stereotypes.

In developing this analysis, the chapter starts with a consideration of previous research relevant to the examination of consensus. A critical idea to emerge from this review is that the sharedness of stereotypes appears to derive not from common experience per se (i.e., exposure to similar information) but rather from common group membership that structures information-processing. As an elaboration of this point it is suggested, following self-categorization theory (Turner, 1985, 1991), that psychological group membership is inextricably bound up with processes of *social influence* which lead people actively to seek agreement with particular others (ingroup members) about the truth or falsity of stereotypes and which therefore lead them (and other ingroup members) to endorse or reject those beliefs. The principles of this theory and its application to stereotyping are briefly summarized prior to the presentation of empirical research which investigates the impact of social influence on both individual and collective components of stereotype form and content. It is concluded not only that social influence is the critical mediator between specific group memberships and stereotype sharedness, but also that it constitutes something of a 'missing link' in previously-advanced cognitive *and* social theories of stereotyping.

2 Previous Research Relevant to the Analysis of Stereotype Sharedness

The measurement tradition

Having observed that consensus is a much-neglected feature of latterday research into stereotyping, it is interesting to remark that up until the 1960s most empirical studies in this area were very much concerned with documenting and monitoring the sharedness of stereotype content within particular groups. Indeed, the degree of sharedness in content was the feature of stereotypes that Katz and Braly (1933) considered most significant when discussing the results of their pioneering study in which subjects assigned five traits from a list of 84 to a range of different nationalities and ethnic groups. For example, 84 per cent of Princeton students described Negroes as superstitious, 78 per cent assigned the trait scientifically-minded to Germans and 48 per cent saw Americans as industrious. The high between-subject uniformity in content was indicated by the fact that on average only 10.1 per cent of the traits on the checklist were needed to account for half of all subjects' trait selections (if selections had been maximally idiosyncratic this figure would have been 50 per cent). Faced with these results, the high level of stereotype sharedness was the first thing the authors sought to explain. Their initial conclusion was that 'the degree of agreement among students in assigning characteristics . . . to different races seems too great to be the sole result of the students' contacts with members of those races' (p. 288). Katz and Braly (1933; see also 1935, p. 185) argued further that stereotype uniformity was an expression of cultural beliefs and norms – what the authors termed 'public attitude' – and was associated with people's 'public social selves', and that as such it could be meaningfully distinguished from 'private attitude' which was more likely to reflect individualized personal experience.

However, as research in this measurement tradition developed, researchers became interested in issues other than stereotype uniformity per se. In particular, they examined if and why stereotypes changed and whether they corresponded to any underlying group reality or were simply indicative of prejudice (for a recent review see Oakes et al., 1994). Studies showed, for example, that different generations of subjects assigned quite different traits to groups (e.g., Gilbert, 1951; Karlins et al., 1969) and that in the short term content also changed as a function both of international upheavals (e.g., war; Dudycha, 1942; Seago, 1947) and of changes in the context of judgement (e.g., variations to the number and types of groups to which subjects assigned traits; Diab, 1963).

In all these studies though, the stereotypes that emerged were still characterized by high levels of inter-subject agreement. So, 46 years after Katz and Braly's original study, although the consensus with which some traits were endorsed had reduced (now 13 per cent described Negroes as superstitious, 47 per cent described Germans as scientifically-minded and 23 per cent assigned the trait industrious to Americans), others had taken their place and the level of stereotype uniformity was much the same. Here an average of 13.0 per cent of traits were needed to include half of subjects' trait selections and now 47 per cent of students saw Negroes as musical, 59 per cent considered Germans to be industrious and 67 per cent believed Americans were materialistic (Karlins et al., 1969).

Although it was not emphasized at the time, the fact of this sharedness was also a necessarily coexistent feature of stereotype content which allowed researchers to address those questions in which they were interested. Thus, conclusions regarding changes or rigidity in stereotypes were based on measures of sharedness (the percentage of subjects who assigned a particular trait at a particular time or in a particular context), and at some juncture this had to be sufficiently high for the content in question to be considered in any sense stereotypic. Similarly, as part of the general quest to establish whether stereotypes were prejudicial (i.e., unjustified and/or negative), researchers looked at the relationships between levels of observed inter-subject agreement and (a) contact with the stereotyped group or (b) unfavourable attitudes towards it.

In this vein, Katz and Braly (1933, p. 289) argued that *lack* of agreement amongst subjects was 'probably explain[ed]' by subjects' personal contact with the stereotyped group in question given that they found more disagreement about the characteristics of Americans, the Irish and the English than about Negroes, Germans, Jews and Italians. Developing the arguments noted above, they thus considered that stereotype sharedness probably was a manifestation of prejudice since consensual images were often not based on actual experience with groups. Katz and Schanck (1938, p. 90) later exemplified this position with the conclusion that 'the absurd stereotype of the cruel Turk, common to American culture, persists because people do not commonly encounter Turks'.

In many respects this analysis was a forerunner to later suggestions that instigating intergroup contact might be a means of breaking down stereotypes (e.g., Triandis and Vassiliou, 1967). Indeed, Katz and Schanck (1938, p. 91) argued that experience with people of other nationalities was a necessary, though not sufficient, condition for prejudice reduction. However, consistent with work showing the limited validity of this 'contact hypothesis' (see Hewstone and Brown, 1986), other studies failed to support this analysis. For example, Schoenfeld (1942) found that Columbia students exhibited most *and* least agreement in their trait selection when describing groups with which they were minimally familiar, while high familiarity was associated with only moderate uniformity. And later, in a study of groups of Asians and Pacific Islanders, Vinacke (1956, p. 121) found exactly the opposite pattern to that observed by Katz and Braly such that in an 'approximately linear relationship' more uniform stereotypes were associated with *more* familiar groups. Both authors were somewhat mystified by these findings: Schoenfeld (1942, p. 28) concluding that 'adequate explanation lies in the social education of . . . subjects', and Vinacke (1956, p. 122) refusing to speculate in any depth 'because familiarity is an elusive variable'. More recently, however, Biernat and Crandall (1994, p. 673) argue on the basis of similar evidence of a positive association between stereotype consensus and familiarity that '*contact may promote learning of consensual reality*' – a conclusion clearly at odds with that reached by Katz and Braly (1933).

Along similar lines, hard-and-fast conclusions as to the relationship between sharedness and stereotype valence also proved elusive. In Katz and Braly's (1933) study there was no clear association between uniformity and stereotype unfavourableness and no clear pattern emerged in the studies by Edwards (1940), Schoenfeld (1942), or Vinacke (1956). On this basis Karlins et al. (1969) argued that consensual stereotypes were certainly not the 'language of prejudice' as had been commonly asserted (e.g., by Katz and Braly, 1935), and in fact they reported significant evidence that the opposite was true insofar as the more favourable stereotypes in their study (of Germans, Jews and the English) were also the most uniform.

On the basis of this early research, any straightforward conclusions about the relationship between the relative consensus of stereotypes and other variables of theoretical interest clearly proved impossible to draw. This was particularly frustrating for researchers given that when Katz and Braly had first embarked on their research, the possibility of identifying links of this nature and thereby understanding the distinct psychological basis and functions of shared stereo-types (public attitude) had seemed both strong and inviting. It was not surprising, then, that, in light of this failure to make significant theoretical progress, researchers grew dissatisfied with the Katz–Braly methodology (e.g., see Brigham, 1971), and that as this was abandoned the field as a whole moved away from the consensus- and content-related issues that it addressed.

The individual cognitive tradition

As has been well-documented elsewhere (e.g., Ashmore and del Boca, 1981; Stroebe and Insko, 1989), the decline of interest in stereotype measurement was attributable in large part to the emergence of a process-based analysis of stereotyping initiated by Tajfel (1969a; Tajfel and Wilkes, 1963). His studies of line judgement showed that some of the key properties of stereotypes – specifically their tendency to accentuate between-group difference and within-group similarity – could be explained in terms of principles of categorization common to all human perception. Although Tajfel had a background in the New Look tradition, and accordingly had been concerned to emphasize the role of group motivations and values in structuring cognition, a large number of researchers who were influenced by his work were attracted to the prospect of a *purely* cognitive analysis of stereotyping. In this vein, the largest part of the vast amount of stereotyping research that has been conducted in the last 25 years has attempted to show how universal strategies of information-processing and categorization might account for the various individual properties of ste-reotypes. Representative work has suggested that stereotype homogeneity, extremity and rigidity arise from inherent cognitive biases that lead perceivers (a) to see outgroups as more homogenous than ingroups (e.g., Linville, Salovey and Fischer, 1986; Judd and Park, 1988), (b) to pay undue attention to infre-quent or extreme behaviours (e.g., Taylor, Fiske, Etcoff and Ruderman, 1978; Hamilton and Gifford, 1976; Rothbart, Fulero, Jensen, Howard and Birrell, 1978) and (c) to engage preferentially in hypothesis confirmation rather than disconfirmation (Snyder, Tanke and Berscheid, 1977; Johnstone and Macrae, 1994).

It is certainly true that in the last ten years there has been an outward softening of this stance, so that it has been explicitly acknowledged that on its own, an individual cognitive approach to stereotyping is not enough to account for its 'real-world manifestations' and that stereotypes are shaped by other 'affective, motivational and socio-cultural variables' (e.g., Hamilton and Trolier, 1986, p. 153; see also Stroebe and Insko, 1989; Stangor and Schaller, 1996). As one commonly-endorsed way forward, it has thus been suggested that researchers

Group Members
(have)

Common Experiences
(that generate)

Similar Information
(that provides common input for)

Generic Processes
(that produce)

Shared Stereotypes

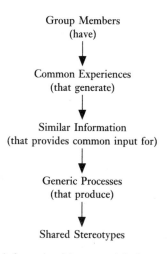

Figure 6.1 The common informational input model of stereotype sharedness.

should examine the manner in which these cognitive and 'non-cognitive' components *combine* in real world contexts (Hamilton and Trolier, 1986, p. 153; Hamilton et al., 1994). Along these lines, a large body of recent research has sought to investigate the manner in which cognition is affected by perceivers' mood states (see Mackie and Hamilton, 1993). Again though, this particular form of interactionism is often profoundly *individualistic* and still leaves examination of the collective aspects of stereotyping (e.g., their sharedness and group functions) out in the cold.

Indeed, within this tradition, considerations of how extra-individual factors structure cognition have tended to suggest rather matter-of-factly that shared stereotypes arise from shared experiences that provide the common informational input upon which generic processes of information-processing and social learning set to work. This explanation is represented schematically in figure 6.1 and is fleshed out by Hamilton and Trolier (1986, p. 154) in the following example:

> When we talk about the effect of media portrayals of blacks on the nature of race stereotypes, we are in essence referring to a learning process in which beliefs develop from exposure to certain kinds of information. In this example, aspects of the social environment shape stereotype development by influencing the content of the information one processes about a particular group.

This model is widely-accepted among cognitive researchers, not least because it demonstrates that a purely cognitive analysis of stereotyping is not *necessarily* incompatible with the phenomenon of stereotype sharedness. For example, in their extensive and influential review, Stangor and Lange (1993, p. 403), identify this idea that 'stereotypes are changed through experience' as a fundamental assumption 'that underlies otherwise diverse analyses of the stereotype development process' (going on to list seven relevant examples, e.g., Eagly and Steffen, 1984; Linville et al., 1986). Moreover, they add that 'because . . . common social processes operate on the same objective data stereotypes must become societally shared'.

However, the common informational input model appears to have at least two major flaws. First, it is not clear that common experience per se satisfies necessary conditions for inter-subjectivity. In particular, and as noted at the start of this chapter, it would appear that in order for cognition to be inter-subjective there must be some form of mutual influence between perceivers and some (at least implicit) *recognition* of a shared basis for influence (in slightly different terms, Ickes and Gonzalez, 1994, p. 305, after Asch, 1952, refer to necessary conditions of 'interaction' and 'interdependence'). Second, and more importantly, there are strong theoretical and empirical grounds for questioning the view that two people who have the same 'objective experience' or who are exposed to identical 'kinds of information' will necessarily have identical reactions. The same racist propaganda, for example, clearly affects racists and non-racists very differently. Along these lines, studies by Bar Tal (1988) demonstrate how the group membership of Israeli Jews and Palestinians provides a belief system and normative structure which leads them to process the very same information about their conflict very differently (e.g., making different attributions and attending to different features; for a similar argument from a social developmental perspective see Keil, 1991; Wellman and Gelman, 1992; Wisniewski and Medin, 1994). As we will see below, this issue resurfaces in studies of stereotyping and social influence which tend to suggest that between-subject response similarity is much more likely to be predicted by shared group membership than by common experience.

The societal tradition

The argument that mainstream cognitive accounts of stereotyping offer only limited explanations of stereotype sharedness has provided impetus for a number of alternative approaches to this issue. Although many of these have been largely speculative (e.g., Condor, 1990; Tajfel, 1981a), some work in the tradition of Moscovici's (1984) theory of social representations has sought to examine processes underpinning the development of a range of shared beliefs and knowledge structures. Broadly speaking, this work is sympathetic to Moscovici's (1984, p. 13) claim that the 'main task of social psychology' is to study the all-pervasive manner in which individuals' subjective interpretations of experience are structured and given meaning by categorical and other schematizing systems that constitute a shared psychological resource within collectives. In contrast to the common informational input model, a central feature of Moscovici's analysis is that it argues that 'objective data' *can only be given meaning* when individuals have access to higher order theories which allow them to interpret similar data in similar ways.

If we look, for example, at the stimulus input in standard cognitive studies (e.g., Hamilton and Gifford, 1976) it is apparent that what constitutes the 'basic' data is potentially negotiable: usually stimuli *could* be categorized in a number of different ways – in much the same way as racists choose to judge people in terms of the colour of their skin, while non-racists may urge discrimination on the basis of the content of people's character. The fact that subjects organize information in a similar way is thus *dependent on*, and not simply a prequel to, shared understanding (one that suggests the appropriateness of differentiating between stimulus sentences in terms of their valence rather than their length, say; McGarty, Haslam, Turner and Oakes, 1993; see also Freyd, 1983). In this sense objectivity is not a given, but is a *product* (and one of the principal functions) of people having shared theories about social reality. As Moscovici (1984, pp. 36–7) puts it:

> The theory of representations ... excludes the idea of thought or perception which is without anchor ... Every system of classifications and of the relations between systems *presupposes* a specific position, a point of view based on consensus. (emphasis added)

Insofar as it is conceived of as 'a science of consensual universes in evolution', Moscovici's theory (and the critique of cognitivism it presents) is clearly relevant to the study of social stereotypes. Having said that though, relatively little work has attempted to spell out the implications of this analysis for improving upon work in the mainstream cognitive tradition. This can be attributed to a number of factors including, on the one hand, the theory's inherent vagueness and, on the other, a keenness amongst researchers to distance themselves from practice (experimental research) that they see to be inherently reductionistic (see Potter and Litton, 1985; Semin, 1985).

One exception to this trend is provided by the work of Augoustinos and Innes (1990; Augoustinos, 1991). In an integrative review of social cognitive and social representations research, they note a number of points of contact between the traditions – including an emphasis on mechanisms of comparison, categorization and classification which serve to organize and simplify the perceiver's stimulus environment. They point out though, that the analysis of belief acquisition that underpins social cognitive research is predicated on models of social learning that are inherently individualistic and neglect the way 'contents arise from and are shaped by social interaction and communication' (p. 225). Questioning the view that the 'acquisition of social knowledge proceeds through logical, sequential and universal stages of development which are controlled by the cognitive capacitates of the individual', Augoustinos and Innes argue for the need to look instead (a) at how attitudes and affective reactions are 'communicated to others so as to be shared reactions and not only idiosyncratic responses to social events' (p. 223) and (b) at the dynamic, context-sensitive nature of representations that change by 'merging, repelling and interacting with other structures' (p. 226).

Evidence bearing on the first of these points is provided by a number of developmental studies which suggest (albeit implicitly) that consensuality is an emergent and socially-negotiated property of social representations and stereotypes. Thus in a study of the development of representations of social structure in Australia, Augoustinos (1991) observed that university students produced more consensual and more uni-dimensional representations of social structure than younger schoolchildren. Using different methodology, Gardner, Kirby and Finlay (1973) found not only that older children were better at recognizing stereotypes of various ethnic groups (e.g., at matching the traits 'scientifically-minded' and 'industrious' with the category label 'Germans'), but also that the perceived difficulty of this task decreased and the likelihood of correct identification increased the more consensual the stereotype. Although some form of 'experience' is clearly essential to the development of such representations, these studies point to the emergent collective meaning given to that experience and to the communicative function served by social beliefs. Moreover, beyond the scope of purely cognitive analysis, the studies suggest that these properties not only contribute to, but also *derive from*, a shared perspective. Thus superior recognition of stereotypes presumably reflects heightened social awareness – including knowledge of, and sensitivity to, the way *other people* structure the world – rather than just (or even) the processing of more 'raw' information about the stereotyped groups.

Other research findings also lend support to the second idea that representations are sensitive to social contextual demands in a manner inconsistent with a simple social learning model. For example, Hrabe, Hagedoorn and Hagedoorn (1989) found that students' shared understanding of the ethnic hierarchy in the Netherlands varied as a function both of the use to which the representation was being put and of subjects' own group memberships: women, for example, were more likely to 'unfold' the ethnic hierarchy (i.e., use a more differentiated representation) when choosing a marital partner and men were more likely to do so when dealing with colleagues. On this basis the authors argue that representations do not constitute rigid 'social facts', but rather are flexible and dynamic enough to allow individuals to use them in different ways according to context.

In a similar manner, Augoustinos (1991) also found evidence that consensual representations of social structure varied as a function of schoolchildren's socio-economic class. While noting that this difference could simply have an experiential base (reflecting the unequal distribution of social knowledge in society), she notes that, beyond this, the different representations appear to serve important social functions for the groups in question. In particular, Augoustinos suggests that each representation may reflect an underlying motivation for group members to maintain a positive social identity – each group achieving this by accentuating *different* status differentials (cf. Tajfel and Turner, 1979; see also Anastasio et al., this volume; Ellemers and van Knippenberrg, this volume).

Points concerning the functional basis of shared representations align this work with Tajfel's (1981a) earlier argument that, while necessary, *it was not enough* to understand the cognitive processes of the individual alone and to assume that inter-individual phenomena like prejudice arose simply because these processes were reproduced in other individuals processing the same information. Instead, he argued that the processing of information about groups was necessarily structured by group life, and determined *inter alia* by group members' needs to provide shared explanations of complex social events, to justify discriminatory intergroup behviour, and to differentiate between ingroups and relevant outgroups in a manner favourable to the former.

Stereotyping research which has built on this social-functional analysis has served to generate data that is again problematic for the common informational input model. Consistent with Tajfel's critique, this suggests that information-processing depends on the perceiver's group membership and not simply the 'objective' properties of information per se. For example, studies where subjects are assigned randomly to so-called 'minimal groups' (after Tajfel, Flament, Billig and Bundy, 1971) show that these group memberships can structure and modify cognition in a way that overrides any biases that might lead perceivers either to represent outgroups more homogeneously than ingroups (Simon and Brown, 1987) or to over-represent distinctive information (Schaller and Maass, 1989). Anticipating such findings, Tajfel (1981a, p. 160) argued that by neglecting to consider *at the outset* the role of groups in shaping cognition, researchers effectively ruled out the possibility of integrating work in the cognitive tradition with earlier studies that had employed the Katz–Braly paradigm.

Overview

For a variety of reasons it can be seen that, to date, progress towards an integrated social psychological analysis of stereotype consensus has been quite unsatisfactory. Research in the measurement tradition points to the reality and significance of the phenomenon but presents no conclusive findings concerning its aetiology and no analysis of psychological process; research in the mainstream cognitive tradition presents analysis of process but a deficient explanation of its inter-subjective properties and social determinants; work in the social tradition supports this critique but provides only a very 'hazy blueprint' for empirical and theoretical progress (Tajfel, 1981a, p. 167; see also Condor, 1990). All these traditions, thus, have something important to offer, but each also has significant shortcomings.

In order to breach this impasse it would appear that there are a number of important points that emerge from existing research which need to be borne in mind. First, it appears that there is a need to recognize between-subject agreement as a central feature of the stereotyping process and to reinstate this as an important dependent variable (Stangor and Schaller, 1996). Second, it seems that an important feature of this agreement is that it not only contributes to group life, but that it also *arises from it*. Partly because of this, third, it is important to see the emergence of consensus as an *active* process that serves necessary communicative and social functions by providing a substrate to collective action.

Following Tajfel's injunction, it thus seems that an appropriate way to enhance the cognitive analysis of stereotype sharedness is to consider the manner in which group life impinges upon information-processing and provides shared and communicable meaning to individual experience. The attempt to delineate such a development in the following sections is an elaboration of self-categorization theory's analysis of stereotyping (Oakes et al., 1994) and extends Tajfel's analysis in a number of ways. Most importantly, it is based on an examination of the way in which as stereotypes develop (and change) shared structure is lent to experience through the process of *social influence* and associated motivations to work *actively* towards agreement with other people who are categorized as similar to the self in particular contexts.

3   Social Identity, Social Influence and Stereotyping

Applications of self-categorization theory to the individual aspects of stereotyping

The following summary of self-categorization theory and its application to stereotyping is intended to be brief, largely because detailed treatments are available elsewhere (especially Oakes et al., 1994; see also Haslam, Oakes, Turner and McGarty, 1996; Oakes and Turner, 1990; Turner, Oakes, Haslam and McGarty, 1994). At the heart of the theory though, is the idea that different forms of behaviour arise from categorical definition of the self (and others) at different levels of abstraction. In particular, it is proposed that group behaviour is made possible by definition of the self in terms of a social identity that is shared with other ingroup members, and which defines that ingroup as different from an outgroup (Turner, 1982). In these terms, stereotyping is seen as the process of perceiving people (including the self) as members of ingroup or outgroup social categories.

An important feature of the theory is that its analysis of stereotyping emphasizes the determination of the social categorization process by features of social context. Particularly relevant to the present discussion are the related ideas both (a) that the salience of a particular social category and (b) that the definition of a given stimulus as a member of a particular category vary as a function of, amongst other things, the perceiver's frame of reference. Both predictions follow from the analysis of comparative fit (Turner, 1985; Oakes, 1987) suggesting that a particular array of stimuli are more likely to the perceived in terms of a shared categorical identity to the extent that their difference from each other is seen to be less than the difference between them and all other stimuli (the principle of meta-contrast). So, for example, an apple and an orange are more likely to be categorized as having a common identity (as fruit) when a perceiver compares them with fish than when they are considered alone. Similarly, a person who is extremely anti-war and another who is moderately anti-war are more likely to see themselves (and to be seen by others) as sharing common group membership in a context that includes other pro-war people rather that just people who are anti-war.

Importantly, the principles of fit are also seen to determine category salience in interaction with perceiver readiness (Oakes et al., 1994). In contrast to the assumptions which underlie a number of individual cognitive models, it seems implausible to suggest that individuals come to social settings waiting to tally up bits of information in a dispassionate, uninvolved manner in order to decide matter-of-factly whether a particular group is good or bad. On the contrary, categorical reaction to a stimulus array is determined not only by the subjectively-perceived features of that array but also by the prior expectations, motives and theories of the perceiver, many of which derive from his or her group membership (Bar Tal, 1988; Sherif and Cantril, 1947; Turner and Giles, 1981b).

These and related principles which suggest that categories are comparative, normative and relative to shared theories, have a number of applications to the analysis of the individual features of stereotypes (see Oakes et al., 1994). First, they generate predictions about *when* a collection of people (one that may or may not include the self) will be perceived in social categorical terms (i.e., as a group) and stereotyped. As well as this, self-categorization theory also generates predictions about the *consequences* of social category salience. In particular (following Tajfel, 1969a), it is argued that when an ingroup–outgroup categorization is salient the extent of individual group members' categorical interchangeability will be reflected in the accentuation of intra-class similarities and inter-class differences. Thus where a woman's anti-war group membership becomes salient, other anti-war people will be seen as more similar to each other (and to her) and more different from pro-war people (whose similarity to each other will also be enhanced) on dimensions that define membership these groups (e.g., attitudes to the use of military force).

A large body of research has demonstrated the utility of this analysis in relation to a number of specific issues in the stereotyping literature. Thus, amongst other things, work has demonstrated the applicability of self-categorization theory to the analysis of distinctiveness (McGarty, et al., 1993; Oakes and Turner,

1986), judgemental polarization (Haslam and Turner, 1992, 1994) and perceived group homogeneity (Haslam et al., 1995, 1996). And in general, empirical work has shown that effects which had previously been considered to result from inherent cognitive biases are in fact context-sensitive responses to stimuli in context. An example of this is provided by research examining the outgroup homogeneity effect: the tendency for perceivers to see ingroups as less homogeneous than outgroups (Linville et al., 1986; see also Ellemers and van Knippenberg, this volume). This asymmetry in ingroup–outgroup representation is seen to arise from the fact that in experimental settings ingroups and outgroups are typically judged under different conditions – the ingroup in in*tra*group contexts on dimensions that are subjectively poorly-defining, and the outgroup in in*ter*group contexts on subjectively better-defining dimensions. These contextual factors impact on the perceived fit of category-based representations of ingroup and outgroups, which in turn determines perceived similarity amongst group members and the subjective applicability of attributes to groups as a whole (for a more detailed account see Haslam et al., 1996).

The central thrust of this research has been to promote an *interactionist* understanding of stereotyping – showing that the cognitive aspects of the process are sensitive to, and shaped by, the realities of group life rather than predetermined and universal. In contrast to the assumptions underpinning the common informational input model, it is thus assumed that the same information is not always processed in the same way (and with similar consequences) by different perceivers or even by the same perceiver in different settings. Consistent with this argument and with specific predictions derived from self-categorization theory, relevant empirical studies have shown, for example, (a) that information-processing is highly dependent on a source's ingroup–outgroup status (McGarty, Haslam, Hutchinson and Turner, 1994), and moreover, (b) that the very same person may be assimilated to an ingroup category and judged favourably by a perceiver in a context that includes other more different people, while in a more restricted context that person will be perceived as an outgroup member and judged relatively negatively (Haslam and Turner, 1992).

All this research suggests that the psychological contribution of the group goes beyond the provision of a common informational base for its members. The idea that white racists share negative stereotypes of blacks because they read the same newspapers and attend the same meetings is attractively simple, but at the most basic level it does not explain either (a) why different people (or the same person at different times) abstract(s) different information from the same 'raw' informational source, or (b) why, even if they did process identical information, it would not affect all people (e.g., pro- and anti-racists) in the same way (Bar Tal, 1988; Schaller and Maass, 1989). In terms of self-categorization theory, it seems reasonable to assert that such variations in information processing need to be explained with reference to the role of social context as a co-determinant both of group definition and individual cognition (e.g., making particular social categorizations accessible and meaningful at particular times and specifying the dimensions on which categorization of social information is based).

Yet even if the common informational input model were to be modified along these lines – noting that similar cognitive processing is only expected when perceivers are acting in terms of similar contextually-defined self-categories – it is still apparent that stereotype sharedness reflects an inter-subjectivity that goes beyond mere correspondence of reaction (cf. Ickes and Gonzalez, 1994). In order to account for this, analysis is needed which examines the psychological links between group membership and mutual influence.

Applications of self-categorization theory to the collective aspects of stereotyping

In the previous section the concept of social identity was introduced as if it was a part of the individual that he or she develops and deploys simply in response to a particular stimulus situation. Yet, while it is true that social identities do determine an individual's interpretation of and behaviour in particular (intergroup) contexts, in those settings they also serve to structure behaviour by creating a basis for mutual influence. Specifically, self-categorization theory (Turner, 1985, 1991; see also Hogg and Turner, 1987; Turner and Oakes, 1989) asserts that an important consequence of people perceiving themselves in terms of social identity (an identity which they share with other ingroup members) is that they agree, and expect to agree, with others who they categorize as similar to themselves. In part this follows from the principle of meta-contrast since clearly the dimension of others' agreement or disagreement with oneself can operate as a powerful basis for social categorization (where the people who agree with us constitute an ingroup whose members differ less from each other than from those with whom we disagree).

As well as this though, it is suggested that those with whom the individual shares a social identity (i.e., ingroup members) are also identified as *sources that can consensually validate his or her subjective beliefs*. This is particularly important, since in social interaction, in order to be confident of the correctness of our beliefs it is generally *not sufficient* simply to engage in personal reality testing – seeking out the truth individually only with reference to our own perceptions and observations. Rather, as Turner (1991) argues, reality testing involves two interdependent and equally important phases, one individual and one collective. Thus while personal testing is important, this is always accompanied (and may be modified) by *social reality testing* – the process of seeking to have our beliefs validated by other people. In other words there is a dynamic between the individual and the group so that for the perceiver:

The psychological processes of relative perception and the social processes of collective discussion and conflict are interdependent means of achieving valid social stereotypes, each building on and correcting for the limitations of the other. (Oakes et al., 1994, p. 210)

A clear implication of self-categorization theory is that it is through this process (of what Turner, 1982, calls *referent informational influence*) that normative beliefs – of which stereotypes are a prime example – are formed and become shared. When a person's social identity is salient, not only does the ingroup provide a common categorical point of view that serves to structure and contextualize their cognitive activity (as suggested in the previous section), but so too it serves an ongoing *regulatory* function as a source of normative information that must be taken into account if potentially idiosyncratic observation is to have any social value. Thus, where *di*sagreement between an individual and other ingroup members emerges (i.e., where a particular belief appears not to be shared) it is anticipated that individuals will be motivated either (a) to *change their views* so that they become consistent with other ingroup members, (b) to attribute the disagreement to perceived relevant differences in the stimulus situation or (c) to recategorize those others as an outgroup, in order to reduce the *subjective uncertainty* that arises from disagreement with people with whom they expect to agree.

Support for these predictions has been provided by a large amount of previous research which indicates that subjects' willingness to endorse another person's views is critically mediated by that person's ingroup–outgroup status (e.g., Abrams and Hogg, 1990; Mackie, Worth and Asuncion, 1990; McGarty, Turner, Oakes and Haslam, 1993; McGarty et al., 1994; Turner, 1991; Wilder, 1991). Nonetheless, there is little or no evidence that similar processes of social influence mediate stereotype formation and development. Moreover, as Condor (1990, p. 236) notes, there has been no direct examination of exactly how these (or any other) processes impact upon stereotype *sharedness*. The research reported in the following section is the result of preliminary attempts to provide more thoroughgoing empirical exploration of these issues and to tie in the present analysis with previous research in measurement, cognitive and social traditions.

Empirical research

As a first stage in examining the processes underpinning emergent stereotype sharedness, some initial studies (Haslam, Oakes, McGarty, Turner, Reynolds and Eggins, in press, Pilot Study and Expt. 1) sought to investigate the manner in which subjects' judgements of the applicability of stereotype content would be affected by the stereotypic beliefs of ingroup and outgroup members. Our most straightforward prediction was that subjects would be more likely to endorse shared stereotypic beliefs under conditions where those beliefs also appeared to be held by other ingroup members than when those beliefs were held by outgroup members or when the ingroup advocated stereotype-inconsistent views.

To this end, Australian students were asked to make judgements about the percentage of members of a given ingroup (Australians) and outgroup (Americans) to whom given attributes applied (this constituting a commonly-employed measure of perceived group homogeneity; see Park and Judd, 1990). They did this after having been randomly assigned to one of six independent conditions in which they were given different feedback about the traits which *other* people had selected to describe these groups (e.g., information that these other people described Americans as extremely nationalistic, materialistic and ostentatious and Australians as happy-go-lucky, pleasure-loving and sportsman-like). These various conditions involved manipulations of (a) the stereotype-consistency of reference group information (consistent, inconsistent or neither – a control condition) and (b) the source of that information (subjects were given information that was said to have emanated either from other students – a relevant ingroup – or from 'closed-minded authoritarians' – a relevant outgroup). The key dependent variable here was the extent of *stereotypic differentiation* in subjects' judgements – the extent to which they perceived stereotype-consistent traits to be applicable to the target group and stereotype-inconsistent traits to be inapplicable.

As predicted, it was found that the relative applicability of stereotype-consistent traits was enhanced where the ingroup source validated these stereotypic beliefs (compared to conditions where it did not; i.e., in inconsistent information and control conditions). As well as this, where information was provided by the authoritarian outgroup, stereotypic differentiation was higher in the condition where the outgroup provided stereotype-*in*consistent information (i.e., disagreed with the subjects) than in consistent-information and control conditions. Consistent with the principles of referent informational influence, and contrary to the common informational input model, these results thus suggest that stereotype sharedness is unlikely to develop from exposure to information per se, but rather is conditioned by the source of that information and the source's relationship to the self. Here information which supported stereotypes strengthened those beliefs *only* when it was provided by an ingroup, while the very same information from an outgroup had the very opposite effect.

Having said this, an important feature of self-categorization theory is its assertion that perceptions of shared identity – and the basis for mutual influence that it provides – are context-sensitive rather than in any sense fixed (David and Turner, 1992). In order to test this prediction, we conducted a second study that incorporated an extra set of source conditions in which the feedback provided to subjects was said to emanate from a more clearly-defined ingroup: students who were not prejudiced rather than just students. In this

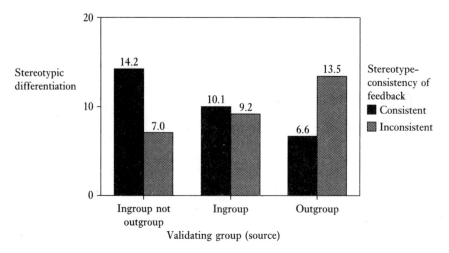

Figure 6.2   Stereotypic differentiation as a function of the stereotype-consistency of feedback and its source (adapted from means presented in Haslam et al., in press, table 1).

study there were, therefore, three levels of the source variable: information being said to have emanated from either (a) an ingroup distinct from an outgroup, (b) an ingroup or (c) an outgroup. We anticipated that in the first of these conditions subjects' identification with the source would be increased since the opportunity to recategorize the source as an outgroup would be reduced (cf. Haslam and Turner, 1992). This enhanced identification was then predicted to heighten the degree to which information provided by the source would bolster stereotypes (where it was consistent with pre existing beliefs) or change them (where it was counter-stereotypic). As can be seen in figure 6.2, the results of the experiment provided very strong support for these predictions.

In these studies, then, greater individual endorsement of shared stereotypes, as brought about through mutual influence, appears to be predicated upon contextually-defined shared identity rather than shared experience. Looking back over the body of research conducted in the measurement tradition it is therefore not surprising that researchers failed to identify a reliable relationship between stereotype uniformity and familiarity since there is no reason why judging a group that one is more familiar with should necessarily make a shared identity more salient for the stereotypers. On the other hand, one might expect (following Oakes, 1987) that uniformity would be enhanced to the extent that the judgement in question was associated with meaningful and relevant intergroup relations between the whole sample of stereotypers on the one hand and the stereotyped group on the other. Amongst other things, this would go some way to explaining why Katz and Braly's (1933) subjects' most uniform stereotypes were of Negroes, Germans and Jews and their least uniform were of Japanese, Chinese and Turks, and why the relative uniformity of Americans' self-stereotypes and their stereotypes of the Japanese increased during the Second World War (Schoenfeld, 1942). By the same token, it also suggests that the greater consensus in older subjects' social representations observed by Augoustinos (1991) may reflect the fact that having to make judgements about the place of groups in society is more likely to make university students act in terms of a shared identity, and does not simply arise from their 'increased contact with and knowledge about social categories' (a conclusion which conflict with earlier findings, e.g., Katz and Braly, 1933; and which, like work in the cognitive tradition, fails to acknowledge the social mediation of contact and knowledge; p. 201).

These preliminary studies break new ground by showing how the perception of group homogeneity – a process that researchers have previously considered to reflect 'basic' cognitive strategies and biases; for example, Linville et al. (1986) – can be structured by processes of social influence. Specifically, in showing how group influence can bolster or suppress an individual's willingness to endorse a particular stereotype, they demonstrate that stereotypes are shaped by (and come to represent) shared ingroup norms. Nonetheless, like all previous cognitive work, they do not provide any *direct* evidence of how these processes impact on sharedness per se. In order to tackle this issue a series of studies were conducted which employed a similar design to these initial experiments, but which reintroduced the Katz–Braly checklist as the primary dependent measure. Despite the limitations of this measure (e.g., see Brigham, 1971), this decision seemed warranted given that it is still the only procedure specifically designed to identify levels of inter-subject consensus (Gardner, 1993).

In the first study (Haslam et al., in press, Expt. 2) Australian subjects were asked to assign traits from a checklist to either Americans or Australians, in the face of information about the traits previously selected by other people. Again these traits were either consistent with preexisting beliefs or inconsistent, and had supposedly been selected either by an ingroup (other students) or an outgroup (prejudiced people). As in the previous studies, our first prediction was that subjects would be more likely to select stereotypic traits where these rather than others had been selected by the ingroup, but that the opposite pattern would emerge when they were given feedback from the outgroup. This prediction was supported by evidence that subjects were likely to select relatively more stereotype-consistent traits when given stereotype-consistent information from the ingroup or stereotype-inconsistent information from the outgroup, than when given stereotype-inconsistent information from the ingroup or stereotype-consistent information from the outgroup.

Importantly, these effects were also reflected in the favourableness of emergent stereotypes as well as in the consensus with which particular traits were selected. For example, when the trait 'extremely nationalistic' had supposedly been chosen by the ingroup to describe the American outgroup it was then selected by 93 per cent of the subjects (far-and-away the highest level of inter-subject agreement we have observed in any study of Australians' stereotypes of Americans), but when that ingroup had selected stereotype-inconsistent (positive) traits, only 38 per cent assigned this trait. On the other hand, where the prejudiced outgroup had selected the trait 'extremely nationalistic' to describe Americans only 46 per cent of subjects did the same, although 61 per cent selected this trait when that outgroup had chosen stereotype-inconsistent traits.

Although on their own such data provide convincing support for the argument that identity-based social influence is a primary determinant of stereotype consensus, it is still clear that there are a number of problems with attempts to obtain aggregate measures of trait selection (e.g., the mean percentage of subjects assigning stereotype-consistent and inconsistent traits). Most importantly, there is a certain amount of ambiguity in the results, as a high level of trait assignment could reflect the fact that all the subjects in one condition agreed on the assignment of some traits or that some subjects agreed on the assignment of all traits. By the same token, it is apparent that previous measures of consensus (e.g., Katz and Braly's, 1933, measure of uniformity) are equally limited in that they are computed for each condition rather than each subject and thus are not generally amenable to statistical analysis (see Gardner, 1993).

In order to address these problems, we devised a new measure which sought to establish the degree to which each subject's trait selections contributed to inter-subject consensus in the stereotypes that emerged in each condition. This *consensus coefficient* was computed for each subject by counting the number of times each trait they had selected was also selected by other subjects in the same condition and dividing it by the maximum number of times those traits could have been selected by those other subjects. In this manner the coefficient had a maximum value of one (i.e., if all subjects in the condition selected all the same traits) and a minimum value of zero. In effect, then, this coefficient can be thought of as the posterior probability that if one took at random any one of the traits selected by any randomly-chosen subject it would also be selected by another randomly-chosen subject in the same condition (in this sense it can be referred to as the *probability of agreement; P_a*). The distribution of the statistic appears to be highly normal, but some caution is warranted where it is subjected to analysis of variance, since, by definition, subjects' scores are not independent.

As predicted, analysis of between-condition variation in values of this consensus coefficient indicated that patterns of inter-subject agreement were interactively shaped by the nature of feedback and its source. Two highly significant effects were particularly relevant to the present discussion (both $ps < .001$). First, following the pattern remarked in previous studies, there was a two-way

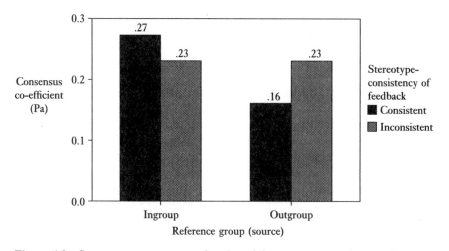

Figure 6.3 Stereotype consensus as a function of the stereotype-consistency of feedback and its source (adapted from means presented in Haslam et al., in press, table 2).

interaction which pointed to there being (a) greater inter-subject agreement when subjects received stereotype-consistent information from the ingroup than when that same feedback came from an outgroup or where the ingroup provided stereotype-inconsistent information; and (b) more consensus where the outgroup provided stereotype-inconsistent information than when it provided stereotype-consistent feedback. As well as this, there was generally much more consensus in stereotypes of Americans than in stereotypes of Australians. It is worth noting that in view of the fact that these subjects had presumably had much more exposure to Australians than Americans, this latter finding again questions the idea that consensus is simply a product of familiarity (cf. Augoustinos, 1991; Biernat and Crandall, 1994). On the other hand, it is quite consistent with the idea that consensus reflects the salience of a shared identity, since, as argued in relation to the analysis of outgroup homogeneity (e.g., Haslam et al., 1996), social identity salience should tend to be enhanced to the extent that subjects are making intergroup rather than intragroup judgements.

Broadly similar findings to these also emerged from a follow-up study which employed a very similar design to this third experiment, but where the outgroup reference group was said to be comprised of Americans rather than prejudiced people. This modification was made because we anticipated that while the general pattern of results would replicate earlier findings (i.e., that consensus would be increased where the ingroup provided stereotype-consistent rather than inconsistent feedback), the provision of stereotype-consistent information from the outgroup *about itself* might here increase rather than reduce consensus.

In the previous study when prejudiced people had described Americans negatively (e.g., as extremely nationalistic and materialistic), this had been associated with a reduction in consensus relative to conditions where that feedback had come from the ingroup. This, we argued, reflected the fact that subjects did not identify (and did not want to be identified) with prejudiced people. In this study though, we anticipated that where negative feedback was given by Americans themselves it might actually *bolster* consensus because subjects would accept Americans as being qualified to comment on this aspect of social reality and hence could recategorize the source as an ingroup at a higher level of abstraction (e.g., seeing them as 'reasonable people'). In relation to this point, it is worth noting that a similar logic has underpinned some previous attempts by social psychologists to establish stereotype accuracy (see Oakes and Reynolds, this volume). Triandis and Vassiliou (1967), for example, accept Americans' negative stereotypes of Greeks as reflecting a higher-level shared reality (rather than than simple ingroup–outgroup prejudice) to the extent that the Greeks themselves endorsed the Americans' negative impression of them as unsystematic and lazy.

This prediction was supported (with the highest consensus in the condition where Americans described themselves as extremely nationalistic, materialistic etc.; P_a = .34 – this being .12 higher than in any other condition). Its attributional base was also confirmed in a follow-up study which looked at the reasons subjects generated in order to account for different patterns of stereotype-relevant feedback. As predicted, when subjects were provided with stereotype-consistent information about Americans (rather than Australians) from Americans (rather than prejudiced people) they were much more likely to attribute this to the fact that this source group was in a good position both to provide the information and to know what the stereotyped group was 'really like'. Subjects in this condition were also most likely to describe Americans as 'generally similar' to themselves, a result consistent with an underlying process of source recategorization (cf. Anastasio et al., this volume).

The significance of these latter studies is that they again point to the sensitivity of ingroup–outgroup definition to social context and to an accompanying fluidity in patterns of mutual influence and stereotype consensus. Importantly too, their findings are also consistent with the idea that under some circumstances people strive to achieve consensus at as high (and broad) a level as possible, rather than simply resting content with a world where one set of ideas are shared by an ingroup and another conflicting set by an outgroup (Turner, 1991). This is not a manifestation of simple-minded cultural imperialism (although clearly we characterize it as such when we are oppressed by the views of outgroups), but rather a feature of the process through which groups strive to correct for the limitations of a perspective which is necessarily partial and thereby 'bootstrap themselves out of their own relativity' (Oakes et al., 1994, p. 210). Clearly further work is needed in order to demonstrate and examine more closely the operation of this process, but this is one of the main directions in which our research is currently progressing (see also Oakes and Reynolds, this volume).

Taken together, the findings from the above experiments thus lend support to the argument that the process of achieving stereotype consensus is substantially structured by the social validation of an individual's beliefs by ingroup sources that are perceived to be qualified to perform that function in a particular context. Consistent with the dual role of social identity, at the same time both a co-ordinator of cognition and a basis for positive mutual influence, they provide extremely strong evidence that consensus is a product of *interactive* individual and collective processes. Thus, while research in the cognitive tradition has focused exclusively on the former, and work in the social tradition (e.g., Moscovici, 1984) largely on the latter, it appears that neither is superfluous and, moreover, that each is dependent on (and structured by) the other. An integrative analysis of these areas suggests that shared stereotypes arise neither from the similar processing of raw experience, nor the unthinking internalization of socio-cultural understanding. Instead they appear to be a product of *socially-structured cognition* that reflects the interrelationship between the psychological processes of the individual and the ongoing realities of group life.

4 Conclusions

This chapter has attempted to broach the perennially difficult issue of how stereotypes come to be shared by members of social groups. The fact that they do seems obvious, not least because it appears that it is largely through their propensity to provide a collective basis for social interpretation and behaviour that stereotypes have justified so much research attention. In spite of this though, it is clear that in most of the social psychological theories of stereotyping that have been developed, attempts to account for sharedness are very much afterthoughts, tacked on to fully developed individual cognitive theories. Here, then, (to borrow a metaphor from Bruner) generic explanations in terms of 'socialization' and 'social learning' arrive on the scene to tie up loose ends much like the long-lost Australian relative in third-rate murder mysteries.

But such solutions are unsatisfactory because evidence points to the fact that these inter-subjective processes are not independent of cognition, but rather a part of it. As Lippmann (1922, p. 55) argued, 'we pick out what our culture has already defined for us, and we tend to perceive what we have picked out in the form stereotyped for us by our culture'. Significantly though, all the evidence suggests that the impact of culture is not fixed but varies a function of our own definition of self and others in a particular context. In some situations (e.g., in a confrontation with physicists) I may define myself as similar to a colleague who teaches cognitive psychology and hence be likely to perceive the world from a common vantage point in terms of a shared identity (as psychologists) and this should lead us to process information in similar ways and to arrive at similar conclusions (e.g., that physicists are narrow-minded and psychologists broad-minded). But in other situations we may see (and expect to see) the world quite differently (in an intra-departmental meeting I may come to see that same cognitive psychologist as narrow-minded).

At the same time though, as well as having specific and contextually-variable effects on our own individual cognitive processes (leading, for example, to variation in the extent to which I see psychologists as a homogeneous group), shared identity *also* serves to structure inter-subjective processes in an ongoing manner. Specifically, it functions to shape patterns of mutual influence, and pressures to *achieve* consensus. In this example, I may seek and expect valida-tion of my views from my colleague in the inter-departmental context, and *actively* strive to co-ordinate our perceptions, while in the intra-departmental setting different expectations prevail – here a failure to achieve consensus will not be so problematic and, while agreement may be sought (to provide higher-level validation of my beliefs), our *dis*agreement can be readily interpreted in terms of contextually-relevant lower-level differences. It is an awareness of this dynamic inter-subjective co-ordination of beliefs and norms that has been most conspicuously absent from previous cognitive and social theorizing (see Haslam, Turner, Oakes, McGarty and Reynolds, in press).

In contrast to the idea that stereotype (or any other normative) consensus arises from generic cultural knowledge or shared unmediated experience, this analysis thus suggests that it arises from recognition and action in terms of contextually-structured shared identity. Accordingly, evidence that the degree and level of consensus varies as a function of context and that the same stereo-type is not expressed in the same way by all members of one group at the same time is not problematic for self-categorization theory in the way that it is for both the theory of social representations and the common informational input model (Condor, 1990; Hrabe et al., 1989; Potter and Litton, 1985; Reicher et al., this volume). Indeed, it follows from the arguments presented above (see also Oakes et al., 1994, chapter 8), that variation in stereotype consensus is to be expected in response to social changes that serve to redefine shared group memberships and intergroup relations.

In the end, then, the fact that stereotype consensus is context-sensitive and often imperfect should not deter us from investigating it, just as it does not deter people from seeking it. Primarily, this is because in studying their sharedness we get to the heart of what makes stereotypes social. However, the present consideration suggests that in order for work in this area to be as rewarding as possible, it is necessary to attend to the manner in which cog-nitive processes are individually structured and collectively co-ordinated by the ongoing realities of group life. By pursuing this form of analysis there is every chance of restoring the investigation of shared content to its initial and rightful place at the forefront of stereotyping research.

Note

This research was funded by a grant from the Australian Research Council, also awarded to Penny Oakes and John Turner. I would like to thank both, as well as Craig McGarty, for their contribution to the chapter.

7

Stereotype Formation: Beyond Illusory Correlation

Craig McGarty and Anne-Marie de la Haye

1 Introduction

It is difficult to imagine anything more fundamental to perception than the ability to detect relationships between objects and events in the environment. The ability to perceive and interpret such relationships is fundamental to making sense of the world: it underlies, for example, our ability to infer cause and effect. There is every reason to suppose that the perception of relationships is especially important for making sense of social environments.

It is a truism of course that people can have great difficulties in distinguishing correlational relationships from causal relationships. However, despite the scope for erroneous inferences to be made about cause, research on the illusory correlation effect (ICE) suggests the possibility for still more basic errors: people can perceive relationships which do not even exist.

The appeal of this simple idea for research on social stereotyping is easy to see. There has been a widely-held view that stereotyping is based on biased processes which lead to distorted perception. This occurs as a consequence of overly selective attention to particularly attention-grabbing stimuli. An unkind critic might suggest that this characterization applies more aptly to much of the social psychological study of stereotyping than to stereotyping itself. However, it certainly is true that the idea that stereotyping is based on the perception of bogus relationships fits in well with the dominant cognitive miser meta-theory: we stereotype because of deficiencies in people's information-processing capabilities. For example, Macrae, Hewstone and Griffiths (1993) state:

As cognitive misers or mental sluggards, perceivers are presumed to activate and apply stereotypes to simplify complex judgemental tasks and to facilitate information processing in sub-optimal environments. (p. 77)

The particular attraction of the illusory correlation effect has been in the explanation of the formation and development of stereotypes of minorities, largely because minority status is held to be attention grabbing due to the relative infrequency (and perceptual novelty) of minority group members. A distinctiveness-based illusory correlation is generally defined as the erroneous perception of the co-occurrence of rare characteristics. Normally, in social psychological usage, the effect is concerned with a perceived linkage between minority group membership and rare (usually undesirable) behaviors.

The view one takes of the illusory correlation effect has important implications for general accounts of stereotype formation. If stereotypes are seen as energy-saving devices involving erroneous perceptions of people as group members rather than as individuals, then an account of stereotype formation as a process of illusory correlation is quite satisfactory. If, on the other hand, stereotypes are seen as ways of veridically representing social contextual realities (as Oakes, Haslam and Turner, 1994, argue following the tradition established by Asch, 1952, and Vinacke, 1957) then the idea that stereotype formation is inevitably based on erroneous perceptions presents an immediate challenge. If stereotypes are not necessarily erroneous how can they be formed on the basis of perceiving illusory correlations?

The details of the illusory correlation effect and paradigm used by Hamilton and Gifford (1976) are now familiar to most social psychologists. In the empirical paradigm which is used to investigate it subjects are presented with a number of statements (usually 36 or 39) describing the behaviour of members of two groups (Group A and Group B). Group B is described as being smaller in the real world than Group A, and, in the stimulus set as a whole, there are twice as many statements about Group A members as about Group B members. Of the statements approximately two-thirds are non-distinctive (normally desirable) and one-third are distinctive (undesirable), but the same ratio of non-distinctive to distinctive behaviours is present in both groups (it is on this basis that any correlation detected by subjects is seen to be illusory). A distinctiveness-based illusory correlation would be said to occur where the distinctive behaviours are overattributed to the minority (distinctive) group and members of this group are hence represented less favourably than the majority. We can see a representation of the stimulus distribution and an example of illusory correlation in table 7.1.

Three main tasks are typically used to provide measures of the effect: (a) the *cued recall* task (also called the *attribution of group membership* task), in which subjects are presented with the original stimuli and asked to remember

Table 7.1   Contingency tables showing the stimulus distribution and a response pattern showing illusory correlation

Stimulus series:

	Group A (majority)	Group B (minority)
nondistinctive (positive)	18 (A$^+$)	9 (B$^+$)
distinctive (negative)	8 (A$^-$)	4 (B$^-$)

Example of illusory correlation favouring Group A:

	Group A (majority)	Group B (minority)
nondistinctive (positive)	20 (A$^+$)	7 (B$^+$)
distinctive (negative)	6 (A$^-$)	6 (B$^-$)

which group was associated with each statement, (b) the *trait rating* task, where subjects rate the groups on a set of evaluative scales and (c) the *frequency estimation* task, where subjects are normally asked to estimate the frequency of the distinctive stimuli. The effect is measured on the first and third tasks by constructing contingency tables and calculating phi (a correlation coefficient for 2×2 contingency tables), where a positive phi, indicating an over association of the minority with the distinctive behaviours, is evidence of illusory correlation. Illusory correlation is shown on the trait rating task where there is evidence of a more favourable evaluation of the majority than the minority.

As we implied above, the effect (as measured in these ways) has provided the basis for an ongoing, but almost implicit debate as to its role in stereotype formation. In crude terms we could characterize this debate as being between those who would argue that illusory correlation is a fundamental aspect of stereotyping and those who would argue that it is a laboratory phenomenon of minimal interest for social psychologists. Beyond these two positions, however, there are still others who might argue that the explanation of the phenomenon is of interest in its own right, regardless of whether it applies to stereotype formation or not (and it is fair to say that much of the more recent work by social psychologists on the effect makes little reference to stereotype formation). In this chapter, however, we develop a rather different position. In short, we develop the argument that, while (a) the ICE does relate to stereotyping, at least to the extent that it involves evaluative contrast or differentiation between groups, and that (b) many of the explanations of the effect do indeed point to processes which determine the laboratory phenomenon, nevertheless (c) most of these processes (and hence explanations) do not themselves relate to stereotype formation. In other words, we are arguing that illusory correlation is an over-determined outcome that can be produced by many different processes. However, we further suggest that most of these hypothesized processes are not implicated in stereotyping, and even when they are, they need not relate specifically to the stereotypes of minorities. To develop this argument though, we first need to consider these existing explanations and factors which qualify the effect.

2 · Explanations of ICE

The original explanation of the effect was Hamilton and Gifford's distinctiveness-based account. The cognitive process underlying ICE is supposed to be as follows. The co-occurrence of two relatively infrequent events is especially noticeable or *distinctive*: it automatically triggers the observer's attention. These jointly infrequent events are hence better encoded, and more accessible to retrieval. Following Tversky and Kahneman's (1973) *availability heuristic*, the more easily they are retrieved, the more the subject perceives them as numerous, and therefore overestimates their frequency.

This model stands out as a strictly 'cognitive' one. The authors do not 'deny, or even question, the importance of socially learned or culturally transmitted bases of stereotypes' (Hamilton and Gifford, 1976, p. 405). However, their core argument is that 'cognitive factors alone can be sufficient to produce differential perceptions of social groups', and this provocative statement is what has come to be most well-known in their theoretical contribution. In this chapter we seek to address how the cognitive approach to the illusory correlation phenomenon can be reconciled with the more general issue of social stereotyping, and in particular with recent work by ourselves and our colleagues.

It is probably helpful to question the restrictive meaning of the word 'cognitive' in these kinds of formulations. When pointing to learning and motivational processes, on the one hand, and to information-processing and cognitive factors, on the other hand, as two distinct (possible) causes of stereotyping, Hamilton and his colleagues introduce a questionable distinction. Are they implying that learning processes are not cognitive? Or that people cease to process information as soon as they are motivated? Obviously, this dichotomy is difficult to sustain. It seems to refer to a distinction, not between what is 'cognitive' and what is not, but between different levels of cognitive functioning. What they seem to be interested in is short-term cognitive functioning, where information-processing is not related to large-scale context nor to long-term experience. The cognitive agent in Hamilton's model mainly reacts to frequencies. Indeed, it might be argued that the model is conceived as if cognition had only to do with numbers and not with meaning. However, it is certainly necessary to activate some pre-established categories of meaning before the subject could perceive anything as rare or frequent. One might object that Hamilton and colleagues' recent work on affect and stereotyping (Stroessner, Hamilton and Mackie, 1992; Mackie and Hamilton, 1993) takes more diverse aspects of cognition into consideration and this is undoubtedly true. However, as far as the ICE itself is concerned, the importance of categorizing behaviours into desirable/undesirable ones has never been explicitly discussed. Would the ICE appear if the subjects could not activate some preexisting schema which contained the information that a crucial attribute of groups is whether they are good or bad?

Nevertheless, the illusory correlation phenomenon has been borne out by a number of studies (see the meta-analytic reviews by Mullen and Johnson, 1990; Johnson and Mullen, 1993). During the first 15 years following Hamilton and Gifford's seminal article, experiments seemed to converge toward the confirmation of Hamilton's model (for a review see Hamilton and Trolier, 1986). Researchers were aware that the phenomenon could result from a number of different mechanisms, and strived toward eliminating several possible counter-explanations, such as preference for the majority, difficulties in integrating complex information or greater availability of the most frequent events instead of the least frequent ones (Hamilton and Sherman, 1989). Hamilton, Dugan and Trolier (1985) showed that jointly infrequent events were in fact more accessible for retrieval. In a free recall task, the highest recall rate was observed for jointly infrequent events, and the number of jointly infrequent items recalled was predictive of the strength of the illusory correlation effect. At the end of the 1980s almost all social psychology textbooks reported illusory correlation as a well-established phenomenon that was best explained in terms of a universal cognitive bias.

Things began to change dramatically in 1991, when two authors independently cast doubt on Hamilton's model (Fiedler, 1991; Smith, 1991). The selective attention hypothesis was challenged by Smith who presented a computer simulation, based on Hintzman's MINERVA2 model, showing that it was possible to obtain results quite similar to the classical ICE without needing to refer to any 'selective attention' hypothesis. The result he obtained was not due to the way information is stored, but to the way the judgement is computed. The simulated subjects are sensitive to the *difference* between the number of positive and negative items recalled, and not to the *proportion* of behaviours that are positive, thus causing the majority group to be seen as more positive than the minority.

In reply to Smith's critique the distinctiveness theorists had to demonstrate that jointly infrequent events did indeed attract greater attention. This was done by Stroessner, Hamilton and Mackie (1992). Instead of setting a fixed presentation time for every item, they let subjects read them at their own pace, and recorded the reading time. This procedure allowed the researchers to show that the subjects allocated more time to jointly infrequent events and this phenomenon can reasonably be taken as an indication of greater attention. Moreover, differential attention toward jointly infrequent events was predictive of illusory correlation.

This experiment casts an interesting light on what happens at the *encoding* stage. An experiment by Johnson and Mullen (1994) applies to the *judgement* stage. They showed that response latencies in the assignment task are shortest for correct assignments of B− (i.e., doubly distinctive) events, compared to all other correct assignments. This result suggests that the retrieval of B− events is easier, or that subjects feel more certain about these assignments. Taken together, both Stroessner et al.'s (1992) and Johnson and Mullen's (1994) results are strong arguments in favour of Hamilton's process model.

Another alternative interpretation of illusory correlation was provided by Fiedler (1991; Fiedler, Russer and Gramm, 1993). The central theme in Fiedler's argument is that illusory correlation is a consequence of information loss. Estimating frequencies is a difficult task, and the subjects in an illusory correlation experiment are generally not in a position to do it perfectly. Thus their performances must inevitably show regression to the mean: in the experiment as a whole low frequencies are correctly perceived as lower than high frequencies, but very low frequencies are perceived as higher than they really are, and very high frequencies are perceived as lower than they really are. Moreover, the information loss mechanism has more severe consequences when the estimations are based on a small number of observations, rather than on a large one. Consequently, regression to the mean must be stronger in responses bearing on a small item-set (the minority group, or the less frequent category of behaviours) than in responses bearing on a large item-set (the majority group, or the more frequent category of behaviours). In short, the subjects do not really show *overestimation* of jointly infrequent events, but greater uncertainty when estimating proportions within small item-sets. Fiedler et al. (1993) provide a very detailed analysis of memory performance in relation to illusory correlation (and argue that there are important, but independently derived, similarities between their approach and that of Smith, 1991). They noted that their results were consistent with the prediction that illusory correlation arises from impaired rather than enhanced memory. In particular, a signal-detection analysis showed that sensitivity was lower for negative (i.e., infrequent) items than for positive ones – a result which hardly seems compatible with the idea that infrequent events are always 'distinctive'.

Recently, McConnell, Sherman and Hamilton (1994a) also presented results which are entirely inconsistent with the original distinctiveness-based account of the effect. They introduced a variation of the standard paradigm where the critical B− (i.e., doubly distinctive) stimuli were presented either early in the sequence of stimuli or late in the sequence. The idea was that when the B− stimuli were presented early in the sequence they would not be distinctive in the context in which they were encountered, but that when the stimuli were presented late in the sequence they would be highly distinctive. In fact, in their first experiment these authors found no evidence of any differences between conditions. They concluded that the original distinctiveness-based explanation could not explain these results, but on the other hand, they concluded that the alternative accounts of Smith and Fiedler could not deal with either the data reported by Johnson and Mullen (1994) or those produced in their own second experiment which showed that the B– items are responded to more rapidly than the other items (though the lack of comparability of the analytical procedures in the two studies raises some concerns about the conclusions).

They instead proposed a new Extended Distinctiveness Based account which adds the possibility that additional post-presentational processing of the B– stimuli occurs as their *ultimate* distinctiveness becomes apparent. In other words these authors conclude that there is not necessarily an automatic bias towards novel stimuli, but rather that enhanced attention to 'ultimately' distinctive items can produce the effect.

3   Factors which Qualify the Illusory Correlation Effect

While alternative theoretical accounts of illusory correlation have only started to proliferate in the last few years, there has been a somewhat longer tradition of research which has sought to establish the conditions under which the illusory correlation effect emerges. Again, the implicit debate here is whether illusory correlation should be considered as an interesting effect which is readily demonstrated in the laboratory but which is hard to generalize outside this setting, or as a fundamental part of social stereotyping. This being the case, much of this research is directly relevant to our concerns in this chapter.

For example, Spears and his colleagues (Spears, van der Pligt and Eiser, 1985, 1986) investigated the extent to which the effect could be generalized. Spears et al. (1985) demonstrated that the effect was moderated by own position. They used as stimuli attitude statements on nuclear power which purportedly expressed the opinions of people from two different towns, one of which was larger than the other. There were twice as many statements labelled as coming from people from Town A as from Town B. The statements varied in their position on the scale from *extremely in favour of*, to *extremely opposed to* the building of a nuclear power station locally.

The stimulus sets were constructed so that either pro or anti statements were infrequent. There were 36 statements in each case, and the study is thus a near replication of the original Hamilton and Gifford studies except for one critical feature. Spears et al. argued that the subjects' own position could affect the amount of illusory correlation because attitude congruent positions would be more self-relevant, and this increased self-relevance would enhance the distinctiveness of those statements. For similar reasons, they expected the illusory correlation effect to be stronger where the subjects had particularly extreme attitudes. To test these ideas they varied whether pro- or anti-nuclear statements were in a majority or minority position in the stimulus set.

They found support for their predictions, but in particular found that people who had positions congruent with the minority attitude position (either pro or anti as the case may be) showed strong illusory correlation. However, the illusory correlation effect was almost non-existent for subjects whose own positions were congruent with the majority position. Thus, these results suggest that the illusory correlation is powerfully moderated by own position.

Research by Sherman, Hamilton and Roskos-Ewoldsen (1989) also suggested that the effect could be reduced when subjects judged more than two groups. In particular when subjects judged statements coming from three different groups (A, B and C) rather than just the usual two, the illusory correlation effect was attenuated. Unfortunately, this study's procedure clearly confounds the number of statements that subjects were exposed to with the number of groups judged. The pattern obtained could therefore have been due to increased cognitive load (cf. Fiedler, 1991; Spears and Haslam, this volume).

Research by Pryor (1986) examined the effects of different sorts of instructions on the illusory correlation effect. Subjects in one condition were given *impression formation* instructions which emphasized forming an overall impression of the groups and, subjects in another condition were given *memory* instructions which emphasized retaining information about individuals. The subjects were given the frequency estimation task and an evaluative rating task after they had completed a recognition task where they had to attempt to recognize the original set of 39 statements out of a longer list of 78 statements. It was found that under the memory instructions there was more illusory correlation (in particular on the frequency estimation and evaluative rating tasks). Pryor interpreted his results as suggesting that illusory correlation might contribute to stereotypes 'only when subjects encounter information in a relatively nonintegrative set – that is, when they have no need to make an immediate judgment' (Pryor, 1986, p. 225). This work was interpreted by Hamilton and Sherman (1989, and more recently by McConnell, Sherman and Hamilton, 1994b) as suggesting that different processes may be involved in forming impressions of groups and individuals. In line with some of the suggestions of Hastie and Park (1986), they suggested that impressions of individuals are made on-line, that is, they form instantaneously as information comes to hand and that impressions of groups are memory-based.

It is also interesting to note that in Pryor's study memory instructions did not lead to improved recognition memory performance, and in fact there was a marginally significant trend ($p < .08$) in the opposite direction. That is, the number of correct identifications was lower in the memory instructions condition. This raises the possibility that it is impression formation instructions which improve memory performance. In any event, these results point to the great difficulty that subjects have in performing illusory correlation tasks, and add weight to Fiedler's (1991) argument that illusory correlation can arise from information loss. Indeed, Pryor's subjects were actually less successful at correctly identifying stimuli from Group A than they would have been if they had simply randomly allocated two-thirds of the traits to Group A and one-third to Group B. However, they were more successful at correctly identifying traits from Group B than this random strategy would suggest.

Another major qualification of the scope of the illusory correlation effect was demonstrated by Schaller and Maass (1989) when they introduced self-categorization into the judgemental context. They did this by asking subjects to process information about groups they had themselves been assigned to. Here they used a variant of the minimal group paradigm (Tajfel, Flament, Billig and Bundy, 1971) whereby the subjects were assigned randomly to one of two groups. They predicted that group membership would qualify the illusory correlation effect because ingroup bias would lead people to develop a positive view of their own group. Broadly speaking, this is what they found in their first study. The illusory correlation effect was wiped out in the cells where illusory correlation would have led subjects to associate their own group with undesirable behaviours. However, this effect was not demonstrated on the trait ratings measures. In their second study Schaller and Maass (1989) added the impression formation instruction set that Pryor (1986) had developed to the ingroup–outgroup context. Here they found very little evidence of illusory correlation in any condition (for further discussion see Ellemers and van Knippenberg, this volume).

Along slightly different lines, Haslam, McGarty, Oakes and Turner (1993) found that introducing real social categorizations into the situation led to variations in the strength of the effect due to particular comparative relations. In this study the cities which the members of Group A and B came from were identified as being Canberra (the subjects' own city in Australia), Perth (another city in Australia) and Detroit (an American city). Previous research had revealed that this population of subjects had relatively negative stereotypes of Americans. Furthermore, at the time of the study Perth (the capital city of western Australia) was receiving very bad publicity as criminal charges (relating to improper conduct and misappropriation of funds) were being prepared against a number of its senior politicians (including the Premier and later the Deputy Premier). Haslam et al. expected the illusory correlation effect to favour the majority when it was identified as the ingroup city (Canberra). However, they expected favouritism for the majority to be less when identified as being from Perth, because even though western Australians shared a national identity with the subjects (in contrast to Americans) they constituted 'black sheep' (Marques, 1990): in other words, ingroup members of low status. This in fact was exactly what they found. The illusory correlation effect did not apply uniformly, nor was there a constant ingroup bias. Rather subjects demonstrated negative stereotypes of the minority that were shaped by features the particular comparative relations had made salient. Put simply, subjects did not display ingroup favouritism towards the 'black sheep' group. Negative stereotypes were deployed selectively rather than in the blanket fashion that the ingroup bias models and distinctiveness-based explanations suggest. Similarly, Berndsen, Spears and van der Pligt (1996) found that an ingroup bias account could not explain the absence of the ICE under conditions where subjects had a vested interest in perceiving an illusory correlation (that is, where the existence of the correlation suited the subjects' own ends).

On the basis of these various demonstrations of factors which attenuate the illusory correlation effect we would draw a number of conclusions. First, it appears that illusory correlation is a contextually-dependent phenomenon. Whatever the nature of the cognitive processes that produce the effect, there is no evidence that these are automatically deployed in every relevant situation. This is apparent from the wide range of variables which appear to qualify it. Secondly, and following from this, it is apparent that the phenomenon is multiply determined. Standard measures of the effect are necessarily insensitive instruments and many different processes could result in patterns which would be classed as the illusory correlation effect. This is because the measures can only reveal three outcomes. They can show favouritism for the majority, favouritism for the minority or no favouritism. When there is such a limited number of outcomes it is difficult to rule out multiple causal processes.

What we propose to do in the remainder of this chapter is to address this recent work and ask how it helps to relate illusory correlation to the stereotyping process. We would argue that by doing this we are bringing consideration of the illusory correlation effect back to the original social psychological interest in this topic: stereotype formation. Hamilton and Gifford's laboratory demonstration of the effect would have attracted far less attention had it not been suggested that negative stereotypes of minorities could arise from a similar process.

4 Is the Illusory Correlation Effect more than just a Laboratory Phenomenon?

Almost paradoxically, it seems that recent interest in the effect has centred not so much on the relationship of the effect to stereotype formation but on the explanation of the effect as a cognitive process. Thus, Mullen and Johnson's (1990) meta-analysis of the illusory correlation effect actually excluded experimental investigations where subjects had been members of the groups judged (most of the subjects in Schaller and Maass', 1989, study were therefore excluded), even though since the work of Tajfel (e.g., Tajfel, 1969a) on stereotyping it seems almost nonsensical to consider the process without reference to the social categorization of the self. Nevertheless, the focus on illusory correlation as a laboratory phenomenon is a perfectly reasonable scientific process. If it were found that the illusory correlation effect is a product of cognitive processes that have little to do with social stereotype formation then this would be an important discovery. One can raise two sorts of objections to the argument that the illusory correlation effect underlies stereotyping. We can term these (a) the cognitive 'quirk' argument and (b) the 'it only works for minorities' argument.

In our experience the cognitive quirk argument is often applied informally by social psychologists who believe that illusory correlation research is concerned with the demonstration of captivating but trivial experimental findings rather than phenomena of genuine social psychological interest. On the other hand, the cognitive quirk argument might be no more than an expression of a difference of opinion about research priorities.

The 'it only works for minorities' argument is in some ways more compelling. The most charitable reading of the possible application of the distinctiveness-based illusory correlation research is that, if it relates to stereotype formation at all, it relates to situations where majorities are forming negative stereotypes of minorities. While this is one extremely important stereotyping context, there are clearly other circumstances where negative stereotypes develop. It is readily apparent that negative stereotypes develop towards both small and large groups. It is not so apparent that these stereotypes would develop by means of different cognitive processes for groups of different size. Nor is it obvious that people tend to have more negative attitudes of minority groups than of other groups. Without in any way denying that there are many minorities that are stereotyped in negative ways, there does not seem to be evidence that stereotypes of low-status minorities are qualitatively different from stereotypes of low-status majorities.

There are at least four possible rebuttals of the 'it only works for minorities' argument. First, proponents of distinctiveness-based illusory correlation as an explanation of stereotype formation would argue it is only one possible contribution to stereotyping (cf. Hamilton and Trolier, 1986). This seems a fair point.

Secondly, the same distinctiveness-based process could apply to majorities if we were to assume that people are more likely to have contact with members of their own group and, therefore, outgroups which are majorities in terms of absolute number can, nevertheless, be novel and infrequent. This implies that as contact increases with outgroup members, ingroup members should develop more favourable impressions of them. One problem with this argument is that it is essentially a statement of the *contact hypothesis* (the idea that contact between groups will of itself produce better relations between the groups). There is no longer any reason to believe that intergroup contact per se leads to more favourable stereotypes (even though the nature of any contact can affect the pattern of intergroup relations, see Hewstone and Brown, 1986).

A third answer to the minorities only argument is that a focus on the perception of minorities is entirely reasonable because of the special psychological significance of minorities. Indeed, the argument has been developed that different psychological processes are engaged in the perception of minorities and majorities. This is apparent in work on minority influence which has suggested that the same behaviour will be perceived differently when it comes from a majority than a minority (e.g., Moscovici, 1980). A related perspective also appears in the work of Simon and Hamilton (1994) and is expressed most clearly in the work of Mullen (1991) who argues that minorities and majorities are actually psychologically represented in different ways. In particular, the distinctiveness and novelty of minorities is held to lead to a prototype (or abstraction-based) representation whereas majorities are more likely to be represented as exemplars. Put another way, the argument is that minorities are more likely to be *entitative* (i.e., having the quality of an entity, after Campbell, 1958) than majorities. However, it should be noted that research on illusory correlation is part of the evidence that Mullen (1991) has assembled in support of this view, and there are good reasons to question whether large and small groups do produce these perceptual differences in entitativity. In fact, McGarty, Haslam, Hutchinson and Grace (1995) have shown, other things being equal, that large groups are more entitative.

The fourth answer to the minorities only argument is the existence of expectancy-based illusory correlations. This research is based on the work of Hamilton and Rose (1980) who found that subjects displayed illusory correlations on the basis of *expectancies*. In other words, people's recollections of the stimulus information were affected by their knowledge of the category memberships of the stimuli. Although these effects are interesting with respect to the maintenance and later development of stereotypes, they tell us very little about stereotype formation. Arguing that expectancies produce stereotypes is equivalent to arguing that stereotypes produce stereotypes. This is far less tautological than it appears. It is entirely reasonable that social stereotypes would be based on socially-mediated prior knowledge rather than simply emerge from direct individual experience with particular groups. In any historical or sociological analysis of stereotypes we would expect that one of the biggest influences on any widely-held stereotype would be preexisting beliefs in that culture about other groups. After all, as Tajfel, (1981a) observed, stereotypes are not just perceptions of social groups, they are perceptions shared by members of groups. Common perceptions may emerge in part from separate but parallel perceptions of the same stimuli but they are also constrained by perspectives shared with ingroup members (see Haslam, this volume).

This is one of the principal lessons to be drawn from the study of social stereotyping according to the perspective introduced by Tajfel. Social stereotyping is different from the perception of other social objects in several important ways. First of all, even though all perception might involve perceptual categorization effects (that is the accentuation of inter-class differences and intra-class similarities as originally envisaged by Tajfel and Wilkes, 1963), in social perception the groups themselves obey these processes. That is, social groups are not just static objects of perception but they also act to differentiate themselves from outgroups, and also become coherent through processes of conformity to social norms. Put simply, categorization is not just something that perceivers do to other people and groups – those people categorize themselves as well (in terms of both their perceptions and behaviours). The second way in which stereotyping is different from other sorts of perception follows from a key insight of social identity theory (Tajfel and Turner, 1979): social stereotyping is informative about our own groups. The process of differentiating between ingroups and outgroups on relevant dimensions tells us things not only about the stereotyped outgroup but about the ingroup and therefore ourselves. Self-categorization theory (Turner, 1985; Turner, Hogg, Oakes, Reicher and Wetherell, 1987) incorporates this idea through the notion of *self-stereotyping*.

This research on differentiation between groups has created a vast body of knowledge about intergroup behaviour which any account of stereotype formation must address. The question is whether the stereotyping process (understood from this intergroup perspective) is in any way connected with the illusory correlation effect.

We believe that there are good reasons to believe that it is. Our work has shown that the illusory correlation effect does relate to functional psychological processes which are implicated in processes of differentiation between social groups, but as yet there is no reason to rule out the previous explanations of the effect, rather they could play complementary roles. In short, the argument here is that the illusory correlation effect is a multiply determined phenomenon. We make the further claim, however, that some of these determining factors are related to stereotype formation, whereas others are not. It is the former class of determining factor, which we term *differentiation* or *evaluative contrast* that we will now discuss.

The argument that illusory correlation reflects the conventional process of differentiation between social groups was developed independently by de la Haye and Lauvergeon (1993) and McGarty, Haslam, Turner and Oakes (1993). In the first case the effect was described as the development of evaluative contrast and in the second case as the accentuation of actual inter-category differences between groups. Our approach is to argue that the standard illusory correlation paradigm can be considered as containing information which actually suggests to the subjects that there are evaluative differences between the groups. We will now turn to a more detailed presentation of these views.

5   Illusory Correlation as Differentiation between Groups

McGarty et al. (1993) argued that the illusory correlation effect can arise through the process of differentiation between groups first articulated in the work of Tajfel, 1969a (Tajfel and Wilkes, 1963). Their argument was based on the idea that the standard illusory correlation task has all the ingredients necessary for the classic categorization effects of the accentuation of differences between groups and the accentuation of similarities within groups to occur, that is, the stimulus situation involves the judgements of two groups in terms of an underlying dimension of social comparison.

It seems reasonable that under these conditions subjects would seek to make sense of the situation by asking how the groups differ. Following Tajfel's original categorization effects perspective, McGarty and Turner (1992) argue that this involves a process of deriving *differentiated meaning* (i.e., meaning which makes categories separable and clear). In the case of the illusory correlation stimulus situation people are likely to make sense of it by asking whether the groups differ by virtue of one group being more positive than the other (as Osgood, Suci and Tannenbaum, 1957, pointed out long ago, evaluation accounts for a great deal of the variance in judgement). We believe, therefore, that people do not come to the task with their minds being blank slates, rather they are armed with the expectation that the groups are different. The subjects might reasonably ask, why would the experimenter be presenting us with information about the groups unless they were meaningfully distinct entities? (see the discussion of related issues by Bless, Strack and Schwariz, 1993). These expectancies can be expressed as subjective hypotheses of the form that the groups differ and that one group is evaluatively better than the other, and that their task is to work out which is which.

Related ideas have been developed in the ongoing tradition of research on the perception of contingency. This tradition is closely related to the issue of illusory correlation. Principal findings in research on this issue are that: (a) The perception of contingency is clearly something that all people can do, but it is a task that is often found to be very difficult, and the way the situation is framed has very strong effects on the task (Alloy and Tabachnick, 1984), and (b) The perception of non-contingency is especially difficult, probably because of the subjects' expectations that their task is to look for an existing relationship, rather than to look for nothing at all (Peterson, 1980).

There are two classes of evidence which suggest that subjects do indeed have these expectations during the illusory correlation task. The more dramatic evidence was provided by the experiments conducted by McGarty et al. (1993) which reproduced the illusory correlation effect without exposing the subjects to standard stimulus information from which they could perceive shared stimulus distinctiveness (as per Hamilton and Gifford's, 1976, account) or from which they could store memory traces (as per the memory-based account of Smith, 1991, and Fiedler, 1991).

The first of these experiments involved simply presenting the subjects with the standard instructions and the response sheets for the three standard tasks. The purpose of this study was to test the possibility that giving general, summary information about the stimuli could produce illusory correlation effects without specific memory traces or stimulus information (this notion has some similarities with ideas previously suggested by Rothbart, 1981, and Fiedler, 1991). Subjects in particular conditions were given additional general information about the stimuli. For example, in the standard paradigm subjects might learn that nearly half of the stimuli (18 out of 39 in Hamilton and Gifford, 1976, Expt. 1) were positive statements about Group A. If the subjects learned this general information and responded to the Group A statements on this basis, but responded randomly to the Group B (minority) statements then we would expect their responses to display illusory correlation. This is one example of general information that might be gleaned from the stimulus situation and in the first experiment the presence or absence of this information was systematically varied. Subjects in some conditions were also told that there were twice as many statements about Group A as about Group B.

Thus a situation was constructed where the subjects were asked to respond to the standard tasks without seeing the stimuli but with the benefit of general information of the kind that they could have picked up had they in fact seen the actual stimuli. The results indicated that illusory correlation did occur under these circumstances. When the subjects were given no additional information there was no evidence of illusory correlation, but when they were given both pieces of information they showed highly significant illusory correlation on all three tasks. The information that there were twice as many statements about Group A as about Group B produced significant illusory correlation on the trait rating and estimation tasks. The information that about half the statements were positive statements about Group A produced significant illusory correlation on the assignment and estimation tasks.

These results were striking because they demonstrated the effect in the absence of the stimulus information, which is so critical to all previous explanations of the effect. The results also suggest the possibility that illusory correlation may be produced not just from the way people encode or retrieve specific pieces of information, but from the way that subjects decide they should respond.

In a second experiment McGarty et al. (1993) found much stronger results to support this conclusion. In this experiment subjects were presented with the statements as in the standard task, but the statements were not individually identified as coming from a particular group. In other respects the experiment was the same as the first one. Here extremely strong illusory correlation occurred in all conditions on all three measures, and the levels of illusory correlation were much stronger than the levels normally obtained in illusory correlation studies (cf. the meta-analysis by Mullen and Johnson, 1990).

It is clear that subjects differentiated between the groups when they were given (a) a task where it was reasonable to differentiate between the social groups and (b) a dimension (evaluation) on which to do so. It also appears that they did so in such a way as to favour the larger group because there was an implicit *fit* between the number of positive statements and the number of statements about the larger group.

To clarify this point we can note that the experimental situation here is analogous to a situation where we have three marbles, two of which are red and one is blue, and we then tell the subjects that two of the marbles were made in Germany and one in Japan. If we were to ask people to guess what colour the Japanese marble was we could expect that they would say 'the blue one' more frequently than one-third of the time. We do not need to attribute this sort of response to a bias towards distinctiveness but rather to the way subjects' expectancies structure the situation. In this hypothetical case the subject may well assume that the question implies a relationship between colour and country of origin: why else would the question be phrased in these terms? Similarly, in the experimental situation created by McGarty et al. it seems reasonable to suppose that the subjects decide the most obvious way to differentiate between the groups is to assign the positive statements to the larger group.

Clearly, these results could not be explained by models based on the role of specific stimulus information. The strength of these results, therefore, leaves only two possibilities: either the effects obtained by McGarty et al. (1993) were not evidence of illusory correlation, or that explanations based on specific stimulus information cannot offer a full account of the illusory correlation effect.

McGarty et al.'s results do, however, suggest that illusory correlation involves processes of differentiation between groups and evaluative contrast. These authors went on to specify how their explanation might apply to the standard paradigm. In particular, they pointed out that there are ways for the subjects to interpret the standard stimulus information to favour the majority over the minority. This depends on the type of reasoning that subjects employ when considering the stimuli.

If, for example, subjects decide that the two groups are likely to differ on the underlying dimension (of evaluation) and see their task as being to decide which of the groups is better than the other, then we are led to view the illusory correlation in a new light. In fact, the illusory correlation effect can then be seen as a reflection of the normal process of differentiation between groups that was identified by Tajfel (1969a; Tajfel and Wilkes, 1963). From this perspective, the question posed by the effect is not: 'how is it that people erroneously come to perceive a correlation when one is not present?' but rather, 'in what ways is it possible to see the stimuli as (for example) favouring the majority over the minority?'

McGarty et al. (1993) suggested two ways in which this was possible. They referred to these as Case X and Case Y. Under Case X it was envisaged that subjects when considering the information might be testing between two hypotheses. These hypotheses were:

H_{X1} Group A members are good and Group B members are bad.
H_{X2} Group B members are good and Group A members are bad.

The point is that the stimulus information in the paradigm can actually be interpreted as favouring H_{X1} as opposed to H_{X2}. In the standard paradigm where there are 39 stimuli presented, 22 of these support H_{X1} (these are the items on the main diagonal, the 18 positive Group A statements and the 4 negative Group B statements) and 17 support H_{X2}.

Put simply, if subjects are trying to find some way of making sense of the task by differentiating between groups then it is possible to interpret the stimuli as showing *real* differences between groups. In a related manner McGarty et al. (1993) suggested an alternative case (Case Y). If we instead assume that subjects entertain competing hypotheses of this form:

H_{Y1} Group A is more positive than negative.
H_{Y2} Group B is more positive than negative.

Then if we were to assume that subjects used conventional statistical logic to test these hypotheses (assuming perfect recall of the information) then they would (at the .05 level of significance) conclude that H_{Y1} was supported and that H_{Y2} was not (i.e., 18 is different from 8 but 9 is not significantly different from 4). In other words, the smaller size of Group B makes it more difficult to draw inferences (this is essentially the same idea as that contained in Fiedler's and Smith's approaches).

Now it is not claimed here that people are actually engaged in applying formal statistical logic in these situations but it is likely that they are using some form of quasi-statistical logic.

Even so, it is unwise to conclude that coming to perceive the two groups as being different is the outcome of a bias-driven process; especially when we have demonstrated that such a conclusion is no more biased or irrational than the (statistical) processes psychologists use to interpret their own research data.

However, the mere detection of differences between groups on its own is not sufficient to explain the direction and magnitude of the illusory correlation effect. McGarty et al. added the argument that, subsequent to the detection of differences between groups, subjects in the illusory correlation paradigm accentuate differences between groups and accentuate similarities within groups (cf. McGarty and Penny, 1988; Tajfel and Wilkes, 1963). The process is held to follow the principle of *meta-contrast*. That is, the effect follows a process of meaningful category formation, which is based, first of all, on the detection of similarities and differences, and the subsequent accentuation of these similarities to arrive at separable, coherent and meaningful categories. Importantly, under this view, these accentuation effects are not distortions but are selective crystallizations of relationships between stimuli (see McGarty and Turner, 1992; Turner, Hogg, Oakes, Reicher and Wetherell, 1987).

Given the importance of these subjective expectations to this explanation it is reasonable to ask whether the illusory correlation effect occurs when we cancel out the expectation that the groups are different. This is what Haslam, McGarty and Brown (1996) sought to do giving Groups A and B social categorical labels such that the subjects would have reason to expect that there would be no evaluative difference between the groups. The social categorization chosen was handedness, with subjects being told that the large group was made up of right-handed people and the small group was made up of left-handed people. This was useful for current purposes because left-handed people constitute a minority in the real world. As predicted, Haslam et al. (in press) found that the illusory correlation effect in the standard paradigm was nullified when the groups were identified in this way. Thus, we have clear evidence that when there is no evaluative basis for differentiating between the groups the illusory correlation effect disappears.

The other class of evidence that bears on the question of subjects' expectations that the task requires them to find differences between groups was reported by McGarty (1993) and Haslam, McGarty and Brown (1996). McGarty (1993) administered questionnaires to subjects in the standard paradigm after they had been presented with the stimuli but before they completed the tasks. The questions attempted to gauge what subjects had been doing while watching the stimuli and what they thought they would be doing next. The questions are shown in table 7.2 along with the mean and standard deviation for each item. McGarty (1993) found that the items relating to forming impressions of the groups and differentiating between the groups had the highest means. Although it might be argued that these sorts of questions are somewhat leading in themselves (and an open response format might be preferable for future investigations) these results do demonstrate that most subjects see the task as being one of impression formation and that they perceive the task to be explicitly comparative. While this evidence does not falsify other explanations it does indicate that subjects have a strongly categorical orientation to the task.

McGarty (1993) and Haslam et al. (1996) also administered post-test questionnaires to subjects. Subjects in general agreed that they had been trying to form impressions of the groups, and that they had been trying to differentiate between the groups. In short, these results indicate that subjects in the standard illusory correlation paradigm see their task as being to form stereotypes of the groups and, therefore, that their subjective impressions of the groups are

Table 7.2   Mean rating (on a 0 to 100 scale) given by subjects in answer to the question: 'What were you doing while watching the stimuli?'

	MEAN	SD
Trying to form a general impression of the groups (Q7)	71.4	35.7
Trying to work out how the groups differed (Q6)	67.2	37.1
Trying to remember which group performed which behavior (Q5)	55.8	39.5
Trying to work out if one group was better (Q3)	54.6	38.6
Trying to work out what the next task would be (Q8)	52.7	40.4
Trying to remember all statements (Q1)	51.5	36.2
Trying to remember which person performed which behavior (Q4)	25.2	34.3
Trying to remember the undesirable behaviors (Q9)	18.1	28.5
Trying to remember just Group B (Q2)	7.9	17.5
	(N = 55)	

categorically-based. While we cannot rule out the possibility that this categorical orientation is itself a by-product of the process of stereotype formation, these data do strongly suggest the possibility that illusory correlation occurs because subjects believe that the groups are different and, therefore, attempt to find some way to understand the information in a manner consistent with this belief.

6   Preference and Evaluative Contrast

Our research groups in Australia and France had been conducting remarkably similar research on illusory correlation independently before an anonymous journal reviewer serendipitously alerted us to this state of affairs, and provided the basis for this collaboration. We have taken the approach of presenting our contributions separately before discussing their integration.

De la Haye and colleagues have developed a very similar approach to that outlined above, and indeed many of the conclusions reached are almost identical. For example, in studies by de la Haye and Lauvergeon (1995; de la Haye, Lauvergeon and Scharnitzky, 1995) the observation that subjects develop contrasted evaluations of the target groups first occurred as an unexpected result in an experiment which had a different goal. The core element of this observation was that subjects tend to form systematically different representations of the two groups. After noticing this phenomenon, de la Haye and her co-authors considered that *evaluative contrast* must be conceptually and descriptively distinguished from *preference* for a predefined group. Their next studies were aimed at specifying whether the standard illusory correlation paradigm specifically induced either preference for a given group, or evaluative contrast, or both, and sought to explore the factors which enhance one or the other process.

The first experiment was originally aimed at exploring the effect of cognitive load on the ICE (de la Haye, Lauvergeon and Scharnitzky, 1995). Item presentation rate was varied, with one item every 5 seconds in the 'Fast' condition, and one item every 9 seconds in the 'Slow' condition.[1] Following the cognitive miser account of stereotyping the hypothesis was that illusory correlation would be stronger when cognitive load was high, thus it would be stronger in the 'Fast' condition; in fact, this manipulation had no effect on any dependent variable (see Spears and Haslam, this volume). An overall ICE was observed in both the assignment and estimation tasks, but not in trait ratings. However, a cursory examination of the data had revealed that many subjects expressed strikingly different judgements of the two groups. Consequently, individual response patterns were analysed. Since the trait judgements had been made on 20 scales, it was possible to test, for each individual subject, whether he/she differentiated between the two groups or not. Out of 167 subjects, almost two-thirds (n = 107, 64.1 per cent) differentiated significantly between the two groups. However, this differentiation did not always favour Group A: 61 subjects showed this pattern, and 46 subjects showed the reverse. Another indication that the subjects systematically perceived the groups to be different from each other was the negative correlation between the mean ratings of Groups A and B.

It follows from this observation that each subject can have strongly biased perceptions of the two groups even when no mean preference for a given group appears. Consequently, evaluative contrast must be conceived as a phenomenon of interest in itself, while the convergence of preferences onto the same target group is another phenomenon, no less interesting of course, but conceptually distinct. The basic process underlying evaluative contrast would seem to be the classic categorization process delineated by Tajfel, to which the experiments of McGarty et al. discussed above refer. The specific importance of the results obtained by de la Haye et al. is that a number of subjects were able to see a significant contrast favouring Group B. This phenomenon raises a crucial question: is it necessary that some objective intergroup difference exists for contrast to appear? If the answer were no, it would not be possible any longer to refer to Tajfel's model, which is based on the idea that people accentuate real differences. McGarty et al.'s (1993) arguments show that differentiation in favour of Group A has some objective basis. Does this imply that favouring Group B is essentially illogical? Such a conclusion is not strictly necessary. Behaviour desirability is not as stable a measure as, for example, line length. Although the illusory correlation item-sets are constructed so as to equate behaviour desirability between target groups, this is only true across subjects, but not for every subject (whereas every subject viewing Tajfel and Wilkes', 1963, stimuli very probably agreed that each of the lines labelled 'A' were shorter than each of the lines labelled 'B' in all conditions). Each subject has his or her own idiosyncratic evaluation of behaviours, and it might very well be that, for some subjects, behaviour desirability is truly higher for Group B, thus lending 'objective' basis to the accentuation process in favour of Group B.

For this discussion, then, we need to distinguish between two conditions: (a) evaluative contrast without converging preferences implies that every individual holds his or her own idiosyncratic stereotype and (b) when convergence of preferences is added to evaluative contrast, true social stereotypes appear, that is, shared perceptions of the target groups. In the following experiments, de la Haye and her co-workers first explored the specificity of the standard illusory correlation paradigm, compared to other stimulus conditions, and then analysed the effects of a number of other factors on contrast and on preference. These additional factors were relative group size, the group letter labels, and focus of attention in the judgment task.

There is something rather surprising in the illusory correlation literature: a lot of experiments have been run with a particular item-set structure, resulting from the crossing of two uneven binary distributions. This particular item-set structure is deemed important in determining the effect of interest. However, the frequency structure of the item-set has never been an independent variable in any experiment. A second experiment (de la Haye and Lauvergeon, 1995) was aimed at examining in what respect the standard illusory correlation paradigm did lead to specific effects. It was mainly exploratory, and addressed two questions: (a) Does the standard paradigm lead to greater preference for the majority than conditions with an equal number of items about each group? and (b) Does it lead to greater contrast? Four different stimulus conditions were used; the two target groups, named A and B, could be either of equal size or unequal, and the two categories of behaviours, desirable/undesirable, appeared in either a 2:1 or 1:1 ratio. When the target groups were unequal the majority was called A and the minority was called B, as in most previous experiments.[2] Obviously, no 'preference for the majority' was possible when the target groups were equal; thus, comparisons between conditions bore on 'preference for Group A'.

The results of this experiment were quite straightforward. The contrast effect appeared in every condition, but was stronger when the groups were not of equal size,[3] and was especially large in the standard 'illusory correlation' condition. An indication that contrast was always more or less present was the fact that, in every condition, the proportion of subjects who expressed significantly different impressions of the two groups was quite large (ranging from 56 per cent to 70 per cent). However, the conditions with unequal groups gave rise to a stronger negative correlation between ratings of Groups A and B; of all the conditions the standard 'illusory correlation' setting stood out as the one where the absolute between-group difference in evaluative ratings was the largest. When it came to the preference effect, this specificity of the standard condition completely disappeared. The classical ICE appeared in the standard condition on all three dependent variables, but this did not make the results for this condition unique. There was no significant difference between the standard condition and the three other ones taken together, on any dependent variable. More specifically, a significant preference for Group A appeared in conditions other than the standard one, revealing an unexpected letter-preference effect.

As the possible effect of group letter labels had not been explored before in the published literature, a complementary experiment was run (Expt. 3), with group labels as an independent variable. For half the subjects, the majority was called A, and the minority was called B; for the other half, the reverse was true. This manipulation had a very strong effect on responses to the assignment task, but no effect on estimations nor on trait ratings. In the assignment task, the number of positive items assigned to the majority was higher, and the number of negative items assigned to the majority was lower, when the majority was called A rather than B. This resulted in a complete inversion of the ICE: the mean phi was positive when the majority was called A, and negative when the majority was called B. However, group letter labels had no effect on the two other dependent variables. In the estimation task, an illusory correlation effect was observed, and did not depend on group labels; in trait ratings, no illusory correlation was found.

That the subjects hold more favourable expectations toward a group called A than toward a group called B is not a phenomenon of great theoretical impact. It is probably rooted in various cultural habits, such as giving an 'A' grade to an excellent piece of work and so on. However, these data serve as a reminder that even seemingly trivial effects of this type might be a source of confusion and should be controlled. In our examination of the illusory correlation literature we found 24 published experiments where the items-set was structured by (a) a categorization into groups called A and B, and (b) a dichotomy into desirable/undesirable behaviours. Out of these 24 experiments, 17 were so designed that a possible 'letter-preference effect' could enhance the illusory correlation effect, that is, where there was a majority group called A and a majority of positive behaviours. Two were so designed that a letter-preference effect would go against the ICE (Hamilton and Gifford, 1976, Expt. 2; Schaller, 1991 – both with a majority of negative behaviours) and five were so designed that a letter-preference effect would be irrelevant (Feldman, Camburn and Gatti, 1986, Expt. 4; Fiedler, 1991, Expt. 2; McConnell, Sherman and Hamilton, 1994b; Schaller and Maass, 1989, both experiments). Thanks to these last seven experiments, we can be fairly confident that the ICE does not boil down to a letter-preference effect (though the ICE was quite weak in some of these studies).

However, it is also quite evident from this count that the conditions where a letter-preference effect could boost illusory correlation occur much more frequently in the literature than other ones. The two experiments by de la Haye and Lauvergeon we described above show that this practice is unwise at best. In fact, a letter-preference effect can occur, and did so in these experiments. As a consequence of it, it was not possible to demonstrate that the standard illusory correlation paradigm really gives rise to *more* preference toward the A majority than did other conditions toward any A group. However, it was shown that the standard paradigm gives rise to more *contrast*. In a fourth experiment, de la Haye, Lauvergeon and Scharnitzky (1995) examined factors which influenced either the preference or the contrast effect.

This fourth experiment was designed as a test of the hypothesis which was untested in the previous one: whether preference for Group A was larger when an ICE can be expected (i.e., when Group A is a majority). In addition to this the focus of the subjects' attention was manipulated as a variable which could be expected to affect the strength of the contrast effect. In line with the evaluative contrast and differentiation perspectives presented here, the hypothesis was that the subjects would be more prone to perceive the groups as different when their attention was directed to the categorization of the target stimuli into groups. Attention focus was manipulated both at the encoding stage and at the judgement stage.

At the encoding stage, the verbal instructions directed the subject to 'try to concretely imagine' either 'each individual person' or 'each one of the two groups'. Attention focus at the judgement stage was manipulated by way of the first task encountered in the series. For half the subjects, the first task was the classical 'attribution of group membership' task, in other words, assignment of behaviours to groups. For the other half of the subjects the first task was to assign the same behaviours to the individual actors – requiring them to recall the actors' first names. The hypothesis was that between-group contrast would be stronger in conditions where the subject's attention was focused on groups rather than on individuals, be it at the encoding or the judgement stage. After performing either assignment-to-groups, or assignment-to-individuals, the subjects completed the two other standard tasks, estimations and trait ratings, in counterbalanced order.

All three hypotheses were confirmed. Preference for Group A was larger when groups were unequal, rather than equal. This phenomenon appeared only in the assignment-to-groups and estimation tasks, but was very clear. In fact, the ICE, as measured by a mean positive phi, appeared only when groups were unequal, and subjects focused on individuals at encoding. Most probably, when subjects were focused on groups at encoding, they tried to form an impression of the groups on-line, and this process is known to attenuate the ICE (see Pryor, 1986). Between-group contrast, as measured by the absolute difference between mean ratings of the two groups, was larger when the subjects were focused on groups, rather than on individuals. Both manipulations, at the encoding and at the judgement stages, had significant main effects. The percentage of subjects who expressed significantly different judgements of Groups

A and B shifted from 40 per cent when subjects were focused on individuals at both stages, to 71 per cent, when subjects were focused on groups at both stages. Contrary to Experiment 2, contrast was stronger when the groups were of equal size, rather than unequal. The effect of this factor must thus be considered unstable.

In this set of experiments, two main questions were raised: (a) Does the standard 'illusory correlation' paradigm give rise to specific effects? and (b) What kind of factors control the contrast effect, as distinguished from the preference effect? To the first question, the answer is clearly yes; in the fourth experiment, de la Haye et al. were able to show that preference for the majority group, which appears in the standard paradigm, is greater than the mere preference for Group A, which appears even when groups are of equal size. This result offers an empirical confirmation of the previously untested assumption that the ICE is in fact specific to the particular stimulus conditions in which it had been repeatedly shown. However, the contrast effect is a much more widespread phenomenon, not at all specific to these particular conditions.

What is specific to the standard paradigm is the relative convergence of preferences toward the majority group, not the biased perception of groups as different. The contrast effect is not restricted to conditions with unequal groups. It is specifically enhanced by any circumstance which draws the subject's attention toward the categorization into groups as such. As a consequence, there are conditions where mean contrast is high, but no overall preference appears. In the fourth experiment, this was the case in conditions where subjects were focused on groups at the encoding stage. These conditions made the ICE disappear, but strengthened the contrast effect.

For these reasons, one must be cautious not to interpret the absence of ICE as an indication of accuracy. Just because there is no ICE this does not mean either that the subjects are responding accurately, or as we have seen, that there is no contrast between the groups. A high level of accuracy is not compatible with the ICE, but a low level of ICE is perfectly compatible with strong inaccuracy. In less technical terms, one must distinguish between personal (i.e., idiosyncratic) stereotypes, which are idiosyncratic biases, and can be quite strong though they do not appear in group analysis, and social stereotypes, which are consensual phenomena.

7 Conclusion

There are several important themes that unify the research that we have reported in this chapter. The most important of these is that many phenomena and many psychological processes are subsumed within what has come to be called the illusory correlation effect. There can now be little doubt that the effect is multiply determined and that there is some scope for many explanations of the effect (though this, of course, raises the question of whether it is proper to speak of 'an effect' as such), at the level of a laboratory phenomenon and as an aspect of social stereotype formation.

Even so, our work reveals evaluative contrast to be a ubiquitous response to the sorts of task that illusory correlation researchers present their subjects with. What the research of de la Haye and her colleagues shows is that evaluative contrast occurs routinely when subjects are asked to judge two groups after being exposed to a series of statements about them. The work of McGarty and his colleagues provides an explanation for why this contrast should be prevalent: contrast is consistent with subjects' expectations that the groups *should* be different. Furthermore, taking these two streams together we have an explanation as to why the majority should be routinely favoured in some circumstances and not in others (and what factors should limit those effects). To recapitulate our argument: our work shows that the stimulus presentation and judgement tasks that are used for investigating the illusory correlation effect actually produce evaluative contrast (or intergroup differentiation) as a routine outcome. However, under the specific circumstances of the standard illusory correlation paradigm one particular group tends to be favoured by most subjects. This special case of evaluative contrast is what has come to be known as the illusory correlation effect.

We thus reject the two competing and narrower views (a) that the effect is of interest of itself purely as a laboratory phenomenon, or (b) that the effect is of minimal interest as it does not relate to the formation of stereotypes of real-life social groups. We have instead argued that while there are aspects of the effect which seem to be highly specific laboratory phenomena, the ICE is an instantiation of the fundamental process of categorization as it relates to differentiation between groups. To that extent, the phenomenon may be of interest not because it reveals anything distinctively new about stereotype formation, but because it reinforces the importance of categorization in stereotype formation, and because it suggests the very great importance of prior knowledge, expectancies and preexisting theories in the stereotyping process. This latter trend is rapidly developing in, for example, work from a self-categorization theory perspective (e.g., Berndsen, McGarty, van der Pligt and Spears, 1994; Brown, forthcoming; McGarty et al., 1995; Oakes, Haslam and Turner, 1994). Following recent work in cognition by writers such as Murphy and Medin (1985), self-categorization theorists have reasserted the argument that social cognition is greatly determined by expectancies and prior knowledge, especially where this knowledge is shared with fellow ingroup members (see Haslam, this volume). Other recent work on illusory correlation has also moved in the direction of taking account of perceiver expectancies and learning (McConnell et al., 1994a).

However, the most central conclusions of this chapter may relate not so much to the relative merits of different explanations of the illusory correlation effect, but to the implications of the work reviewed here for our understanding of social stereotyping. It would appear from the present findings that the illusory correlation effect does have important implications for social stereotype formation. In this regard it is worth noting that, even though the implications of the effect for stereotype formation originally guided Hamilton and Gifford's (1976) research, much recent work has focused on the relative merits of different explanations of illusory correlation, or on factors which mediate it. Thus, it is apparent that in recent times the illusory correlation effect has become a topic of interest in its own right, rather than being of interest because it informed us about stereotyping. This trend is not an unreasonable one, for if it can be shown that the effect is created by processes that are probably not directly implicated in everyday stereotype formation (such as information loss due to the nature of skewed contingency tables) then social psychologists will be forced to find new explanations of stereotype formation.

Our work suggests a somewhat different conclusion. While it provides no evidence for the role of an automatic bias towards distinctiveness in explaining the illusory correlation effect, it does suggest that the effect may instead reflect the more general process of differentiation between social groups that has been held to underlie stereotyping since the pioneering research of Tajfel, (e.g. 1969a; Tajfel and Wilkes, 1963). Under this view, the illusory correlation effect is not something to do with minorities or distinctiveness as such, it is simply that the experiments designed to test for it involve creating implicit fit between the minority and the distinctive stimuli (due to the skewed contingency tables used).

At the time the illusory correlation effect in stereotyping was first proposed it was the paradigmatic case of the social cognitive approach. It was argued that erroneous social perceptions emerged due to the operation of cognitive processes which involved the automatic attention of the perceiver to distinctive stimuli. This was attributed to perceivers not having enough processing capacity to arrive at accurate perception. This distinctiveness-based limited information processing view came to dominate social cognition, and in particular, the study of social stereotyping (see Hamilton, 1981). Despite the early promise of this approach, it seems that, based on the research discussed here, it is very difficult to sustain the argument that *automatic* biases towards novelty lead to the formation of negative stereotypes of minorities. On the contrary, the full picture of the ICE seems to involve normal sense-making processes involving differentiation between groups which can be seen as both sensible and logical in the unusual contexts in which subjects are asked to make judgements. If we take the further step to argue that what is deemed sensible and logical for any individual can only be defined relative to some social context, then we are forced to conclude that the explanation of stereotype formation must make reference to the social mediation of cognitive processes rather than to individualistic cognitive biases.

Notes

The authors would like to thank the editors and in particular Alex Haslam and Mariette Berndsen for their insightful comments on an earlier draft of this chapter.

1   However, very recently Spears and van Knippenberg (1995) found that illusory correlation has an inverted U-shaped relationship with load such that the amount of illusory correlation was greater with a 5 second presentation rate than with 2.5 and 10 second presentation rates (see Spears and Haslam, this volume).
2   To our knowledge there was only one previous experiment (Schaller and Maass, 1989, Expt. 2) where the group letter label had been controlled.
3   This effect was not replicated in Experiment 4; on the contrary, we found greater between-group contrast when the groups were equal.

8
Stereotyping and the Burden of Cognitive Load

Russell Spears and S. Alexander Haslam

1   Introduction: Economy versus Meaning

In this chapter we consider the basis for social stereotyping: what causes us to perceive others in terms of the social categories to which they belong rather than as unique individuals? An increasingly common answer to this question concerns cognitive load and our information processing capacity. Following the currently dominant cognitive approach, social categorization and stereotyping tend to be seen as the default option for social judgement that is resorted to when people are unable to give their full attention to social perception. This analysis in fact dates back to the very first detailed treatment of stereotyping and was expressed succinctly by the journalist Walter Lippmann (1922, p. 59) when he wrote:

> There is no shortcut through, and no substitute for, an individualized understanding . . . but modern life is hurried and multifarious. There is neither time nor opportunity for intimate acquaintance. Instead we notice a trait which marks a well-known type, and fill in the rest of the picture by means of the stereotypes we carry about in our heads.

According to this view, then, we categorize others and apply stereotypes associated with these categories, when we do not have sufficient cognitive resources (the time, the ability and the motivation) to perceive them as individuals or in individuating terms.

In its more recent instantiation this analysis is closely associated with a characterization of the social perceiver as a '*cognitive miser*' who compromises accurate perception in the face of the 'overwhelming stimulus complexity' of the social world (Taylor, 1981a; Fiske and Taylor, 1984, 1991). As such it is an extension of approaches in cognitive psychology and decision making that regard human information-processing as generally adaptive but nevertheless prone to systematic error. According to this view, social judgements and decisions are guided by a range of heuristics and biases that serve to render the judgement situation manageable (e.g., Kahneman, Slovic and Tversky, 1982) but which also introduce error unintentionally. In relation to stereotyping, the cognitive tradition has therefore tended to view stereotypes as the products of information-processing biases or judgemental heuristics, applied when there is too much information to process optimally or individually (see e.g., Hamilton and Trolier, 1986; Hamilton and Sherman, 1994, for reviews). The implication is that if life was longer or less demanding, and perceivers were able to process and recall all the social stimuli they encountered perfectly, the use of cognitive heuristics would be unnecessary, and hence the error associated with stereotypic beliefs would be avoided.

There is now a growing body of studies which would seem to demonstrate that the application or use of stereotypes is indeed a function of cognitive load or 'busyness' (e.g., Bodenhausen, 1988; Bodenhausen, 1990; Bodenhausen and Lichtenstein, 1987; Bodenhausen and Wyer, 1985; Gilbert and Hixon, 1991; Kaplan, Wanshula and Zanna, 1993; Macrae, Hewstone and Griffiths, 1993; Macrae, Milne and Bodenhausen, 1994; Stangor and Duan, 1991). On this basis, Gilbert and Hixon (1991, p. 509) claim in an influential article that the assertion that 'a stereotype is the sluggard's best friend' enjoys 'near perfect consensus' and that modern theorists have 'raised the notion of cognitive economy to a first principle' (see also Macrae et al., 1994, p. 37).

However, as these authors point out, this principle of cognitive parsimony in the realm of stereotyping is not a new discovery of the cognitive era but can be traced back to the earliest writings on stereotyping. Indeed, as noted above, this analysis can be identified in Lippmann's (1922) original definition of stereotypes as 'pictures in our heads' and it was later elaborated by Allport (1954, p. 21) when he argued that:

So long as we can 'get away' with coarse over-generalizations we tend to do so. (Why? Well it takes less effort).

For Allport stereotyping was a direct consequence of the fact that 'life is just too short to have differentiated concepts about everything' and so 'to consider every member of a group as endowed with the same traits saves us the pains of dealing with them as individuals' (1954, p. 173).

Yet in arguing that stereotyping is above all an economical effort-saving process, both Lippmann and Allport's analyses also served as clear articulations of the individualistic *meta-theory* which underpins the mainstream cognitive approach and which holds that the truth about people lies in the things that differentiate them from each other rather than in the things they have in common. This belief (which is widespread in western culture) necessarily defines stereotyping as error at the outset and effectively blocks the path to any more sympathetic understanding of the process. The legacy of these early writers was thus twofold, for as we will argue below, individualism and cognitivism have tended to buttress each other throughout the evolution of the currently dominant (individual-based) cognitive approach to stereotyping.

Another important figure often identified with the cognitive approach to stereotyping is Henri Tajfel. His paper on the cognitive aspects of prejudice (Tajfel, 1969a) has been widely regarded as a landmark contribution to the field (e.g., Hamilton, 1981). Indeed, like Allport before him, his early research and theorizing on social categorization can be seen to have contributed to subsequent cognitive miser meta-theory, for he also regarded an important function of social categorization to be the simplification of our social world (e.g., Tajfel and Forgas, 1981). In spite of this though, it is misleading to identify Tajfel with the current directions being taken in the individual cognitive tradition as his own work advocated a much more integrative and non-reductionist approach to stereotyping which was based on an awareness of the manner in which the cognitive aspects of this process were structured by intergroup relations and other social factors (see Tajfel, 1981a, 1981b). Thus Tajfel believed that an important aspect of categorization was the meaningful organization of the stimulus world, but unlike other researchers he did not reduce the idea of organization purely to an issue of simplification, or see individual-based perception as functionally superior to perception and judgement in social categorical terms.

In stressing the meaningful and functional aspects of social categorization, Tajfel followed Bruner (1957b). Despite being one of the key forefathers of social cognition, in much the same way as Tajfel, Bruner (1990) became critical of the information-processing metaphor and rejected it in favour of a more agentic and meaning-based approach to cognition. In this he argued that categorization was not a mechanism of information reduction, but rather the opposite, in fact (in his famous phrase) allowing perceivers to go 'beyond the information given'. Interestingly, this idea (and its opposition to the metaphor of the categorizer as a cognitive miser) has recently been elaborated by researchers working from a mainstream cognitive perspective. For example Medin (1988, pp. 121–2) has stated:

> One common answer to the question of why people might categorize is that it is in the interests of cognitive economy. That is, categorization is a way of coping with information overload. I confess to being very sceptical about this answer . . . I think that categorization, including social categorization, is primarily to cope with the problem of too little rather than too much information.

However, references to Bruner's work in the current stereotyping literature have tended to be one-sided. For example, his research on perceiver readiness and category accessibility has been developed by stereotyping researchers to demonstrate that social cognition can be coloured by primed categories and their associated stereotypes of which we may be unaware and over which we may have little control (e.g., Devine, 1989; Greenwald and Banaji, 1995). It is interesting to note, however, that the other half of the categorization process originally studied by Bruner, namely the 'fit' of the category system to the stimulus array, has tended to receive much less attention by stereotyping researchers in the mainstream cognitive tradition. One of the consequences of this selectivity has been an emphasis of the top-down (cognitive, individually located) aspects of stereotyping at the expense of the bottom-up (real, socially derived).

Importantly though, not all researchers have adopted this strategy. In particular, self-categorization theorists have emphasized both (a) the group-based aspects of the stereotyping process found in Tajfel's work, and (b) after Bruner, the role of stimulus fit as well as perceiver readiness in determining category salience (e.g., Oakes, 1987).[1] Furthermore, this work has led to the development of an alternative analysis of stereotyping which regards it as a socially meaningful and appropriate activity, structured by the social realities of group life (Oakes, Haslam and Turner, 1994).

In this chapter, we attempt to take a closer look at the assumptions and findings on which the mainstream cognitive approach is based and ask whether, as the vast majority of researchers contend, stereotyping really is a strategy of individually-based simplification necessitated by a high ratio of cognitive demands to cognitive resources. As a first stage in this process we start by providing a brief review of the fast-growing body of research which has argued for the cognitive miser or heuristic approach to stereotyping, and focus specifically on the role of cognitive load in this analysis. We follow this with sections critiquing and reinterpreting this work which build upon the view of stereotyping as a meaning-seeking process. Evidence from additional stereotyping research which relates to this alternative view is then presented, prior to a more detailed discussion of findings from some of our own research. From these, as from our considerations as a whole, we are led to question the relationship between cognitive load and stereotyping proposed by the cognitive miser model on both theoretical and empirical grounds. Amongst other things, we suggest that it is unclear that stereotyping necessarily lightens perceivers' cognitive load (or that this is its primary function). More fundamentally perhaps, we take a critical stance towards the very meaning of 'load' and suggest that manipulations of it may reduce to the 'choices of attention' that are arguably a feature of all perception and cognition. We propose that the relationship between load and stereotyping is therefore more complex than the miser model would suggest and may be better accounted for in terms of a meaning-oriented analysis.

2 The Case for the Miser Hypothesis

At first glance the empirical case for the argument that cognitive load produces or facilitates stereotyping seems as overwhelming as the apparent nature of the social stimulus field itself. The aim of this section is to briefly review some of the most important contributions to this recent research although space limitations prevent an exhaustive coverage. Before we begin however, it is perhaps important to distinguish the different sorts of paradigm which are relevant to research into this issue. These can be roughly divided into three categories: (a) studies in which a stereotype label is activated or rendered accessible, but in which little or no relevant data pertaining to the validity of the stereotype is presented, (b) studies where no specific stereotype is primed, but where stereotype-relevant information is contained within the stimuli and social categories in the data, and (c) studies where both a stereotype is activated *and* participants are required to process stereotype-relevant information bearing on the validity of this stereotype. The first category (a) involves a (top down) application of a stereotype, (b) involves (bottom-up) generation of a stereotype and (c) involves elements of both. Accordingly, it can be seen that differentiation between paradigmatic variations is pertinent to the distinction between the role of (1) accessibility and (2) fit in determining the salience of categories and the use of associated stereotypes. Despite the fact that is not always easy to neatly categorize studies according to this taxonomy (and most studies come into the last category, although fit is rarely manipulated), it is nonetheless useful to be aware of these paradigmatic variations, and of the distribution of reported studies into each – for, as we will see, of those that support the load hypothesis very few are of the second type.

In a series of studies which fall into the first of these categories, Bodenhausen and his colleagues have argued that stereotypes operate as judgemental heuristics (e.g., Bodenhausen, 1988; 1990; Bodenhausen and Lichtenstein, 1987; Bodenhausen and Wyer, 1985). For example, Bodenhausen and Wyer (1985) showed that participants tended to use a primed stereotype (implied by the target's name and address) to guide their judgements when a depicted transgression was stereotypic of that group, and to ignore other relevant information that would otherwise be used if the stereotypic label was not activated (i.e., if the crime was counterstereotypic). So when a target was identified as Ashley Chamberlain from Cambridge rather than Carlos Ramirez from Alberquerque subjects were more likely to suspect him of fraud than of attacking a man in a bar. Moreover, additional research indicated that the use of such heuristics seemed to increase for ostensibly more complex judgemental tasks, such as judging the guilt of the target, rather than rating aggressiveness (Bodenhausen and Lichtenstein, 1987). On this basis the authors suggested that load, defined as task complexity, can increase our reliance on simplifying heuristics, such as stereotypes. In subsequent research similar arguments have been advanced for the resource-depleting effects of mood and (suboptimal) arousal which have also been shown to increase stereotypic biases (Bodenhausen, 1990; Bodenhausen, 1993; Bodenhausen, Kramer and Süsser, 1994).

Perhaps a more direct manipulation of cognitive load is provided in the studies of Gilbert and Hixon (1991). They varied 'cognitive busyness' by requiring participants to rehearse and recall an eight-digit number during an experimental task which involved completing word fragments presented by a Caucasian or an Asian woman. For example, she held up a card bearing the fragment 'RI_E' which might (stereotypically for the Asian prime) be completed as 'rice'. The authors showed that when subjects had to recall the digit this could prevent activation of an Asian stereotype. However, when the stereotype was *already* activated subsequent busyness on a concurrent task (where participants listened to an Asian or Caucasian assistant describe a day in their life) increased use of the stereotype as measured by ratings of the assistant. This study led the authors to a modified version of the basic cognitive miser model, whereby the tendency for load to increase stereotyping is dependent on the stereotype having already been activated. Significantly, the study thus suggests that mere exposure to a category exemplar does not necessarily lead to automatic activation of this category or an associated stereotype (see also Bargh, 1994).

Rothbart, Fulero, Jensen, Howard and Birrell (1978; Expt. 1) conducted one of the first studies to examine the effect of load on the representation and recall of information presented about experimentally created groups (category b above). In their first study participants were presented with 16 (low load) or 64 (high load) person–trait pairings and the proportion of negative to positive traits and the distribution of traits over targets were also manipulated experimentally. They found that under low load conditions participants were able to distinguish those individuals who were associated with a number of negative traits from other individuals who were each associated with a single negative trait. In the high load condition by contrast, people tended to form more group-level impressions such that recall and judgements were simply influenced by the number of traits, without taking into account whether these were concentrated in individuals or dispersed over the group. In other words, people were perceived more in terms of their group membership under high load, or at least less in terms of individual attributes. This finding was later taken as evidence that people's ability to make intra-category differentiations is mediated by cognitive load and associated pressures on cognitive resources.

Stangor and Duan (1991) investigated the hypothesis that load defined as multiple task demands would influence the processing of stereotype consistent versus inconsistent information. They proposed that under optimal (low load) conditions information inconsistent with a stereotype might be well recalled and influence judgement (cf. Rojahn and Pettigrew, 1992; Stangor and MacMillan, 1992) because people would have time to resolve this inconsistent information and work it into their impression (see also Srull and Wyer, 1989; Schaller and Maass, 1989). However, they proposed that where demands on attention and information-processing were high, there would be no time for such inconsistency resolution and hence consistent information would have a recall advantage, and unduly influence stereotypic judgements. They obtained support for this idea in two studies. In the first, they manipulated demands by having participants form impressions of one, two or four experimentally devised groups, which varied on either of two dimensions (honest vs. friendly) and found a decrease in the recall of the incongruent behaviours as a function of the number of judged groups. The second study replicated the two-group condition from the first experiment and introduced a different manipulation of load, namely a concurrent distraction task in which subjects had to listen to a news broadcast while forming their impression of target groups. An interaction between the recall of consistent versus inconsistent behaviour and load/distraction was found such that in the distraction condition the recall of consistent behaviour clearly exceeded that of inconsistent behaviour, with the reverse pattern in the no-distraction condition.

Macrae, Hewstone and Griffiths (1993) combined aspects of Gilbert and Hixon's (1991) and Stangor and Duan's (1991) studies and used the digit memorization paradigm to study the effects of cognitive load on recall for stereotype-consistent versus stereotype-inconsistent behaviour (an example of c above). In their paradigm (addressed in greater detail below) they used stereotypes of real-life groups. Participants were presented with a video of a conversation between two women, in which the target for subsequent judgement was described either as a hairdresser or as a doctor. Half of the statements made by this target woman were consistent with the hairdresser stereotype and half with a doctor stereotype. As predicted, cognitive busyness (memorization of an eight-digit number) resulted in better recall for prime-consistent than prime-inconsistent information, reversing the effect for low load. There was also evidence of a significant correlation between recall and judgement in the high load condition (i.e., more stereotypic ratings were associated with recall of a higher proportion of stereotypic items), an effect which had not been obtained in Stangor and Duan's (1991) earlier study.

Macrae, Milne and Bodenhausen (1994) have recently provided further evidence that stereotypes can act as 'energy-saving devices' in line with the cognitive miser meta-theory. In three studies they showed that priming a stereotype could lead participants to recall more information presented and have more residual cognitive resources to perform a concurrent task. Participants also recalled more stereotype-consistent than neutral behaviour in these studies. However, while there was some evidence that supraliminal priming differentially facilitated recall of stereotype-consistent over neutral information (Studies 1 and 3), subliminal priming appeared simply to facilitate the recall of both consistent and neutral information (Studies 2 and 3).

No review of stereotyping and the cognitive miser model would be complete without consideration of the continuum model developed by Susan Fiske and her associates (e.g., Fiske and Neuberg, 1990; see also the dual processing model of Brewer, 1988, which shares many theoretical assumptions and similarities). The basic idea of this is that there is a continuum of information-processing and impression formation ranging from the (social) categorical to a more individuated level of perception and judgement which focuses on a more piecemeal integration of attribute information. It is proposed that perceiving people in terms of a social category is the easiest and default mode of perception and impression formation (premise 1), although movement towards the individuating end of the continuum will increase as the correspondence of the target to the category decreases (premise 2).[2] Moreover, piecemeal processing and thus individuated impressions (in contrast to category-based impressions) are seen to require a degree of motivation and cognitive resources and hence are predicted to be more common when these resources are available. A basic procedure used to test this model involves measuring attention to information consistent versus inconsistent with a category or stereotype. Typically, when people are not motivated to pay a great deal of attention to the target, they are predicted to pay relatively little attention to inconsistent information (although inconsistent information can also shift perception and judgment towards the individuating pole).[3] However, when they are more motivated (for example, when they learn that they will be expected to work together with the target) they are expected to attend to and recall more inconsistent information.

A recent study by Pendry and Macrae (1994) is representative of research in this tradition and involved an attempt directly to manipulate load or busyness. Under conditions of outcome-dependence with a target, resource depletion caused by cognitive busyness (memorizing an eight-digit number in Study 1, a probe reaction task in Study 2) reduced participants' ability to individuate the target woman, as revealed by more stereotypic ratings on consistent traits (though not less on inconsistent traits) while there was no evidence of differential recall for inconsistent over consistent in the non-busy cell in Study 1 (all participants were busy in Study 2). Once again, then, social categories and the stereotyping and categorization process are seen as simplifying but functional heuristics that aid information processing, and that typically result in better recall of consistent than inconsistent information. In sum, categorization is conceptualized as a cognitive default which is activated under conditions of busyness but which is happily overridden where motivation and capacity allow for more accurate processing (Fiske and Neuberg, 1990, p. 33).

To summarize research in the cognitive miser tradition, it is possible to characterize the relationship between load (defined by task complexity, concurrent tasks, cognitive busyness, etc.) and the sort of information-processing (individuating vs. social categorical) in terms of a trade-off function. That is, as load increases, the use of individuating or stereotype-incongruent information is likely to decrease, while the use of category relevant and/or stereotype consistent information is likely to increase.[4] The hypothesized relation between load and stereotyping can thus be depicted as a linear or asymptotic function with category use and stereotyping rising with load, presumably to a limit where it cannot increase any more, and levelling off (but importantly not decreasing).[5]

3 From Cognitive Misers to Meaning Seekers

Although the evidence generated in support of the load hypothesis has been widely accepted by stereotyping researchers (e.g., Hamilton et al., 1994; Stangor and Lange, 1994), the tradition of research from Bruner via Tajfel to self-categorization theory that we sketched in the introduction articulates a different meta-theory of social categorization and stereotyping that can be contrasted with that of the cognitive miser model (see Oakes and Turner, 1990). In extending this specifically for the purpose of analysing issues of cognitive load, we will refer to this alternative model as the rational meaning-seeking or 'meaning' model for short. In contrast to the continuum model, this approach starts by arguing that all perception is categorical at some level. This idea is not new. Philosophers have long argued that all thought is both categorical (Kant) and social (Wittgenstein), or both (Marx, Vygotsky, Volisinov). The general point that the social world is to some extent interpreted or constructed through categories is now widely accepted in psychology. The question then, is whether the 'social categories' typically accessed in studies of cognitive load (e.g., gender, 'race', etc.) should have a special status in facilitating social information-processing.

When we are perceiving an individual as 'an individual' we are also categorizing him or her in a number of senses. First, we may be perceiving the person in terms of attributes (e.g., friendly–unfriendly, pro- vs. anti-abortion) and these attributes (e.g., traits) can themselves be thought of as cognitive categories (e.g., Pratto and Bargh, 1991; see also Simon, this volume). It thus seems pertinent to ask how perceiving someone in terms of trait-based (individuating) categories is qualitatively different from perceiving them in terms of social categories (cf. Fiske and Neuberg, 1990), and whether one generally requires more effort than the other (see e.g., Pratto and Bargh, 1991). The example of personal attributes underlines this argument, because an attribute can itself very quickly become the basis for a social categorization: a property like intelligence defines someone as a unique individual in one context, but also defines them as a group member in another (Simon, this volume). Rather than being an issue of individuation versus categorization, this is arguably an issue of *level* of categorization, whereby the individual can be categorized either as a unique individual, as a group member or as a member of the human race (Turner et al., 1987). Here individuation implies the perception of similarity and difference relative to a categorical frame of reference at the next higher level of self-categorization (Turner, 1987b), suggesting a close interdependence between processes of categorization and 'particularization' (Billig, 1985). In this sense, individuation and stereotyping are simply *two sides of the same coin* as exactly the same comparative and contrastive processes are required in order to perceive someone as a unique individual (different from other individuals) as to perceive them as a member of a particular group (different from other groups). It might be argued that social categories are more simple (and hence more economical) by virtue of being more inclusive than the individuals they comprise and because they relate these individuals to group stereotypic dimensions. This advantage would presumably only hold for the representation of the group as a whole (as opposed to an aggregate of individuals), and not for the judgement of any particular individual, as required in many stereotyping paradigms (e.g., as in research using the continuum model). However, once again it can be argued that the idea that it is more difficult to perceive a group of individuals as individuals (and emphasize difference) rather than as a common group (and emphasize similarity) still makes the assumption that to perceive mutual difference is different from and more effortful than perceiving mutual similarity. This assumption is particularly problematic if difference and individuation are just as much defined in relation to the stereotypic dimension as are similarity and stereotyping (as in paradigms where individuation is predefined as preference for information inconsistent with the category stereotype).

In the abstract, then, it requires just as much effort to perceive someone as an individual as to perceive them as a member of a group since both are products of the same process. In practice, one may demand more 'effort' than the other, but this is not simply a function of level of abstraction. Thus, it may take more effort to perceive a policeman in a baton charge as a pet-lover, but so too it may take more effort to perceive a professor wearing a swimming costume at a graduation ceremony as an academic or a person wielding a knife in a lecture as just another student. The lesson to be drawn from these examples is that level of categorization (individuated vs. social categorical) is closely bound up with meaning-in-context rather than being primarily the product of a trade-off with effort.

To summarize, social perception is intrinsically categorical in at least two senses. First, the constructs of perception (e.g., traits) can be viewed as meaningful social categories for perceiving people. Second, even perceiving people as individuals, implies some reference to other levels of (social) categorization without which individuality cannot be appreciated. As with commonality and consistency, individuality and inconsistency are in themselves categorically defined.

Having questioned the possibility of non-categorical social perception, and the opposition of individual versus categorical perception, it is important to elaborate further the nature and function of categorization from a meaning-seeking perspective. In terms of the meaning model, categorization can be understood as a process of interpretation which is likely to require a degree of attention if not effort, rather than an information-processing short-cut. This interpretative effortful element is likely to be particularly apparent when the categories are not pre-given, but have to be determined in relation to the social stimulus or data (categories b and c in the previous section) – in short where perceivers have to take into account stimulus 'fit' and to choose between alternative categorizations to see which is most appropriate in making sense of the stimulus. Importantly too, even familiar or 'accessible' categories may be highly provisional in the sense that they are being continually revised in context, as a function of motivation, goals and the fit with the environment (Barsalou, 1987; Oakes et al., 1994), or even in negotiation or dispute with others (Edwards, 1991). In these terms the act of social categorization might represent as much a *gain of meaning*, as *information loss* (Oakes et al., 1994; Spears, 1995). The vaunted laziness of categorical processing is thus partly a product of the pre-definition of categories as fixed schemas or cognitive grooves that ease cognition. If categorization is seen as a more flexible on-line construction in context, then the heuristic advantages of social categorization as a short-cut (and the associated implication of bias) are less evident. At the same time, categories become much more functional and appropriate to context and provide us with local understanding. In short, the meaning model emphasizes the role of fit as well as perceiver readiness (Bruner, 1957a; Oakes, 1987), whereas the miser model tends to privilege the processing advantages associated with accessible but rigid images ('tools that jump out of a metaphorical cognitive toolbox'; Macrae et al., 1994, p. 37), and neglect their relation or fit to the stimulus (see also Stroebe and Insko, 1989; Tajfel, 1981b).

The dominant conception of the relationship between categorization and cognitive capacity is reflected in, and reinforced by, information-processing and memory paradigms that use information recall as the primary dependent variable or indicator of stereotyping. This focus can be contrasted with earlier judgement-based approaches that demonstrate category accentuation and stereotyping effects even when cognitive capacity is not at issue (e.g., Eiser and Stroebe, 1972; Tajfel and Wilkes, 1963; Tajfel, 1981a). The meaning model regards stereotyping first and foremost as the product of an ongoing judgemental process rather than of memory biases. Clearly memory *is* involved in the stereotyping process; although again we believe it operates in an active ongoing way and does not simply provide a passive unmediated window onto past experience. From this perspective, therefore, we should be wary of using memory data uncritically. For example, as we will argue below, the lack of memory for individuating information cannot always be taken to indicate an increase in stereotyping. The poor correlation between recall and judgement measures in social information processing (e.g., Bargh and Thein, 1985; Hastie and Park, 1986) tends to reinforce the argument that memory does not always reflect judgement and that these can be independent. Moreover, people have meta-cognitive insight into their memory and may attempt to correct for any 'biases' they observe in their own recall behaviour (e.g., Stapel, Reicher and Spears, 1995).

From the meaning perspective it is thus important to stress (a) that categorization is often an active, effortful process insofar as it is based on fit as well as accessibility, and (b) that the relation between memory indicators and stereotyping is unlikely to be straightforward or unmediated. With these points in mind it is now perhaps useful to consider the predictions of the meaning model in relation to the impact of load on stereotyping in memory paradigms, and contrast this with predictions from the miser perspective outlined earlier. As we have argued, the meaning model does not assume that treating people as individuals is the preferred or superior mode of perception – this will depend on the relevance of the particular level of categorization in context. Indeed, because people's behaviour and our substantive relations with them can be determined by their group membership (e.g., as bus drivers, lecturers, skinheads) to perceive them as individuals would in many contexts be highly inappropriate (Asch, 1952; Oakes and Turner, 1990). Furthermore, given that all categorization relies upon identification of relevant similarities and differences in the stimulus field, the ability to 'categorize' people both as unique individuals or as social category members is likely to be higher under low load and to decrease as load increases, because as attention becomes stretched (or refocused) meaningful category-based discrimination is subject to information loss and impaired (cf. Fiedler, 1991). Thus we can characterize the relationship between load and information use as more or less the same for individuating and categorical information, with both degrading as a function of load. Most critically, even if there was a processing advantage for perception in terms of social categories rather than 'as individuals' (e.g., because categories are more inclusive and help to organize information at this level – see above) there would be no a priori reason to assume that these processing curves will cross over or interact as a function of load. At most this implies a fairly constant memory advantage for categorical information and processing.

What, then, are the predicted consequences of load manipulations for categorization and stereotyping under this model? This will depend partly on the specific nature of the paradigm and the measures it employs. To make things concrete, we will therefore focus our analysis on the example of the category confusion paradigm developed by Taylor, Fiske, Etcoff and Ruderman (1978) which has become one of the classic methods for studying categorization effects in social information-processing, and which also forms the basis of research reported later below (see section 5). In this paradigm, perceivers see, hear or read statements made by members of two groups (e.g., men and women), and have to remember 'who said what'. The proportion of intra-category to inter-category confusions then provides an indication of the strength of social categorization as an organizing principle.

For the meaning approach, then, such categorization effects (and related stereotypic judgements) are first and foremost not predicted to be primarily a product of load, but should be more related to the perceived appropriateness and meaning of the categorization prescribed by the context. One important determinant of category salience and use is the fit between the category and the stimuli.[6] If fit is high, and people are able to detect this fit, stereotyping and categorization effects may result irrespective of load. However, it is possible that load manipulations may block the detection of fit in which case thay should *reduce* stereotyping and the proportion of stereotypic or intra-category memory errors (see section 7 below). On the other hand, if fit is detected but load prevents perfect recall, perceivers may employ rational guessing strategies to go beyond the information given and infer information from category membership or vice versa (cf. van Knippenberg, van Twuyver and Pepels, 1994; Spears and Doosje, 1996), thereby resulting in a relative increase in intra-category errors as a function of load. This is rational (e.g., following Bayesian principles) because as the category attribute is diagnostic of the category (and vice versa), if information cannot be remembered perfectly it makes sense to use this knowledge in attributing information to category targets rather than responding randomly. In the case of high fit, then, the effect of load on stereotyping is likely to depend heavily on fit detection (note that this is different to Gilbert and Hixon's (1991) distinction between stereotype activation and stereotype application in relation to load effects; in the present case load may affect the detection of fit in the data, rather than the activation and accessibility of a stereotypic label).

An equally interesting test case however is that of low or no fit between a social category and its content (i.e., in terms of behaviour, expressed opinions, etc.). Under these conditions people may be less likely to use accessible social categories as a strategy for making sense of the stimulus array when (a) performance on the the recall task is easy allowing retention of all identifying information (i.e., under low memory demands or low load), or (b) attention to all stimulus relevant information is undermined because the task is too debilitating (i.e., under high memory demands, or high load). Thus where there is no clear fit between stimuli and category both high and low load may, for different reasons, reduce the ratio of intra-category to inter-category recall errors. Under moderate load conditions, however, it may be both (1) *possible* to organize information according to social category cues (although not so easily as when the fit is high), and (2) *meaningful* and useful to do so. This is because storing all the information in terms of separate individuals is likely to exceed the 'chunking' ability of memory, and may encourage a *search for meaningful regularities* at a higher level of abstraction (although again this would be easier and more successful with at least a moderate degree of category fit). In the case of no or low fit in this memory paradigm we, therefore, predict a curvilinear relationship between 'load' and categorization effects. Moderate load represents the case where organization in terms of more abstract social categories as opposed to individuals will tend to be both be *useful* (unlike low load) and *possible* (unlike high load). This hypothesis is investigated in section 6 below.

This curvilinear hypothesis of the meaning model clearly differs from the linear or asymptotic function predicted by the cognitive miser analysis. Although the meaning approach does address the limitations of memory, a key difference is that the categorization (and stereotyping) process is regarded as effortful, strategic and sense-seeking, rather than effortless, automatic and sluggardly. Moreover it allows for meta-cognitive accommodation to these memory limitations on the part of the perceiver (cf. Bless, Strack and Schwarz, 1993; Stapel, Reicher and Spears, 1995). The contextual appropriateness of category use, therefore, includes knowledge that social categorical as well as more individual cues can aid the encoding and retrieval of information, especially in paradigms where memory is at issue. It should also be noted that the use of social category cues to aid encoding and recall also leaves open the question of whether perceivers will actually *judge* the individuals more in terms of their social category or stereotype. If perceivers recognize that they are employing social categories as part of a recall strategy, there is little reason to suppose that they will necessarily view the individuals to be more (stereo)typical of their category than under low load.

From this analysis, it should also be noted that a reduction in memory for individuating characteristics, specific individuals or inconsistent information, cannot necessarily be taken as positive evidence of categorization or stereotyping – instead this may (and often will) merely reflect the decay of individuating information, and information generally under load. Put another way, the inability to individuate may be quite independent of the motivation to stereotype. Positive evidence of increases in stereotyping should involve, at minimum, the enhanced recall of stereotype-consistent information as a function of load, or a greater tendency to make intra-category compared to inter-category errors. Conversely, if both intra- and inter-category errors rise with load, this would only provide general evidence of information loss, and not evidence for the heuristic value of social categories under load.

Finally, it is important to note that for this meaning-based approach, the perceived meaning of the task is crucial, and so it is essential to ensure that attempted load manipulations do not also alter the task orientation of perceivers. We will argue in more detail below that a number of load manipulations can mislead participants as to the true nature of the experimental task, and thus disrupt otherwise goal-directed social perception and judgement (cf. Stapel et al., 1995). At the very least, and as Bargh (1982) and Kantowitz (1974) have argued, research should control for this possibility by ensuring that the task orientation for different levels of load is similar. This point raises the more general issue that different manipulations of load (i.e., time pressure, set-size, task complexity, the presence of concurrent tasks) may have subtly different effects on the stereotyping process, by varying task meaning, and/or intervening at different stages of this process (e.g., activation, fit detection, application). A consideration of the effects of any given load manipulation will therefore require a task analysis of its effect in any given paradigm or setting.

To summarize this quite complex analysis, in examining the relationship between load and stereotyping it is important to emphasize a number of points:

1   Categorization and stereotyping are interpretative processes that require at least some attention and cognitive activity even when this occurs outside awareness (see Bargh, 1994, for a discussion of the different components of automaticity) and can often be more effortful than implied by the cognitive miser analysis.

2   Reduced memory for individuating information should not be taken as hard evidence for an increase in stereotyping with load; stronger evidence for the miser position is for the increase (with no subsequent decrease) in the use of category-based or stereotype-consistent information as a function of load.

3   It is necessary to measure more than two levels of load, and to be sure of tapping beyond only a moderate level of load (see also Bargh and Tota, 1988). Low levels of load can also produce ceiling effects associated with high recall of individual (i.e., identifying) information.

4   In determining the degree of stereotyping it is important to take the degree of fit into account, factors affecting its detection and the possibility of rational guessing strategies for measures that involve recognition or cued recall.

5   It is important to consider whether the load manipulations could influence the perceived meaning of the task and disrupt otherwise goal-directed, selective perception, and whether different load manipulations have different effects by affecting different aspects of the stereotyping process.

4   Re-examining the Evidence for the Load Hypothesis

Having taken another look at, and presented an alternative to, the assumptions that underpin the load hypothesis, we are now in a position to re-examine that body of research which has previously been offered as evidence in its favour (as in section 2 above). Although it is not possible to reinterpret the multitude of findings in the cognitive miser tradition it would also be unsatisfactory to ignore those studies that appear most inconsistent with our alternative approach. We, therefore, briefly present a range of theoretical arguments addressing apparent contradictions between the meaning approach and support for the heuristic explanations of stereotyping. This is followed by a more specific critical response to the load literature.

The first general issue concerns a question of interpretation. Rather than doubt the validity of the various findings described in section 2 above, we argue that many are quite compatible with a more rational meaning-based approach to stereotyping. For example, evidence that stereotypes function as cognitive energy-saving devices (e.g., Macrae et al., 1994; Macrae, Stangor and Milne, 1994) might seem problematic for a more interpretative or meaning-based account, which implies elaboration of the stimulus and information gain, rather than information reduction. However, the argument that categorization and stereotyping involves meaningful interpretation and elaboration of the social stimulus does not necessarily mean that this is an inefficient or sluggardly process. On the contrary, when stereotypes are meaningful this should allow people to encode much more information within a single unit or 'chunk' (Miller, 1956). For example, research on chess players has shown that experts can memorize positions at a glance because they can meaningfully categorize larger constellations than novices, allowing them to remember more quickly (Chase and Simon, 1973). In these terms, stereotypes do not have to be seen as reflecting simplifying heuristics, but may be considered elaborated units of meaning incorporating background knowledge (Medin and Wattenmaker, 1987), and it is this very meaningful elaboration in terms of prior knowledge that can account for efficient processing and recall of relevant information. After all, the idea that efficiency can be a product of effort rather than laziness, is widely accepted in other fields of human endeavour.

In theoretical terms it is also possible to accept that stereotypes facilitate information-processing under demanding conditions, without necessarily accepting that even if this did reduce information (which we question in the sense normally implied), this was its main function. Indeed, to define a function by means of its apparently beneficial effects or outcomes to the perceiver in information-processing terms would be to fall into the teleological trap of functionalism. Sparing energy or capacity could thus be regarded as an incidental by-product of meaningful processing rather than a motivating function per se. By analogy whilst we can recognize that going to hospital saves energy because people do not have to cook for themselves, it would be misleading to suggest that is what hospitals are for. The point is that in these contexts expending effort by doing otherwise would not only be wasteful but also irrational in terms of current purposes and goals. Some intriguing evidence that stereotypes do not always save energy has recently been obtained in an unpublished study by Yzerbyt, Rocher and Coull (1995) using the paradigm of Macrae et al. (1994; see also Yzerbyt, Rocher and Schadron, this volume). This study, found some support for the finding of Macrae et al. that primed stereotypes would enhance information-processing, but this only occurred when the stimulus displayed a moderate degree of prototypicality. When the target was inconsistent with the stereotype (i.e., low prototypicality) the stereotype actually interfered with information-processing ability. Thinking back to our earlier examples, this suggests that it may take just as much effort ('of the imagination') to perceive the academic in a swimming costume at graduation as a professor, as to perceive the baton-wielding policeman as a pet-loving individual. In other words, the perception of (normatively ill-fitting) individuals in terms of their category creates just as many problems as perceiving (normatively highly fitting) category members as distinct individuals. This point questions the generality of the conclusion that stereotypes act as energy-saving devices, as well as reinforcing the importance of fit in our general analysis. Moreover, evidence of processing efficiency, and even enhanced recall of stereotype-consistent information under conditions of load neither demonstrate the heuristic function of stereotypes, nor rule out more meaning-based explanations of their functions – namely veridical perception of the social level properties of groups and members (e.g., Asch, 1952; Oakes et al., 1994).

More generally, the recurring finding that people bias their judgements in line with a stereotype, when that stereotype is activated or primed is quite compatible with a more rational meaning-based account, according to which it is often appropriate to perceive and judge others in terms of their social level properties (stereotypes). Because the miser meta-theory tends to view the individual as the appropriate basis for accurate perception and analysis, stereotypes are more or less defined a priori as biases (e.g., Oakes and Reynolds, this volume; Spears, 1995). This framing in terms of bias is often facilitated by the fact that experimental contexts are chosen in which it is normatively inappropriate for people to let their judgement of a given individual be swayed by that person's group membership (e.g., sitting in judgement as a member of a jury). On the other hand, if stereotypes associated with different groups (including our own) are sensitive to differences in the context-specific base rates associated with these groups, normative decision theory argues it can be rational and meaningful to use this information (e.g., Locksley, Borgida, Brekke and Hepburn, 1980; Locksley, Hepburn and Ortiz, 1982).

This raises one of the more fundamental issues in psychology generally, namely when is it rational to rely on our prior expectations (or base rates), and when to rely on currently available data (cf. Alloy and Tabachnik, 1984). If our expectations are based on a lot of previously processed data (past 'fit'), then expectations may provide the basis for a more reliable judgement. Of course, any given experiment can define the use of stereotypes as erroneous for any given case and point to the 'pernicious' effects of social categorization, but stereotype application may be justified over more representative sampling of the object domain (Brunswik, 1943; Hammond, 1978), where stereotypes might reflect important category-based reality. A consistent feature of experimental studies is that the data are often designed a priori to disconfirm a stereotypic expectation (e.g., the illusory correlation paradigm), but if we accept the validity of stereotypes for a moment this may be unnatural and unrepresentative. It is possible to argue that it is largely the validity of stereotypes which explains how they arise and are maintained (Oakes et al., 1994). However, these deliberations about accuracy also partly miss the point, namely that stereotypes reflect the meaningful realities of the intergroup perspectives, that this reality *changes* with a shift from an individual to an intergroup context, and that stereotypes are highly sensitive to the specific nature of that context. Whether it is correct to apply particular stereotypes in making judgements can be considered an issue of politics (e.g., social debate), but from a psychological perspective it is only meaningful to append the heuristic tag when it is clear there is error in the perceiver's perceptual and judgemental processes.

A central issue is also the degree to which certain categories, and their associated stereotypes, are automatically activated upon contact with a category member, the implication being that, even if we can control and repress the negative contents of our stereotypes (e.g., Devine, 1989), any degree of busyness or load will lay them bare. The research of Gilbert and Hixon (1991) cited earlier would seem to suggest that activation is not automatic (or at least not always). This may be partly to do (a) with the question of the meaning in context of this category and (b) the fact that this requires some degree of attention or resources. Gilbert and Hixon highlight an important difference between their studies and those of others who have made this strong automaticity claim, namely that many of these other studies have used verbal labels and descriptions to make salient the categories, whereas they used a video display of the target person. Such minimal linguistic information may load the dice in favour of eliciting that category whereas a more complete and natural presentation of the target would provide the perceiver with the opportunity to perceive and categorize the person in a range of other ways (by assessing fit), including at the personal level (see also Bargh, 1994; Zárate and Smith, 1990). Reicher (1988) has made a similar point with regard to the 'spontaneous' salience of 'race' in studies using visual stimulus materials. Race was much more spontaneously salient in a study where the participants were presented with (facial) photo portraits of children of different ethnic backgrounds but this was much less the case when full pictures were provided of the children engaged in different activities. Naturalistic contexts may, therefore, provide more uncertainty about the appropriate level and form of categorization than many experimental paradigms give credit. These paradigms may, therefore, underestimate interpretative work involved in categorization, and overestimate probability of using 'chronic' social categories.

We now turn more directly to the issue of load. The central question here is whether stereotype activation and use is itself a necessary or unwilled consequence of cognitive load. In particular, do people routinely apply stereotypes inappropriately (independently of intentional goals consistent with salient self-categorizations), and *purely* because they are overloaded or because the task is too complex? The studies of Bodenhausen and others reported above would seem to suggest that this is the case. Although manipulating load by increasing the amount of information expected did not elicit greater heuristic stereotype-based judgements, a manipulation of task complexity did (Bodenhausen and Lichtenstein, 1987). However, in this study other aspects of the meaning of the task were varied as well as task complexity. To judge someone's guilt rather than their aggressiveness may be a more complex decision, but it is also a different sort of decision in other ways. Judgements of guilt may establish an adversarial role for participant judges which makes aspects of the intergroup relationship more salient and makes stereotypic differentiation on value-laden content dimensions more likely (see Haslam, Oakes, McGarty, Turner and Onorato, 1995). Moreover, to the extent that judgements of guilt are less straightforward than judgements of aggressiveness, they may also provide more latitude for the expression of aversive racism (Gaertner and Dovidio, 1986). Along these lines, Kunda (1990) has shown that motivational biases (e.g., those favouring the ingroup over the outgroup; Tajfel and Turner, 1986) can be enhanced when the stimulus is rich or complex, because of the scope this provides for self-serving construal. More information also provides fertile ground for people to confirm their stereotypic theories about groups (Kunda and Oleson, 1995; see also Yzerbyt et al., this volume). Manipulations of mood and arousal may also vary more than just load, and affect the perceived relationship between perceiver and target, thus altering the social categorical meaning of that target (cf., Esses, Haddock and Zanna, 1993).

A number of other load manipulations may also subtly influence the perceived meaning of the task or context in ways which influence the degree of stereotyping. For example, in the studies by Stangor and Duan (1991) load was manipulated by increasing the *number* of groups (as well as the number of items) to be judged, with the single group condition showing greater recall of incongruent information, and no significant difference between proportions of congruent and incongruent information recalled for two-group and four-group conditions.[7] Here load can be seen to be confounded to some extent with the intragroup versus intergroup nature of the judgemental context; self-categorization theorists have argued that we are more likely to focus on stereotypic or group attributes in intergroup contexts, while individual differences (e.g., idiosyncratic or incongruent behaviour) may be more relevant in intragroup contexts where no additional group is present (Oakes et al., 1994, pp. 106–7; Haslam, Oakes, Turner and McGarty, 1995). Combining these points, it follows that just as manipulations of outcome-dependence impact upon a perceiver's categorical relationship with a target, thereby affect stereotyping (Oakes and Reynolds, this volume), so too these processes will be affected by the imposition of additional tasks that suggest it is appropriate for perceivers to attend to different features of the total stimulus context (as in Pendry and Macrae, 1994).

In this regard it is worth noting that in Stangor and Duan's studies the number of groups affected load and recall whereas the set size or number of behaviours did not (see Rothbart et al., 1978; Stangor and McMillan, 1992). This overall pattern of results suggests that meaning, and not just the amount of information is important. In Stangor and Duan's (1991) second study participants were asked to 'pay as much attention as possible' to a radio broadcast while simultaneously receiving the group information. Once again this could have affected task orientation such that participants made the inference that the task was less concerned with group impression formation and more of a memory task and allocated attentional resources accordingly. This point also applies to the research by Gilbert and Hixon (1991) and Macrae et al. (1993) and we explore more directly, below, exactly how such supplementary concurrent tasks might affect task meaning and thereby produce results of the type obtained by these authors.

An important aspect of this question of task meaning concerns the issue of intentional goals, and how people choose to deploy their attentional resources. Many experimental situations do not allow this to become an issue by requiring subjects to direct their attention to concurrent tasks which effectively prevent them from encoding or elaborating stimulus information. It is not surprising, then, that knowledge about the category, recently primed and stored in memory, enjoys a judgement advantage over data-driven processing and the information contained therein. Information integration is logically likely to be weighted in favour of the stereotype if other information is prevented from entering consciousness or being optimally processed (e.g., see Kaplan, Wanshula and Zanna, 1993). A more conservative and theoretically interesting test of the miser model would involve looking at whether people choose to stereotype or attend to stereotype-consistent information when there is competing stimulus information in the environment ('load'), but when they have the possibility of attending to individuating target information and, moreover, have reason to believe this is relevant for the task at hand. Busyness as it is often manipulated not only leads away from relevant information but also often misleads as to the nature of the task (see Stapel, Reicher and Spears, 1995, for a similar argument concerning the availability heuristic, and also Bless et al., 1993).

However, the stronger version of the miser position does not claim that load simply blocks the processing of some incoming (individuating) information but more strongly that it leads to a reliance on or use of stereotypes (e.g., Macrae et al., 1994). Stereotype-consistent information is processed more efficiently at the expense of incongruent or individuating information because this is held to be easier to process and hence energy saving. Evidence to this effect would indeed provide more compelling support for the status of stereotypes as simplifying heuristics implied in the miser model. Yet, from many priming studies it is not always clear that greater recall or use of the stereotype reflects the superior processing of consistent information or the 'gist' of the primed stereotype itself (see Bellezza and Bower, 1981).

Although the study by Macrae et al. provides evidence of this we have been unable to replicate this effect (see below). Another important study which has claimed to demonstrate a truly data-based preferential recall of stereotype consistent information under multiple task demands is that reported by Stangor and Duan (1991). This is indeed an important test case because their studies did not require the priming of a prior learned stereotype, but rather the stereotype was contained in the data (case b in section 2 above). As such this study might be seen to provide strong evidence that load can result in biased information-processing favouring consistent information and hence to afford evidence of the cross-over function depicted by the miser model. However, a close look at data from Stangor and Duan's first study indicates that this provides strong evidence for the reduced recall of incongruent information, but much less compelling evidence that the recall of congruent information increases with load (they do not report the simple effects which would test this in their second study). Indeed, while the proportion of incongruent items recalled fell (from .45 to .07) as the number of groups increased from one to four, *so too* did the proportion of congruent items (from .32 to .09). Their conclusion that in demanding contexts 'recall for information about social groups is more likely to be congruent with expectations about those groups' (p. 374), is therefore debatable.

Although the study by Rothbart et al. (1978) cited earlier provided evidence that increasing the amount of group information affected the *representation* of group-level information, there was little evidence that higher load increased the proportion of stereotype congruent to incongruent information recalled (see also Stangor and Duan, 1991). In a more recent study Dijksterhuis and van Knippenberg (1995) examined the effect of load on memory for stereotype-consistent and stereotype-inconsistent information by varying the processing pace (cf. Bargh and Thein, 1985). Once again, the recall data provide much stronger evidence of a diminution in memory for inconsistent information under time pressure than for an increase in memory for consistent information (the relevant simple effect is absent). Greater stereotypic scores in the high paced condition could also reflect reduced stereotype-inconsistent rather than increased stereotype-consistent judgements.

A review of the literature on memory for expectancy congruent and incongruent information by Stangor and McMillan (1992) provides meta-analytic evidence relevant to evaluation of the hypothesis that load increases memory for congruent (i.e., stereotypic) information. Although certain indices (recall and response bias) do provide evidence of such a positive relation between load and recall, the pattern seems to vary with the indicator of load (e.g., number of individuals, groups or traits). It is also difficult to evaluate evidence for linear versus more curvilinear relationships between load and stereotyping from these indices.

Other research not reviewed earlier has failed to obtain unequivocal support for the predicted effects of load according to the miser hypothesis. Pratto and Bargh (1991) found an equal influence of the target sex on stereotyping in both low and high load conditions, whereas the sex-typedness of behaviour influenced global masculine–feminine rating in both non-overload and overload (manipulated by time pressure). There was also evidence here (as in the Stangor and Duan's, 1991, research) of more moderate stereotypic judgements under high load (table 4, p. 38). In Taylor et al.'s (1978) classic category confusion study there was no evidence that load, defined as the number of statements to be recalled (Expt. 2), enhanced the proportion of intra-category to inter-category recall errors. Furthermore, similar research by McGarty (1990) indicated that categorization effects were actually reduced by task complexity, and that categorization was associated with higher levels of judgemental accuracy.

Along slightly different lines, Hewstone, Hantzi and Johnston (1991) combined the 'who said what' procedure of Taylor et al. with predictions derived from the continuum model of Fiske and Neuberg (1990). In one condition a relation of interdependence was established by telling participants that they would be expected to work with the stimulus person depicted in the slides. In line with the continuum model it was predicted that interdependence would produce greater individuation and thereby reduce stereotyping as indicated by the difference between intragroup and intergroup errors. Although people made fewer errors overall in the interdependence condition, there was no significant diminution of the error-based stereotyping effect as a function of interdependence. Thus, just as load does not appear to increase stereotyping in this paradigm, a manipulation designed to increase attention did not appear to reduce it either.

One of the problems with the continuum model highlighted by this finding is that the paradigm typically involves judgements of individuals in interpersonal contexts (e.g., Pendry and Macrae, 1994). Following self-categorization theory, in such contexts it is often contextually appropriate to perceive others in individual-based or unique terms (Tajfel, 1979; Turner et al., 1987), which in turn would help explain subjects' tendency to prefer inconsistent or idiosyncratic information in a relation of interdependence (Fiske and Neuberg, 1990). In this regard it is worth noting too that the studies conducted by Pendry and Macrae (1994) actually present very little evidence of stereotyping per se, for if evaluation on consistent and inconsistent information was treated as a within-subjects variable (rather than being analysed separately) a sizeable main effect would undoubtedly reveal a preference for inconsistent (i.e., counterstereotypic) evaluation (e.g., see Pendry and Macrae, 1994, tables 1 and 2). Regardless of their state of interdependence, it is thus not true that subjects' reactions to targets were heavily contaminated by stereotype-based preconceptions and inferences.

It is possible, then, that if studies created more clearly intergroup contexts, stereotypic or group-relevant information would become more relevant and informative and would be more likely to be attended to under optimal process-ing conditions (Spears, 1993). Indeed, in the few studies in this paradigm that have explicitly manipulated the intergroup dimension, participants tend to give more attention to category-consistent information of outgroup members under conditions of interdependence (e.g., competition) thereby reversing the usual effect (Ruscher and Fiske, 1990; Ruscher, Fiske, Miki and Van Manen, 1991). Ruscher et al. (1991) explain this effect in terms of information overload, but evidence that in their study no less attention overall was devoted to the outgroup target, is inconsistent with a heuristic explanation based on limited capacity. It is, however, in line with self-categorization theory's argument that stereotype-consistent information should tend to be more relevant in intergroup contexts (Reynolds, 1994; Spears, 1993).

On the basis of evidence reviewed in this section we would thus conclude that at this stage it is hard to sustain the claim that there is a direct or simple causal relation between load and stereotyping, and that previous statements or inferences to this effect have been premature. At a theoretical level, research that apparently demonstrates stereotypic bias under load, and its energy-saving functions, does not prove either that it is biased, or that its primary function is saving energy. What is biased at an individual level, may be valid at a social level, and to the extent that it occurs, the saving of cognitive effort may be an incidental aspect of meaningful cognition. Some of the problems that have bedevilled this research include the contextual issues concerning the nature of the paradigm or stereotyping context (as detailed in section 2 above), the potential shifts of meaning and task orientation produced by load manipula-tions, together with the mixed findings from the literature itself. Apart from anything else, we know of few studies that have systematically manipulated load at more than two levels (but see Stangor and Duan, 1991), ruling out tests of more complex, non-linear relations. It is with these problems in mind that we now turn to some of our own attempts to tease out these issues.

5   Load and Social Categorization Effects in the 'Who said what' Paradigm

As we indicated above, Taylor et al. (1978) found no evidence for an effect of cognitive load on the use of social categories in their classic 'who said what' study. However, in the preceding section we also argued that meaning-based models may predict a more complex, curvilinear relationship between these vari-ables, especially within memory paradigms that do not rely on the salience of a primed stereotype. A more useful test between the meaning and miser models should, therefore, involve at least three conditions (e.g., low, moderate and high load). This was the purpose of the following studies. In these, people were presented with a series of six males and six females reading statements.

There was no stereotypic relationship (in terms of either comparative or normative fit) between the statements and the gender categories. In this paradigm then we are concerned with the use of social categories as organizing principles, rather than the application of stereotypic content to a particular target. Following the arguments developed in section 3 above, the predictions of the miser model were for an increasing linear or asymptotic relationship between load and stereotyping such that people would make more intra-category than inter-category errors as a function of load. The meaning model, on the other hand, predicts a more complex curvilinear relation such that whereas the total number of errors may increase with load, it is possible that the relative proportion of intra-category to inter-category errors will increase from low to moderate load, but should recede again under high load. This is because under moderate load it is both useful and possible to use on social categories as organizing principles when the number of individuals exceed the limits of memory.

As a first stage of research we re-analysed some data from a study that had not originally been designed to test our hypothesis (Brink, 1993; Spears, 1993). In this study six males and six females read the statements which had to be remembered 'live' in front of other 'observer' participants (they drew the statements from an envelope just prior to reading them, replacing them immediately afterwards). Both readers and observers had to remember 'who said what'. The 'readers' had previously been categorized into two separate 'debating teams' (K and L) of three females and three males each, the aim being to undermine the use of sex as an organizing principle by means of a cross-cutting category. The readers were each allocated an individual code number (e.g., K3, L6) and seated in their debating groups, with males and females mixed up within groups, so that everybody could see each other. Load was determined by two between-subjects factors, namely (a) the amount of information to be remembered (24 vs. 36 statements) and (b) whether participants were reading or simply observing. The latter was not originally intended as a load manipulation, but subsequent analysis revealed that it had this effect (by reducing the number of statements attributed correctly), with there being greater load for people who read out the statements. It seems likely that in this condition performance anxiety, and concentration on actual features of the performance distracted attention from the content of statements and reduced overall memory for statements. The combination of these two load manipulations thus generated a high, a low and two intermediate levels of load. Participants had to remember who said what by matching the reader's code number to the statements in an answer booklet and the degree of category-based stereotyping is given by comparing the number of intra-sex to the number of inter-sex category errors (after correcting for the greater chance of making an inter-category error).

The results are presented in figure 8.1. Overall people made more intra-sex than inter-sex errors indicating the categorization effect. However, the number

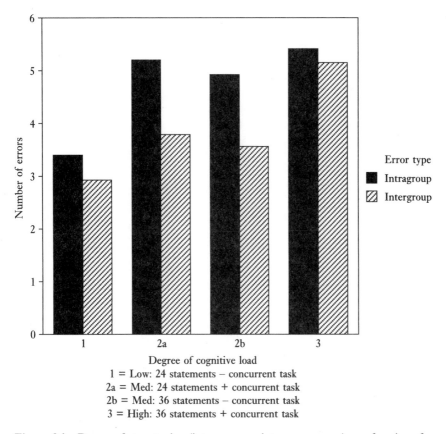

Figure 8.1 Degree of stereotyping (intragroup vs. intergroup errors) as a function of cognitive load: Study 1.

of intra-sex errors increased from the low to the moderate conditions, but did not increase further in the high load condition whereas inter-sex errors increased from low through moderate to high load, such that there was no difference between the number of intra-sex and inter-sex errors in the high load condition. Putting these two patterns together, there was most category-based stereotyping in the moderate load conditions, and least (actually none) in the low and high load conditions. In short, these data provide support for the predicted curvilinear relation between load and the use of social categories.

Although these data provided encouraging support for our hypothesis, there are some problems with this experiment. First, this represented a re-analysis of a study that was not originally designed to test this load hypothesis. In this regard, our reliance on the two different manipulations of load to generate four load levels was far from elegant and may have introduced confounds.

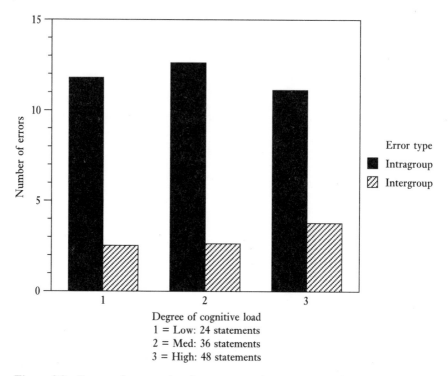

Figure 8.2   Degree of stereotyping (intragroup vs. intergroup errors) as a function of cognitive load: Study 2.

Accordingly, we conducted a new study in which we used a single method of manipulating cognitive load, namely set size, or the amount of information to be remembered (see Spears, Haslam and Jansen, 1996, for a fuller account).

For this study we made a videotape of six male and six female students reading out a fixed number of statements in random order, a more conventional procedure in this paradigm than the live performance of the previous study. Participants were allocated to one of three conditions: (1) Low load (24 statements, 2 per target person), (2) Intermediate load (36 statements, 3 per target person), and (3) High load (48 statements, 4 per target person). This time participants had to remember 'who said what' by matching the photographs of the targets to the statements in an answer booklet. Once again our measure of the extent to which people were using social categories in their information-processing was the number of intra- to inter-sex errors (correcting for chance and for set size). The results are presented in figure 8.2.

There was a strong overall categorization effect for sort of error. Participants made many more intra- than inter-sex errors and this difference is much stronger than in the previous study, reflecting the fact that no cross-cutting category was employed to undermine the use of sex as an organizing principle. Intra-sex errors increased slightly from low to moderate load conditions, but decreased again from the moderate to high load condition. However, inter-category errors increased from low through to high load conditions (a significant linear trend) and this overall pattern resulted in a significant two-way interaction between load and type of error. From the means it is clear that social categorization was most pronounced in the moderate load condition (where there was the biggest difference between intra- and inter-sex errors), and least social categorization occurred in the high load condition (where there was the smallest difference between intra- and inter-sex errors). A similar pattern was found when we restrict our analysis to errors on the first 24 items common to all three load manipulations. (We have now also recently replicated this basic pattern using time pressure rather than set size to manipulate load: Spears et al., 1996).

In conclusion, neither of these studies lends any support to the argument that stereotyping, as defined by category recall errors, simply increases with load, as would be predicted by the cognitive miser analysis. At the same time both studies provide some support for the curvilinear prediction of the meaning model. This suggests that people may be less likely to use social categories as a strategy for making sense of a complex stimulus array (i.e., in the absence of any strong manipulation of fit; cf. McGarty et al., 1993) when (a) encoding and recall are unlikely to be significantly improved by their elaboration and use (i.e., under low memory demands or low load), or (b) attention to all stimulus-relevant information is undermined because the task is too debilitating (i.e., under high memory demands, or high load). There are aspects of these studies that are still unsatisfactory insofar as it is not clear that there was a lot of social meaning in the task for perceivers to uncover. Manipulating fit is thus an important next step for this research programme and indeed recent research by Nolan (1995) showed that under conditions of high fit, increasing load by means of time pressure and concurrent task demands actually undermined category-based recall in this paradigm. He also found a positive correlation between stereotypic recall and resource availability, further supporting the present analysis. Overall, as with the original work of Taylor et al. (1978), results from these studies fail to generate support for the basic cognitive miser position in one of the classic categorization paradigms.

6 Load and Stereotyping in the Illusory Correlation Paradigm

Since its original development by Hamilton and Gifford (1976), work in the illusory correlation paradigm has been a central feature of the cognitive approach to stereotyping (see McGarty and de la Haye, this volume). Part of the reason for this is that it presents a model of stereotype formation, which asserts that stereotypes need not reflect any categorical realities whatsoever (i.e., differences between groups) but can arise purely from an information-processing bias. Illusory correlation refers to the perception of a covariation between two classes of events where none actually exists and is typically demonstrated by means of a procedure whereby participants are presented with a series of moderately positive and negative behaviours performed by members of two groups (named A and B to prevent the influence of prior expectations associated with existing groups). In the original study (Hamilton and Gifford, 1976, Expt. 1) more behaviours were attributed to people from Group A (which was described as the larger group) and there were also more positive behaviours but, importantly, the proportion of positive to negative behaviours was the same (9:4) for both groups. Here though, as in many replications, participants overestimated the proportion of distinctive (i.e., negative) behaviours performed by members of the smaller (minority) group.

The explanation for this effect favoured by Hamilton and his co-workers has been in terms of a paired distinctiveness mechanism, whereby the infrequent behaviours of the minority group (i.e., the rarest combinations) are the most distinctive, and therefore the most available in memory during retrieval, disproportionately influencing subsequent judgements (Hamilton and Gifford, 1976; Hamilton, Dugan and Trolier, 1985; Johnson and Mullen, 1994; McConnell, Sherman and Hamilton, 1994b). According to this view illusory correlations are believed to be produced by the differential processing and retrieval of distinctive events, and are explained in terms of an availability heuristic (Tversky and Kahneman, 1973). In recent research which has cast some doubt on the enhanced processing of distinctive co-occurrences at the early stages of encoding, McConnell, Sherman and Hamilton (1994b) have argued that the distinctiveness effect is due to post-presentational processing (see also McGarty and de la Haye, this volume). Thus, the effect is seen to originate in biased elaboration and memory processes, rather than to result from encoding biases occurring on-line.

It is important to note that although cognitive load is not directly manipulated (i.e., over different levels), it plays a crucial role in the original explanation of this effect. Presumably, if the set size were small enough so that all behaviours could be recalled, no illusory correlation would result; hence the availability heuristic should only come into play in situations of uncertainty or overload, where information-processing is suboptimal, and distinctiveness-based elaboration comes into play. One inference that might be drawn from this is that load is causally implicated in illusory correlation, and that increasing cognitive load should increase the memory advantage of infrequent and distinctive minority behaviours. In short, this again implies a linear or 'level-off' relationship between load and stereotyping (but see Stroessner, Hamilton and Mackie, 1992).

Such predictions can be contrasted with those derived from a more meaning-based approach that views illusory correlation effects as the product of motivated category accentuation processes founded on real fit-based categorical differences (McGarty, Haslam, Turner and Oakes, 1993; see the chapter by McGarty and de la Haye, this volume). According to this view, the greater absolute number of behaviours, and notably positive behaviours in Group A, gives a *real* basis for perceivers to presume that Group A is more positive than Group B (see also Smith, 1991). Combined with the proposed motivational tendency for perceivers to seek meaningful evaluative differences between the groups, the perception and accentuation of this difference can help to explain the effect. There is now a growing body of literature providing support for this categorical meaning-based view (e.g., Berndsen, van der Pligt, Spears, and McGarty, 1996; Haslam, McGarty and Brown, 1996; McGarty, Haslam, Turner and Oakes, 1993; see McGarty and de la Haye, this volume). Thus, if illusory correlation is based on meaningful and motivated categorical processing, similar to the reasoning outlined above for the 'who said what' memory paradigm, we might predict a curvilinear relationship between load and illusory correlation. Again under very low load, people should be able to remember the behaviours adequately so that little category-based differentiation should result. Moderate load should preclude on-line processing, and in subjects' quest to identify meaning in the stimulus array the tendency to make categorical contrasts based on evaluative fit should come to the fore. However, if the process of categorical contrast is a meaningful and effortful one based on the detection of fit, then high load should undermine this effortful categorical differentiation and weaken the illus-ory correlation effect. In this memory paradigm, as in others where perceivers are engaged in a search after meaning, there should thus be an optimal window within which stereotyping is most likely to occur.

Interestingly, we know of very few studies which manipulate load in the illusory correlation paradigm. Yet those that have again tend to argue against a simple positive relation between load and illusory correlation. For example, an unpublished study by Slugoski, Sarson and Krank (1991) manipulated load in two ways, namely by means of set size, doubling the standard number of behaviours presented (from 36 to 72), and by employing a concurrent digit memorization procedure (easy vs. hard; cf. Gilbert and Hixon, 1991). Con-trary to the paired distinctiveness explanation, no evidence was found for an increase in illusory correlations as indicated by the frequency or evaluative trait ratings in the easy, hard or double conditions over a standard baseline control condition. Moreover, on the cued recall measure the two highest load condi-tions (hard and double) actually exhibited significantly less illusory correlation than the baseline condition, again at odds with derivations from the distinct-iveness hypothesis. Another study by Stroessner et al. (1992) manipulated load by means of mood (positive, neutral, negative). It was reasoned here that for a variety of reasons, positive or negative affective states might use up cognitive

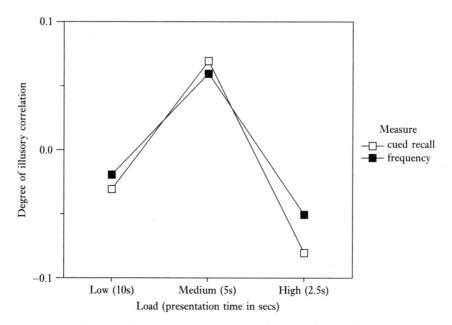

Figure 8.3   Degree of illusory correlation as a function of load for cued recall and frequency estimate indices.

resources (see e.g., Bodenhausen, 1993; Isen, 1984). In this study, significant illusory correlations were only obtained in the neutral mood condition, which would seem to argue against the heuristic distinctiveness explanation. However, Stroessner et al. argued that the distinctiveness explanation requires at least a moderate level of attention to enable recognition of differential frequencies, and thus interpreted this finding in line with the distinctiveness account. It should be noted though, that this argument runs counter to the prevailing wisdom (e.g., that of Fiske and Neuberg, 1990; Pendry and Macrae, 1994; Hamilton et al., 1994) that attention *reduces* stereotyping.

In our own study (see Spears and van Knippenberg, 1995, for a fuller account) we manipulated load in a third fashion, namely in terms of the presentation time of the behaviours: 10s, 5s, or 2.5s (cf. Bargh and Thein, 1985; Pratto and Bargh, 1991). Pretesting confirmed that participants had time to read the statements (and thus encode infrequency) in the fast exposure or high load condition. Other aspects of the experiment were similar to those reported by Hamilton and Gifford (1976, Expt. 1). The results for the phi scores calculated from the cued recall and frequency estimates are presented in figure 8.3 and a positive phi score represents the predicted illusory correlation whereby the small group (B) is more strongly associated with the infrequent (negative) behaviours. As can be seen from this figure, the only condition where there was a positive illusory correlation was in the moderate (5s) load condition, although this only reached significance (difference from zero) on the cued recall measure, where there was also a significant main effect (and curvilinear trend) of the load manipulation. On this cued recall measure the moderate load condition differed significantly from the other two conditions, but these did not differ from each other. Although evaluative differentiation between group A and B on the trait rating measure did not vary significantly with load, Group A was rated more positively in the moderate load condition (see Spears and van Knippenberg, 1995, for further details).

To summarize, our results provided some support for the categorization-based meaning hypothesis. On the basis of our earlier analysis we would expect ·stronger effects for the memory-based measure, with weaker effects on more judgement-based measures. Interestingly also, despite the load manipulation, there was no significant difference across conditions in terms of accuracy of recall. These accuracy data suggest that it is unlikely that participants were actually unable to detect differential frequencies in the high load condition as suggested by Stroessner et al. (1992). The motivated categorical differentiation argument, however, implies that cognitive and interpretative work is necessary to produce the illusory correlation, and our data are consistent with the claim that time pressure undermined this effortful meaning-seeking process.

7   Load and Stereotyping in the Digit Rehearsal Paradigm

The findings from studies discussed in the foregoing sections serve to question the load hypothesis under conditions where load manipulations were added to existing research paradigms. In a final series of studies, though, we sought to test between competing cognitive miser and meaning hypotheses in a paradigm specifically developed to test load-related issues. In our first study (see Haslam, Oakes, Rainbird and Spears, 1994, for a full account) we attempted to replicate the study by Macrae et al. (1993) which reported a positive relationship between load and stereotyping and at the same time to address the possibility that requiring participants to recall an eight-digit number may change the inferred meaning given to the experimental task. To recap, Macrae et al. found that perceivers were more likely to recall information consistent with a primed stereotype (doctor or hairdresser) when they also had to recall an eight-digit number, than when there was no concurrent task. However, as an alternative to Macrae et al.'s account, we reasoned that in a no load condition participants may ('correctly' from the experimenter's perspective) define their goal as being to attend to the interviewee, but that in the high load condition they may define their goal (at least partly) as being to remember the digit and ('incorrectly') see the interview (not the digit) as a distraction. If in the latter case subjects *choose* to attend to the interview less (believing it to be irrelevant), it is perhaps appropriate and reasonable that their judgements only reflect the fact that particular social categories are accessible (based on the experimenter's prime). By contrast, if in the no load condition they put themselves in a position to detect the actual lack of category fit in the stimulus information, the salience of those categories should logically be reduced (though not completely eliminated).

In order to investigate this possibility that the load manipulation affected subjects' 'task orientation' we, therefore, added a further *low load* condition to the design of Macrae et al. In this, participants were required to rehearse and recall a two-digit number. In this way, we were able to provide a load manipulation (low vs. high) which was not confounded with task orientation (no vs. high load). If task orientation had contributed to the original results of Macrae et al., we would expect more stereotyping under low load than no load, even though having to remember a two-digit number should have minimal impact on cognitive capacity.

Analysis of our results indicated that in contrast to the pattern of findings reported by Macrae et al. (1993), load had no clear effects upon the recall of stereotype-consistent or stereotype-inconsistent information, either on its own or in interaction with the prime. The only effect to emerge from this analysis indicated that subjects given the hairdresser prime recalled more stereotype-consistent items than those given the doctor prime. In terms of stereotypic trait ratings of the target, analysis of variance provided no evidence to suggest that the load manipulation had any straightforward effects upon the perceived stereotypicality of the target. Interestingly, though, there was an indication that the stereotypicality of target rating varied as an interactive function of load and prime ($p < .10$). Moreover, this interaction was significant ($p < .03$) if analysis was confined to a comparison of those conditions that were included in Macrae et al.'s original study (i.e., no load and high load). Specifically, stereotyping of the 'hairdresser' increased with load, but if anything stereotyping of the 'doctor' decreased. On the other hand, the interaction was non-significant when based on a comparison between low and high load conditions. The only significant difference uncovered by comparisons between conditions indicated that in the no load condition the target was rated more stereotypically when she was said to be a doctor ($M = .87$) than when she was said to be a hairdresser ($M = -.43$).

This attempted replication, therefore, provided no evidence to support the claim that high load inhibits the recall of stereotype-disconfirming information or that it enhances recall of stereotype-confirming information, or the stereotypicality of target ratings. The results, thus, question the robustness of the earlier findings and suggest that the load manipulation may have affected task orientation. Nonetheless, the reasons for the exact pattern obtained here also require elucidation. Evidence from other measures that indicated that the target used in the video, in our study, was more *fitting* with the doctor stereo-type allow an albeit post hoc explanation in terms of the interaction between accessibility and fit in line with self-categorization theory. If we assume that in the no load conditions the extent to which subjects perceived the target in social categorical terms was an interactive function of the particular category's fit and accessibility, then subjects should have been more likely to judge the target stereotypically when a category was both accessible and fitting (as in the case of the doctor prime) than when the category was accessible but ill-fitting (as in the case of the hairdresser prime). On the other hand, if in high load conditions subjects attended less to the interview, because they were dis-tracted or believed it to be irrelevant, they would not be in an ideal position to detect the extent of the target's fit with the primed category. Their judge-ments should then reflect the accessibility of the particular primed categories leading to moderate levels of prime-consistent stereotyping in each case. It is apparent that this analysis corresponds very closely to the actual pattern of stereotypic ratings that were observed across no load and high load conditions.

In a follow-up study we explored this interpretation further. In this study all participants watched the same video and all were given the eight-digit number to recall. However, half were told that it was more important that they attended to the interview than that they remembered the digit (although checks on digit recall showed that these participants still recalled digits with few errors and to the same extent as those in the other condition, suggesting they were equally 'loaded' and did not simply ignore this task). Our reasoning was that if parti-cipants believed that it was more important that they attend to the interview, this should put them in a better position to detect the relatively good fit be-tween the target and the doctor stereotype, or her poor fit with the hairdresser stereotype (depending on the stereotypic prime they received). We therefore predicted that perceived stereotypicality should vary as an interactive function of task orientation (whether the interview was most important or not) and prime. The results supported this prediction; stereotyping increased in the digit irrelevant condition, but only for the (well-fitting) doctor prime. In short, it seems that when participants were aware of the importance of the interview, they were able to devote attention to it, and the information it contained in-fluenced their stereotypic judgements accordingly (in line with the fit of the target with the stereotype), independent of cognitive load (all participants showed good recall of the eight-digit number).

These data provide further evidence of the importance of perceived task orientation in determining the allocation of attentional resources and suggest that stereotyping is not just the product of a 'biasing' prime or stereotypic label (accessibility), but is also sensitive to the *actual content* of behaviour ('fit'; see also Pratto and Bargh, 1991). In this sense our analysis confirms the point that distraction does not always enhance stereotyping. If the available information serves to enhance the fit of an accessible social category, distraction from the central task may actually undermine otherwise more stereotypic judgements, as occurred when subjects were given the doctor prime here. This outcome thus reinforces our contention that the stereotyping process (as opposed to the reporting of a stereotypic base rate when focused on another task) will typically reflect the *combination* of both the accessibility of prior beliefs and the fit of the available data. If there is any inherent tendency for accessible primed stereotypes to elicit more stereotyping than processing of actual stimulus data, this arguably reflects the fact that the accessible prime will by definition usually be stereotypic (or 'prototypical') of the social category, whereas this is not necessarily the case for the specific stimulus information or exemplar (especially if, as in the present paradigm, this has been pretested to be equally stereotypic and non-stereotypic).

8 Conclusions

Taken as a whole, perhaps the most striking feature of our first attempts at empirical research on this topic is that it provides no clear evidence to support the miser-based load hypothesis. In none of our studies in a range of classical categorization and stereotyping paradigms did the addition of load (by way of extra tasks, more information or faster exposure) lead to a straightforward increase in stereotyping, despite claims elsewhere that such a relationship is both robust and highly generalizable (e.g., Macrae et al., 1993). In this, our studies present obvious empirical problems for the miser model and the associated theoretical belief that stereotypes function primarily as energy-saving devices.

On the other hand, this research, together with reappraisal of existing findings, does lend support to the claim that stereotyping arises from a rational process of detecting and representing social meaning. This approach is the only one, so far as we are aware, that allows for the possibility of more complex curvilinear relationships between load and stereotyping in memory paradigms, as obtained in both 'who said what' and illusory correlation studies. The meaning model also provides a general framework within which to address apparent tensions within more heuristic-based approaches. Specifically, it resolves the contradiction whereby in some circumstances (e.g., in standard recall paradigms) load is predicted to facilitate the processing of consistent information, but in others it is expected to enhance the processing of infrequent or distinctive information (e.g., in the illusory correlation paradigm). In terms of the meaning-based approach, effects in both paradigms can be viewed as products of a process of meaningful categorical differentiation. Although load may facilitate this to a degree (by preventing recall of individuals or individuating information), increasing load further can also impair this process by interfering with meaningful categorization and category use.

This process, and the curvilinear relationship between load and stereotyping, is consistent with our argument that categorization and stereotyping are not always effortless and automatic especially where the relationship between the stimulus and the category (the fit) must be determined. It is still possible to see stereotyping as an energy-saving activity, but this is true only in the restricted sense that it does not actually involve energy waste by leading the perceiver to engage in contextually-irrelevant and purposeless activity. We contend though, that it is much more appropriate to see stereotyping as the manifestation of a concern to uncover social meaning and thereby enrich social perception (Oakes and Turner, 1990; Spears, 1993).

In relation to this argument, a recurring shortcoming of the heuristic approach to stereotyping is its emphasis on the accessibility of a primed stereotype and its relative neglect of the role of fit detection in the stereotyping process. Many of the experimental manipulations used in previous investigations of the relationship between load and stereotyping serve, we would argue, to enhance the former at the expense of the latter, often by affecting task orientation in a way that changes what is construed as the central goal of social judgement. Consistent with this argument, in our third set of studies we showed that load can actually reduce stereotyping when the fit present in the data would otherwise render stereotyping appropriate (see also Yzerbyt, Rocher and Coull, 1995, and Yzerbyt, Rocher and Schadron, this volume). Moreover, when people had a perception of the task more consistent with that of the experimenter, their judgements were more likely to reflect the interaction between the accessible prime and fit-relevant data.

The emphasis in the literature on accessibility at the expense of fit (especially at the level of experimental manipulations) also speaks to the distinction between stereotype activation and application. Many studies of stereotyping take stereotype activation for granted, or only start investigating the effects of load once activation has occurred (an exception being Gilbert and Hixon, 1991). To us, however, this may miss out the most interesting and important point, namely how and why categories and stereotypes get activated in the first place. We have argued that fit and its detection are central in this regard, a key difference with the continuum model being that 'fit' or 'applicability' are only introduced *after* the category and its stereotype are already made up and on stage (see note 1). From the perspective of the present approach (and in contrast to Gilbert and Hixon) the whole separation of activation and application becomes less central. This is because we do not view stereotypes or categories as generally coming off the peg 'ready-to-wear' (which, however, is not to deny that some social categories or stereotypes can be so chronically used that they are very easily activated for use). Indeed, the whole question of application (to what extent are they useful and can they be applied to the stimulus), is likely to be a *determinant* of their ongoing activation in context. In questioning the sharp distinction between activation and application it is, then, also necessary to question the dualism of accessibility and fit in the sense that accessibility is likely to be at least partly a product of meaningful fit perceived in the past. The point that social categorization is also a bottom-up process makes it clearer why it is effortful and can be disrupted by cognitive load (just as 'individuated' perception can), rather than constituting a cognitive shortcut.

In summary, the present chapter has tried to provide a more complete picture of the whole stereotyping process, and not just examine the application of a pre-given accessible belief or stereotype label under constrained conditions. We would argue that the one-sided focus on accessibility and top-down processes is a product of a perspective that assumes at the outset that stereotypes are pre-established, simplifying structures rather than psychologically meaningful reflections of ongoing (and sometimes shifting) social reality. For us the functionality of stereotyping lies in detecting this reality, not in saving cognitive energy. Following this view, we would thus argue that it is not the case, as is commonly supposed (after Allport, 1954; Fiske and Neuberg, 1990; Lippmann, 1922) that in a 'perfect' world or given a longer life free from cognitive demands, people would always treat and perceive everyone else as individuals. For to do so would involve missing out on reality and effectively preclude social activities which necessarily rely upon group-based social categorical perception (e.g., playing sport, driving, voting . . .). Harking back to Lippmann, we would argue that stereotyping *is* a response to the demands of life, but that those demands are to pursue meaning rather than efficiency and hence the response is of a very different form to that commonly envisaged by stereotyping researchers.

Notes

We would like to thank John Bargh, Ap Dijksterhuis, Naomi Ellemers, Jolanda Jetten, Penny Oakes and Diederik Stapel for their comments on an earlier draft. Responsibility for the present text is of course our own.

1   However, the concept of fit does play an important role in the continuum model of Fiske and Neuberg (1990) although it is important to note that its definition and theoretical status is somewhat different to that accorded to it by Bruner and self-categorization theorists. In the continuum model the category-based processes form the default mode of perception (premise 1) and the subsequent 'fit' between the target stimulus (i.e., a person) to the category may determine whether more attribute-based processing will result (premise 2). Greater difficulty in fitting the attributes to the category (e.g., in terms of a low proportion of category consistent information) will result in more attribute-based processing and 'individuated' impressions. According to this model, then, categorization is separate from and prior to perceived fit, but may also be undone by it. Self-categorization theory on the other hand, does not define fit in terms of the match of an individual exemplar to a category prototype. Rather categorization itself is at least partly determined by the fit

of the relevant range of stimuli to a system of classification (which may but does not have to be indicated by a category label), as determined by the principle of meta-contrast (Turner et al., 1987; see Oakes and Reynolds, this volume). In this sense, categories and their contents are not pre-given, but are often constructed in situ in response to the stumuli. Fit is thus not a property of the stimulus defined in relation to a category, but a property of the context-specific relation between stimuli (i.e., plural) and category. In other words, fit determines categorization as much as vice versa and is intrinsic to the categorization process rather than being inferred from it. To avoid confusion it is appropriate to refer to fit as used in the continuum model as 'applicability' (see Higgins, 1995).

2   See note 1.

3   See note 1.

4   It is a moot point whether the continuum model actually suggests that people use category information less as they move up the continuum. Fiske and Neuberg (1990) argue that individuating processing is mediated by the increased use of attribute information (p. 34) but that the use of category information remains high (p. 35). On the other hand, categories 'function to discourage individuation' and categorization is associated with the enhanced processing of stereotype-consistent information (pp. 15–19). However, other approaches in the cognitive miser tradition already reviewed, which view stereotypes as cognitive heuristics, imply not only that individuation will be more possible and likely under low load, but that busyness or load should increase relative reliance on the use of categories and stereotyping in order to save energy and to simplify (see e.g., Macrae et al., 1994; Pendry and Macrae, 1994). It is perhaps worth noting that the notion that there is a continuum between individuating and categorical processes, characteristic of the miser model of stereotyping, is not a view shared by other cognitive models outside the realm of stereotyping. For example, Bargh's research on automaticity proposes that both processes can operate in parallel with no necessary hydraulic trade off (Bargh, 1989, 1994).

5   This assumes of course at least a minimal degree of attention to the stimuli to allow category/stereotype activation (cf. Gilbert and Hixon, 1991); overload must not be so great that it prevents people actually 'seeing' the stimuli.

6   See note 1.

7   Although the difference between the proportion of incongruent minus congruent information recalled was significantly different for two-group (.04) and four-group (−.02) conditions, the clearer difference was between these multiple group conditions and the single group condition (.13).

9
Stereotyping in Social Context

Naomi Ellemers and
Ad van Knippenberg

1 Introduction

The adaptive nature of stereotypes

Contrary to common conceptions in psychology textbooks, where stereotypes are described as fixed and enduring beliefs about groups of people (see for instance Brehm and Kassin, 1990), in this chapter we want to focus on the *flexibility* of stereotypes.

In the *Handbook of Social Psychology*, stereotypes are defined as: 'sets of traits attributed to social groups' (Stephan, 1985, p. 600). Although this does not necessarily imply that the same traits are always associated with a specific group, stereotypes are often conceived of in precisely this way (see Worchel and Rothgerber, this volume). Consequently, within the social cognitive research tradition, a large body of research has been devoted to the question of how various cognitive processes may help people process behavioural information in such a way that they can maintain pre-existing stereotypical beliefs (see for instance, Borgida, Locksley and Brekke, 1981; Fyock and Stangor, 1994; Fiske and Taylor, 1984). Accordingly, the conceptualization of stereotypes in the literature on social stereotyping to date has in large part focused on the rigidity or cross-situational stability of social stereotypes.

In the present chapter we want to argue that stereotypes or group perceptions are essentially context-dependent. That is, we want to focus on the flexible, adaptive nature of group perceptions (cf. Oakes and Turner, 1990; Oakes, Haslam and Turner, 1994), and present recent research in order to demonstrate that perceptions of group members and attributions of group traits may vary as a function of social context.

When we take a closer look at the differences between the 'social-cognitive' approach on the one hand, and the adaptive or 'socio-motivational' approach on the other hand (see Leyens, Yzerbyt and Schadron, 1994; van Knippenberg, 1992), it seems that social-cognitive research on stereotyping has focused on developing theories that describe *the processing of information about, and mental representations of, social groups and group members.* A related feature of research in this tradition is the use of sophisticated experimental paradigms and advanced measurement techniques, usually borrowed from research in cognitive psychology (e.g., lexical decision tasks, interferences in Stroop tests, response latencies, memory data).

At a meta-theoretical level, an underlying assumption of social-cognitive research on stereotyping seems to be that stereotypes are useful as tools for individual perceivers to cope with the complexities of the social information they are confronted with (the 'cognitive miser' metaphor; cf. Fiske and Neuberg, 1990; Hamilton, 1979; Stephan, 1985). The adaptive or 'socio-motivational' approach, on the other hand, explicitly treats the social nature of stereotypes as an object of investigation (cf. Oakes et al., 1994; Tajfel, 1981b; Turner, Hogg, Oakes, Reicher and Wetherell, 1987). As a result, researchers working from this tradition not only see stereotypes primarily as socially shared images of social categories, and investigate effects of social context, but also focus on the functional nature of stereotypes in a broader sense (cf. Yzerbyt, Rocher and Schadron, this volume). This theoretical focus is essentially based on the idea that people not only passively observe social situations, but are also active participants in these situations. Consequently, strategic considerations stemming from their self-categorizations and self-stereotypes influence the way they perceive their social environment.

Although for analytical purposes we may distinguish between these two approaches in general terms, this distinction is not as clear-cut as it may seem. Researchers who have been working from a social cognitive perspective have recently turned their attention to motivational aspects of stereotyping (cf. Mackie and Hamilton, 1993), while investigations of the adaptive or motivational nature of stereotyping have increasingly started to employ methodologies that stem from the social-cognitive research tradition (cf. Oakes, et al., 1994). The present chapter illustrates this development: we will try to gain further understanding of the strategic nature of stereotyping by explicitly investigating the interplay between socio-motivational and cognitive processes involved in group perceptions.

Stereotype rigidity and stereotype flexibility

Researchers working from a social cognitive tradition feel that the information-processing approach: '. . . has shifted our conceptualization of stereotypes from examples of irrational, unusual social beliefs to examples of normal, everyday social beliefs' (Borgida, et al., 1981, p. 155; see also Stangor and Lange, 1994). This claim may seem valid when we compare information processing models to early motivational theories of social stereotypes (particularly psychodynamic theories, see also Tajfel, 1969a), that focused on personality factors and tried to explain extreme examples of social attitudes and behaviour (e.g., Adorno, Frenkel-Brunswick, Levinson and Sanford, 1950). Nevertheless, it also evokes the suggestion that motivational approaches to stereotypes are by definition not concerned with normal or everyday social processes.

Our position, however, is that it is precisely the everyday adaptive function of social stereotypes that causes group perceptions to vary across social situations. The point of departure for our argument is that people make sense of their every-day social environment by activating those social categories, or by selecting those stereotypic group traits, *that are most meaningful or informative given the specific social context*. In general terms, we want to argue that social stereotypes comprise a collection of possibly relevant group attributes, which delimit the boundaries within which the stereotype may vary. From this collection, people may then adaptively select those traits that best fit the specific situation, and/or best serve motives that are relevant given the situation. In this way, different social contexts may prescribe the rationality according to which certain aspects of social stereotypes become activated.

In a sense, the image of a group that emerges in a given situation, may be seen as reflecting a compromise between the consensual understanding of social situations and stereotypical group characteristics on the one hand, and the chronic or situationally evoked goals and motives of the perceiver on the other hand. To the extent that there exists consensus about the social situation (e.g., because one group is generally perceived as having lower status than the other), this restricts the nature of the social stereotype that may credibly be maintained. Conversely, variations in social situations (e.g., when the same group is perceived in a different comparison context), and the varying positions of parties involved in it, may affect the extent to which different aspects of the stereotype become salient as relevant group characteristics.

Sources of stereotype variation

When we systematically compare stereotypes or group perceptions held by different perceivers, and in different social contexts, we should be able to see more clearly which aspects of stereotypes are flexible, and to what extent they remain rigid. In principle, we can conceive of a great variety of social situations, in which contextual differences may be relatively subtle (e.g., a slight difference in the wording used to describe relevant stereotypic dimensions), or rather dramatic (e.g., natural groups with a long-standing history of conflict and mutual hostility versus relatively value-free artificial groups with no clear expectations of each other). For our present purpose, we will distinguish four general sources of variation that may influence the way people perceive social groups. These are:

1   *The salience of social categorizations.* The same group may be perceived differently, depending on the social categorization that is most salient in a particular social context. Variations may occur in the salience of a specific level of categorization, the salience of competing categorizations at the same level of abstraction or the salience of a specific categorization given the nature and number of available comparison groups.

2   *The degree of involvement or the perspective of the perceiver.* Secondly, variations in group perceptions may stem from differences in the extent to which the perceiver's own social identity is at stake. Therefore, we have to consider to what extent the perceiver can be regarded as a detached observer, or is an active participant in the social situation to be judged.

3   *Established differences between groups.* The existing status relations between groups impose constraints on the group perceptions of the parties involved. Thus, consensual agreement about stereotypic group characteristics may reveal the tension between motivational considerations on the part of group members on the one hand, and restrictions posed by the social context on the other hand.

4   *The relevance of stereotypic dimensions.* A final important issue concerns the number and kind of relevant dimensions on which groups or group members are judged. Specifically, perceptions of the same groups may differ, depending on whether unidimensional or multidimensional intergroup comparisons are made, and whether groups are judged in rather general or more specific terms.

In the following we will further develop the theoretical argument with respect to each of these sources of contextual variation, and examine the validity of our approach in empirical research.

2   The Salience of Social Categorizations

Individuals or members of social groups?

An important question in stereotyping research is under what conditions people are viewed as separate individuals, and in which situations they are primarily regarded as members of social groups (see Brewer, 1988; Fiske and Neuberg, 1990; Simon, this volume; Tajfel, 1978b). In the literature on stereotyping, it is generally assumed that the group membership of the people concerned as either ingroup members or outgroup members is of crucial importance. The 'outgroup homogeneity' phenomenon, for instance (cf. Linville,

Fischer and Salovey, 1989; Park and Judd, 1990), is usually taken as an indication that people tend to see members of their own group as separate individuals, while they are more likely to perceive people who belong to another group as interchangeable members of the same social category (but see Simon, 1992a, for a different perspective on this issue).

In our discussion of contextual influences on stereotyping, the first hypothesis we want to propose is that it is the *social context*, rather than people's group membership per se, that determines whether people are primarily perceived at an individual level, or categorized as members of social groups. We will empirically examine the validity of this hypothesis using a research paradigm recently developed by Ostrom and his colleagues (Ostrom, Carpenter, Sedikides and Li, 1993) as a tool to investigate whether people process and recall group relevant information separately for each individual, or combine information at a group level.

On the basis of a series of experiments investigating differential perceptions of ingroup and outgroup members with this paradigm, Ostrom et al. have advanced their 'differential processing hypothesis'. Their basic argument is that, since people are more familiar with ingroup members than with outgroup members, they have a richer mental repertoire of ingroup exemplars and, therefore, they find it less difficult to distinguish between individual ingroup members than between individual outgroup members. On the basis of this 'familiarity' argument, Ostrom et al. predict that people are more likely to process ingroup information separately for individual members, while outgroup information is processed primarily in terms of common group attributes.

Ostrom et al. presented subjects with information about four ingroup members and four outgroup members. Each target person was described in terms of four relevant attributes, for example, 'Diane was a fashion model, did the mending, read romance novels and was a member of the country club' (see Ostrom et al., 1993, p. 25). In this way, subjects received information that could be ordered either in terms of individual persons (e.g., Diane) with their own characteristic attributes, or in terms of relevant attribute categories (e.g., professions, reading preferences, etc.) for a group of people as a whole. In a free recall task, subjects were asked to reproduce the information they had received.

The central dependent variable was a measure of sequential clustering of information, the so-called 'adjusted ratio of clustering index', which theoretically varies from zero (chance clustering) to 1 (maximum use of a certain category structure). The assumption underlying this measure is that the order in which information about individuals and attributes is reproduced during recall informs us about the way this information is stored and accessed in memory. In other words, when a subject consecutively reproduces all available information about a specific person, and then continues with the next person, this is taken as an indication for a cognitive representation in terms of separate individuals.

Clustering in terms of attributes (for instance, first all different professions are mentioned, then the different reading preferences, etc.), presumably denotes a tendency to process and retrieve information for a group of people as a whole. The results of the three experiments Ostrom et al. report, indeed, indicate that subjects are more likely to cluster information about ingroup members according to person categories, while they tend to organize outgroup information in terms of attribute categories.

Although the results described by Ostrom et al. seem quite convincing, there remains some uncertainty as to whether their explanation in terms of differential familiarity with members of ingroup and outgroup is the most plausible one. An alternative explanation for the results obtained by Ostrom et al. may be derived from self-categorization theory (see Oakes et al., 1994; Turner, et al., 1987). According to self-categorization theory, all other things being equal, outgroups tend to be perceived more as a group, and as a consequence will be categorized on a higher level of abstraction than ingroups (unless specific circumstances evoke ingroup homogeneity). Although, in our view, familiarity with ingroup and outgroup may play a role as a cognitive constraint, and people may have some difficulty with the mental representation of individual outgroup 'persons' (cf. Vonk and van Knippenberg, 1995), the 'level of abstraction' hypothesis constitutes a plausible alternative.

A critical test of the latter idea would be to show that person versus attribute clustering in memory depends on the intragroup versus intergroup context of stimulus presentation, rather than the group membership of individuals. On the basis of self-categorization theory, one would predict that the way in which people are perceived – as individuals or as group members – is a function of comparative context (cf. Haslam, Oakes, Turner and McGarty, 1995). When only one group has to be considered, that is, when the stimulus persons are exclusively ingroup *or* outgroup members, perception and memory should, following the meta-contrast principle (Turner, 1987b), be primarily organized in terms of persons, although, as suggested above, this may be more difficult to achieve in the case of outgroup members. An intergroup context, however, implying simultaneous consideration of both ingroup and outgroup persons should evoke a group level of information organization in perception and memory.

In a recent experiment, Young, van Knippenberg, Ellemers and de Vries (1995) manipulated the intragroup versus intergroup context of four 'target' ingroup or outgroup members about each of whom information was given on four attributes (cf. the paradigm used by Ostrom et al., 1993). In this study, subjects were either law or psychology students, and the four target stimuli were either law or psychology students, while four other stimulus persons, constituting the stimulus context, were either from the same group as the targets (intragroup context), or from the other group (intergroup context). In a subsequent free recall task subjects had to reproduce what they remembered from the information presented. Measures of person clustering and attribute clustering revealed that in the memory of ingroup target information, person clustering was prevalent over attribute clustering in the *intragroup* context (cf. the findings described by Ostrom et al., 1993). In the *intergroup context*, however, the reverse effect was found, in the sense that memory of ingroup information revealed more attribute clustering than person clustering. These data suggest that although person clustering occurs for ingroup information in an *intragroup* context, an *intergroup* context leads people to organize ingroup information in terms of group attributes. Memory data about outgroup information showed no effect of context, in the sense that neither person nor attribute clustering was observed (as was the case in the outgroup data of Ostrom et al.'s Expt. 3, which also used university major as criterion for group membership).

These results confirm that, at least in the perceptions of the ingroup, intragroup versus intergroup context affects the way in which information about persons is processed and stored in memory. Consistent with predictions from self-categorization theory, it seems that ingroup members are more seen as individual persons in an intragroup context and more as group members in an intergroup context, and that it is this comparative context rather than differential familiarity which determines how information about group members is processed and retrieved from memory. Thus, our empirical data suggest that cognitive processing of group relevant information is adapted to the social context and the ensuing level of categorization.

Relevance and fit of alternative categorizations

Contextual variables not only affect 'individuation' versus categorization of people, they may also have a strong impact on which of two or more competing categorizations becomes salient in a particular social situation. Using a modified version of the name confusion paradigm (cf. Taylor, Fiske, Etcoff and Ruderman, 1978), van Knippenberg, van Twuyver and Pepels (1994) studied determinants of social categorizations used in the perception of a group discussion. In the name confusion paradigm, subjects are shown discussion statements of a number of persons belonging to different social groups. The main prediction addressed by van Knippenberg et al. is that contextual variables such as the discussion topic and people's positions with regard to this topic result in differential 'fit' (cf. Oakes, 1987) of different alternative categorizations, and hence determine which categorization seems most appropriate to structure the information.

Van Knippenberg et al. used male and female students and teachers as stimulus persons. Gender and academic status of the stimulus persons were uncorrelated (i.e., they constituted crossed categorizations; cf. Vanbeselaere, 1991). After the presentation of the statements made by the stimulus persons (discussion participants), subjects were again presented with each statement and asked to indicate which of the stimulus persons had made that statement. The number and type of errors made in allocating statements to stimulus persons constituted the dependent variable. For each categorization criterion the numbers of within-category and between-category errors were calculated. A subject could for instance erroneously allocate a statement of a female participant to another female participant (within-gender error) or to one of the male participants (between-gender error). The relative prevalence of within-category over between-category errors in the memory of 'who said what', is taken as an indication of the use of that categorization in the perception and storage in memory of the discussion information.

One of the manipulations in the van Knippenberg et al. (1994) experiment was simply to vary the relevance of the topic of the group discussion for the two social categorizations involved: it was either about 'positive discrimination favouring women' (gender relevant), concerned 'consequences of course evaluations' (relevant to academic status) or addressed 'measures against social welfare fraud' (neutral). First, it was found that, irrespective of which categorization was used, subjects made more within-category than between-category errors, indicating that social categorizations were used to process the discussion information. Second, across discussion topics, the male–female categorization was much stronger than the student–teacher categorization, indicating that the former categorization, being more embedded in our culture, is more chronically used than the latter (see Messick and Mackie, 1989). More importantly, the 'contextual' manipulation of the discussion topic had a strong effect on the categorization used. Given the gender relevant topic, the greatest proportion of within- relative to between-gender errors was observed, while the prevalence of within- rather than between-academic status errors was relatively small. In the academic status relevant topic condition, however, the results indicated significantly more use of the categorization according to academic status than the gender categorization (although the latter categorization still played a substantial role). The results in the neutral condition were in between. On the whole, these results confirm the general notion that, in addition to the chronic prevalence of the gender categorization, there is an adaptive flexibility in the use of social categorizations as a function of contextual relevance.

In a similar vein, van Knippenberg et al. (1994) showed that the 'fit' between positions taken in the discussion (namely, pro versus con) and the gender and academic categorizations (male–female fit, student–teacher fit, no fit) affected strength of categorization as well. When the gender of participants in the discussion coincided systematically with a particular stance (male–female fit), strong gender categorizations emerged in the memory data. Conversely, student–teacher fit evoked a stronger academic status categorization, while in the no fit condition the (more chronically salient) gender categorization was stronger than the academic status categorization.

The above described effects of topical relevance and fit on the use of social categorizations demonstrate the hypothesized adaptive function of social categorizations. It seems reasonable that perceivers pay attention to what students and teachers have to say when the discussion is about 'consequences of course evaluations'. Similarly, the gender categorization seems more useful when trying to capture what is going on when all females turn out to be in favour of 'more severe measures against social welfare fraud', while all males are against (or vice versa). These phenomena support our general argument that social categorizations serve to make sense of social situations, and, therefore, as social situations vary, categorizations must be flexible.

While the above described experiments show how people spontaneously adapt their level of categorization or shift from one categorization to the other when this seems to make more sense, the use of specific social categorizations can also be elicited by active 'priming'. Although Stangor, Lynch, Duan and Glass (1992) failed to establish such priming effects in a name confusion experiment, it seems likely that the categorizations they used (gender and race) are chronically so strong that priming cannot be expected to further enhance these categorization effects. Therefore, van Twuyver and van Knippenberg (1995), in their attempt to investigate effects of priming on social categorizations, took care to select categorizations that would be equally strong and, normally, not very salient (in this case, the stimulus person's university town and major subject).

Subjects in this experiment were presented with a series of statements, allegedly from a discussion between psychology students and law students from the University of Amsterdam and the University of Nijmegen. Thus, the discussion participants could be classified in terms of two cross-cutting categorizations. During a previous task, which was presented as a different experiment, subjects had either been asked to focus on differences between psychology students and law students (major prime), or between students from Amsterdam and Nijmegen (city prime). As expected, the analysis of within-and between-category errors when ascribing statements to discussion participants at a later stage, revealed significant priming effects; the 'major prime' enhanced the psychology–law categorization of the discussion information, while the 'city prime' enhanced the Amsterdam–Nijmegen categorization. Although they were significant, the observed priming effects were rather weak.

The results of a recent experiment carried out by Blanz and colleagues (Blanz, 1995) suggest that the priming of social categorizations would be much more effective if there is at least some degree of fit in the discussion stimulus material between the primed categorization and the positions taken in the discussion. This seems to indicate that the salience of social categorizations is essentially jointly determined by the accessibility of the categorization in question (which may be enhanced through priming) and the fit between content and categorization (see Oakes, 1987).

Differential ranges of relevant outgroups

In their investigation, van Twuyver and van Knippenberg (1995) actively enhanced the salience of a specific categorization by inviting subjects, prior to the discussion, to elaborate on differences between members of specific social categories, in order to induce their use of these categories. A more subtle or indirect way to study differential salience of group memberships is by confronting subjects with a different range of relevant comparison groups, and see whether this 'spontaneously' alters their perception of the same target group.

Doise, Deschamps and Meyers (1978) have used such an indirect manipulation of relevant social context, which confirmed that perceptions of the same group may vary, depending on the relevant comparison groups. In their study, subjects either rated German-speaking, French-speaking and Italian-speaking Swiss, or they were asked to rate two of these groups (for instance German- and French-speaking Swiss) together with a group who spoke the third language, but had a different nationality (e.g., Italian-speaking Italians). The results of this study show that, in the presence of a group of foreigners, different groups of Swiss are perceived as more similar than when three groups of Swiss are rated. In the latter case, that is, when all three groups can be subsumed under the more general category of 'Swiss citizens', people seem to focus on differences between these three groups.

Similar results were reported by Wilder and Thompson (1988), who used a 'mock jury' paradigm, in which verdicts from different groups of subjects had to be compared. After being told that another group had reached a judgement that was moderately similar to the verdict of their own group, people tended to accentuate the contrast between these two groups. When, however, a third group was introduced, which had reached a more extreme verdict, the more similar group was assimilated with the subjects' own group.

When the comparison context is broadened by the introduction of a more *similar* outgroup, however, a reverse effect may occur. This was demonstrated in a study by Spears and Manstead (1989; Expt. 2). Students of the University of Manchester were either asked to rate their own group and a moderately dissimilar outgroup, namely Manchester polytechnic students, or were presented with a comparison context that also incorporated a more similar outgroup, namely another group of university students (either from Oxford or from Exeter). The main results of this study indicate that the relevant categorization was shifted by the introduction of a more similar outgroup. Specifically, the presence of another group of university students made the distinction between university students on the one hand, and polytechnic students on the other hand more salient, causing Manchester University students to differentiate the ingroup from the group of Manchester Polytechnic students, while assimilating the ingroup with the other groups of university students. Thus, at a more general level, it appears that people may either assimilate or differentiate the same groups, depending on the categorization that seems most useful given the specific comparison context (see also van Knippenberg and Ellemers, 1990).

This general idea was addressed in a series of studies by Haslam and Turner (1992), which investigated whether these assimilation and contrast principles (which may be predicted from the meta-contrast ratio), in addition to influencing the perceived similarity of different groups, may also affect stereotype *content*. Indeed, the results of three experiments demonstrated that people attribute different characteristics to the same group, depending on their frame of reference in terms of the range of attitudinal positions of different group members, and the relative similarity of the target and the perceiver.

Doosje, Spears, Haslam, Koomen and Oakes (1995) further pursued the question of how the presence of similar or different outgroups affected subjects' stereotypic judgements. A novel aspect of their approach is that they not only looked at shifts in the *content* of stereotypic traits, but also in the *perceived homogeneity* of the groups under consideration. In their first study, psychology students at the University of Amsterdam had to rate the ingroup (psychology students) only, a similar outgroup (students of sociology) only, psychology *and* sociology students or both these groups together with a dissimilar outgroup (consisting either of business students or of physics students). Pretesting had confirmed that psychology and sociology students were considered more similar to each other than to the other groups. The main dependent variable consisted of group ratings in terms of central tendency and variability on a number of stereotype-relevant dimensions. These ratings reveal that subjects perceive their own group differently, depending on the social context. More specifically, psychology students were seen as less intelligent when physics students also had to be judged, while on a number of dimensions differences between psychology and sociology students were neglected under these circumstances. Moreover, when other groups were present in the comparison context, the ingroup was seen as more homogeneous than when it was the only group that had to be rated, underlining the importance of distinguishing intragroup from intergroup contexts, that was previously discussed. A second study carried out by Doosje et al., replicated these findings with psychology students at the Australian National University either comparing the ingroup with drama students only, with physics students only or with drama *and* physics students. Additionally, this study revealed differential evaluations of the same comparative dimensions, depending on the social context.

The findings reviewed above support our general argument by demonstrating that the (inter)group comparison context affects the perceptions and judgement of the ingroup as well as perceived differences between groups. First, as in the study by Young et al. (1995) described earlier, the perception of the ingroup is more heterogeneous in an intragroup context than in an intergroup context. Second, the estimated central tendency of ingroup characteristics (in accordance with general predictions from stimulus context theories) is a function of the relative position of the ingroup *vis-à-vis* salient comparison groups. Third, when the ingroup is compared with a relatively similar outgroup, people tend to focus on the way the ingroup differs from this comparison group. However, the mere presence of a more dissimilar outgroup enhances the perceived resemblance between the ingroup and the more similar outgroup. In sum, in line with predictions from self-categorization theory, perceptions of central tendency and homogeneity of ingroup, as well as perceptions of intergroup similarity, vary as a function of the intergroup comparative context.

3 Passive observers versus active agents

An 'outside' or 'inside' perspective

An important principle underlying the argument in this chapter, is that group perceptions are by definition subjective images of social reality. Hence, the *perspective* from which the group is perceived, that is, from the 'outside' or from the 'inside' of the group, should also influence the resulting group image. Thus, in our view, it is important to take into account that in many social situations people do not perceive groups as detached observers. Instead, they are often active participants in the situations that are being judged, and as such, may have a vested interest in holding favourable perceptions of groups they are personally involved in. Therefore, they should be more inclined to depict their own group positively. As a consequence, certain patterns in group perception which are generally seen as robust phenomena, might turn out to be appreciably different when the perceiver's own social identity is at stake.

Illusory correlation and ingroup favouritism

An illustration can be found in the literature on stereotype formation, and specifically the 'illusory correlation' phenomenon. The term illusory correlation (see Hamilton and Gifford, 1976; Hamilton and Trolier, 1986) is used to indicate that people may associate infrequent traits or behaviours with infrequently occurring group memberships, even though in reality these traits or behaviours are not correlated with group membership. Further investigations seemed to indicate that the overassociation of minority group membership with infrequently occurring behaviours is a general and robust phenomenon (see Hamilton and Sherman, 1989; Mullen and Johnson, 1990, for overviews). Moreover, the perception of illusory correlations is seen as an important cognitive mechanism in stereotype formation, which is attributed to the relative accessibility in memory of infrequent and hence distinctive information (see Hamilton, Dugan and Trolier, 1985).

Recently, however, there has been some dispute about the validity of this 'paired distinctiveness' explanation (see also McGarty and de la Haye, this volume). More important from our present point of view, is that recent research has revealed that the perspective from which people judge the situation plays a crucial role, and that people may primarily display the illusory correlation when processing information about groups they are not personally involved with.

In two studies, Spears and his colleagues (Spears, van der Pligt and Eiser, 1985, 1986) demonstrated how self-relevance and personal involvement may affect the illusory correlation effect. Participants in these studies were presented with attitudes to nuclear power held by people from two towns, such that more statements came from one town (A) than from the other (B). Furthermore, both studies also assessed participants' own attitudes towards nuclear power. An illusory correlation effect would in this situation entail overestimating the occurrence of the most distinctive opinion, that is, the opinion held in the least frequently occurring town. However, it turned out that participants in the study also systematically overestimated the frequency of the stance that corresponded to their *own attitude* in the disctinctive town, and this increased as a function of attitude involvement. This effect was accounted for by the salience of self-relevant positions, which was greater for people with stronger views. Related findings were reported by Berndsen, Spears and van der Pligt (1996), who observed that perceptions of illusory correlation were influenced by people's vested interests regarding the issue at hand. Thus, it appears that, in addition to distinctiveness, other factors such as self-relevance may influence the way people process and recall information about social groups.

In a series of experiments, Maass and Schaller (1991) have presented further evidence suggesting that the illusory correlation phenomenon disappears when the perceiver is a member of one of the groups under consideration. In their first experiment (Schaller and Maass, 1989, Expt. 1), they used the 'standard' illusory correlation paradigm (see Hamilton and Gifford, 1976) and presented participants with a set of desirable and undesirable behaviours, which were ascribed to members of two different groups. As in previous illusory correlation research, Schaller and Maass systematically varied the relative infrequency of either desirable or undesirable behaviours, as well as the relative size of the two groups, while keeping the *proportion* of desirable and undesirable behaviours equal for each group. Their main adaptation of this standard paradigm, consisted of an instruction that led some of the participants to believe that they themselves were members of one of the groups under consideration. The three dependent variables Schaller and Maass used consisted of a cued recall measure (asking participants to indicate the correct group membership for each behaviour they had been shown), the estimated frequency of desirable and undesirable behaviours within each group and evaluative ratings of the two groups.

For participants who had no vested interest in either group, the usual illusory correlation effects were obtained, namely an overassociation of infrequently occurring behaviours with minority group membership, which, furthermore, resulted in a more positive impression of the group that was thought to display more positive behaviour. However, participants who considered themselves a member of one of the groups, did not systematically associate desirable or undesirable behaviours with either group, but allocated the behaviours more or less accurately to the stimulus groups. Nevertheless, these participants showed ingroup biases in estimated frequencies of behaviours and also held a more favourable impression of their own group than of the other group.

As a possible explanation for this differential response of group members and non-members, Schaller and Maass suggest that they may process social information differently. More specifically, detached observers might be inclined to make *memory-based* judgements, which are more likely to be biased and reflect their memory of the most distinctive information they recall about the group. Group members, however, may tend to form *on-line* impressions of the groups, which are continuously adapted on the basis of incoming information, and are hence more accurate. In a second study, Schaller and Maass (1989, Expt. 2) investigated the validity of this argument by explicitly asking group members as well as non-members to form an impression of the two groups as they received the behavioural information; the further design and procedure of this study by and large resembled their first experiment described above, although this time undesirable behaviours were always less frequently presented than desirable behaviours.

The main results of this second study show that, in spite of the information-processing instruction, group members showed more accurate recall of the presented information than non-members. At the same time, however, group members consistently held a more favourable impression of their own group than the other group, that is, regardless of whether they were minority or majority group members. The aim of a third experiment was to rule out the alternative explanation for this finding that group members simply ascribed desirable behaviours to the ingroup because they occurred most frequently in all conditions of the second experiment. In this third study (Schaller, 1991), participants always received more information about undesirable than desirable behaviours. Again, although non-members showed the pattern predicted by the 'illusory correlation' hypothesis, that is, they overassociated infrequently presented behaviours with the minority group, group members consistently held more favourable perceptions of their own group.

In their research, Maass and Schaller employed experimentally created groups, and systematically varied the information about group members that was presented. It is not self-evident, however, that similar processes will occur with real-life groups, or in more natural situations. Nevertheless, on the basis of a further series of experiments employing natural groups, Schaller (1992) suggests that group members tend to process group relevant information selectively, in order to derive a more positive image of their own group than other groups. Moreover, the results of a recent study of D. van Knippenberg, A. van Knippenberg and Dijksterhuis (1994) provide additional support for the idea that members of natural groups will show ingroup favouring tendencies, at least under appropriate conditions. In their study, students of two disciplines (law students and management students) served as subjects, who were led to believe that they either constituted a minority or formed a majority group. Behavioural information about ingroup and outgroup members was presented, in which either desirable or undesirable behaviour occurred infrequently. Furthermore, there were two processing goal conditions, that is, an impression condition (induced with similar instructions as used by Schaller and Maass 1989, Expt. 2) and a 'memory' condition (which explicitly emphasized that subjects only had to memorize the behavioural information, cf. Pryor, 1986).

It was found that proportionally more positive behaviours were allocated to the ingroup than to the outgroup, but only when subjects were induced to memorize the information. Furthermore, subjects in this condition gave higher frequency estimates of positive behaviour of the ingroup than of the outgroup, and evaluated the ingroup more positively than the outgroup, while such ingroup favouring biases were not observed in the 'impression' condition. Unexpectedly, independently of these effects, there was an overall paired distinctiveness effect (regardless of processing goal), that is, subjects generally overassociated the minority group with infrequent behaviours. In other words, contrary to the results obtained by Schaller and Maass (1989) a paired distinctiveness illusory correlation was observed which, in the 'memory' condition, was *amplified* when the direction of the illusory correlation favoured the ingroup (namely, by majority group members when undesirable behaviours were infrequent and by the minority group members when desirable behaviours occurred infrequently) and *mitigated* when the direction of the illusory correlation favoured the outgroup (namely, in the two complementary conditions). Thus, although the classic illusory correlation effect reappeared in this study, ingroup favouritism occurred in the condition facilitating the occurrence of memory biases.

In sum, empirical data from several studies indicate that the vested interests that group members have in holding a favourable image of their own group, lead them to differentiate their own group positively from relevant outgroups, at least when the circumstances foster the occurrence of such biases.

Generalization of self-relevant information

Additional indications that people do not 'objectively' process information about groups when their own social identity is at stake, may be found in a recent investigation of Doosje, Spears and Koomen (1995). In their investigation they divided participants into groups of 'inductive' and 'deductive' thinkers, and addressed the question to what extent information about a *sample* of group members, would be generalized to the whole *population* of 'inductive' or 'deductive' thinkers. The sample information either contained positive ingroup behaviours and negative outgroup behaviours, or paired negative behavioural episodes with ingroup members and gave positive descriptions of outgroup members. Additionally, the reliability of the sample information was manipulated by means of sample variability (Expt. 1) and sample size (Expt. 2). The main dependent measures asked participants to indicate their general impression of the two groups of thinkers, as well as the perceived variability within each group.

Overall, the results of both experiments confirm that group members tend to selectively generalize sample information so that they can derive a positive image of their own group. When the presented information described ingroup members favourably but was unfavourable for the outgroup, group members' evaluations always favoured the ingroup, regardless of the reliability of the sample. However, when the sample information described the ingroup less positively than the outgroup, the behavioural information was only reflected in the general group image when the sample had been homogeneous or large. In the conditions where the sample information seemed less reliable, group members held equally favourable perceptions of both groups, which suggests that they used the hetereogeneity or the small size of the relevant sample as an 'excuse' not to generalize the unfavourable information they received about ingroup members to the group as a whole. This interpretation is supported by the perceived group variability measure, which indicates that group members emphasize intragroup differences when the information is unfavourable for the ingroup *and* this information is based on small or heterogeneous behavioural samples.

The results of this study further support the argument that people may draw different inferences from behavioural information, depending on the extent to which their own identity is at stake. More specifically, they seem to look for ambiguities in the available information that may help them neutralize or even negate information that depicts the group to which they belong unfavourably. Again, this points at the adaptive nature of group perceptions, and motivational processes that may affect the stereotyping process.

In a more general sense, we may not only distinguish between ingroups and outgroups. Even when comparing people who are all members of a certain group, they may differ in the extent to which they feel their self-image is implicated in this social group, and this is assumed to be reflected in the strength of their identification with that group. We want to take the above argument one step further, and suggest that as people's group identification becomes stronger, their social identity becomes more intertwined with their personal identity, causing group traits to be more consequential for their personal self-image. Accordingly, the motivation to hold a positive group image should become more pressing, the stronger people identify with the group under consideration.

In the context of social identity theory, various researchers have taken the above argument as an indication that there should be a direct relation between the extent to which group members identify with their group, and the positivity of the image they hold of this group. Although the degree of ingroup identification has not systematically been included as an explicit measure in research investigating group perceptions, a recent overview of studies which did incorporate both types of measures (Hinkle and Brown, 1990) failed to establish a straightforward relation between group identification and the occurrence of positive ingroup ratings. In the literature, several explanations have been advanced which may account for the complex nature of the relation between group identification and group perceptions. To some extent, the lack of a simple relation may be attributed to restrictions posed by the social context, or more specifically, by existing differences between groups (see also Doosje and Ellemers, this volume), as well as the number and nature of relevant dimensions on which groups are rated (cf. Ellemers, van Rijswijk, Roefs and Simons, in press). Both these issues will be discussed more extensively in the remaining sections of this chapter.

4   Established Differences between Groups

Group status and group identification

So far, we have discussed the ways in which contextual variations may influence the way a group stereotype takes shape. In this section we want to take a somewhat different perspective and look at the ways in which consensually agreed upon differences between groups may *restrict* the flexibility of group perceptions. As we have argued previously, people are generally motivated to hold favourable perceptions of the groups to which they belong. As a result, they will try to depict stereotypical group characteristics positively, and/or 'claim' positive traits as typical for their own group. However, these strategic perceptions are delimited by consensual agreement about which traits are characteristic for which group, as well as a shared definition of what 'positive' and 'negative' group traits are. In a more general sense, we may distinguish between groups that are generally perceived positively, high-status groups, and groups with a more negative overall image, low-status groups. In this section, we will take a closer look at lower status groups. Specifically, the main focus will be on the tension between the motivation to hold a favourable group image on the one hand, and the generally held negative perception of lower status groups on the other hand.

As briefly indicated above, to the extent that people derive their self-conceptions from social groups to which they belong, they should be motivated to hold favourable perceptions of these groups. Moreover, it would seem that the necessity to establish a positive group image is most pressing for members of groups that are generally held in low regard, namely low status groups. Although members of lower status groups should consequently be most motivated to hold perceptions that are favourable for their own group, research to date has failed to reveal consistent support for the hypothesis that ingroup favouring biases are stronger the less favourable the current status of the group. On the contrary, several studies report greater ingroup favouritism by members of dominant or superior groups than by members of lower status groups (e.g., Sachdev and Bourhis, 1985, 1987, 1991).

One possible explanation for this lack of an inverse relation between status and the display of ingroup favouring biases may be found in the observation that members of lower status groups can respond to this identity threat by lowering their ingroup identification (cf. Ellemers, 1993). Thus, instead of upgrading their group's social standing, members of lower status groups may display little group identification, indicating their pursuit of individualistic strategies as a means of coping with the inferior position of their group, for instance, by opting for membership in another group (cf. Ellemers, van Knippenberg, de Vries and Wilke, 1988). Nevertheless, it is important to note that these effects were obtained with people who had no long-term commitment to their group (namely, with randomly created laboratory groups), and the tendency to show an individual level response to a group threat was less pronounced when group members had some common characteristic or shared a common fate (Ellemers, Doosje, van Knippenberg and Wilke, 1992; Ellemers, Wilke and van Knippenberg, 1993). Indeed, recent research reveals that only uninvolved group members easily set themselves apart from the group, while strongly committed group members are more likely to show a group-level response in situations that threaten their group's positive distinctiveness (see Doosje and Ellemers, this volume, for an overview).

The importance of distinctiveness

Thus, although we may conclude on the one hand that low group status does not necessarily result in the display of ingroup favouring biases, it seems on the other hand that decreased ingroup identification, and a resulting preference for individual-level strategies, cannot be regarded as a standard response to low group status either. Recent research (see Mlicki and Ellemers, 1996) indicates that people may even accentuate the low status position of their group in order to protect their common identity as a distinct group. Mlicki and Ellemers carried out a series of four studies with Polish and Dutch psychology students as natural groups. The first study revealed that, when asked to generate distinctive national traits, Polish students generated substantially more negative than positive traits, while these were mentioned in equal proportions by Dutch students. Moreover, Polish students mentioned five negatively evaluated traits as most characteristic for their nation (boozy, quarrelsome, disorderly, vulgar and intolerant), whereas the five most typical national traits generated by the Dutch students were rated positively (sober, frugal, achievement-oriented, well-educated and serious).

In their second study, Mlicki and Ellemers investigated how these national self-stereotypes were related to feelings of national identity of Polish and Dutch students. The main results of this study revealed much stronger national identification among Polish students, as well as an accentuation of the distinctiveness of their (positive *and* negative) national traits. Thus, it seemed that the Polish students at the same time hold a negative self-stereotype, *and* identify strongly with the Poles as a distinct national group.

In a third study, Mlicki and Ellemers tested an alternative explanation for the occurrence of strong national identification displayed by Polish students, by investigating whether Polish students attenuated the negative valence of their distinctive national traits, and/or would 'claim' non-typical positive attributes as characteristic for their own national group, as alternative strategies to establish a positive national identity. The results of this study reveal that Polish students seemed to decline these opportunities to establish a favourable national image. Contrary to what was expected, Polish students accentuated their national distinctiveness as well as the negative valence of 'typical' Polish traits relative to the perceptions held by Dutch students. Furthermore, instead of Polish students claiming non-typical traits as characteristic for their own national group, Polish and Dutch students alike rated these positive traits as more typical for the Dutch than for Poles. Moreover, while maintaining their negative national self-stereotype, the Polish students again displayed much stronger national identification than the Dutch students.

Mlicki and Ellemers carried out a fourth study, to check whether Polish students attributed their (negative) national traits to external circumstances (e.g., as stemming from political and economical historical developments). It was hypothesized that such a group-serving attribution (cf. Hewstone, 1990) would make it easier to combine a negative national self-stereotype with strong feelings of national identity. However, the results of this fourth study again indicate that Polish students did not display group-protective attributional patterns (cf. Taylor and Doria, 1981; Taylor, Doria and Tyler, 1983). Consistent with the findings of the first three studies, the main results of this study revealed that Polish students considered traits they evaluate negatively as typical for their national group, while Dutch students selected positively evaluated traits to describe their own national self-stereotype. Nevertheless, compared to the Dutch students, Polish students did not display a tendency to attribute these (negative) national traits to external circumstances. Furthermore, as was the case in the previous studies, the Polish students in this study reported much stronger feelings of national identity than the Dutch students.

Taken together, the results of these four studies indicate that Polish students hold a more negative national self-stereotype than Dutch students, but simultaneously show relatively strong national identification. For these Polish students, establishing a *distinctive* national identity is of paramount importance, which is evident from their strong sense of national identity. At the same time, this concern apparently causes them to prefer a *negative* self-stereotype to a more favourable but less distinctive national identity.

Self-categorization and self-esteem components of social identity

The studies summarized above further support our argument that ingroup identification and the favourability of ingroup perceptions may be relatively independent of each other. However, as indicated previously, the general prediction usually derived from social identity theory is that negative intergroup comparisons may threaten group members' self-esteem, as a result of which they tend to identify less with their (lower status) group (see Hinkle and Brown, 1990; Hogg and Abrams, 1990). Thus, these processes are generally expected to display a relatively straightforward covariation (but see Long and Spears, this volume). As a result, both in theoretical definitions and in frequently used operationalizations, social identity measures usually incorporate both satisfaction with group membership or social self-esteem (cf. Luhtanen and Crocker, 1991) and self-categorization as a group member (see Ellemers and Mlicki, 1990; Hinkle, Taylor, Fox-Cardamone and Crook, 1989). This makes it more difficult to distinguish between these two components, and to investigate the possibility that they are affected differentially by characteristics of the group or the social context.

Our attempt to disentangle *strength* of group identification from the *value connotation* of the resulting social identity was the rationale for an experiment (Ellemers, Kortekaas and Ouwerkerk, 1995) which tried to distinguish between self-categorization, commitment to the group and social self-esteem, as related but distinct responses to group membership. Thus, the first aim of this study was to see whether such a distinction can not only be made at a conceptual level, but can also be demonstrated empirically. Furthermore, it is important to determine whether these different aspects of people's social identity are differentially affected by characteristics of the group to which they belong. Therefore, the second aim of this investigation was to assess how the group formation criterion (self-selected vs. assigned group membership), as well as the relative size (minority vs. majority) and status (high vs. low) of artificially created groups influence these three aspects of social identity.

The main results of this study confirm that self-categorization, commitment to the group and social self-esteem can be distinguished as separate aspects of social identity; the questions relevant to these concepts emerge as three orthogonal factors in a principal components analysis. The significance of this distinction was, furthermore, supported by the differential effects the independent variables had on these three components. It turned out that group members' self-categorizations were only affected by the relative *size* of the group: minority group members showed stronger self-categorization as a group member than majority group members (cf. Simon and Hamilton, 1994). Social self-esteem, however, was only influenced by group *status*: members of high status groups reported a more positive social self-esteem than members of low status groups. Finally, commitment to the group depended on group status and on the group formation criterion. Commitment was relatively high when the group had high status as compared to the low-status condition, and when group membership was self-selected rather than assigned. In sum, the results of this study support our previous argument that identification or self-categorization as a group member may occur relatively independently from social self-esteem derived from relative group status.

Coping with social restrictions

The research presented above indicates that group members may identify strongly with a group, and at the same time acknowledge this group's inferiority in terms of comparative status. This does not necessarily imply that members of lower status groups abandon their desire for positive identity altogether (see also Ellemers, van Knippenberg and Wilke, 1990). However, the fulfillment of their identity needs will have to take place within the restrictions that are imposed by the social environment. In other words, we argue that members of lower status groups are motivated to display ingroup favouring biases on the one hand, but on the other hand feel restricted in displaying claims of ingroup superiority because of their current lower status.

Van Dyck, Ellemers and Hinkle (1995) explicitly investigated the nature of these restrictions in a study using university sports clubs as natural groups. The main purpose of this investigation was to find out whether members of lower status groups would also hold the *private* conviction that their group is inferior, or only refrain from displaying ingroup favouring biases because of social restrictions in *public* situations. Thus, we argued that the private expression of ingroup favouring biases would inform us about peoples' *motivation* to regard their own group favourably, while public displays of ingroup favouritism are subject to perceived social *restrictions*.

In this study, participants of different sports clubs were first divided into groups with high or low self-perceived group status, by means of a median split on items from the public collective self-esteem scale developed by Luhtanen and Crocker (1992). Subsequently, all participants performed a 'spot-the-ball' task that supposedly measured their insight into sports situations. As a dependent measure, participants were given the opportunity to display ingroup favouring biases when rating the performance of a member of their own sports club and a member of a relevant other sports club. The manipulation consisted of instructions either indicating that these ratings would remain strictly anonymous, *or* that participants would later have to report their ratings publicly in front of the other participants in the study.

The results of this study underscore the role of both motivations and social restrictions in the display of ingroup favouritism. Participants who perceived their group's status positively, apparently felt no need to accentuate their group's superiority in the present situation, hence they did not display evidence of ingroup favouritism in either condition. The responses of participants who considered themselves members of a lower status group, however, were affected by the experimental manipulation. As predicted, these group members rated their *own group* more favourably than the other group when they could do so *anonymously*, while they tended to favour the *outgroup* in the *public* condition. Thus, the results of this study indicate that, although members of low status groups may be motivated to establish a positive social identity, and may privately believe in their group's superiority, their expression of this conviction is restricted by the social reality of their low-status position.

It is important to note that it is not so much the distinction between public and private responses per se that is relevant in this discussion (cf. Reicher, Spears and Postmes, 1995). However, in this particular case, subjects in the 'public' condition would have to defend their ratings of the two groups in front of ingroup as well as outgroup members. Members of the lower status group presumably refrained from publicly displaying ingroup favouritism, out of concern that members of the other group would not accept their judgements. In a more general sense, it is argued that the specific norms held by a particular group shape people's perceptions and behaviours (cf. Turner, 1991; see also Haslam, this volume). Thus, a different situation may occur when group members adapt their responses to expectations held by their own group. In fact, a recent investigation by Noel, Wann and Branscombe (1995) suggests that the confrontation with an *ingroup* audience may also *enhance* the expression of ingroup favouritism.

In two studies, Noel et al. investigated the hypothesis that members of artificially created, as well as natural groups, would adapt their responses to *ingroup* norms, and as a result would be more inclined to derogate relevant outgroups in a public situation (i.e., in front of an ingroup audience) than in private. Furthermore, in each study they distinguished between different forms of group membership. In Experiment 1, people who were led to believe they just met the criteria for group assignment (peripheral members) were compared with 'near perfect examples' (core members) of the personality type that was allegedly used to categorize participants. In experiment 2, a distinction was made between fraternity and sorority pledges (marginal members) and active members of these organizations (core members). The results of both studies revealed that peripheral (or marginal) group members showed more outgroup derogation when this was displayed in front of other ingroup members than they did privately. Thus, when confronted with an ingroup audience, people whose standing as group members was insecure, publicly displayed their solidarity with the group. At a more general level, then, these empirical findings support our position that group ratings may vary depending on people's identity concerns on the one hand, and on the relevant social context on the other hand.

5   Relevance of Stereotypic Dimensions

The use of indirect strategies

The tension between the restrictions of low ingroup status on the one hand, and the motivation to establish a positive identity on the other hand, may be resolved in different ways. Group members may acknowledge their group's inferiority in certain respects, while claiming ingroup superiority on alternative dimensions ('social creativity'; cf. Lemaine, 1974; van Knippenberg, 1984). In a more general sense, we may argue that the ingroup's relative standing is reflected in direct measures of social status, nevertheless, group members may try to establish a positive identity in more indirect ways (cf. Brown, Collins and Schmidt, 1988).

A similar argument has been put forward in the literature on individual-level comparisons (see Goethals, Messick and Allison, 1991), where it appears that people try to resolve self-enhancement *and* self-consistency motives when responding to self-relevant social information (e.g., Shrauger, 1975; Swann, Griffin, Predmore and Gaines, 1987). As we will argue in this next section, for members of low status groups, the number and nature of available comparison dimensions may provide some scope for the use of indirect strategies, as a means to simultaneously cope with social identity and social reality.

Unidimensional and multidimensional comparisons

More subtle or indirect patterns of positive ingroup perception are likely to emerge when groups are not just compared in terms of their generalized status. As Mummendey and her colleagues (Mummendey and Schreiber, 1983, 1984; Mummendey and Simon, 1989) demonstrated, competing claims for ingroup superiority, indicating 'social competition' (Turner, 1975) are likely to emerge when only one dimension is available to express differences between groups. When, however, there is an opportunity to make more refined judgements, because the groups are rated in terms of multiple specific traits, members of different groups tend to concede that each group may have its own characteristic abilities or features (Spears and Manstead, 1989; van Knippenberg, 1978, 1984; van Knippenberg and van Oers, 1984; van Knippenberg and Wilke, 1979).

This mutual acknowledgement of each group's differential superiority has been termed 'social cooperation' (van Knippenberg, 1984; van Knippenberg and Ellemers, 1990; see also Anastasio, Bachman, Gaertner and Dovidio, this volume).

Thus, patterns of differentiation in multidimensional comparison situations seem to be aimed at achieving positive group distinctiveness within the context of consensual definitions of social reality. To the extent that certain comparison dimensions are specifically characteristic for a certain group, members of different groups may reach consensus as to the relative position of their group, acknowledging the consensually defined 'social reality' of group stereotypes. At the same time, however, members of different groups may competitively claim ingroup superiority with respect to more ambiguous aspects of the intergroup comparison, for instance, when 'alternative' characteristics can be assigned to the group, or when the relative importance of specific group characteristics is at stake.

Ambiguous aspects of the intergroup comparison

Ellemers, van Rijswijk, Roefs and Simons (in press), carried out a study with members of natural groups, to systematically test the hypothesis that members of a lower status group would correctly indicate their group's inferior status, but at the same time try to use more ambiguous aspects of the intergroup comparison to establish a positive group image. Participants in this study were members of two student associations ('Group A' and 'Group B'), of which one ('Group B') held inferior status, and students who did not belong to either group. The ratings of these non-members confirmed the lower perceived status of Group B. Furthermore, a pilot study, as well as the ratings provided by the non-members, helped us to distinguish between traits that were considered typical for Group A, typical for Group B and non-typical traits.

The main results of this study confirm our prediction that members of both groups acknowledge the established differences between the groups. Consequently, members of both groups indicated that 'typical A-traits' were more characteristic for Group A, while 'typical B-traits' were generally considered more typical for Group B. Nevertheless, members of the lower status group (Group B) evaluated their group's typical traits more positively, and typical A-traits more negatively, than did members of Group A or non-members (cf. Doosje et al., 1995, Expt. 2). Moreover, members of the lower status group indicated that they considered the positively evaluated 'non-typical traits' more characteristic for their own group, while non-members and members of the high-status group perceived these traits as equally characteristic for both groups. Finally, correlational analyses indicated that the tendency to hold favourable group perceptions with respect to these ambiguous aspects is more pronounced the stronger people identify with that group. In other words, although social reality restrictions prevent a simple relation between strength of group identification and the tendency to positively differentiate the ingroup on all available dimensions (as we have seen previously), people do display a greater tendency to hold favourably biased group perceptions the more they feel their social identity is at stake.

Status related and alternative dimensions

The results of the study by Ellemers et al. (in press) indicate that group members may give biased judgements when rating 'ambiguous' aspects of the intergroup comparison, but take 'real' differences between the groups into account while doing this. A recent investigation by van Rijswijk and Ellemers (1996) further supports this argument. In this study, subjects were allocated to groups of 'underestimators' and 'overestimators', allegedly on the basis of an estimation task. The subject's group constituted a minority or a majority of participants in the session. More importantly for our present argument, subjects were either led to believe that their group had performed relatively poorly on a 'group creativity' task, or they were informed that that their group's performance on this task was relatively good. Subjects were first asked ten questions (e.g., I feel involved with my group) to assess to what extent they identified as members of their group. The main dependent measures consisted of ratings of both groups on the status-defining dimension (creativity), a number of status-related dimensions (competent, motivated) and an alternative dimension (honest). Furthermore, subjects were asked to indicate the similarity among members of both groups (i.e., the intragroup homogeneity) with respect to each of these dimensions. Additionally, subjects were asked how they would divide a sum of money (100 Dutch guilders) between a member of their own group and a member of the other group.

The main findings of this study were that, overall, ingroup identification was higher in the high group status condition than under low status, which confirms results from previous experiments (see Ellemers, 1993). When we look at how group status affects the allocation of 'money' and the ratings of the groups on different dimensions, an interesting pattern emerges. Firstly, results of the allocation task reveal that both groups allocate more 'money' to the high-status group than to the low-status group. In the same vein, the ratings of the two groups on the status defining dimension reveal that both groups consider the high-status group superior to the low-status group. In other words, regardless of their own group affiliation, members of both groups seem to agree that the high status group is superior on the status-defining dimension, and hence 'deserves' larger outcomes in the allocation task.

When we turn to the status related dimensions, this pattern changes somewhat. Although members of the high status group still consider their own group superior, members of the low-status group rate the two groups equally favourably on these dimensions. Finally, the ratings on the alternative dimension indicate that members of the high-status group accord equal ratings to both groups, while members of the low-status group claim ingroup superiority. In other words, these group ratings indicate that as the dimension under consideration is further removed from the status-defining criterion, members of the low status group feel less restricted by 'real' status differences, and are more at liberty to claim equal value or even superiority of the ingroup (cf. Mummendey and Schreiber, 1983, 1984; Mummendey and Simon, 1989).

Further support for the use of indirect strategies among members of a lower status group can be found in the group homogeneity ratings, which indicate that group members systematically perceive greater homogeneity of the ingroup on dimensions on which they consider their group superior, while they accentuate the relative heterogeneity of the ingroup on dimensions on which the ingroup is considered inferior. A similar pattern of perceived ingroup homogeneity on typical ingroup attributes and perceived outgroup homogeneity on outgroup attributes has been described by Simon (1992b). In a more general sense, a recent investigation by Lee and Ottati (1995) corroborates the notion that group members may either accentuate intragroup homogeneity or heterogeneity, depending on the social context and the resulting consequences for their identity as group members.

The results of these studies confirm that, although members of a lower status group may feel compelled to acknowledge 'real' differences between the groups (i.e., in terms of mean differences on the status defining dimension), they may nevertheless bolster their group's image when more ambiguous aspects of the intergroup comparison are rated. These latter claims may either consist of perceived ingroup superiority on some alternative dimension, or refer to the differences between individual group members in case the inferiority of the ingroup as a whole cannot be evaded. Again, this supports our general argument that people's group perceptions, both with respect to the relative typicality of certain group characteristics and with respect to the intragroup similarities or differences in terms of these characteristics, may vary as a function of the implications of the social context and the extent to which this affects their own identity.

Correlational analyses of the results obtained by van Rijswijk and Ellemers (1996) further extend the picture that emerges from this study. It turns out that, as members identify more strongly with the high-status group, they are more likely to differentiate their group from the other group in terms of the status-defining and status-related dimensions. Conversely, stronger identification with the lower status group is related to a stronger tendency to differentiate this group positively with respect to the status-related and alternative dimensions. This supports our previous conclusion from the study by Ellemers et al. (in press), namely that the tendency to hold favourable group perceptions can be related to strength of ingroup identification, although the present data indicate that this relation only occurs with respect to comparative dimensions on which group members have some scope to hold strategic perceptions.

In sum, the results of the studies reviewed above point to the strain between the social restrictions members of lower status groups are faced with on the one hand, and their motivation to maintain a favourable social identity on the other hand. Depending on the specific comparison dimensions, group members may simultaneously show their awareness of these 'real' differences between groups, and creatively take advantage of the ambiguity of the intergroup comparison in other respects.

6   Conclusions

Social context and social perspective

Our aim in this chapter was to argue that group perceptions should not be conceptualized as fixed or enduring 'pictures in our heads' (cf. Lippmann, 1922). Instead, we presented empirical results from different research paradigms systematically indicating that group images are continually adapted as a function of relevant aspects of the social context, as well as the perspective of the perceiver. At the conclusion of this chapter, we want to summarize the main points of our argument, and identify the factors that play a central role in these adaptive processes.

A first important factor is the *categorization* that is being used. The empirical results presented support the theoretical position (cf. Oakes et al., 1994) that an intragroup context may cause people to be considered as separate individuals, while an intergroup context fosters the perception of these people as members of social groups. At the group level, we have demonstrated how contextual characteristics (such as category fit or the presence of different comparison groups) determine which of several alternative categorizations is most likely to guide people's perceptions of these groups.

As a second factor, we argued that the *identity* of the perceiver plays a crucial role. The data we presented show that the motivation to hold favourable ingroup perceptions may cause people to adapt the way they deal with information about social groups. Specifically, when the situation is conducive of strategic group perceptions, motivational considerations may affect or even override the occurrence of a seemingly robust phenomenon, namely the illusory correlation effect.

The third important issue we dealt with is how *consensual agreement* about intergroup differences defines the boundary conditions that delimit the extent to which group perceptions may vary. To support this position we presented research showing that, especially for members of groups with lower social status, there is a tension between motivational concerns on the one hand, and social restrictions posed by their inferior standing on the other hand.

Finally, we turned to the *multidimensionality* of stereotypes. We argued that the availability of multiple comparative dimensions provides some opportunity to acknowledge established intergroup differences on the one hand, while enabling people on the other hand to adapt group images flexibly to motivational concerns when it comes to more ambiguous aspects of the intergroup comparison. It was further argued that it is this very multidimensional nature of stereotypes that offers lower status groups scope to pursue various indirect strategies in order to maintain a positive group image.

To come back to the distinction between social cognitive and motivational approaches to stereotyping, our conclusion is that group images are characterized by an interplay between stabilizing and adaptive forces, which may either stem from factors in the social situation, or from perceiver-related factors. Our attempt to gain a more profound understanding of the motivational nature of group perceptions by investigating cognitive processes is guided by the conviction that an integrative approach is the most fruitful way to study the stereotyping process in its social context.

Note

The authors would like to thank Alex Haslam, Penny Oakes and Russell Spears for their helpful comments on a previous draft of this chapter.

10

Categorization, Recategorization and Common Ingroup Identity

Phyllis Anastasio, Betty Bachman, Samuel Gaertner and John Dovidio

Whether studied within the laboratory or encountered in more naturalistic social settings, intergroup attitudes and social stereotypes have proven to be highly resistant to change (Fiske and Taylor, 1991; Hewstone, 1989; Rothbart and John, 1985; Weber and Crocker, 1983; Wilder, 1984). From a social cognition perspective, which has traditionally focused on intrapersonal and interpersonal processes, one reason why stereotypes may be resistant to change is that they are functional for reducing the complexity, and thus increasing the comprehensibility, of the social environment. However, motivational factors and intergroup processes, as well as cognitive processes, may contribute to stereotyping and bias and may, therefore, be instrumental in changing or breaking down stereotypes.

Although there has been a long tradition of research on how people form impressions of individuals (e.g., Anderson, 1981; Asch, 1946), there is also strong social psychological interest in how group membership influences impressions formed of individual members (e.g., Allport, 1954; Katz and Braly, 1933; Tajfel, 1969a). The salience of individual versus group identity, for example, critically influences both cognitive and affective processes and consequently one's responses to others (Brewer, 1988; Fiske and Neuberg, 1990). The role and function of stereotypes and bias may, thus, be critically shaped by the intergroup social context. In the present chapter, bias refers to systematic differences in the favourability of characteristics attributed to groups, and stereotyping involves also the association of specific traits (e.g., loud) with groups.

The purpose of this chapter is to consider recent evidence on the Common Ingroup Identity Model (Gaertner, Dovidio, Anastasio, Bachman and Rust 1993; Gaertner, Rust, Dovidio, Bachman and Anastasio, 1994) which identifies cognitive and motivational intragroup and intergroup processes that can contribute to reducing intergroup biases and stereotypes. We first examine how cognitive and motivational processes associated with social identity influence bias and stereotyping within an intergroup social context. In the second section, we outline the Common Ingroup Identity Model and provide evidence concerning how cognitive and motivational intragroup and intergroup processes can contribute to the reduction of bias and the acceptance of counterstereotypic impressions of outgroup members. Third, we summarize the results of laboratory and field studies that provided initial evidence for the model. Then we describe two more recent studies that extend the model in different directions. One of these focuses on intergroup processes during corporate mergers between organizations that may have different status within the new corporate entity. The other study focuses on how cognitive and motivational intergroup processes may influence the likelihood that an interaction with a counterstereotypic outgroup member can be used to change the stereotype of the group.

1 Intergroup Cognitive and Motivational Processes

The mere act of classifying individuals into social categories not only guides people's cognitive impressions of others, but impacts upon their affective reactions as well. The minimal group paradigm (Tajfel, Billig, Bundy and Flament, 1971) illustrates that even categorization along arbitrary dimensions leads to bias, assuming that the categories include an ingroup ('us') and an outgroup ('them'). Bias is consistently demonstrated by people's higher ratings of ingroup members than of outgroup members on affective dimensions and in the allocation of more resources to the ingroup than to the outgroup (Billig and Tajfel, 1973; Brewer and Silver, 1978; Tajfel and Billig, 1974).

Social Identity Theory (Tajfel and Turner, 1979; Turner, 1975) explains the incidence of bias as a two-step process that includes both cognitive and motivational factors. First, the perceiver must cognitively divide the social world into at least two distinguishable social categories that separate the self from others ('us' vs. 'them'). Second, the desire for positive self-esteem, derived in part from the social categories to which individuals belong, motivates people to view the ingroup as superior to the outgroup (see Long and Spears, this volume). Social Identity Theory, therefore, utilizes the human propensity to categorize individuals into groups and then offers a logical rationale for the development and maintenance of intergroup bias.

Social Identity Theory also offers a plausible and parsimonious explanation for the readiness with which humans are inclined to embrace negative social stereotypes of the outgroup. The motivation to view one's ingroup as superior to the outgroup may influence the type of information that is encoded and stored about the outgroup. That is, ingroup favouritism may predispose the perceiver to form relatively negative impressions of the outgroup (Doise et al., 1972; Rothbart and John, 1985). Downward comparison can enhance self-esteem and feelings of well-being (Wills, 1981). For example, Schaller (1991) found that group membership systematically influenced how group traits were remembered. When an observer was not affiliated with either a majority or minority group, memory for traits was biased to associate distinctive traits with the minority group, regardless of the desirability of the traits. However, belonging to either the majority or the minority group biased memory for traits in quite a different manner: memory for desirable and undesirable traits was biased to favour one's ingroup.

Beyond influencing evaluative biases, social identity can also affect the attribution of stereotypic characteristics to outgroup members. Wilder and Shapiro (1991) found, for instance, that when ingroup identity was enhanced by the presence of other ingroup members, the ambiguous behaviours of an outgroup member were rated as significantly more stereotypical than when the subjects rated the same behaviours while alone. Moreover, when the outgroup target's behaviours clearly disconfirmed the outgroup stereotype, presence of fellow ingroup members attenuated the perception of the disconfirming behaviour and biased perception of the behaviour in the direction of the outgroup stereotype. Clearly, social identity with one's ingroup not only influences the affective judgements of outgroup members, but also prejudices the cognitive impressions of the outgroup in ways that reinforce the persistence of stereotypes.

Because of this apparent positive relationship of salience of group identity with bias and stereotyping, for many researchers (e.g., Bettencourt, Brewer, Croak and Miller, 1992; Brewer and Miller, 1984; Miller, Brewer and Edwards, 1985) the problem of changing intergroup attitudes and stereotypes involves the cognitive strategy of decategorization. Decategorization involves short-circuiting the tendency for people to categorize other people in terms of their group identities. When social identities are less salient, people may be perceived more as individuals and less as representative group members. Thus, perceivers would no longer be influenced by the stereotypic expectations associated with the target person's group membership. As a consequence, decategorization may produce more accurate and potentially more favourable impressions of outgroup members. Increasing the salience of group identities, however, may not *necessarily* increase stereotyping and bias. That is, it may be possible to combine the forces of group dynamics and motivation with social cognition to produce alternative strategies for reducing stereotypical thinking and intergroup bias. In the next section, we discuss a body of research that points to the efficacy of such a strategy and the social contexts in which it is effective.

2 Reducing Intergroup Bias: The Common Ingroup Identity Model

In this section of the chapter, we consider the potential for reducing inter-group bias and stereotypical thinking by utilizing an approach based upon two powerful human tendencies: (1) the cognitive tendency to categorize the social world into ingroups ('us') and outgroups ('them'), and (2) the motivational tendency to perceive the ingroup more positively than the outgroup (Tajfel and Turner, 1979).

The Common Ingroup Identity Model (Gaertner et al., 1993) asserts that inducing two separate groups to recategorize their perceptions of group boundaries so as to perceive themselves as two parts of a whole or as sharing a common identity (e.g., 'Koreans' and 'blacks' become 'Americans') will effectively reduce the bias typically felt between two groups. This model is derived from the social identity and self-categorization approaches to intergroup behavior (Brown and Turner, 1981; Tajfel and Turner, 1979; Turner, Hogg, Oakes, Reicher and Wetherell, 1987) and from two conclusions of Brewer's (1979) analysis. First, Brewer (1979) and Turner (1975) concluded that intergroup bias frequently takes the form of ingroup enhancement rather than outgroup devaluation. Also, group formation brings ingroup members closer to the self while the distance between the self and outgroup members remains relatively unchanged. Together, these conclusions suggest that behaviour towards other people is strongly regulated by perceptions of their closeness to the self as gauged by their ingroup membership.

Categorization of a person as an ingroup member rather than as an outgroup member has been demonstrated to produce greater perceptions of shared beliefs (Brown, 1984; Brown and Abrahms, 1986; Hogg and Turner, 1985; Stein, Hardyck and Smith, 1965; Wilder, 1984) which increases interpersonal attraction (Byrne, 1971); to facilitate empathic arousal, whereby a person's motivational system becomes coordinated to the needs of another (Hornstein, 1976; Piliavin, Dovidio, Gaertner and Clark, 1981); and to enhance memory for positive information about others (Howard and Rothbart, 1980). Thus, we propose that recategorizing original outgroup members as ingroup members enables the cognitive and motivational processes, that initially contribute to pro-ingroup bias and stereotyping, to be redirected towards developing more positive intergroup relations.

From our perspective, intergroup cooperation toward the achievement of superordinate goals among Sherif and Sherif's (1969) groups of summer campers, reduced the intensity of intergroup bias by altering members' representations of the memberships from 'us' and 'them' to a more inclusive 'we' (see also, Brown and Turner, 1981; Feshbach and Singer, 1957; Hornstein, 1976; Turner, 1981; Worchel Axsom, Ferris, Samaha and Schweitzer, 1978).

Further, we propose that many of the conditions of contact situations (e.g., equal status and cooperative interaction, self-revealing interaction and egalitarian norms; see Allport, 1954, and Cook, S. W., 1984) that are necessary to reduce intergroup bias, are effective, at least in part, because they can contribute to recategorization and the development of a more inclusive common ingroup identity. A series of laboratory studies has provided initial evidence for the validity of the Common Ingroup Identity Model.

3 Empirical Evidence for the Model

The Common Ingroup Identity Model identifies antecedents and outcomes of recategorization as well as the mediating processes (see Gaertner et al., 1993). In general, it is hypothesized that environmental factors that influence group differentiation (e.g., proximity) and dimensions of the social context (e.g., interdependence) that shape intergroup relations can independently or in concert alter cognitive representations of the aggregate (e.g., as one group). These resulting cognitive representations are then proposed to result in specific affective, cognitive and overt behavioral consequences. This section of the chapter provides an overview of selected research that illustrates these hypothesized relationships between environmental and social factors and representations of the aggregate (i.e., one group, two subgroups within one group, two different groups or separate individuals) and between these representations and intergroup bias and stereotyping (see figure 10.1). The first experiment examined the benefits of recategorization induced in part through the configuration of the environmental context. The second experiment focused specifically on the influence of intergroup cooperation. The third and fourth studies investigated the relationships among the conditions of contact, cognitive representations of the groups and intergroup bias in natural settings. The fifth study, investigated how an authority's framing of the intergroup boundary as (1) two subgroups within one group, (2) two separate groups or (3) separate individuals (i.e., no groups) influences stereotyping. In particular, this experiment explored the likelihood that group members will generalize counterstereotypic information revealed during an interaction with one outgroup member to the entire outgroup.

The benefits of recategorization (Study 1)

The first of the series examined the relative benefits and the mediational processes involved in both recategorization and decategorization strategies (Gaertner, Mann, Murrell and Dovidio, 1989). Members of two separate laboratory-formed groups were induced through various structural interventions (e.g., seating arrangement) either to recategorize themselves as one superordinate entity or to decategorize themselves and to conceive of themselves as separate

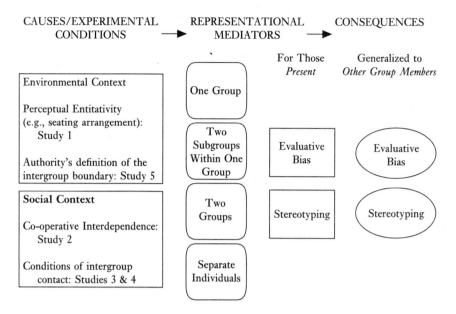

Figure 10.1 Overview of the hypothesized relationship between envionmental and socal factors and intergroup bias and stereotyping in the five studies.

individuals. In both cases these changes in the perceptions of the intergroup boundaries reduced bias. Furthermore, as expected, these strategies reduced bias in different ways. Recategorizing outgroup members as members of the ingroup reduced bias by *increasing* liking for these former outgroup members. Decategorizing members of the two groups so that they conceived of themselves as separate individuals reduced bias by *decreasing* liking for former ingroup members. Thus, as specified by Turner et al. (1987), 'the attractiveness of an individual is not constant, but varies with ingroup membership' (p. 60).

As ingeniously demonstrated by Sherif's series of Robbers' Cave field studies (Sherif and Sherif, 1969), cooperation between two groups can reduce intergroup tension and foster increased liking towards the outgroup. But how does cooperation effect these changes? The mechanism by which cooperative interaction works to reduce bias was explored in a second laboratory study (Gaertner, Mann, Dovidio, Murrell and Pomare, 1990). It was hypothesized that cooperation may work in part through cognitive means: by inducing members of two separate groups to conceive of themselves as one superordinate entity or as sharing a common ingroup identity. Thus, we propose that the relationship between cooperative intergroup interaction and reduced bias may be mediated, in part, by changes in cognitive representations of the memberships from separate groups to one, more inclusive group.

How does cooperation reduce intergroup bias? (Study 2)

To test these hypotheses, cooperative interaction was manipulated independently of perceptions of the aggregate. A 2 (presence/absence of cooperation) × 2 (perceptions of the aggregate as one group or two groups) design allowed the effects of cooperation to be experimentally separated from the effects of cognitive representations of the aggregate. Cooperation was manipulated by having two separately formed laboratory groups of three individuals interact to achieve a common goal which determined their shared fate; groups in the non-cooperation condition merely sat together and listened to a recording of a third group's discussion. Perceptions of the two memberships (Group A and B) as two groups or one were manipulated through seating arrangements (AAA BBB vs. ABABAB), the use of the groups' different names or the assignment of a new group name to represent the six participants and other structural factors used in the previous study. Measures of bias ('How much did you like each participant? How cooperative, honest and valuable was each person during the interaction?'), as well as perceptions of the aggregate (how much the aggregate of six felt like one group, two groups or separate individuals) were the main dependent measures.

The results supported the hypothesis that cooperation works to reduce intergroup bias by changing participants' cognitive representations of the aggregate from two separate groups to one group. First, in the absence of cooperative interaction (i.e., in the No Cooperation Conditions), groups that were induced to conceive of themselves as one group rather than two groups had lower levels of intergroup bias. This finding supports the assumed causal relationship between members' cognitive representations of the memberships and intergroup bias. Second, when the groups initially conceived of themselves as two groups (i.e., the Two Groups Condition), the introduction of cooperation increased the extent to which members perceived the aggregate as one group (and less as two groups) and also decreased bias in evaluative ratings. Also, consistent with the effects of recategorization in the earlier study (Gaertner et al., 1989), cooperation reduced bias primarily by increasing the favourable evaluations of (former) outgroup members. Finally, and directly supportive of the hypothesis, the causal relation between intergroup cooperation and more favourable evaluations of outgroup members was, in part, mediated by increased perceptions of the aggregate as one group. Thus, cooperative interaction reduced bias partially through cognitive means.

This support for the Common Ingroup Identity Model highlights the importance of both cognitive and motivational processes for reducing biases and potentially for changing stereotypes. As Turner's (1981) analysis of the literature indicates, it is 'difficult to explain discrimination on the basis of ingroup–outgroup divisions solely in terms of cognitive processes; motivational factors need to be superimposed' (p. 82). The Common Ingroup Identity Model assumes that viewing former outgroup members as part of a larger ingroup provides the motivation to evaluate these members in a more positive light while relying on (rather than undermining) the tendency for people to categorize. Also, this study of how cooperation reduces bias is important because it *experimentally* demonstrates the direction of causality proposed by the model. Thus, we can be more confident about the plausibility of the direction of causality suggested in our subsequent correlational studies.

But this does not necessarily mean that a one-group identity is necessary or even desirable in every situation. For instance, a one-group identity would require participants to forsake their former group identity, an approach which does not promote the multicultural environment many groups are striving for today. Furthermore, taking on a new, common ingroup identity that does not include one's former group identity may not be possible to implement in many social contexts. And what effect would a one-group representation have upon impressions of the outgroup in general?

Is a one-group representation desirable for the purpose of generalizing positive impressions and changing negative stereotypes of the outgroup as a whole? Or are the new-found positive impressions of those former outgroup members within the contact situation limited to only those within the immediate setting? It is possible that a common one-group identity (or even seeing people only as individuals) may sever cognitive associations with one's former outgroup identity to some extent; should that occur, then it is also possible that the resulting positive evaluations of former outgroup members have few if any links to the original outgroup (see Rothbart and John, 1985; Hewstone and Brown, 1986). A one-group representation therefore may not be desirable for purposes of generalization. However, if members of different groups maintained their ethnic identities, but conceived of themselves as having a dual identity (as though they were members of different groups but all playing on the same team or two subgroups within one larger group), the intergroup consequences may be more favourable than if they only regarded themselves as separate groups. The next study served to extend the Common Ingroup Identity Model to a naturalistic social setting while also exploring the potential value of the dual identity for influencing intergroup attitudes.

Common ingroup identity in a multi-ethnic high school (Study 3)

A survey study was conducted in a multi-ethnic high school in which a sample of 1,357 black, Chinese, Hispanic, Japanese, Korean, Vietnamese and Caucasian students, closely matching the school's diversity, participated (Gaertner, Rust, Dovidio, Bachman and Anastasio, 1994). The major purpose of this study was to determine if the pattern of findings obtained in our laboratory experiment study (in which the direction of causality was reasonably clear-cut) would be conceptually replicated in this more complex school setting. Would students' perceptions of the student body as one group or separate groups mediate the relationship between their perceptions of the favourableness of the conditions of contact (e.g., cooperation, equal status) and their intergroup attitudes?

The survey instrument asked students to identify the groups (as many as were appropriate) that applied to themselves: American, black, Chinese, Jewish, etc. Questionnaire items that were modifications of those developed by Green, Adams and Turner (1988) were designed to measure four distinct conditions hypothesized by the Contact Hypothesis (see Allport, 1954; Cook, S. W., 1984) to be necessary for successful intergroup contact: equal status, cooperative interdependence, the degree of interaction between the groups and egalitarian norms. Scores on these four scales were combined to form an overall measure of intergroup contact. Additional items, similar to those used in our laboratory work, were included to measure students' perceptions of the student body as one group ('Despite the different groups at school, there is frequently the sense that we are all just one group'), separate groups ('At school, it usually feels as though we belong to different groups') and separate individuals ('At school, it usually feels as though we are individuals and not members of a particular group'). Also, we included a dual-identity item ('Although there are different groups of students at this school, it feels as though we are all playing on the same team'). The distinction between the one group and the dual-identity items may appear subtle, but they were significantly correlated with one another (r = .44), suggesting that they were perceived to be related but not identical concepts. An index of intergroup bias was obtained by including several items designed to assess feelings towards one's own ethnic group and towards other ethnic groups. Evaluation of the 'outgroups' was indexed by averaging feelings towards all ethnic groups of which students did not indicate membership. The index measuring bias in affective reactions was then obtained by calculating the difference between feelings for one's ingroup and feelings for the 'outgroups'.

The results of this study converged with the findings from the laboratory. The conditions of contact significantly predicted both cognitive representations of the groups and intergroup bias. Cognitive representations, in turn, predicted bias. The more the student body was perceived to be 'one group' or 'different groups all on the same team', the lower the bias. Furthermore, providing evidence of the mediating role of cognitive representations, the relationship between conditions of contact and bias was significantly reduced when cognitive representations were statistically controlled. These results parallel the findings of our laboratory study and indicate the applicability of the Common Ingroup Identity Model to naturalistic settings.

Furthermore, while the mediation analyses provided support for the theoretical model, this study offered an additional opportunity to examine the value of a dual identity in which subgroup identities are maintained within the context of a superordinate entity. Those minority students who indicated that they were members of a minority group (e.g., Korean) and also American had lower bias compared to those minority students who did not use the superordinate American identity but only identified themselves using their minority subgroup identity. Whereas there may be many differences between these two groups of students (e.g., American citizenship) that could explain their different levels of bias, they did have different perceptions of the student body. As we might expect if the item 'different groups but all on the same team' did measure a dual identity, minority students who identified themselves both as American and as a member of their minority group endorsed this item (but not the other representation items) more strongly than minority students who only identified themselves with their minority group.

Additional analyses of these data examined the moderating role of status, defined in terms of majority or minority group status (see Gaertner, Rust, Dovidio, Bachman and Anastasio, 1994). Consistent with Islam and Hewstone's (1993) research and the idea that social-contextual factors influence intergroup attitudes, majority (i.e., Caucasian) students relative to the minority group students (disregarding whether they used a dual identity) perceived the conditions of contact more favourably. They also had stronger representations of the student body as 'all playing on the same team' and had lower degrees of bias in affective reactions, primarily because their attitudes toward outgroup members were more favourable. These results suggest that status can moderate the processes involved in intergroup bias (see Sachdev and Bourhis, 1991), and as suggested by Fiske (1993a), processes involved in stereotyping.

Overall, these findings offer further support for the Common Ingroup Identity Model in a rich and complex setting containing many different groups, so that bias involving ingroups and the outgroups was not limited to any specific pair possessing a unique history. The results also revealed that 'one group' and 'same team' cognitive representations each had independent effects in the reduction of bias. This is encouraging, for there may be situations in which facilitating the development of a dual identity or a conception of 'different groups on the same team' may be preferable to simply establishing a one-group representation without reference to prior group membership. Furthermore, generalization of positive feelings to other outgroup members outside of the common ingroup (for example, members of ethnic outgroups not attending one's school) is desirable in many circumstances and may best be facilitated by retaining some sort of associative link with the original outgroups. Keeping one's original group identity while simultaneously perceiving an inclusive superordinate group may create such an associative link.

In addition to demonstrating the generalizability of the processes outlined in the Common Ingroup Identity Model and illustrating the potential role of dual identities, our more recent analyses reconfirmed the importance of another aspect of the social context – the *status* of the groups (see Sachdev and Bourhis, 1991). Status is a fundamental form of social organization for both individuals and groups (Berger, Wagner and Zeldtich, 1985). In many social contexts it is the primary distinguishing factor. For example, in corporate mergers, the acquiring company, by virtue of its action, establishes its status relative to the company that was acquired. The following study tested the Common Ingroup Identity Model within such corporate structures where again groups are real and intergroup attitudes are rich and complexly determined.

Corporate mergers and ingroup identity (Study 4)

In another effort to extend the model to situations outside of the laboratory, Bachman (1993; see also, Bachman, Gaertner, Anastasio and Rust, 1993) investigated the impact of intergroup processes in corporate mergers. Mergers embody in a rich and complex fashion the goals that we have attempted to study in our laboratory research – making two groups into one – and thus represent fertile ground for examining the processes of social categorization, stereotyping and intergroup biases.

People who work in organizations that have merged are frequently resistant to post-merger integration (Marks and Mirvis, 1985). The negative consequences of these intergroup dynamics could be devastating for the newly formed organizational entity if allowed to go unchecked. After all, the survival and growth of any organization is dependent upon the commitment of all of its members to work together in order to achieve organizational goals. Research reveals, in fact, that many merged organizations experience lags in productivity, high turnover and absenteeism, and decreased profits (Jemison and Sitkin, 1986).

Categorization and its consequences are expected to be particularly influential during mergers because the process of merging is essentially a group-level phenomenon. Mergers increase the salience of group identity for organizational members because the focus of a merger is on the redefinition of organizational groups and their boundaries. Thus, awareness of the ingroup (own organization) and outgroup (the other organization) is heightened and likely to affect the judgements and interactions of merger participants. Ingroup favouritism, stemming from the need for positive social identity, should also motivate employees to protect their self-esteem by perceiving themselves (and their group) as 'better' than the outgroup on important dimensions. Another important contextual dynamic that is quite prevalent in mergers – competition – should increase cohesion within groups and polarize perceived differences between them (Blake and Mouton, 1979). Given all of the pressures that tend to keep organizational groups apart, we wanted to investigate the factors that we hypothesized would promote more harmonious intergroup relationships.

The Common Ingroup Identity Model suggests that if group members' mental representations of separate groups could be recategorized into a 'one-group' representation, then the fundamental biases and conflicts between groups should diminish. Following the work in the multi-ethnic high school, Bachman et al. (1993) proposed that, to the extent that Contact Hypothesis variables were favourable in the merged organization, differentiation between groups would be reduced resulting in a more unified conceptualization of the merged organization. A more unified representation of the merged organization was predicted to be associated with lower levels of bias between the groups. Also, as suggested by the high-school study, the relative status of the groups in contact was expected to moderate members' perceptions and reactions to the merger. Within the context of the mergers, status relates to the roles each organization played in the merger. Because of group differences in power and control in the merged organization, acquiring organizations typically have higher status than organizations that were acquired. Some of the participants in our sample were members of an acquiring organization (high-status group), some were from organizations that had been acquired (low-status group), while others indicated that theirs was a merger of equals. Bachman et al. (1993) proposed that status differentials between acquired and acquiring organizational members may affect their perceptions of the conditions of contact. Higher status groups may view the conditions of contact more favourably and, thus, may have a more inclusive representation of the merged organization and lower levels of intergroup bias.

The participants in this survey study were 229 banking executives who were students or alumni of a three-year long summer graduate banking programme. We were fortunate to have the opportunity to study bankers because the banking industry has engaged in a high rate of merger activity over the past several years (Business Week, 1992). Our participants came from many geographical locations and financial institutions across the United States. Some of the participants in our sample were members of an acquiring organization, some were from organizations that had been acquired, while others indicated that theirs was a merger of equals.

Each of the participants completed a 126-item survey that contained items relating to perceptions of intergroup contact, conceptions of the merged organization and intergroup bias. Specifically, similar to the items in the high-school study, the participants' mental representations of the merged organization were assessed as well as the conditions of contact (equal status contact, positive interdependence, opportunities for intimacy and egalitarian norms) in the merged organization. Seven-point rating scales, which required the respondents to compare the outgroup (the 'other' organization in the merger) with their ingroup, were used to assess intergroup bias on characteristics related to the work setting (e.g., skilled, hard-working, intelligent, creative, sociable, cliquish and helpful).

Overall, mediation analysis revealed a pattern of findings that suggested that employees' cognitive representations of their merged organizations mediated the relationship between their perceptions of the conditions of contact and intergroup bias. As in the high-school study, the pattern of four sets of relationships indicated mediation. First, conditions of contact significantly predicted intergroup bias [beta = −.38]; more favourable perceptions of the contact conditions predicted lower bias. Second, conditions of contact significantly predicted a more inclusive organizational representation [beta = .62]. Third, the effect of conditions of contact was reduced when the cognitive representation of merged organization was entered simultaneously in the regression equation [beta = −.20]. Fourth, the more inclusive representations of the merged organization significantly predicted lower levels of bias over and above conditions of contact [beta = −.28]. The more the organization was perceived to be one group the lower the bias.

Additional analyses examined the moderating role of relative group status in more detail. While the results of this study were very interesting, they were also quite complex. Supportive of the assumed link between organizational role in a merger and status, participants rated their organizations as equivalent in status before the merger, but significant differences existed after the merger. Members of acquiring organizations perceived their group to be of higher status than did members of organizations that were acquired. Members of organizations involved in mergers perceived to be of equals reported an intermediate degree of status. Furthermore, as expected and consistent with the high-school study, status was positively related to perceptions of the conditions of contact. Members of acquiring organizations perceived the conditions of contact significantly more favourably ($p < .001$) than did members of companies that were acquired in a merger. Members of organizations seen as equal partners in a merger viewed the conditions of contact at an intermediate level of favourability, although also more favourably ($p < .01$) than did members of acquired organizations.

In addition to perceptions of status and conditions of contact, members' representations of the merged organization also varied as a function of merger conditions. Members of organizations that acquired another company or who perceived the merger as involving equal partners had a less differentiated, more inclusive, one-group representation of the merged organization than did members of organizations that were acquired in a merger ($p < .001$). These findings parallel the results of majority and minority status in the recent analyses of the high-school study.

As it did in the multi-ethnic high school, intergroup bias varied as a function of status. The picture is a bit more complex, however, because we divided the bias measure into two different indices based largely on the factor loadings of the items: sociability bias (including the traits sociable, helpful and cliquish), and work-competence bias (including the traits skillful, creative, intelligent and hard-working). When bias is measured in terms of sociability, members of acquiring organizations demonstrated lower levels of bias than members of the acquired organizations. Also members of groups perceived to be equal in status did not show significant ingroup favouritism. Thus, supportive of the processes hypothesized in the Common Ingroup Identity Model, lower levels of sociability bias corresponded with more favourable perceptions of the conditions of contact and more inclusive representations of the merged organization. When bias is measured in terms of work competence, however, a different pattern emerges. In contrast to the results for sociability bias, members of acquiring organizations exhibited significantly higher levels of ingroup favouritism on the work-competence index than did either members of acquired organizations or members of equal-status organizations. Thus, higher work-related status, in terms of organizational role in a merger, was related to lower sociability bias but to greater ingroup bias in their perceptions of work competence. The effects of status on our bias measures are consistent with other studies that have found that high-status groups tend to emphasize their superiority on 'power' and 'competence' dimensions (we are cleverer, richer, stronger) while low-status groups tend to emphasize the importance of social (we are nicer) dimensions (see Cheyne, 1970; Doojse and Ellemers, this volume; Ellemers, van Knippenberg and Willie, 1990; Mummenday and Schreiber, 1983; Spears and Manstead, 1989). These effects of status suggest the importance of considering the relevance and centrality of the dimensions on which bias is assessed – that is, the social context of the dependent measures as well as the social context of the intergroup contact and the relative status of the groups. It is possible, for instance, that members of acquired organizations, recognizing their disadvantage in the work situation, were particularly motivated to seek positive distinctiveness on an alternative dimension – manifested in this case as higher levels of sociability bias than exhibited by members of acquiring organizations (see also, Brewer, Manzi and Shaw, 1993; Mullen, Brown and Smith, 1992; Sachdev and Bourhis, 1991).

There are still many more important questions to answer in future research. We do not know, for example, if integration in mergers would be better assisted by preserving and respecting previous organizational boundaries (procedures, traditions, etc.), by blending the two organizations (allowing pockets of the previous organization to exist) or by attempting to degrade former alliances by forming a totally new organization (see Bachman and Gaertner, 1995; Mottola, Bachman and Gaertner, 1995; Schoennauer, 1967). In a merger context, is it beneficial in the long term, to foster the conceptualization of two subgroups within a superordinate identity? It may be useful on a short-term basis to allow employees to cling to their previous groups as a way of finding solace in a time of great change, but should this be encouraged on a long-term basis if the goal is to have employees make a psychological investment in the newly merged entity?

Generalization and reduction of stereotypical thinking (Study 5)

From the results of our laboratory and field studies, it appears that perceiving a common identity reduces intergroup bias by increasing evaluations of outgroup members who are immediately present within the contact setting. But what happens to evaluations of those outgroup members with whom one does not have direct contact? In our study within the multi-ethnic high school, students responded to items which asked how they felt about certain ethnic groups in general (e.g., 'Koreans') rather than any specific member of the outgroup. However, the field study did not specifically examine the model's potential for generalization.

Additionally, tests of the model have been limited to changing affective evaluations of outgroup members ('How much do you like . . .') and examining work-related cognitions (e.g., intelligent, hard-working) rather than specific, learned beliefs about the outgroup, such as stereotypes. The next study was undertaken in an attempt to answer the following questions: Is the reduction of bias resulting from a common ingroup identity generalized to other members of the outgroup with whom one has not had direct contact? Does induction of a common ingroup identity also attenuate stereotypical thinking? The research findings presented next provide a tentative 'yes' to both questions.

The model's potential for changing outgroup stereotypes was tested in an experiment (Anastasio, Gaertner, Bachman and Rust, 1992) by using a traditionally stereotyped outgroup for students at the University of Delaware: young adults who live within the area but who do not attend college (colourfully referred to as 'Townies'). Subjects (n = 72), who were University of Delaware students, 'interacted' with a member of the 'Townie' outgroup under one of three conditions. These conditions related to the two group, common ingroup and separate individuals manipulations used in experiments previously described in this chapter. In the Two-Group condition, the separate group memberships as university students and townspeople were emphasized; in the Superordinate (i.e., common ingroup) condition, both these separate group memberships and their common identity as 'Delawareans' were made salient. The third condition promoted decategorization by encouraging the perception of the participants as separate individuals (interpersonal condition). In lieu of actual face-to-face interactions between subjects and the outgroup member(s), the same videotape of an individual purported to be a 'Townie' was shown in each condition.

In the Interpersonal condition subjects participated individually and viewed the video target while sitting by themselves. These subjects were told that the study was designed to study communication between individuals having different vocational goals and that after the viewing the videotape they would interact face-to-face with the video target on a one-to-one basis. In the Two Group and the Superordinate Group conditions, students were run in groups of three and together viewed the videotape of the 'Townie' outgroup member. These subjects were seated at a three-person table and were told that after viewing the video target they would interact face-to-face with the target plus two other 'Townie' outgroup members. In these conditions, the instructions stated that the experiment was designed to study communication between groups with different vocational goals. In the Superordinate Group condition, subjects were additionally told that the identical study was being run at the University of Rhode Island and that the two groups of students and townspeople participating here would be representing the Delaware sample. Therefore, a common superordinate group identity, that of 'Delawarean', was emphasized. Prior to viewing the videotaped target, participants were asked to indicate their expectancies of the target on a number of traits.

The videotaped individual was an actor who outwardly appeared to be a 'typical' member of the 'Townie' outgroup (long hair, thick beard, flannel shirt, jeans) and who portrayed (as determined in pilot testing) several counterstereotypical traits (such as creativity, intelligence, sensitivity, ambition) as well as stereotypical traits (such as sloppiness and noisiness). After viewing the videotape, subjects were asked to rate on seven-point scales both the video target and the entire 'Townie' outgroup on the same traits. Therefore, three separate measures were obtained: expectancies for the target individual, actual impressions of the target individual and impressions of the outgroup in general. All three measures were indexed by combining ratings on counterstereotypical traits and reverse-scored ratings of stereotypical traits, so that higher values on each index indicated less stereotypical impressions overall.

It was expected that subjects, regardless of the condition, would share the same stereotypical expectations of the Townie partner and that they would recognize his counterstereotypic traits similarly. It was hypothesized, however, that exposure to the counterstereotypic target would be most effective in changing negative stereotypes of the outgroup as a whole when the intergroup boundary was maintained and subjects and the target shared a common superordinate identity as Delawareans – that is, in the Superordinate Identity condition. The maintenance of the intergroup boundary in the Two-Group condition and the lack of associative link between the model and other outgroup members when subjects were encouraged to conceive of themselves as *individuals* in the Interpersonal condition were hypothesized to limit the effectiveness of the counterstereotypic model for changing group stereotypes.

As anticipated, across the three experimental conditions participants had similar expectations of the Townie partner before they interacted and had similar perceptions of the person after he exhibited a range of non-stereotypic characteristics. That is, they equally held stereotypic expectations of a particular Townie and equivalently recognized the counterstereotypic traits of this particular member of that outgroup. However, as predicted, the manipulated conditions of interaction (i.e., Two Groups, Superordinate Group, Interpersonal) systematically affected counterstereotypic impressions of the outgroup in general. Specifically, the Superordinate Group (Delaware: students and townspersons) condition yielded higher counterstereotypical ratings of the outgroup than either the interpersonal (5.22 vs. 3.86) or the intergroup conditions (5.22 vs. 4.00), and was the only condition which effected significant changes from a baseline rating (3.54) obtained from a control group of students who did not view the video or expect to interact with members of the outgroup in the context of this study.

Additional analyses even more directly supported the hypothesis that shared identity is a critical element for changing stereotypes of the outgroup. As expected, subjects in the Superordinate Group condition more strongly thought of themselves as being a Delawarean (mean = 4.25) relative to those in the Interpersonal (mean = 2.71) and Two Groups (mean = 2.88) conditions. Moreover, analyses revealed that the perception of oneself as a Delawarean statistically mediated the relation between the interaction conditions and the generalized counterstereotypic impressions of the Townie outgroup. Further, supportive of the role of the superordinate Delawarean representation for influencing beliefs about the 'Townie' outgroup more generally, separate correlational analyses revealed that only within the Superordinate Group condition was there a reliable correlation between the rating of oneself as a Delawarean and the strength of the counterstereotypic impression of the outgroup [r = .92]. Thus, changes in outgroup stereotypes occurred primarily in the condition in which a common superordinate identity between subjects was salient, and within that condition changes were strongly directly related to the salience of that identity.

Overall, the results of this study indicate that a common ingroup identity was successful in attenuating stereotypical impressions of the outgroup. It is especially important to consider the fact that the stereotypical impressions that were affected by the interaction condition were those of the entire outgroup rather than the individual(s) directly involved in contact. In fact, the interaction condition did not influence what the video target was expected to be like or how he was actually perceived. This finding runs counter to theory (Brewer and Miller, 1984) and previous research findings (Anastasio, Gaertner, Bachman and Rust, 1992; Wilder and Shapiro, 1991) which predict and demonstrate that individuated interactions are superior to group-level interactions for promoting counterstereotypical impressions of those directly involved in contact.

Why the results of this study did not replicate this phenomenon is not clear at the present time. It is possible that contemplating the video target's traits prior to actually 'meeting' him may have attenuated the relatively negative effects of intergroup interaction. This hypothesis is consistent with the finding that the video target was perceived in a moderately positive manner across all conditions. In any event, this study demonstrated that despite the fact that the target individual was not viewed differently across interaction conditions, the general outgroup was. The fact that the common ingroup identity was successful in reducing stereotypical thinking with real groups rather than with artificially-created laboratory groups demonstrates that this approach can alleviate longstanding negative outgroup impressions. Additionally, it appears as if the benefits of a common identity stem primarily from motivational, rather than cognitive mechanisms: impressions of the target individual did not predict impressions of the general outgroup, while the nature of the interaction conditions did. Positive impressions of the target were the same across interaction conditions and, therefore, had the same opportunity to be generalized to the outgroup. Equal generalization should have occurred if the only factors influencing stereotypical thinking are cognitive in nature; the fact that only the Superordinate Group condition promoted generalization indicates that other factors are at work besides cognition. Motivation must be a factor since the default stereotype remains in place regardless of how positively the target individual is perceived, and a common ingroup identity is assumed to provide that motivation. Again, motivation plays a major role in forming cognitive as well as affective impressions. Indeed, it appears that the social context directly affects motivation which in turn colours cognitions. The social context draws and redraws the intergroup boundary, changing not the motivation for self-esteem itself but the people and groups whom we are motivated to view in a positive light, both affectively and cognitively. In summary, the principles of social cognition need to be explored within varying social contexts in order to gain a clearer picture of prejudicial and stereotypical thinking.

4 Conclusions

We began this chapter with the supposition that any strategy which is aimed at alleviating intergroup tension and reducing stereotypical thinking should incorporate motivational as well as cognitive phenomena. Our model attempts to capture both cognitive and motivational components of impression formation, and is based on a very basic premise of Tajfel and Turner's (1979) Social Identity Theory: needs for self-esteem motivate people to view members of the ingroup as superior to those of the outgroup. Social situations that induce members of two groups to conceive of themselves as sharing a common identity (whether it be primarily as one superordinate group or as two subgroups within a larger whole) can capitalize on this motivational process to reduce bias. That is, motivational as well as cognitive mechanisms that can contribute to intergroup bias may be harnessed and redirected to enhance evaluations of former outgroup members and to undermine negative stereotypes of the outgroup.

In general, the research reported in this chapter provides further support for the basic tenet of the Common Ingroup Identity Model – that recategorization from two groups to one group can have a fundamental beneficial influence on intergroup relations. Across a variety of laboratory and field studies, factors that facilitate a more inclusive representation of the ingroup reduced bias and negative stereotyping. These changes were, in particular, mediated by the conception of the aggregate as one group.

This research also identified important moderating influences in the social context of intergroup interaction. Status, which was operationalized as membership in the majority or minority racial and ethnic groups in the high-school study and as the acquiring or acquired organization in the merger study, was systematically related to perceptions of intergroup contact, representations of the groups and bias. Perhaps because high-status groups are presumed to have more control over the contact situation, high-status groups may have more of a vested interest in perceiving the conditions of contact favourably (see Sachdev and Bourhis, 1991; Tajfel, 1972). These perceptions, in turn, predicted more inclusive representations of the groups and lower levels of bias. These findings are consistent with Mullen, Brown and Smith's (1992) meta-analytic review of the ingroup bias literature. They found that ingroup bias increased with status in laboratory groups but, as in our field studies, it tended to decrease as a function of relative status in real groups.

The merger study in the present chapter, however, further indicates that the dimension of evaluation is also critical. The higher status group exhibited less bias only when the dimension, sociability, was not directly related to the work dimension that distinguished the groups. When the evaluative dimension was related to the status distinction (work-related characteristics) the higher status group, perhaps to justify its position, demonstrated higher levels of bias than did lower status group members. From the perspective of low-status group members, their relatively greater ingroup favouritism on the sociability measure might also reflect a motivation to achieve positive distinctiveness (see Doojse and Ellemers, this volume). Thus, the fact that sociability is an alternative basis for comparison, rather than sociability per se, may be a determining factor. It is possible that after a merger, those within the groups who have been taken over do not necessarily view themselves as more sociable specifically, but rather may view themselves as superior to the acquirers on any non-work-related, positive dimension, such as 'family-oriented' or 'altruistic'.

The research presented in this chapter also demonstrates the value of fostering a common ingroup identity for altering cognitive impressions of outgroups (i.e., stereotypes), as well as enhancing global evaluations. In particular, negative stereotypes of the outgroup can be undermined by experience with an outgroup member who reveals some counterstereotypic characteristics when the original intergroup boundary is salient within the context of a more inclusive, superordinate entity. In this study, the experimental condition that made the superordinate group identity as a Delawarean salient significantly reduced the negative stereotyping by University of Delaware students of Townies. Generalization from a counterstereotypic member to the outgroup did not occur to the same extent when the salience of the original group boundaries was simply reinforced. Furthermore, degrading group boundaries in itself was not sufficient to reduce outgroup stereotyping significantly. When the salience of the boundaries was decreased by inducing participants to conceive of themselves as individuals (i.e., decategorization) the effects of exposure to the counterstereotypic model were also weak. Decategorization may weaken the perceived link between the particular outgroup member who displayed counterstereotypic characteristics and other members of the group. The basis for generalization may therefore be weakened. Thus, decategorization alone, without any concomitant cognitive or motivational change, may not be sufficient to generalize reductions in bias beyond the immediate contact situation.

Developing a common superordinate identity, however, does not require group members to forsake their original group identity nor to ignore the sub-group identities of other members. For example, the high-school study revealed that a dual identity, such as conceiving of oneself simultaneously as a minority group member and as an American, or regarding the different groups as 'play-ing on the same team', is not only possible, but is associated with lower inter-group bias. In addition, this dual identity can maintain a link for generalizing positive affect or counterstereotypical impressions to other group members. The strength of the superordinate identity mediates positive attitudes toward members of the outgroup and the strength of the subgroup identity provides a mechanism by which generalization can occur. Additionally, because the dual identity maintains the integrity of the subgroup identities, it may reduce the likelihood that members of higher status groups would resist coalescence with lower status groups.

We caution, however, that there may be limiting conditions, not yet ex-plored, to the stereotype-reducing effect we obtained. In our study, although the outgroup was a real group possessing an established stereotype, very little actual contact takes place between ingroup (students) and outgroup ('Townies'). In such a situation, the common ingroup identity of Delawarean may have made enhancing outgroup impressions a desirable end, particularly since this shared identity posed no threat to either subgroup. Furthermore, it is difficult to estimate just how long, and in which specific situations generalization will persist. A more complete test of the Common Ingroup Identity Model's poten-tial for attenuating outgroup stereotypes will come when it is tested among real groups with established stereotypes who experience continued contact with one another in potentially threatening contexts. Such a situation may be sim-ilar to that of a corporate merger in which intergroup contact is maintained for continued periods of time and in which there is usually implicit competition between the groups. If so, then we can learn from the merger study: promoting a one-group representation through egalitarian norms and positive interdepend-ence should only make it easier to embrace the outgroup.

In summary, this chapter has emphasized the potential importance of cog-nitive and motivational dynamics associated with group identity for initiating and reversing intergroup biases and stereotyping. Also, we have emphasized how the social context, such as the conditions of intergroup contact, can in-fluence whether people maintain categorized, decategorized or recategorized impressions of people who were initially ingroup and outgroup members. Although we do not regard a common ingroup identity to be a panacea, we have presented evidence from a variety of situational contexts that perceiving a more inclusive, shared identity with former outgroup members can reduce bias and negative stereotyping.

Note

Preparation of this chapter was facilitated by a grant from the National Institutes of Mental Health (Grant RO1MH48721) to Samuel Gaertner and John Dovidio. We wish to extend our deep-felt thanks to the editors, Russell Spears, Penny Oakes, Naomi Ellemers and Alex Haslam for their very helpful suggestions and insights on an earlier version of this chapter.

11
Stereotyping under Threat: The Role of Group Identification

Bertjan Doosje and Naomi Ellemers

> After attending the candlelight vigil in Seattle in memory of Kurt Cobain, a young man returned to his home and abruptly ended his own life with a single bullet. In Southern Turkey a teenage girl was suffering from depression since hearing about Cobain's death. She put on a Nirvana song, locked her bedroom door, and shot herself in the head. In Australia, a teenager committed suicide as a tribute to Cobain. A twenty year old man in Tracy California was with friends when he put a shotgun in his mouth and said, 'Look, I'm just like Kurt Cobain.' Now he is. There have been several other reports of 'copy-cat' suicides since Cobain's death.
>
> (Grant, 1995, p. 4)

The suicide of Kurt Cobain in April 1994 received world-wide media attention. Kurt Cobain, the 27-year-old lead singer of the popular band Nirvana, was regarded as leader of the alternative grunge movement. The untimely death of this young and successful artist not only caused emotional distress among his mostly adolescent followers, but also resulted in uneasiness among their parents. During his lifetime, Kurt Cobain had exerted an important influence on their children's behaviour in terms of music preferences, clothing and hair-style, and even regarding their general outlook on life. In view of their children's display of strong identification with the grunge movement in general and with Kurt Cobain in particular, parents were afraid that their children might also follow him in this ultimate act and take their own lives. The examples given above indicate that this concern may not have been totally irrational. Thus, an important issue that was pursued in the media revolved around the question of how far people would go in expressing their identification with this pop idol and the movement he represented.

In this chapter, we focus on the consequences of group identification for stereotyping and intergroup behaviour. The central aim of our analysis is to uncover the circumstances under which people will act as group members or pursue their individual interests when the image of their group is threatened. Applying an often-reported distinction between sport fans (i.e., 'die-hard' fans vs. 'fair-weather' fans; cf. Wann and Branscombe, 1990), to our reasoning, we propose that 'die-hard' *members* (i.e., those people who identify strongly with their group) are more predisposed to act in terms of their group, and make sacrifices for it, than are 'fair-weather' members. The latter are more likely to take a much more opportunistic and individualistic stance towards group membership. Thus, in the context of stereotyping we suggest that, when faced with a group threat, low identifiers will perceive themselves less in group stereotypical terms than high identifiers.

In our argument, we first make a distinction between straightforward and subtle identity management strategies. We then move on to factors that may threaten the image of a group to which one belongs. Subsequently, we consider how these factors, in interaction with the level of group identification, may affect stereotypical judgements as well as self-stereotyping of group members. The validity of our theoretical argument is tested in a review of experimental studies focusing on these issues. The main conclusions that can be drawn from the present analysis are formulated in terms of identity management strategies that may help people cope with threats to the image of their group.

1   Identity Management Strategies: Straightforward or Subtle

According to social identity theory (Tajfel, 1978a; Tajfel and Turner, 1986), people are motivated to perceive themselves as individuals favourably in relation to others. In other words, people aim to uphold a relatively favourable self-esteem. In addition, it is assumed that people partly derive their self-image from membership in groups, and that they will therefore try to favourably compare a group to which they belong (an ingroup) with other relevant groups to which they do not belong (outgroups). In our view, this can be achieved by means of employing two different kinds of identity management strategies: straightforward and/or subtle. In the context of stereotyping, simply ascribing positive characteristics to the ingroup is perhaps the most straightforward strategy to achieve positive group distinctiveness.

Although examples of straightforward intergroup conflict and discrimination are not hard to find in real-life groups (e.g., the violence towards foreign refugees or immigrants in western European countries), perhaps a more surprising feature of intergroup relations is that group favouring strategies can be very subtle. There is considerable evidence that groups do not always differentiate themselves positively from outgroups – at least not on all possible dimensions (Mummendey and Schreiber, 1983; Spears and Manstead, 1989). One reason for this is that members of low-status groups in real life are often constrained by the consensual social reality of the status hierarchy, especially when these status differences are stable and secure (Tajfel and Turner, 1986). For example, in a study by Spears and Manstead (1989, Expt. 2), Manchester University students had to compare themselves with, amongst others, students from a more prestigious university (Oxford). It was observed that participants acknowledged the superiority of the Oxford University students in terms of perceived status and prestige. Thus, in some conditions, it is difficult to challenge real-life differences that can exist between groups. For this reason, members of low-status groups are likely to display indirect or subtle identity management strategies (e.g., Ellemers and van Knippenberg, this volume; Lemaine, 1974; van Knippenberg and Ellemers, 1990).

These subtle identity management strategies can take various forms (see also Tajfel and Turner, 1986). Emphasizing the importance of positive ingroup dimensions is one form of a subtle strategy (cf. van Knippenberg, 1978). For example, members of a soccer team may stress their team's quality in terms of scoring a lot of goals (and consider this characteristic the most important one in intergroup comparisons), while de-emphasizing the fact that their team's defence is relatively weak. Comparing the ingroup and outgroup on a new dimension can be considered another subtle identity management strategy (cf. 'social originality', Lemaine, 1974). Imagine a sports team that is ranked low in a league. Members of this team probably feel themselves inferior to other teams in terms of achievement, but they may consider themselves superior to other teams with respect to other comparison dimensions, 'playing fair' for instance. A third subtle way to deal with unfavourable comparison contexts is to change the value connotation of dimensions attributed to the ingroup (e.g., the 'black-is-beautiful' movement). For example, Peabody (1968) demonstrated that members of different groups may agree about the type of traits ascribed to a group, but may disagree about the evaluation of those traits. In his classic study, both Chinese and Filipino students agreed that Chinese people tend to spend less money than people from the Philippines. However, Chinese were more likely to describe themselves as 'thrifty' than Filipinos did, whereas Filipinos were more likely to refer to Chinese as 'stingy' than Chinese did. A different kind of strategy to save face in threatening comparative contexts is to lower the aspiration level of the group, and to seek out other lower status groups to compare one's own group with. Thus, instead of comparing their team with the present European and national soccer champion Ajax Amsterdam, teams that are ranked relatively low are more likely to compare themselves with teams possessing equivalent qualities. In addition to these various forms of subtle identity management strategies, a relatively novel form has been identified by Doosje, Spears and Koomen (1995). They observed that group members may accentuate intragroup differences when the image of their group is threatened. To explain this argument, we need to discuss the relation between intergroup differentiation and intragroup variability in more detail.

Although the vast majority of studies on social stereotyping has focused on *inter*group differentiation, recent research has also increasingly begun to consider the issue of perceived *intra*group differences, both in terms of conceptualization and measurement of stereotypes (e.g., Park, Judd and Ryan, 1991). Until the beginning of the 1980s, in most definitions, stereotypes were considered to be personality traits or other characteristics ascribed to a group (e.g., Ashmore and Del Broca, 1981). However, more recently, researchers have started to focus on differences between individual group members with respect to the relevant stereotype (i.e., perceived intragroup variability). In other words, the stereotyping process not only involves ascribing (negative) characteristics to a group of people, but also the perception that this applies to the *group as a whole*. Most research to date that has addressed this issue of perceived group variability has concentrated on the so-called outgroup homogeneity effect, that is the tendency to perceive more intragroup variation within an ingroup than within an outgroup (e.g., Park and Rothbart, 1982; Park et al., 1991; but see for critical discussions Haslam, Oakes, Turner and McGarty, 1996; Simon, 1992). However, we would argue that the perception of intragroup variability may differ as a function of social identity concerns. In particular, it is argued that members of groups with a negative stereotype may stress the heterogeneity of the ingroup and possibly the outgroup (Doosje, Spears and Koomen, 1995). This can be interpreted in at least two ways. First, it is possible to conceptualize this in terms of a subtle identity management strategy to protect the image of the ingroup. Indeed, it could be argued that by perceiving much intragroup variation, the unfavourable intergroup difference becomes less clear. Alternatively, stressing intragroup variation in unfavourable intergroup comparative contexts can also be considered a *personal*-identity protection mechanism. To the extent that people hold a favourable self-image, the idea that there is considerable variation within the ingroup offers scope to maintain this self-image, even when their group as a whole is seen as inferior to other groups. Two studies by Doosje, Spears and Koomen (1995) offer support for these arguments. In these studies, participants were categorized allegedly on the basis of an association task, and received information about the ingroup and the outgroup which was either favourable or unfavourable for the ingroup. It was found that participants in the unfavourable conditions perceived more intragroup variability than in the favourable conditions. This perception of considerable intragroup variability is argued to result most likely from personal identity concerns as described above.

In contrast to people who are inclined to use individual-coping strategies and probably do not feel strongly committed to their group, it is likely that people who are strongly involved with their group may prefer to deal with low group status collectively (Ellemers, 1993). In this sense, we would argue that in the face of a threatening intergroup context, members who differ with respect to their involvement with their group may react in different manners. We would argue that low identifiers are more likely to dissociate themselves as an *individual* from their group, whereas high identifiers may be more inclined to instigate action to the benefit of their *group as a whole* (cf. Tajfel's [1978b, p. 46] distinction between individual and social mobility). In other words, our central prediction is that people who do not feel strongly involved with their group will attempt to protect their personal identity at the expense of the rest of their group when faced with a group threat, which may ultimately result in the group falling apart. Conversely, highly committed group members should stick together and try to improve the fate of their group as a whole.

2   Individual and Collective Responses to Low Group Status

The identity of a group can be threatened in different ways. Tajfel and Turner (1986, p. 16) suggest that 'the evaluation of one's group is determined with reference to specific other groups through social comparisons in terms of value-laden attributes and characteristics'. When this comparison process results in an unfavourable perception of the ingroup, this poses a threat to the image of the group, and, therefore, indirectly a threat to the individual members of the group. This kind of threat is typical of low-status groups, in particular when the status criteria are fair and legitimate (Ellemers, Wilke and van Knippenberg, 1993). A soccer team ranked low in a league may serve as a good example: the team's image may be seriously damaged by the unfavourable comparison with the other teams in terms of group performance, that is, a clear status criterion. In a series of laboratory studies, Ellemers (1993) demonstrated that members of an artificially-created group that performed relatively poorly on a group performance task, were inclined to address to this threat to their social identity either in individual or collective terms, depending on other socio-structural factors (e.g., permeability of group boundaries and stability of group status). Thus, a relative *low group status* position can be considered as a potential threat to the image of a group and its members.

In general terms, we would argue that people who differ in their level of identification with a group may employ different identity management strategies to deal with a threatening group situation. In particular, our argument is that low identifiers may 'turn their back' on their group in a difficult situation, while high identifiers may still 'keep faith' with their group. Using different argumentation and focusing on another dependent variable (i.e., outgroup derogation), Branscombe and Wann (1994) found evidence of an interaction between group-identity threat and identification with one's group. They made a distinction between low- and high-identifying female Americans by dividing undergraduates into groups on the basis of their pride in being American. The participants were shown different versions of the video of *Rocky IV* (which they had not seen before). In the no-threat condition, in the crucial boxing match Rocky (the American fighter) defeated the Russian fighter, whereas in the threat condition the Russian won. Although the authors themselves frame the results somewhat differently, one interpretation of the observed interaction between threat and identification is that in the threat condition the amount of Russian derogation was higher for high identifiers (4.26) than for low identifiers (2.52), whereas in the no-threat condition this difference was absent (2.92 vs. 2.52 for high and low identifiers respectively).

Similar ideas were tested in a study by Turner, Hogg, Turner and Smith (1984, Expt. 2). In this experiment, 13- and 14-year-old Bristol schoolgirls were divided into two groups of four, and were either told that the composition of the groups would remain the same during the experiment, or that they would be recategorized after the first part of the investigation. In the authors' terms, this manipulation created a respectively high and low commitment to the group. Bogus feedback on an anagram task induced the relative ingroup status, which was either low or high. A significant interaction showed that in the low-commitment condition, a high-status position led to increased ingroup favouritism (and liking for the group members), whereas the opposite pattern was observed in the high-commitment condition: a low-status position increased ingroup favouritism (and liking for the group members). The results of these studies offer some support for the notion that people who differ in their level of involvement with their group, may react differently to threats to the image of the group in terms of status.

Another line of research has focused on the relation between ingroup identification and group variability. This line of research indicates that high identifiers generally perceive the ingroup as more homogeneous than low identifiers (cf. Kelly, 1989; Simon, 1992; Wann and Branscombe, 1993). For example, Kelly (1989) showed that among supporters of the British Labour Party, those who were at the same time *members* of the party (and were assumed to identify relatively strongly with their party) perceived their party as more homogeneous than mere supporters of the party (i.e., low identifiers).

In our own research, however, we try to determine more specifically how group members with different levels of identification deal with group threats, that is, whether they employ individual- and/or group-level strategies (Doosje, Ellemers and Spears, 1995). In our view, when facing an uncomfortable intergroup situation, low identifiers may want to 'break free' from the group, and focus on individual differences between group members. In contrast, high identifiers may be more inclined to still try to deal with the situation at the group level, and thus focus on similarities within their group. In other words, the tendency to employ specific subtle strategies under unfavourable conditions is expected to be reflected in intragroup variability judgements. Whereas low identifiers are expected to stress the heterogeneity within the ingroup, high identifiers, on the other hand, may be motivated to emphasize the homogeneity within the ingroup, in order to keep up the group spirit ('United we stand, divided we fall'; cf. Brown, 1978; Simon and Brown, 1987; Turner, Hogg, Turner and Smith, 1984).

In a first study explicitly addressing this issue (Doosje, Ellemers and Spears, 1995, Expt. 1), first-year Dutch psychology students were categorized as either low or high identifiers on the basis of a median split on the mean of a four-item identification scale that measured the level of involvement with psychology students. Participants received false feedback that their group was either less *or* more intelligent than business students. Results indicated elements of both straightforward and subtle strategies. In general, participants ascribed more (positively evaluated) characteristics to the ingroup than to the outgroup, a pattern that can be interpreted as a straightforward strategy to favour the ingroup over an outgroup. Additionally, evidence of more subtle strategies was observed. Firstly, those dimensions that participants had associated with psychology students (the ingroup) were perceived as more important than the dimensions ascribed to business students (the outgroup). The analysis further revealed that when group status was low, low identifiers displayed a decrease in perceived importance of their group's typical dimensions compared to the other three conditions (see table 11.1). Interestingly, this result is further supported by the same interaction and similar pattern of means on perceived ingroup variability (see table 11.2). Thus, low identifiers in the low-status condition perceived the ingroup as significantly more heterogeneous than participants in the other three conditions. These responses from low identifiers may indicate their letting the group 'fall apart': lowering perceived importance of ingroup

Table 11.1 Perceived importance of ingroup dimensions

Ingroup Identification	Ingroup Status	
	Low	*High*
Low	4.98[a]	5.50[b]
High	5.51[b]	5.54[b]

Table 11.2 Perceived intragroup similarity

Ingroup Identification	Ingroup Status	
	Low	*High*
Low	3.57[a]	4.00[ab]
High	4.49[b]	4.08[ab]

Note. Higher values indicate higher importance and intragroup similarity (from 1 to 7). Only cells with different superscripts differ significantly from each other ($p < .05$) in an analysis of simple main effects. Adapted from Doosje, Ellemers, and Spears (1995).

attributes and giving up ingroup homogeneity may eventually result in group decay. In contrast, high identifiers in a group with a negative image still regard ingroup attributes as important and perceive the ingroup as homogeneous: as predicted, these members still want to hold on to their group membership and try to 'stick together' (cf. Worchel, Coutant-Sassic and Grossman, 1992).

Although this experiment delivered preliminary support for our arguments, two methodological weaknesses could be identified. First, because identification was measured rather than manipulated, the observed covariation between identification and intragroup variability does not allow us to infer causality. In addition, the measurement of perceived variability could have been more sophisticated than the general question that was used to measure perceived variability in the first study. Thus, in a second laboratory experiment (Doosje, Ellemers and Spears, 1995, Expt. 2), we tried to avoid these two problems by *manipulating* group identification (as well as group status), and by using more reliable indices of perceived group variability (i.e., range scores; Park and Judd, 1990).

Because group identification has (at least to our knowledge) never been experimentally manipulated before, it seems useful to describe the procedure we developed in some detail. Basically, a bogus pipeline procedure (Gerard, 1964; Jones and Sigall, 1971) was used to directly manipulate group identification. At the beginning of the experiment, first- and second-year Dutch students were instructed to position three electrodes on their hand, ostensibly in order to measure the level of arousal in the body. Participants were categorized allegedly on the basis of their problem-solving style. Next, they performed an intergroup task. They were further required to answer some questions with regard to group membership and relations with other people in general. It was stated that on the basis of both the answers on these questions *and* the measurement of the level of arousal in their body by means of the electrode while performing the intergroup task, it was established that they either weakly or strongly identified with their group. Subsequently, they received bogus feedback on their group's performance on the group task in relation to the other group (status manipulation).

Although the analyses revealed an overall pattern of straightforward ingroup bias in terms of central tendencies, the theoretically more interesting findings are concerned with a more subtle strategy that was displayed in response to low group status: perceived group variability in terms of range scores. The pattern of results closely parallels the findings observed in our first study with natural groups: in the high-status condition, identification had no effect on perceived group variability. However, in the low-status condition, low identifiers perceived the ingroup (see table 11.3) as well as the outgroup (see table 11.4) as more heterogeneous than did high identifiers.

Again, we would argue that this indicates that members who differ in their level of group involvement employ different strategies to cope with a group-identity

Table 11.3 Perceived range ingroup		
Ingroup Identification	*Ingroup Status* *Low*	*High*
Low	72.82^c	63.10^{bc}
High	48.34^a	61.22^{ab}

Table 11.4 Perceived range outgroup		
Ingroup Identification	*Ingroup Status* *Low*	*High*
Low	72.09^c	63.91^{bc}
High	47.86^a	62.24^b

Note. Higher values indicate more intragroup variability (from 1 to 100). Only cells with different superscripts differ significantly from each other ($p < .05$) in an analysis of simple main effects. Adapted from Doosje, Ellemers and Spears (1995).

threat. People who feel little commitment to their group are more inclined to focus on comparisons between themselves as individuals and other individuals in their group, resulting in a rather heterogeneous ingroup perception. In addition, the finding that these members also perceive the *out*group as relatively heterogeneous may stem from the desire to accentuate the overlap between the different groups. In contrast, people who strongly identify as group members still want to deal with group identity threats collectively. This solidarity appears to be reflected in a relatively homogeneous perception of the ingroup (cf. Simon and Brown, 1987). Additionally, their perceptions of both the ingroup and outgroup as relatively homogeneous may be interpreted as a means to accentuate the distinctiveness of the group, and their identity as group members. To summarize the above argument: while 'fair-weather' members may respond to low group status individually, 'die-hard' members seem more inclined to deal with this situation at the group level (cf. Wann and Branscombe, 1990).

3 Self-stereotyping in Response to an Unfavourable Group Stereotype

If the findings with respect to perceived group variability indeed point to a preference for individual or collective strategies to cope with group threat, this should also be evident in a more direct measure. To this end, we conducted two further studies using a measure of self-stereotyping, that is the extent to which participants perceive themselves as similar to other ingroup members as the central dependent variable. This measure of self-ingroup similarity or prototypicality can be considered as a relatively direct measure of self-categorization (Turner, Hogg, Oakes, Reicher and Wetherell, 1987). The more important a group membership is to a person's social identity, the more prototypical members should perceive themselves to be.

Interestingly, a similar measure of self-stereotyping was also administered in a recent study by Simon and Hamilton (1994, Expt. 1). In this experiment, American undergraduates were shown slides of paintings by two painters. They were told that preference for one painter rather than the other was related to being an introvert or an extrovert, and that this preference was associated with belonging to either a minority or a majority. Simon and Hamilton observed stronger self-stereotyping (e.g., higher perceived self-ingroup similarity) for members of a minority group than for members of a majority group. These results were explained in terms of salience of group membership: presumably group membership is more important for members of a minority than for members of a majority group (cf. Ellemers, Doosje, Van Knippenberg and Wilke, 1992; McGuire and Padawer-Singer, 1976).

In a similar vein, by definition group membership is more important for high identifiers than for low identifiers, and thus we expect that high identifiers will perceive more self-ingroup similarity than low identifiers. In addition, it is expected that this difference between low and high identifiers may become particularly apparent when the identity of the ingroup is relatively unfavourable (cf. Doosje, Ellemers and Spears, 1995). In other words, we expect low identifiers to dissociate more from their group than high identifiers, in particular when the group's image is threatened. This idea was tested in two studies. In the first experiment (Spears, Doosje and Ellemers, 1995, Expt. 1), first-year Dutch psychology students were categorized as either low or high identifiers on the basis of the same identification scale we used in the studies described above. Next, as a status induction, participants were requested to judge both the ingroup and an outgroup on eight dimensions. These dimensions and the groups were selected in such a way that the ingroup either compared favourably (i.e., in terms of intelligence with art college students, or in terms of creativity with physics students), or unfavourably to the relevant outgroup (i.e., in terms of intelligence with physics students, or in terms of creativity with art college students). Pilot research had revealed the perceived positions of the groups on these dimensions. Thus, in this experiment, the identity of the ingroup was manipulated by inducing a favourable or unfavourable *self*-perception of the group. The pattern of means confirms our hypothesis with respect to self-stereotyping. In the unfavourable group comparison condition, low identifiers perceived themselves as less similar to the other psychology students than did high identifiers, whereas there was no significant difference in terms of self-stereotyping between low and high identifiers in the favourable comparison condition (see table 11.5). Thus, low and high identifiers differed in their reaction to an unfavourable group stereotype. Whereas low identifiers do not see themselves in terms of their group membership, high identifiers are still prepared to perceive themselves as similar to other group members even when the ingroup stereotype is unfavourable.

In a second study (Spears et al., 1995, Expt. 2), the central aim was to investigate whether an unfavourable group identity due to *public* perception (rather

Table 11.5   Self-stereotyping as a function of ingroup identification and self-perceived ingroup status

Ingroup Identification	Self-Perceived Ingroup Status	
	Low	High
Low	2.64[a]	3.03[b]
High	3.47[c]	3.20[b]

Table 11.6   Self-stereotyping as a function of ingroup identification and public-perceived ingroup status

Ingroup Identification	Public-Perceived Ingroup Status	
	Low	High
Low	3.28[a]	3.62[b]
High	4.00[b]	3.84[b]

Note. Higher values indicate higher self-stereotyping (from 1 to 7). Only cells with different superscripts differ significantly from each other ($p < .05$) in an analysis of simple main effects. Adapted from Spears, Doosje and Ellemers (1995).

than *self*-perception as in the first experiment) would render the same results. First, as in the previous study, we solicited the level of identification, and divided the participants in low and high identifiers on the basis of a median split. Then, participants who were first-year Dutch psychology students, received information comparing psychology to business students, in which they were informed that the general public either perceived psychology students as more favourable (e.g., in terms of empathy) or as less favourable (e.g., less efficient) than business students. Once again, the expected interaction between identification and group threat was found: in the unfavourable comparative condition (in this case due to public perception), low identifiers perceived less similarity between themselves and other psychology students than did high identifiers. As expected, this difference between low and high identifiers was again absent in the favourable comparison condition (see table 11.6).

Taking these studies together, we can draw two important conclusions. First, group favourableness inductions through self-perception and public perception seem to have similar effects as more direct status threats such as described in our earlier work (i.e., Doosje, Ellemers and Spears, 1995). Furthermore, by focusing on the measure of self-stereotyping, these experiments have more directly tested our central hypotheses about individual- and group-level responses to low group status. Thus, a central point of our argument is that when a group finds itself in an unfavourable comparison situation, members who are strongly involved with their group react by drawing together as group members in contrast to members who feel little commitment to their group.

4   Low Distinctiveness as a Group-identity Threat

In the previous section, we have illustrated the different strategies group members may use to cope with threats to the image of their group in terms of relative group status. In this section, we will further explore how various identity management strategies may be employed, while focusing on a different kind of group threat. In particular, in this section, we will discuss reactions to an endangered image of one's group in terms of *group distinctiveness* (cf. Turner, 1978a), implying that the unique identity of the group is at stake.

As individuals, people feel attraction to others with similar attitudes (Byrne, 1971). At the same time, however, people are motivated to perceive themselves as unique human beings, possessing a rare set of qualities and personality characteristics which distinguishes them from other people (Brewer, 1993; Snyder and Fromkin, 1980). At the group level, the same arguments may hold: on the one hand, people may feel attraction to other groups who are similar, as postulated by Rokeach's (1960) belief congruence theory. On the other hand, however, people may prefer membership in groups that are different than other groups, in particular if those groups can be differentiated from other groups in a positive manner (Tajfel and Turner, 1986; Turner, 1978a). Consider for example the Dutch, who in general do not like to be confused with Germans when they travel abroad. Although this may be explained in historical terms (e.g., the German occupation of the Netherlands in the Second World War), the reason also partly is that the Dutch (a very small country and population) may fear that their distinctive identity is threatened by the Germans (a very large country and population), who in many respects are very similar to the Dutch (e.g., in terms of physical appearance and language). Thus, in situations such as this, group members are motivated to insist on a distinctive group identity.

This has also profound consequences for changing group stereotypes by trying to bring members of different groups together. Traditionally, it was assumed that bringing group members in close inter-individual contact with each other would help to change negative attitudes about each other, a notion referred to as the contact hypothesis (e.g., Allport, 1954; Hewstone and Brown, 1986). The central assumption was that contact between members of two groups would help them discover mutual similarities that might diminish the salience of the intergroup differences. More recently, however, it has become increasingly clear that trying to lessen the importance of group membership by focusing on intragroup differences and/or accentuating intergroup similarities may not always be the ideal strategy (cf. Anastasio, Bachman, Gaertner and Dovidio, this volume). Some researchers have argued that people like to be or remain members of groups with a distinctive identity (Turner, 1978a). These researchers have also argued that in order to make intergroup contact successful, it is necessary to respect and secure each other's group membership (Hewstone and Brown, 1986). This then leads to the counter-intuitive hypothesis that changing stereotypes by bringing group members in contact with each other is most likely to be successful when differential group affiliations are both salient and secure. Indeed, empirical evidence supports the notion that members are motivated to perceive their group as *different* (Mummendey and Schreiber, 1983), and recent findings suggest that group members are even willing to accentuate negative ingroup traits, as long as this enables them to clearly distinguish their group from relevant outgroups (Mlicki and Ellemers, 1996; cf. Ellemers and Van Knippenberg, this volume).

A study by Brown (1984, Expt. 2) illustrates the importance of a unique group identity. In that experiment, 12- and 13-year-old Bristol schoolchildren expected to interact with a team that was either similar or dissimilar to them in terms of attitudes. When distinguishing between the children on the basis of their cooperative or competitive orientation, a clear pattern was found: for children low in competitiveness, attitude similarity led to an increased attraction to the other team, but for highly competitive children, attitude similarity led to rejection (see also Brown and Abrams, 1986; Diehl, 1990). Thus, at least for some group members, increasing the salience of similarities between the ingroup and an outgroup can lead to more intense intergroup discrimination, in contrast to what was traditionally expected in the stereotyping literature.

Similar ideas were tested in a recent study by Roccas and Schwartz (1993). They told Israeli high-school students that their school was either a little bit similar, rather similar, or very similar to another school on a number of characteristics (e.g., success in national examination, choices of careers and academic success). In support of their hypotheses, their results showed that ingroup favouritism on group-relevant dimensions was highest in the very high similarity condition. Thus, there is at least some support for the notion that intergroup similarity can pose a threat to the distinctive image of a group, and that group members may respond to this threat by displaying stronger intergroup discrimination.

An important goal of the study by Roccas and Schwartz was to investigate the role of distinctiveness threat on *inter*group judgements. However, in our view, it is also important to investigate predictions with respect to the effects of outgroup similarity and ingroup identification on *intra*group judgements, because, as we have seen in previous sections of this chapter, this may be indicative of the inclination to respond individually or collectively to a group threat. We would argue that in response to a threat to group distinctiveness, members who identify strongly with their group may want to accentuate their prototypicality as group members, in order to reassert their common identity as members of a distinct group. Low identifiers, however, would perceive the similarity of an outgroup as less of a threat, and are hence less likely to respond by displaying increased prototypicality. Thus, in our view, outgroup similarity, in combination with ingroup identification, is expected to affect perceived prototypicality. As a result, we would argue that effects of enhanced salience of intergroup similarities as a means to reduce intergroup discrimination are conditional on ingroup identification. Translating previously advocated arguments in this domain, we would maintain that in a group distinctiveness threatening condition, low identifiers should be more prepared to give up the distinctive role of their group, and may refrain from describing themselves as prototypical group members. In contrast, high identifiers in a group distinctiveness threatening situation should be more likely to reassert the group's distinctive identity, and may perceive themselves as relatively representative for their group. Finally, when the image of the group is not threatened, we expect no difference between low and high identifiers with respect to self-stereotyping, as was the case with threats to group status. In order to test these ideas, two further studies were conducted.

In the first study (Spears, Doosje and Ellemers, 1995, Expt. 3), an ingroup identification measure was obtained, in order to enable us to divide first-year Dutch psychology students into low and high identifiers. Next, they were informed that previous research had revealed that psychology students were either very similar or dissimilar to business students. As expected, the results show that, in general, high identifiers perceived themselves as more similar to other ingroup members than did low identifiers. Additionally, in support of our hypotheses, planned contrasts revealed that this effect was stronger in the similar condition than in the dissimilar condition, albeit that in both distinctiveness conditions the main effect of ingroup identification remained significant. Thus, this first study offered some preliminary support for the notion that low and high identifiers respond differently to an outgroup similarity threat in terms of self-stereotyping.

In the second study along this line (Spears et al., 1995, Expt. 4), the same design was used. However, while in the first study group distinctiveness was varied by inducing a similar or different *self*-perception, the second study focused on differences in group distinctiveness due to *public* perception. Again, the first-year Dutch psychology students were divided into low and high identifiers on the basis of a median split on the identification measure. However, in this study, outgroup similarity was manipulated by providing information that the general public in the Netherlands either perceived no difference or a clear difference between psychology students and business students. The results revealed the predicted interaction between ingroup identification and outgroup similarity on perceived prototypicality. As expected, in the similar outgroup condition, high identifiers perceived themselves as more prototypical for their group than low identifiers, whereas the difference in self-stereotyping was not significant in the dissimilar condition.

Taken together, these two studies illustrate the importance of ingroup identification, in this case in combination with outgroup similarity, in accounting for differential responses of group members with respect to self-stereotyping or perceived prototypicality. In our view, the level of ingroup identification determines whether group members respond individually or collectively to group distinctiveness threats. We would argue that for high identifiers, a similar outgroup may indeed posit a real threat to their distinctive group image. Hence, they respond to this threat by accentuating the self-ingroup similarity, as a means of reasserting their identity as group members. In other words, these members appreciate relatively clear boundaries between the ingroup and similar outgroups. Low identifiers, on the other hand, seem less motivated to stress their group membership, even when confronted with a similar outgroup. The low proto-typicality reported by these members seems to indicate that they think they might as well have been members of the other group. To them, the boundaries between the ingroup and the outgroup seem less important, and they seem more prepared to 'merge' the groups.

5 Conclusions

The present chapter focuses on identity management strategies as a function of group identity threats and ingroup identification. In general terms, it can be argued that either in straightforward or subtle ways, people may try to achieve or maintain a positive social identity. More specifically, the studies discussed in this chapter have demonstrated that group members may react differently to group–identity threats that impinge upon group status or group distinctiveness. In both cases, it was observed that in a threatening situation, high identifiers tend to engage in collective strategies, whereas low identifiers are inclined to search for a solution in individual terms (cf. Ellemers, 1993; Tajfel and Turner, 1986). Only when the group affects one's social identity positively are low and high identifiers equally prepared to perceive themselves in group terms. In other words, responses to a negative group stereotype and attempts to accen-tuate intragroup similarity depend on ingroup identification. The difference between low and high identifiers under threatening situations was evident both from judgements of group variability and from self-stereotyping measurements. Low identifiers seem quite prepared to let the group fall apart and to dissociate themselves from it when under threat, as indicated by low perceived ingroup homogeneity and low perceived self-prototypicality. In contrast, high identi-fiers are inclined to protect the group's distinctiveness, even when the group has a negative image (cf. Mlicki and Ellemers, 1996), as was evident from the relatively high ingroup homogeneity perceptions and high perceived self-ingroup similarity.

These conclusions relate to the discussion on personal and collective self-esteem (Crocker and Luhtanen, 1990; see Long and Spears, this volume). To be more specific, low identifiers may be more concerned with their personal iden-tity, whereas high identifiers are more likely to derive their self-esteem to a considerable extent from their collective or social identity. However, we do think it is important to make a distinction between general collective self-esteem meas-ures as developed by Crocker and Luthanen and our group-specific measure of ingroup identification (Doosje, Ellemers and Spears, 1995; Spears et al., 1995). We agree with James and Cropanzano (1994), who advocate making ingroup identification measures more group-specific than is the case with the global collective self-esteem measure of Crocker and Luthanen. In our view, ingroup identification is precisely that aspect of a person's social identity that can account for substantial differences in coping style to threatening situations for group members. It seems that low identifiers prefer individually oriented strategies: 'Only if the group is any good, I feel like I'm part of it'. In contrast to these 'fair-weather' members, high identifiers opt for more group-level identity management strategies by making clear that they are 'die-hard' members, as in other relationships to which one feels committed: 'For richer for poorer, in sickness and in health, until death do us part'.

Note

The authors would like to thank Alex Haslam, Penny Oakes and Russell Spears for their useful comments on a draft of this chapter. The authors are also grateful to Russell Spears for collaborating on the studies reported here. This research was partially funded by the Dutch organization for scientific research (NWO), SGW grant 560–270–053, awarded to R. Spears.

12
Interdependence, Social Identity and Discrimination

Richard Y. Bourhis, John C. Turner and André Gagnon

1 Introduction: Stereotypes and Intergroup Relations

A major theme of this book is that stereotypes are not only an outcome of individual cognitive functioning, but are always at the same time a social product of group life. Stereotypes are not idiosyncratic creations of particular personalities. They are collective representations of one's own and other groups, shared by members of the stereotyping group and reflecting intergroup relationships (Oakes, Haslam and Turner, 1994; Tajfel, 1981a). They are collective in origin, evolving from within-group interaction and influence to become normatively shared beliefs, consistent with group values and ideologies. They are also collective in object, representing the socially shared properties of group members, their varying intragroup similarities and intergroup differences.

Moreover, the social context in which they develop is a specifically intergroup one. Stereotypes function to represent intergroup realities, defining groups in contrast to others, creating images of the outgroup (and the ingroup) that explain, rationalize and justify the intergroup relationship and one's past, present and future behaviour within it. They play an active and not merely passive role in the conduct of intergroup behaviour. 'They are the oppressors, we the oppressed' is a call for political and social revolt; 'We stand for civilization and progress, they are inferior and backward' is a description of the intergroup relationship which contains a political analysis, justifying the pursuit of group interests. Stereotypes are political weapons in conflicts and other kinds of relationships between groups (Oakes et al., 1994; Tajfel, 1981a).

An inescapable fact is that *stereotypes represent and reflect intergroup relations.* There is much relevant evidence for this assertion. An early and clear demonstration was provided by Sherif and his colleagues (see Sherif, 1967) in the late

1940s and early 1950s, as an aspect of their pioneering research into the causes of social conflict. Sherif originated what has been called the 'intergroup' perspective on prejudice, discrimination and social conflict (Turner and Giles, 1981b). He rejected the idea that social conflict was a product of individual or interpersonal attitudes and processes and saw it as a lawful reflection of the character of the relationships between the relevant social groups. He pointed to the psychological discontinuities between people acting as group members and people acting as individuals.

Sherif's research showed that as groups formed and intergroup relationships changed, so did stereotypes of own and other groups. They emerged to glorify the ingroup and consolidate group cohesion and to denigrate the outgroup, placing it and its members at a definite social distance where relations were conflictual. This work illustrated that stereotypes are the collective representational aspect of intergroup relations and that, therefore, *theories of intergroup conflict are central to understanding stereotyping*. Stereotyping is in effect intergroup perception. The same social psychological processes which determine intergroup behaviour also play a crucial role in determining stereotyping.

Sherif's specific theory offered an 'interdependence' perspective on intergroup relations and stereotyping. It was the structure of the objective relationship between groups' goals that was decisive in stereotyping. Conflict of interests between groups produced intergroup competition and negative outgroup stereotypes. Superordinate group goals generated intergroup cooperation and mutually positive stereotypes. Sherif's anti-reductionist and anti-individualistic meta-theory, his 'intergroup' perspective, has subsequently been developed by Social Identity Theory (Tajfel and Turner, 1979). Whilst fully embracing Sherif's thesis that social conflict and related phenomena must be explained as a function of group-level relationships and processes, Social Identity Theory has nevertheless focused on a different set of processes at work in intergroup relationships. Where interdependence theories emphasize the structure of relationships between group goals, Social Identity Theory points to the complementary role of ingroup identity formation, collective self-evaluation and social comparison in producing discriminatory behaviour and ethnocentric evaluation of ingroup and outgroup members. It is particularly relevant to the ethnocentric, evaluative aspect of social stereotyping.

Social Identity Theory originated as an explanation of findings obtained in the 'minimal group paradigm' (Tajfel, 1972; Turner, 1975). The paradigm seemed to suggest that interdependence relationships were not a necessary condition for the appearance of discriminatory intergroup behaviour and stereotyping. Social identity processes seemed able to play an autonomous role in intergroup behaviour. However, this interpretation has been challenged in recent years by interdependence theorists. In this chapter we focus on the competing interpretations of this paradigm and its results. We ask whether it is possible, as claimed, to explain these results solely in terms of interdependence relationships. In effect, the paradigm serves as an experimental vehicle for considering whether and the degree to which both social identity and interdependence processes are required to explain intergroup behaviour and stereotyping. Unravelling the nature of the minimal psychological conditions for intergroup discrimination is a research task with direct and major implications for the analysis of stereotyping.

2 Theories of Intergroup Behaviour and the Minimal Group Paradigm

Social scientists have sought to explain prejudice and discrimination from a variety of perspectives which taken together offer complementary accounts of these intergroup phenomena (Allport, 1954). For instance, sociologists have tended to view prejudice and discrimination as the product of social stratification based on the unequal distribution of power, status and wealth between rival groups (Marger, 1991). In stratified societies dominant groups can maintain their power position by imposing an ideology which justifies the discriminatory practices needed to maintain their advantaged position within the social structure (Taguieff, 1987). In the field of ethnic group relations, a number of sociologists concur in considering differential power between ethnic groups as one of the more important determinants of discriminatory practices in multi-ethnic societies (Marger, 1991; Schermerhorn, 1970).

In contrast to the societal models adopted in the sociological literature, social psychology has sought to integrate both psychological and collective explanations of prejudice and discrimination (Brown, 1986; Bourhis and Gagnon, 1994; Tajfel, 1978b; Turner and Giles, 1981b). As noted by Billig (1976) much of the early work on the social psychology of intergroup relations stressed intra-individual and interpersonal psychological processes contributing to prejudiced attitudes and discriminatory behaviour. The authoritarian personality (Adorno, Frenkel-Brunswick, Levinson and Sanford, 1950; Altermeyer, 1987) and scapegoat theory (Campbell, 1947) represent classic examples of intra-individual accounts of prejudice and discrimination. Social learning theory combined developmental and socio-cultural processes as explanations for prejudice and discrimination across the lifespan (Aboud, 1988). However, as seen earlier, it was the interdependence approach of Sherif (see Sherif, 1967, for a summary) stressing the competitive nature of intergroup relations which provided a fully social psychological framework for the study of prejudice and discrimination (Dovidio and Gaertner, 1986; Turner and Giles, 1981b).

The well-known field experiments of Sherif and his colleagues showed how competition for scarce resources (negative interdependence) could lead to discrimination and antagonistic intergroup relations while positive interdependence between groups in terms of a superordinate goal could lead to more favourable intergroup attitudes and behaviours. Though Sherif's Realistic Conflict Theory received much empirical support in the literature (Jackson, 1993), results from minimal group paradigm experiments showed that conflicting group interests were not a necessary condition for intergroup discrimination (Tajfel and Turner, 1979). Over two decades of research, using variations of the minimal group paradigm, have shown that under certain conditions the mere categorization of people into two groups is sufficient to foster intergroup discrimination (Diehl, 1990; Tajfel, Flament, Billig and Bundy, 1971; Turner, 1975, 1981, 1983). Thus, within the last two decades social psychologists have focused mainly on cognitive and motivational explanations of prejudice and discrimination (Bourhis and Leyens, 1994; Dovidio and Gaertner, 1986; Hogg and Abrams, 1988; Oakes et al., 1994; Tajfel, 1978a; Turner, Hogg, Oakes, Reicher and Wetherell, 1987; Turner and Giles, 1981a; Worchel and Austin, 1986; Zanna and Olson, 1994).

Under what conditions is mere categorization sufficient to trigger intergroup discrimination? Typically, the minimal group paradigm involves members of two arbitrary groups allocating valued resources to anonymous members of the ingroup and the outgroup. There is no previous history of relations between the groups; there is no social interaction within- or between-group members and there are no instrumental links between subjects' responses and their personal self-interest (Tajfel and Turner, 1979). Although these procedures were designed to eliminate grounds for discriminatory behaviour, results show that categorized subjects, nevertheless, discriminate in this ' "empty", almost Kafkaian' situation (Tajfel, 1972, p. 282).

The effect of social categorization is robust and has been replicated with subjects from different nationalities, age and sex groups, occupational groups and with different dependent measures including intergroup perceptions, evaluative ratings, and the distribution of valued resources such as symbolic points, course marks and money (Brewer, 1979; Diehl, 1990; Messick and Mackie, 1989; Tajfel, 1982a; Turner, 1975, 1981). Social categorization has led to intergroup discrimination on various resource distribution scales including free choice (Ng, 1981), binary allocations (Bornstein, Crum, Wittenbraker, Harring, Insko and Thibaut, 1983), multiple allocation matrices (Brewer and Silver, 1978), as well as the 'Tajfel' matrices (Bourhis, Sachdev and Gagnon, 1994; Turner, 1983; Turner, Brown and Tajfel, 1979).

Social Identity Theory (Tajfel, 1972, 1978c; Tajfel and Turner, 1979; Turner, 1975) proposes that the minimal group findings reflect a competition for a positive social identity. Social identity is conceptualized as those aspects of an individual's self-concept that derive from their social group or category memberships together with their emotional and evaluative significance (Tajfel and Turner, 1979; Turner and Oakes, 1989). According to the theory, the arbitrarily imposed categorization into group members provides subjects with their social identity within the minimal group paradigm. Group members' desire for a positive social identity is translated into seeking favourable social comparisons between the ingroup and the outgroup on the only available dimensions of comparison in the experiment, namely, choices on resource distribution scales such as the Tajfel matrices. Thus, by discriminating in their resource distributions, subjects in minimal group studies are able to achieve a positive social identity within the intergroup situation. Subsequently, Self-Categorization Theory (Turner et al., 1987) was developed to provide a broader, complementary analysis of the cognitive processes underlying group formation which allow even categorized individuals within the minimal group paradigm to define and identify themselves as members of a psychological group.

In line with Social Identity Theory, studies suggest that discriminatory behaviour is related to degree of ingroup identification and the achievement or maintenance of a positive social identity within the minimal situation (Sachdev and Bourhis, 1984, 1987, 1991; Turner, 1978b). Furthermore, a number of studies provide evidence that minimal group subjects who discriminated had higher self-esteem than those who did not (Chin and McClintock, 1993; Lemyre and Smith, 1985; Oakes and Turner, 1980). However, the theory does not suggest that intergroup discrimination is the only means of achieving a positive social identity and lays down specific conditions for predicting when this will occur (Tajfel and Turner, 1979). Also, positive social identity, representing the collective, group-level of self-esteem, is quite distinct from the traditional global, individual difference construct of self-esteem. Indeed, Self-Categorization Theory strongly questions the usefulness of any fixed, global or unitary concept of the individual self (Turner, Oakes, Haslam and McGarty, 1994). Not surprisingly, therefore, recent reviews of laboratory and field studies suggest that the relationship between discriminatory behaviour and self-esteem is complex (Crocker, Blaine and Luhtanen, 1993; Hogg and Abrams, 1990; Hogg and Sunderland, 1991; see Long and Spears, this volume).

Summarizing the results of social identity research on the minimal group effect, Oakes et al. (1994) conclude that whether social categorization is likely to lead to intergroup discrimination depends on the following conditions:

(1) the degree to which subjects identified with the relevant ingroup and (2) the salience of the relevant social categorization in the setting, (3) the importance and relevance of the comparative dimension to ingroup identity, (4) the degree to which the groups were comparable on that dimension (similar, close, ambiguously different), including in particular, (5) the ingroup's relative status and the character of the perceived status differences between the groups (Tajfel, 1978b; Turner, Brown and Tajfel, 1979; Sachdev and Bourhis, 1987). (Oakes et al., 1994, p. 83)

Taken together, social identity research in both laboratory and field settings emphasizes the subtlety of the discrimination process and its sensitivity to the realities of social context and the dynamics of intergroup relations in specific situations (Bourhis, 1994; R. J. Brown, 1995; Oakes et al., 1994; Tajfel, 1978c).

Several explanations other than Social Identity Theory have been proposed to account for minimal intergroup discrimination. However, these alternative interpretations – based on conformity to cultural or social norms (Billig, 1973; Turner, 1981), the type of criterion used to categorize subjects such as intragroup similarity (Billig and Tajfel, 1973), the unfamiliar character of the minimal group situation (Tajfel and Billig, 1974), demand characteristics within the paradigm (St. Claire and Turner, 1982), social norms related to fairness and discrimination (Brown, Tajfel and Turner, 1980), and anticipated discrimination from outgroup members (Diehl, 1990) – do not provide a complete explanation or have not been supported by research results. Research suggests that factors such as specific group norms or perceived similarity can certainly affect intergroup discrimination (e.g., Jetten, Spears and Manstead, 1995), but they are probably better conceptualized as additional interactive causes of ingroup bias rather than as explanatory alternatives to the role of social identity in minimal discrimination.

Recently in a series of papers, Rabbie and his colleagues have argued against the analysis of the social group and minimal intergroup discrimination provided by social identity and self-categorization theories (Horwitz and Rabbie, 1989; Rabbie, 1991; Rabbie and Horwitz, 1988; Rabbie, Schot and Visser, 1989). Rabbie et al. (1989) propose an alternative explanation of the minimal group effect based on their analysis of group behaviour known as the Behavioural Interaction Model. One of its main propositions is that group cohesion, social identification, discrimination, cooperative and affiliative group interaction result from mutual interdependence for the achievement of some rewarding outcome related to the satisfaction of individual needs (Rabbie, 1991). Rabbie et al. (1989) argue and claim to provide data to demonstrate that ingroup favouritism in the minimal group paradigm is not a function of social categorization or social identification but is purely rational, instrumental, utilitarian and economically self-interested. Thus, contrary to Social Identity Theory, they propose that social categorization is *not* a sufficient condition for group formation and intergroup discrimination. They maintain instead that perceived interdependence

> is a crucial pre-condition for the formation of social groups from which other processes may follow such as the emergence of specific group norms, interpersonal attraction, ingroup–outgroup differentiation, group identification. (Rabbie et al., 1989, p. 175)

Rabbie et al. (1989) propose that allocation behaviour in the minimal group paradigm, as any other behaviour, is a function of both the external environment and the psychological orientations of individuals. According to the Behavioural

Interaction Model, the external environment of the paradigm includes the interdependence structure between the two groups within the experimental situation. This interdependence structure elicits an indirect instrumental link between subjects' personal fate and that of ingroup and outgroup others on whom they depend within the intergroup structure. The psychological orientations of group members in the paradigm include self-interest, expectations of reciprocity from ingroup members and social and cultural norms about appropriate intergroup behaviour. It is the interaction of the external environment and the psychological orientations of individuals which leads group members to choose actions that contribute most to the satisfaction of their own personal needs. Thus, for the Behavioural Interaction Model, there is a rational, instrumental link between subjects' discriminatory behaviour and their personal fate: subjects will allocate more money to group members upon whom they feel dependent for maximizing their own personal self-gain (Rabbie et al., 1989, p. 187). In contrast, the social identity explanation is that social categorization along with the process of ingroup identification leads to discrimination uncontaminated by any rational link between subjects' personal self-interest and ingroup favouritism (Tajfel, 1972; Turner, 1975). As shown in figure 12.1 it is clear that the Behavioural Interaction Model and Social Identity Theory offer fundamentally opposed explanations for discriminatory behaviour within the minimal group paradigm.

3 The Rabbie, Schot and Visser 'Interdependence' Study

One single published article (Rabbie et al., 1989) forms the empirical backbone of the Behavioural Interaction Model explanation of discrimination in the minimal group paradigm. The present chapter analyses the empirical evidence provided by Rabbie et al. (1989) in support of their interdependence interpretation of the minimal group effect. The more general critique of social identity theory made by Rabbie and colleagues will not be discussed here, since Turner and Bourhis (in press) have provided a comprehensive analysis and rebuttal of this critique. In line with their model, Rabbie and his colleagues state that the goal of their 1989 experiment is to show that there is a self-interest link explaining discrimination within the minimal group paradigm:

> The main aim of this paper is to show that in the standard MGP [minimal group pradigm], there *is* a rational link between economic self-interests and the two major allocation strategies which are often found in MGP experiments: the strategy of ingroup favouritism and the 'influential strategy of fairness' (Tajfel and Turner, 1979, 39): to give the ingroup about as much as the outgroup. (Rabbie et al., 1989, pp. 175–6)

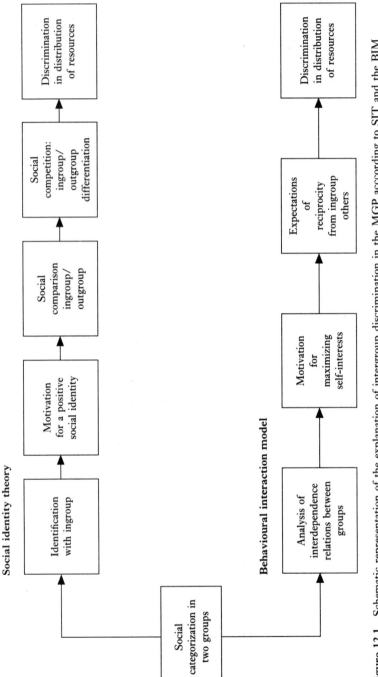

Figure 12.1 Schematic representation of the explanation of intergroup discrimination in the MGP acccording to SIT and the BIM (Rabbie et al., 1989; Tajfel and Turner, 1979, 1986).

The most important feature of the Rabbie et al. (1989) experiment is a manipulation of the interdependence structure between ad hoc groups in a standard minimal group situation. Undergraduate students took part in a decision-making task in which they were categorized into two groups ostensibly on the basis of their preferences for styles of paintings. The decision task consisted of the allocation of money to anonymous members of the ingroup and the outgroup using the Tajfel matrices (Tajfel et al., 1971). In the ingroup dependence condition (ID) subjects were told that 'they would receive, at the end of the experiment the amount of money the ingroup members had awarded them' (Rabbie et al., 1989, p. 182). In the outgroup dependence condition (OD) subjects were told they would receive the money outgroup members had awarded them. In the 'two-sided interdependence' condition subjects were told they would receive the amount of money awarded by both ingroup and outgroup others (IOD, i.e., ingroup and outgroup dependence). The IOD condition represents the objective interdependence structure of the standard minimal group paradigm experiment.

In line with the Behavioural Interaction Model, the prediction for the ID condition was that the greater the perceived dependence of outcomes on the ingroup, the more subjects would use ingroup favouritism (FAV) in their resource distribution. Likewise the greater the perceived dependence on the outgroup, the more subjects should favour the outgroup (O FAV) in their monetary allocations. However the authors make a prediction inconsistent with their model in the IOD control condition:

> The ingroup favouritism in the standard IOD condition will occupy an inter-mediate position between these two poles of the perceived interdependence continuum since subjects perceive themselves to be dependent on both groups. (Rabbie et al., 1989, p. 179)

However, it remains unclear why subjects should discriminate in favour of their own group in the IOD control condition if favouritism reflects interdependence. On the basis of the Behavioural Interaction Model, one should expect maximal use of parity (P) and *no ingroup favouritism whatsoever* in the IOD condition since subjects depend equally on both ingroup and outgroup others and favouritism towards one group rather than the other would destroy the expectation of mutual reciprocity with one of the groups, thus undermining the subject's ultimate financial self-interest in the experiment. Furthermore, the interdependence analysis should also predict strong use of the maximum joint profit (MJP) strategy in the IOD condition, since this strategy of giving as much money as possible to *both* ingroup and outgroup others maximizes financial self-interest on the assumption that others in the experiment will have done likewise (Bourhis et al., 1994).

Manipulation checks showed that subjects in the Rabbie et al. (1989) study correctly perceived the interdependence structure established in each of the three experimental conditions. For instance, subjects in the IOD control condition did perceive their own fate to be equally dependent on both ingroup and outgroup members. However, contrary to the Behavioural Interaction Model, subjects expected to gain more money from ingroup than outgroup members in the IOD control condition. Also, subjects expected to gain more money from the ingroup in the OD condition than from the outgroup in the ID condition. Taken together, these results suggest a tendency to expect more from ingroup than outgroup members regardless of the interdependence structure established in the three conditions. These results are inconsistent with the Behavioural Interaction Model and Rabbie et al. (1989) invoke the following post hoc explanation:

> These findings may reflect the operation of a normative orientation to expect more of one's own group than from an outgroup, e.g., according to the generic 'groupness' norm of Tajfel et al. (1971), or the moral notion that more weight should be given to the desires of the ingroup and its members than to the outgroup and its members . . . (p. 186)

Implicit in both explanations offered by Rabbie is the assumption that psychological group formation has already taken place following the ad hoc categorization of subjects, regardless of the interdependence structure established in the three conditions. As Self-Categorization Theory predicts, social categorization per se is sufficient to produce an expectation of mutual cooperation between ingroup members: in a 'we-group', others' interests become 'our own interests' (Turner, 1981, 1982, 1985).

As regards resource distribution, results obtained by Rabbie et al. (1989) showed that discrimination varied as a function of the interdependence structure established between the groups in the ID and OD conditions, while results obtained in the control condition (IOD) remain open to interpretation. Group members whose outcome was determined exclusively by ingroup others (ID condition) not only used ingroup favouritism (FAV) but also maximum differentiation (MD). MD is the discrimination strategy 'par excellence' as it represents a choice that maximizes the difference in money awarded to ingroup and outgroup recipients but at the cost of sacrificing maximum ingroup profit. 'The maximum differentiation strategy is not economically rational, although it offers the greatest possible differentiation outcome between ingroup and outgroup fate, this differential being in favour of the ingroup' (Bourhis et al., 1994, p. 211). Thus there is no obvious interdependence explanation for the use of the MD strategy in the ingroup dependence (ID) condition established by Rabbie et al. (1989).

Group members whose fate was exclusively determined by outgroup others (OD condition) used outgroup favouritism (O FAV), allocating more money to outgroup members than ingroup members. As predicted by the Behavioural Interaction Model, these results suggest that total dependence on outgroup others can reverse the usual minimal group effect.

In the standard minimal group condition in which subjects were equally dependent on ingroup and outgroup others (IOD), subjects used more parity (P) than in the other two conditions, thus supporting the Behavioural Interaction Model prediction. However, subjects in the IOD condition ALSO used BOTH ingroup favouritism (FAV) and maximum differentiation (MD) to favour members of their own group. Clearly the latter results are not in line with the model, which should predict that dependence on both ingroup and outgroup others would eliminate the need to discriminate on FAV and should certainly not predict use of the economically irrational MD strategy. Nevertheless, Rabbie et al. (1989) conclude:

> In their early work Tajfel et al. (1971, p. 174) emphasized the 'non-rational', 'non-instrumental' and 'non-utilitarian' character of the allocation behaviour in their experiments. In contrast with this view we have shown that the allocation behaviour in the MGP is perfectly rational, instrumental and utilitarian at least when monetary outcomes are involved. (Rabbie et al., 1989, p. 197)

However on the same page the authors must acknowledge the non-instrumental nature of the discriminatory responses they obtained in their IOD and ID conditions, though the authors propose ad hoc explanations for these non-supportive results:

> Even in subgroups within the same preference group, some ingroup favouritism was observed, although this strategy did not have any utilitarian value to the subjects in maximizing their outcomes, but can probably be best understood as a consequence of the normative orientation to give greater weight to the desires of ingroup than outgroup members . . . (Rabbie et al., 1989, p. 197)

In their paper Rabbie et al. (1989) maintain that discrimination (FAV) in their 'two-sided interdependent' IOD condition is consistent with the Behavioural Interaction Model. They suggest that this model is more parsimonious than social identity theory because it can explain the greater parity (P) obtained in the IOD than the ID and OD conditions, as well as the more moderate levels of FAV in IOD than ID and OD. However, the authors predicted greater parity in the IOD condition for the same reason that they should *not predict* any discrimination whatsoever (FAV or MD) in the IOD condition. As in the usual minimal situation, there is no differential dependence on the ingroup and the outgroup in the IOD condition and, thus, according to the Behavioural Interaction Model, subjects would not serve their self-interest if they discriminated against either group in this condition.

4   The Sachdev and Bourhis 'Power Differential' Study

Do the Rabbie et al. (1989) results warrant the conclusion that interdependence of fate and self-interest offer a better explanation of minimal intergroup discrimination than Social Identity Theory? In fact many of the issues raised in the Rabbie et al. study were earlier addressed by Sachdev and Bourhis (1985), who approached the question of ingroup/outgroup dependence from a 'power differential' perspective using Social Identity Theory as a conceptual framework (Ng, 1980, 1982). As is evident from the sociological literature, Sachdev and Bourhis (1984) noted that, unlike the usual minimal group studies, real-life intergroup relations usually occur between groups of unequal power, status and demographic strength. Consequently, Sachdev and Bourhis (1984, 1985, 1987, 1991) conducted a series of minimal group studies specifically designed to investigate the independent and combined effect of group power, group status and group numbers on intergroup discrimination.

In their power differential study, Sachdev and Bourhis (1985) created ad hoc minimal groups whose degree of control over the allocation of course credits to ingroup and outgroup members varied systematically from 0 per cent to 100 per cent power. Intergroup power was defined as the degree of control one group has over its own fate and that of outgroups. Three types of intergroup power differential were created: (1) a situation in which both the ingroup and outgroup had 50 per cent power as in the usual minimal group study; (2) a situation in which one group had 70 per cent control over the distribution of resources while its outgroup had only 30 per cent control; (3) an extreme power differential situation in which one group had total 100 per cent control while its outgroup had 0 per cent or no control. The decision task consisted of distributing an extra course credit for taking part in the study. The extra credit was distributed to anonymous ingroup and outgroup others using the Tajfel matrices. These behavioural measures were supplemented with perceptual items including subjects' degree and quality of ingroup identification, intergroup perceptions and self-reports of strategies used with the Tajfel matrices.

It is clear that Rabbie et al.'s (1989) ID condition corresponds closely to the Sachdev and Bourhis (1985) 100 per cent power condition, since relevant subjects in both studies are in complete control of their own fate and need not depend at all on the outgroup for the resources they obtain in the study. Similarly, subjects in the OD condition are in the same situation as the 0 per cent power group since subjects in both situations are at the total mercy of the dominant outgroup for the resources they receive in the experiment. As in the standard minimal studies, the IOD condition corresponds to the 50 per cent power condition in Sachdev and Bourhis's (1985) study, since subjects' fate in each experiment depend equally on ingroup and outgroup decisions.

Sachdev and Bourhis (1985) proposed that 'usable power' enables group members to actualize and achieve a positive social identity through discriminatory behaviour (Ng, 1982). Thus, power was conceptualized as a discrimination tool needed to attain a more positive social identity. Increasing ingroup power should lead to concomitant increases in discrimination such that dominant group members (100%, 70% groups) should discriminate more than subordinate group members (0%, 30% groups), while equal power groups (50%) should discriminate as much as in the usual minimal group studies. It is through the use of discrimination strategies such as ingroup favouritism (FAV) and especially the 'economically irrational' maximum differentiation (MD) strategy that positive social identity can be achieved under such power differential conditions.

Sachdev and Bourhis (1985) did find that dominant group members discriminated more than subordinate group members. On both FAV and MD the 70 per cent high power group was most discriminatory, closely followed by the 100 per cent power group. These are essentially the results obtained by Rabbie et al. (1989) showing that ID subjects, in complete control of their own fate, discriminated using both the FAV and MD strategies. As expected in the power differential study, low power groups (0%, 30%) were less discriminatory than dominant (70%, 100%) and equal power (50%) groups. Importantly, the no (0%) power group members were overwhelmingly fair (P) and did not discriminate at all on either the FAV or MD strategy, demonstrating that 'usable power' is a necessary condition for intergroup discrimination. Likewise, OD subjects, totally dependent on outgroup others in the Rabbie et al. study, did not discriminate at all against the outgroup and in some cases showed outgroup favouritism. Corroborating the usual minimal group results, equal power groups (50%) in the Sachdev and Bourhis study discriminated against outgroup members using both FAV and MD, a result also obtained in the 'two-sided interdependence' IOD condition of Rabbie et al. Taken together, the pattern of discrimination obtained by Rabbie et al. to support their Behavioural Interaction Model is quite similar to that found in the earlier power differential study of Sachdev and Bourhis (1985) which used Social Identity Theory as a conceptual framework. Basically similar empirical results are used to support two rival theories.

Unlike Rabbie et al. (1989), Sachdev and Bourhis (1985) did use extensive post-session questionnaire items to further test basic conceptual issues relevant to their study. As expected from Social Identity Theory, post-session questionnaire results showed that absolute (100%), high (70%) and equal (50%) power group members felt more comfortable, satisfied and happy about their group membership than did low (30%) and no power (0%) group members. Thus dominant and equal power groups seemed to enjoy a more positive social identity than subordinate group members in the experiment. Furthermore, the high power group (70%) which was the most discriminatory also reported the highest level of identification with their own group. Finally, regardless of their group power (0%–100%), subjects felt they liked ingroup members more than outgroup members. The latter result is clearly an effect of a general cognitive process of self-categorization (consistent with social identity ideas) which is at work in intergroup perceptions, over and above any effects due to the 'interdependence structure' of power differentials established between dominant and subordinate groups. Sachdev and Bourhis (1985) conclude by noting that whereas minimal group categorization may lead to more ingroup than outgroup liking, power differentials may be more predictive of discriminatory behaviour. Very similar patterns of discrimination and intergroup perceptions have been obtained in other 'power differential' studies conducted with mixed sex groups, same sex and opposite sex groups (Bourhis, 1994; Sachdev and Bourhis, 1991).

Rabbie et al. (1989) use their results to dispute Social Identity Theory while claiming their findings support the Behavioural Interaction Model. However, aside from a number of open-ended questions which could not be and were not systematically content-analysed, Rabbie et al. did not include any post-session questionnaire items to address the social identity issues they claimed their results spoke to. Likewise they provide no post-session questionnaire data to document their claim that results inconsistent with their model can be explained (post hoc) by the 'generic groupness norm'. If appropriate post-session questionnaires had been used, then Rabbie et al. (1989) would have had better empirical grounds for claiming that their study was adressing the relative merits of their model and Social Identity Theory as accounts of minimal intergroup discrimination.

In a subsequent chapter, Horwitz and Rabbie (1989) finally abandon their original line of argument to the effect that discrimination in the 'two-sided interdependence' condition (i.e., IOD) is consistent with the Behavioural Interaction Model. Summarizing the results of the Rabbie et al. (1989) experiment they state:

> The results should not be taken to mean that subjects in the minimal intergroup situation act only to maximize their individual gains and are indifferent to the outcomes of others in their groups. Biases in favour of ingroup members remain evident in these data. In the condition in which subjects were dependent on both the ingroup and outgroup, they allocated as usual more money to ingroup than outgroup members. In the conditions in which subjects were solely dependent on either the ingroup or outgroup, they allocated significantly more money to ingroup than outgroup members. Their behaviour could reflect the fact that they expected ingroup members to be more likely than outgroup members to cooperate with themselves (Hornstein, 1982). It could also reflect the other side of this 'generic' norm, namely that as group members they ought to give more consideration to the interests of the ingroup and its members than to the interests of the outgroup and its members. (Horwitz and Rabbie, 1989, p. 111)

Thus Rabbie and colleagues focus on the ID and OD data of the 1989 experiment to claim that their predictions are confirmed and that minimal group responses are perfectly rational and self-interested. As seen above, the authors are also aware that ingroup favouritism (FAV) in the IOD condition and stronger ingroup bias in the ID than outgroup bias in the OD condition are findings at odds with the interdependence structure they established to test the Behavioural Interaction Model. But they invoke the 'generic groupness norm' to rescue their position from demonstrable falsification. This supposed 'generic groupness norm' was first proposed by Tajfel et al. (1971) in the paper reporting the original minimal group experiments. Rabbie et al.'s version of the groupness norm, which has no obvious conceptual link with the Behavioural Interaction Model, is that people give more weight to the desires of ingroup members than outgroup members. This 'norm' in effect acknowledges a fundamental result of their study: that it is the social categorization of subjects into ingroup and outgroup, as well as the manipulated reward structure, which determines how subjects define their 'self-interests' and with whom they expect to cooperate or compete. Thus, the invocation of the 'groupness norm' is a restatement of the psychological effect of social categorization and redescribes a causal process more consistent with Social Identity Theory than with the Behavioural Interaction Model. If there were no social categorization effect (no FAV and MD in the IOD condition, etc.), if responses were purely instrumental, rational and self-interested, why would Rabbie need to add the 'groupness norm' to their model? The Tajfel et al. (1971) notion of a 'groupness norm' was a first attempt to explain the minimal group effect but was quickly discarded as unsatisfactory (Billig, 1976; Tajfel, 1978b; Turner, 1975). As Tajfel and others have noted, any number of norms can be invoked to explain results 'after the fact'. Normative accounts remain unsatisfactory to the extent that one cannot predict 'before the fact' *which norm* will prevail as the determinant of intergroup behaviour. Thus the 'generic groupness norm' is unsatisfactory *as an explanation* of the minimal group effect, precisely because it is largely a redescription of the effect (Tajfel, 1978b; Turner, 1975, 1980).

5   The Gagnon and Bourhis 'Autonomous' versus 'Interdependence' Study

Another difficulty with the Rabbie et al. study is the fact that the collective interest of the group and the personal self-interest of individual members were confounded. As in the usual minimal group experiment, subjects were dependent on ingroup or outgroup others both for their personal gain and for what their group as a whole would gain. Subjects expected to give and receive resources from anonymous others both as *individual persons* and as members of their *assigned group membership*. So even if subjects were actually seeking to favour their group as a whole rather than themselves personally, their responses inevitably appear as self-interested. What is required to test the self-interest explanation proposed by Rabbie et al. is a manipulation of the degree to which subjects are *personally* dependent, or not, on group outcomes whilst allowing them to favour their own group if they wish.

Using the minimal group paradigm, Gagnon and Bourhis (1992, 1996) categorized undergraduates as members of ad hoc groups on the basis of a random criterion (the toss of a coin). The study was presented as a decision-making task in which subjects made decisions about how to distribute an extra five percentage points which could be added to their final grade in the psychology course in which they were enrolled. The percentage grade distribution was made using the Tajfel matrices. The first condition consisted of the usual minimal group situation in which subjects' final grades depended on the combined allocation decisions of anonymous ingroup and outgroup others. For the specific purpose of this study this 'two-sided interdependent' (i.e., IOD) situation was labelled the 'interdependent' condition. The second condition was exactly the same as the first except for one important difference. Prior to their decision task, individual subjects were privately told that in their personal case the experimenter had already decided to give them the total possible five-extra points for taking part in the study. Individuals who are assured by the experimenter that they will personally receive the *maximum* points possible within the experiment are 'autonomous'; because their individual fate no longer depends on the decisions of ingroup or outgroup others.

According to the Behavioural Interaction Model, full satiation of the individual's self-interested need for maximum gain should remove the basis for the expectation of ingroup reciprocity which supposedly accounts for discrimination in the minimal group paradigm. There is no longer any self-interest basis for favouring ingroup others since there is nothing to gain. Thus 'autonomous' individuals should *not* engage in discriminatory behaviour in this condition. In contrast, according to Social Identity Theory, both 'autonomous' subjects as much as 'interdependent' subjects should discriminate under these conditions. For 'autonomous' subjects, the satiation of personal self-interest should not affect the desire to compare favourably with the outgroup, which, in the minimal group paradigm, can best be achieved through discrimination against outgroup members. Even when personal self-interest is satisfied, Social Identity Theory predicts that subjects who identify with their own group will discriminate as a way of comparing favourably with the outgroup and thus satisfy their need for a positive social identity (Tajfel and Turner, 1986).

According to Social Identity Theory, the determining process in the minimal group paradigm is not interdependence of outcomes, but subjects' identification with their assigned social category membership (Turner, 1985). In order to evaluate the effect of social identification, degree of ingroup identification was measured after completing the resource allocation task. Scores on the group identification measure permitted the formation of two groups: the Low and High ingroup identifiers. Social Identity Theory predicts a positive correlation between degree of ingroup identification and intensity of intergroup discrimination in this paradigm. Under appropriate conditions, the more individuals identify with their own group, the more favourably they want to compare with the outgroup and the more strongly they are likely to discriminate (cf. Hinkle and Brown, 1990). Thus, regardless of their condition as 'autonomous' or 'interdependent' subjects, individuals who identify strongly with their own group (high ingroup identifiers) should be those who discriminate most, while subjects who identify weakly with their own group (low ingroup identifiers) should be those who discriminate least. Thus the Gagnon and Bourhis (1995) study consisted of a 2 × 2 design (Interdependent/Autonomous × Low/High ingroup identifiers) which tested competing predictions derived from the Behavioural Interaction Model and Social Identity and Self-Categorization theories.

Manipulation checks showed that autonomous subjects did expect to receive the maximum number of percentage points at the end of the study and felt much less dependent on ingroup and outgroup others than did independent subjects. Discrimination results showed no significant main effect for the interdependence manipulation and there was no significant interaction effect. Autonomous subjects were as strongly discriminatory on FAV and MD as interdependent subjects. Contrary to the Behavioural Interaction Model prediction, satisfaction of individual self-interest did not stop autonomous subjects from engaging in discriminatory behaviour.

As predicted by Social Identity Theory, the main effect for degree of ingroup identification on intergroup discrimination was highly significant. As can be seen in figure 12.2, high ingroup identifiers discriminated on the relevant FAV and MD strategies while low ingroup identifiers discriminated only weakly on the MD strategy. Conversely low ingroup identifiers were much more parity-oriented (P) than high ingroup identifiers. Thus identification with the minimal ingroup category, not personal self-interest, best predicted discrimination in this minimal group situation. Since degree of identification was not experimentally manipulated but measured after resource allocation, it is also possible that subjects who discriminated more were also those who identified more with their ingroup category. Social Identity Theory suggests that identification can be both an effect and a cause of ingroup bias under certain conditions (see below). The present data do not establish a causal direction from degree of ingroup identification to discrimination. However, the positive and significant correlation ($r = .48$) obtained between degree of ingroup identification and discrimination (FAV, MD) was more consistent with Social Identity Theory than with the Behavioural Interaction Model.

For Self-categorization Theory 'social identity is the social-cognitive basis of group behaviour, the mechanism that makes it possible'. (Turner et al., 1987,

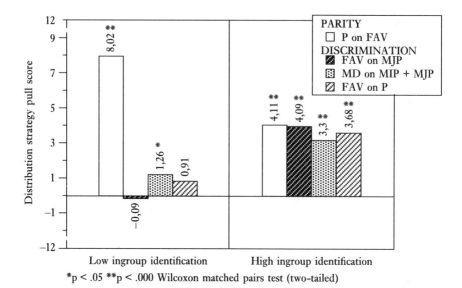

*p < .05 **p < .000 Wilcoxon matched pairs test (two-tailed)

Figure 12.2   Mean pull scores of subjects' matrix distribution strategies, as a function of degree of ingroup identification.

p. ix). As a consequence of self-categorization at the intergroup level, people who identify strongly with their own group tend to perceive themselves in a stereotypical fashion, attributing to themselves the attitudes and behaviours which best define their ingroup membership (the depersonalization process; Turner, 1982). From this perspective, high ingroup identifiers in the Gagnon and Bourhis (1996) study should perceive their own resource distribution behaviour to be more similar to the behaviour of other ingroup members than to that of outgroup members. In contrast, low ingroup identifiers were expected to view their behaviour in a less stereotypical way, seeing little difference between their own behaviour and that of ingroup or outgroup others. In contrast, no such differential predictions can be made from the point of view of the Behavioural Interaction Model.

Subjects were asked to report on the resource distribution strategies they used in their respective experimental conditions: ingroup favouritism, maximum differentiation, parity, maximum joint profit and/or outgroup favouritism on the Tajfel matrices (Bourhis et al., 1994). Subjects were also asked to report on how much they thought ingroup and outgroup others had used each of these strategies in the experiment. Composite difference scores were calculated for perceptions of *self*, *ingroup* and *outgroup* resource distribution behaviours. In line with Self-Categorization Theory, results showed that low ingroup identifiers did not perceive their own resource distribution behaviour as being significantly different from either ingroup or outgroup behaviour.

However, high ingroup identifiers perceived their own distribution behaviour to be much more similar to the behaviour of other ingroup members than to that of outgroup members. These results are supportive of the role of self-categorization in psychological group formation. Most of the previous evidence confirming this self-categorization effect has been obtained with attitudes, opinions or stereotypes (Oakes et al., 1994), whereas the present results show that the effect can also be obtained on overt intergroup behaviours such as discrimination and parity towards ingroup and outgroup members.

A fundamental premise of Social Identity Theory is that group members discriminate in order to achieve or maintain a positive social identity within the intergroup structure (Tajfel, 1978a). Unlike the Behavioural Interaction Model, Social Identity Theory predicts that favourable feelings associated with ingroup membership (quality of social identity) should be positively related to degree of discriminatory behaviour under certain conditions. Within the Gagnon and Bourhis (1996) study, quality of social identity (positive/negative social identity) was operationalized as a single measure consisting of the following items: how happy, satisfied and comfortable subjects felt about their group membership and how much they liked being members of their own group in the experiment. Results of correlations between subjects' quality of social identity and discriminatory behaviour supported the social identity predictions. Results showed a positive and significant correlation ($r = .30$) between intensity of discriminatory behaviour (on FAV, MD) and quality of social identity. Thus, in line with a fundamental premise of Social Identity Theory, the more group members discriminated the more positive they felt about their social identity (cf. Hinkle and Brown, 1990; Tajfel, 1978b).

An important aspect of the explanation of minimal group discrimination provided by the Behavioural Interaction Model is the idea that subjects favour ingroup members because they expect that these ingroup others will reciprocally favour them (Rabbie and Horwitz, 1988; cf. Diehl, 1990). If expectations of reciprocity play a central role in the minimal group paradigm, then there should be a positive and significant relationship between 'interdependent' subjects' use of ingroup favouritism and their expectations that other ingroup members will favour them. Social Identity Theory might expect subjects in general to expect ingroup others to behave similarly to self but no strong and definite link between ingroup bias and reciprocity expectations is required.

Subjects in the Gagnon and Bourhis (1996) study rated how many points they expected to receive from ingroup members and outgroup others. Results showed that interdependent subjects expected to receive significantly more points from ingroup members than from outgroup members, thus corroborating findings obtained in the Rabbie et al. (1989) study. However, a further analysis showed that there was no significant correlation between how many points interdependent subjects expected to receive from ingroup members and subjects' actual use of discriminatory strategies on the Tajfel matrices (FAV on

P, FAV on MJP). The lack of a significant and positive correlation between interdependent subjects' expectation of reciprocity from ingroup others and their actual discriminatory behaviour does not support Rabbie et al.'s (1989) assertion that

> although subjects in the standard minimal group paradigm cannot directly allocate money to themselves, they can do it indirectly, on the reasonable assumption that the other ingroup members will do the same to them. (p. 176)

The Behavioural Interaction Model posits that perceived interdependence is a pre-condition for psychological group formation including ingroup identification (Rabbie and Horwitz, 1988). Thus interdependent subjects, whose personal fate depends on ingroup others, should identify strongly with their own group. In contrast, with their personal gain maximized, autonomous subjects do not depend on ingroup others to safeguard their self-interest and consequently need not identify strongly with their assigned ingroup membership. Did subjects in the interdependent condition identify more strongly with their own group than subjects in the autonomous condition? Results showed that interdependent subjects did not identify more with their own group than did subjects in the autonomous condition. These results suggest that interdependence does not play the central role in psychological group formation proposed in the Behavioural Interaction Model.

Did autonomous subjects, whose personal self-gain was assured, enjoy a more positive social identity than interdependent subjects? Results showed that autonomous subjects were no more positive about their social identity than subjects whose fate remained dependent on ingroup and outgroup others. These results suggest that the satisfaction of personal self-interest enjoyed by autonomous subjects had little if any effect on the quality of their social identity as *group members*. Satisfaction of personal self-interest neither directly nor indirectly seemed to affect psychological group formation in this study. However, results showed that high ingroup identifiers were more positive about their social identity than low ingroup identifiers. These patterns are more in line with Social Identity Theory than the Behavioural Interaction Model. As noted above, results showed that high ingroup identifiers discriminated more than low ingroup identifiers and that discriminatory behaviour was associated with a positive social identity.

Overall, results of the Gagnon and Bourhis (1996) study support the explanation of discrimination based on Social Identity Theory. However, one concern that could be raised is that Gagnon and Bourhis used resource allocations based on percentage grade points rather than money. Rabbie and colleagues assert that individuals' concerns for self-interest might be more salient when monetary rewards are at stake and that: 'the norm to give more weight to the desires of ingroup members than to outgroup members is considerably weakened when economic rather than when symbolic incentives are at stake' (Rabbie, 1991, p. 258). Secondly, the relatively advantaged nature of the autonomous subjects' personal outcomes (receiving all the possible resources in the study) might have led them to associate their group membership with positive outcomes, even though results showed that 'interdependent' and 'autonomous' subjects felt equally positive about their group membership.

Consequently, Perreault, Senécal and Bourhis (1994) conducted a minimal group study in which subjects allocated money to ingroup and outgroup others using the Tajfel matrices in one of the following three conditions: an 'interdependent' condition in which the financial fate of subjects depended equally on ingroup and outgroup allocations as in the standard minimal group paradigm; and two 'autonomous' conditions: one positive and one negative. Subjects in both autonomous conditions were privately informed that their personal financial fate was completely independent of ingroup and outgroup allocations. As in the Gagnon and Bourhis (1996) study, subjects in the 'positively autonomous' condition were privately told that in their case they would receive the maximum amount of money possible in the experiment. In the 'negatively autonomous' condition, subjects were privately told that they would personally receive no money at all, regardless of allocations made by ingroup or outgroup others. According to the Behavioural Interaction Model, both the 'positive' and 'negative' autonomy conditions annul the expectation of ingroup reciprocity and consequently subjects in these conditions should discriminate less than subjects in the interdependent condition, if at all. In contrast, Social Identity Theory predicts that subjects in both autonomy conditions should discriminate as much as subjects in the interdependent condition, since in each case subjects will use discrimination as a way of achieving a positive social identity. Results corroborated those obtained by Gagnon and Bourhis (1996): positively and negatively autonomous subjects discriminated as much (FAV, MD) as subjects in the interdependent condition, further supporting the social identity explanation of discrimination in the minimal group paradigm.

6 Conclusions

The combined results of the Gagnon and Bourhis (1992, 1996) and Perreault et al. (1994) studies offer greater support for Social Identity and Self-Categorization theories than for the Behavioural Interaction Model. As proposed by Social Identity and Self-Categorization Theories, social categorization, ingroup identification, social comparison and the need for a positive social identity remain the most plausible explanation for discrimination in the minimal group paradigm (Tajfel and Turner, 1979, 1986). Our analysis of the only published experiment claiming that interdependence of fate and self-interest are central to the explanation of minimal intergroup discrimination (Rabbie et al., 1989) shows that the empirical evidence it provides is mixed at best, while interpretation of the results is logically weak and self-contradictory.

Rabbie et al. themselves acknowledge that *they did find* in their study that social categorization per se produced ingroup favouritism irreducible to personal self-interest, interdependence or expectations of reciprocal favouritism. To account for these inconsistent results they are forced to resort to ad hoc and post hoc additions to their model such as the 'generic groupness norm' or the 'moral notion' of giving greater weight to the desires of ingroup than outgroup members. These additions merely weaken the Behavioural Interaction Model as a plausible, genuinely heuristic, alternative explanation of the minimal group effect.

Nevertheless, as pointed out by Turner and Bourhis (in press), criticism of Rabbie's interdependence and self-interest explanation of the minimal group effect does not imply rejection of classic group interdependence perspectives such as Realistic Conflict Theory (Sherif, 1967). We are not suggesting that social identity is the sole principle at work in intergroup relations. Social Identity Theory was always meant to *complement* Realistic Conflict Theory, to help account both for (a) intergroup situations in which there was a lack of an objective conflict of interests between groups but intergroup attitudes and behaviours were still antagonistic; and (b) intergroup situations in which an actual conflict of group interests did not lead to antagonistic intergroup attitudes and behaviours (Billig, 1976; Tajfel and Turner, 1979). Similarly, Self-Categorization Theory provides a detailed analysis of the relationship between group formation and perceived interdependence (Turner and Bourhis, in press).

There is a need for a more pluralistic theoretical and empirical approach to intergroup relations, integrating cognitive, motivational and socio-structural factors in the explanation of prejudice, stereotyping and discrimination (Bourhis, 1994; Leyens and Bourhis, 1994; Turner, in press). As Tajfel (1981a) argued, stereotypes serve both individual and social functions. The former relate to the needs of individuals for cognitive simplicity and coherence and to maintain their systems of values. The latter relate to the *collective* needs of groups to make sense of, explain and justify the intergroup relationship and their place in it. In making sense of the intergroup relationship and pursuing their goals, individuals, as group members, are driven not merely by instrumental considerations, but also by a need for positive distinctiveness, for positive social identity. Stereotypes do not represent and explain intergroup relations from a neutral, disinterested point of view; they are fundamentally oriented to and driven by the stereotyping group's collective definition of itself and its place in the order of things. They originate from a particular perspective (Oakes et al., 1994) and define the group to itself. In this respect a pervasive function which they serve is to describe intergroup relationships in such a way as to ensure, where possible, that ingroup identity is evaluated positively.

To understand stereotypes we need to place analysis of their individual cognitive and motivational functions in the context of their wider social role in intergroup relations. This role embraces *inter alia* the pursuit of both collective self-interest and positive social identity. However, a particular advantage of the social identity perspective for studying stereotypes as products of group life is its two-fold emphasis on (a) understanding intergroup relations as an expression of an interaction between general social psychological processes and the macro-social structure and (b) demonstrating that group life is characterized by emergent social and psychological processes which cannot be reduced to an individualistic algebra of personal gain or loss (Turner and Bourhis, in press). A continuing theme of our research has been that shared social identity is a means by which people are able to act as psychological group members rather than as individual persons. It is highly doubtful that something as socially systematic and large scale as intergroup conflict could ever be reduced to the operation of 'personal' self-interest. The crucial point is that as we move from interpersonal to intergroup behaviour the nature of self and, therefore, the nature of self-interest are redefined at a collective level.

Note

This chapter was made possible thanks to a grant to the first author from the Social Science and Humanities Research Council of Canada and to the second author from the Australian Research Council. Comments or requests for reprints should be addressed to: Richard Y. Bourhis, Département de psychologie, Université du Québec à Montréal, C.P. 8888, Succursale Centre-Ville, Montréal, Québec, Canada, H3C 3P8; or: John C. Turner, Division of Psychology, The Australian National University, Canberra, ACT 0200, Australia; or: André Gagnon, Département des sciences du comportement, Université du Québec en Abitibi-Témiscamingue, 42, rue Mgr Rhéaume Est, C.P. 700, Rouyn-Noranda, Québec, Canada, J9X 5E4.

13
The Self-esteem Hypothesis Revisited: Differentation and the Disaffected

Karen Long and Russell Spears

1 Introduction

Over recent years interest in the concept of self-esteem has blossomed in a number of different areas in social and clinical psychology. In the realm of intergroup relations it has assumed a particularly important role at the centre of the social identity account of intergroup discrimination, as a linchpin of the motivational motor underlying this phenomenon (Tajfel, 1978a; Tajfel and Turner, 1979, 1986). According to social identity theory, one important reason why people display ingroup bias is that this enhances positive group distinctiveness and social identity, thereby elevating the self-esteem of these group members. This account is all the more important here given the increasing challenge to purely cognitive explanations of stereotypic and prejudiced beliefs that forms a central theme of the present volume. This chapter is, therefore, concerned with the motivational dimensions of intergroup differentiation (although it is not our purpose to provide a comprehensive overview of this literature; see e.g., Hogg and Abrams, 1990).

The 'self-esteem hypothesis' as it has become known is no stranger to controversy, both in terms of its conceptualization and its ability to account for diverse empirical findings. These findings have led some theorists close to abandoning the hypothesis altogether or at least to modify and extend it to the point where it loses much of its original explanatory punch (Hogg and Abrams, 1990). In contrast, another recent review of the literature has maintained that the hypothesis has not yet even been properly tested (Farsides, 1995). This disagreement about how extensive the relevant literature is, or what it actually tells us, barely conceals deeper dispute about the very formulation of this hypothesis itself. In an influential elaboration of the original hypothesis Hogg and Abrams (1990) identify two corollaries, namely (1) that successful intergroup discrimination elevates self-esteem, and (2) that low or threatened self-esteem motivates intergroup discrimination to restore self-esteem (p. 33). This re-specification makes clear that self-esteem can be viewed as a predictor as well as a product of intergroup differentiation. However, although much research attention has been devoted to both corollaries, the second is somewhat controversial in that it was never contained in the original statements of the self-esteem hypothesis (e.g., Tajfel, 1978a; Tajfel and Turner, 1979) nor has it been endorsed by its surviving author.

It is perhaps, therefore, no surprise that much of the recent controversy and debate concerning the self-esteem hypothesis has centred largely around this second corollary. The research reported in the present chapter also focuses on the role of self-esteem as a predictor rather than as a product of intergroup differentiation. Specifically, we attempt to reformulate this second corollary in a manner that speaks to both personal and group agendas of those involved in the intergroup context, addressing some important criticisms of the conceptualization of self-esteem in the process. In contrast to other theoretical analyses we argue that certain dimensions of self-esteem may motivate compensatory ingroup bias by 'disaffecting' the individual in the intergroup context.

First, it is important to mention in passing evidence from three studies supporting corollary (1) which best represents the original formulation of the self-esteem hypothesis. A pioneering study by Oakes and Turner (1980) showed that the opportunity to differentiate by completing the Tajfel matrices resulted in higher levels of self-esteem in line with social identity theory. The argument is that successful intergroup differentiation produces elevated self-esteem as a result of the more positive social identity. A subsequent study by Lemyre and Smith (1985) confirmed that the ability to discriminate, rather than category salience per se, enhanced self-esteem, in line with corollary (1). Branscombe and Wann (1994) also found that differentiation elevated subsequent self-esteem under threat. Farsides (1995) has argued that other failures to find evidence for corollary (1) can often be related to the fact that researchers have simply looked for a positive correlation between intergroup discrimination and self-esteem, whereas this corollary specifies that the discrimination must be *successful* in order for self-esteem to be elevated. Other problems have arisen from the manner in which self-esteem has been conceptualized and measured which we will consider in further detail below.

Turning now to the research on self-esteem as an *independent* variable, the most widely-held interpretation of the way in which self-esteem *motivates* intergroup differentiation is very closely linked to the prediction based on the original self-esteem hypothesis or corollary (1). By reversing the original causal direction whereby differentiation increases self-esteem, it is inferred that those individuals with low self-esteem should be most strongly motivated to engage in intergroup differentiation. They do this in order to attain a more positive social identity and thereby increase their self-esteem. For example, Hogg and Sunderland (1991) manipulated subjects' self-esteem by providing either positive or negative feedback on task performance. They found that those subjects who had received negative feedback (and who, therefore, should have lower self-esteem) engaged in intergroup discrimination to the greatest extent (although this did not translate into a consequent increase in self-esteem). Overall, however, the evidence in support of this position is not particularly overwhelming (Abrams and Hogg, 1988; Hogg and Abrams, 1990) and this lack of consistency has led some researchers to rethink the possible role of self-esteem as a possible motivator for differentiation.

Lemyre and Smith (1985) propose that intergroup differentiation is best thought of as a strategy for restoring or maintaining self-esteem following threat, which they see as intrinsic to any intergroup situation. This idea, then, does not assume that only those with low self-esteem will be inclined to engage in ingroup bias. Threat is also central to Hogg and Abrams' second corollary, and our own analysis. Meanwhile, other researchers (e.g., Luhtanen and Crocker, 1991) take this notion to another extreme, and argue that individuals with high rather than low self-esteem will be more likely to differentiate in favour of the ingroup. We will return to this prediction and the reasons for it in some detail below. First, however, we turn from the status of self-esteem as product versus predictor to consider perhaps even more basic issues of conceptualization and measurement that have fuelled (and dogged) recent debates about the self-esteem hypothesis.

2   Distinguishing Personal and Collective Self-esteem

A further complication is that the conceptual framework provided by both social identity theory and self-categorization theory states clearly that the identity which is enhanced through favourable intergroup comparisons is the *social* identity of the individual as a social category member. However, the vast majority of research on self-esteem has employed measures of esteem deriving from personal rather than social identity (or, more accurately, this is often unspecified, but tapped by items framed in the first person). For example, Hogg and Sunderland (1991) measured personal self-esteem, and found no evidence that categorization (or discrimination) increased this. It is perhaps not so surprising that such research has been inconclusive if the type of measure used is inappropriate for the theoretical question being addressed. Self-categorization theory stresses this point clearly; intergroup behaviour is supposed to involve individuals interacting in terms of a social identity, and, therefore, measures of personal self-esteem are at the wrong level of abstraction to account for behaviour and cognition at the intergroup level (see also Branscombe and Wann, 1994, p. 645).

A more appropriate focus for testing the predictions derived from social identity theory outlined above should, therefore, presumably incorporate self-esteem deriving from the social category in terms of which the people are currently acting. For this reason it is possible to argue that the vast majority of research on the relationship between self-esteem and intergroup differentiation is individualistic in suggesting that collective comparisons are driven by purely personal motives, and can be reduced to an individual difference variable. This is particularly ironic given the original objective of social identity theory to transcend individualistic hydraulic motivational explanations of intergroup behaviour (Billig, 1976; Tajfel, 1978a). While we would not wish to argue that personal self-esteem is irrelevant to the context of intergroup judgement and behaviour (and we will return to this point later), it is clearly important to measure collective self-esteem at a level which maps onto the social identity concerned.

A possible solution to this problem has been provided by Luhtanen and Crocker (1992) who have developed a scale specifically for the purpose of measuring what they refer to as trait *collective* self-esteem (CSE) defined as self-esteem deriving from one's membership of social groups. The 16-item scale consists of four subscales: *membership esteem*, which refers to a person's attitude towards their performance as a member of the group; *private CSE*, which refers to a person's attitude towards the group and their membership of it; *public CSE*, which refers to a person's perception of the general regard in which their group is held by non-members; and *importance to identity*, which refers to the contribution made by the group membership to the person's self-concept overall. Luhtanen and Crocker see private CSE as mapping most directly onto Tajfel's (e.g., 1978) conceptualization of social identity and most of their interesting findings have been demonstrated most strongly, if not exclusively, on this subscale. They also report (Crocker and Luhtanen, 1990; Luhtanen and Crocker, 1992) that their scale is relatively independent of conventional personal self-esteem scales such as Rosenberg's (1965), and elsewhere only low correlations between these two measures have been found (e.g., Ellemers, Doosje and Spears, 1994; Long, Spears and Manstead, 1994).

However, in contrast to Hogg and Abrams' second corollary, Crocker and Luhtanen (1990) proposed that under certain circumstances people *high* in collective self-esteem would be more likely to show ingroup bias than those low in collective self-esteem. In deriving this hypothesis, they extrapolated from an earlier study by Crocker, Thompson, McGraw and Ingerman (1987) in which they found that people who were high in personal self-esteem *indirectly* enhanced the self by upgrading high scorers who (similarly) succeeded on a test whereas people low in personal self-esteem did not. They reasoned that collective self-esteem might moderate reactions to collective threat (group success vs. failure) in a similar way. Analogous to Crocker et al. (1987), participants high or low in CSE were required to rate above average and below average scorers on a test, after receiving group success or failure feedback. In line with predictions, high collective self-esteem participants whose group succeeded enhanced their ratings of above average scorers compared to those high in CSE who received group failure feedback, whereas there was no difference for people low in CSE.

Although, going against the self-esteem hypothesis deriving from social identity theory, evidence for greater ingroup bias for people high in collective self-esteem fits with other research on the relationship between (personal) self-esteem and positive illusions. Clinically-orientated research on personal self-esteem suggests that positive self-esteem is desirable for general well-being and this is served by various interpersonal comparisons and perceptual biases (e.g., Taylor and Brown, 1988; see also section 6 below). In other words, those individuals who have high personal self-esteem are more likely to engage in positive interpersonal comparisons whereas those with low self-esteem are less inclined to self-enhance and may be more concerned with self-protection (e.g., Baumeister, Tice and Hutton, 1989) or self-consistency (e.g., Swann, 1987).

In developing this line of argument Crocker and colleagues have started to differentiate the motivations of people who are high and low in self-esteem (Crocker, Blaine and Luhtanen, 1993). However, the basic isomorphism between the personal and the collective levels of self-esteem remains: both personal and collective self-esteem as a personality or trait variable are predicted to have analogous or *parallel* effects in the domains of interpersonal and intergroup comparisons. It is argued that people who are high in personal and/or collective self-esteem are motivated to seek enhancement for themselves and their ingroups respectively. Conversely, people scoring low on these constructs will be motivated to be self-protective of themselves and their ingroups, in order to avoid failure and humiliation (Crocker, Blaine and Luhtanen, 1993, p. 58). As a result of this analysis they predict that people high in collective self-esteem are more likely to enhance the ingroup (self-enhancement motive) whereas people low in collective self-esteem should be more likely to derogate the outgroup (self-protection motive). Thus, whereas trait collective self-esteem predicts the absolute level of ingroup and outgroup ratings, low collective self-esteem may be associated with greater outgroup derogation.

Moreover, Crocker, Blaine and Luhtanen (1993) suggest that people low in collective self-esteem are particularly unlikely to make positive public claims about their ingroup (fearing being tested or contested on these claims), but are likely to risk public derogatory claims about outgroups which imply no judgement of the self or ingroup. On this reading, the relationship between collective self-esteem and ingroup bias is complex if not unclear. The analysis allows for the possibility of ingroup bias from people both high and low in collective self-esteem, but sees this as being produced differently and for different reasons.

Although people high in collective self-esteem may enhance the ingroup, they do not need to derogate the outgroup, and although people low in collective self-esteem derogate the outgroup, they also play down ingroup attributes relative to those high in collective self-esteem. This analysis suggests absolute differences in the levels of ratings of both ingroups and outgroups for people high and low in collective self-esteem, but it is not entirely clear whether ingroup bias (i.e., the difference score of ingroup minus outgroup ratings) should be more evident for people high or low in collective self-esteem. All in all then, although earlier research predicts positive ingroup differentiation to be more a product of high collective self-esteem (Crocker and Luhtanen, 1990), the most recent analysis suggests that this may be unclear.

The conclusions of the review by Hogg and Abrams (1990) seem no more clear-cut. They claim there is inconclusive empirical support for either corollary of the self-esteem hypothesis (namely that discrimination enhances identity, or that threatened self-esteem promotes discrimination). They suggest that the self-esteem hypothesis has lost its group-specificity and has been over-extended to domains where other processes and aspects of social identity theory are perhaps as, if not more, relevant. They then broaden their conceptualization of the motivational factors that could underlie discrimination, such as the need for structure and meaning, as satisfied by the categorization process (and presumably discrimination).

3 The End of the Self-esteem Hypothesis?

In the previous section we found that despite some clarification about the appropriate ways to conceptualize (collective) self-esteem, there is still considerable confusion as to the relation between self-esteem and intergroup differentiation or ingroup bias. The arguments presented by Crocker and her associates that high collective self-esteem can drive ingroup bias or at least enhancement implies the very reverse of the second corollary. According to Hogg and Abrams, the conclusion is even more pessimistic: the impetus for the role of self-esteem as a mediator or even a moderator seems to have finally dissipated in a mixed bag of findings and can best be replaced by other motivationally tinged principles such as the search for meaning.

However, we would argue that it is premature to abandon consideration of the effects of self-esteem as an independent variable on intergroup discrimination especially as the quest to find evidence with the new and further refined measures is far from exhausted. First of all, let us briefly return to the work of Crocker and her associates. In the study by Crocker and Luhtanen (1990) no evidence was actually found of a relationship between collective self-esteem and direct ingroup bias. Rather their main dependent variable (following Crocker et al., 1987) was an indirect measure of enhancement relating to high and low scorers on the test in question. In other words, the claim of any general relation between high collective self-esteem and ingroup bias seems overstated.

Second, Crocker and Luhtanen used their global measure of collective self-esteem, which was not linked to the particular group membership in question, but refers to *all* the groups to which the person belongs. They attempt to measure 'a general cross-group tendency to have a positive social identity' (Luhtanen and Crocker, 1992, p. 304). It seems very unlikely that we think of ourselves in terms of all of our numerous possible social identities simultaneously, if indeed this is even possible. Social identity researchers (e.g., Abrams and Hogg, 1988; Kelly, 1988) have argued for *specificity* of analyses applied to intergroup discrimination, and suggested that predictions and measurement be framed in terms of the specific social identity which is salient in the experiment (see Crocker, Luhtanen, Blaine and Broadnax, 1994, for a discussion of the pros and cons of using global vs. specific measures). In terms of the original self-esteem hypothesis, it can be argued that differentiation causes changes primarily in the positivity of the social identity being enhanced and in the esteem which derives from that specific identity.

Third, the conceptualization of collective self-esteem as a relatively stable trait raises further theoretical and methodological problems. At a theoretical level, despite the collective nature of the object of esteem, this analysis would seem to suggest that intergroup processes can reduce to a stable individual difference variable, suggesting quite an individualistic analysis and explanation for intergroup behaviour (see above). Moreover, if we accept that the nature of the social comparative context (the relevant comparison group and comparison dimension) is highly situation-specific and thus inherently variable, it follows that the nature of our collective self-esteem should depend not only on the specific social identity or self-categorization, but also on the specific social comparison being made in situ. In these terms collective esteem is unlikely to be a stable feature of the individual, but rather a contingent feature of the comparative context. Indeed, the idea that esteem fluctuates would seem to be inherent in the original self-esteem hypothesis, that is, corollary (1). If we do regard esteem associated with one's group as a relatively stable trait, the question also arises of how distinguishable this is from identification with this group. Evidence from our own research suggest correlations between these constructs is high ($rs = .4–.5$; e.g., Ellemers, Doosje and Spears, 1994; Jetten, Spears and Manstead, 1995). If social identity theory predicts a positive relationship between group identification and ingroup bias (see e.g., Hinkle and Brown, 1990), it is perhaps hardly surprising that high trait-based collective self-esteem can be associated with enhancement or intergroup differentiation.

Finally, Crocker and Luhtanen (1990) used a minimal group classification with which participants had no history of participation, and which presumably had little meaning for them. Certainly the link between the global collective self-esteem measure, and the esteem attached to this particular group was far from evident in their study. All in all, then, on the basis of this research it seems premature to conclude that high collective self-esteem should necessarily be associated with greater ingroup bias in a general sense. In order to evaluate the relationship between collective self-esteem and ingroup bias it would at the very least be necessary to investigate the influence of social self-esteem specific to the social identity made salient in the intergroup context.

There has also now been some very recent empirical work by Branscombe and Wann (1994) which has reasserted the position of corollary (2) using measures of collective self-esteem. This research moves away from the personality-based approach of Crocker and her co-workers whilst providing scope for the refinements concerning self-protection versus self-enhancement. Specifically, Branscombe and Wann (1994) have argued that the notion that low collective self-esteem results in greater outgroup derogation may apply particularly under conditions of situational *threat* (e.g., a collective or ingroup failure) such that people most responsive to failure (low collective self-esteem) should derogate the outgroup for self-protective purposes. This concurs with the view that some form of threat is a pre-condition of the second corollary as formulated by Hogg and Abrams (1990), although Farsides (1995) has argued that tests of this corollary have often paid lip-service to this point. People more responsive to success (high in collective self-esteem) on the other hand, should be most likely to self-enhance when threat is replaced with collective success over the outgroup. In their research, and in contrast to Crocker and Luhtanen (1990), Branscombe and Wann used a natural social categorization for their American student participants that already had a clear history of relevant and competitive social comparison (US vs. Soviet Union). Using structural modelling techniques they confirmed that the classical social identity prediction of low self-esteem resulting in greater derogation in response to threat was upheld, corollary (2), and moreover that derogation of the relevant outgroup (but not other outgroups) led to enhanced collective self-esteem, corollary (1). Less support was forthcoming for the predicted positive relation between (high) collective self-esteem and derogation under no-threat conditions.

This study would seem to offer some hope of resolving not only conflicting empirical findings, but also conflicting theoretical accounts. It is possible that the differentiation associated with high collective self-esteem reported by Crocker and Luhtanen (1990) may simply be used to 'reflect' status superiority under no- or low-threat social comparisons (although we would argue that the lack of threat implied by high collective self-esteem, at least in the absence of an additional threat to identity, should render identity secure enough not to resort to differentiation – see below). The groups used by Crocker and Luhtanen (minimal groups) may have been less threatening compared to the more relevant and involving national categories (US vs. Soviet Union) employed by Branscombe and Wann. Level of identification and threat may therefore be important moderating factors in evaluating the self-esteem hypothesis (see also Spears, Doosje and Ellemers, 1995, and Doosje and Ellemers, this volume).

Despite the value of this study, some issues remain unresolved and unexplored. First, as in other studies, Branscombe and Wann used the global measure of collective self-esteem. Second, although these recent studies have made important conceptual and methodological advances by switching from personal to the collective level of esteem, we think it would be unfortunate to neglect the importance of personal identity and personal esteem in the group context altogether. Although we have argued that personal esteem is measured at the wrong level to evaluate either corollary of the self-esteem hypothesis, the fact that it has sometimes produced effects (albeit often contradictory; see Hogg and Abrams, 1990) suggests that it is still worthy of study. Moreover, in more theoretical terms, there are many group and intergroup contexts where personal identity, interpersonal comparison and personal esteem may still be relevant, and this may account for some of the effects of personal esteem. This is particularly likely to be the case in task groups where personal contributions and thus personal credit are at issue. For this reason we consider it interesting but also theoretically important to consider how both collective and personal esteem might contribute to intergroup evaluations, both independently and in mutual interaction.

The basic aim of the following research is to address these issues. We use existing social categories and measure collective self-esteem with respect to these categories so that there is a meaningful relationship between the category and the level of self-esteem. We also consider the role of personal self-esteem within the same paradigm, and use a context (evaluation of group performance to which individuals have contributed) in which this variable is likely to play a role. In the following section we provide the theoretical rationale for this research. It should be stressed that our analysis developed partly 'retroductively' in the course of conducting the studies and in order to make sense of findings (Sayer, 1983), crystallized prior to conducting the follow-up to the first experiment. However, for the sake of clarity and brevity, we introduce the research within the resulting theoretical framework rather than reiterating all stages of our thinking. We have also been selective in presenting those comparisons from the first study in particular that are relevant to the evaluation of this general framework.

4   The Role of (Personal and Collective) Self-esteem in Ingroup Bias Reconsidered

In line with the critique of Crocker and her associates, we agree that self-esteem has often been measured at the wrong level of abstraction (the individual level) and that this has contributed to some of the conceptual confusion. However, as we have argued, studies that have measured or manipulated personal self-esteem have produced interesting and significant findings that are difficult to ignore or leave unexplained. An additional objective of the present research, then, is to clarify the relationship between personal self-esteem and ingroup bias. More specifically we argue that it is important to examine the role of personal and collective self-esteem in an integrated fashion, and to see how these factors combine and interact. Unlike Crocker and her associates, we have come to the conclusion that personal and collective esteem will not necessarily have similar or isomorphic effects, at least at the intergroup level, and this is partly *because* collective self-esteem is matched to the level of social categorization whereas personal self-esteem is not. The way we have begun to rethink the role of personal and collective esteem in our research is to consider their consequences, in isolation and in combination, for the perceived threat to the individual group member.

What is, then, the relationship between the different levels of self-esteem and ingroup bias? First, in line with social identity theorists, we do not regard ingroup bias as a universal or inevitable feature of intergroup relations but rather primarily as a response to threats to identity (usually but not exclusively social identity) and thus esteem. We agree with Lemyre and Smith (1985) that ingroup bias may arise partly as an attempt to address threat to the self implied by categorization in a social category (cf. Lemyre and Smith, 1985), especially where this categorization is imposed rather than self-sought (cf. Ellemers, Kortekaas and Ouwerkerk, 1995; Hinkle and Brown, 1990; Roccas and Schwartz, 1993). We are not assuming that social categorization is intrinsically threatening to the self, but people who have low identity-specific collective self-esteem are especially likely to be threatened by the particular social categorization (and the social comparisons that derive from this), and one strategy to compensate for this is by displaying ingroup bias (cf. Branscombe and Wann, 1994; Lemyre and Smith, 1985). People who are high in identity-specific collective self-esteem on the other hand, already derive a positive image from their group, and should be relatively secure in their identity and should not need to address this by means of positive differentiation (e.g., outgroup derogation).

Against this view it is possible to argue that people who are low in collective self-esteem are likely to view this category as simply unimportant to their self-concept. If this is the case, it could be argued that immersion in the category may not actually be threatening at all, in the same way that people are not threatened by outgroup superiority on unimportant or non-central dimensions (e.g., Mummendey and Schreiber, 1983, 1984; Spears and Manstead, 1989; see also Anastasio et al., this volume). This point demands further refinement and specification of the nature of the threat involved. What is arguably threatening about being categorized as a member of group X, especially where this categorization is imposed, is the resulting self-image (more generally) that this presents to ourselves but also to others, rather than its threat to an internalized collective identity per se. In other words, we may be uncomfortable with the categorization precisely because we are being seen in terms of something which is not valued, which is alien to us, which is in short not 'us'. This conceptualization of experienced threat can thus perhaps best be thought of comprising two necessary components, namely a threat to the evaluation or status of the group within which one is categorized (e.g., by means of low status; cf. Spears et al., 1995) combined with a lack of faith in that given social identity (e.g., because of a low identification, a preference for personal identification, etc.; cf. Spears et al., 1995; see also Doosje and Ellemers, this volume). These elements should especially contribute to the 'disaffection' of the group member when this social categorization and its negative attributes are inescapable because membership and its resulting evaluation are publically acknowledged. In these terms, the public collective self-esteem subscale is likely to be the most relevant indicator of collective esteem for our purposes because this captures the threat to public respect caused by group membership rather than relating to the intrinsic value of that membership (cf. private collective self-esteem, membership self-esteem and importance to identity). Any effects of a negative relation between collective self-esteem and ingroup bias should, therefore, be largely due to differences on the public self-esteem subscale. Again, previous research has failed to address this possibility by either leaving out items from this subscale altogether, and/or by using a global rather than an identity-specific measure (e.g., Branscombe and Wann, 1994).

But what about personal self-esteem? Once again, we can consider the effect of this factor in relation to perceived threat within the intergroup context. However, unlike the case for collective self-esteem, we argue that (particularly imposed) social categorization and social comparison is likely to be threatening for people *high* in personal self-esteem, especially in groups requiring personal contributions or inputs. Our reasoning here is that immersion in a group for someone who has a strong sense of personal regard will be threatening because this is the wrong level of abstraction for them to display their positive (personal) self-image, and is thus unlikely to satisfy a need to shine or stand out in terms of their personal worth. Not only is taking personal credit more difficult at the group level than at the individual level, but the group may be regarded as not showing them in a good light, and they are likely to have less control over collective than individual outcomes. Compared to the case of individual performance and interpersonal comparisons, this is a potentially threatening situation. This leads to the prediction, contra the original formulation of the self-esteem hypothesis (which albeit failed to distinguish personal and collective self-esteem), of increased compensatory ingroup bias with high *personal* self-esteem.

It is important to note that although this last prediction is similar to that of Crocker et al. (1987), the rationale is quite different. This difference is made

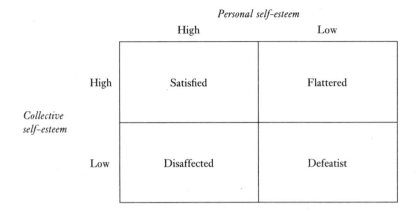

Figure 13.1   A typology of the combined effects of personal and collective self-esteem.

more empirically discernable when we consider the effects of personal and collective self-esteem in combination. Putting the two tendencies outlined above together, we argue that the most threatening combination is of low collective self-esteem, and high personal self-esteem. For people who fall into this category (be it chronically or momentarily) the intergroup context is likely to provide them little solace at either a collective or a personal level, and this aversive and restrictive situation is likely to result in most compensatory inter-group differentation or ingroup bias. For ease of reference, but also because we think it captures their psychological predicament described above, we refer to these high personal self-esteem/low (public) collective self-esteem individuals as the 'disaffected'[1] (see figure 13.1). People in all other three quadrants of the personal × collective self-esteem combinations should experience less threat: people who are high CSE/high PSE are 'satisfied' because group-derived esteem is consistent with their percieved personal self-worth; people who are high CSE/low PSE are 'flattered' because their group raises them above their perceived personal self-worth, and people who are low CSE/low PSE are 'defeatist' in that their group membership offers them no more and no less than their personal self-worth, so that these tend to legitimate each other ('we deserve our group and it deserves us').

Although elements of our analysis have been tested before, as we have argued above, a lack of appropriate measures, failure to tune measures to levels of categorization and specific identities, failure to distinguish properly the differential effects of personal and collective self-esteem and failure to examine the interactive effects of the two, have arguably contributed to the messiness of results and theoretical conclusions. In the following studies we tie levels of collective esteem to the actual groups with which individuals are likely to identify, and in which they have an investment in terms of personal and collective performance. We provide some evidence for our general analysis in a first study, and then attempt to replicate the effect in a simpler design in a follow-up study.

5   Study 1

Although the first study discussed here utilized a natural social categorization (Dutch psychology students) we employed a design in which the person's 'owngroup' was distinguished from another ingroup deriving from the same social category (an 'ingroup' also made up of Dutch psychology students) as well as 'outgroups' deriving from a different social category (Swiss vs. German students). This design was originally used to distinguish direct from indirect forms of ingroup bias (cf. Brown, Collins and Schmidt, 1988), with indirect discrimination being defined as favouring an 'ingroup' solution with which the person has had no direct involvement over that of an outgroup. However, these different forms of differentiation are of little concern to the present analysis although we maintain the distinction between owngroup and ingroup to remain faithful to the original data.

Participants were divided into small groups at the beginning of the sessions in order to work together on a collective brainstorming task and were later invited to evaluate various solutions to this task (within subjects) including their owngroup product, other ingroup products, and products produced by the outgroup. These group product ratings formed the main measure of ingroup bias (cf. Hinkle and Schopler, 1986). In sum, participants (Dutch psychology students) were asked to evaluate *three* group solutions – one produced by their owngroup, one produced by another ingroup (i.e., another group of Dutch psychology students) and one produced by an outgroup (psychology students of another nationality).

The main independent variables in this study were level of identity-specific collective self-esteem (as measured by the Crocker and Luhtanen 16-item scale) and level of personal self-esteem (as measured by the Rosenberg scale). In the case of collective self-esteem, all items were modified to refer to the relevant social category, namely Dutch psychology students. On the basis of responses to these two scales, median splits were performed allowing division of participants into four separate groups, representing the various high and low scores on the two scales (i.e., high PSE/high CSE, high PSE/low CSE, low PSE/high CSE, low PSE/low CSE).

A further experimental manipulation of the comparison outgroup was also included. A prerequisite for ingroup bias is that the ingroup should perceive the outgroup as a relevant comparison group for the purposes of the task, so that ideally some degree of social threat should exist between them, laying the foundation for competitive intergroup comparisons (cf. Branscombe and Wann, 1994; Farsides, 1995; Spears, Doosje and Ellemers, 1995). Subsequent analysis and post-testing showed that the Swiss outgroup used in our study fulfilled these criteria, but the German outgroup did not (see Long, Spears and Manstead, 1994). To simplify the results we will therefore confine ourselves to a discussion of the data concerning the Swiss outgroup conditions.

In order to obtain an independent evaluation of each of the three solutions used during the experiment, judges (from the same subject population but who had not participated in the experiment) evaluated them on scales identical to those used by the original subjects. A 'quality index' was computed for each solution by summing ratings across all eight dimensions for each judge, and calculating the mean. These indices were used as covariates in the main analyses.

Both CSE and PSE interacted with the ratings of the targets, and these two interactions were also qualified by a significant higher order interaction involving all three factors. It is easiest to describe the two-way interactions followed by the three-way interaction. In terms of PSE, people high in PSE demonstrated ingroup bias whereas people low in PSE did not. For the high PSE participants ratings of both the owngroup and the other ingroup ($M = 51.7$ and $M = 51.5$) significantly exceeded those of the Swiss outgroup ($M = 44.8$). For the low PSE participants' ratings, means across the three groups did not differ significantly ($Ms = 49.5$, 45.6 and 47.1 for the owngroup, ingroup, and Swiss outgroup respectively). In terms of CSE, in contrast, the reverse patterns occurred: people low in CSE showed ingroup bias but people high in CSE did not. For the ratings of high CSE people, means across the three groups did not differ significantly ($Ms = 51.5$, 46.6 and 47.0 for the owngroup, ingroup, and Swiss outgroup respectively). However, for the low CSE people, the rating of the ingroup ($M = 50.6$) significantly exceeded that of the Swiss outgroup ($M = 44.2$), although the owngroup ($M = 49.8$) was not quite significantly higher than the outgroup. In terms of the three-way interaction, when we split the combinations of CSE and PSE into the four cells, only the 'disaffected' (high PSE/low CSE) combination results in significant ingroup bias, with both owngroup and ingroup ratings ($Ms = 50.6$ and 52.1 respectively) higher than the Swiss outgroup rating ($M = 41.3$).

To supplement the above analysis, separate similar ANCOVAs of product ratings were carried out using the four CSE subscales. Interactions involving CSE were significant only for the public CSE subscale, which interacted significantly with PSE and target. The pattern of means for the interactions involving public CSE are almost identical to those for the CSE scale as a whole, and it can thus be concluded that this subscale is largely responsible for this effect.

Overall then, this pattern of findings is in line with our analysis of the relationship between the two different levels of self-esteem and ingroup bias described earlier. That is, low CSE and high PSE and particularly the combination of the two produces the most intergroup differentiation or ingroup bias.

Moreover, it appears to be public collective self-esteem which is responsible for the effect on the overall CSE measure. This finding is in line with the general analysis that ingroup bias resulting from low CSE is a response to the threat of this categorization and social comparison to one's self-image generally. It is also worth noting that this interaction, and the pattern of ratings for owngroup, ingroup and outgroup as a function of PSE and CSE provide no clear support for the prediction of Crocker et al. (1993; cf. Baumeister et al., 1989) that people high in PSE or CSE should self-enhance (i.e., the owngroup, and possibly the ingroup), whereas those low in esteem would be more likely to display outgroup derogation. A close inspection of the cell means suggest that greater ingroup bias in the 'disaffected' cell is comprised of both enhancement and derogation elements (see also Long et al., 1994), and the remaining cells show that other combinations of both high and low PSE and CSE produce little or no enhancement or derogation.

6   Study 2

In the following study (see Long and Spears, 1995, for a more complete account) we attempted to replicate the findings of the previous experiment concerning the opposing effects of PSE and CSE on intergroup differentiation in a simpler design, in order to provide further independent evidence for our analysis. We simplified the contextual factors by eliminating the outgroup manipulation and the owngroup versus ingroup manipulation originally designed to investigate direct versus indirect ingroup bias (cf. Brown et al., 1988). In the present study the salient social category was stressed in order to discourage intra-category comparisons between the various *in vivo* groups participating in the experiment.

The most important addition of the present study, however, is that we allowed for comparisons made at an interpersonal level. Given that our analysis distinguishes personal from collective esteem, and that threat to identity, even social identity, is personally experienced, it seems appropriate to examine whether participants also respond to comparisons at the intergroup level in terms of interpersonal evaluations. Historically, most of the explanations of ethnocentrism have focused on intrapersonal and interpersonal explanations of intergroup relations (see Billig, 1976, and Tajfel, 1978a, for critiques), so it is perhaps appropriate to turn the tables and see whether intergroup relations can influence or even determine interpersonal evaluations (see also Turner, 1988, and Simon, this volume). By including interpersonal as well as intergroup comparisons, we hope, therefore, not only to clarify the separate effects of identity enhancement at the personal and social levels, but also to investigate the influence of the social on the interpersonal level.

As with intergroup comparisons, in the realm of interpersonal comparisons there is some debate regarding the link between (personal) self-esteem and evaluation of self relative to other individuals. The self-evaluation approach (e.g., Shrauger, 1975) proposes that the further a person's self-concept falls short of a positive ideal, the stronger the motivation to reduce this discrepancy through self-enhancement. Consequently, people with low self-esteem should self-enhance to a greater extent than people with high self-esteem because their negative self-image is more discrepant from the ideal. In a similar vein, Wills' (1981) theory of downward comparison argues that subjective well-being may be increased through comparison with a less fortunate other and suggests that such comparisons are particularly likely for people with low or threatened self-esteem.

However, in common with the research on intergroup comparisons, the reverse prediction has also been suggested. Taylor and Brown (1988) conclude that a general positively enhanced perception of self is psychologically adaptive such that high levels of self-esteem characterize healthy mental functioning. Swann (1987) has argued that a positive relation between self-esteem and self-enhancement does not have to reflect a positive illusion but may be more grounded in reality than its reverse. From a self-consistency viewpoint, individuals are motivated to maintain a self-image that is consistent over time and situation in order to have some basis for the prediction and control of behaviour. This is manifested as a preference for self-confirmation or self-validation in social interaction, in other words a preference for accuracy over flattery. Self-consistency theory predicts that people with high self-esteem will be likely to self-enhance in order to confirm a positive identity whereas people with low self-esteem cannot realistically or credibly do so (cf. Baumeister, Tice and Hutton, 1989; Brown, Collins and Schmidt, 1988; Crocker, Blaine and Luhtanen, 1993).

In line with the majority of recent research, outlined above, we expect that the self-serving bias associated with high personal self-esteem will be apparent in the interpersonal comparisons made by these participants, whereas no such bias should be evidenced in the comparisons made by participants with low self-esteem. However, we should not forget the intergroup context in which these interpersonal evaluations take place, and our more motivational analysis in terms of threatened identity relating to this context. Extending our argument with respect to ingroup bias, the mismatch between the intergroup context and personal-identity concerns should exacerbate the self-enhancement motive for those high in self-esteem. Specifically, if people high in personal self-esteem are threatened by being judged in terms of a poorly valued group, they may attempt to compensate for this by displaying more self-serving interpersonal enhancement bias as well as ingroup bias. If this argument holds, we would again expect the combination of low public collective self-esteem and high personal self-esteem to be the most threatening combination (the 'disaffected'), resulting in a higher order interaction between personal and collective self-esteem in terms of self-enhancement. This predicted interaction also allows us to distinguish our analysis from the more individualistic self-enhancement hypothesis, outlined above, which does not predict any interaction with collective self-esteem.

To summarize, the aim of our second experiment was to examine the relationship between self-esteem deriving from both personal and social identity and comparisons at both interpersonal and intergroup level. The study was presented as an investigation of group performance of student groups compared to non-student groups and employed a cover story which referred to job selection procedures. The method used was very similar to that used in the previous experiment, with a few important variations. We actively tried to avoid the division of the ingroup category by leading subjects to believe that their task group was the only ingroup that would be performing those particular tasks under those specific conditions, and that there was one non-student group who would be tested in exactly the same way. The intention here was to make intra-category comparisons between student groups irrelevant. In addition, it was hoped that this cover story would stress to the participants that their particular task group of students was representing the student category as a whole.

Self-esteem scales were administered as previously, and the same brainstorming task was used. However, as we wanted to include interpersonal comparisons in the design, it was necessary to administer a second brainstorming task that subjects worked on individually. This task was similar to the group task in nature while avoiding possible overlap in content. The order in which these tasks were performed was counterbalanced. Because of the additional brainstorming task, the evaluation stage of the experiment was also modified. This time, subjects evaluated *five* solutions. For the individual task, they were asked to evaluate their own solution, a solution produced by another ingroup member and one produced by an outgroup member. These three solutions were included to enable us to examine whether interpersonal comparisons operated independently of group boundaries. For the group solution, both ingroup and outgroup solutions were evaluated. The outgroup solution was the same for all groups, and the quality of the ingroup solution was assessed as in the previous experiment by independent judges. This was not feasible for the individual task solutions due to the sheer number involved. Thus ratings of individual solutions measured interpersonal differentiation, and ratings of group solutions measured intergroup differentiation. In summary, the design was a 2 (high vs. low PSE) × 2 (high vs. low CSE) × 3 (own individual solution, ingroup individual solution, outgroup individual solution) for the interpersonal evaluation, and a 2 × 2 × 2 (ingroup vs. outgroup) design for the group task ratings, in both cases with repeated measures on the last factor.

We consider first the data for the intergroup comparisons. PSE was found to influence the relative evaluations of ingroup and outgroup solutions as reflected by a significant interaction. Participants with high PSE significantly differentiated the ingroup solution ($M = 55.4$) from the outgroup solution ($M = 39.7$), whereas participants with low PSE did not ($Ms = 41.4$ and 44.9 for ingroup and outgroup respectively). There was no overall effect of the CSE scale on group task ratings. However, analysis of the separate subscales revealed the predicted interaction for the public CSE subscale. Participants with low levels, who therefore think that others hold their group in low regard, differentiated significantly ($Ms = 50.0$ and 39.8 for ingroup and outgroup respectively), whereas those with high levels did not (equivalent $Ms = 49.5$ and 46.5). There was no higher order interaction between PSE and public CSE on the intergroup ratings as in the previous study.

Now we address the results for the interpersonal ratings. Considering PSE first, there was a significant interaction between PSE and the source of the solution evaluated. High PSE participants rated their own solution more positively ($M = 43.3$) than low PSE participants ($M = 32.6$), however, they did not differentiate it significantly from other solutions ($Ms = 39.2$ and 41.0 for solutions of ingroup and outgroup members respectively). Participants with low PSE rated their solutions ($M = 32.6$) significantly less positively than both ingroup ($M = 42.3$) and outgroup ($M = 42.0$) members. In addition, there was an interaction between participants' level of CSE and their evaluations of the various individual solutions. The striking thing here is that participants with high CSE rate outgroup member's solutions ($M = 45.3$) more positively than their own ($M = 33.8$) with ratings of the ingroup member in between ($M = 39.0$). On the other hand, the means for participants low in CSE show a trend towards ingroup bias. These participants awarded similar ratings to both their own and the ingroup member's solution ($Ms = 42.2$ and 42.1 respectively), whereas the outgroup member's solution was rated more negatively ($M = 38.0$). It is also noteworthy that low CSE participants were more positive about their own individual solutions than were high CSE participants. More importantly, however, analyses using public CSE revealed the predicted interaction between PSE and *public* CSE, summarized in figure 13.2. The most striking contrast in differentiation is between the 'disaffected' (those with low public CSE and high PSE) who differentiate their own solutions from ingroup and especially outgroup members, whereas for people with low public CSE and low PSE (the 'defeatists'), the reverse effect is obtained: the outgroup member's solution is rated more positively than their own. For 'satisfied' participants high in both types of self-esteem, the pattern of bias in favour of the outgroup member's solution was also in evidence.

To summarize these results, data for the intergroup and interpersonal comparisons show some degree of consistency and overlap. High PSE participants differentiated at the intergroup level, rating the ingroup solution as significantly higher than the outgroup. Participants with high PSE rated their individual solutions more positively than low PSE participants, although they did

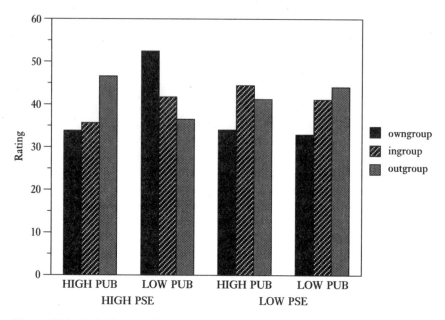

Figure 13.2   Individual product ratings by PSE and public CSE.

not in fact significantly differentiate between solutions. Thus, as in the first study, the evidence was that high PSE was a predictor of ingroup bias, certainly at the explicitly intergroup level.

In terms of collective self-esteem low scorers on the the public CSE subscale differentiated more than high scorers. Thus, those participants who thought the public image of their group was more negative awarded more favourable ratings to the ingroup. In addition, CSE also had some influence on interpersonal comparisons. The disaffected combination produced most self-serving bias, at the expense of other ingroup and outgroup members' solutions whereas in all other cells the individual's own solution was rated lowest. This effect, is similar to the combined (main) effects for PSE and CSE on the intergroup ratings, and also the higher order interaction in the first study, where the disaffected group also produced the most self-serving bias. However, it is notable that in the interpersonal ratings disaffected participants also rate themselves higher than ingroup as well as outgroup members, suggesting that this is an interpersonal rather than an intergroup strategy. Once again, however, it seems that the high PSE/low CSE participants are most threatened by the intergroup judgemental context, and when they are able, resolve this by showing a self-serving bias on the interpersonal ratings. In other words, this interaction implies that people who are high in PSE are not simply self-enhancing for individualistic and cognitive reasons (cf. Brown et al., 1988; Swann, 1987; Swann et al., 1987), but are at least partly also responding to the threat implied in the intergroup comparative context, in line with our analysis. Moreover, as in Study 1, the pattern of these data provides little clear evidence of any general sense in which people high in PSE or CSE self-enhance, and still less that people low in self-esteem derogate the outgroup (cf. Crocker et al., 1993).

7 Conclusions

Taking the two experiments together, the results of the second study clearly reinforce the findings of the first study while at the same time avoiding some of the additional complications of that design. The opposing effects of personal and collective self-esteem that were demonstrated in our first study appear to be robust as a similar pattern was found in the second study. Participants with high personal self-esteem clearly differentiated more at the intergroup level in the second study, and in the Swiss outgroup condition of the first study. Conversely, subjects with low collective self-esteem scores differentiated more, and again this was shown in both the second study and the Swiss outgroup condition of the first study. However, it should be noted that this effect was largely if not entirely due to the effects of public collective self-esteem. Low scores on this subscale indicate that participants view their group as having a relatively negative public image, and the data suggests that such individuals are particularly strongly motivated to differentiate in favour of the ingroup. This is in line with our analysis that the disaffection derives not so much from low 'intrinsic' collective self-esteem (i.e., private CSE, membership CSE and importance to identity) but from the lack of regard associated with a group lacking in 'group respect' (cf. Smith and Tyler, 1995).

Overall, these findings provide some support for a modified version of the second corollary of the self-esteem hypothesis, and illustrate the opposing effects that personal and collective self-esteem can have in this regard. We proposed an analysis of the effects of self-esteem in terms of threat to identity, with ingroup bias increasing under conditions of threat. However, instead of personal and collective self-esteem producing similar or isomorphic effects (cf. Crocker and Luhtanen, 1990; Crocker, Blaine and Luhtanen, 1993) our analysis suggests their effects will be quite different. The notion that low collective self-esteem should be threatening and result in attempts to compensate for this by means of ingroup bias is perhaps the aspect of our research that comes closest to the original formulation of corollary (2). Our support for this prediction is consistent with the recent study by Branscombe and Wann (1994), but appears to contradict the theorizing of Crocker and her colleagues. The fact that the research by Branscombe and Wann and ourselves employed natural groups may have much to do with this difference. In addition, we would argue that the failure to specify the object of collective self-esteem in this earlier research can lead to problems of interpretation, and we echo the plea of other social identity researchers to relate this to the specific category involved (cf. Abrams and Hogg, 1988; Hogg and Abrams, 1990; Kelly, 1988).

However, we should not disguise differences between our analysis and findings with regard to CSE and those of earlier interpretations of the self-esteem hypo- thesis either. Our effects were obtained on the public collective self-esteem subscale of Luhtanen and Crocker (1992), and not on the 'private' subscale employed by others (e.g., Branscombe and Wann, 1994). In terms of our ana- lysis, people may not so much be trying to restore the stock associated with a valued social self (cf. Branscombe and Wann, 1994), but to compensate the opprobrium attached to a negative and not particularly valued social identity. Of course we are not claiming this effect is general or universal. Although the social categories we worked with were natural and long-standing enough, the performance groups were ad hoc, and both these and the categorization were imposed by the experimenter rather than chosen by the participants. Although this may represent the reality of many groups and categorizations, we would not claim that our analysis holds for more valued or chosen group member- ships. It is possible to conceive of many low-status groups (low in public CSE) which are also important to their members, and in which private collective self-esteem may play a more central role in motivating ingroup bias in line with the classical self-esteem hypothesis (the study of Branscombe and Wann may be an example).

The second feature of our research that distinguishes it from earlier treat- ments of the self-esteem hypothesis concerns the predicted effect of personal self-esteem. First of all our findings confirm that although this variable may be at the wrong level of abstraction for a group-level analysis, this does not mean that its effects disappear when judgements are made in this context. We argue that people who are high in trait-based personal self-esteem may be particularly threatened by social categorization into groups, especially when an element of task performance and evaluation is involved. This context may limit the possibility to demonstrate or claim credit in line with personal image, and the result may be to enhance the ingroup or derogate the outgroup to com- pensate for this threat to identity, especially if other identity enhancing strat- egies are limited. Results from both studies provide support for this analysis and suggest the 'disaffecting' combination of high personal self-esteem with low collective self-esteem may be the most potent of all in evoking ingroup bias. Results from the first study show that this combination did indeed result in greatest ingroup bias, although the opportunity for interpersonal comparison in the second study also allowed this effect to manifest itself as enhanced self- serving bias. In sum, the present analysis provides an interesting twist to the self-esteem hypothesis in that people who think they are better than their group worth are most likely to show ingroup bias. Other recent research suggests that *insecure* group members may also be threatened for different reasons, and under appropriate conditions will exhibit greater ingroup bias in order to prove themselves to the group (Noel, Wann and Branscombe, 1995). Perhaps it is the 'average' group members who are neither insecure nor 'better than thou' who will feel most at home with their group and least need to discriminate against outgroups. This is perhaps a comforting thought that questions further the assumption that ingroup bias is a universal feature of intergroup relations (cf. Spears et al., 1995).

These findings indicate that we should be cautious before ruling out the role of more personal motives in collective contexts and the personal agendas that can be served by judgements at this level. Just as we should be wary of reducing social-level effects to individual differences and motives, we should be equally wary of ruling out the role of interpersonal processes in the intergroup context purely on a priori theoretical grounds (cf. Stephenson, 1981). Perhaps one of the more intriguing theoretical implications of this work, is the idea that the intergroup context can also influence judgements at the interpersonal level. In a field which has been long wedded to the idea that prejudice against groups may reflect the displacement of intra-psychic and individualistic processes (see e.g., Billig, 1976 for a review and critique), this reversal provides an interesting new slant for research (see Tajfel, 1981a). Hopefully, as well as providing a contribution to the debate on the self-esteem hypothesis, we have also illustrated the value of a multi-level, non-reductionist and integrative approach, sensitive to the specific identities and aims of the participants involved.

Notes

We would like to thank Tony Manstead, Nanne de Vries, and Sandie van Beuningen for their help on the research conducted here; and Nyla Branscombe, Naomi Ellemers, Alex Haslam, Penny Oakes and Heather Smith for commenting on an earlier draft.

1 Note that we are employing a complex and compound definition of threat here which includes the combination of three elements, namely the threat to public identity caused by low status, and the threat of social categorization, exacerbated by the greater importance attached to personal self-worth and identity. These are to be distinguished from at least two other types of threat that are relevant in the intergroup context, namely the 'defensive' threat caused by negative intergroup comparisons for people who strongly identify with the group (the difference with the first being that because of high identification social identity rather than just the person's public image is being threatened). A further form of threat is that caused by insecurity due to peripheral membership in the group (Noel, Wann and Branscombe, 1995). We are grateful to Nyla Branscombe for making this taxonomy explicit.

14

Self and Group in Modern Society: Ten Theses on the Individual Self and the Collective Self

Bernd Simon

1 Introduction

There is wide agreement among both lay persons and social psychologists that people behave differently in interpersonal settings than in collective or group settings. In fact, there is ample empirical evidence for what appears to be a 'discontinuity' between the behaviour of people acting as individuals on the one hand and the behaviour of people acting as group members on the other (e.g., Roger Brown, 1954; Rupert Brown and Turner, 1981; Schopler and Insko, 1992). A 'master problem' of social psychology is, therefore, to specify and conceptualize the psychological processes which underlie the individual–group discontinuity (Floyd Allport, 1962; Brown and Turner, 1981).

Tajfel and Turner (1979, 1986) initiated a school of theorizing and empirical research which focuses on the role of self-definition or self-interpretation processes in mediating the transition from individual (interpersonal) perception and behaviour to collective or group (intergroup and intragroup) perception and behaviour and vice versa. A key element of that approach is the distinction between the *individual self* (or personal identity) and the *collective self* (or social identity) (see Turner, Hogg, Oakes, Reicher and Wetherell, 1987; Turner, Oakes, Haslam and McGarty, 1994).[1] The individual self and the collective self are conceptualized as two different forms of self-interpretation with each being responsible for particular types of perceptual and behavioural phenomena. Reflecting self-interpretation as a unique individual, the individual self is the psychological basis of individual phenomena, that is, patterns of perception and behaviour characterized by inter-individual variation. Conversely, the collective self reflects self-interpretation as an interchangeable group member and thus provides the psychological basis for collective or group phenomena, that is, patterns of perception and behaviour characterized by inter-individual uniformity. It follows that, from a social psychological perspective, the occurrence of individual and group phenomena depends on the relative weighting of the individual self and the collective self in people's self-images. That is, the likelihood of individual phenomena (e.g., egotism) increases relative to the likelihood of group phenomena (e.g., intragroup altruism or stereotyping) to the extent that the individual self is more salient in people's current self-images than the collective self (and vice versa).

In this chapter I present ten theses which elaborate on the conceptual distinction between the individual self and the collective self. These theses build on the distinction between the individual self (or personal identity) and the collective self (or social identity) as specified within the framework of social identity theory and self-categorization theory (Tajfel and Turner, 1979, 1986; Turner et al., 1987). Thus the conceptualization of the individual self and the collective self presented below is clearly rooted within that framework. In fact, it attempts to bring (back) into focus many important aspects of the individual self and the collective self which have certainly been recognized, but not systematically analyzed so far, within the framework of social identity and self-categorization theory. For that purpose, theses are presented here that often go beyond that framework in provocative ways. This is especially true for the proposed conceptualization of the individual self and its relation to the collective self in modern society. Given their focus on group phenomena, social identity as well as self-categorization theorists have so far invested most of their conceptual (and empirical) efforts in promoting our understanding of the collective self. The individual self has received only scant attention. The theses presented below are thus also a reaction to some lacunae within the framework of social identity and self-categorization theory.

Before turning to the specific theses, a brief comment on the present terminology is in order. In this chapter, the term 'self-interpretation' is preferred to the term 'self-definition', because the former better connotes the flexibility of the corresponding process (see Simon, 1994). Moreover, to forestall 'homuncular regression in our thinking' (Gordon Allport, 1968, p. 25), I want to emphasize that the terms 'individual self' and 'collective self' are used here merely as short-cut expressions for self-interpretation as a unique individual and self-interpretation as an interchangeable group member, respectively. They are not meant to refer to some unalterable, hard-wired mental structures, but serve as convenient labels for two different forms of context-dependent representation of oneself and associated modes of psychological functioning. All this does not exclude the possibility, however, that (individual or collective) self-interpretations can also solidify under appropriate conditions. For example, self-interpretations may indeed become chronic due to prolonged periods of social contextual invariance. Then, they may very well function as rather stable self-definitions or even identities. I can now turn to the first thesis.

I   *The collective self is centred on a single dominant self-aspect, whereas the individual self is centred on a unique configuration of many non-redundant self-aspects.*

It is proposed here that a collective self is activated whenever a person interprets her or his own experiences, perceptions and behaviours as well as the (re)actions of other people towards her or him primarily in terms of a particular self-aspect that person shares with other, but not all other people in the relevant social context. Following Linville (1985, 1987), a self-aspect may be considered a cognitive category or concept which serves to process and organize information and knowledge about the own person. Self-aspects can refer, amongst others, to generalized psychological characteristics or traits (e.g., introverted), physical features (e.g., red hair), roles (e.g., father), abilities (e.g., bilingual), tastes (e.g., preference for strawberry ice cream), attitudes (e.g., against the death penalty) and explicit group or category membership (e.g., member of the communist party).[2]

Being centred on a single dominant self-aspect, self-interpretations in terms of a collective self are thus basically one-dimensional. Interpersonal differences on other dimensions (self-aspects) then become irrelevant and the similarity or interchangeability of oneself with other people sharing the same self-aspect moves into the foreground (Turner et al., 1987). On the other hand, the individual self is activated to the extent that self-interpretations are based on a more comprehensive set or configuration of different self-aspects. The more comprehensive that set, the more complex that configuration and the less likely it is that another person possesses the identical set of aspects. Consequently, activation of the individual self implies that one's own uniqueness moves into the foreground.

Note that, although the collective self is centred on a single dominant self-aspect, it is not maintained here that no additional self-aspects can be involved in collective self-interpretations. They certainly can. The important point however is that such 'secondary' self-aspects should directly be implied by the dominant self-aspect. They should be (stereo)typically associated with it and thus be redundant. For example, if someone sees her- or himself in terms of her or his collective self as a 'German' (dominant self-aspect), that person should, by implication, see her or himself also as dependable and hard-working (redundant self-aspects). Conversely, the individual self is based on several non-redundant self-aspects. For example, one's individual self may comprise, amongst others, the self-aspects 'psychologist', 'female', 'German' and 'red hair' which are not mutually redundant, because they are not (stereo)typically associated with each other.

II   *Both the individual self and the collective self are social selves.*

The insight that with the activation of the individual self socially shared similarities recede into the background does not imply that the individual self denotes any 'asocial' form of self-interpretation. First, all self-aspects are social products in that they acquire their meaning and significance only within a context of social relations between people. Self-aspects are never absolute features of an isolated monad, but relational features (e.g., 'young' vs. 'old') of interdependent social beings. This is true for self-aspects which serve as a basis for a collective self and are thus explicitly recognized as socially shared with some other (but not all other) people, but also for self-aspects which are construed as more personal or individual features and thus contribute to the individual self (Simon, 1993, p. 141). That is, the individual self is not based on special 'asocial' self-aspects, but on *a unique configuration or combination of social self-aspects.* In fact, it will be argued even more radically later that there is no inherent difference between self-aspects on which the individual self is based and self-aspects on which the collective self is based. Second, both self-interpretation in terms of the individual self and self-interpretation in terms of the collective self arise under specific social conditions. In other words, the relative weighting of the individual self and the collective self in a person's current self-image is *a function of the relevant social context* (e.g., Turner et al., 1987; Simon and Hamilton, 1994). Third, self-interpretation in terms of the individual self is as social in its consequences as is self-interpretation in terms of the collective self. Each form of self-interpretation is responsible for *a particular type of social behaviour and perception.* The former for individual behaviour and perception, the latter for group behaviour and perception. Taking all three points together, it can be concluded that the individual self is as social 'in terms of its content, origin and function' as the collective self (Turner et al., 1987, p. 46).

III   *The individual self and the collective self are not based on different types of self-aspects.*

It is often assumed that the individual self and the collective self are construed with reference to quite different types or classes of self-aspects. For example, a person's sex, skin colour, nationality, political affiliation or religion are frequently thought of as almost 'natural' bases for collective selves. On the other hand, physical features, psychological characteristics, tastes, abilities, etc. are often assumed to be personal or individual in nature and therefore genuine components of the individual self (Gergen, 1971; Gordon, 1968; Triandis, 1990).

It is argued here that there is no reason to assume that the individual self and the collective self are based on *inherently* different types of self-aspects.

Although some self-aspects may appear to have more potential than others to provide a basis for a collective self, it is important to note that such potential is highly context-specific. Religious denomination, for example, has great potential for collective self-interpretation in Northern Ireland, whereas in Germany it may be viewed more as contributing to an individualized self-image. Also, most of us would be inclined to think that wearing spectacles is more likely to be associated with one's individual self. But imagine that all people who wear spectacles were suddenly singled out for the same special treatment (perhaps because they were considered literate and therefore dangerous), 'wearing spectacles' should soon acquire great potential for collective self-interpretation (see also Tajfel, 1976, for another illustration of the same point).

The important point is that each self-aspect can be experienced as socially shared and thus serve as a basis for a collective self *under the appropriate social conditions*. This fact has long been acknowledged, or at least been capitalized on, by experimental social psychologists working in the area of group processes. Following the minimal group paradigm (Tajfel, Billig, Bundy and Flament, 1971), it has become a standard procedure in experimental group research to create ad hoc groups by informing subjects that they allegedly share a particular self-aspect with other, but not all other subjects. This procedure has proven very successful in inducing subjects to act in terms of their collective self as group members. It is especially noteworthy, that this procedure has successfully been employed with a diverse variety of self-aspects such as artistic preference (e.g., preference for Klee vs. Kandinsky paintings), perceptual sensitivity (e.g., blue vs. green sensitivity), psychological characteristics (e.g., introverted vs. extroverted) or cognitive styles (e.g., analytical vs. holistic) (e.g., Judd and Park, 1988; Oakes and Turner, 1980; Simon and Hamilton, 1994). Evidently, the success of this procedure does not hinge so much on the specific type of self-aspect used for psychological group formation, but on the meaning which the particular social context affords the socially shared self-aspect: the social microcosm created in the minimal group paradigm affords the particular self-aspect (e.g., preference for Klee) special meaning because its possession (or non-possession) is the only criterion available under such social conditions which can provide a basis for meaningful self–other distinctions and interpretations.

In conclusion, the same self-aspect (e.g., 'German') can provide the basis for a collective self at one time ('We, the Germans'), whereas at another time it may be construed as a component of the individual self ('I am a psychologist, male, German, have brown eyes, etc.'). In the first case the particular self aspect defines a social category of which oneself is one member amongst others, whereas in the other case it is one feature amongst several other features of oneself the ensemble of which represents the individual self. In the first case the own person is allocated to the self-aspect, in the second case the self-aspect is allocated to the own person. Whether a particular self-aspect is construed as a social category or as one feature amongst others is thus subject to variation. Such variation is not random, however. Instead, research on the relative salience of the collective self and the individual self strongly suggests that it can systematically be tied to social contextual variables (e.g., Oakes, 1987; Simon, Pantaleo and Mummendey, 1995). (Note that, at a more general level, a similar argument could be advanced against an essentialistic distinction between categories and attributes; cf. Fiske and Neuberg, 1990; pp. 9–12; also Spears and Haslam, this volume).

IV   *Self-aspects referred to by nouns are especially likely to serve as a basis for the collective self.*

The assumption here is that self-aspects referred to by nouns are particularly likely to serve as a basis for a collective self because nouns (e.g., worker, woman, psychologist) suggest that the respective self-aspects define discrete social types or categories with relatively clear boundaries. More specifically, when thinking about aspects of the self (and other people), the use of nouns is likely to imply underlying essence and hence essential similarities with other people sharing the critical self-aspect as well as essential or qualitative differences between self and other people not sharing the self-aspect (Medin and Ortony, 1989; Rothbart and Taylor, 1992; Yzerbyt, Rocher and Schadron, this volume). Nouns thus appear to cut the (social) world 'at its joints' (Roger Brown, 1986, pp. 468–82).

On the other hand, self-aspects referred to by other linguistic terms or expressions (e.g., verbs) should be less likely to serve as a basis for the collective self. This applies also to self-aspects referred to by adjectives, even though adjectives may be very similar to nouns with respect to many other cognitive functions (Semin and Fiedler, 1988). Yet, unlike nouns, adjectives suggest that self-aspects to which they refer (e.g., strong, short, extroverted) vary along underlying continua (e.g., from not very strong to extremely strong) (Gordon, 1968). 'Adjective self-aspects' are therefore seen more as a matter of degree or quantity than as a matter of quality. Accordingly, similarities and differences are viewed merely as quantitative in nature and are thus less likely to trigger essentialistic beliefs.

The belief that nouns denote qualities or underlying essences may incite us, to a greater extent than in the case of adjectives or other linguistic expressions, 'to go beyond the information given' (Bruner, 1957b), that is, to make additional inferences about the target (Hamilton, Gibbons, Stroessner and Sherman, 1992; Rothbart and Taylor, 1992; Yzerbyt et al., this volume). Accordingly, self-interpretations in terms of noun self-aspects should be richer and more saturated. Even a *single* noun self-aspect may then be able to provide an exhaustive self-interpretation (e.g., 'I am a socialist'.). In the case of self-interpretations in terms of other self-aspects, however, more comprehensive sets of self-aspects would be necessary for satisfactory self-interpretation (e.g., 'I am male, quite friendly, not very religious, usually not very punctual, I like my work, etc.').

To summarize, it seems more likely that self-interpretations are centred on a single noun self-aspect than on a single self-aspect referred to by other linguistic expressions because single noun self-aspects are more likely to allow for exhaustive and essential(istic) self-interpretations. Noun self-aspects should, therefore, be particularly good candidates for a basis of the collective self. Self-aspects referred to by other linguistic expressions should be more representative for the individual self.

Finally, in line with Thesis III it should be emphasized here that one does not need to postulate inherent (essential) differences in the *content* of noun self-aspects and self-aspects referred to by other linguistic expressions (e.g., adjectives) which would make the former better candidates for a basis of the collective self. For example, while at some times 'being extroverted' or 'being intellectual' may just be one component of the individual self, it is certainly possible that, at other times, interpreting oneself primarily as 'an extravert' or as 'an intellectual' defines a collective self. Two directions for future research thus suggest themselves at this point. First, one could examine the extent to which reference to noun self-aspects in self-descriptions can serve as a reliable and valid indicator of the collective self, and reference to other self-aspects as an indicator of the individual self. And second, we need to specify the antecedent conditions and mediating processes which determine when a particular self-aspect is referred to either by a noun or any other linguistic expression.

V   *Modernization favours the individual self over the collective self.*

Traditional ('classical') sociological theories have conceptualized modernization as *functional differentiation* which in turn is based, amongst others, on division of labour, urbanization, mass communication, literacy and nation-building. Functional differentiation together with social permeability and mobility, formal equality, individualized interests and universalistic competition are thus viewed as characteristic conditions of modern societies (Esser, 1988). It follows from such a conceptualization that in the course of modernization traditional collectives (e.g., family, village, class, ethnic community) should lose their capacity to sustain close social ties among people (Beck, 1994). For instance, Max Weber predicted that modernization would erode any kind of community:

> With the multiplication of life chances and opportunities, the individual becomes less and less content with being bound to rigid and undifferentiated forms of life prescribed by the group. Increasingly he desires to shape his life as an individual and to enjoy the fruits of his own abilities and labor as he himself wishes. (Weber, 1978, p. 375)

Similarly, Karl Marx (and Friedrich Engels) pointed out in the Manifesto of the Communist Party that (economic) modernization would set people progressively free from their traditional social ties:

> Constant revolutionising of production, uninterrupted disturbance of all social conditions, everlasting uncertainty and agitation distinguish the bourgeois epoch from all earlier ones. All fixed, fast frozen relations, with their train of ancient and venerable prejudices and opinions, are swept away, all new-formed ones become antiquated before they can ossify. All that is solid melts into air, all that is holy is profaned, and man is at last compelled to face with sober senses, his real conditions of life, and his relations with this kind. (Marx, 1978, p. 476)

At the same time that traditional collectives lose their importance in modern society, the complexity of the social fabric increases. The system of social coordinates necessary to locate each person increases in complexity. People no longer belong to a single dominant collective or social group which for a lifetime affects all or most aspects of their lives ('from the cradle to the grave'). Instead, they belong simultaneously to an increasing number of different, often mutually independent, but sometimes also conflicting social groups (professional groups, political parties, neighbourhoods, sports teams, etc.). Just as a group incorporates many individuals, so does 'an individual incorporate[s] many groups' (F. Allport, 1962, p. 25).

The important point here is that by virtue of the increasing complexity of the system of social coordinates the individuality of each person becomes increasingly well-defined in modern society. Or in Georg Simmel's words:

> The groups with which the individual is affiliated constitute a system of coordinates, as it were, such that each new group with which he becomes affiliated circumscribes him more exactly and more unambiguously. To belong to any one of these groups leaves the individual considerable leeway. But the larger the number of groups to which an individual belongs, the more improbable is it that other persons will exhibit the same combination of group-affiliations, that these particular groups will 'intersect' once again [in a second individual]. Concrete objects lose their individual characteristics as we subsume them under a general concept in accordance with one of their attributes. And concrete objects regain their individual characteristics as other concepts are emphasized under which their several attributes may be subsumed. To speak Platonically, each thing has a part in as many ideas as it has manifold attributes, and it achieves thereby its individual determination. There is an analogous relationship between the individual and the groups with which he is affiliated. (Simmel, 1955, p. 140)

From a psychological perspective, the placement of the self within a more differentiated and thus more complex system of social coordinates implies the cognitive differentiation of additional non-redundant (independent) self-aspects. It follows that modern society offers access to additional non-redundant self-aspects. It thereby expands the basis for the individual self, that is, for self-interpretation as a unique individual. The individual self, which as a psychological matrix reflects the complex social positioning of the own person in modern society, should therefore assume a privileged status (be more salient) *vis-à-vis* the collective self in people's self-images.

This conclusion is also supported by Elias's (1988, 1990) socio-historical analysis of changes in people's self-images. Elias notes that, since the European Middle Ages, the balance between the collective self ('we-identity') and the individual self ('I-identity') has undergone a remarkable change towards an increasing pre-potency of the individual self (Elias, 1988, especially pp. 209–315). According to Elias, this process, the starting point of which he sees symbolized by Descartes' famous 'Cogito, ergo sum', is still developing in the same direction. It is sustained by the decreasing permanence and increasing interchangeability of 'we-relations' in modern society and the accompanying civilizing process which fosters interpretations of the own person as a self-contained entity separated from other people 'outside' (Elias, 1988, p. 168).[3]

VI   *Though not obsolete, the collective self is highly variable and fragile in modern society.*

The thesis that modern society favours the individual self over the collective self does not imply that the collective self has simply been rendered obsolete in modern society. The relationship between the individual self and the collective self is more complicated than that. It will be remembered that each self-aspect can be experienced as socially shared and thus serve as a basis for a collective self *under the appropriate social conditions*. As modern society gives access to additional (non-redundant) self-aspects, the number of potential or latent collective selves increases accordingly. The ensuing pluralism of potential collective selves confines the activation or instantiation of each particular collective self to specific social conditions, however. The collective self is, therefore, highly context-dependent and variable, and self-interpretations in terms of a particular collective self are transitory and fragile.

Quite a body of social psychological research conducted within the framework of self-categorization theory is now available which demonstrates the dependency on social contextual variables of the collective self (Turner et al., 1994). For instance, Simon and Hamilton (1994) examined self-interpretations in terms of the collective self as a function of the numerical distinctiveness and social status associated with particular self-aspects. In one experiment, they showed that the likelihood that a particular self-aspect (e.g., preference for a particular painter) would serve as a basis for a collective self increased when that self-aspect was shared with only a minority of people in the relevant social context. In a second experiment, they found that a high as opposed to a low social status associated with a particular self-aspect also increased the likelihood that the self-aspect would serve as a basis for a collective self, but only if at the same time, the self-aspect was numerically distinct (i.e., shared by a minority).

Additional evidence of the context-dependency of the collective self stems from a series of studies by Simon et al. (1995). They focused on several social contextual variables which prior work in the social identity and self-categorization theory tradition suggested should be positively or negatively related to self-interpretation in terms of a collective self. These variables were the temporarily salient value connotations of a self-aspect, the more stable or chronic attractiveness of a self-aspect, and finally awareness of common fate due to a shared self-aspect. An important novel feature of those studies was the measurement of perceived intragroup similarities and differences as an indicator of the salience in subjects' current self-images of the collective self relative to the individual self. More specifically, it was suggested that a predominance of perceived similarities relative to differences among people sharing the relevant self-aspect (including the self) would be indicative of greater salience of the collective self. On the other hand, greater salience of the individual self would be indicated by the perception of more intragroup differences than similarities.

In the first two studies, the temporarily salient value connotations of the critical self-aspect (i.e., nationality) were manipulated simply by asking subjects to list either positively or negatively valenced attributes that they thought were typical of people sharing that self-aspect (including themselves). It was predicted that subjects would be more willing to engage in collective self-interpretations, and view themselves as interchangeable group members, to the extent that the particular group membership was based on a positively connoted self-aspect. If the critical self-aspect was negatively connoted, however, self-interpretation as a unique individual (the individual self) would be more likely, because it would dilute the negative impact of the unattractive self-aspect on self-evaluation. As predicted, the salience of the collective self relative to the individual self (indicated by the perception of intragroup similarities relative to differences) increased when value connotations were positive as opposed to negative. Similar, although somewhat weaker, results were found in a third study which examined the impact of the more *stable* or *chronic* attractiveness of a self-aspect (i.e., membership in the socially stigmatized group of gay men or in the dominant group of straight men).

In a fourth study, Simon et al. (1995) manipulated awareness of common fate due to a shared self-aspect (i.e., sexual orientation) experimentally by asking gay men either to recall episodes of categorical treatment of gays by the outside world or simply to answer some irrelevant filler questions. It was hypothesized that gay men would view themselves in terms of their collective self to the extent that they were made aware of their common fate as recipients of special treatment by the outside world (i.e., the heterosexual majority). The results confirmed the hypothesis. When not made aware of their common fate, gay subjects clearly accentuated intragroup differences relative to intragroup similarities. In other words, they stressed their individual selves. That tendency was significantly reduced or even (non-significantly) reversed, however, when common fate was made salient.

Finally, the results reported by Simon et al. (1995) pointed to an interesting asymmetry. Although the hypothesized variation in the perception of intragroup similarities relative to differences was obtained across all four studies, subjects appeared to be more ready to report a predominance of perceived intragroup differences than a predominance of perceived intragroup similarities. This asymmetry is in line with the assumption that in modern society the individual self is granted a privileged status *vis-à-vis* the collective self whereby the latter is rendered rather fragile.

VII   *There is no simple antagonistic relationship between the individual self and the collective self, but rather a dynamic, dialectic interaction between the two.*

I have argued that a collective self is activated whenever self-interpretations are centred on a single dominant, socially shared self-aspect, whereas the individual self is activated to the extent that self-interpretations are based on a more comprehensive set or configuration of non-redundant self-aspects. Furthermore, the same self-aspect (e.g., 'gay') can provide the basis for a collective self at one time (e.g., during a Gay Pride March), whereas at another time it may be construed as just one component, amongst others, of the individual self ('I am a psychologist, male, German, gay, have brown eyes, etc.'). Consequently, to the extent that it includes self-aspects that have previously served as bases for collective selves, the individual self imports, or better, incorporates past experiences with the corresponding collective selves. The individual self is, therefore, at least partly composed of the sediments of formerly activated collective selves which in turn are thus preserved by the individual self. Moreover, as each self-aspect can – under the appropriate conditions – provide the basis for a collective self, the individual self is in an extreme sense the synthesis of all possible (formerly activated and yet-to-be-activated) collective selves.

In conclusion, the relationship between the individual self and the collective self is not simply an antagonistic one. It is a dialectic relationship in that there is a continual, dynamic dialogue between the two in the course of which they make each other possible. Although in modern society the individual self tends to obstruct the collective self, it simultaneously incorporates and synthesizes the ensemble of possible collective selves thereby preserving their potential for realization under appropriate conditions. On the other hand, although each of the collective selves may be able to temporarily suspend the individual self, the (ensemble of) collective selves also play(s) an important role in the maintenance of the individual self. They do so by virtue of their diversity which reflects and highlights the complexity of the system of social coordinates within which the self is located and thus defined as unique. In a similar vein, Georg Simmel pointed out that it is in fact the tension or even conflict arising from the diversity of collective selves ('group affiliations') which contributes positively to the individual self:

> But it is also true that multiple group-affiliations can strengthen the individual and reenforce the integration of his personality. Conflicting and integrating tendencies are mutually reenforcing. Conflicting tendencies can arise just because the individual has a core of inner unity. The ego can become more clearly conscious of this unity, the more he is confronted with the task of reconciling within himself a diversity of group interests. (Simmel, 1955, pp. 141–2)

Finally, a slight asymmetry implicit in the conceptualization of the individual self and the collective self presented so far needs to be rectified. It is evident that a person can have more than one collective self. Hypothetically, there can be as many collective selves for a given person as there are self-aspects available to her or him. Conversely, it may seem at first glance as if a person can have only one unique ensemble of self-aspects and thus only one individual self. It should be noted however that different subconfigurations or subsets of the entire ensemble of possible self-aspects may be processed and used for self-interpretation in different situations. Consequently, it is also justified to speak of different individual selves of a person.

VIII *The individual self and the collective self may be cognitively represented by 'placeholders'.*

In modern society, the complex social positioning of the self should foster self-interpretation as a unique individual as opposed to self-interpretation as an interchangeable member of a social category or group. Accordingly, researchers have suggested – particularly with reference to modern western societies – that:

> The self is clearly a unique cognitive structure, different in nature from those structures representing others . . . The self may well be the largest and most rich prototype in our cognitive arsenal. (T.B. Rogers, 1981, p. 203; see also Markus and Kitayama, 1991)

Note however that the exact form of cognitive representation of the self as a unique individual is debatable. For example, it may not be necessary to assume that the individual self corresponds directly to a fixed cognitive structure in long-term memory consisting of a complex configuration of cognitively represented self-aspects. The sheer number of possible self-aspects which would need to be stored and later retrieved makes such an assumption not very plausible. Instead, one could speculate that all that is needed is a cognitive 'placeholder', possibly with the (meta-)feature 'unique' tagged to it (as to the concept of 'placeholder' see also Medin and Ortony, 1989). Its function would be to reserve a cognitive place for context-dependent representations or instantiations of the individual self. Instead of retrieving an invariant representation from long-term memory, context-dependent representations could be constructed in working memory drawing both on specific information salient in the concrete situation and more general knowledge retrieved from long-term memory (Barsalou, 1987). Each time the person experiences her- or himself as being more different from than similar to other people in her or his usual social milieu, the placeholder and its tag would be reinforced. Such reinforcement may also provide at least some rudimentary sense of unity or coherence regarding the individual self.

People may also hold cognitive placeholders for collective selves, especially for those that are frequently or even chronically activated. It is very likely that such placeholders would be associated with essentialistic beliefs implying that the self shares some essence with other ingroup members (Rothbart and Taylor, 1992). In other words, such placeholders may be tagged with the (meta-) feature 'essentially interchangeable with other ingroup members'. As with the belief in the essence of categories in other domains, people need not know exactly what the shared essence is to hold such a belief (Medin, 1989; Medin and Ortony, 1989). It is sufficient to believe that such essence is knowable. For example, it would be sufficient to believe that there are other people, experts (e.g., psychologists or biologists), who really know or at least will know some day what the particular essence is. For the time being, people may quite happily take the shared self-aspect (e.g., being German) as a 'surface' indicator of an underlying, 'deeper' essence (e.g., genetic make-up) shared by the self and other ingroup members.

As with the placeholder for the individual self (or selves), the placeholder for a particular collective self would reserve a cognitive place for context-dependent representations (instantiations) of that collective self. Note that it is the very fact that the placeholder is rather content-free that allows for context-dependent flexibility or variability in the content of the collective self. For instance, the concrete instantiation of the collective self as a German can vary with the presence of a particular outgroup. In the presence of an American outgroup the feature 'formal' may be viewed as an important characteristic of the collective self as a German, whereas in the presence of a Polish outgroup the feature 'prosperous' may be viewed as particularly characteristic of that collective self (see also Haslam, Turner, Oakes, McGarty and Hayes, 1992). At the same time, the belief that the collective self is tied to some deeper, not necessarily known essence assures that the collective self is still attributed sufficient coherence despite all context-dependent variation.

IX   *The individual self and the collective self are phenomen(ologic)ally equally valid variants of the self.*

Even though (or actually because) it has been suggested earlier on that in modern society the individual self may hold a privileged status *vis-à-vis* the collective self, it is important to highlight the descriptive or phenomenological character of that suggestion. There are good reasons to assume that in modern society the individual self is often *experienced* as primary *vis-à-vis* the collective self, perhaps even as the authentic or true self (e.g., Elias 1988; Simon, 1993). This must not be (mis)understood as an *ontological* or even normative postulate, however. It is not maintained that the individual self possesses or should be granted a priori context-independent priority over the collective self. Quite on the contrary, it shall be warned here explicitly against any such individualistic bias in social psychological theory and research.

The important point is that modern society appears to promote experiences, or interpretations thereof, that strengthen the individual self (or its placeholder). The ensuing predominance of the individual self is thus not an ontological invariant, but a specific outcome of specific social conditions prevalent especially in modern (western) societies (Markus and Kitayama, 1991; Triandis, 1990). What is more, the relative weighting of the individual self and the collective self remains variable even in modern societies, despite the chronic advantage they may afford the individual self. Metaphorically speaking, though the general 'climate' may favour the individual self, we also have variable 'weather conditions'. The relative weighting of the individual self and the collective self still varies with the more proximate social conditions within the immediate social context.

In other words, whether the self is interpreted as either a unique individual or as an interchangeable group member is dependent on the position of the self in the relevant social context (Turner et al., 1994). This should be so because similarities with and differences from other people acquire significance and thus become relevant as a function of the social positioning of the self (see also Popper, 1982, p. 375, for a similar argument concerning the role of the perceiver's position and/or interests for the perception of similarities and differences). For example, being a target of prejudice and discrimination by virtue of possessing a particular feature or self-aspect (e.g., religious denomination in Northern Ireland) highlights the similarity (difference) between self and those people (not) sharing the same self-aspect. Under such circumstances (in such a social position), it may be more appropriate to interpret one's own experiences, perceptions and behaviours as well as the (re)actions of other people towards oneself in terms of the collective self than in terms of the individual self. Under different circumstances, sharing the same self-aspect (e.g., religious denomination in Germany) may not constitute a relevant similarity or difference. Self-interpretation in terms of the individual self or some other collective self may then be more appropriate.

In conclusion, both the individual self and the collective self can have psychological or phenomenological validity to the extent that they adequately reflect the social positioning and related experiences of the self. It also follows from this analysis that self-interpretation in terms of the collective self must not be viewed as a simple distortion of objective reality, whereas self-interpretation in terms of the individual self would reflect reality quite accurately. By the same token, perceptual and behavioural consequences of the collective self (e.g., the accentuation of intragroup similarities relative to differences) are in no way less legitimate offsprings of 'normal' psychological functioning than the corresponding consequences of the individual self (e.g., the accentuation of intragroup differences relative to similarities) (see also Oakes and Turner, 1990). It would therefore be misleading at best, and ideological at the worst, to view the individual self and its consequences as some kind of objective standard against which to judge the validity or accuracy of the collective self and its consequences (for a divergent viewpoint on this issue, see Judd and Park, 1993). The latter approach is most likely motivated by the misconception that only self-interpretation in terms of the collective self is categorical and thus abstract, whereas self-interpretation in terms of the individual self is concrete and thus closer to reality. Yet, as discussed more thoroughly by Oakes, Haslam and Turner (1994, pp. 114–16), self-interpretation in terms of the individual self, too, involves abstraction, namely, abstraction of self-aspects across time and/or situations which accentuates similarities (consistency) within the own person. If so, it should then make little sense to regard the outcome of one abstraction process as the objective baseline against which to assess the alleged distortion involved in another abstraction process (for a more detailed discussion of the accuracy issue, see the chapter by Oakes and Reynolds, this volume).

X   *There may exist quasi-intergroup situations such that (out)group phenomena can occur even when people weigh the individual self more heavily than the collective self.*

If the collective self overrides the individual self, it is not just self-interpretation that is centred on a single socially shared self-aspect (e.g., 'I am a democrat'.). Interpretations (by the self) of other people, their experiences, perceptions and behaviours are similarly focused. People sharing the relevant self-aspect are then interpreted primarily in terms of that self-aspect. Together with the self, they are cognitively construed as a homogeneous *ingroup* (e.g., 'We are democrats'.). Analogously, people not sharing the relevant self-aspect are interpreted primarily in terms of the opposite or complementary self-aspect. They are cognitively construed as a homogeneous *outgroup* (e.g., 'They are not democrats, but fascists'). Following Brown and Turner (1981, p. 37) such presence of two salient social categories or groups of which one represents an ingroup and the other an outgroup is a basic characteristic of (truly) intergroup situations.

Conversely, if the individual self possesses a privileged status *vis-à-vis* the collective self, the salience of socially shared self-aspects is reduced and no phenomenally relevant ingroup is (cognitively) construed. Note however that the cognitive construal of outgroups is not necessarily inhibited under such conditions. This should be so, because features which other people share with each other, but not with the self (i.e., socially shared *other*-aspects) tend to be more salient than features which the self shares with other people (i.e., socially shared *self*-aspects), especially when the self is viewed as a unique individual (McGuire, 1984; McGuire and McGuire, 1988; Simon, 1993). Research on perceived group homogeneity in fact supports this line of reasoning, as it strongly suggests that people *not* sharing a given self-aspect with the social perceiver (i.e., outgroup members) are more readily construed as a homogeneous social category or group than people actually sharing that self-aspect (for reviews, see Ostrom and Sedikides, 1992; Park, Judd and Ryan, 1991; but see also Haslam, Oakes, Turner and McGarty, 1996).

Taken together, this gives rise to the interesting possibility that people may actually construe a clear-cut outgroup (i.e., people sharing a particular feature not shared by the self) without necessarily interpreting themselves in terms of a collective self. Then, only the outgroup is a salient social entity and, consequently, only outgroup members are perceived and treated as group members, whereas (potential) 'ingroup members' are perceived and treated more as individuals. Situations characterized by such an asymmetry can be called *quasi*-intergroup situations (Simon, 1993; see also Allen, 1985). They should be especially likely in modern (western) societies by virtue of the privileged status these societies tend to grant to the individual self (Simon, 1993).

At the outset of this chapter, the individual self was classified as the psychological basis for individual phenomena and the collective self as the psychological basis for collective or group phenomena. That classification now needs some specification. The analysis presented in this section does not question the role of the collective self. It is still responsible for group phenomena. Such phenomena are characterized by self-interpretation as an interchangeable group member who is engaged in intragroup relations with other ingroup members and intergroup relations with outgroup members. The role of the individual self needs to be expanded, however. It can be responsible not only for individual phenomena, but also for certain group phenomena. More specifically, self-interpretation as a unique individual can result both in individualized perception and treatment of people who do not differ conspicuously from oneself, but also in the perception and treatment as an outgroup of those who do share a relevant difference *vis-à-vis* the self. Thus, quasi-intergroup situations can arise in which phenomena like outgroup stereotyping, outgroup derogation or outgroup discrimination may be observed even when the individual self is not overridden by the collective self. In the light of this analysis, it then appears less surprising that measures of the collective self (or of identification with the ingroup) have often failed as predictors of attitudes and behaviour towards outgroups (see Hinkle and Brown, 1990; Hinkle, Taylor, Fox-Cardamone and Crook, 1989; also Doosje and Ellemers, this volume).

2   Conclusions

I began this chapter by referring to the difference or even discontinuity between the perception and behaviour of people acting as individuals on the one hand and the perception and behaviour of people acting as group members on the other. Following the social identity and self-categorization approach, I argued that the shift from individual to collective self-interpretations (from the individual self to the collective self) is the crucial *psychological* process which makes group life possible (Turner et al., 1987). The distinction between the individual self and the collective self as well as their relationship was then elaborated in ten theses with particular reference to modern society.

As group life has its psychological basis in the shift from the individual to the collective self, the nature of the relationship of the individual self and the collective self in modern society is an important psychological parameter shaping (and constraining) contemporary group life. The major theme underlying the analysis presented in this chapter is that in modern society the collective self gains flexibility, but also loses stability and thus provides more room for the evolution of the individual self. The collective self no longer reflects people's permanent social positioning in a rigidly stratified social environment. Instead, it becomes increasingly contingent upon the immediate (and highly variable) social context, while the individual self is progressively reinforced as it unfolds as the integrative synthesis of constantly fluctuating collective self-interpretations.

To be sure, groups (and, for that matter, collective selves) are still alive in modern society. But they are doing better in some contexts than in others. Consequently, the analysis of group life and its manifestations such as intergroup discrimination and stereotyping need to be contextualized. This whole volume testifies to the potential of the social identity and self-categorization framework to lead the way in this undertaking. The theses presented in this chapter address some under-researched issues and lacunae within that framework. To the extent that they should not provide satisfactory answers themselves, I certainly hope that these theses are controversial enough to provoke challenging antitheses, both inside and outside the framework of social identity and self-categorization theory. The goal is to set in motion a *dialectic* dynamic of thesis and antithesis concerning the individual and collective self as well as their relationship that should eventually provide us with a better understanding of group life at a higher level of theoretical synthesis.

Notes

In writing this chapter, I benefited greatly from the extensive discussions with Penny Oakes and Mrs Bil Potsdam. Though those discussions did not lead to consensus in every case, they were always enlightening and constructive.

1   A similar, though more specific, distinction was suggested by Marx about 150 years ago when he differentiated between the personal individual ('persönliches Individuum') and the class individual ('Klassenindividuum') (Marx, 1978, p. 199).

2   The development of self-aspects is a function of a person's experiences in various social roles, relationships and situations. The relation between a self-aspect (as a cognitive concept) and experiences (as empirical examples) is analogous to the relation between theory and data (see Medin, 1989, p. 1474, for a more general treatise on the relation between cognitive concepts and empirical examples). Thus, self-aspects can help us to interpret or explain our experiences (e.g., 'I don't like parties. That's because I am introverted'.) in a way very similar to our use of more formal theories to explain scientific observations (e.g., the use of genetic theories to explain a mental or physical handicap). Yet scientific observations or data may also force us to modify our theories. Similarly, experiences can lead to a change in one's self-aspects (e.g., 'I come to like parties more and more. Maybe I am not so introverted after all'.). Finally, theories guide data collection or data production. In a similar way, self-aspects can increase the likelihood of certain experiences (e.g., 'I am an extroverted person, so perhaps I should do something to cheer this crowd up'.). In short, self-aspects can be viewed as theories or mini-theories about the self.

3   Though its operation is certainly not limited to modern societies, another factor should be mentioned here which may also contribute to a predominance of the individual self. That is, self-interpretation as a unique individual can adhere directly to one's own individual body. The individual self is thus provided with a well-defined natural (biological) anchor in time and space (see G. Allport, 1968, pp. 27–8; also Markus and Kitayama, 1991, p. 225). Such a direct anchor or embodiment is not available for the collective self, however. It must, therefore, fall back on more remote constructions (i.e., symbols such as monuments, flags, songs, etc.).

15
Commentary: Individual, Group and System Levels of Analysis and their Relevance for Stereotyping and Intergroup Relations

Charles Stangor and John T. Jost

Research on social stereotyping continues to flood the social psychological literature. This is reflected not only in an expanding stream of empirical reports, but also by a spate of recent monographs and edited books, including this one (see also Lee, Jussim and McCauley, 1995; Leyens, Yzerbyt and Schadron, 1994; Mackie and Hamilton, 1993; Oakes, Haslam and Turner, 1994; Macrae, Stangor and Hewstone, 1996). Such intense interest in stereotypes among social psychologists is probably not surprising, given that person attributes such as traits are among the most significant ways in which people characterize others (Fiske and Cox, 1979). Stereotypes are fundamental to interpersonal relations, both determining the course of social interaction (Devine, Evett and Vasquez-Suson, 1996; Jussim and Fleming, 1996; Neuberg, 1989) and developing out of social interaction (Reicher, Hopkins and Condor, this volume). Stereotypes are integral to the study of intergroup relations, relating to both prejudice (Dovidio, Brigham, Johnson and Gaertner, 1996; Yzerbyt, Rocher and Schadron, this volume) and discriminatory intentions (Stangor, Sullivan and Ford, 1991). Stereotypes are also highly functional for the perceiver – they are used to create social identity (Ellemers and van Knippenberg, this volume), to inform social reality (Oakes, Haslam and Turner, 1994), to justify existing social orders (Jost and Banaji, 1994) and to simplify information-processing (Macrae, Milne and Bodenhausen, 1994).

Two general approaches have dominated the social psychological study of stereotyping, and the influence of both pervades the contributions collected here. The first approach is recognizable as the social cognition approach, and it has dominated the North American scene since the late 1970s (Hamilton, 1981; Hamilton and Sherman, 1994; Macrae et al., 1996). In many ways, this approach owes its development to Gordon Allport (1954), who first articulated the extent to which stereotyping and prejudice are fundamental cognitive processes. The second approach is primarily European, based upon social identity theory (Tajfel and Turner, 1986) and self-categorization theory (Turner, Hogg, Oakes, Reicher and Wetherell, 1987), and it is indebted to the personal and professional contributions of Henri Tajfel (1978a, 1981b; see Oakes et al., 1994).

Both the social cognition and social identity perspectives have come of age during the past two decades. Research in social cognition has effectively validated Allport's major proposals concerning the primacy of cognition and categorization, and work on social identification has similarly validated many of Tajfel's main theses pertaining to social categorization, ingroup favouritism and outgroup derogation. Yet in both cases the empirical and theoretical work has gone well beyond the original insights of the founding fathers. This is because each approach has been informed not only by the original assumptions of its own framework, but also by recent advances in cognitive and motivational theorizing.

Perhaps primarily due to the geographic separation in the centres of training and research in these two approaches, there has heretofore been little contact between them. But this has changed in recent years, and we are beginning to see attempts to integrate and reconcile these two distinct approaches (cf. Leyens et al., 1994). And as this integration continues, it is becoming increasingly clear that, although the two approaches have focused upon different underlying motivational functions for stereotyping, and to some degree they have relied upon different methodologies to test their hypotheses, these differences are now yielding to a general sense that both identification and categorization are indispensable to the study of stereotyping and group life.

Although the tendency of many analysts has been to focus on their differences (cf. Spears, Oakes, Ellemers and Haslam, this volume) our analysis suggests that these may be overshadowed by fundamental similarities between the two approaches. Both social cognition and social identity approaches espouse social categorization as the basic foundation of intergroup relations and as a necessary antecedent to ingroup favouritism and social stereotyping (Taylor, Fiske, Etcoff and Ruderman, 1978; Tajfel, Billig, Bundy and Flament, 1971). The principles and paradigms followed by each perspective have been fueled by work in cognitive psychology and have drawn on general principles of person perception and judgement.

Furthermore, both approaches are committed to integrating cognitive and motivational factors, sharing the goal of understanding how motivations influence and are influenced by cognitive processes. European researchers have grown increasingly cognitive, shifting their focus from the effects of social status and other macro-social variables on group identification (Tajfel, 1978) to the effects of 'meta-contrast ratios' and perceived group variability on self-categorization (Turner, 1991). Thus, researchers have adopted information-processing paradigms to study group-related phenomena of interest (Haslam; McGarty and De La Haye; Spears and Haslam, this volume). At the same time, North American social cognitivists have exhibited an increased interest in motivational factors, with a renewed emphasis on the relationships among affect, social identity, self-esteem and stereotyping (Crocker and Major, 1989; Ethier and Deaux, 1994; Mackie and Hamilton, 1993). Differences in methodology and theoretical emphasis are giving way to a broader sense that processes of categorization and evaluation are compatible in the end.

The social identity and social cognition approaches share another basic similarity, and that is that they are each limited in the range of issues that they deem appropriate for study. Both approaches have focused upon one or two underlying functions or motivations – typically either cognitive economy or identity enhancement – and neither approach has adequately expanded the study of social stereotyping to its broadest level – the institutional or systemic level.

The goal of the present chapter is to develop the notion that stereotypes can be studied at (at least) three different levels of analysis (the *individual* level, the *group level* and the *system level*), that each of these levels provides a partial picture of the overall stereotyping process, and that scientific progress may be made by addressing all of the possible paths among levels. Although predictions made at different levels may sometimes conflict with one another, this does not mean that any one set of assumptions is necessarily more correct or appropriate. Social behavior is notoriously complex, and it may be understood adequately only by aggregating across a wide variety of theoretical and empirical perspectives (e.g., McGuire, 1989). We begin by outlining the levels of analysis we have in mind and describing in some detail the possible paths among these levels, using the contributions of this volume to illustrate. Finally, we discuss some benefits of extending social psychological analyses to the systemic level and of adopting a multi-level approach to the study of stereotyping and group life.

1   Three Levels of Analysis: Individual, Group and System

A theme that is central to virtually all of the chapters of this book, and one that forms a basis of this concluding chapter, is that stereotypes and stereotyping can and should be studied at different levels of analysis. However, it is our contention that there are at least three, rather than two, relevant levels of analysis, and that existing research, from both the social cognition and the social identity traditions, have restricted themselves to the level of the individual and, less frequently, to the level of the group. We propose that the system level is as informative and predictive as the other two and that attending to it may help to resolve conceptual and empirical difficulties faced at other levels.

A distinction between individual and group levels of analysis in social identity theory provides the basis for Tajfel's (1981b) distinction between individual-level functions of the stereotype such as organizing and simplifying perception and preserving important social values, on the one hand, and group-level functions such as explaining social events, justifying collective action, and creating positive distinctiveness, on the other hand (see Stangor and Schaller, 1996). This distinction also underlies Tajfel and Turner's (1986) notion of a 'behavioural continuum' between individual and group action, a formulation that reaches new levels of sophistication in self-categorization theory (see Turner, Oakes, Haslam and McGarty, 1994) and in many of the contributions to this volume (Simon; Worchel) It also forms the theoretical rationale for Luhtanen and Crocker's (1992) distinction between personal and collective self-esteem, a topic that is extremely well summarized by Long and Spears (this volume).

Jost and Banaji (1994) argued, however, that stereotypes may also develop through the operation of macro-social systems and structures. For instance, the stereotype that 'blacks are lazy' may be viewed as an ideological justification for the socio-economic disadvantage of people of African descent (cf. Ashmore and Del Boca, 1976; Stroebe and Insko, 1989). Through the formation and use of stereotypes such as these, the legitimacy of the social and economic system is preserved and blame is placed instead on the group that 'fails' (see Yzerbyt et al., this volume).

Social identity theorists may be tempted to regard the 'social system', as we have been using the term, as merely a broader, more inclusive group identification – a categorization at some superordinate level. Tyler's (1989, 1990) 'group-value model', for instance, draws on notions of social identity and group membership to explain citizens' loyalty to legal and governmental institutions. However, we feel that the systemic level must be treated as distinct from the group level (see also Doise, 1986). For one thing, a system may be a set of ideas or practices such as capitalism, patriarchy or slavery, and these ideas and practices may be rather different from the ideas or practices of a specific group of people. And, even more importantly, some beliefs do not refer specifically to a social group, but rather to a set of relationships among groups. The inclusion of a systemic level seems particularly appropriate for this volume, as several of the contributors address issues pertaining to status, power, politics, ideology and society (see especially Bourhis, Turner and Gagnon; Ellemers and van Knippenberg; Reicher et al.; Simon; Yzerbyt et al., this volume). As Spears, Oakes, Ellemers and Haslam note in their introduction, 'the nature of specific stereotypes has as much to do with the social system as with the cognitive system' (p. 23).

In our analysis, adopting an individual level of analysis is to seek explanations of stereotyping in terms of unique properties of an individual person, as when researchers attempt to explain stereotyping and prejudice in terms of motivations for cognitive economy (Fiske and Neuberg, 1990), or as personality responses to childhood experiences (Adorno, Frenkel-Brunswik, Levinson and Sanford, 1950). According to a group level of analysis, explanations are sought in terms of social beliefs that are shared by members of a particular group, as when stereotyping and prejudice are understood as ways in which members of one group attempt to advance their own interests at the expense of other groups (e.g., Billig, 1976; Brewer, 1986). Finally, the system level of analysis implies that explanations should be given in terms of structural and ideological features associated with particular types of social arrangements, as when stereotyping and prejudice are explained in terms of highly stratified and competitive economic systems that require justification (e.g., Jackman and Senter, 1983), or as cultural systems that promote racism and discrimination (Jones, 1972). Thus, one may identify causal factors that originate with a given individual, a particular social group or an existing social system.[1]

In addition to serving as the source of social psychological effects, the individual, group, and system levels may also be used to specify objects or targets of social cognition and behaviour. Thus an individual, a group or a social system may give rise to beliefs and actions that are about or are directed at individuals, groups and systems. This formulation results in the identification of nine distinct relational paths, as outlined in figure 15.1. In what follows, we consider the unique contributions of each path to the study of stereotyping and social life.

Path 1   *Effects of the individual on perceptions of and reactions to individuals.*

The most common path of study within contemporary social psychology is certainly Path 1, which describes the effects that one individual's beliefs or behaviour have on another individual. With regard to stereotyping, Path 1 highlights factors about an individual perceiver that contribute to the likelihood that he or she will categorize a target person as a member of a given social group and subsequently apply stereotypes in judgements of or behaviour toward the individual.

Whereas the social cognition approach has relied heavily on goals of cognitive economy as a determinant of category activation and use (cf. Fiske and Neuberg, 1990), social identity and self-categorization approaches have focused especially on the contextual 'fit' between the stereotype and its social context (Oakes et al., 1994), the informational goal of 'enriching' the social

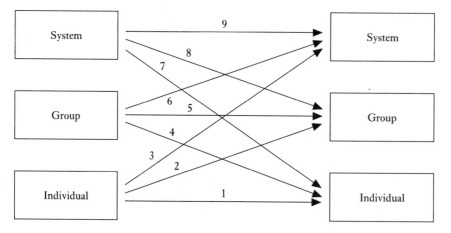

Figure 15.1   Individual, Group, and System Levels of Analysis (Causes and Effects).

environment (Oakes and Turner, 1990; Turner et al., 1994) and motivational needs for individual or collective self-enhancement (Hogg and Abrams, 1988).
There continues to be lively debate about which of these functions is the most important determinant of stereotype activation. Although some analyses have taken the stance that one particular motivation is involved to a greater degree in stereotyping than another (cf. Oakes and Turner, 1990), it seems to us more likely that all of these functions determine category activation and use, and the true challenge is to determine which motivations activate which stereotypes for which people under which conditions (cf. Snyder and Miene, 1994). Spears and Haslam (this volume) have taken a step in this direction by distinguishing between motivations for 'enrichment of the social environment' and for 'cognitive economy'. Although there would appear to be at this point virtually overwhelming evidence to support the contention that stereotypes serve, in part, to promote cognitive efficiency, Spears and Haslam make it clear that categorization may serve in some cases to elaborate on information rather than to reduce it.

Path 2   *Effects of the individual on perceptions of and reactions to social groups.*

Studies of the application of social stereotypes in judgements of individuals are Path 1 phenomena, whereas the measurement of stereotypes has almost always occurred via Path 2. Nearly all existing measures of stereotype centrality and variability require individuals to express their opinions about a group of people (e.g., 'I believe that most blacks are musical'; 'Asians are all the same'). Social cognition research on stereotyping has frequently followed a Path 2 approach, with a particular interest in how individuals develop social stereotypes through differential attention to and encoding of social stimuli. This approach has been based to a large degree on the assumption that group-level perceptions will be distorted or biased as the result of information-processing errors such as illusory correlations (McGarty and De La Haye, this volume), preferential memory for stereotype-consistent information (Fyock and Stangor, 1994) and behavioural confirmation effects (Jussim and Fleming, 1996; Word, Zanna and Cooper, 1974).

Another of the fundamental goals of social cognition research has been to elucidate how information about social groups is stored by individuals in long-term memory. The prevailing theories of representation have followed developments in cognitive psychology – moving from schema models (Fiske and Taylor, 1991; Fiske and Linville, 1980) to prototype models (Stangor and Lange, 1994) to exemplar models (Smith and Zárate, 1992). Most recently, parallel-distributed-processing (PDP) approaches have become the rage in cognitive psychology, and now (a few years later) are being developed as models of stereotype representation (Smith, in press).

In part because of their reliance upon methods of cognitive psychology, however, current models of stereotype representation have remained exclusively at the level of stereotypes held by the individual (Path 2 effects), and have not dealt with shared group representations (Path 4 and above). But, as noted eloquently by Haslam (this volume) individuals do not merely develop their own unique beliefs and explanations – these beliefs are group, societal and cultural constructions that are widely shared (e.g., Jost and Banaji, 1994; Stangor and Schaller, 1996; Tajfel, 1981b). As Haslam (this volume) points out, social psychology desperately needs to move beyond existing models of stereotype representation to include those that represent shared social reality.

Social identity theorists have also investigated Path 2 effects to account for stereotyping and evaluation. In these models, individuals hold group-level stereotypes (Path 2) and apply them to individuals (Path 1) to serve the motivational function of elevating personal self-esteem (Chin and McClintock, 1993; Lemyre and Smith, 1985; Oakes and Turner, 1980). Although social identity theorists frequently criticize 'individualistic' approaches to intergroup relations, social identity theory frequently relies on individual-level predictors such as self-enhancement, self-categorization and environmental enrichment, suggesting that it, too, might be classified as 'individualistic', at least in terms of independent and mediating variables (Abrams and Hogg, 1988). Examinations of the influence of 'collective self-esteem' on intergroup perception and behaviour (see Long and Spears, this volume) also fit, Path 2, insofar as collective self-esteem refers to an individual's sense of the importance of his or her own membership in a particular social group.

Whereas social identity theory suggests that ingroup identification should be related positively and straightforwardly to ingroup favouritism, self-stereotyping, and the perception of ingroup homogeneity, studies have failed to provide strong support for these hypotheses (e.g., Hinkle and Brown, 1990; Hogg and Abrams, 1988; Leyens et al., 1994). Long and Spears (this volume) offer important insights into this problem in terms of the relationship between self-esteem and ingroup favouritism. They find that personal and collective self-esteem have opposite effects on ingroup favouritism, such that personal self-esteem is positively related – whereas collective self-esteem is negatively related – to ingroup favouritism. In their research, the greatest degree of ingroup favouritism was observed among people who were high in personal self-esteem and low in collective self-esteem, suggesting that ingroup favouritism may represent a specific strategic response to feeling that one's social identification is being threatened, rather than a blanket strategy for maintaining or enhancing self-esteem.

Doosje and Ellemers (this volume) provide another important clarification of this general prediction in their research which shows that ingroup identification interacts with the social status of the ingroup to determine self-stereotyping and the perception of intragroup variability. Among members of high-status groups, there seems to be no relation between ingroup identification and these dependent variables. Among members of low-status groups, however, stronger ingroup identification is associated with greater self-stereotyping and the perception of increased ingroup homogeneity. Doosje and Ellemers interpret this pattern of findings as evidence for an indirect strategy of dissociation from the group on the part of weakly identified, low-status group members. These chapters represent fine examples of the types of advances that are being made in social identity theory and contribute to a fuller understanding of how individuals perceive the social groups in their environments.

Path 3   *Effects of the individual on perceptions of and reactions to social systems.*

Just as Path 2 deals with individuals' perceptions and evaluations of the social groups around them, Path 3 deals with individuals' perceptions and evaluations of existing social systems. For instance, people hold both descriptive and evaluative beliefs about economic forces, governmental institutions, political procedures, social customs, and so on, and they frequently base their behaviour on these beliefs. Systems of social, economic and political arrangements are developed and transformed in part through attitudes and behaviours of individuals who either do or do not support them. Perceptions of social systems are thus created and constructed, just as are perceptions of individuals and groups. In this sense, they are similar to social stereotypes, and they are certainly amenable to social psychological investigation.

The theory of system justification (Jost, 1996; Jost and Banaji, 1994) has incorporated a system level of analysis into the study of stereotyping by focusing upon the social and psychological tendency to understand particular distributions of costs and benefits, divisions of labour and social roles, and differences in success or prestige between groups or individuals in such a way that the essential nature of these arrangements seem justified, rational, legitimate, and perhaps even necessary. This theory assumes that individuals are motivated to maintain a sense that social outcomes are predominantly fair and just (e.g., Crosby, 1982; Lerner, 1980; Major, 1994; Tyler, 1990). Such processes may be said to operate at the level of Path 3, insofar as individual motivations and cognitions are directed toward the social system as an object of perception and behaviour.

One well-known example of a Path 3 analysis is to be found in Lerner's (1980) defense of the hypothesis that individuals are motivated to preserve a sense that the 'world' is a fair and just place and that people in general get what they deserve. Similarly, Tyler's (1990) work on how individuals' experiences with legal and political institutions impact their perceptions of legitimacy and loyalty towards those institutions adopts a Path 3 level of analysis. For instance, Tyler finds that pleasant interpersonal interactions with law enforcement officials lead one to develop a sense of procedural justice, which in turn leads one to profess satisfaction with legal institutions and to obey the law. A growing body of research indicates that the types of attributions that individuals make for economic hardship affect their global evaluations of governmental and economic systems (e.g., Iyengar, 1987; Kluegel, 1988; Lewis, Snell and Furnham, 1987). Thus, the personal beliefs that people hold concerning social systems may have important ramifications for the stability of those systems.

Attending to individuals' perceptions and reactions to the social system (Path 3) reflects a needed return to theoretical and research interest in classic social psychological questions concerning the relation between the individual and the social order (e.g., Brown, 1936). In terms of stereotyping, the goal of this research should be to investigate how beliefs about social groups are related to and are influenced by beliefs about social systems. The system-justification approach provides one such direction. Other potential avenues for theory and research involving systemic variables include Cox's (1948/1959) 'exploitation theory of prejudice', Jones' (1972) work on 'cultural racism', Jackman and Senter's (1983) application of dominant ideology theory to the development of stereotypic beliefs, and Hoffman and Hurst's (1990) 'stereotypes as rationalization' hypothesis.

Path 4   *Effects of the group on perceptions of and reactions to individuals.*

The most important difference between the social identity and the social cognition approach involves assumptions about the level of analysis at which stereotyping is assumed to occur. As demonstrated by the very title of this book, social identity theory assumes that stereotyping is a reflection of 'group life'. This approach suggests that stereotypes originate from shared group membership and shared group perceptions, and thus follow along Paths 4–6. Social cognition approaches, by contrast, have generally confined their analyses to stereotyping that occurs at the individual level, along Paths 1–3.

Although there is a large body of research indicating that individuals frequently bring their attitudes and beliefs into line with shared group norms (see Abrams and Hogg, 1990; Turner et al., 1994; Haslam, Reicher et al. and Simon, this volume), there is relatively little direct evidence regarding the importance of shared group memberships and shared group beliefs as determinants of stereotyping. For example, there are few actual demonstrations that stereotypes develop as a result of shared group memberships rather than through personal observation of the behaviour of others (but see Augoustinos, 1991). And, as we have seen earlier, the basic functions of stereotyping assumed to be important in social categorization theory (self-enhancement and informational enrichment) are ultimately individual-level phenomena and do not depend upon social sharing of beliefs.

It would seem, therefore, that strong statements about the importance of 'group life' should involve corresponding demonstrations of the importance of shared reality as a determinant, as well as an outcome, of intergroup behaviour. It is precisely such issues that form the basis of Paths 4–6. Although the idea that stereotypes represent consensually-shared beliefs formed the basis of much of the early work on stereotyping (Katz and Braly, 1933; Vinacke, 1957), issues of consensus have recently been understudied and, in some cases, their importance has been denied (Hamilton, Stroessner and Driscoll, 1994). Yet there is reason to think that, as proposed by social identity theory, beliefs that are perceived to be shared by other members of the ingroup may hold a special force for the individual (e.g., Bar-Tal, 1990). Haslam (this volume) argues that 'those with whom the individual shares a social identity (i.e., ingroup members) are also identified as *sources that can consensually validate his or her subjective beliefs*' (p. 133). Our own research (Stangor, Sechrist, Jost and Bar-Tal, 1996), as well as that of Haslam (this volume), suggests that altering perceptions of the consensuality with which certain stereotypic beliefs are held may change individual's endorsements of those stereotypic beliefs. However, the full significance of shared beliefs for individual, group and system life remains to be studied.

Path 5   *Effects of the group on perceptions of and reactions to social groups.*

Path 5 addresses the extent to which attitudes and behaviours are derived from ingroup norms and, especially in the case of stereotypes and evaluations, are directed at groups *qua* groups. Twenty years of research using the 'minimal group paradigm' characterizes the development of stereotypes and other evaluative social judgements in ethnocentric terms. People are assumed to hold attitudes toward ingroup and outgroup members that are relatively favourable to the former and unfavourable to the latter. The minimal group paradigm was designed for the expressed purpose of evoking Path 5 relations by emphasizing research participants' experimental group memberships and de-emphasizing their individual differences. This research is summarized well and expanded upon in the present volume by Anastasio et al., Bourhis et al., Ellemers and van Knippenberg, and Worchel and Rothberger.

Although a main premise of social identity theory is that ingroup members will favour their own group over other groups, this contention has been challenged of late. Evidence indicates that groups that are low in status, power, prestige or success frequently evaluate the outgroup more favourably than they evaluate their own group (e.g., Hinkle and Brown, 1990). Nevertheless, many contributors to the present volume retain the notion that there is a nearly ubiquitous tendency to favour members of the ingroup. For instance, Anastasio et al. assume a motivation to 'view the ingroup as superior to the outgroup' (p. 237), Haslam describes a need 'to differentiate between ingroups and relevant outgroups in a manner favourable to the former' (p. 129), and Oakes and Reynolds note that stereotypes may be 'little more than self-serving rationalizations of intergroup discrimination' (p. 64).[2] The strongest statement is made by Bourhis et al., who write that: 'social identity theory points to the complementary role of ingroup identity formation, collective self-evaluation and social comparison in producing *inherent tendencies to discriminatory, ethnocentric evaluation* in intergroup perception' (p. 274, emphasis added).

Although the tendency toward ingroup favouritism may be strong under some circumstances, research conducted by Sachdev and Bourhis (1985, 1987, 1991) provides enough evidence of outgroup favouritism among groups low in status and power to belie the notion that ethnocentrism is an inherent tendency. A recent dissertation by Jost (1996) indicated, further, that, contrary to the claims of Mullen, Brown, and Smith (1992) and others, outgroup favouritism among low-success groups is not confined to group memberships created in the laboratory, it cannot be dismissed as a 'demand characteristic', and it is not necessarily weaker in magnitude than the degree of ingroup favouritism displayed by high-success groups.

Several writers have concluded that social identity theory presently lacks the theoretical apparatus to adequately explain the phenomenon of outgroup favouritism among groups low in social standing (e.g., Hinkle and Brown, 1990; Jost and Banaji, 1994; Sidanius and Pratto, 1993). This is because group-level variables such as the need for positive social identity are capable of accounting only for behaviour that is group-serving in some way; behaviours that are contrary to the interests or needs of the ingroup cannot be accounted for in terms of membership in that group. To the extent that social identity theory and other perspectives succeed in rendering a complete account, it is by making reference to system-level variables, such as those discussed by Ellemers and van Knippenberg and Yzerbyt et al. We will discuss these issues more fully in our discussion of Paths 7 and 8.

Path 6   *Effects of the group on perceptions of and reactions to social systems.*

Although shared group beliefs may impact stereotyping of individuals and groups, group members may also share beliefs about the social systems in which they exist. One exciting example of such research is recent work by Crocker, Broadnax, Luhtanen and Blaine (1993) on the relation between group-consciousness raising and the tendency to believe in conspiracy theories at a systemic level. They report that African Americans are far more likely than European Americans to endorse items such as the following: 'the government deliberately singles out and investigates black elected officials in order to discredit them'; and 'the government deliberately makes sure that drugs are easily available in poor black neighbourhoods in order to harm black people'. Belief in conspiracy theories such as these is correlated with ingroup identification and self-esteem among African Americans, indicating that there are important effects of group membership on perceptions and evaluations of the social system.

Work by Augoustinos (1991) and others on the 'social representations' that people hold concerning economic systems also reflects an interest in Path 6 effects, emphasizing the collective or shared nature of people's beliefs about social systems. Although they did not measure group consensus directly, several studies suggest that members of the same social class tend to hold many (but not all) of the same beliefs about the causes and consequences of economic inequality (e.g., Emler and Dickinson, 1985).

Attention to the social and psychological factors contributing to how groups perceive and react to perceptions of injustice and disadvantage has been relatively scant in the social psychological literature, largely because perceived legitimacy has been treated almost exclusively as an independent variable and not as a dependent variable (e.g., Ellemers, Wilke and van Knippenberg, 1993). There is some evidence that members of low-status groups do perceive the system of status differences to be less fair and legitimate in general than do members of high-status groups (Jost, 1996; Sachdev and Bourhis, 1987, 1991), but we know little about how these perceptions impact upon group behaviour. There is a substantial body of evidence in the field of justice research which tells us that individuals (Path 3) and groups (Path 6) frequently perceive situations to be justified or legitimate, even when there is good reason to think that they are not (for a review, see Jost, 1995). It is worth noting in the context of this book that Tajfel (1982c) presaged this line of thought when he wrote that:

> [an] important requirement of research on social justice would consist of establishing the link between social myths and the general acceptance of injustice,

and research which would attempt to specify the sociopsychological conditions which could be expected to contribute to the dissolution of these patterns of acceptance. (p. 164)

The kind of research Tajfel calls for here would follow Path 6 from group attitudes to the acceptance or rejection of particular social systems. Years later, this path is still extremely under-studied, although work by Crocker and others on 'group-consciousness raising' provides a good starting point. An important difference between social identity theory's use of the concept of ingroup identification and system justification theory's use of the concept of group-consciousness raising has to do with levels of analysis. Whereas identification with the ingroup may occur at Path 5 or below and need not involve any beliefs at all about the social system, group-consciousness raising implies that, in addition to a sense of group belonging, members of low-status groups possess a sense that the social system is unjust and in need of change. In other words, ingroup identification may be a necessary but not a sufficient cause of group-consciousness raising.

Path 7   *Effects of the social system on perceptions of and reactions to individuals.*

Given that most, if not all, existing social systems possess some degree of inequality among different groups (e.g., Sidanius and Pratto, 1993) and that this inequality is one important basis for the development of stereotypes and prejudice (Eagly and Steffen, 1984), any adequate theory of group life must address the potential effects of social systems on the stereotypic beliefs of individuals in that system. In our model, Paths 7–9 capture the extent to which perceptions of social systems are bound up in everyday life, and the implications of these beliefs for the functioning of individuals, groups and social systems. One implication of bringing systemic factors into the study of social stereotypes is the recognition that structural and ideological aspects of the social system may lead people to develop favourable or unfavourable attitudes about themselves (Path 7), their social groups (Path 8) and various social systems (Path 9). Simon (this volume) implicitly adopts this approach when he proposes that 'Modernization favours the individual self over the collective self' (Thesis V).

Social psychological research addressing the effects of low socio-economic status on self-stereotyping and self-esteem (e.g., Crocker and Major, 1989; Porter and Washington, 1993) follows Path 7 from the system of economic stratification to the individual. The theoretical expectation has been that perceiving oneself to be socially and economically disadvantaged within an existing system should lead to deficits in self-esteem (e.g., Clark and Clark, 1947). By and large, however, there is relatively little evidence that low-status groups possess lower self-esteem than members of high-status groups. Attributional factors have been shown to moderate the effects of social systems on individuals and groups (cf. Crosby, 1982; Ruggiero and Taylor, 1995), so that if one is able to blame his or her disadvantage on the prejudice of others, then it is possible to escape negative consequences for the self-concept (Crocker and Major, 1989).

However, social systems may affect people in extremely subtle ways, often outside of conscious awareness (Jost and Banaji, 1994). Examples include females' unconscious acceptance of the devaluation of women's roles and abilities (Bem and Bem, 1970) and African American college students' internalization of others' stereotypic expectations that they will fail academically (Steele and Aronson, 1995). This is an insidious way in which the effects of social systems may differ from the effects of group memberships, the latter of which seem to occur most strongly at a conscious level when group membership is highly accessible or 'salient' (e.g., Turner et al., 1994). Stereotypes, including self-stereotypes, may be so ingrained in the consciousness (and unconsciousness) of individuals by the educational system, the media and by political leaders, that their effects may scarcely be recognized. Because such beliefs may be so fundamental to the smooth operation of the social system, they are challenged infrequently; people who do challenge these beliefs often are dismissed as extremist.

According to system justification theory (Jost and Banaji, 1994), people often accommodate, consciously and unconsciously, to the demands of the system. In Marxian and feminist theory, the internalization of system-justifying attitudes on the part of the disenfranchised is referred to as 'false consciousness' (see Jost, 1995, for a defense of the psychological utility of this concept). Consciousness raising, therefore, refers in part to the overcoming of Path 7 and Path 8 effects, by individuals and groups respectively. One of the strengths of the present volume is that it underscores the socially progressive role of stereotypes and group beliefs in bringing about social and political change (e.g., Reicher et al., this volume). In other words, 'stereotypes may also play a part in *challenging* aspects of stability or the status quo' (Spears et al., this volume p. 7).

Path 8   *Effects of the social system on perceptions of and reactions to social groups.*

Path 8 analyses involve the conditions under which features of the social system lead groups to develop shared perceptions and behaviours. As has already been suggested, there is reason to believe that some low-status groups develop relatively unfavourable images of themselves and relatively favourable images of higher status groups. Examples include phenomena such as women's widespread failure to support the Equal Rights' Amendment (Mansbridge, 1986) and the significant lack of support among the American working class for policies of economic redistribution (Kluegel and Smith, 1986). As well summarized by Ellemers and van Knippenberg (this volume), one way in which social identity theory has dealt with the phenomenon of outgroup favouritism is by arguing that 'subordinate groups will seek positive distinctiveness from dominant groups to the degree that their inferiority is not perceived as inherent, immutable or fully legitimate' (Turner and Brown, 1978, p. 207). However, the system-level concepts of perceived legitimacy and stability seem rather post hoc in the context of the theory, as they are not derivable from the central group and individual-level tenets concerning self-esteem and ingroup identification. There is also nothing in social identity theory that predicts when a given social system will be perceived as 'inherent, immutable, or fully legitimate' and when it will not.

Furthermore, it is not clear from social identity theory how or why members of low-status groups would perceive the status differences to be legitimate in the first place, because such a perception itself favours the interests and position of the outgroup (Jost and Banaji, 1994). Hinkle and Brown (1990) similarly note that 'the problem of how groups seek and maintain positive social identities whilst simultaneously espousing out-group favouritism remains unresolved by the legitimacy and stability notions' (p. 53). The guiding assumption of social identity theory, that people are motivated to favour their own group over other groups, seems conspicuously lacking when outgroup favouritism occurs, even if it is under conditions of legitimacy and stability.

Another way in which social identity theorists have attempted to deal with the problem of outgroup favouritism is by postulating that members of low-status groups tend to disidentify with their own group and to identify themselves instead with higher status outgroups (e.g., Tajfel and Turner, 1986). Jost (1996) found no evidence that high- and low-status group members differed in terms of identification with the ingroup. Ellemers and van Knippenberg report new evidence which calls into question this account as well. They find that while Polish students exhibit stronger identification with their national group than do Dutch students, they also hold relatively unfavourable stereotypes of their own group (boozy, quarrelsome, disorderly, vulgar and intolerant) and relatively favourable stereotypes of the Dutch outgroup (sober, frugal, achievement-oriented, well-educated and serious).

Our own view is that just as some group-level beliefs are derived from needs for positive social identity, still others are the result of systemic factors. These may include both direct effects of the social system as well as subjective perceptions of those structures. Thus, the relative failure in recent years of the Polish economy, as well as ideological justifications for that failure, may best explain the outgroup favouring and ingroup-derogating beliefs held by Ellemers and van Knippenberg's Polish sample. Explanations for the perceived legitimacy and immutability of social structures seem better derived from a system-level analysis than from a group-level analysis such as that provided by social identity theory. We are arguing, therefore, that theory and research in the social identity tradition may be supplemented by investigating systemic factors such as those described by Paths 3 and 6–9. Just as social identity theory should be viewed as a complement to realistic conflict theory (see Bourhis et al., this volume), and to social cognition approaches, perspectives stressing system-level variables should be regarded as complementary to social identity theory.

Path 9   *Effects of the social system on perceptions of and reactions to the social system.*

We turn at last to Path 9, according to which structural and ideological aspects of social systems contribute to perceptions of and reactions to social systems. Such effects may occur either when the characteristics of a social system act to maintain or change that same system, or when one system impacts upon another. These relations have been little studied within psychology, and they overlap considerably with the disciplines of sociology and political science. But because system-level relations have a profound impact upon the lives of the individuals who live in those systems, they are far from irrelevant to social psychological analysis.

System justification theory provides one way of thinking about system–system relations, arguing that many behaviours occur to meet the needs of the social system, rather than to meet the needs of individuals or groups per se. These behaviours often lead systems to perpetuate themselves, sometimes harming individuals and groups in the process. An illustration of this point is provided by Deutsch's (1985) 'crude law of social relations', according to which '*the characteristic processes and effects elicited by a given type of social relationship also tend to elicit that type of social relationship*' (p. 69, emphasis in original). Thus, competitive systems breed the sort of behaviour that tends to reproduce competitive systems, cooperative systems breed the sort of behavior that tends to reproduce cooperative systems, and so on.

In many cases, behaviour that maintains a societal structure may also meet the needs of the individual, such as when a person pays school taxes and receives an education in return. In other cases, the needs of individuals are at odds with the demands of the social system. People may possess 'false consciousness' and engage in maladaptive behaviour, in which case their needs would be better met by behaving differently (see Jost, 1995). But in both of these cases, people are acting because the system requires such action, not necessarily because they or their social groups require it.

Not all effects of the social system tend to result in greater support for that system. An extreme or unjustifiable degree of inequality or exploitation may lead people to reject the system and participate in processes of social change. Kluegel (1988), for example, concludes that: 'Economic problems do encourage people to doubt that the economic order is working as it should' (p. 294). According to Marxian theory, social systems such as capitalism possess inherent flaws and contradictions that are the seeds of their own demise. But the success or failure of a particular social system depends not only on its structural properties but also on the extent to which it is able to provide ideologies that are effective in producing a sense of legitimacy. Stereotypes and other social beliefs may be used to maintain social systems, deflecting blame away from the social system and onto actors within that system (Jackman and Senter, 1983; Jost and Banaji, 1994). Although these processes have not heretofore been fully analysed within social psychology, it would seem to be important to study how perceptions and behaviours of individuals and groups contribute to stability and change within social systems (cf. Tyler, 1990).

Aspects of one social system may also have an impact upon how individuals perceive and react to other social systems. People who have been socialized under a capitalist system, for instance, are likely to find alternative economic or social schemes (e.g., socialist, communist) undesirable or even incomprehensible. In this way, social systems may render some 'cognitive alternatives' unavailable (cf. Tajfel, 1978a), hindering the development of certain ways of thinking about social arrangements. Conversely, the tenets of one social system may be especially conducive to acceptance of other systems. For instance, political systems that espouse racial segregation or patriarchy may be more compatible with some religious systems than with others. And cultures that foster inividualistic or collectivistic values may develop differential social and political relationships with other systems stressing individualism or collectivism.

In general, then, an analysis at the level of Path 9 focuses upon the effects that social systems have on the same or on other social systems. These would be integral to the psychological study of the social order (Brown, 1936). Avenues of investigation concern how the characteristics of one social system influence people's cognitive and behavioural responses to social systems, and the consequences of these responses for the maintenance or change of those systems. The extent to which the characteristics of a social system bring about predictable effects on perceptions of social systems, the success or failure of those systems, and the psychology of the groups and individuals within those systems seem important avenues for future research.

2   Conclusions

Although our nine-fold analysis results in an unusual degree of complexity, we believe that considering stereotyping and group life according to individual, group and system levels of analysis and the relations among these levels is a necessary precursor to the development of comprehensive models of social relations. Our analysis makes clear that stereotypes are relevant to more than one level, and that conclusions about the causes and consequences of stereotypes may vary according to the level at which they are conceptualized. In addition, this conceptualization elucidates both the strengths as well as the limitations of existing theoretical approaches. Most importantly, however, our approach stresses that the three levels of analysis are ultimately compatible and mutually instructive, and that analyses at each level can and must be informed by analyses at other levels. In this concluding section we address three specific content areas (stereotype formation and change, stereotype accuracy and inaccuracy, and the effects of stereotyping on targets) which provide illustrative examples of how our analysis may be applied to important issues in stereotyping.

Stereotype formation and change

Social psychology has not, in general, developed particularly useful models of stereotype development and change. Virtually all existing models have emphasized 'bottom-up learning' – the observation of others in everyday life – as demonstrated by, for instance, illusory correlation models of stereotype development (see McGarty and De La Haye, this volume) and contact models of stereotype change (Hewstone and Brown, 1986; Stephan, 1985). Yet these models of 'common informational input', as Haslam (this volume) refers to them, are clearly limited, both because individuals develop stereotypes about groups with which they have had no direct contact, and because contact is notoriously ineffective at changing stereotypes.

Our approach suggests that it may be useful to broaden our models of stereotype development and change, taking into consideration that many important social beliefs are important precisely because they are shared with relevant reference groups and exist within social institutions. Some stereotypes certainly develop, not through interpersonal contact, but rather through communication with members of relevant reference groups. They come to be shared with others because they satisfy motivations for belief validation (Hardin and Higgins, 1996) and for identification with relevant ingroups (Haslam, this volume). In our own research we have found that altering perceptions of the consensuality with which stereotypic beliefs are held can change individuals' endorsements of those stereotypic beliefs (Stangor, Sechrist, Jost and Bar-Tal, 1996). Also along this line, Worchel and Rothgerber (this volume) note that stereotypes are more likely to be changed (and, we would add, developed) through 'top-down' group-level processes (via Paths 4 and 5) in collectivistic, as compared with individualistic, cultures. It would, therefore, be useful for social identity theorists to go further in developing models of stereotype formation and change that explicitly incorporate the notion of shared beliefs and 'group life'.

System justification theory provides another account of the origin of stereotypes. If stereotypes are developed to rationalize inequalities of the social system (see Yzerbyt et al., this volume), then it is no surprise that stereotypes of particular groups are persistent and consensual for as long as the structural inequalities remain intact. The system justification perspective thus proposes an ideological or rationalization function for the development of stereotypes which does not rely on the assumption that social perception is 'accurate' or 'veridical' (see Jost and Banaji, 1994). Yzerbyt et al. expand interestingly on this argument by proposing that ideological 'rationalization is best served by an essentialistic approach to social categories' (p. 23), according to which social and material inequalities between groups are justified in terms of 'inherent' characteristics of the groups in question, especially physical or biological differences between the groups.

It seems likely that a variety of underlying motivations contribute to the development and change of specific stereotypes about different groups, and research must ultimately address this complexity. As models of social stereotyping are extended from individual to group to system levels of analysis, new models of stereotype representation must also be developed. Social psychologists must opt for representational models that are most explanatory in terms of phenomena of interest, rather than merely drawing our representational models from those that have been developed by cognitive psychologists. Cognitive psychology focuses exclusively upon individual perceptions (Paths 1–3), but social psychology must extend to Path 4 and above. Thus, the implicit critique of individualism in social cognition that permeates the chapters of this book is, in our opinion, particularly well-founded when it comes to stereotype formation and change.

Accuracy and inaccuracy at all three levels of analysis

Distinguishing among various levels of analysis may help to clarify some controversial issues pertaining to stereotype accuracy and inaccuracy (cf. Lee et al., 1995; Oakes et al., 1994). Most generally, inaccuracy may occur within a single level of analysis, or it may be the result of the inappropriate use of beliefs that are developed at one level of analysis to relationships at another level of analysis. It is our contention that focus on any one level of analysis to the exclusion of others will necessarily provide an incomplete picture of stereotype accuracy.

In terms of stereotype content, no one level of analysis may be specified a priori as being more accurate than any other. Individuals, groups and systems may hold true or false beliefs about individuals, groups or systems. Furthermore, the standards by which a stereotype is considered accurate may change across levels, and this makes criteria for accuracy difficult to develop. For instance, stereotypes directed at groups of people may be different than those that are applied to individual group members (see Stangor and Lange, 1994). In addition, individuals may express different stereotypes when they are in groups than when they are alone, and the context of other comparison groups may influence the expression of stereotypes. Taking into account multiple levels of analysis adds another layer of complexity to issues concerning stereotype accuracy.

The issue of accuracy may be considered not only in terms of content, but also in terms of application (Stangor, 1995). This issue has been a primary focus of social cognition researchers who have been concerned about the potential inaccuracy that may result when beliefs about social groups (Path 2) are carried over to interpersonal relationships (Path 1). This situation may be especially damaging when shared stereotypic beliefs are applied to individual targets (Path 4), because stigmatized targets will be subjected to the same stereotypes by an entire group of people. In cases such as this, it does not matter much whether the content of the belief is accurate or not, because even accurate stereotypes may be applied unfairly (Stangor, 1995).

Although it has been argued within the social cognition approach that Path 1 judgements based upon 'individuating' information are more accurate than Path 2 judgements based upon categorical information (cf. Fiske and Neuberg, 1990), Oakes and Reynolds (this volume) are correct in pointing out that the use of one type of information is logically no more accurate or rational than the use of another. For instance, relying on 'individuating' as opposed to 'categorical' information is no guarantee of accuracy because when category-based information is accompanied by individuating information, the individuating information may actually be used to amplify existing stereotypes (Brewer, 1996; Darley and Gross, 1983; Sagar and Schofield, 1980; Yzerbyt et al., 1994).

In contrast to social cognition researchers who have emphasized stereotype inaccuracy, social identity theorists have focused upon the 'meaning-seeking' functions of stereotypes which may lead them to be 'adaptive', 'valid', 'pragmatic' and possibly even 'veridical' (Oakes and Reynolds; Spears and Haslam; Yzerbyt et al., this volume). The development of stereotypes about social groups may indeed inform one's reality, guide behaviour and provide important information about the social relationships among individuals, groups and systems. But social stereotypes should not be granted validity or accuracy simply because they are the result of the same social and cognitive processes that are responsible for individual impression formation or because they help individuals and groups to 'make sense of their world'. In general, stereotypes are even subjectively experienced as valid, insofar as research indicates that people frequently find the application of stereotypic attributes to particular individuals to be socially inappropriate (Yzerbyt, Schadron, Leyens and Rocher, 1994) and to produce negative emotional consequences on the part of many stereotypers (Monteith, Devine and Zuwerink, 1993). Under some circumstances at least, people recognize that there is unfairness in applying the stereotype to individual group members who may not fit the stereotype (Yzerbyt et al., 1994).

A focus upon system-level variables that may contribute to false conscious-ness leads the system justification approach to draw still different conclusions about the potential for accuracy and inaccuracy in stereotyping than those that are drawn from individual- or group-level analyses. If stereotypes are used as ideological devices to bolster social systems that are harmful to groups and individuals, then there are important ways in which stereotypes are misrep-resentations of social reality. When a political party employs a stereotype (for instance, that 'blacks are aggressive') as a rhetorical 'weapon' to change or justify social policy concerning crime (cf. Reicher et al., this volume), the basis for the stereotype is not to interpret or enhance the perception of reality. Rather, the genuine purpose of such stereotypes may be to mislead people.

A focus on the targets of stereotyping

One of the most dramatic limitations of both social cognition and social iden-tity approaches is an almost exclusive focus on stereotypers and the prejudiced, with little attention to the targets of stereotyping and prejudice. Until very recently, we knew very little about how stigmatized group members perceive stereotyping and discrimination, and how they react to it (but see Branscombe and Wann, 1994; Cohen and Swim, 1995; Crocker and Major, 1989; Ethier and Deaux, 1994; Steele and Aronson, 1995; Swim and Stangor, in press). Long and Spears (this volume) provide an important contribution to this literature in their analysis of those disaffected individuals who have high personal self-esteem, but who cannot gain collective esteem through memberships in import-ant reference groups. This work bears striking similarity to Steele's (1992) work on academic 'dis-identification' among African Americans.

Issues concerning the effects of stereotypes on groups and individuals have gained social and political significance as a result of increased attention to issues of diversity and multiculturalism, particularly in North America. There are growing and insistent demands by minority group members not to ignore group memberships, but rather to celebrate them. Thus, as social identity theorists have long pointed out, group affiliations may have desirable as well as undesirable consequences. Contributors to this volume are correct that the meaningfulness of social group memberships presents a real challenge to social cognitive theorists who have argued that judgements that incorporate social category memberships are inferior to judgements based on 'individuating' information.

According to the system justification perspective, there are at least three important and distinct responses that targets of stereotyping and prejudice might adopt. For instance, a woman might respond to sexist discrimination by: (a) protecting her own self-esteem and distancing herself from the plight of her group, (b) attempting to enhance her group's social identity and fighting for the rights of women or (c) accepting her own and her group's alleged inferiority and developing a reactionary or 'right-wing' ideology that justifies sexism against women (cf. Dworkin, 1983). Our perspective provides a clear classification of these different types of responses as reflecting ego justification, group justification and system justification, respectively (Jost and Banaji, 1994). Not only does this classification help to distinguish among patterns of behaviour that have long been of interest to researchers of social identity and intergroup relations (e.g., see Ellemers and van Knippenberg, this volume), but it also underscores the cognitive and behavioural complexity that results from the fact that human beings are interactive products of personal, group and systemic factors. The purpose of laying out distinct levels of analysis, of course, is to introduce some order into the complexity.

As we have seen, stereotypic beliefs have far-reaching implications for the self, the group, and the social system, and these implications may be either welcome or unwelcome for the individuals who are the targets of these beliefs. Like all social beliefs, stereotypes suffer from grave limitations of fallibility, but they also offer undeniably important opportunities for interpreting and changing reality. It is our hope that considering causes and effects of stereotypes at multiple levels of analysis will focus and clarify theoretical and research attention to profoundly important issues of stereotyping and group life.

Notes

Funding for this project was provided to C.S. by a Lilly Foundation fellowship and to JTJ by NIMH Grant # R01-MH52578-01A1 to Arie W. Kruglanski. We are grateful to the editors of this volume and to Curtis D. Hardin and Erik Thompson for helpful comments on an earlier version of this chapter.

1   In exploring causal relations among variables at distinct levels of analysis, it is possible to adopt either a subjective or an objective approach. Social psychologists frequently gravitate toward subjectivist explanations (e.g., Jones, 1990; Ross and Nisbett, 1991; Turner, 1982), taking seriously Thomas and Znaniecki's famous dictum that 'if men define situations as real, they are real in their consequences'. From a subjective or phenomenological perspective, our three levels of analysis may be characterized as referring to perceptions of 'self' and 'other', perceptions of 'my ingroup' and perceptions of 'my world-view'.

However, there are also good reasons to adopt also an objective or structural perspective (see Spears et al., this volume), according to which certain types of variables might exert their effects quite independently of subjective awareness. From this perspective, the three levels of analysis refer to the impact of unique personal experiences, the impact of social group memberships and other collectively shared experiences and the impact of reward and punishment structures in social, economic, political and sexual domains. We mean to include both subjective and objective factors in our analysis of individual, group and system variables (see also Yzerbyt et al., this volume).

2   In the present volume, only Long and Spears explicitly question 'the assumption that ingroup bias is a universal feature of intergroup relations' (p. 26).

References

Abate, M. and Berrien, F. K. (1967). Validation of stereotypes: Japanese versus American students. *Journal of Personality and Social Psychology*, 7, 435–8.

Aboud, F. E. (1988). *Children and Prejudice*. Oxford: Blackwell.

Abrams, D. and Hogg, M. (1988). Comments on the motivational status of self-esteem in social identity and intergroup discrimination. *European Journal of Social Psychology*, 18, 317–34.

Abrams, D. and Hogg, M. A. (1990). Social identification, self-categorization and social influence. In W. Stroebe and M. Hewstone (eds), *European Review of Social Psychology* (vol. 1, pp. 195–228). Chichester: Wiley.

Adorno, T. W., Frenkel-Brunswick, E., Levinson, D. J. and Sanford, R. N. (1950). *The Authoritarian Personality*. New York: Harper & Row.

Allen, V. L. (1985). Infra-group, intra-group and inter-group: Construing levels of organisation in social influence. In S. Moscovici, G. Mugny and E. van Avermaet (eds), *Perspectives on Minority Influence* (pp. 217–38). Cambridge: Cambridge University Press.

Alloy, L. B. and Tabachnik, N. (1984). Assessment of covariation by humans and animals: The joint influence of prior expectations and current situational information. *Psychological Review*, 91, 112–49.

Allport, F. H. (1962). A structuronomic conception of behaviour: Individual and collective. *Journal of Abnormal and Social Psychology*, 64, 3–30.

Allport, G. W. (1954). *The Nature of Prejudice*. Cambridge, MA: Addison-Wesley.

Allport, G. W. (1961). *Pattern and Growth in Personality*. New York: Holt, Rinehart & Winston.

Allport, G. W. (1968). Is the concept of self necessary? In C. Gordon and K. J. Gergen (eds), *The Self in Social Interaction* (vol. I: Classic and Contemporary Perspectives, pp. 25–32). New York: John Wiley & Sons, Inc.

Altemeyer, B. (1987). *Enemies of Freedom: Understanding right-wing authoritarianism*. London: Jossey-Bass.

Althusser, L. (1970). Idéologie et appareils idéologiques d'Etat. *Lapensée*.

Anastasio, P. A., Gaertner, S. L., Bachman, B. A. and Rust, M. C. (1992). Generalization of positive impressions: Interpersonal, intergroup, and common ingroup interactions. Unpublished manuscript, University of Delaware.

Andersen, S. M. and Klatzky, R. L. (1987). Traits and social stereotypes: Levels of categorisation in person perception. *Journal of Personality and Social Psychology*, *53*, 235–46.

Andersen, S. M., Klatzky, R. L. and Murray, J. (1990). Traits and social stereotypes: Efficiency differences in social information processing. *Journal of Experimental Social Psychology*, *59*, 192–201.

Anderson, C. A. (1982). Inoculation and counterexplanation: Debiasing techniques in the perseverance of social theories. *Social Cognition*, *1*, 126–39.

Anderson, C. A. (1983). Abstract and concrete data in the perseverance of social theories: When weak data lead to unshakable beliefs. *Journal of Experimental Social Psychology*, *19*, 93–108.

Anderson, C. A., Lepper, M. R. and Ross, L. (1980). Perseverance of social theories: The role of explanation in the persistence of discredited information. *Journal of Personality and Social Psychology*, *39*, 1037–49.

Anderson, C. A. and Sedikides, C. (1991). Thinking about people: Contributions of a typological alternative to associationistic and dimensional models of person perception. *Journal of Personality and Social Psychology*, *60*, 203–17.

Anderson, N. H. (1965). Averaging versus adding as a stimulus-combination rule in impression formation. *Journal of Experimental Psychology*, *70*, 394–400.

Anderson, N. H. (1981). *Foundations of Information Integration Theory*. New York: Academic Press.

Aristotle (1991). *Rhétorique*, Le Livre de Poche, Coll. Classiques de la Philosophie.

Aronson, E. and Carlsmith, J. M. (1963). Effect of the severity of threat on the devaluation of forbidden behavior. *Journal of Abnormal and Social Psychology*, *66*, 584–8.

Aronson, E. and Mills, J. (1959). The effect of severity of initiation on liking for a group. *Journal of Abnormal and Social Psychology*, *59*, 177–81.

Asch, S. E. (1946). Forming impressions of personality. *Journal of Abnormal and Social Psychology*, *41*, 258–90.

Asch, S. (1952). *Social Psychology*. New York: Prentice Hall.

Asch, S. E. and Zukier, H. (1984). Thinking about persons. *Journal of Personality and Social Psychology*, *46*, 1230–40.

Ashmore, R. D. and Del Boca, F. K. (1976). Psychological approaches to understanding intergroup conflict. In P. A. Katz (ed.), *Towards the Elimination of Racism*. New York: Pergamon.

Ashmore, R. D. and Del Boca, F. K. (1981). Conceptual approaches to stereotypes and stereotyping. In D. Hamilton (ed.), *Cognitive Processes in Stereotyping and Intergroup Behavior* (pp. 1–35). Hillsdale, NJ: Erlbaum.

Augoustinos, M. (1991). Consensual representations of social structure in different age groups. *British Journal of Social Psychology*, *30*, 193–205.

Augoustinos, M. and Innes, J. M. (1990). Towards an integration of social representations and social schema theory. *British Journal of Social Psychology*, *29*, 213–31.

Avigdor, R. (1953). Etude expérimentale de la genèse des stéréotypes. *Cahiers Internationaux de Sociologie*, *14*, 154–68.

Bachman, B. A. (1993). An intergroup model of organizational mergers. Unpublished Ph.D. Dissertation, University of Delaware.

Bachman, B. A. and Gaertner, S. L. (1995). The urge to submerge: The consequences of the absorb merger pattern. Presented at the American Psychological Society meetings, Washington, D.C.

Bachman, B. A., Gaertner, S. L., Anastasio, P. and Rust, M. (1993). When corporations merge: Organizational identification among employees of acquiring and acquired organizations. Paper presented at the 64th Eastern Psychological Association Convention, Crystal City, VA.

Bar-Tal, D. (1988). Delegitimizing relations between Israeli Jews and Palestinians: A social psychological analysis. In J. Hoffman (ed.), *Arab–Jewish Relations in Israel* (pp. 217–48). Bristol, IN: Wyndam Hall.

Bar-Tal, D. (1990). *Group Beliefs: A conception for analyzing group structure, processes, and behavior.* New York: Springer-Verlag.

Bargh, J. A. (1982). Attention and automaticity in the processing of self-relevant information. *Journal of Personality and Social psychology, 43,* 425–36.

Bargh, J. A. (1989). Conditional automaticity: Varieties of automatic influence in social perception and cognition. In J. S. Uleman and J. A. Bargh (eds) *Unintended Thought* (pp. 3–51). New York: Guilford.

Bargh, J. (1994). The four horsemen of automaticity: Awareness, intention, efficiency, and control in social cognition. In R. S. Wyer, Jr. and T. K. Srull (eds), *Handbook of Social Cognition* (2nd edn) (pp. 1–40). Hillsdale, NJ: Erlbaum.

Bargh, J. A. and Thein, R. D. (1985). Individual construct accessibility, person memory, and the recall-judgment link: The case of information overload. *Journal of Personality and Social Psychology, 49,* 1129–46.

Bargh, J. A. and Tota (1988). Context-dependent automatic processes in depression: Accessibility of negative constructs with regard to self but not others. *Journal of Personality and Social Psychology, 54,* 925–39.

Barsalou, L. W. (1987). The instability of graded structure: Implications for the nature of concepts. In U. Neisser (ed.), *Concepts and Conceptual Development: Ecological and intellectual factors in categorization* (pp. 101–40). Cambridge: Cambridge University Press.

Baumeister, R. F., Tice, D. M. and Hutton, D. G. (1989). Self-presentational motivations and personality difference in self-esteem. *Journal of Personality, 57,* 547–79.

Bayton, J. A. (1941). The racial stereotypes of Negro college students. *Journal of Abnormal and Social Psychology, 36,* 97–102.

Beauvois, J.-L. (1984). *La psychologie quotidienne.* Paris: PUF.

Beauvois, J.-L. (1995). *Traité de la servitude libérale: Analyse de la soumission.* Paris: Dunod.

Beauvois, J.-L. and Dubois, N. (1988). The norm of internality in the explanation of social events. *European Journal of Social Psychology, 18,* 299–316.

Beauvois, J.-L. and Joule, R. V. (1981). *Soumission et idéologies.* Paris: Presses Universitaires de France.

Beck, U. (1994). Jenseits von Stand und Klasse? (Beyond class?). In U. Beck and E. Beck-Gernsheim (eds), *Riskante Freiheiten* (Risky freedoms) (pp. 43–60). Frankfurt: Suhrkamp.

Bellezza, F. S. and Bower, G. H. (1981). Person stereotypes and memory for people. *Journal of Personality and Social Psychology, 41,* 856–65.

Bem, S. L. and Bem, D. J. (1970). Case study of a nonconscious ideology: Training the woman to know her place. In D. J. Bem (ed.), *Beliefs, Attitudes, and Human Affairs.* Belmont, CA: Brooks/Cole Publishing Co.

Berger, J., Wagner, D. G. and Zelditch, M., Jr. (1985). Introduction: Expectation states theory. In J. Berger and M. Zelditch, Jr. (eds), *Status, Rewards, and Influence* (pp. 1–72). San Francisco: Jossey Bass.

Berlin, I. (1978). *Karl Marx: His life and environment.* Oxford: Oxford University Press.

Berndsen, M., Spears, R. and van der Pligt, J. (1996). Illusory correlation and attitude-based vested interest. *European Journal of Social Psychology, 26,* 247–64.

Berndsen, M., van der Pligt, J., Spears, R. and Mcgarty, C. (in press). Expectation-based and data-based illusory correlation: The effects of confirming versus disconfirming evidence. *European Journal of Social Psychology.*

Berresford Ellis, P. and Mac a'Ghobhainn, S. (1989). *The Scottish Insurrection of 1820.* London: Pluto.

Bettelheim, B. and Janowitz, M. (1964). *Social Change and Prejudice.* New York: Free Press of Glencoe.

Bettencourt, B. A., Brewer, M. B., Croak, M. R. and Miller, N. (1992). Co-operation and the reduction of intergroup bias: The roles of reward structure and social orientation. *Journal of Experimental Social Psychology, 28,* 301–19.

Biernat, M. and Crandall, C. R. (1994). Stereotyping and contact with social groups: Measurement and conceptual issues. *European Journal of Social Psychology, 24,* 659–78.

Billig, M. (1976). *Social Psychology and Intergroup Relations.* London: Academic Press.

Billig, M. (1985). Prejudice, categorization and particularization: From a perceptual to a rhetorical approach. *European Journal of Social Psychology, 15,* 79–103.

Billig, M. (1987). *Arguing and Thinking.* Cambridge: Cambridge University Press.

Billig, M. (1992). *Talking of the Royal Family.* London: Routledge.

Billig, M. (1995). *Banal Nationalism.* London: Sage.

Billig, M. G. (1973). Normative communication in a minimal group situation. *European Journal of Social Psychology, 3,* 339–44.

Billig, M., Condor, S., Edwards, D., Gane, M., Middleton, D. and Radley, A. (1988). *Ideological Dilemmas: A social psychology of everyday thinking.* London: Sage.

Billig, M. G. and Tajfel, H. (1973). Social categorization and similarity in intergroup behaviour. *European Journal of Social Psychology, 3,* 27–52.

Blake, R. R. and Mouton, J. S. (1979). Intergroup problem solving in organizations: From theory to practice. In W. Austin and S. Worchel (eds), *The Social Psychology of Intergroup Relations.* Monterey, CA: Brooks/Cole.

Blanz, M. (1995). When persons are perceived as group members: Experiments on the salience of social categories. Paper presented at the Third Muenster Workshop on the Social Identity Approach, Muenster/Rothenberge, March 22–24.

Bless, H., Strack, F. and Schwarz, N. (1993). The informative functions of research procedures: Bias and the logic of conversation. *European Journal of Social Psychology, 23,* 149–66.

Bodenhausen, G. V. (1988). Stereotypic biases in social decision making and memory: Testing process models of stereotype use. *Journal of Personality and Social Psychology, 55,* 726–37.

Bodenhausen, G. V. (1990). Stereotypes as judgmental heuristics: Evidence of circadian variations in discrimination. *Psychological Science, 1,* 319–22.

Bodenhausen, G. V. (1993). Emotions, arousal, and stereotypic judgments: A heuristic model of affect and stereotyping. In D. M. Mackie and D. L. Hamilton (eds), *Affect, Cognition and Stereotyping: Interactive processes in group perception* (1993).

Bodenhausen, G. V., Kramer, G. P. and Süsser, K. (1994). Happiness and stereotypic thinking in social judgment. *Journal of Personality and Social Psychology*, *66*, 621–32.

Bodenhausen, G. V. and Lichtenstein, M. (1987). Social stereotypes and information-processing strategies: The impact of task complexity. *Journal of Personality and Social Psychology*, *52*, 871–80.

Bodenhausen, G. V. and Wyer, R. S. (1985). Effects of stereotypes on decision making and information processing strategies. *Journal of Personality and Social Psychology*, *48*, 267–82.

Bogardus, E. S. (1950). Stereotypes versus sociotypes. *Sociology and Social Science Research*, *34*, 286–91.

Borgida, E., Locksley, A. and Brekke, N. (1981). Social stereotypes and social judgement. In N. Cantor and J. F. Kihlstrom (eds), *Personality, Cognition, and Social Interaction* (pp. 153–69). Hillsdale, NJ: Lawrence Erlbaum.

Bornstein, G., Crum, L., Wittenbraker, J., Harring, K., Insko, C. and Thibaut, J. (1983). On the measurement of social orientations in the minimal group paradigm. *European Journal of Social Psychology*, *13*, 219–43.

Bouchard, T. J., Jr. (1995). Breaking the last taboo. *Contemporary Psychology*, *40*, 415–18.

Boudon, R. (1990). *L'art de se persuader des idées douteuses, fragiles ou fausses*. Paris: Seuil.

Bourhis, R. Y. (1994). Power, gender and intergroup discrimination: Some minimal group experiments. In M. P. Zanna and J. M. Olson (eds), *The Social Psychology of Prejudice: The Ontario symposium, vol. 7* (pp. 209–32). Hillsdale, NJ: Erlbaum.

Bourhis, R. Y. and Gagnon, A. (1994). Les préjugés, la discrimination et les relations intergroupes. In R. J. Vallerand (ed.), *Les Fondements de la Psychologie Sociale*. Boucherville, Canada: Gaetan Morin.

Bourhis, R. Y. and Leyens, J. P. (eds) (1994). *Stéréotypes, discrimination et relations intergroupes*. Liège, Belgique: Mardaga.

Bourhis, R. Y., Sachdev, I. and Gagnon, A. (1994). Intergroup research with the Tajfel matrices: Methodological notes. In M. P. Zanna and J. M. Olson (eds), *The Social Psychology of Prejudice: The Ontario symposium, vol. 7* (pp. 209–32). Hillsdale, NJ: Erlbaum.

Branscombe, N. R. and Wann, D. L. (1994). Collective self-esteem consequences of outgroup derogation when a valued social identity is on trial. *European Journal of Social Psychology*, *24*, 641–58.

Brehm, S. S. and Kassin, S. M. (1990). *Social Psychology*. Boston: Houghton Mifflin Company.

Brewer, M. B. (1979). Ingroup bias in the minimal intergroup situation: A cognitive-motivational analysis. *Psychological Bulletin*, *86*, 307–24.

Brewer, M. B. (1986). The role of ethnocentrism in intergroup conflict. In S. Worchel and W. Austin (eds), *Psychology of Intergroup Relations*. Chicago: Nelson-Hall.

Brewer, M. B. (1988). A dual process model of impression formation. In T. K. Srull and R. S. Wyer (eds), *Advances in Social Cognition* (vol. 1, pp. 1–36). Hillsdale, NJ: Erlbaum.

Brewer, M. B. (1993). Social identity, distinctiveness, and in-group homogeneity. *Social Cognition, 11*, 150–64.

Brewer, M. B. (1996). When stereotypes lead to stereotyping: The use of stereotypes in person perception. In C. N. Macrae, C. Stangor and M. Hewstone (eds), *Stereotypes and Stereotyping* (pp. 254–75). New York: Guilford Press.

Brewer, M. B., Dull, V. and Lui, L. (1981). Perception of the elderly: Stereotypes as prototypes. *Journal of Personality and Social Psychology, 41*, 656–70.

Brewer, M. B. and Lui, L. (1989). The primacy of age and sex in the structure of person categories. *Social Cognition, 7*, 262–74.

Brewer, M. B., Manzi, K. J. and Shaw, J. (1993). In-group identification as a function of depersonalization, distinctiveness, and status. *Psychological Science, 4*, 88–92.

Brewer, M. and Miller, N. (1984). Beyond the contact hypothesis: Theoretical perspectives on desegregation. In N. Miller and M. B. Brewer (eds), *Groups in Contact: The psychology of desegregation* (pp. 281–302). Orlands: Academic Press.

Brewer, M. B. and Silver, M. (1978). Ingroup bias as a function of task characteristics. *European Journal of Social Psychology, 8*, 393–400.

Brigham, J. C. (1971). Ethnic stereotypes. *Psychological Bulletin, 76*, 15–38.

Brink, M., (1993). Seksecategorisatie en herinnering van personen. Unpublished Masters dissertation, University of Amsterdam.

Brislin, R. (1993). *Understanding Culture's Influence on Behavior*. Fort-Worth: Harcourt Brace College Publishers.

Brown, J., Collins, R. L. and Schmidt, G. W. (1988). Self-esteem and direct vs. indirect forms of self-enhancement. *Journal of Personality and Social Psychology, 55*, 445–53.

Brown, J. F. (1936). *Psychology and the Social Order*. New York: McGraw-Hill.

Brown, P. M. (1994). The role of diagnosticity and normative fit in stereotype formation. Paper presented at the 23rd Meeting of Australian Psychologists, Cairns, 28 April–1 May.

Brown, P. M. (forthcoming). Category fit and theories in the formation of stereotype content. Unpublished Ph.D. thesis, Australian National University.

Brown, R. (1965). *Social Psychology*. New York: Free Press.

Brown, R. (1986). *Social Psychology: The second edition*. New York: Free Press.

Brown, R. J. (1978). Divided we fall: An analysis of relations between sections of a factory work force. In H. Tajfel (ed.), *Differentiation Between Social Groups: Studies in the social psychology of intergroup relations*, London: Academic Press.

Brown, R. J. (1984). The effects of intergroup similarity and cooperative vs. competitive orientation on intergroup discrimination. *British Journal of Social Psychology, 23*, 21–33.

Brown, R. J. (1988). *Group Processes: Dynamics within and between Groups*. Oxford: Blackwell.

Brown, R. J. (1995). *Prejudice: Its social psychology*, Oxford: Blackwell.

Brown, R. J. and Abrams, D. (1986). The effects of intergroup similarity, and goal interdependence on intergroup attitudes and task performance. *Journal of Experimental Social Psychology, 22*, 78–92.

Brown, R. J., Tajfel, H. and Turner, J. C. (1980). Minimal group situations and intergroup discrimination: Comments on the paper by Aschenbrenner and Schaefer. *European Journal of Social Psychology, 10*, 399–414.

Brown, R. J. and Turner, J. C. (1981). Interpersonal and intergroup behavior. In J. C. Turner and H. Giles (eds), *Intergroup Behavior* (pp. 33–64). Chicago: University of Chicago Press.

Brown, R. W. (1954). Mass phenomena. In G. Lindzey (ed.), *Handbook of Social Psychology* (pp. 833–76). Reading: Addison-Wesley.

Bruner, J. S. (1957a). On perceptual readiness. *Psychological Review*, *64*, 123–52.

Bruner, J. S. (1957b). Going beyond the information given. In H. E. Gruber, K. R. Hammond and R. Jessor (eds), *Contemporary Approaches to Cognition* (pp. 41–69). Cambridge, MA: Harvard University Press.

Bruner, J. S. and Tagiuri, R. (1954). The perception of people. In G. Lindzey (ed.), *Handbook of Social Psychology* (vol. 2). Cambridge: Addison-Wesley.

Bruner, J. S. (1990). *Acts of Meaning*. Cambridge, MA: Harvard University Press.

Brunswik, E. (1943). Organismic achievement and environmental probability. *Psychological Review*, *50*, 255–72.

Buchanan, W. (1951). Stereotypes and tensions as revealed by the UNESCO international poll. *International Social Science Journal*, *3*, 515–28.

Burnstein, E. and Schul, Y. (1982). The informational basis of social judgments: Operations in forming an impression of another person. *Journal of Experimental Social Psychology*, *18*, 217–34.

Business Week (1992). The prize catches being eyed by big banks. 27 July, 64–5.

Byrne, D. (1971). *The Attraction Paradigm*. New York: Academic Press.

Campbell, D. (1947). Factors associated with attitudes towards Jews. In T. Newcomb and E. Hartley (eds), *Readings in Social Psychology*. Cambridge: Cambridge University Press.

Campbell, D. T. (1958). Common fate, similarity, and other indices of the status of aggregates of persons as social entities. *Behavioral Science*, *3*, 14–25.

Campbell, D. T. (1967). Stereotypes and the perception of group differences. *American Psychologist*, *22*, 817–29.

Cantor, N. and Mischel, W. (1977). Traits as prototypes: Effects on recognition memory. *Journal of Personality and Social Psychology*, *35*, 38–48.

Cantor, N. and Mischel, W. (1979). Prototypes in person perception. In L. Berkowitz (ed.), *Advances in Experimental Social Psychology* (vol. 12, pp. 3–52). New York: Academic Press.

Cauthen, N. R., Robinson, I. E. and Krauss, H. H. (1971). Stereotypes: A review of the literature 1926–1968. *Journal of Social Psychology*, *84*, 103–25.

Chase, W. G. and Simon, H. A. (1973). Perception in chess. *Cognitive Psychology*, *4*, 55–81.

Cheyne, W. M. (1970). Stereotyped reactions to speakers with Scottish and English regional accents. *British Journal of Social and Clinical Psychology*, *9*, 77–9.

Chin, M. G. and McClintock, C. G. (1993). The effect of intergroup discrimination and social values on level of self-esteem in the minimal group paradigm. *European Journal of Social Psychology*, *23*, 63–75.

Cialdini, R. B. (1988). *Influence: Science and practice* (2nd edn). Glenview, IL: Scott, Foresman and Co.

Cialdini, R. B., Borden, R. J., Thorne, A., Walker, M., Freeman, S. and Sloane, L. R. (1976). Basking in reflected glory: Three (football) field studies. *Journal of Personality and Social Psychology*, *34*, 366–75.

Clark, K. B. and Clark, M. P. (1947). Racial identification and preferences in Negro children. In T. M. Newcomb and E. L. Hartley (eds), *Readings in Social Psychology*. New York: Holt.

Cohen, L. L. and Swim, J. K. (1995). The differential impact of gender ratios on women and men: Tokenism, self-confidence, and expectations. *Personality and Social Psychology Bulletin, 21,* 876–84.

Cohn, N. (1970). *The Age of the Millennium*. London: Paladin.

Condor, S. (1986). Sex role beliefs and 'traditional women': feminist and intergroup perspectives. In S. Wilkinson (ed.), *Feminist Social Psychology*. Milton Keynes: Open University Press.

Condor, S. (1988). Race stereotypes and racist discourse. *Text, 8,* 69–89.

Condor, S. (1989). Biting into the future: Social change and the social identity of women. In S. Skevington and D. Baker (eds), *The Social Identity of Women*. London: Sage.

Condor, S. (1990). Social stereotypes and social identity. In D. Abrams and M. Hogg (eds), *Social Identity Theory: Constructive and Critical Advances*. Hemel Hempstead: Harvester Wheatsheaf.

Condor, S. (1993). Denken over sekse als sociale categorie. *Tijdschrift voor vrouwenstudies, 55,* 280–94.

Condor, S. (in press). On having history: A social psychological account of Anglo British autostereotypes. In C. Barfoot (ed.), *National Stereotypes and Racial Purity*. DQR Studies in Literature.

Cook, M. (1984). *Issues in Person Perception*. London: Methuen.

Cook, S. W. (1984). Cooperative interaction in multiethnic contexts. In N. Miller and M. B. Brewer (eds), *Groups in Contact: The psychology of desegregation* (pp. 291–302). Orlando, FL: Academic Press.

Corneille, O. and Leyens, J.-Ph. (1994). Catégories, catégorisation sociale et essentialisme psychologique. In R. Y. Bourhis et J.-Ph. Leyens (eds), *Stéréotypes, discrimination et relations intergroupes* (pp. 42–68). Liège: Mardaga.

Cox, O. C. (1948/1959). *Caste, Class, and Race: A study in social dynamics*. New York: Monthly Review Press.

Crocker, J., Blaine, B. and Luhtanen, R. (1993). Prejudice, intergroup behaviour and self-esteem: Enhancement and protection motive. In M. Hogg and D. Abrams (eds), *Group Motivation: Social psychological perspectives* (pp. 52–67). New York: Harvester-Wheatsheaf.

Crocker, J., Broadnax, S., Luhtanen, R. and Blaine, B. (1993). Belief in U.S. government conspiracies against blacks: Powerlessness or group consciousness? Unpublished manuscript, State University of New York at Buffalo.

Crocker, J., Hannah, D. B. and Weber, R. (1983). Person memory and causal attributions. *Journal of Personality and Social Psychology, 44,* 55–66.

Crocker, J. and Luhtanen, R. (1990). Collective self-esteem and ingroup bias. *Journal of Personality and Social Psychology, 58,* 60–7.

Crocker, J., Luhtanen, R., Blaine, B. and Broadnax, S. (1994). Collective self-esteem and psychological well-being among White, Black and Asian college students. *Personality and Social Psychology Bulletin, 20,* 503–13.

Crocker, J. and Major, B. (1989). Social stigma and self-esteem: The self-protective properties of stigma. *Psychological Review, 96,* 608–30.

Crocker, J., Thompson, L. L., McGraw, K. M. and Ingerman, C. (1987). Downward comparison, prejudice, and evaluation of others: Effects of self-esteem and threat. *Journal of Personality and Social Psychology, 52*, 907–16.

Cronbach, L. J. (1955). Processes affecting scores on 'understanding of others' and 'assumed similarity'. *Psychological Bulletin, 52*, 177–93.

Crosby, F. J. (1982). *Relative Deprivation and Working Women*. New York: Oxford University Press.

Darley, J. M. and Gross, P. H. (1983). A hypothesis-confirming bias in labelling effects. *Journal of Personality and Social Psychology, 44*, 20–33.

David, B. and Turner, J. C. (1992). Studies in self-categorization and minority conversion. Paper presented at the joint EAESP/SESP meeting, Leuven/Louvain-la-Neuve, Belgium, 15–18 July.

de la Haye, A.-M. (1993, September). Illusory correlation, evaluative contrast, and how to tell them apart. Paper presented at the Xth General Meeting of the European Association of Experimental Social Psychology, Lisbon.

de la Haye, A.-M. and Lauvergeon, G. (1995). Is illusory correlation distinctiveness-based? Unpublished manuscript, Université René Descartes.

de la Haye, A.-M., Lauvergeon, G. and Scharnitzky, P. (1995). On distinguishing preference from contrast in the illusory correlation paradigm. Unpublished manuscript, Université René Descartes.

Deaux, K. and Emswiller, T. (1974). Explanations for successful performance on sex-linked tasks: What is skill for the male is luck for the female. *Journal of Personality and Social Psychology, 29*, 80–5.

Deaux, K. and Lewis, L. L. (1984). Structure of gender stereotypes: Interrelationships among components and gender label. *Journal of Personality and Social Psychology, 46*, 991–1004.

Deutsch, M. (1985). *Distributive Justice*. New Haven: Yale University Press.

Devine, P. G. (1989). Stereotypes and prejudice: Their automatic and controlled components. *Journal of Personality and Social Psychology, 56*, 680–90.

Devine, P. G. and Baker, S. M. (1991). Measurement of racial stereotype subtyping. *Personality and Social Psychology Bulletin, 17*, 44–50.

Devine, P. G., Evett, S. R. and Vasquez-Suson, K. A. (1996). Exploring the interpersonal dynamics of group contact. In R. M. Sorrentino and E. T. Higgins (eds), *Handbook of Motivation and Cognition: The interpersonal context* (vol. 3). New York: Guilford.

Diab, L. N. (1963). Factors determining group stereotypes. *Journal of Social Psychology, 61*, 3–10.

Diehl, M. (1990). The minimal group paradigm: Theoretical explanations and empirical findings. *European Review of Social Psychology, 1*, 263–92.

Dijksterhuis, A. and van Knippenberg, A. (1995). Memory for stereotype-consistent and stereotype-inconsistent information as a function of processing pace. *European Journal of Social Psychology, 25*, 689–93.

Doise, W. (1986). *Levels of Explanation in Social Psychology*. Cambridge: Cambridge University Press.

Doise, W. (1988). Individual and Social identities in intergroup relations. *European Journal of Social Psychology, 18*, 999–1111.

Doise, W., Csepeli, G., Dann, H.-D., Gouge, G. C., Larsen, K. and Ostell, A. (1972).

An experimental investigation into the formation of intergroup representations, *European Journal of Social Psychology*, 2, 202–4.

Doise, W., Deschamps, J. C. and Meyers, G. (1978). The accentuation of intracategory similarities. In H. Tajfel (ed.), *Differentiation between Social Groups* (pp. 159–68). London: Academic Press.

Dollard, J. Doob, L. W., Miller, N. E., Mowrer, O. H. and Sears, R. R. (1939). *Frustration and Aggression*. New Haven, CT: Yale University Press.

Doosje, B., Ellemers, N. and Spears, R. (1995). Perceived intragroup variability as a function of group status and identification. *Journal of Experimental Social Psychology*, *31*, 410–36.

Doosje, B., Spears, R., Haslam, S. A., Koomen, W. and Oakes, P. J. (1995). The effect of comparative context on central tendency and variability judgments and the evaluation of group characteristics. Unpublished manuscript.

Doosje, B., Spears, R. and Koomen, W. (1995). When bad isn't all bad: The strategic use of sample information in generalization and stereotyping. *Journal of Personality and Social Psychology*, *69*, 642–55.

Dorfman, D. D. (1995). Soft science with a neoconservative agenda. *Contemporary Psychology*, *40*, 418–21.

Dovidio, J. F., Brigham, J. C., Johnson, B. T. and Gaertner, S. L. (1996). Stereotyping, prejudice, and discrimination: Another look. In C. N. Macrae, C. Stangor and M. Hewstone (eds), *Stereotypes and Stereotyping* (pp. 276–322). New York: Guilford Press.

Dovidio, J. F., Evans, N. and Tyler, R. B. (1986). Racial stereotypes: The contents of their cognitive representations. *Journal of Experimental Social Psychology*, *22*, 22–37.

Dovidio, J. F. and Gaertner, S. (1986). Prejudice, discrimination and racism: Historical trends and contemporary approaches. In J. Dovidio and S. L. Gaertner (eds), *Prejudice, Discrimination and Racism*. New York: Academic Press.

Dubois, N. (1994). *La norme d'internalité et le libéralisme*. Grenoble: PUG.

Duckitt, J. H. (1992). Psychology and prejudice: A historical analysis and integrative framework. *American Psychologist*, *47*, 1182–93.

Dudycha, G. Y. (1942). The attitudes of college students toward war and the Germans before and during the Second World War. *Journal of Social Psychology*, *15*, 317–24.

Duncan, B. (1976). Differential social perception and attribution of intergroup violence: Testing the lower limits of stereotyping Blacks. *Journal of Personality and Social Psychology*, *34*, 590–8.

Dweck, C. S., Hong, Y.-Y. and Chiu, C.-Y. (1993). Implicit theories: Individual differences in the likelihood and meaning of dispositional inference. *Personality and Social Psychology Bulletin*, *19*, 644–56.

Dworkin, A. (1983). *Right-wing Women*. New York: Perigree.

Eagly, A. H. (1987). *Sex Differences in Social Behavior: A social-role interpretation*. Hillsdale, NJ: Erlbaum.

Eagly, A. H. and Chaiken, S. (1993). *The Psychology of Attitudes*. Ft. Worth: Harcourt Brace Jovanovich College Publishers.

Eagly, A. H. and Kite, M. E. (1987). Are stereotypes of nationalities applied to both women and men? *Journal of Personality and Social Psychology*, *53*, 451–62.

Eagly, A. H. and Steffen, V. J. (1984). Gender stereotypes stem from the distribution of women and men into social roles. *Journal of Personality and Social Psychology*, *46*, 735–54.

Easterbrook, J. A. (1959). The effect of emotion on cue utilization and the organization of behavior. *Psychological Review*, *66*, 183–201.

Eco, U. (1984). *The Name of the Rose*. London: Picador.

Edwards, A. L. (1940). Four dimensions in political stereotypes. *Journal of Abnormal and Social Psychology*, *35*, 566–72.

Edwards, D. (1991). Categories are for talking: On the cognitive and discursive bases of categorization. *Theory and Psychology*, *1*, 515–42.

Edwards, D. and Potter, J. (1992). *Discursive Psychology*. London: Sage.

Eiser, J. R. and Stroebe, W. (1972). *Categorization and Social Judgment*. London: Academic Press.

Elias, N. (1988). *Die Gesellschaft der Individuen* (The society of the individuals). Frankfurt am Main: Suhrkamp.

Elias, N. (1990). *Über den Prozeß der Zivilisation* (zwei Bände). Frankfurt am Main: Suhrkamp. (Translated into English by Edmund Jephcott: The civilizing process. Vol. 1, New York: Urizen Books, 1978; Vol. 2, New York: Pantheon Books, 1982).

Ellemers, N. (1993). The influence of socio-structural variables on identity enhancement strategies. *European Review of Social Psychology*, *4*, 27–57.

Ellemers, N., Doosje, B. and Spears, R. (1994). A measure of group identification. Unpublished data, Free University/University of Amsterdam.

Ellemers, N., Doosje, B., van Knippenberg, A. and Wilke, H. (1992). Status protection in high status minority groups. *European Journal of Social Psychology*, *22*, 123–40.

Ellemers, N., Kortekaas, P. and Ouwerkerk, J. (1995). Self-categorization, commitment to the group and social self-esteem as related but distinct aspects of social identity. Paper presented at the Third Münster Meeting on Social Identity.

Ellemers, N. and Mlicki, P. (1991). Refining the social identity concept: Some theoretical and empirical complexities. Unpublished manuscript.

Ellemers, N., van Knippenberg, A., De Vries, N. K. and Wilke, H. (1988). Social Identification and permeability of group boundaries. *European Journal of Social Psychology*, *18*, 497–513.

Ellemers, N., van Knippenberg, A. and Wilke, H. (1990). The influence of permeability of group boundaries and stability of group status on strategies of individual mobility and social change. *British Journal of Social Psychology*, *29*, 233–46.

Ellemers, N., van Rijswijk, W., Roefs, M. and Simons, C. (in press). Bias in intergroup perceptions: Balancing group identity with social reality. *Personality and Social Psychology Bulletin*.

Ellemers, N., Wilke, H. and van Knippenberg, A. (1993). Effects of the legitimacy of low group or individual status on individual and collective identity enhancement strategies. *Journal of Personality and Social Psychology*, *64*, 766–78.

Emler, N. and Dickinson, J. (1985). Children's representations of economic inequalities: The effects of social class. *British Journal of Social Psychology*, *3*, 191–8.

Esser, H. (1988). *Ethnische Differenzierung und moderne Gesellschaft*. Zeitschrift für Soziologie, *17* (4), 235–48.

Esses, V. M., Haddock, G. and Zanna, M. P. (1993). The role of mood in the expression of intergroup stereotypes. In M. P. Zanna and J. M. Olson (eds), *The Psychology of Prejudice: The Ontario Symposium, vol. 7* (pp. 77–101). Hillsdale, NJ: Erlbaum.

Ethier, K. A. and Deaux, K. (1994). Negotiating social identity when contexts change: Maintaining identification and responding to threat. *Journal of Personality and Social Psychology*, *67*, 243–51.

Eysenck, H. J. (1983). Is there a paradigm in personality research? *Journal of Research in Personality*, *17*, 369–97.

Farr, R. and Moscovici, S. (1984). *Social Representations*. Cambridge: Cambridge University Press.

Farsides, T. (1995). Why social identity theory's self-esteem hypothesis has never been tested – and how to test it. Paper presented at BPS Social Section Conference, York, September.

Feldman, J. M., Camburn, A. and Gatti, M. (1986). Shared distinctiveness as a source of illusory correlation in performance appraisal. *Organizational Behavior and Human Decision Processes*, *37*, 34–59.

Feldman, R. (1968). Response to compatriot and foreigner who seek assistance. *Journal of Personality and Social Psychology*, *10*, 202–14.

Feshbach, S. and Singer, R. (1957). The effects of personality and shared threats upon social prejudice. *Journal of Abnormal and Social Psychology*, *54*, 411–16.

Festinger, L. and Carlsmith, J. M. (1959). Cognitive concequences of forced compliance. *Journal of Abnormal and Social Psychology*, *58*, 203–10.

Fiedler, K. (1991). The tricky nature of skewed frequency tables: An information loss account of distinctiveness-based illusory correlations. *Journal of Personality and Social Psychology*, *60*, 26–36.

Fiedler, K., Russer, S. and Gramm, K. (1993). Illusory correlations and memory performance. *Journal of Experimental Social Psychology*, *29*, 111–36.

Fishman, J. A. (1956). An examination of the process and function of social stereotyping. *Journal of Social Psychology*, *43*, 27–64.

Fiske, S. T. (1993a). Controlling other people: The impact of power on stereotyping. *American Psychologist*, *48*, 621–8.

Fiske, S. T. (1993b). Social cognition and social perception. *Annual Review of Psychology*, *44*, 155–94.

Fiske, S. T., Bersoff, D. N., Borgida, E., Deaux, K. and Heilman, M. E. (1991). Social science research on trial: Use of sex stereotyping research in *Price Waterhouse v. Hopkins*. *American Psychologist*, *46*, 1049–60.

Fiske, S. T. and Cox, M. G. (1979). Person concepts: The effect of target familiarity and descriptive purpose on the process of describing others. *Journal of Personality*, *47*, 136–61.

Fiske, S. T. and Linville, P. W. (1980). What does the Schema Concept buy us? *Personality and Social Psychology Bulletin*, *6*, 543–57.

Fiske, S. T. and Neuberg, S. L. (1990). A continuum of impression formation, from category-based to individuating processes: Influences of information and motivation on attention and interpretation. In M. P. Zanna (ed.), *Advances in Experimental Social Psychology* (vol. 23, pp. 1–74). New York: Random House.

Fiske, S. T. and Stevens, L. E. (1993). What's so special about sex? Gender stereotyping and discrimination. In S. Oskamp and M. Costanzo (eds), *Gender Issues In Contemporary Society* (pp. 173–96). Newbury Park, CA: Sage.

Fiske, S. T. and Taylor, S. E. (1984). *Social Cognition*. Reading, MA: Addison-Wesley.

Fiske, S. T. and Taylor, S. E. (1991). *Social Cognition* (2nd edn). New York: McGraw-Hill.

Foote, N. N. (1951). Identification as the basis for a theory of motivation. *American Sociological Review, 16,* 14–21.

Ford, T. E. and Stangor, C. (1992). The role of diagnosticity in stereotype formation: Perceiving group means and variances. *Journal of Personality and Social Psychology, 63,* 356–67.

Forsyth, D. (1990). *Group Dynamics.* Pacific Grove: Brooks/Cole.

Fraser, S. (1995) (ed.). The Bell Curve Wars: Race, Intelligence and the Future of America. NY: Basic Books.

Frazer, J. G. (1959). *The New Golden Bough.* New York: Criterion books.

Freedman, J. L. (1965). Long-term behavioral effects of cognitive dissonance. *Journal of Experimental Social Psychology, 1,* 103–20.

Freedman, J. L. and Fraser, S. C. (1966). Compliance without pressure: The foot-in-the-door technique. *Journal of Personality and Social Psychology, 4,* 195–202.

Freyd, J. F. (1983). Shareability: The social psychology of epistemology. *Cognitive Science, 7,* 191–210.

Friedman, D. (1983). Normative and rational explanations of a classic case: Religious specialization in academia. In M. Hechter (ed.), *The Microfoundations of Macrosociology.* Philadelphia: Temple University Press.

Fyock, J. and Stangor, C. (1994). The role of memory biases in stereotype maintenance. *British Journal of Social Psychology, 33,* 331–43.

Gaertner, S. L. and Dovidio, J. F. (1986). The aversive form of racism. In J. F. Dovidio and S. L. Gaertner (eds), *Prejudice, Discrimination and Racism* (pp. 61–89). Orlando, FL: Academic Press.

Gaertner, S. L., Dovidio, J. F., Anastasio, P. A., Bachman, B. A. and Rust, M. C. (1993). Reducing intergroup bias: The common ingroup identity model. In W. Stroebe and M. Hewstone (eds), *European Journal of Social Psychology* (vol. 4, pp. 1–26). Chichester: Wiley & Sons.

Gaertner, S. L., Mann, J. A., Dovidio, J. F., Murrell, A. J. and Pomare, M. (1990). How does cooperation reduce intergroup bias? *Journal of Personality and Social Psychology, 59,* 692–704.

Gaertner, S. L., Mann, J., Murrell, A. and Dovidio, J. F. (1989). Reducing intergroup bias: The benefits of categorization. *Journal of Personality and Social Psychology, 57,* 239–49.

Gaertner, S., Rust, M., Dovidio, J., Bachman, B. and Anastasio, P. (1994). The contact hypothesis: The role of a common ingroup identity on reducing intergroup bias. *Small Group Research, 25,* 224–9.

Gaertner, S. L., Rust, M. C., Dovidio, J. F., Bachman, B. A. and Anastasio, P. A. (1995). The contact hypothesis: The role of a common ingroup identity of reducing intergroup bias among majority and minority group members. In J. L. Nye and A. Brower (eds), *What's Social about Social Cognition?* Newbury Park, CA: Sage Publications.

Gage, N. L. and Cronbach, L. J. (1955). Conceptual and methodological problems in interpersonal perception. *Psychological Bulletin, 62,* 411–22.

Gagnon, A. and Bourhis, R. Y. (1992). Discrimination intergroupe: Identité sociale ou intérêt personnel? Paper presented at the Annual Congress of the Canadian Psychological Association, Québec, Canada. Abstract in *Canadian Psychology, 33,* 508.

Gagnon, A. and Bourhis, R. Y. (1996). Discrimination in the minimal group paradigm: Social identity or self-interest? *Personality and Social Psychology Bulletin,* (in press).

Gardner, R. C. (1993). Stereotypes as consensual beliefs. In M. P. Zanna and J. M. Olson (eds), *The Psychology of Prejudice: The Ontario symposium, vol. 7*. Hillsdale, NJ: Erlbaum.

Gardner, R. C., Kirby, D. M. and Finlay, J. C. (1973). Ethnic stereotypes: The significance of consensus. *Canadian Journal of Behavioural Science, 5*, 4–12.

Gerard, H. B. (1964). Physiological measurement in social psychological research. In P. H. Leiderman and D. Shapiro (eds), *Psychobiological Approaches to Social Behavior*. Stanford: Stanford University Press, 43–58.

Gergen, K. J. (1971). *The Concept of Self*. New York: Holt, Rinehart and Winston, Inc.

Gervey, B. M., Chiu, C.-Y., Hong, Y.-Y. and Dweck, C. S. (1993). Processing and utilizing information in social judgment: The role of implicit theories. Paper presented at the Fifth Annual Convention of the American Psychological Society, Chicago.

Gilbert, D. T. and Hixon, J. G. (1991). The trouble of thinking: Activation and application of stereotypic beliefs. *Journal of Personality and Social Psychology, 60*, 509–17.

Gilbert, D. T. and Malone, P. S. (1995). The correspondence bias. *Psychological Bulletin, 117*, 21–38.

Gilbert, G. M. (1951). Stereotype persistence and change among college students. *Journal of Abnormal and Social Psychology, 46*, 245–54.

Goethals, G. R., Messick, D. M. and Allison, S. T. (1991). The uniqueness bias: Studies of constructive social comparison. In J. Suls and T. A. Wills (eds), *Social Comparison: Contemporary theory and research* (pp. 149–76). Hillsdale, NJ: Lawrence Erlbaum.

Goffman, E. (1961). *Asylums*. Garden City: Doubleday Anchor.

Gordon, C. (1968). Self-conceptions: Configurations of content. In C. Gordon and K. J. Gergen (eds), *The Self in Social Interaction* (vol. I: Classic and contemporary perspectives, pp. 115–36). New York: John Wiley & Sons, Inc.

Gould, S. J. (1981). *The Mismeasure of Man*. New York: W. W. Norton & Company.

Grant, P. R. and Holmes, J. G. (1981). The integration of implicit personality theory schemas and stereotypic images. *Social Psychology Quarterly, 44*, 107–15.

Grant, T. (1995). *Update #4 of Tom Grant's theories* [On-line]. Available: http://www.oswego.edu/~jmcrae/nirvana/update.4.

Graumann, C. F. and Wintermantel, M. (1989). Discriminatory speech acts: A functional approach. In D. Bar-Tal, C. F. Graumann, A. W. Kruglanski and W. Stroebe (eds), *Stereotyping and Prejudice: Changing conceptions* (pp. 183–204). Berlin: Springer-Verlag.

Green, C. W., Adams, A. M. and Turner, C. W. (1988). Development and validation of the School Interracial Climate Scale. *American Journal of Community Psychology, 16*, 241–59.

Greenwald, A. G. and Banaji, M. R. (1995). Implicit social cognition: Attitudes, self-esteem, and stereotypes. *Psychological Review, 105*, 4–27.

Guimond, S., Begin, G. and Palmer, D. L. (1989). Education and causal attributions: The development of 'person-blame' and 'system-blame' ideology. *Social Psychology Quarterly, 52*, 126–40.

Gurwitz, S. B. and Dodge, K. A. (1977). Effect of confirmations and disconfirmations on stereotype-based attributions. *Journal of Personality and Social Psychology, 39*, 578–89.

Hamilton, D. L. (1979). A cognitive-attributional analysis of stereotyping. *Advances in Experimental Social Psychology*, *12*, 53–84.

Hamilton, D. L. (1981). Stereotyping and intergroup behavior: Some thoughts on the cognitive approach. In D. L. Hamilton (ed.), *Cognitive processes in stereotyping and intergroup behavior*. Hillsdale, NJ: Erlbaum.

Hamilton, D. L. (ed.) (1981). *Cognitive Processes in Stereotyping and Intergroup Behavior*. Hillsdale, NJ: Erlbaum.

Hamilton, D. L., Dugan, P. M. and Trolier, T. K. (1985). The formation of stereotypic beliefs: Further evidence for distinctiveness-based illusory correlations. *Journal of Personality and Social Psychology*, *48*, 5–17.

Hamilton, D. L., Gibbons, P. A., Stroessner, S. J. and Sherman, J. W. (1992). Stereotypes and language use. In G. R. Semin and K. Fiedler (eds), *Language, Interaction and Social Cognition*. London: Sage.

Hamilton, D. L. and Gifford, R. K. (1976). Illusory correlation in intergroup perception: A cognitive basis of stereotypic judgments. *Journal of Experimental Social Psychology*, *12*, 392–407.

Hamilton, D. L. and Rose, T. L. (1980). Illusory correlation and the maintenance of stereotypic beliefs. *Journal of Personality and Social Psychology*, *39*, 832–45.

Hamilton, D. L. and Sherman, J. W. (1994). Stereotypes. In R. S. Wyer and T. K. Srull (eds), *Handbook of Social Cognition* (2nd edn, vol. 2, pp. 1–68). Hillsdale, NJ: Erlbaum.

Hamilton, D. L. and Sherman, S. J. (1989). Illusory correlations: Implications for stereotype theory and research. In D. Bar-Tal, C. F. Graumann, A. W. Kruglanski and W. Stroebe (eds), *Stereotyping and Prejudice: Changing conceptions* (pp. 127–63). New York and London: Springer Verlag.

Hamilton, D. L., Stroessner, S. J. and Driscoll, D. M. (1994). Social cognition and the study of stereotypes. In P. G. Devine, D. L. Hamilton and T. M. Ostrom (eds), *Social Cognition: Contributions to classic issues in social psychology* (pp. 291–321). New York: Springer-Verlag.

Hamilton, D. L. and Trolier, T. K. (1986). Stereotypes and stereotyping: An overview of the cognitive approach. In J. F. Dovidio and S. L. Gaertner (eds), *Prejudice, Discrimination, and Racism* (pp. 127–63). New York and Orlando, FL: Academic Press.

Hammond, K. R. (1978). Psychology's scientific revolution: Is it in danger? Report No. 211, Center for research on Judgement and Policy, University of Colorado.

Hardin, C. and Higgins, E. T. (1996). Shared reality: How social verification makes the subjective objective. In R. M. Sorrentino and E. T. Higgins (eds), *Handbook of Motivation and Cognition: Foundations of social behavior*. New York: Guilford.

Haslam, S. A., McGarty, C. and Brown, P. M. (1996). The search for differentiated meaning is a precursor to illusory correlation. *Personality and Social Psychology Bulletin*, *22*, 611–19.

Haslam, S. A., McGarty, C., Oakes, P. J. and Turner, J. C. (1993). Social comparative context and illusory correlation: Testing between ingroup bias and social identity models of stereotype formation. *Australian Journal of Psychology*, *45*, 97–101.

Haslam, S. A. and Oakes, P. J. (1995). How context dependent is the outgroup homogeneity effect? A response to Bartsch and Judd. *European Journal of Social Psychology*.

Haslam, S. A., Oakes, P. J., McGarty, C., Turner, J. C. and Onorato, R. (1995). Contextual changes in the prototpyicality of extreme and moderate outgroup members. *European Journal of Social Psychology*, *22*, 509–30.

Haslam, S. A., Oakes, P. J., McGarty, C., Turner, J. C., Reynolds, K. J. and Eggins, R. A. (in press). Stereotyping and social influence: The mediation of stereotype applicability and sharedness by the views of ingroup and outgroup members. *British Journal of Social Psychology*.

Haslam, S. A., Oakes, P. J., Rainbird, K. and Spears, R. (1994). What is cognitive load and how does it affect stereotyping? Unpublished manuscript, Australian National University.

Haslam, S. A., Oakes, P. J., Turner, J. C. and McGarty, C. (1995). Social categorization and group homogeneity: Changes in the perceived applicability of stereotype content as a function of comparative context and trait favourableness. *British Journal of Social Psychology*, *34*, 139–60.

Haslam, S. A., Oakes, P. J., Turner, J. C. and McGarty, C. (1996). Social identity, self-categorization and the perceived homogeneity in ingroups and outgroups: The interaction between social motivation and cognition. In R. M. Sorrentino and E. T. Higgins (eds), *Handbook of Motivation and Cognition* (vol. 3). Guilford: New York.

Haslam, S. A. and Turner, J. C. (1992). Context-dependent variation in social stereotyping 2: The relationship between frame of reference, self-categorization and accentuation. *European Journal of Social Psychology*, *22*, 251–78.

Haslam, S. A. and Turner, J. C. (1995). Context-dependent variation in social stereotyping 3: Extremism as a self-categorical basis for polarized judgment. *European Journal of Social Psychology*, *25*, 341–71.

Haslam, S. A., Turner, J. C., Oakes, P. J., McGarty, C. and Hayes, B. K. (1992). Context-dependent variation in social stereotyping 1: The effects of intergroup relations as mediated by social change and frame of reference. *European Journal of Social Psychology*, *22*, 3–20.

Haslam, S. A., Turner, J. C., Oakes, P. J., McGarty, C. and Reynolds, K. J. (in press). The group as a basis for emergent stereotype consensus. In W. Stroebe and M. Hewstone (eds), *European Review of Social Psychology* (vol. 9). Chichester: Wiley.

Hastie, R. and Park, B. (1986). The relationship between memory and judgment depends on whether the judgment task is memory-based or on-line. *Psychological Review*, *93*, 258–68.

Hastie, R. and Rasinski, K. A. (1988). The concept of accuracy in social judgment. In D. Bar-Tal and A. W. Kruglanski (eds), *The Social Psychology of Knowledge*. Cambridge: Cambridge University Press.

Herrnstein, R. J. and Murray, C. (1994). *The Bell Curve Intelligence and Class Structure in American Life*. New York: Free Press.

Hewstone, M. (1989). Changing stereotypes with disconfirming information. In D. Bar-Tal, C. G. Grauann, A. W. Kruglanski and W. Stroebe (eds), *Stereotyping and Prejudice* (pp. 207–23). New York: Springer-Verlag.

Hewstone, M. (1990). The ultimate attribution error: A review of the literature on intergroup causal attribution. *European Journal of Social Psychology*, *20*, 311–55.

Hewstone, M. (1994). Revision and change of stereotypic beliefs: In search of the elusive subtyping model. In W. Stroebe and M. Hewstone (eds), *European Review of Social Psychology* (vol. 5, pp. 69–109). Chichester: Wiley.

Hewstone, M. R. C. and Brown, R. J. (1986). Contact is not enough: An intergroup perspective on the contact hypothesis. In M. R. C. Hewstone and R. J. Brown (eds), *Contact and Conflict in Intergroup Encounters* (pp. 1–44). Oxford: Basil Blackwell.

Hewstone, M. and Brown, R. J. (eds) (1986), *Contact and Conflict in Intergroup Encounters*. Oxford: Basil Blackwell.

Hewstone, M., Hantzi, A. and Johnston, L. (1991). Social categorization and person memory: The pervasiveness of race as an organizing principle. *European Journal of Social Psychology*, *21*, 517–28.

Hewstone, M., Hopkins, N. and Routh, D. (1992). Cognitive models of stereotype change (1): generalization and sub-typing in young people's views of the police. *European Journal of Social Psychology*, *22*, 219–34.

Hewstone, M. and Jaspars, J. (1982). Intergroup relations and attribution processes. In H. Tajfel (ed.), *Social Identity and Intergroup Relations*. Cambridge, Cambridge University Press and Paris, Maison des Sciences de l'Homme.

Hewstone, M., Johnston, L. and Aird, P. (1992). Cognitive models of stereotype change (2): perceptions of homogenous and heterogenous groups. *European Journal of Social Psychology*, *22*, 235–49.

Hewstone, M., Macrae, C. N., Griffiths, R., Milne, A. and Brown, R. J. (1994). Cognitive models of stereotype change (5): Measurement, development and consequences of subtyping. *Journal of Experimental Social Psychology*, *30*, 1–22.

Higgins, E. T. (1995). Knowledge activation: Accessibility, applicability and salience. In E. T. Higgins and A. W. Kruglanski (eds), *Social Psychology: Handbook of basic principles*. New York: Guilford.

Higgins, E. T. and King, G. (1981). Accessibility of social constructs: Information processing consequences of individual and contextual variability. In N. Cantor and J. F. Kihlstrom (eds), *Personality, Cognition and Social Interaction* (pp. 69–121). Hillsdale, NJ: Erlbaum.

Hinde, R. A. (1979). *Towards Understanding Relationships*. London: Academic Press.

Hinkle, S. and Brown, R. J. (1990). Intergroup comparisons and social identity: Some links and lacunae. In D. Abrams and M. A. Hogg (eds), *Social identity theory. Constructive and critical advances* (pp. 48–70). London: Harvester Wheatsheaf.

Hinkle, S. and Brown, R. (1990). Intergroup comparisons and social identity: Some links and lacunae. In D. Abrams and M. A. Hogg (eds), *Social Identity Theory: Constructive and critical advances* (pp. 48–70). New York: Springer-Verlag.

Hinkle, S. and Schopler, J. (1986). Bias in the evaluation of ingroup and outgroup performance. In S. Worchel and W. Austin (eds), *Psychology of Intergroup Relations*. Monterey: Brooks/Cole.

Hinkle, S., Taylor, L. A., Fox-Cardamone, D. L. and Crook, K. F. (1989). Intragroup identification and intergroup differentiation: A multicomponent approach. *British Journal of Social Psychology*, *28*, 305–17.

Hintzman, D. L. (1986). 'Schema abstraction' in a multiple-trace memory model. *Psychological Review*, *93*, 411–28.

Hoffman, C. and Hurst, N. (1990). Gender stereotypes: Perception or rationalization? *Journal of Personality and Social Psychology*, *58*, 197–208.

Hofstede, G. (1980). *Culture's Consequences*. Beverly Hills, CA: Sage.

Hofstede, G. (1991). *Cultures and Organizations*. London: McGraw Hill.

Hogg, M. A. and Abrams, D. (1988). *Social identifications: A social psychology of inter-group relations and group processes*. London: Routledge.

Hogg, M. A. and Abrams, D. (1990). Social motivation, self-esteem and social identity. In D. Abrams and M. A. Hogg (eds), *Social Identity Theory. Constructive and critical advances* (pp. 28–47). London: Harvester Wheatsheaf.

Hogg, M. A. and Sunderland, J. (1991). Self-esteem and intergroup discrimination in the minimal group paradigm. *British Journal of Social Psychology*, *30*, 51–62.

Hogg, M. A. and Turner, J. C. (1985). Interpersonal attraction, social identification and psychological group formation. *European Journal of Social Psychology*, *15*, 51–66.

Hogg, M. A. and Turner, J. C. (1987). Intergroup behaviour, self-stereotyping and the salience of social categories. *British Journal of Social Psychology*, *26*, 325–40.

Hornstein, H. A. (1976). *Cruelty and Kindness: A new look at aggression and altruism.* Englewood Cliffs, NJ: Prentice Hall.

Hornstein, H. A. (1982). Promotive tension: Theory and research. In V. J. Derlega and J. Grzelak (eds), *Cooperation and Helping Behaviour* (pp. 231–48). New York: Academic Press.

Horwitz, M. and Rabbie, J. (1989). Stereotypes of groups, group members, and individuals in categories: A differential analysis. In D. Bar-Tal, C. F. Grauman, A. W. Kruglanski and W. Stroebe (eds), *Stereotyping and Prejudice: Changing conceptions.* New York: Springer Verlag.

Hovland, C. and Sears, D. C. (1940). Minor studies of aggression: Correlations of lynchings with economic indices. *Journal of Psychology*, *9*, 301–10.

Howard, J. M. and Rothbart, M. (1980). Social categorization for ingroup and outgroup behavior. *Journal of Personality and Social Psychology*, *38*, 301–10.

Hrabe, J., Hagedoorn, L. and Hagedoorn, R. (1989). The ethnic hierarchy in the Netherlands: Social distance and social representations. *British Journal of Social Psychology*, *28*, 57–69.

Huici, C. (1984). The individual and social functions of sex-role stereotypes. In H. Tajfel (ed.), *The Social Dimension: European developments in social psychology*. Cambridge: Cambridge University Press.

Humphrey, R. (1985). How work roles influence perception: Structural-cognitive processes and organizational behavior. *American Sociological Review*, *50*, 242–52.

Ibañez, T. (1994). Idéologie et relations intergroupes. In R. Y. Bourhis and J.-Ph. Leyens (eds), *Stéréotypes, discrimination et relations intergroupes* (pp. 321–45). Bruxelles: Mardaga.

Ickes, W. and Gonzalez, R. (1994). 'Social' cognition and *social* cognition: From the subjective to the intersubjective. *Small Group Research*, *25*, 294–315.

Isen, A. M. (1984). Toward understanding the role of affect in cognition. In R. S. Wyer and T. K. Srull (eds), *Handbook of Social Cognition* (pp. 179–236). Hillsdale, NJ: Erlbaum.

Islam, M. R. and Hewstone, M. (1993). Dimensions of contact as predictors of intergroup anxiety, perceived outgroup variability and outgroup attitude: An integrative model. *Personality and Social Psychology Bulletin*, *19*, 700–10.

Israel, J. and Tajfel, H. (1972). *The Context of Social Psychology*. London: Academic Press.

Iyengar, S. (1987). Television news and citizens' explanations of national affairs. *American Political Science Review, 81*, 815–31.

Jackman, M. R. and Senter, M. S. (1983). Different, therefore unequal: Beliefs about trait differences between groups of unequal status. *Research in Social Stratification and Mobility, 2*, 309–35.

Jackson, J. W. (1993). Realistic group conflict theory: A review and evaluation of the theoretical and empirical literature. *The Psychological Record, 43*, 395–414.

Jahoda, G. (1986). Nature, culture and social psychology. *European Journal of Social Psychology, 16*, 17–30.

James, K. and Cropanzano, R. (1994). Dispositional group loyalty and individual action for the benefit of an ingroup: Experimental and correlational evidence. *Organizational Behavior and Human Decision Making, 60*, 179–205.

Jaspars, J. and Hewstone, M. (1984). La théorie de l'attribution. In S. Moscovici (ed.), *Psychologie Sociale*. Paris: Presses Universitaires de France.

Jellison, J. M. and Green, J. (1981). A self-presentation approach to the fundamental attribution error: The norm of internality. *Journal of Personality and Social Psychology, 40*, 643–49.

Jemison, D. B. and Sitkin, S. B. (1986). Corporate acquisitions: A process perspective. *Academy of Management Review, 11*, 145–63.

Jetten, J., Spears, R. and Manstead, A. S. R. (1995). Intergroup norms and intergroup discrimination: Distinctive self-categorization and social identity effects in experimental and natural groups. Unpublished manuscript, University of Amsterdam.

Johnson, C. and Mullen, B. (1993). The determinants of differential group evaluations in distinctiveness-based illusory correlation in stereotyping. *British Journal of Social Psychology, 32*, 253–63.

Johnson, C. and Mullen, B. (1994). Evidence for the accessibility of paired distinctiveness in distinctiveness-based illusory correlation in stereotyping. *Personality and Social Psychology Bulletin, 20*, 65–70.

Johnston, L. and Hewstone, M. (1992). Cognitive models of stereotype change 3: Subtyping and the perceived typicality of disconfirming groups members. *Journal of Experimental Social Psychology, 28*, 360–86.

Johnston, L., Hewstone, M., Pendry, L. and Frankish, C. (1994). Cognitive models of stereotype change: IV. Motivational and cognitive influences. *European Journal of Social Psychology, 24*, 237–65.

Johnston, L. and Macrae, C. N. (1994). Changing social stereotypes: The case of the information seeker. *European Journal of Social Psychology, 24*, 581–92.

Jones, E. E. (1990). *Interpersonal Perception*. New York: Freeman.

Jones, E. E. and Pittman, T. (1982). Toward a general theory of strategic self presentation. In J. Suls (ed.), *Psychological Perspectives of the Self*. Hillsdale, NJ: Erlbaum.

Jones, E. E. and Sigall, H. (1971). The bogus pipeline: A new paradigm for measuring affect and attitude. *Psychological Bulletin, 76*, 349–64.

Jones, J. M. (1972). *Prejudice and Racism*. New York: Random House.

Jost, J. T. (1995). Negative illusions: Conceptual clarification and psychological evidence concerning false consciousness. *Political Psychology, 16*, 397–424.

Jost, J. T. (1996). Ingroup and outgroup favoritism among groups differing in socioeconomic success: Effects of perceived legitimacy and justification processes. Unpublished doctoral thesis, Yale University.

Jost, J. T. and Banaji, M. R. (1994). The role of stereotyping in system-justification and the production of false consciousness. *British Journal of Social Psychology*, *33*, 1–27.

Joule, R. V. and Beauvois, J.-L. (1987). Internalité, comportement et explication du comportement. In J.-L. Beauvois, R. V. Joule and et J.-M. Monteil (eds), *Perspectives cognitives et conduites sociales* (vol. 1). Cousset: Delval.

Judd, C. M. and Park, B. (1988). Out-group homogeneity: Judgments of variability at the individual and group levels. *Journal of Personality and Social Psychology*, *54*, 778–88.

Judd, C. M. and Park, B. (1993). Definition and assessment of accuracy in social stereotypes. *Psychological Review*, *100*, 109–28.

Jussim, L. and Fleming, C. (1996). Self-fulfilling prophecies and the maintenance of social stereotypes: The role of dyadic interactions and social forces. In C. N. Macrae, C. Stangor and M. Hewstone (eds), *Stereotypes and Stereotyping* (pp. 161–92). New York: The Guilford Press.

Kahneman, D., Slovic, P. and Tversky, A. (1982). *Judgment under Uncertainty: Heuristics and biases*. Cambridge: Cambridge University Press.

Kantowitz, B. H. (1974). Double stimulation. In B. H. Kantowitz (ed.), *Human Information Processing: Tutorials in performance and cognition*. Hillsdale, NJ: Erlbaum.

Kaplan, M. F., Wanshula, L. T. and Zanna, M. P. (1993). Time pressure and information integration in social judgment. In O. Svenson and J. Maule (eds), *Time Pressure and Stress in Human Judgment and Decision Making* (pp. 255–67). New York: Plenum Press.

Karlins, M., Coffman, T. L. and Walters, G. (1969). On the fading of social stereotypes: Studies in three generations of college students. *Journal of Personality and Social Psychology*, *13*, 1–16.

Katz, D. and Braly, K. (1933). Racial stereotypes of one hundred college students. *Journal of Abnormal and Social Psychology*, *28*, 280–90.

Katz, D. and Braly, K. (1935). Racial prejudice and racial stereotypes. *Journal of Abnormal and Social Psychology*, *30*, 175–93.

Katz, D. and Schanck, R. L. (1938). *Social Psychology*. New York: Wiley.

Keil, F. C. (1991). The emergence of theoretical beliefs as constraints and concepts. In S. Corey and R. Gelman (eds), *The Epigenesis of Mind: Essays on biology and cognition* (pp. 237–56). Hillsdale, NJ: Erlbaum.

Kelly, C. (1988). Intergroup differentiation in a political context. *British Journal of Social Psychology*, *27*, 321–7.

Kelly, C. (1989). Political identity and perceived intragroup homogeneity. *British Journal of Social Psychology*, *28*, 239–50.

Kenny, D. A. and La Voie, L. (1984). The social relations model. In L. Berkowitz (ed.), *Advances in Experimental Social Psychology* (vol. 18, pp. 141–82). New York: Academic Press.

Kidder, L. H. and Stewart, V. M. (1975). *The Psychology of Intergroup Relations: Conflict and consciousness*. New York: McGraw-Hill.

Klineberg, O. (1951). The scientific study of national stereotypes. *International Social Science Bulletin*, *3*, 505–15.

Kluegel, J. R. (1988). Economic problems and socioeconomic beliefs and attitudes. *Research in Social Stratification and Mobility*, *7*, 273–302.

Kluegel, J. R. and Smith, E. R. (1986). *Beliefs about Inequality: Americans' views of what is and what ought to be*. New York: Aldine de Gruyter.

Koehler, D. J. (1991). Explanation, imagination, and confidence in judgment. *Psychological Review*, *110*, 499–519.

Komatsu, L. K. (1992). Recent views on conceptual structure. *Psychological Bulletin*, *112*, 500–26.

Kruglanski, A. W. (1989). The psychology of being 'right': The problem of accuracy in social perception and cognition. *Psychological Bulletin*, *106*, 395–409.

Krull, D. S. (1993). Does the grill change the mill? The effect of the perceiver's inferential goal on the process of social inference. *Personality and Social Psychology Bulletin*, *19*, 340–48.

Kulik, J. A. (1983). Confirmatory attribution and the perpetuation of social beliefs. *Journal of Personality and Social Psychology*, *44*, 1171–81.

Kunda, Z. (1990). The case for motivated reasoning. *Psychological Bulletin*, *108*, 480–98.

Kunda, Z., Miller, D. T. and Claire, T. (1990). Combining social concepts: The role of causal reasoning. *Cognitive Science*, *14*, 551–77.

Kunda, Z. and Oleson, K. C. (1995). Maintaining stereotypes in the face of disconfirmation: Constructing grounds for subtyping deviants. *Journal of Personality and Social Psychology*, *68*, 565–79.

Kunda, Z. and Sherman-Williams, B. (1993). Stereotypes and the construal of individuating information. *Personality and Social Psychology Bulletin*, *19*, 90–9.

La Mettrie (1748). *L'homme-machine*. Edition présentée et établie par P. L. Assoun (1981). Paris, Denoël-Gonthier, 'Médiations'.

Lee, Y. T., Jussim, L. J. and McCauley, C. R. (eds) (1995). *Stereotype Accuracy: Toward appreciating group differences*. Washington, D.C.: American Psychological Association.

Lee, Y. T. and Ottati, V. (1995). Perceived in-group homogeneity as a function of group membership salience and stereotype threat. *Personality and Social Psychology Bulletin*, *21*, 610–19.

Lemaine, G. (1974). Social differentiation and social originality. *European Journal of Social Psychology*, *4*, 17–52.

Lemyre, L. and Smith, P. M. (1985). Intergroup discrimination and self-esteem in the minimal group paradigm. *Journal of Personality and Social Psychology*, *49*, 660–70.

Lerner, M. J. (1980). *The Belief in a Just World: A fundamental delusion*. New York: Plenum.

LeVine, R. A. and Campbell, D. T. (1972). *Ethnocentrism*. New York: Wiley.

Lewis, A., Snell, M. and Furnham, A. (1987). Lay explanations for the causes of unemployment in Britain: Economic, individualistic, societal, or fatalistic? *Political Psychology*, *8*, 427–39.

Leyens, J. P. and Bourhis, R. Y. (1994). Epilogue: Perception et relations intergroupes. In R. Y. Bourhis and J. P. Leyens (eds), *Stéréotypes, discrimination et relations intergroupes*. Bruxelles: Mardaga.

Leyens, J.-Ph., Yzerbyt, V. and Schadron, G. (1992). Stereotypes and social judgeability. In W. Stroebe and M. Hewstone (eds), *European Review of Social Psychology* (vol. 3, pp. 91–120). Chichester: Wiley.

Leyens, J.-P., Yzerbyt, V. and Schadron, G. (1994). *Stereotypes and Social Cognition.* London: Sage.

Linville, P. W. (1982). The complexity-extremity effect and age-based stereotyping. *Journal of Personality and Social Psychology, 42,* 193–211.

Linville, P. W. (1985). Self-complexity and affective extremity: Don't put all your eggs in one cognitive basket. *Social Cognition, 3,* 94–120.

Linville, P. W. (1987). Self-complexity as a cognitive buffer against stress-related illness and depression. *Journal of Personality and Social Psychology, 52,* 663–76.

Linville, P. W., Fischer, G. W. and Salovey, P. (1989). Perceived distributions of the characteristics of in-group and out-group members: Empirical evidence and a computer simulation. *Journal of Personality and Social Psychology, 57,* 165–88.

Linville, P. W. and Jones, E. E. (1980). Polarized appraisals of outgroup members. *Journal of Personality and Social Psychology, 38,* 689–703.

Linville, P. W., Salovey, P. and Fischer, G. W. (1986). Stereotyping and perceived distribution of social characteristics: An application to ingroup–outgroup perception. In J. Dovidio and S. L. Gaertner (eds), *Prejudice, Discrimination and Racism* (pp. 165–8). New York: Academic Press.

Lippmann, W. (1922). *Public Opinion.* New York: Harcourt, Brace, Jovanovitch.

Locksley, A., Borgida, E., Brekke, N. and Hepburn, C. (1980). Sex stereotypes and social judgment. *Journal of Personality and Social Psychology, 39,* 821–31.

Locksley, A., Hepburn, C. and Ortiz, V. (1982). Social stereotypes and judgments of individuals: An instance of the base-rate fallacy. *Journal of Experimental Social Psychology, 18,* 23–42.

Long, K. and Spears, R. (1995). Opposing effects of personal and collective self-esteem on interpersonal and intergroup evaluations. Unpublished manuscript, Sussex University.

Long, K. M., Spears, R. and Manstead, A. S. R. (1994). The influence of personal and collective self-esteem on strategies of social differentiation. *British Journal of Social Psychology, 33,* 313–29.

Luhtanen, R. and Crocker, J. (1991). Self-esteem and intergroup comparisons: Toward a theory of collective self-esteem. In J. Suls and T. A. Wills (eds), *Social Comparison: Contemporary theory and research* (pp. 211–34). Hillsdale, NJ: Lawrence Erlbaum.

Luhtanen, R. and Crocker, J. (1992). A collective self-esteem scale: Self-evaluation of one's social identity. *Personality and Social Psychology Bulletin, 18,* 302–18.

Maass, A. and Schaller, M. (1991). Intergroup biases and the cognitive dynamics of stereotype formation. *European Review of Social Psychology, 2,* 189–209.

Mackie, D. M. and Hamilton, D. L. (eds) (1993). *Affect, Cognition, and Stereotyping: Interactive processes in group perception.* Academic Press: San Diego.

Mackie, D. M., Worth, L. T. and Asuncion, A. G. (1990). Processing of persuasive ingroup messages. *Journal of Personality and Social Psychology, 58,* 812–22.

Mackie, M. (1973). Arriving at 'truth' by definition: The case of stereotype inaccuracy. *Social Problems, 20,* 431–47.

Macrae, C. N., Hewstone, M. and Griffiths, R. J. (1993). Processing load and memory for stereotype-based information. *European Journal of Social Psychology, 23,* 77–87.

Macrae, C. N., Milne, A. B. and Bodenhausen, G. V. (1994). Stereotypes as energy-saving devices: A peek inside the cognitive toolbox. *Journal of Personality and Social Psychology, 66,* 37–47.

Macrae, C. N., Stangor, C. and Hewstone, M. (eds) (1996). *Stereotypes and Stereotyping*. New York: Guilford Press.

Macrae, C. N., Stangor, C. and Milne, A. B. (1994). Activating social stereotypes: A functional analysis. *Journal of Experimental Social Psychology, 30*, 370–89.

Major, B. (1994). From social inequality to personal entitlement: The role of social comparisons, legitimacy appraisals, and group memberships. *Advances in Experimental Social Psychology, 26*, 293–355.

Major, J. (1992). *Trust the People: Keynote speeches in the 1992 election campaign*. London: Conservative Political Centre.

Mansbridge, J. (1986). *Why We Lost the E.R.A.* Chicago: University of Chicago Press.

Marger, M. N. (1991). *Race and Ethnic Relations* (2nd edn). Belmont, CA: Wadsworth.

Marks, M. L. and Mirvis, P. (1985). Merger syndrome: Stress and uncertainty. *Mergers & Acquisitions, Summer*, 50–5.

Markus, H. R. and Kitayama, S. (1991). Culture and the self: Implications for cognition, emotion, and motivation. *Psychological Review, 98*, 224–53.

Markus, H. and Zajonc, R. (1985). The cognitive perspective in social psychology. In G. Lindzey and E. Aronson (eds), *Handbook of Social Psychology* (vol. 1, pp. 137–230). New York: Random House.

Marques, J. M. (1990). The black-sheep effect: Outgroup homogeneity in social comparison settings. In D. Abrams and M. A. Hogg (eds), *Social Identity Theory: Constructive and critical advances* (pp. 131–51). Hemel Hempstead: Harvester Wheatsheaf.

Marr, A. (1992). *The Battle for Scotland*. Harmondsworth: Penguin.

Martin, C. L. and Parker, S. (1995). Folk theories about sex and race differences. *Personality and Social Psychology Bulletin, 21*, 45–57.

Marx, K. (1978). The German Ideology/Manifesto of the Communist Party. In R. C. Tucker (ed.), *The Marx–Engels Reader* (2nd edn). New York: W. W. Norton & Company.

Marx, K. and Engels, F. (1846/1968). *L'idéologie allemande*. Paris: Editions Sociales.

McCauley, C. (1988). The content of awareness and top-down versus bottom-up processing. In T. K. Srull and R. S. Wyer (eds), *Advances in Social Cognition* (vol. 1, pp. 119–26). Hillsdale, NJ: Erlbaum.

McCauley, C., Jussim, L. and Lee, Y. T. (1995). The time is now: Stereotype accuracy and intergroup relations. In Y. T. Lee, L. Jussim and C. McCauley (eds), *Stereotype Accuracy: Toward appreciating group differences*. Washington, D.C.: American Psychological Association.

McCauley, C. and Stitt, C. L. (1978). An individual and quantitative measure of stereotypes. *Journal of Personality and Social Psychology, 36*, 929–40.

McConnell, A. R., Sherman, S. J. and Hamilton, D. L. (1994a). On-line and memory-based aspects of individual and group target judgments. *Journal of Personality and Social Psychology, 67*, 173–85.

McConnell, A. R., Sherman, S. J. and Hamilton, D. L. (1994b). Illusory correlation in the perception of groups: An extension of the distinctiveness-based account. *Journal of Personality and Social Psychology, 67*, 414–29.

McCrone, D. (1992). *Understanding Scotland: The sociology of a stateless nation*. London: Routledge.

McGarty, C. (1990). Categorization and the social psychology of judgment. Unpublished Ph.D. thesis, Macquarie University.

McGarty, C. (1993, September). Illusory correlation as the accentuation of actual differences between groups. Paper presented to the Xth General Meeting of the European Association of Experimental Social Psychologists, Lisbon.

McGarty, C., Haslam, S. A., Hutchinson, K. J. and Grace, D. M. (1995). Determinants of perceived consistency: The relationship between group entitativity and the meaningfulness of categories. *British Journal of Social Psychology, 34*, 237–56.

McGarty, C., Haslam, S. A., Hutchinson, K. J. and Turner, J. C. (1994). The effects of salient group memberships on persuasion. *Small Group Research, 25*, 267–93.

McGarty, C., Haslam, S. A., Turner, J. C. and Oakes, P. J. (1993). Illusory correlation as accentuation of actual intercategory difference: Evidence for the effect with minimal stimulus information. *European Journal of Social Psychology, 23*, 391–410.

McGarty, C. and Penny, R. E. C. (1988). Categorization, accentuation and social judgement. *British Journal of Social Psychology, 27*, 147–57.

McGarty, C. and Turner, J. C. (1992). The effects of categorization on social judgement. *British Journal of Social Psychology, 31*, 253–68.

McGarty, C., Turner, J. C., Oakes, P. J. and Haslam, S. A. (1993). The creation of uncertainty in the influence process: The role of stimulus information and disagreement with similar others. *European Journal of Social Psychology, 23*, 17–38.

McGuire, W. J. (1984). Search for the self: Going beyond self-esteem and the reactive self. In R. A. Zucker, J. Aronoff and A. I. Rabin (eds), *Personality and the prediction of behavior* (pp. 73–120). New York: Academic Press.

McGuire, W. J. (1989). A perspectivist approach to the strategic planning of programmatic scientific research. In B. Gholson, W. R. Shadish, Jr., R. A. Niemeyer and A. C. Houts (eds), *The Psychology of Science: Contributions to metascience* (pp. 214–45). New York: Cambridge University Press.

McGuire, W. J. and McGuire, C. V. (1988). Content and process in the experience of self. In L. Berkowitz (ed.), *Advances in Experimental Social Psychology* (vol. 21, pp. 97–144). New York: Academic Press, Inc.

McGuire, W. J. and Padawer-Singer, A. (1976). Trait salience in the spontaneous self-concept. *Journal of Personality and Social Psychology, 33*, 743–54.

Medin, D. L. (1988). A commentary on 'a dual process model of impression formation' by M. Brewer. In T. K. Srull and R. S. Wyer (eds), *Advances in Social Cognition, vol. 1* (pp. 119–26). Hillsdale, NJ: Erlbaum.

Medin, D. L. (1989). Concepts and conceptual structure. *American Psychologist, 44*, 1469–81.

Medin, D. L., Goldstone, R. L. and Gentner, D. (1993). Respects for similarity. *Psychological Review, 100*, 254–78.

Medin, D. L. and Ortony, A. (1989). Psychological essentialism. In S. Vosniadou and A. Ortony (eds), *Similarity and Analogical Reasoning* (pp. 179–95). Cambridge: Cambridge University Press.

Medin, D. L. and Shaffer, M. M. (1978). Context theory of classification learning. *Psychological Review, 85*, 207–38.

Medin, D. L. and Shoben, E. J. (1988). Context and structure in conceptual combination. *Cognitive Psychology, 20*, 158–90.

Medin, D. L. and Wattenmaker, W. D. (1987). Category cohesiveness, theories, and cognitve archeology. In U. Neisser (ed.), *Concepts and Conceptual Development. Ecological and intellectual factors in categorization*. Cambridge: Cambridge University Press.

Meenes, M. (1943). A comparison of racial stereotypes of 1935 and 1942. *Journal of Social Psychology*, *17*, 327–36.

Merton, R. (1957). *Social Theory and Social Structure*. Glencoe: Free Press.

Messick, D. M. and Mackie, D. M. (1989). Intergroup relations. In M. R. Rosenzweig and L. W. Porter (eds), *Annual Review of Psychology* (vol. 40, pp. 45–81). Palo Alto, CA: Annual Review.

Milgram, S. (1974). Soumission à l'autorité. Paris: Calmann-Lévy.

Miller, G. A. (1956). The magic number seven, plus or minus two. *Psychological Review*, *63*, 81–97.

Miller, J. G. (1984). Culture and the development of everyday social explanation. *Journal of Personality and Social Psychology*, *46*, 961–78.

Miller, N., Brewer, M. B. and Edwards, K. (1985). Cooperative interaction in desegregated settings: A laboratory analogue. *Journal of Social Issues*, *41*(3), 63–79.

Mischel, W. (1981). *Introduction to Personality* (3rd edn). New York: Holt, Rinehart and Winston.

Mlicki, P. and Ellemers, N. (1996). Being different or being better? National stereotypes and identifications of Polish and Dutch students. *European Journal of Social Psychology*, *26*, 97–114.

Monteith, M. J., Devine, P. G. and Zuwerink, J. R. (1993). Self-directed versus other-directed affect as a consequence of prejudice-related discrepancies. *Journal of Personality and Social Psychology*, *64*, 198–210.

Morris, M. W., Nisbett, R. E. and Peng, K. (1994). In G. Lewis, D. Premack and D. Sperber (eds), *Causal Understanding in Cognition and Culture*. Oxford: Oxford University Press.

Morris, M. W. and Peng, K. (1994). Culture and cause: American and Chinese attributions of social and physical events. *Journal of Personality and Social Pscyhology*, *67*, 949–71.

Moscovici, S. (1961). *La Psychanalyse: Son Image et Son Public*. Paris: Presses Universitaires de France.

Moscovici, S. (1980). Towards a theory of conversion behavior. In L. Berkowitz (ed.), *Advances in Experimental Social Psychology* (vol. 13, pp. 209–39). New York: Academic Press.

Moscovici, S. (1984). The phenomenon of social representations. In R. M. Farr and S. Moscovici (eds), *Social Representations*. Cambridge: Cambridge University Press.

Mottola, G. R., Bachman, B. A. and Gaertner, S. L. (1995). How groups merge: The effects of merger integration patterns on expectations of organizational commitment. Unpublished manuscript, University of Delaware.

Mullen, B. (1991). Group composition, salience, and cognitive representations: The phenomenology of being in a group. *Journal of Experimental Social Psychology*, *27*, 297–323.

Mullen, B., Brown, R. and Smith, C. (1992). Ingroup bias as a function of salience, relevance, and status: An integration. *European Journal of Social Psychology*, *22*, 103–22.

Mullen, B. and Johnson, C. (1990). Distinctiveness-based illusory correlations and stereotyping: A meta-analytic integration. *British Journal of Social Psychology*, *29*, 11–28.

Mummendey, A. and Schreiber, H. J. (1983). Better or just different?: Positive social identity by discrimination against or differentiation from outgroups. *European Journal of Social Psychology*, *13*, 389–97.

Mummendey, A. and Schreiber, H.-J. (1984). Different just means better: Some obvious and some hidden pathways to ingroup favouritism. *British Journal of Social Psychology*, *23*, 363–68.

Mummendey, A. and Simon, B. (1989). Better or just different? III: The impact of comparison dimension and relative group size upon intergroup discrimination. *British Journal of Social Psychology*, *28*, 1–16.

Murphy, G. L. and Medin, D. L. (1985). The role of theories in conceptual coherence. *Psychological Review*, *92*, 289–316.

Mussen, P. H. (1950). Some personality and social factors related to children's attitudes towards Negroes. *Journal of Abnormal and Social Psychology*, *45*, 423–41.

Neuberg, S. L. (1989). The goal of forming accurate impressions during social interactions: Attenuating the impact of negative expectancies. *Journal of Personality and Social Psychology*, *56*, 374–86.

Neuberg, S. L. and Fiske, S. T. (1987). Motivational influences on impression formation: Outcome dependency, accuracy-driven attention, and individuating processes. *Journal of Personality and Social Psychology*, *53*, 431–44.

Newman, L. S. (1991). Why are traits inferred spontaneously? A developmental approach. *Social Cognition*, *9*, 221–53.

Newman, L. S. (1993). How individualists interpret behavior: Idiocentrism and spontaneous trait inference. *Social Cognition*, *11*, 243–69.

Ng, S. H. (1980). *The Social Psychology of Power*. New York: Academic Press.

Ng, S. H. (1981). Equity theory and the allocations of rewards between groups. *European Journal of Social Psychology*, *11*, 439–43.

Ng, S. H. (1982). Power and intergroup discrimination. In H. Tajfel (ed.), *Social Identity and Intergroup Relations*. Cambridge: Cambridge University Press.

Ng, S. and Bradac, J. (1993). *Power in Language: Verbal communication and social influence*. Newbury Park, CA: Sage.

Nisbett, R. E. and Ross, L. (1980). *Human Inference: Strategies and shortcomings of social judgment*. Englewood Cliffs, NJ: Prentice Hall.

Noel, J. G., Wann, D. and Branscombe, N. (1995). Peripheral ingroup membership status and public negativity toward outgroups. *Journal of Personality and Social Psychology*, *68*, 127–37.

Nolan, M. (1995). Testing between resource-based and fit-based theories of stereotyping: Challenging the cognitive miser metaphor. Honours thesis, Department of Psychology, Australian National University.

Oakes, P. J. (1987). The salience of social categories. In J. C. Turner, M. A. Hogg, P. J. Oakes, S. D. Reicher and M. S. Wetherell (eds), *Rediscovering the Social Group* (A self-categorization theory, pp. 117–41). Oxford: Basil Blackwell.

Oakes, P. J. (1993). Stereotype accuracy: Is measurement the route to enlightenment? Paper presented at the General Meeting of the European Association of Experimental Social Psychology, Lisbon, September 15–20.

Oakes, P. J. (in press). The categorization process: Cognition and the group in the social psychology of stereotyping. In W. P. Robinson (ed.), *A Festschrift for Henri Tajfel*. Oxford: Butterworth Heineman.

Oakes, P. J., Haslam, S. A. and Turner, J. C. (1994). *Stereotyping and Social Reality*. Oxford: Blackwell.

Oakes, P. J. and Reynolds, K. J. (1995). Resources, reality and the relationship between stereotyping and individuation. Paper presented at the Third Münster Workshop on the Social Identity Approach, Muenster/Rothenberge, March 22–24.

Oakes, P. J. and Turner, J. C. (1980). Social categorization and intergroup behaviour: Does minimal intergroup discrimination make social identity more positive? *European Journal of social Psychology*, *10*, 295–301.

Oakes, P. J. and Turner, J. C. (1986). Distinctiveness and the salience of social category memberships: Is there a perceptual bias towards novelty? *European Journal of Social Psychology*, *16*, 325–44.

Oakes, P. J. and Turner, J. C. (1990). Is limited information processing the cause of social stereotyping? In W. Stroebe and M. Hewstone (eds), *European Review of Social Psychology* (vol. 1, pp. 111–35). Chichester, UK: Wiley.

Oakes, P. J., Turner, J. C. and Haslam, S. A. (1991). Perceiving people as group members: The role of fit in the salience of social categorizations. *British Journal of Social Psychology*, *30*, 125–44.

Osgood, C. E., Suci, H. J. and Tannenbaum, P. H. (1957). *The Measurement of Meaning*. Urbana, IL: University of Illinois Press.

Ostrom, T. M., Carpenter, S. L., Sedikides, C. and Li, F. (1993). Differential processing of in-group and out-group information. *Journal of Personality and Social Psychology*, *64*, 21–34.

Ostrom, T. M. and Sedikides, C. (1992). Outgroup homogeneity effects in natural and minimal groups. *Psychological Bulletin*, *112*, 536–52.

Ottati, V. and Lee, Y.-T. (1995). Accuracy: A neglected component of stereotyping research. In Y.-T. Lee, L. Jussim and C. McCauley (eds), *Stereotype Accuracy: Toward appreciating group differences*. Washington, D.C.: American Psychological Association.

Park, B., DeKay, M. L. and Kraus, S. (1994). Aggregating social behavior into person models: Perceiver-induced consistency. *Journal of Personality and Social Psychology*, *66*, 437–59.

Park, B. and Judd, C. M. (1990). Measures and models of perceived group variability. *Journal of Personality and Social Psychology*, *59*, 173–91.

Park, B., Judd, C. M. and Ryan, C. S. (1991). Social categorization and the representation of variability information. In W. Stroebe and M. Hewstone (eds), *European Review of Social Psychology* (vol. 2, pp. 211–45). Chichester: Wiley.

Park, B. and Rothbart, M. (1982). Perception of out-group homogeneity and levels of social categorization: Memory for the subordinate attributes of in-group and out-group members. *Journal of Personality and Social Psychology*, *42*, 1051–68.

Peabody, D. (1968). Group judgments in the Philippines: Evaluative and descriptive aspects. *Journal of Personality and Social Psychology*, *10*, 290–300.

Pendry, L. F. and Macrae, C. N. (1994). Stereotypes and mental life: The case of the motivated but thwarted tactician. *Journal of Experimental Social Psychology*, *30*, 303–25.

Perreault, S., Senécal, S. and Bourhis, R. Y. (1994). Discrimination intergroupe: La théorie de l'identité sociale vs le modèle de l'interaction comportementale. Paper presented at the 17th Annual Congress of the Société Québécoise pour la recherche en psychologie, Montréal, Canada.

Peterson, C. R. (1980). Recognition of noncontingency. *Journal of Personality and Social Psychology*, *38*, 727–34.

Piliavin, J. A., Dovidio, J. F., Gaertner, S. L. and Clark, R. D., III. (1981). *Emergency Intervention*. New York: Academic Press.

Popper, K. R. (1982). *Logik der Forschung* (7. Auflage). Tübingen: Mohr.

Porter, J. R. and Washington, R. E. (1993). Minority identity and self-esteem. *Annual Review of Sociology*, *19*, 139–61.

Potter, J. and Litton, I. (1985). Some problems underlying the theory of social representations. *British Journal of Social Psychology*, *24*, 81–90.

Potter, J. and Wetherell, M. (1987). *Discourse and Social Psychology: Beyond attitudes and behaviour*. London: Sage.

Pratto, F. and Bargh, J. A. (1991). Stereotyping based on apparently individuating information: Trait and global components of sex stereotypes under attention overload. *Journal of Experimental Social Psychology*, *27*, 26–47.

Prothro, E. T. and Melikian, L. H. (1955). Studies in stereotypes: V. Familiarity and the kernel of truth hypothesis. *Journal of Social Psychology*, *41*, 3–10.

Pryor, J. B. (1986). The influence of different encoding sets upon the formation of illusory correlations and group impressions. *Personality and Social Psychology Bulletin*, *12*, 216–26.

Quattrone, G. A. (1982). Overattribution and unit formation: When behavior engulfs the person. *Journal of Personality and Social Psychology*, *42*, 593–607.

Rabbie, J. M. (1991). Determinants of instrumental intra-group cooperation. In R. A. Hinde and J. Groebel (eds), *Cooperation and Prosocial Behaviour*. Cambridge: Cambridge University Press.

Rabbie, J. M. and Horwitz, M. (1988). Categories versus groups as explanatory concepts in intergroup relations. *European Journal of Social Psychology*, *18*, 117–23.

Rabbie, J. M., Schot, J. C. and Visser, L. (1989). Social identity theory: A conceptual and empirical critique from the perspective of a behavioural interaction model. *European Journal of Social Psychology*, *19*, 171–202.

Read, S. J. (1987). Constructing causal scenarios: A knowledge structure approach to causal reasoning. *Journal of Personality and Social Psychology*, *52*, 288–302.

Reicher, S. D. (1988). From 'race' to racialization: Changing the object of psychological enquiry. Paper presented at the BPS Social Section Conference, September.

Reicher, S. D. (1993a). The national constitution: An argumentative approach to the definition and salience of national identities. Worshop on 'National Identities in Europe', Lisbon.

Reicher, S. D. (1993b). On the construction of social categories: From collective action to rhetoric and back again. In B. Gonzalez (ed.), *Psicologia Cultural*. Seville: Eudema.

Reicher, S. D. (1995). Three dimensions of the social self. In A. Oosterwegel and R. Wicklund (eds), *The Self in European and North American Culture*. Amsterdam: Kluwer.

Reicher, S. D. (1996). The Battle of Westminster: Developing the social identity model of crowd behaviour in order to deal with the initiation and development of collective conflict. *European Journal of Social Psychology*, *26*, 115–34.

Reicher, S. D. (in press, a). Social identity and social change: Rethinking the context of social psychology. In W. P. Robinson (ed.), *A Festschrift for Henri Tajfel*. Oxford: Butterworth Heinemann.

Reicher, S. D. (in press, b). What is critical in critical psychology? In T. Ibañez and L. Iñiguez (eds), *Critical Social Psychology*. London: Sage.

Reicher, S. D. and Hopkins, N. (in press, a). Seeking influence through characterising self-categories: An analysis of anti-abortionist rhetoric. *British Journal of Social Psychology*.

Reicher, S. D. and Hopkins, N. (in press, b). Constructing categories and mobilising masses: An analysis of Thatcher's and Kinnock's speeches on the British miner's strike 1984–5. *European Journal of Social Psychology*.

Reicher, S. D., Hopkins, N. and Condor, S. (in press). The lost nation of psychology. In C. Barfoot (ed.), *National Stereotypes and Racial Purity*. DQR Studies in Literature.

Reicher, S. D., Spears, R. and Postmes, T. (1995). A social identity model of deindividuation phenomena. *European Review of Social Psychology*, 6, 161–98.

Reynolds, K. J. (1995). Beyond the information given: Capacity, context and the categorization process in impression formation. Unpublished Ph.D. thesis, The Australian National University.

Reynolds, K. J. and Oakes, P. J. (1995). When do we stereotype and individuate others? An examination of context and attentional resources. Paper presented at the 24th Meeting of Australian Social Psychologists/ Inaugural meeting of the Society of Australasian Social Psychologists, Tasmania, 22–25 April.

Riley, T. and Fiske, S. T. (1991). Interdependence and the social context of impression formation. *European Bulletin of Cognitive Psychology*, 11, 173–92.

Roccas, S. and Schwartz, S. H. (1993). Effects of intergroup similarity on intergroup relations. *European Journal of Social Psychology*, 23, 581–95.

Rogers, T. B. (1981). A model of the self as an aspect of the human information processing system. In N. Cantor and J. F. Kihlstrom (eds), *Personality, Cognition, and Social Interaction* (pp. 193–214). Hillsdale, NJ: Erlbaum.

Rojahn, K. and Pettigrew, T. F. (1992). Memory for schema-consistent and schema-inconsistent information: A meta-analytic resolution. *British Journal of Social Psychology*, 31, 81–109.

Rokeach, M. (1960). *The Open and the Closed Mind*. New York: Basic Books.

Rokeach, M., Smith, P. and Evans, R. (1960). Two kinds of prejudice or one? In M. Rokeach, *The Open and the Closed Mind* (pp. 132–68). New York: Basic Books.

Rosch, E. (1978). Principles of categorization. In E. Rosch and B. Lloyd (eds), *Cognition and Categorization* (pp. 28–49). Hillsdale, NJ: Erlbaum.

Rosch, E. and Mervis, C. B. (1975). Family resemblances: Studies in the internal structure of categories. *Cognitive Psychology*, 7, 573–605.

Rosenberg, M. (1965). *Society and the Adolescent Self-Image*. Princeton, NJ: Princeton University Press.

Rosenberg, S., Nelson, C. and Vivekanathan, P. S. (1968). A multidimensional approach to the structure of personality impressions. *Journal of Personality and Social Psychology*, 9, 283–94.

Rosenberg, S. and Sedlak, A. (1972). Structural representations of implicit personality theory. In L. Berkowitz (ed.), *Advances in Experimental Social Psychology* (vol. 6, pp. 235–97). New York: Academic Press.

Ross, L. (1977). The intuitive psychologist and his shortcomings: Distortions in the attribution process. In L. Berkowitz (ed.), *Advances in Experimental Social Psychology* (vol. 10, pp. 173–220). New York: Academic Press.

Ross, L. and Nisbett, R. E. (1991). *The Person and the Situation: Perspectives of social psychology*. New York: McGraw-Hill.

Ross, L., Amabile, T. M. and Steinmetz, J. L. (1977). Social roles, social control, and biases in social-perception processes. *Journal of Personality and Social Psychology*, *35*, 485–94.

Ross, L., Lepper, M. R. and Hubbard, M. (1975). Perseverance in self-perception: Biased attributional processes in the debriefing paradigm. *Journal of Personality and Social Psychology*, *32*, 880–92.

Rothbart, M. (1981). Memory and social beliefs. In D. Hamilton (ed.), *Cognitive Processes in Stereotyping and Intergroup Relations* (pp. 145–81). Hillsdale, NJ: Erlbaum.

Rothbart, M., Evans, M. and Fulero, S. (1979). Recall for confirming events: Memory processes and the maintenance of social stereotypes. *Journal of Experimental Social Psychology*, *15*, 343–55.

Rothbart, M., Fulero, S., Jensen, C., Howard, J. and Birrell, P. (1978). From individual to group impressions: Availability heuristics in stereotype formation. *Journal of Experimental Social Psychology*, *14*, 237–55.

Rothbart, M. and John, O. (1985). Social categorization and behavioral episodes: A cognitive analysis of the effects of intergroup contact. *Journal of Social Issues*, *41*, 81–104.

Rothbart, M. and Taylor, M. (1992). Category labels and social reality: Do we view social categories as natural kinds? In G. Semin and K. Fiedler (eds), *Language, Interaction and Social Cognition* (pp. 11–36). London: Sage.

Rothgerber, H. and Worchel, S. (1995). Relations between disadvantaged groups. Unpublished manuscript: Texas A&M University.

Ruggiero, K. M. and Taylor, D. M. (1995). Coping with discrimination: How disadvantaged group members perceive the discrimination that confronts them. *Journal of Personality and Social Psychology*, *68*, 826–38.

Ruscher, J. B. and Fiske, S. T. (1990). Interpersonal competition can cause individuating processes. *Journal of Personality and Social Psychology*, *58*, 832–43.

Ruscher, J. B., Fiske, S. T., Miki, H. and Van Manen, S. (1991). Individuating processes in competition: Interpersonal versus intergroup. *Personality and Social Psychology Bulletin*, *17*, 595–605.

Sachdev, I. and Bourhis, R. Y. (1984). Minimal majorities and minorities. *European Journal of Social Psychology*, *14*, 35–52.

Sachdev, I. and Bourhis, R. Y. (1985). Social categorization and power differentials in group relations. *European Journal of Social Psychology*, *15*, 415–34.

Sachdev, I. and Bourhis, R. Y. (1987). Status differentials and intergroup behaviour. *European Journal of Social Psychology*, *17*, 277–93.

Sachdev, I. and Bourhis, R. Y. (1991). Power and status differentials in minority and majority group relations. *European Journal of Social Psychology*, *21*, 1–24.

Sagar, H. A. and Schofield, J. W. (1980). Racial and behavioral cues in black and white children's perceptions of ambiguously aggressive acts. *Journal of Personality and Social Psychology*, *39*, 590–98.

Sande, G. N., Ellard, H. J. and Ross, M. (1986). Effect of arbitrarily assigned status labels on self-perceptions and social perceptions: The mere position effect. *Journal of Personality and Social Psychology*, *50*, 684–9.

Sani, F. (1995). *The Social Psychology of Schisms*. Unpublished Ph.D. thesis, University of Exeter.

Sani, F. and Reicher, S. (1995). Genesis of a schism: arguing about women priests and the identity of the church of England. Paper presented at the Annual Conference of the Social Section of the British Psychological Society, York.

Sayer, D. (1983). *Marx's Method: Ideology, science & critique in 'Capital'*, Sussex: Harvester.

Schadron, G., Morchain, P. and Yzerbyt, V. (1994). Le rôle de la fonction explicative dans le développement des stéréotypes. Manuscript submitted for publication, Catholic University of Lille.

Schadron, G. H. and Yzerbyt, V. Y. (1993). Les stéréotypes et l'approche de la jugeabilité sociale: un impact des stéréotypes sur le jugement indépendant de leur contenu. In J. L. Beauvois, R. V. Joule and J. M. Monteil (eds), *Perspectives cognitives et conduites sociales* (vol. 4, pp. 15–35). Neuchâtel-Paris: Delachaux & Niestlé.

Schaller, M. (1991). Social categorization and the formation of group stereotypes: Further evidence for biased information processing in the perception of group-behavior correlations. *European Journal of Social Psychology*, *21*, 25–35.

Schaller, M. (1992). In-group favoritism and statistical reasoning in social inference: Implications for formation and maintenance of group stereotypes. *Journal of Personality and Social Psychology*, *63*, 61–74.

Schaller, M. and Maass, A. (1989). Illusory correlation and social categorization: Toward an integration of motivational and cognitive factors in stereotype formation. *Journal of Personality and Social Psychology*, *56*, 709–21.

Schermerhorn, R. A. (1970). *Comparative Ethnic Relations: A framework for theory and research*. New York: Random House.

Schoenfeld, N. (1942). An experimental study of some problems relating to stereotypes. *Archives of Psychology*, No. 270.

Schoennauer, A. W. (1967). Behavior patterns of executives in business acquisitions. *Personnel Administration*, *(Jan.–Feb.)*, 27–32.

Schopler, J. and Insko, A. (1992). The discontinuity effect in interpersonal and intergroup relations: Generality and mediation. In W. Stroebe and M. Hewstone (eds), *European Review of Social Psychology* (pp. 121–51). Chichester: John Wiley & Sons, Inc.

Schuman, H. (1966). Social change and the validity of regional stereotypes in East Pakistan. *Sociometry*, *29*, 428–40.

Schwarz, B. (1982). 'The people' in history: The Communist Party Historians' Group, 1946–56. In R. Johnson, G. McLennan, B. Schwarz and D. Sutton (eds), *Making History: Studies in history writing and politics*. London: Hutchinson.

Seago, D. W. (1947). Stereotypes: Before Pearl Harbour and after. *Journal of Social Psychology*, *23*, 55–63.

Sedikides, C. and Anderson, C. A. (1994). Causal perceptions of intertrait relations: The glue that holds person types together. *Personality and Social Psychology Bulletin*, *20*, 294–302.

Semin, G. R. (1985). The 'phenomenon of social representations'. *British Journal of Social Psychology*, *24*, 93–4.

Semin, G. R. and Fiedler, K. (1988). The cognitive functions of linguistic categories in describing persons: Social cognition and language. *Journal of Personality and Social Psychology*, *54*, 558–68.

Semin, G. R. and Krahé, B. (1987). Lay conceptions of personality: Eliciting tiers of a scientific conception of personality. *European Journal of Social Psychology*, *17*, 199–209.

Sherif, M. (1948). *An Outline of Social Psychology*. New York: Harper and Row.

Sherif, M. (1967). *Group Conflict and Co-operation: Their social psychology*. London: Routledge and Kegan Paul.

Sherif, M. and Cantril, H. (1947). *The Social Psychology of Ego-involvements, Social Attitudes and Identifications*. New York: Wiley.

Sherif, M. and Sherif, C. W. (1969). *Social Psychology*. New York: Harper & Row.

Sherman, S. J., Hamilton, D. L. and Roskos-Ewoldsen, D. R. (1989). Attenuation of illusory correlation. *Personality and Social Psychology Bulletin*, *15*, 559–71.

Shipman, P. (1994). *The Evolution of Racism: Human differences and the use and abuse of science*. New York: Simon & Schuster.

Shrauger, J. S. (1975). Responses to evaluation as a function of intitial self-perceptions. *Psychological Bulletin*, *82*, 581–96.

Sidanius, J. and Pratto, F. (1993). The inevitability of oppression and the dynamics of social dominance. In P. Sniderman, P. E. Tetlock and E. G. Carmines (eds), *Prejudice, Politics, and the American Dilemma* (pp. 173–211). Stanford, CA: Stanford University Press.

Simmel, G. (1955). *The Web of Group-affiliations* (Translation of 'Die Kreuzung sozialer Kreise', Soziologie (München: Duncker & Humblot) by Reinhard Bendix). New York: The Free Press.

Simon, B. (1992a). The perception of ingroup and outgroup homogeneity: Reintroducing the social context. *European Review of Social Psychology*, *3*, 1–30.

Simon, B. (1992b). Intragroup differentiation in terms of ingroup and outgroup attributes. *European Journal of Social Psychology*, *22*, 407–13.

Simon, B. (1993). On the asymmetry in the cognitive construal of ingroup and outgroup: A model of egocentric social categorization. *European Journal of Social Psychology*, *23*, 131–47.

Simon, B. (1994). *Individuelles und kollektives Selbst: Zur selbst-interpretatorischen Grundlage von Individuum und Gruppe in modernen Gesellschaften*. Berichte aus dem Psychologischen Institut IV, Universität Münster, Oktober 1994 (auch: Positionsreferat auf dem 39. Kongreß der Deutschen Gesellschaft für Psychologie in Hamburg, 25.–29. September 1994).

Simon, B. and Brown, R. J. (1987). Perceived intragroup homogeneity in minority–majority contexts. *Journal of Personality and Social Psychology*, *53*, 703–11.

Simon, B. and Hamilton, D. L. (1994). Self-stereotyping and social context: The effects of relative in-group size and in-group status. *Journal of Personality and Social Psychology*, *66*, 699–711.

Simon, B., Pantaleo, G. and Mummendey, A. (1995). Unique individual or interchangeable group member? The accentuation of intragroup differences versus similarities as an indicator of the individual self versus the collective self. *Journal of Personality and Social Psychology*, *69*, 106–19.

Slugoski, B. R., Sarson, D. A. and Krank, M. D. (1991). Cognitive load has paradoxical effects on the formation of illusory correlations. Unpublished manuscript, Mount Allison University.

Smith, E. E. and Medin, D. L. (1981). *Categories and Concepts.* Cambridge, MA: Harvard University Press.

Smith, E. R. (1991). Illusory correlation in a simulated exemplar-based memory. *Journal of Experimental Social Psychology, 27,* 107–23.

Smith, E. R. (in press). What do connectionism and social psychology offer each other? *Journal of Personality and Social Psychology.*

Smith, E. R. and Zárate, M. A. (1990). Exemplar and prototype use in social categorization. *Social Cognition, 8,* 243–62.

Smith, E. R. and Zárate, M. A. (1992). Exemplar-based model of social judgment. *Psychological Review, 99,* 3–21.

Smith, H. J. and Tyler, T. R. (1995). No disrespect: Social reputations, self-esteem and group behavior. Unpublished manuscript, University of California, Berkeley.

Smith, J. and Russell, G. (1984). Why do males and females differ: Children's beliefs about sex differences. *Sex Roles, 11,* 1111–20.

Snyder, C. R. and Fromkin, H. L. (1980). *Uniqueness: The human pursuit of difference.* New York: Plenum Press.

Snyder, M. (1984). When belief creates reality. In L. Berkowitz (ed.), *Advances in Experimental Social Psychology* (vol. 18, pp. 248–306). New York: Academic Press.

Snyder, M. (1992). Motivational foundations of behavioral confirmation. In M. P. Zanna (ed.), *Advances in Experimental Social Psychology* (vol. 25, pp. 67–114). San Diego, CA: Academic Press.

Snyder, M. and DeBono, K. G. (1989). Identifying attitude functions: Lessons from personality and social behavior. In A. R. Pratkanis, S. J. Breckler and A. G. Greenwald (eds), *Attitude Structure and Function* (pp. 339–59). Hillsdale, NJ: Erlbaum.

Snyder, M. and Miene, P. K. (1994). Stereotyping of the elderly: A functional approach. Special Issue: Stereotypes: Structure, function and process. *British Journal of Social Psychology, 33,* 63–82.

Snyder, M. and Swann, W. B. (1978). Hypothesis-testing processes in social interaction. *Journal of Personality and Social Psychology, 36,* 1202–12.

Snyder, M., Tanke, E. D. and Berscheid, E. (1977). Social perception and interpersonal behaviour: On the self-fulfilling nature of social stereotypes. *Journal of Personality and Social Psychology, 35,* 656–66.

Spears, R. (1993). Isolating the collective self: The social context and content of identity, rationality and behaviour. NWO Pionier grant application, University of Amsterdam.

Spears, R. (1994). Why depopulation should not (necessarily) be taken personally: A reply to 'Repopulating the depopulated pages of Social Psychology' by Michael Billig. *Theory and Psychology, 4,* 337–44.

Spears, R. (1995). 'Social categorization'. In A. S. R. Manstead and M. Hewstone (eds), *The Blackwell Encyclopedia of Social Psychology,* Oxford: Blackwell.

Spears, R. and Doosje, B. (1996). Categorization and individuation: The effect of group identification and encoding set. Paper presented at SASP Conference, ANU, Canberra, Australia, May.

Spears, R., Doosje, B. and Ellemers, N. (1995). Self-stereotyping in the face of threats to group status and distinctiveness: The role of group identification. Unpublished manuscript, University of Amsterdam.

Spears, R., Haslam, S. A. and Jansen, R. (1996). Category errors in social stereotyping: Getting a load off your mind. Unpublished manuscript, University of Amsterdam.

Spears, R. and Lea, M. (1994). Panacea or panopticon? The hidden power in computer-mediated communication. *Communication Research, 21,* 427–59.

Spears, R. and Manstead, A. S. R. (1989). The social context of stereotyping and differentiation. *European Journal of Social Psychology, 19,* 101–21.

Spears, R. and van Knippenberg, D. (1995). Illusory correlation and cognitive load. Unpublished manuscript, University of Amsterdam/University of Leiden.

Spears, R., van der Pligt, J. and Eiser, J. R. (1985). Illusory correlation in the perception of group attitudes. *Journal of Personality and Social Psychology, 48,* 863–75.

Spears, R., van der Pligt, J. and Eiser, J. R. (1986). Generalizing the illusory correlation effect. *Journal of Personality and Social Psychology, 51,* 1127–34.

Srull, T. K. and Wyer, R. S. (1989). Person memory and judgment. *Psychological Review, 96,* 58–83.

St. Claire, L. and Turner, J. C. (1982). The role of demand characteristics in the social categorization paradigm. *European Journal of Social Psychology, 12,* 307–14.

Stangor, C. (1988). Stereotype accessibility and information processing. *Personality and Social Psychology Bulletin, 14,* 694–708.

Stangor, C. (1995). Content and application inaccuracy in social stereotyping. In Y. T. Lee, L. J. Jussim and C. R. McCauley (eds), *Stereotype Accuracy: Toward appreciating group differences* (pp. 275–92). Washington, D.C.: American Psychological Association.

Stangor, C. and Duan, C. (1991). Effects of multiple task demands upon memory for information about social groups. *Journal of Experimental Social Psychology, 27,* 357–78.

Stangor, C. and Lange, J. (1994). Mental representation of social groups: Advances in understanding stereotypes and stereotyping. In M. P. Zanna (ed.), *Advances in Experimental Social Psychology* (vol. 26, pp. 357–416). New York: Academic Press.

Stangor, C., Lynch, L., Duan, C. and Glass, B. (1992). Categorization of individuals on the basis of multiple social features. *Journal of Personality and Social Psychology, 62,* 207–81.

Stangor, C. and McMillan, D. (1992). Memory for expectancy-congruent and expectancy-incongruent information: A review of the social and developmental literatures. *Psychological Bulletin, 111,* 42–61.

Stangor, C. and Schaller, M. (1996). Stereotypes as individual and collective representations. In C. N. Macrae, C. Stangor and M. Hewstone (eds), *Stereotypes and Stereotyping* (pp. 3–40). New York: Guilford Press.

Stangor, C., Sechrist, G., Jost, J. T. and Bar-Tal, D. (1996). *Diagnosticity and Consensuality in Stereotype Change.* Unpublished data, University of Maryland.

Stangor, C., Sullivan, L. A. and Ford, T. E. (1991). Affective and cognitive determinants of prejudice. *Social Cognition, 9,* 359–80.

Stapel, D. A., Reicher, S. D. and Spears, R. (1995). Contextual determinants of strategic choice: Some moderators of the availability bias. *European Journal of Social Psychology, 25,* 141–58.

Steele, C. M. (1992, April). Race and the schooling of black Americans. *The Atlantic Monthly*, 68–78.

Steele, C. M. and Aronson, J. (1995). Stereotype threat and the intellectual test performance of African Americans. *Journal of Personality and Social Psychology*, 69, 797–811.

Stein, D. D., Hardyck, J. A. and Smith, M. B. (1965). Race and belief: An open and shut case. *Journal of Personality and Social Psychology*, 1, 281–89.

Steinberg, S. (1974). *The American Melting Pot*. New York: McGraw Hill.

Stephan, W. G. (1985). Intergroup relations. In G. Lindzey and E. Aronson (eds), *Handbook of Social Psychology*. New York: Random House.

Stephenson, G. M. (1981). Intergroup bargaining and negotiation. In J. C. Turner and H. Giles (eds), *Intergroup Behaviour*. Oxford: Blackwell.

Stroebe, W. and Insko, C. A. (1989). Stereotype, prejudice and discrimination: Changing conceptions in theory and research. In D. Bar-Tal, C. F. Graumann, A. W. Kruglanski and W. Stroebe (eds), *Stereotyping and Prejudice: Changing conceptions* (pp. 3–34). New York and London: Springer-Verlag.

Stroessner, S. J., Hamilton, D. L. and Mackie, D. M. (1992). Affect and stereotyping: The effect of induced mood on distinctiveness-based illusory correlation. *Journal of Personality and Social Psychology*, 62, 564–76.

Swann, W. B., Jr. (1984). Quest for accuracy in person perception: A matter of pragmatics. *Psychological Review*, 91, 457–77.

Swann, W. B. (1987). Identity negotiation: Where two roads meet. *Journal of Personality and Social Psychology*, 53, 1038–51.

Swann, W. B., Grifffin, J. J., Predmore, S. C. and Gains, B. (1987). The cognitive-affective crossfire: When self-consistency confronts self-ehnancement. *Journal of Personality and Social Psychology*, 52, 881–9.

Swim, J. K. (1994). Perceived versus meta-analytic effect sizes: An assessment of the accuracy of gender stereotypes. *Journal of Personality and Social Psychology*, 66, 21–36.

Swim, J. T. and Stangor, C. (eds) (in press). *Prejudice from the target's perspective*.

Taguieff, P. A. (1987). *La force du préjugé: Essai sur le racisme et ses doubles*. Paris: Gallimard.

Tajfel, H. (1969a). Cognitive aspects of prejudice. *Journal of Social Issues*, 25, 79–97.

Tajfel, H. (1969b). Social and cultural factors in perception. In G. Lindzey and E. Aronson (eds), *Handbook of Social Psychology, vol. 3*. Cambridge, MA: Addison-Wesley.

Tajfel, H. (1972). La catégorisation sociale. In S. Moscovici (ed.), *Introduction à la psychologie sociale* (vol. 1, pp. 272–302). Paris: Larousse.

Tajfel, H. (1973). The roots of prejudice: Cognitive aspects. In. P. Watson (ed.), *Psychology and Race*. Harmondsworth: Penguin.

Tajfel, H. (1976). Against 'biologism'. *New Society*, 29 (July), 240–2.

Tajfel, H. (ed.) (1978a). *Differentiation between Social Groups: Studies in the social psychology of intergroup relations*. London: Academic Press.

Tajfel, H. (1978b). Interindividual behaviour and intergroup behaviour. In H. Tajfel (ed.), *Differentiation between Social Groups* (pp. 27–60). New York: Academic Press.

Tajfel, H. (1978c). Social categorization, social identity and social comparison. In H. Tajfel (ed.), *Differentiation between Social Groups* (pp. 61–76). London: Academic Press.

Tajfel, H. (1979). Individuals and groups in social psychology. *British Journal of Social and Clinical Psychology*, *18*, 183–90.

Tajfel, H. (1981a). Social stereotypes and social groups. In J. C. Turner and H. Giles (eds), *Intergroup Behaviour* (pp. 144–67). Oxford: Blackwell; Chicago: University of Chicago Press.

Tajfel, H. (1981b). *Human Groups and Social Categories*. Cambridge: Cambridge University Press.

Tajfel, H. (1982a). Social psychology of intergroup relations. In M. R. Rosenzweig and L. W. Porter (eds), *Annual Review of Psycholoy* (vol. 33, pp. 1–39). Palo Alto, CA: Annual Reviews.

Tajfel, H. (1982b). *Social Identity and Intergroup Relations*. Cambridge, Cambridge University Press and Paris, Maison des Sciences de l'Homme.

Tajfel, H. (1982c). Psychological concepts of equity: The present and the future. In P. Fraisse (ed.), *Psychologie de demain*. Paris: Presses Universitaires de France.

Tajfel, H. and Billig, M. G. (1974). Familiarity and categorization in intergroup behavior. *Journal of Experimental Social Psychology*, *10*, 159–70.

Tajfel, H., Billig, M. G., Bundy, R. F. and Flament, C. (1971). Social categorization and intergroup behaviour. *European Journal of Social Psychology*, *1*, 149–77.

Tajfel, H. and Forgas, J. P. (1981). Social categorization: Cognitions, values and groups. In J. P. Forgas (ed.), *Social Cognition: Perspectives in everyday understanding* (pp. 113–40). London: Academic Press.

Tajfel, H. and Turner, J. (1979). An integrative theory of intergroup conflict. In W. G. Austin and S. Worchel (eds), *The Social Psychology of Intergroup Relations* (pp. 33–48). Monterey, CA: Brooks/Cole.

Tajfel, H. and Turner, J. C. (1986). The social identity theory of intergroup behavior. In S. Worchel and W. G. Austin (eds), *The Psychology of Intergroup Relations* (pp. 7–24). Chicago: Nelson-Hall.

Tajfel, H. and Wilkes, A. L. (1963). Classification and quantitative judgement. *British Journal of Psychology*, *54*, 101–14.

Taylor, D. M. and Doria, J. R. (1981). Self-serving van group-serving bias in attribution. *The Journal of Social Psychology*, *113*, 201–11.

Taylor, D. M., Doria, J. R. and Tyler, J. K. (1983). Group performance and cohesiveness: An attribution analysis. *The Journal of Social Psychology*, *119*, 187–98.

Taylor, D. M. and Jaggi, V. (1974). Ethnocentrism and causal attribution in a south Indian context. *Journal of Cross-Cultural Psychology*, *5*, 162–71.

Taylor, S. E. (1981a). The interface of cognitive and social psychology. In J. Harvey (ed.), *Cognition, Social Behaviour and the Environment* (pp. 189–211). Hillsdale, NJ: Erlbaum.

Taylor, S. E. (1981b). A categorization approach to stereotyping. In D. L. Hamilton (ed.), *Cognitive Processes in Stereotyping and Intergroup Behavior* (pp. 88–114). Hillsdale, NJ: Erlbaum.

Taylor, S. E. and Brown, J. D. (1988). Illusion and well-being: A social psychological perspective on mental health. *Psychological Bulletin*, *103*, 193–210.

Taylor, S. E., Fiske, S. T., Etcoff, N. L. and Ruderman, A. J. (1978). Categorical and contextual bases of person memory and stereotyping. *Journal of Personality and Social Psychology*, *36*, 778–93.

Terman, L. M. (1916). *The Measurement of Intelligence*. Boston: Houghton Mifflin.

Terman, L. M. (1923). *Intelligence Tests and School Reorganization.* Yonkers-on-Hudson, NY: World Book Company.

Triandis, H. C. (1990). Cross-cultural studies of individualism and collectivism. In J. Berman (ed.), *Nebraska Symposium on Motivation* (1989, pp. 41–133). Lincoln, NB: University of Nebraska Press.

Triandis, H. C. (1994). *Culture and Social Behavior.* New York: McGraw-Hill.

Triandis, H. C. and Vassiliou, V. (1967). Frequency of contact and stereotyping. *Journal of Personality and Social Psychology, 7,* 316–28.

Turner, J. C. (1975). Social comparison and social identity: Some prospects for intergroup behaviour. *European Journal of Social Psychology, 5,* 5–34.

Turner, J. C. (1978a). Social comparison, similarity, and in-group favouritism. In H. Tajfel (ed.), *Differentiation between Social Groups: Studies in the social psychology of intergroup relations* (pp. 235–50). London: Academic Press.

Turner, J. C. (1978b). Social categorization and social discrimination in the minimal group paradigm. In H. Tajfel (ed.), *Differentiation between Social Groups: Studies in the social psychology of intergroup relations.* London: Academic Press.

Turner, J. C. (1980). Fairness or discrimination in intergroup behaviour? A reply to Branthwaite, Doyle and Lightbown. *European Journal of Social Psychology, 10,* 131–47.

Turner, J. C. (1981). The experimental social psychology of intergroup behaviour. In J. C. Turner and H. Giles (eds), *Intergroup Behaviour* (pp. 66–101). Oxford: Blackwell.

Turner, J. C. (1982). Towards a cognitive redefinition of the social group. In H. Tajfel (ed.), *Social Identity and Intergroup Relations.* Cambridge: Cambridge University Press.

Turner, J. C. (1983). Some comments on . . . 'the measurement of social orientations in the minimal group paradigm'. *European Journal of Social Psychology, 13,* 351–67.

Turner, J. C. (1985). Social categorization and the self-concept: A social cognitive theory of group behavior. In E. J. Lawler (ed.), *Advances in Group Processes: Theory and research* (vol. 2). Greenwich, CT: JAI Press.

Turner, J. C. (1987a). Introducing the problem: Individual and group. In J. C. Turner, M. A. Hogg, P. J. Oakes, S. D. Reicher and M. S. Wetherell, *Rediscovering the Social Group: A Self-categorization Theory.* Oxford: Blackwell.

Turner, J. C. (1987b). A self-categorization theory. In J. C. Turner, M. A. Hogg, P. J. Oakes, S. D. Reicher and M. S. Wetherell, *Rediscovering the Social Group: A self-categorization theory* (pp. 42–67). Oxford: Blackwell.

Turner, J. C. (1987c). The analysis of social influence. In J. C. Turner, M. A. Hogg, P. J. Oakes, S. D. Reicher and M. S. Wetherell (1987), *Rediscovering the Social Group: A self-categorization theory.* Oxford: Blackwell.

Turner, J. C. (1991). *Social Influence.* Milton Keynes: Open University Press.

Turner, J. C. (in press). Henri Tajfel: An introduction. In W. P. Robinson (ed.), *A Festschrift for Henri Tajfel.* Oxford: Butterworth Heinemann.

Turner, J. C. and Bourhis, R. Y. (in press). Social identity, interdependence and the social group: A reply to Rabbie et al. In W. P. Robinson (ed.), *A Festschrift for Henri Tajfel.* Oxford: Butterworth Heinemann.

Turner, J. C. and Brown, R. (1978). Social status, cognitive alternatives, and intergroup relations. In H. Tajfel (ed.), *Differentiation between Social Groups* (pp. 201–34). London: Academic Press.

Turner, J. C., Brown, R. J. and Tajfel, H. (1979). Social comparison and group interest in ingroup favouritism. *European Journal of Social Psychology*, *9*, 187–204.

Turner, J. C. and Giles, H. (1981a) (eds). *Intergroup Behaviour*. Oxford: Blackwell.

Turner, J. C. and Giles, H. (1981b). Introduction: The social psychology of intergroup behaviour. In J. C. Turner and H. Giles (eds), *Intergroup behaviour*. Oxford: Blackwell; Chicago: University of Chicago Press.

Turner, J. C., Hogg, M. A., Oakes, P. J., Reicher, S. D. and Wetherell, M. S. (1987). *Rediscovering the Social Group: A self-categorization theory*. Oxford and New York: Blackwell.

Turner, J. C., Hogg, M. A., Turner, P. J. and Smith, P. M. (1984). Failure and defeat as determinants of group cohesiveness. *British Journal of Social Psychology*, *23*, 97–111.

Turner, J. C. and Oakes, P. J. (1989). Self-categorization theory and social influence. In P. B. Paulus (ed.), *The Psychology of Group Influence*. Hillsdale, NJ: Erlbaum.

Turner, J. C., Oakes, P. J., Haslam, S. A. and McGarty, C. A. (1994). Self and collective: Cognition and social context. *Personality and Social Psychology Bulletin*, *20*, 454–63.

Tversky, A. (1977). Features of similarity. *Psychological Review*, *84*, 327–52.

Tversky, A. and Gati, I. (1978). Studies of similarity. In E. Rosch and B. Lloyds (eds), *Cognition and Categorization* (pp. 79–98). Hillsdale, NJ: Erlbaum.

Tversky, A. and Kahneman, D. (1973). Availability: A heuristic for judging frequency and probability. *Cognitive Psychology*, *4*, 207–32.

Tyler, T. R. (1989). The psychology of procedural justice: A test of the group-value model. *Journal of Personality and Social Psychology*, *57*, 830–8.

Tyler, T. R. (1990). *Why People Obey the Law*. New Haven, CT: Yale University Press.

Van Dyck, C., Ellemers, N. and Hinkle, S. (1995). Ingroep favoritisme en sociaal self-esteem: Behoeften versus mogelijkheden. *Fundamentele Sociale Psychologie*, *9*, 67–76.

Van Knippenberg, A. (1978). Status differences, comparative relevance and intergroup differentiation. In Tajfel, H. (ed.), *Differentiation between Social Groups: Studies in the social psychology of intergroup relations* (pp. 171–99). London: Academic Press.

Van Knippenberg, A. (1984). Intergroup differences in group perceptions. In H. Tajfel (ed.), *The Social Dimension: European developments in social psychology* (pp. 560–78). Cambridge: Cambridge University Press.

Van Knippenberg, A. (1992). Sociale categorisatie en sociale cognitie. *Fundamentele Sociale Psychologie*, *6*, 5–24.

Van Knippenberg, A. and Ellemers, N. (1990). Social identity and intergroup differentiation processes. *European Review of Social Psychology*, *1*, 137–70.

Van Knippenberg, A. and van Oers, H. (1984). Social identity and equity concerns in intergroup perceptions. *British Journal of Social Psychology*, *23*, 351–61.

Van Knippenberg, A., Van Twuyver, M. and Pepels, J. (1994). Factors affecting social categorization processes in memory. *British Journal of Social Psychology*, *33*, 419–32.

Van Knippenberg, A. and Wilke, H. (1979). Perceptions of collégiens and apprentis re-analyzed. *European Journal of Social Psychology*, *9*, 427–34.

Van Knippenberg, D., Van Knippenberg, A. and Dijksterhuis, A. (1994). Illusoire correlatie en zelfcategorisatie: aandacht als moderator van ingroup bias in groepsimpressies. *Fundamentele Sociale Psychologie*, *8*, 21–33.

Van Rijswijk, R. and Ellemers, N. (1996). De invloed van groepsstatus en relatieve groepsgroote op het gebruik van directe en indirecte intergroepsdifferentiatie stratagieën. *Fundamentele Sociale Psychologie*, 10.

Van Twuyver, M. and van Knippenberg, A. (1995). Social categorization as a function of priming. *European Journal of Social Psychology*, 25, 695–702.

Vanbeselaere, N. (1991). The different effects of simple and crossed categorizations: A result of the category differentiation process or of differential category salience? *European Review of Social Psychology*, 2, 247–78.

Vinacke, W. E. (1949). Stereotypes among national-racial groups in Hawaii: A study in ethnocentrism. *Journal of Social Psychology*, 30, 265–91.

Vinacke, W. E. (1956). Explorations in the dynamic process of stereotyping. *Journal of Social Psychology*, 43, 105–32.

Vinacke, W. E. (1957). Stereotypes as social concepts. *Journal of Social Psychology*, 46, 229–43.

Vonk, R. and van Knippenberg, A. (1995). Processing attitudes from ingroup and outgroup members: Effects of within-group and within-person inconsistencies. *Journal of Personality and Social Psychology*, 68, 215– .

Wann, D. L. and Branscombe, N. R. (1990). Die hard and fair-weather fans: Effects of identification on BIRGing and CORFing tendencies. *Journal of Sport and Social Issues*, 14, 103–17.

Wann, D. L. and Branscombe, N. R. (1993). Sport fans: Measuring degree of identification with their team. *International Journal of Sport Psychology*, 24, 1–17.

Wattenmaker, W. D., Nakamura, G. V. and Medin, D. L. (1988). Relationships between similarity-based and explanation-based categorization. In D. J. Hilton (ed.), *Contemporary Science and Natural Explanation: Common sense conceptions of causality* (pp. 204–40). Brighton: Harvester Press.

Weber, M. (1964). *L'éthique protestante et l'esprit du capitalisme*. Paris: Plon.

Weber, M. (1978). The disintegration of the household: The rise of the calculative spirit and of the modern capitalist enterprise. In G. Roth and C. Wittich (eds), *Max Weber: Economy and society* (vol. I). Berkeley, CA: University of California Press.

Weber, R. and Crocker, J. (1983). Cognitive processes in the revision of stereotypic beliefs. *Journal of Personality and Social Psychology*, 45, 961–77.

Wellman, H. M. and Gelman, S. A. (1992). Cognitive development: Foundational theories of core domains. *Annual Review of Psychology*, 43, 337–75.

Wetherell, M. and Potter, J. (1992). *Mapping the Language of Racism*. Hassocks: Harvester Wheatsheaf.

Wilder, D. A. (1978). Perceiving persons as a group: Effects on attributions of causality and beliefs. *Social Psychology*, 1, 13–23.

Wilder, D. A. (1984). Intergroup contact: The typical member and the exception to the rule. *Journal of Experimental Social Psychology*, 20, 177–94.

Wilder, D. A. (1986). Social categorisation: Implications for creation and reduction of intergroup bias. In L. Berkowitz (ed.), *Advances in Experimental Social Psychology* (vol. 19, pp. 291–355). New York: Academic Press.

Wilder, D. A. (1991). Some determinants of the persuasive power of ingroups and outgroups: Organization of information and attribution of independence. *Journal of Personality and Social Psychology*, 59, 1202–13.

Wilder, D. A. and Shapiro, P. (1991). Facilitation of outgroup stereotypes by enhanced ingroup identity. *Journal of Experimental Social Psychology*, *27*, 431–52.

Wilder, D. A. and Thompson, J. E. (1988). Assimilation and contrast effects in the judgments of groups. *Journal of Personality and Social Psychology*, *54*, 62–73.

Williams, J. and Giles, H. (1978). The changing status of women in society: An intergroup perspective. In H. Tajfel (ed.), *Differentiation Between Social Groups*. London, Academic Press.

Wills, T. A. (1981). Downward comparison principles of social psychology. *Psychological Bulletin*, *90*, 245–71.

Wishner, J. (1960). Reanalysis of 'impressions of personality'. *Psychological Review*, *67*, 96–112.

Wisniewski, E. and Medin, D. L. (1994). On the integration of theory and data in concept learning. *Cognitive Science*, *18*, 221–82.

Wittenbrink, B., Gist, P. and Hilton, J. (1994). Tools for explanation: Stereotypes in a knowledge-based approach to categorization. Unpublished manuscript, University of Michigan.

Wittgenstein, L. (1953). *Philosophical Investigations*. New York: Macmillan.

Worchel, S. (1979). Cooperation and the reduction of intergroup conflict: Some determining factors. In W. Austin and S. Worchel (eds), *The Social Psychology of Intergroup Relations*. Monterey, CA: Brooks/Cole.

Worchel, S. (1986). The role of cooperation in reducing intergroup conflict. In S. Worchel and G. Austin (eds), *Psychology of Intergroup Relations*. Chicago, IL: Nelson-Hall.

Worchel, S. (1994). You can go home again: Returning group research to the group context with an eye on development issues and supporting data. *Small Group Research*, *25*, 205–23.

Worchel, S. and Austin. W. G. (1986) (eds). *Psychology of Intergroup Relations*. Chicago, IL: Nelson-Hall.

Worchel, S., Axsom, K., Ferris, F., Samaha, C. and Schweitzer, S. (1978). Factors determining the effect of intergroup attraction. *Journal of Conflict Resolution*, *22*, 428–39.

Worchel, S., Coutant-Sassic, D. and Grossman, M. (1992). A developmental approach to group dynamics: A model and illustrative research. In S. Worchel, W. Wood and J. A. Simpson (eds), *Group Process and Group Productivity* (pp. 181–202). Newbury Park: Sage.

Worchel, S., Coutant-Sassic, D. and Wong, F. (1993). Toward a more balanced view of conflict: There is a positive side. In S. Worchel and J. A. Simpson (eds), *Conflict between People and Groups* (pp. 76–89). Chicago: Nelson-Hall.

Worchel, S., Grossman, M. and Coutant, D. (1994). Minority influence in the group context: How group factors affect when the minority will be influential. In S. Moscovici, A. Mucchi-Faina and A. Maass (eds), *Minority Influence* (pp. 97–114). Chicago, IL: Nelson Hall.

Worchel, S. and Hills, M. (1995). The impact of culture on the self-concept and aspirations for self and country. Unpublished manuscript, Texas A&M University.

Word, C. G., Zanna, M. P. and Cooper, J. (1974). The nonverbal mediation of self-fulfilling prophecies in interracial interaction. *Journal of Experimental Social Psychology*, *10*, 109–20.

Wyer, R. S. and Srull, T. K. (1980). The processing of social stimulus information: A conceptual integration. In R. Hastie, T. M. Ostrom, E. B. Ebbesen, R. S. Wyer, Jr., D. L. Hamilton and D. E. Carlston (eds), *Person Memory: The cognitive basis of social perception* (pp. 227–300). Hillsdale, NJ: Erlbaum.

Wyer, R. S. and Srull, T. K. (1981). Category accessibility: Some theoretical and empirical issues concerning the processing of social information. In E. T. Higgins, C. P. Herman and M. P. Zanna (eds), *Social Cognition: The Ontario symposium on personality and social psychology* (vol. 1, pp. 161–97). Hillsdale, NJ: Erlbaum.

Wyer, R. S. and Srull, T. K. (1984). *Handbook of Social Cognition* (vols 1–3). Hillsdale, NJ: Erlbaum.

Wyer, R. S. and Srull, T. K. (1989). Understanding social knowledge: If only data could speak for themselves. In D. Bar-Tal and A. Kruglanski (eds), *The Social Psychology of Knowledge* (pp. 142–92). Cambridge: Cambridge University Press.

Young, H., van Knippenberg, A., Ellemers, N. and de Vries, N. (1995). Is vertrouwdheid genoeg? De effecten van groepslidmaatschap en sociale context of informatie-organisatie. *Fundamentele Sociale Psychologie*, *9*, 53–66.

Yzerbyt, V. Y., Coull, A. and Rocher, S. J. (1995). Stereotype maintenance in the face of disconfirmation: The role of resource availability. Unpublished manuscript, University of Louvain at Louvain-la-Neuve.

Yzerbyt, V. Y., Rocher, S. J. and Coull, A. (1995). Stereotypes, inconsistency management, and cognitive economy. Unpublished manuscript, University of Louvain at Louvain-le-Neuve.

Yzerbyt, V. Y. and Schadron, G. H. (1994). Stéréotypes et jugement social. In R. Bourhis and J.-Ph. Leyens (eds), *Stéréotypes, discrimination et relations entre groupes* (pp. 127–60). Bruxelles: Mardaga.

Yzerbyt, V. Y. and Schadron, G. (1996). *Connaître et juger autrui: Une introduction à la cognition sociale*. Grenoble: Presse Universitaire de Grenoble.

Yzerbyt, V. Y., Schadron, G., Leyens, J.-P. and Rocher, S. (1994). Social judgeability: The impact of meta-informational cues on the use of stereotypes. *Journal of Personality and Social Psychology*, *66*, 48–55.

Yzerbyt, V. Y., Schadron, G. and Morchain, P. (1994). Stereotypes and the function of rationalization in social categorization. Unpublished manuscript, University of Louvain at Louvain-la-Neuve.

Zanna, M. P. and Olson, J. M. (eds) (1994). *The Psychology of Prejudice: The Ontario symposium, vol. 7*. Hillsdale, NJ: Lawrence Erlbaum.

Zárate, M. A. and Smith, E. R. (1990). Person categorization and stereotyping. *Social Cognition*, *8*, 161–85.

Zawadzki, B. (1942). Limitations of the scapegoat theory of prejudice. *Journal of Abnormal and Social Psychology*, *43*, 127–41.

Author Index

Subject Index